Nuevos amigos

A functional approach to proficient communication!

- **Emphasis on interactive communication in everyday situations!**
- **Cultural authenticity!**
- **Consistent organization for effective instruction!**
- **A rich collection of teaching and learning resources!**

Functional language for proficient communication

From greeting others to inviting friends, from seeking information to expressing opinions, ***Nuevos amigos*** introduces students to the world of *real* language in *real* situations!

Learning activities that develop basic concepts

Through a variety of activities, ***Nuevos amigos*** provides specific practice for basic vocabulary and grammar concepts.

Each section opens with an appealing situation rich in ideas for lively communication.

Application activities for proficient communication

Motivating activities invite students to apply what they have learned to real-life situations.

A balance of activities for learning and application helps students become proficient in listening, speaking, reading, and writing in Spanish.

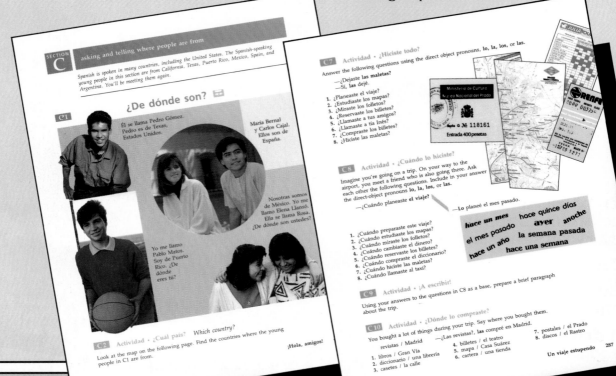

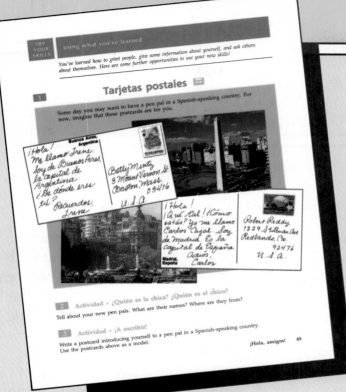

Application activities in **Try Your Skills** provide "real-life" opportunities for students to use their new language skills.

Reading selections in a variety of formats—including comic strips, letters, interviews, character sketches, and articles, as well as narratives—help students develop reading skills in Spanish. Activities, following each selection, check comprehension and relate reading to students' personal experiences.

Sample pages are reduced.
Actual sizes are 8"x10". All pages are from *Level 1*.

Cultural awareness to broaden understanding

Positive cultural attitudes

To help students understand and appreciate Spanish-speaking people and countries, **Nuevos amigos** interweaves cultural insights and information. Teaching more than just the language, the program depicts everyday life, such as family and peer relations and social customs, in Spanish culture.

Cultural authenticity

To surround students with vibrant, authentic Spanish culture, the textbook includes such special features as an introduction to the language and culture, colorful photographic essays, and cultural notes. To ensure authenticity, the textbook was written by native speakers of Spanish. In addition, the annotated *Teacher's Edition* and *Teacher's ResourceBank* ™ provide an abundance of cultural resources, realia, and insights to further enhance learning experiences.

Strikingly illustrated, **Spanish and You** introduces students to Spanish people, language, and culture.

INTRODUCTION

Spanish and You

Welcome to the Spanish-speaking world! Today you are embarking on a new journey—the exploration and learning of Spanish. This trip will take you to many lands, where you will meet different people. The route you will take is the Spanish language; the destination is an understanding of how speakers of Spanish think, behave, and interact with others. You will discover their values, history, and traditions. Are you ready to start your trip?
Let's go!   ¡Vamos!

In this introduction you will learn:

1 where Spanish is spoken around the world

2 how Spanish and English are related

3 about Spanish-speaking areas in the United States

4 about Spanish and your leisure time activities—hobbies, sports, travel

5 about the knowledge of Spanish and your future career

6 suggestions for studying Spanish

Depicting the lifestyles of Spanish-speaking people, colorful photo essays enhance students' understanding of Spanish attitudes and customs.

Each section includes a cultural note—**¿Sabes que...?**—that provides interesting facts about Spanish-speaking people to increase students' cultural awareness.

Viñeta cultural 1

Pueblos y ciudades

In the large, bustling cities of the Spanish-speaking world, and the many small villages that dot the countryside, visitors can find great contrasts and a wide variety of cultures. In Spain, medieval castles, Gothic cathedrals, and ancient aqueducts are dramatic reminders of the past amidst the modern life of today.

❶ Iglesia de la Sagrada Familia en Barcelona, España
❷ Un café al aire libre en Barcelona, España
❸ El parque del Retiro en Madrid, España
❹ La hermosa ciudad de Ávila, España

Pueblos y ciudades 125

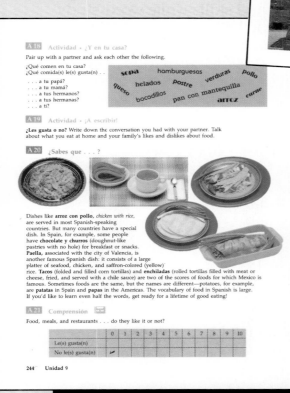

A 18 Actividad · ¿Y en tu casa?

Pair up with a partner and ask each other the following.

¿Qué comen en tu casa?
¿Qué comida(s) le(s) gusta(n) . . .

. . . a tu papá?
. . . a tu mamá?
. . . a tus hermanos?
. . . a tus hermanas?
. . . a ti?

sopa   hamburguesas
queso   helados   postre   verduras   pollo
bocadillos   pan con mantequilla   arroz   carne

A 19 Actividad · ¡A escribir!

¿Les gusta o no? Write down the conversation you had with your partner. Talk about what you eat at home and your family's likes and dislikes about food.

A 20 ¿Sabes que . . . ?

Dishes like **arroz con pollo,** *chicken with rice,* are served in most Spanish-speaking countries. But many countries have a special dish. In Spain, for example, some people have **chocolate y churros** (doughnut-like pastries with no hole) for breakfast or snacks. **Paella,** associated with the city of Valencia, is another famous Spanish dish: it consists of a large platter of seafood, chicken, and saffron-colored (yellow) rice. **Tacos** (folded and filled corn tortillas) and **enchiladas** (rolled tortillas filled with meat or cheese, fried, and served with a chile sauce) are two of the scores of foods for which Mexico is famous. Sometimes foods are the same, but the names are different—potatoes, for example, are **patatas** in Spain and **papas** in the Americas. The vocabulary of food in Spanish is large. If you'd like to learn even half the words, get ready for a lifetime of good eating!

A 21 Comprensión

Food, meals, and restaurants . . . do they like it or not?

	0	1	2	3	4	5	6	7	8	9	10
Le(s) gusta(n)											
No le(s) gusta(n)	✓										

244 Unidad 9

Sample pages are reduced. Actual sizes are 8"x10". All pages are from *Level 1.*

Consistent organization for effective teaching and learning

Manageable content

Designed as a one-year course, **Nuevos amigos** promotes active learning at a comfortable pace. Instruction progresses logically without overwhelming students, introducing a manageable amount of new grammar and vocabulary to support the communicative functions.

Clear learning objectives

Consistent unit organization with clearly defined objectives ensures success in learning. As students move through each new lesson, they build self-confidence and self-motivation.

Frequent review

Periodic review helps students apply what they have learned to new and different situations. Self-checks in each unit allow students to monitor their grasp of important concepts and skills while word-study activities help students review vocabulary effectively. Review units provide numerous activities that teachers may select to reinforce learning and satisfy special needs.

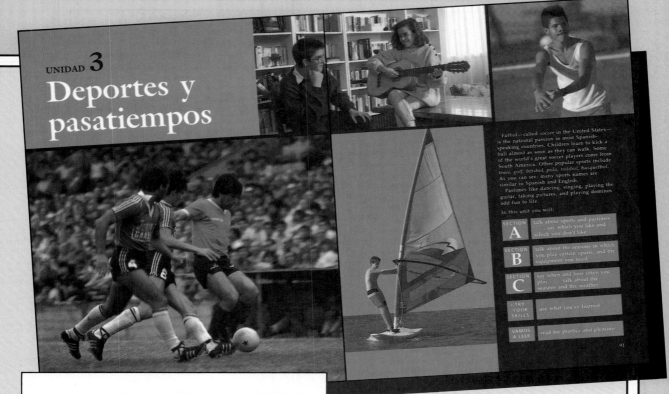

UNIDAD 3
Deportes y pasatiempos

Fútbol—called *soccer* in the United States—is the national passion in most Spanish-speaking countries. Children learn to kick a ball almost as soon as they can walk. Some of the world's great soccer players come from South America. Other popular sports include *tenis, golf, béisbol, polo, vólibol, basquetbol*. As you can see, many sports names are similar in Spanish and English.

Pastimes like dancing, singing, playing the guitar, taking pictures, and playing dominos add fun to life.

In this unit you will:

SECTION A	talk about sports and pastimes . . . say which you like and which you don't like
SECTION B	talk about the seasons in which you play certain sports, and the equipment you need
SECTION C	say when and how often you play . . . talk about the seasons and the weather
TRY YOUR SKILLS	use what you've learned
VAMOS A LEER	read for practice and pleasure

91

¿LO SABES?

Let's review some important points you have learned in this unit.

SECTION A

When talking about sports and pastimes in Spanish, can you name a few?
Name five. Add the definite article if necessary or use an infinitive.

Can you talk about your likes, dislikes, or preferences in sports?
Answer the following questions, expressing your preferences and say why you feel that way.

¿Qué deporte te gusta? ¿Por qué?
¿Cuál es tu pasatiempo favorito? ¿Por qué?
¿Qué deporte practican en tu escuela?
¿Te gusta? ¿Por qué?

SECTION B

Can you tell in which seasons you play different sports?
Make up four sentences.
En (name of season) jugamos / practicamos (name of sport).

Do you know what equipment is needed for different sports?
Say what sport needs the following equipment. Start your sentences with **Necesitamos . . .**

una raqueta	un bate	bastones
esquís	botas	unas pelotas
un balón	una canasta	un guante

SECTION C

Can you say how often you practice a sport or pastime, and whether you practice in the morning, in the afternoon, or at night?
Write four sentences. Say how often and when you practice two sports and two pastimes.
Siempre juego tenis por la tarde.

Can you talk about the weather?
Answer these questions.
¿Qué tiempo hace hoy?
¿Llueve?
¿Nieva?
¿Para qué está bueno el tiempo?

114   Unidad 3

Clearly delineated sections with specific communicative functions provide a "purpose" for language learning.

Cross-referenced to the communicative functions, **¿Lo sabes?** helps students monitor their progress.

Sample pages are reduced. Actual sizes are 8"x10". All pages are from *Level 1*.

A wealth of teaching resources for a range of needs

Flexible resources

Nuevos amigos provides a range of resources to satisfy a variety of teaching preferences and individual learning rates and styles.

Teacher's Edition

The easy-to-use annotated *Teacher's Edition* contains numerous convenient features:

- A scope and sequence chart for each unit
- Detailed teaching suggestions— including ideas for cooperative learning—conveniently located before each unit
- Cultural background notes for each section of every unit
- Provisions for students of different abilities
- Scripts and answers for listening comprehension exercises
- Annotated pupil's pages with answers to exercises

UNIDAD 3

SECTION A

A1-3

OBJECTIVES To express feelings and emotions: talk about what you and others like and don't like to do

CULTURAL BACKGROUND When Mexico hosted the World Cup Soccer Championship in 1986, millions of people from different parts of the world attended or watched on television. Argentina won the games, and the Argentinians celebrated along with their Spanish-speaking neighbors in all of Spanish America.

Soccer, or **fútbol**, is the most popular sport in Spanish-speaking countries. Children can be seen playing **fútbol** at all hours of the day in the streets of Mexico, Spain, or Argentina. On weekends, parks are filled with amateur soccer teams. In Mexico City, the **Estadio Azteca** is one of the largest stadiums in the world, holding more than 100,000 people.

MOTIVATING ACTIVITY Have the students decorate the bulletin board with pictures illustrating popular sports in Spanish-speaking countries. As they learn the Spanish name for each sport, they may label each picture.

A1 ¿Qué deporte te gusta?

Display magazine pictures of the sports depicted in this section. Point to each picture illustrating a sport and name the sport with its article (el tenis). Have the students repeat. Then hold up the picture illustrating tennis and, while pointing to yourself, say **Me gusta el tenis.** Then ask the students ¿Qué deporte te gusta?

To introduce **no me gusta . . . ,** you may wish to follow the same procedure, adding a gesture of thumbs down or shaking your head and saying **No me gusta . . .**

Now play the cassette or read aloud while the students listen. Have them practice the lines in groups of three. One student may be Miguel, and the other two may talk about Olga and Pedro. Have the students exchange roles so that everyone has the opportunity to practice each role.

A2 Actividad • ¡Para completar!

Have the students complete the sentences with a partner. Then, for writing practice, assign this activity as written homework.

CHALLENGE Have the students make up five original questions based on the dialog in A1. Then have them exchange papers and answer each other's questions.

A3 Actividad • Y ahora, tú

Call on individuals to say which sports they like and don't like. Point out to the students that the infinitives **nadar, correr,** and **montar** do not take an article.

To re-enter the days of the week, have the students say what sport or pastime they like or dislike on a particular day.

Me gusta patinar el lunes.
No me gusta estudiar el sábado.

SLOWER-PACED LEARNING Use magazine pictures illustrating the sports mentioned in the box. Write on the board or a transparency the names of the sports with their appropriate articles. Have the students choose a picture

T70 Teacher's Notes Unidad 3

Teacher's Notes provide specific strategies for each part of the unit—including basic material, activities, and reading selections. Notes include special projects, variations of textbook exercises, and suggestions for accommodating different learning styles. Tabbed pages allow quick location of **Teacher's Notes.**

Challenge and **Slower-Paced Learning** activities satisfy individual learning needs.

Sample pages are reduced. Actual sizes are 8"x10". Pages are from *Level 1, Teacher's Edition.*

Teacher's ResourceBank™

The *Teacher's ResourceBank™* includes useful *Teacher's Resource Materials* —proficiency practice situations, games, songs, vocabulary lists with exercises, realia, component correlation charts, a glossary of grammatical terms, and a pronunciation guide. The *Teacher's ResourceBank™* also contains posters; an Overhead Transparencies Sampler and Planning Guide; the *Student's Test Booklet* in copying-master form; the *Teacher's Test Guide;* and the *Unit Cassette Guide.* A three-ring binder with convenient tabbed dividers provides organized storage for these teaching resources.

Additional components for students and teachers

Exercise Workbook with Teacher's Edition

The *Exercise Workbook* contains activities that provide practice in grammar concepts and vocabulary. The accompanying *Teacher's Edition* contains answers for all activities.

Activity Workbook with Teacher's Edition

Rich in illustrations and realia, the *Activity Workbook* provides entertaining and challenging activities to develop communication skills. The accompanying *Teacher's Edition* contains answers for all activities.

Testing Program

The comprehensive *Testing Program*—consisting of the *Student's Test Booklet, Teacher's Test Guide,* and *Test Cassettes*—assesses both achievement and proficiency in Spanish. The perforated *Student's Test Booklet* includes section quizzes, unit tests, review unit tests, mid-year and final examinations, and proficiency tests. The *Teacher's Test Guide* includes recording scripts for the listening portions of all quizzes and tests, speaking tests for each unit, suggestions for administering and scoring tests, and an answer key. *Test Cassettes* contain the listening portions of all quizzes and tests as well as a model for administering the speaking portion of a proficiency test.

Teacher's Resource Materials

Teacher's Resource Materials provide a variety of copying masters, including:
- Proficiency practice situations—activities for use with each review unit—to help students improve communication skills
- Games to help develop fluency in Spanish
- Spanish songs for group singing activities
- Vocabulary lists and exercises
- Realia—including authentic menus, transportation schedules, and invitations—with teaching suggestions and cross-references to textbook units
- Components correlation charts
- A glossary of grammar terms with examples
- A pronunciation guide with drills for pronunciation practice

Unit Cassettes

Cassettes for instructional and review units include basic material, selected activities, listening comprehension and pronunciation exercises, and reading selections—all recorded by native speakers with pauses for student repetition and response, where appropriate. They also provide Spanish songs.

Unit Cassette Guide

The *Unit Cassette Guide* includes an index to the *Unit Cassettes,* recording scripts for all *Unit Cassettes,* and copying masters for the listening comprehension exercises in the textbook.

Overhead Transparencies

Overhead Transparencies, with copying masters, accompany each instructional and review unit. Full-color map transparencies include overlays with geographical names. In addition, a Planning Guide contains suggestions for classroom use.

Unit Theme Posters

Colorful posters feature captivating photographs to enhance each unit in the textbook.

Nuevos amigos

Teacher's Edition

HBJ HARCOURT BRACE JOVANOVICH, PUBLISHERS
Orlando   San Diego   Chicago   Dallas

Printed in the United States of America
ISBN 0-15-388301-4

We do not include a Teacher's Edition automatically with each shipment of a classroom set of textbooks. We prefer to send a Teacher's Edition only when it is part of a purchase order or when it is requested by the teacher or administrator concerned or by one of our representatives. A Teacher's Edition can be easily mislaid when it arrives as part of a shipment delivered to a school stockroom, and, since it contains answer materials, we would like to be sure it is sent directly to the person who will use it, or to someone concerned with the use or selection of textbooks.

If your class assignment changes and you no longer are using or examining this Teacher's Edition, you may wish to pass it on to a teacher who may have use for it.

CONTENTS

TO THE TEACHER

SCOPE AND SEQUENCE CHARTS AND TEACHER'S NOTES

TO THE TEACHER

In creating the new Harcourt Brace Jovanovich Spanish Program, we have incorporated suggestions from foreign language teachers in all parts of the country. We are grateful to you for talking and writing to us. We feel that, based on your suggestions and on what we have observed about general trends in foreign language teaching, we have produced a program that you and your students will profit from and enjoy.

Philosophy and Goals

The primary goal of the Harcourt Brace Jovanovich Spanish Program is to help students develop proficiency in the four basic skills: listening, speaking, reading, and writing. At the same time, it aims to increase the students' knowledge and appreciation of the diverse cultures of the countries whose language they are learning.

In order to become proficient in a foreign language, students must not only learn the vocabulary and structures of the language, but also apply what they have learned. Thus, students learn and practice the material in each unit; they also have many opportunities to apply their skills. Given ample opportunity for creative expression, students are on their way to developing proficiency.

The emphasis is on communication. The approach is based on the communicative purposes of young people at this level—to invite, inform, inquire, exclaim, agree, disagree, compliment, express emotions and opinions, and so on. These communicative purposes, or functions, in turn determine the selection and the amount of vocabulary and grammar that students need to learn. The communicative functions, grammar, and vocabulary are presented in culturally authentic situations that appeal to young people. They are followed by a variety of activities that promote both learning and application of the language, ultimately leading students to function with increasing proficiency in many new situations. The question to be asked constantly in measuring students' success is, "What can they do with the language they are learning, and how well?"

Description of the HBJ Spanish Program

We have designed the materials of this program to be highly adaptable. You will be able to offer a variety of experiences in learning and using the foreign language, choosing materials that correspond to the learning needs of each student. The various parts of the program are:

Components of the program

- Pupil's Edition
- Teacher's Edition
- Activity Workbook
- Activity Workbook, Teacher's Edition
- Exercise Workbook
- Exercise Workbook, Teacher's Edition
- Overhead Transparencies
- Unit Theme Posters
- Testing Program
    Student's Test Booklet
    Teacher's Test Guide
    Test Cassettes
- Audio Program
    Unit Cassettes
    Unit Cassette Guide
- Teacher's Resource Materials

Pupil's Edition

The student textbook is the core of the program. The opening pages, entitled "Getting to Know Your Textbook," take students on a guided, illustrated "walk-through" of the book. The introductory photo essay, "Spanish and You," familiarizes students with the countries where Spanish is spoken, provides information on the origin of the language and its influence on English, explores the application of a foreign language in careers, and gives students hints on how to study a foreign language.

Organization of the textbook

The book contains twelve units, grouped into three Parts. Each Part consists of three instructional units *(Unidad)*, one review unit *(Unidad de repaso)*, and one photo essay *(Viñeta cultural)*. The book ends with a reference section. Here students will find summaries of the communicative functions, grammar, and vocabulary. Culturally authentic photographs, art, and realia appear throughout the book.

Organization of Instructional Units

Each instructional unit starts with two pages of photographs that illustrate the theme of the unit. Also appearing on these pages are a brief introduction and an outline of the unit that lists, section by section, the performance objectives, or communicative functions, that the students should expect to achieve.

Communicative functions

The instructional portion of each unit is divided into three sections—Section A, Section B, and Section C. The communicative functions are repeated at the beginning of the section, followed by a brief introduction to the theme of the section. Each section includes basic material, presented in the form of a dialog, narrative, or letter; a grouping of the words and phrases necessary to the communicative function *(Se dice así)*; grammar *(Estructuras esenciales)*; a cultural note *(¿Sabes que . . . ?)*; a listening comprehension exercise *(Comprensión)*; and numerous activities *(Actividades)*, both oral and written. The activities range from those that help students acquire new skills and knowledge through practice to those that provide opportunities for them to apply their newly acquired skills in simulated real-life situations. Personalized questions encourage students to relate the material to their own experiences. Many of the activities recommend that students work in pairs or groups.

Color coding

All headings are color-coded. Blue signifies new material, communicative functions, and grammar. Orange signals activities. Green calls attention to the cultural notes.

Application

Following Section C is another section called Try Your Skills. The activities in this section are generally open-ended. They create situations in which students can apply what they have learned, bringing together the communicative functions, grammar, and vocabulary presented in the preceding sections. The Try Your Skills section is essential to the development of proficiency. At the end of the Try Your Skills section there are pronunciation, letter-sound correspondence, and dictation exercises that help students isolate and practice the sounds and spelling of Spanish.

Self-check

A one-page self-check *(¿Lo sabes?)* follows the Try Your Skills section. Here a few key questions and check-up exercises help students assess their achievement of the objectives listed on the opening pages of the unit. You may use the self-check after completing Sections A, B, and C and Try

Your Skills, or you may choose to use the appropriate part of the self-check after completing the corresponding section of the unit.

Vocabulary

On the page opposite the self-check is a list of active vocabulary words (*Vocabulario*) and their English equivalents, grouped by section. Below the list, a word-study exercise (*Estudio de palabras*) focuses attention on the vocabulary list; it gives students practice in developing word-attack skills while expanding their Spanish vocabulary.

Reading

The unit closes with one or more short reading selections (*Vamos a leer*) linked to the theme of the unit. The selections may be in the form of a poem, short story, article, or cartoon. The activities accompanying the reading selections seek to develop reading skills in the foreign language and to encourage critical thinking through open-ended questions.

The basic material, some of the activities, the listening comprehension and pronunciation exercises, and the reading selections of each unit are recorded on the Unit Cassettes.

Organization of Review Units

The three review units (*Unidad de repaso*)—Units 4, 8, and 12—are considerably shorter than the nine instructional units. A review unit presents familiar material in a different context. No new vocabulary, grammar, or communicative functions are presented. Like the Try Your Skills section within an instructional unit, a review unit contains activities that encourage students to combine and apply the skills they acquired in the preceding instructional units. The situations presented in the review unit may differ from those the students encountered previously; using skills in new situations is crucial to developing proficiency. Selected material from the review units is also recorded on the Unit Cassettes.

Teacher's Edition

Annotations

The Teacher's Edition is designed to be of maximum assistance to you. It includes the pages of the Pupil's Edition, fully annotated with background notes, answers to activities, teaching suggestions, and variations.

Teacher's Notes

In addition, special Teacher's Notes—pages tabbed in blue—accompany each unit. For your convenience the Teacher's Notes for each unit are placed immediately before the annotated pupil pages of that unit. The Teacher's Notes address not only each section of the unit but every item within the section. The teaching suggestions are cross-referenced to the corresponding material (A1, A2, etc.) in the pupil pages.

Scope and Sequence chart

The Teacher's Notes begin with a detailed Scope and Sequence chart for the unit that also contains suggestions for the consistent re-entry of previously learned material. Below the chart is a list of the relevant ancillary components of the program and suggested materials that you may wish to prepare or gather. The Teacher's Notes state objectives, provide cultural background, suggest motivating activities, and offer teaching suggestions for all basic material, for the functions, grammar, and culture notes, and for each activity. To help you adapt instruction to meet different learning styles, suggestions are given on how to accommodate slower-paced learning and how to provide a challenge. Also included are suggestions for using cooperative learning and TPR (Total Physical Response) techniques

(see page T7) and for combining the different language skills. The scripts of the listening comprehension exercises and the pronunciation exercises also appear in the Teacher's Notes.

Activity Workbook

The Activity Workbook (*Manual de actividades*) offers additional activities, puzzles, and games that give students practice with communicative functions, vocabulary, and structure in a variety of entertaining and challenging ways. Culturally authentic photographs, art, and realia add an appealing visual dimension. All the exercises and activities are cross-referenced to those in the textbook.

The Teacher's Edition of the Activity Workbook provides you with the answers to the activities, printed in place.

Exercise Workbook

The Exercise Workbook (*Manual de ejercicios*) contains exercises of a more structured nature, all of which are cross-referenced to the textbook. The grammar points taught in the textbook are restated in the Exercise Workbook, where they are followed by extensive practice.

The Teacher's Edition of the Exercise Workbook, like that of the Activity Workbook, contains the answers to the exercises, printed in place.

Testing Program

Student's Test Booklet

Section quizzes

Unit tests

Proficiency-based tests

The Student's Test Booklet has three parts. The first part contains quizzes based on every section of the nine instructional units in the textbook. The second part includes a unit test for each instructional unit, three review tests covering the three Parts of the textbook, a midterm test, and a final exam. Listening comprehension is an integral part of each quiz and test. The third part of the Student's Test Booklet contains three proficiency-based tests that are designed to assess students' levels of proficiency in all four language skills. You may wish to use the first two tests for practice during the second half of the school year and the third proficiency-based test at the end of the year. Although related to the content of the textbook, the proficiency-based tests do not measure students' mastery of specific material. Rather, they present a variety of situations in which students are expected to demonstrate their ability to function in Spanish.

Teacher's Test Guide

Speaking tests

The Teacher's Test Guide consists of several parts. The introduction describes the testing program and offers suggestions on how you may administer and score the quizzes and tests.

Following the introduction are the recording scripts of the listening parts of the quizzes, tests, and proficiency-based tests.

The next section of the Teacher's Test Guide presents speaking tests for each unit in the textbook. Although these tests are optional, you are

urged to administer them at the appropriate times. Suggestions for administering and scoring the speaking tests are given in the introduction to the Teacher's Test Guide.

The answer key to the entire testing program forms the final part of the Teacher's Test Guide.

Test Cassettes

The listening parts of the quizzes, tests, and proficiency-based tests are recorded on cassettes. Included is a recording of an examiner administering the speaking portion of a proficiency-based test to a student; it is intended to serve as a model if you are not familiar with proficiency testing.

Audio Program

Unit Cassettes

For each unit the recordings include the new or basic material, some of the activities, the listening and pronunciation exercises, and the reading selections. The texts of the three photo essays are also recorded. Where appropriate, pauses are provided for student repetition or response. In the textbook, items that are recorded are designated by means of a cassette symbol ▭ . The scripts of the recordings are provided in the Unit Cassette Guide. One of the Unit Cassettes contains several songs; the lyrics are provided in the Teacher's Resource Materials.

Unit Cassette Guide

The Unit Cassette Guide includes the reference index to the Unit Cassettes, the scripts of the Unit Cassettes, and student answer forms for the listening exercises in each unit.

Overhead Transparencies

Copying
masters

A set of overhead transparencies with copying-master duplicates supplements the textbook. The set includes one transparency for each section of the nine instructional units, one for each of the three review units, and three maps. Each transparency depicts a situation that is closely related to the one in the corresponding section of the unit. The transparencies are accompanied by a Planning Guide booklet that offers suggestions on how to use them effectively.

Teaching
suggestions

The transparencies are a valuable teaching aid. Students may be asked to describe what they see and then to imagine themselves in the situation and converse appropriately. Used in this manner, the transparencies serve to involve students in interactive communication. You may wish to use the transparencies in your presentation of basic material. As students learn new vocabulary and communicative functions, transparencies from previous units may be reintroduced to provide additional situations for the practice of the new material. When students view a new transparency, they may be encouraged to re-enter previously learned communicative functions and vocabulary. The copying masters enable you to distribute copies of the transparencies for use in cooperative learning groups, for individual or group writing assignments, and for homework.

Unit Theme Posters

Twelve full-color posters are available. Each poster displays one or more photographs relevant to the theme of the corresponding unit in the textbook. An accompanying guide suggests ways in which you might use the posters. Aside from creating a cultural ambiance in the classroom, they can be an effective teaching aid when you present and review a unit.

Teacher's Resource Materials

The Teacher's Resource Materials booklet contains numerous teaching aids. One section discusses learning and teaching strategies, such as Total Physical Response (TPR), group learning, study hints, and suggestions for

Proficiency practice

planning total immersion experiences. Another provides copying masters for role-playing situations to be used with each review unit. You may reproduce and distribute them to the students to stimulate extemporaneous communication, oral or written.

Vocabulary exercises

Also included in the Teacher's Resource Materials are the vocabulary lists of the nine instructional units with the words regrouped according to their parts of speech. Supplementary vocabulary exercises complement each list. Enrichment vocabulary and useful classroom expressions complete the vocabulary section.

Realia

The booklet contains several pages of realia, authentic documents that you may reproduce for classroom use. In addition, there are suggestions

Games/songs

for classroom games and the lyrics of favorite songs. The music has been recorded on one of the Unit Cassettes. Also included are a pronunciation guide, a glossary of grammar terms, and a listing of additional sources of instructional materials (magazines, films, software, etc.).

Contents of Teacher's Resource Materials booklet

- Learning and Teaching Strategies
- Proficiency Practice Cards
- Realia
- Games
- Songs
- Unit Vocabulary Lists
- Unit Vocabulary Exercises
- Enrichment Vocabulary

- Classroom Expressions
- Pronunciation Guide
- Stress and Accent Marks
- The Spanish Alphabet
- Glossary of Grammar Terms
- References
- Component Correlation Charts
- Answer Forms for Listening Exercises

Using the HBJ Spanish Program

The following procedures and techniques are suggested to meet diverse learning styles and classroom circumstances and to help students achieve communicative competence.

Developing Proficiency in the Four Skills

Listening

From the beginning, students are eager to say things in the foreign language, but they should also hear authentic language, even if they do not grasp the meaning of every word. You will wish to provide an abundance of listening activities.

For this purpose, the textbook is a primary source. The basic material and selected activities in each unit are recorded so that students may hear authentic language spoken by a variety of native speakers. In addition, each section of every unit contains a listening exercise. When playing the recordings in class, consider that students need time to listen to the new material before you ask them to repeat it or apply it.

Listening requires active mental participation. You may want to share these listening strategies with your students: (1) they should listen for key words that tell what the situation is about; (2) they should not feel that they must understand every word; (3) they should make guesses and verify their hunches by repeated listening.

The TPR (Total Physical Response) technique is an effective means of developing proficiency in listening. TPR is a physical response to an oral stimulus. Students listen to instructions or commands and give nonverbal responses according to their comprehension of the message. These responses may include moving about the classroom, interacting silently with classmates, drawing, or arranging pictures in sequence. Some activities in the student textbook call for TPR responses. Suggestions for applying the TPR technique to other activities are given in the Teacher's Edition.

By minimizing the use of English in the classroom from the beginning, you provide more opportunity for students to hear the foreign language. You may want to make a practice of relating personal experiences and local or world happenings to the students in the foreign language. Students will pick up a great deal of this "incidental" language.

Side notes:
Authentic input

Listening strategies

TPR (Total Physical Response)

Speaking

Students want most to be able to speak the foreign language they are studying. Keep in mind that the speaking skill is the most fragile; it takes careful nurturing and encouraging, uninhibited by rigid standards. It is more important to encourage fluency first; accuracy will follow.

Each of the units in the textbook focuses on the speaking skill. The majority of the activities are designed to lead to interaction and communication among students. Managed properly, these activities will provide the optimum speaking experiences for the students. The use of various grouping techniques will facilitate this procedure (see page T13).

The development of the speaking skill follows this pattern: (1) repeating after adequate listening; (2) responding, using words and expressions of the lesson (up to this point no degree of proficiency should be expected); (3) manipulating learned material and recombining parts; (4) using what was previously learned in a new context.

When students use a previously learned expression spontaneously in a simulated situation as a natural thing to say at that time, they are truly beginning to speak the language. Students must be engaged in the application phase in order to develop proficiency beyond the novice level. Application activities are found particularly in the Try Your Skills section of each unit and in each review unit.

Side notes:
Interactive communication

Developing speaking proficiency

Reading

It is appropriate for students to read material they have been practicing, but they should also develop their reading skills using unfamiliar material. Require students to skim, scan, draw inferences, determine the main

idea, and so forth. They should begin their reading by extracting the general ideas before they approach the details of a reading selection. The aim should be global comprehension in reading just as in listening.

You may help students approach reading selections through prereading strategies. Key words or expressions that might cause difficulty may be clarified, preferably in the foreign language. Students may be encouraged to examine the title and illustrations of a reading selection in search of clues to its meaning. You may elicit students' background knowledge of the subject of the reading through preliminary discussion; comprehension is definitely influenced by the prior information that students bring to a reading selection.

Also consider conducting directed reading lessons, requiring students to read selected passages silently with a purpose: to find answers to questions; to find reasons for actions and events; to find descriptions of characters. Students may be asked to write down all they recall of the content of a passage they have just read silently. In the follow-up lesson, you will wish not only to inquire about the who, what, and where of the content, but also to encourage critical thinking by asking why.

The TPR technique may be used to develop reading proficiency as well as listening proficiency. In the case of reading, students are expected to respond nonverbally to directions they have read.

Writing

The development of the writing skill is analogous to that of the speaking skill. Although the first stage may consist of copying, learning to spell, filling in the blanks, and writing from dictation, this training does not constitute writing. Writing is transferring thoughts to paper. Hence, students should progress from directed writing to more creative expression. To this end, a variety of controlled and open-ended writing activities appear in the textbook. The Teacher's Notes identify other activities suitable for writing practice and suggest additional writing activities.

Communicative Functions

When people communicate with each other—either orally or in writing—they use language for a specific purpose: to describe, persuade, argue, express emotions and opinions, praise, complain, agree, and so on. The term "communicative functions." or simply "functions," is used to refer to these purposes for which people communicate.

In the HBJ Spanish Program, the objectives of each instructional unit are phrased as communicative functions. They are clearly stated on the unit opener and are repeated on the section openers so that students can readily see the purpose for learning the language. Within the sections, the communicative functions are presented in new, or basic, material in a culturally authentic situation of interest to young people.

New (Basic) Material

Each section of an instructional unit opens with the presentation of basic material. In some sections there may be more than one piece of new material. The basic material may take different forms; it may be a dialog, an

interview, a monolog, or a narrative. Its purpose is to introduce the expressions, grammar, and vocabulary necessary to the communicative function(s) to be learned in the section. Previously learned functions may reappear in the basic material where appropriate. Also, in any basic material there will necessarily appear new functions besides those to be practiced in the section. Another purpose of the basic material is to provide cultural information, either directly or indirectly.

Before introducing any basic material, consult the list of communicative functions in the Scope and Sequence chart in the Teacher's Notes for that unit. The new material should be presented in ways that emphasize these communicative functions.

Students should approach basic material with these questions in mind, "What is the communicative purpose of the native speakers in the particular situation, and how are they using their language to accomplish it?" Students should not be required to memorize the basic material. The dialogs and narratives in the textbook are only samples of what a particular speaker of Spanish might say in a given situation; they should not be taught as fixed and rigid sentences. The aim should be to transfer the communicative functions from the basic material to other situations. Students should use the language functions to communicate naturally and spontaneously in real situations.

To help students, the communicative function is restated and the expressions necessary to achieve it are grouped together under the heading *Se dice así*. As the title suggests, this is how you say it, how you accomplish the communicative purpose or function. The expressions listed are primarily those introduced in the basic material. There may also be expressions from previous units that are appropriate to the communicative function; expressions that are learned to carry out one function may also be applied to carry out others. *Se dice así*, then, is a statement of a communicative function and the expressions to accomplish it.

After students have read the basic material and done the related activities, direct their attention to the expressions in *Se dice así*. You might make some statements in Spanish and have students choose appropriate responses from the expressions listed. Or, you might have students suggest ways to use Spanish to elicit the expressions from classmates.

The activities that follow *Se dice así* give students opportunities to carry out the intended communicative function by applying the expressions in real-life situations.

You will find detailed suggestions on how to present basic material and *Se dice así* in the Teacher's Notes preceding each unit. All basic material is recorded on the Unit Cassettes.

Activities

**Practice/
application**

The heading *Actividad* identifies the exercises in the textbook. There are two basic types of activities: (1) those that reinforce learning of the new material through practice and (2) those that require students to apply what they have learned.

The activities that follow the basic material are arranged in a planned progression from practice to application of the communicative functions, grammar, and vocabulary. Try Your Skills sections and review units contain only activities of the application type. Many application activities

are designed to have the students converse in pairs or groups in order to foster communication and encourage creative expression.

The activities in the textbook may take many different forms. Those that relate to the basic material include questionnaires, sentence completions, true and false statements, identifications, and the sequencing of events. Personalized questions encourage students to relate the basic material to their own experiences. (Be careful to respect the privacy of individuals.) Grammar explanations are followed by practice exercises. Then, since the grammar is meant to support the communicative function(s), additional activities lead students to use the grammar in communicative situations.

Writing

Writing activities of two kinds appear throughout the textbook. Controlled exercises provide practice in writing the forms and structures of the language. Others provide opportunities for creative written expression. For further writing practice, many of the oral activities may be assigned to be written.

Listening

One or more listening comprehension activities, identified by the heading *Comprensión* appear in each instructional section of a unit. These listening exercises are recorded on the Unit Cassettes, and student answer forms for them are located in both the Unit Cassette Guide and the Teacher's Resource Materials booklet. The scripts of the listening exercises are reproduced in the Teacher's Notes preceding each unit in the Teacher's Edition, as well as in the Unit Cassette Guide.

Optional activities

A few activities have been identified in the Teacher's Notes as optional. Usually found at the end of a section, these activities are intended to enrich vocabulary. You may choose to use them or not, as time permits.

Pronunciation

In each instructional unit, at the end of the Try Your Skills section, you will find a pronunciation exercise. This exercise, called *Pronunciación, lectura y dictado,* is designed to teach the most difficult sounds of Spanish. The sounds are presented first in a listening-speaking exercise that gives the students practice in saying them. Then a letter-sound correspondence exercise provides practice in reading the symbols that represent the sounds. Finally, sentences to be written from dictation afford practice in transcribing the sounds. These exercises are recorded on the Unit Cassettes; the scripts are located in the Teacher's Notes preceding each unit in the Teacher's Edition and in the Unit Cassette Guide.

Recordings

This cassette symbol ⬚ signals the activities that are recorded on the Unit Cassettes. Frequently, activities have been modified to adapt them for recording. You will find that a communicative activity in the textbook may be more structured when recorded. For this reason, you will want to consult the scripts in the Unit Cassette Guide before you play the cassettes. In certain circumstances, you may wish to play the recorded version of an activity first and then have the students perform the activity as it was intended for the classroom.

Answers to all activities are indicated (in blue) in the annotated pupil pages of the Teacher's Edition.

Grammar

In each section of every unit except the review units, the main grammar points relating to the functional objectives of the unit are summarized.

Grammar may be approached inductively or deductively, depending on

the nature of the item and on student learning styles. Younger students, in general, respond favorably to an inductive approach that leads them to draw conclusions about the forms they have been practicing and applying.

On the other hand, because of the relative complexity of some structures, there may be a need to explain them before the students practice and apply them. In this case, the deductive approach may be more effective. You will want to determine which approach is more suitable.

Grammar and proficiency

Regardless of the approach, it is important to remember that in the development of proficiency, grammar is a means and not an end. Only the grammar that is relevant to the communicative function is necessary.

Vocabulary

Vocabulary and proficiency

As in the case of grammar, consider the extent to which the amount and type of vocabulary presented serves the communicative purpose at hand. The introduction of excessive or irrelevant vocabulary, however interesting, may only complicate the task. The goal is to use vocabulary to communicate. Like grammar, vocabulary is a means, not an end.

Vocabulary is presented in context and listed at the end of each unit. A word-study activity following the list helps students understand and remember the vocabulary by pointing out word families, relationships, derivations, and so on.

You may use word games, puzzles, and mnemonic aids to teach vocabulary. An effective motivational practice is to have students devise their own games, puzzles, illustrative posters, and picture dictionaries to be used by their classmates.

Culture

Cultural expression

We hope to instill cultural awareness by exposing students to different kinds of cultural expression—authentic written and spoken language, a rich collection of photographs showing a cross-section of people and places, an abundance of realia, and special culture notes in English. We want students to get to know what Spanish-speaking young people are like and to develop a feel for the everyday life in the foreign culture.

Throughout this Teacher's Edition we have noted additional cultural points that may interest you and your students or that clarify situations depicted in the units. The Teacher's Notes preceding each unit provide additional background information on the unit themes. You may want to consult these pages as you prepare to introduce each unit. Include in your teaching as much of this information as you find helpful.

Photo essays

Sources for cultural awareness are present on almost every page of the textbook. They are especially concentrated, however, in the photo essays that follow every review unit. To help you in presenting the photo essays, we have included background information on the various topics and some details about specific photographs in the Teacher's Notes preceding the review units.

Projects

Encourage your students to personalize the Spanish-speaking cultures as they study and practice the themes and vocabulary of the units. Suggestions for projects are given in the units and in the Teacher's Notes; assign

as many projects as possible. In doing projects, students not only practice their skills, but they also share in an experience that helps them learn about the particular country's culture in a direct and personal way.

You can enhance students' cultural awareness and appreciation by utilizing community resources and, if possible, by taking school trips to regions or countries where the foreign language is spoken.

Review

Frequent feedback is essential to assess your students' progress toward proficiency and their need for review. The quizzes based on each section of a unit are one means of assessment. They are short and are best checked immediately during the same class period.

The textbook itself is structured to ensure adequate review. The self-check (*¿Lo sabes?*) and the Try Your Skills section at the end of each unit, as well as the three review units, provide opportunities for students to review and recombine previously presented material.

In addition, you will want to make a practice of systematically re-entering material from previous units, especially during warm-up activities at the beginning of a class period. You will find suggestions for the re-entry of previously learned material in the Scope and Sequence chart in the Teacher's Notes preceding each instructional unit.

Testing and Evaluation

Evaluation is an ongoing process. Informal assessment should take place in the classroom on an almost daily basis, whether by observing students during their group work or by engaging individuals or groups briefly in conversation. The section quizzes and the unit tests in the Student's Test Booklet provide a formal check on progress in the areas of listening, reading, and writing. You may wish to administer a short speaking test after each unit. To save you preparation time, speaking tests are supplied in the Teacher's Test Guide.

Unlike achievement, which is the realization of the immediate objectives of a lesson, proficiency develops slowly. Therefore, assessments of proficiency should be made less frequently. Proficiency-based tests are a vital part of this program. There are two practice tests and a final test. Meant to be given during the second half of the year, they require students to demonstrate their abilities in all four language skills in situations beyond—but not completely unrelated to—the textbook.

Suggestions for Classroom Management

Classroom Climate

As you know, students are more enthusiastic and responsive in a friendly, nonthreatening atmosphere of mutual respect that fosters self-confidence. A tense atmosphere may inhibit the spontaneous use of the foreign language which is so necessary to the development of proficiency.

You may wish to consider the importance of organization and keeping students on task. Ground rules for classroom procedures will help you

create an effective environment for learning. These procedures should include an explanation of how English is to be used and the distribution of a list of classroom expressions in Spanish that students will gradually begin to use with confidence.

Another—but not the least—consideration is the positive effect of a classroom decorated with posters, maps, pictures, realia, and students' papers and projects.

English in the Classroom

The use of the foreign language in the classroom is basic to helping students develop listening proficiency. Students should become accustomed to hearing classroom directions in the foreign language. You will find lists of classroom expressions in Spanish on page 28 of the Pupil's Edition and in the vocabulary section of the Teacher's Resource Materials.

It is natural for students to ask for explanations and want to make comments in English. You may wish to set aside a short segment of time at the end of a class period for clarifications in English.

Classroom Strategies

Two fundamental approaches to classroom instruction can be described as teacher-centered and student-centered. Both have a place in the foreign language classroom. In either approach the student is the primary focus.

A teacher-centered approach is most effective in the learning phase. You may wish to use this approach for directed teaching activities, such as presenting new material and conducting drills and question/answer sessions. Consider using various student-centered activities, such as simulated social situations and conversations, in the application phase to develop the independence that eventually leads to proficiency beyond the novice stage.

Grouping

Grouping maximizes opportunities for interaction among students in life-like situations. It is an especially useful strategy in classes that have combined levels of students with varied learning styles and abilities.

Cooperative learning

Cooperative learning is one way in which students and teachers can achieve learning goals. In cooperative learning, small groups of students collaborate to achieve a common goal. There are four basic benefits of a cooperative learning group: (1) positive interdependence; (2) face-to-face interaction; (3) individual accountability; (4) appropriate use of interpersonal skills. Following are some suggestions for structuring cooperative learning activities.

Forming cooperative learning groups

1. Be sure the task is clear to everyone.
2. Set a time limit. Completion of the task and reporting to the class should take place during the class period.
3. Circulate among the students and assist them as needed.
4. Assign specific tasks to each group member.
5. Clarify any limitations of movement during the activity.
6. Select the group size most suited to the activity. Pairs are appropriate for many activities.

7. Assign students to groups. Heterogeneous groups are more desirable. Groups should not be permanent.
8. Evaluate the group's task when completed and discuss with the group the interaction of the members.

Many activities in the textbook lend themselves to cooperative learning.

Providing for Different Learning Styles

Different students learn best in different ways. Some learn new material most easily when they are allowed to listen to it and repeat it. Others do best when they see it in writing. Still others respond best to visual experiences—photographs, drawings, overhead transparencies. And some students need to be involved physically or emotionally with the material they are learning and to respond concretely and personally. Moreover, all students need variety in the learning experience; the same student may respond differently on different days.

Slower-paced learning

Slower-paced learning requires that you present and adapt materials differently than you do when a greater challenge is called for. The Teacher's Notes that precede each unit contain numerous suggestions for teaching strategies to be used in a slower-paced learning environment and in a challenge situation.

Challenge

In general, you may wish to consider strategies for slower-paced learning that involve breaking down an activity into smaller tasks and then rebuilding it gradually. Accept short answers and elicit passive, non-linguistic responses more often. On the other hand, when you deal with students who need a greater challenge, consider expanding activities and adding new twists that require critical thinking and creativity.

Forming heterogeneous cooperative learning groups and pairing students of different abilities can be effective means of assisting all students, both academically and socially.

Homework

Differentiated assignments

Homework that reinforces and enriches class work should be an integral part of instruction. You may want to consider giving differentiated homework assignments to suit the varied needs of students instead of issuing identical assignments to all. For this purpose, the Activity Workbook and the Exercise Workbook provide numerous exercises of various types that are designed to meet different learning styles.

Homework should be collected and checked; otherwise students will not respect the practice. You may devise a system for students to check their own homework, but you must take care to avoid spending an entire class period checking homework. Long-term homework projects as well as short-term assignments are effective.

Use of Audio-Visual Materials

Audio-visual components

Students need to hear a variety of voices speaking Spanish. The Unit Cassettes provide an auditory program to develop listening proficiency.

Students also need to see authentic representations of the foreign culture. The photographs in the textbook—in each unit and in the photo

essays—can be used to motivate students before they launch into new material and also to increase cultural awareness. In addition, the unit theme posters and the transparencies related to each section of a unit depict culturally authentic situations.

Additional materials

You may want to use an overhead projector with a transparency instead of writing on the board to focus students' attention more directly. Where the facilities exist, students may create their own skits based on the units and record them on a videocassette for classroom viewing. Showing rented films, displaying posters, and sharing realia are other means you may consider to add a visual dimension to classroom instruction.

Planning

Pacing

Controlling the pace

It is helpful to devise a schedule of instruction for the year. Planning ahead is essential to setting the pace most appropriate for your classroom. The textbook is designed to be completed in one school year. Where needed, you can control the time spent on each unit by including or omitting optional exercises, by reading all or only one of the reading selections at the end of the unit, by doing some or all of the activities in the review unit, by insisting on total mastery of material before progressing or relying on the cumulative acquisition of the language.

Unit planning

Your schedule will vary according to the grade and ability level of your students and the number of interruptions in your school program. In general, an instructional unit can be taught in three weeks; in some cases an additional day may be needed for the unit test. A review unit will take one week, including the review test. Sufficient time should remain for discussing the cultural notes and photo essays, administering midterm, final tests, and proficiency-based tests, and conducting optional enrichment activities.

Lesson Plans

You will probably want to prepare a daily lesson plan that incorporates various language skills. Plans may vary, but the basic lesson should include the following to some degree, at least over a span of two days.

Planning sequence

- A warm-up activity, usually involving review
- A quiz or test when appropriate
- The presentation of new material preceded by a motivating activity and a statement of objectives
- Developmental activities and guided practice
- Application by the students of what they have learned
- Summarizing statements, preferably elicited from the students
- Closure (review with students what they have learned)
- Assignment, planning ahead, or previewing the next lesson
- Periodic long-range planning with the students

Unit Planning Guide

The following plan suggests how the material in Unit 2 may be distributed over fifteen days. You may wish to prepare similar lesson plans, adjusting them to suit the needs and interests of your students. For a faster pace, the exercises in parentheses might be assigned as homework or omitted.

	Daily Plans	Unit Resources

Day 1	Objective: To talk about how you come to school
	  Unit opener: discussion
	  Section A: motivating activity
	  Basic material A1
	  Actividades A2, A3
	  Comprensión A4
	  Estructuras esenciales A5
	  Actividades A6, A7
	  ¿Sabes que . . . ? A9
	  Assign Actividad A8
		Unit 2 Poster
		Overhead Transparency 4
		Unit 2 Cassette
		Activity Workbook
		Exercise Workbook

Day 2	Objective: To ask for and give an explanation
	  Se dice así A10
	  Estructuras esenciales A12
	  Actividades A11, A13
	  Comprensión A13
	  Actividades A15, A16
	  Assign review of Section A
		Unit 2 Cassette
		Activity Workbook
		Exercise Workbook
		Overhead Transparency 4

Day 3	Objective: To talk about school subjects
	  Quiz on Section A
	  Section B: motivating activity
	  Basic material B1
	  Actividad B2
	  ¿Sabes que . . . ? B3
	  Estructuras esenciales B4
	  Actividades B5, B6, (B7)
		Quiz 4
		Overhead Transparency 5
		Unit 2 Cassette
		Activity Workbook
		Exercise Workbook

Day 4	Objective: To talk about school subjects, giving days of the week
	  Basic material B8
	  Actividad B9
	  Estructuras esenciales B10
	  Actividades B11, B12
	  Estructuras esenciales B13
	  Actividades B14, B15, B16, B17, (B18)
		Unit 2 Cassette
		Activity Workbook
		Exercise Workbook

Day 5	Objective: To talk about your school schedule, giving times
	  Estructuras esenciales B19
	  Actividad B20
	  Comprensión B21
	  Actividades B22, (B23), B24
	  Basic material B25
	  Actividades B26, B27
		Unit 2 Cassette
		Activity Workbook
		Exercise Workbook

	Daily Plans	Unit Resources

Day 6	Objective: To say how you feel about school subjects
	    Se dice así B28
	    Actividades B29, (B30), (B31)
	    ¿Sabes que . . . ? B32
	    Comprensión B33
	    Actividades B34, B35
	    Assign review of Section B
		Unit 2 Cassette
		Activity Workbook
		Exercise Workbook
		Overhead Transparency

Day 7	Objective: To say what you need for school
	    Quiz on Section B
	    Section C: motivating activity
	    Basic material C1
	    Actividad C2
	    Estructuras esenciales C3
	    Actividades C4, C6
	    Comprensión C5
		Quiz 5
		Overhead Transparency 6
		Unit 2 Cassette
		Activity Workbook
		Exercise Workbook

Day 8	Objective: To buy what you need for school
	    Basic material C7
	    Se dice así C8
	    Actividades C9, C10
	    Estructuras esenciales C11
	    Actividad C12
	    ¿Sabes que . . . ? C13
		Unit 2 Cassette
		Activity Workbook
		Exercise Workbook

Day 9	Objective: To buy what you need for school
	    Basic material C14
	    Estructuras esenciales C16
	    Actividades C15, C17, C18
		Unit 2 Cassette
		Activity Workbook
		Exercise Workbook

Day 10	Objective: To buy what you need for school
	    Actividades C19, C20, C21
	    Comprensión C22
	    (Actividad C23)
	    Assign review of Section C
		Unit 2 Cassette
		Activity Workbook
		Exercise Workbook
		Overhead Transparency 6

Day 11	Objective: To use what you've learned
	    Quiz on Section C
	    Basic material Try Your Skills 1
	    Actividad 2
		Quiz 6
		Unit 2 Cassette
		Activity Workbook

Day 12	Objective: To use what you've learned Actividades 3, 4, (5), 6	Unit 2 Cassettes Activity Workbook

Day 13	Objective: To prepare for Unit 2 Test
	    ¿Lo sabes?
	    Vocabulario
	    Estudio de palabras
		Activity Workbook
		Exercise Workbook
		Overhead Transparencies
		    4, 5, 6
		Unit 2 Poster

Day 14	Objective: To assess progress Unit 2 Test	Unit 2 Test

	Daily Plans	**Unit Resources**
Day 15	Objective: To read for practice and pleasure Vamos a leer: Libros para la escuela, ¡Socorro!, El regalo Actividades (Choice of other reading selections)	Unit 2 Cassette

Beyond the Classroom

In School

A vibrant foreign language program extends outside the classroom to other disciplines, the entire school, the community, and beyond.

Relating to other disciplines

By its very nature, the study of foreign languages is interdisciplinary. You may wish to consider cooperating with social studies teachers to promote global education. Since you deal with the art, music, and literature of the foreign culture, you complement the work of the art, music, and English teachers. Foreign language study raises students' level of general linguistic awareness, thereby reinforcing their work in English language arts. Learning about sports in other countries may increase the enthusiasm for sports among your students.

Foreign language classes should have an impact on the total school environment. You may have the students label areas of the building and prepare public address announcements in the foreign language. Staging assemblies, participating in school fairs, and celebrating foreign festivals schoolwide are other ways to provide students with opportunities to use their knowledge and skills outside the classroom, particularly during National Foreign Language Week in March.

Outside School

Your efforts to heighten enthusiasm for foreign language study might reach out into the community through field trips to ethnic restaurants, museums, embassies, and local areas where the foreign language is spoken. Encourage your students to present special foreign language programs in nursing homes and hospitals. If you receive radio and television programs in Spanish, or if foreign movies are shown in your region, you will want your students to take advantage of them to improve their language skills as well as their cultural awareness.

The ultimate extension of foreign language study is a trip to or a stay in a country where the language is spoken. Working with school authorities, you may be able to arrange trips abroad for your students.

Total immersion

However, a total foreign language experience need not require travel outside the area. For a day, a weekend, or a longer period during a school vacation, the foreign culture can be recreated at the school, at a camp, or at a university to provide a total immersion experience. This

activity requires detailed planning and preparation. Suggestions for planning total immersion experiences are presented in the Teacher's Resource Materials.

Whatever the nature of the endeavor to extend foreign language study beyond the classroom, you will need to develop guidelines with the students in addition to any school rules governing such activities. Adherence to an organized plan results in a more productive experience.

Career Awareness

For many students, foreign language study will form the basis of their life's work or enhance it.

Career awareness activities can be a strong motivating force to learn a foreign language. Students should be made aware of the types of professions and occupations prevailing in the foreign culture and those in their own culture that either depend on foreign language skills or are enhanced by such skills. The Introduction to the Pupil's Edition is a good place to start. It contains segments and activities dealing with career awareness.

You may want to collaborate with guidance counselors in your school to provide up-to-date information concerning career opportunities related to foreign languages. Many schools have career fairs in which you might consider participating.

Conclusion

Many teachers have found the following guidelines practical in planning their foreign language courses. You, too, may find them useful.

- Establish a positive climate.
- Have a classroom decor that reflects the foreign culture.
- Establish a fair-but-firm policy for classroom management.
- Take student interests into consideration when planning.
- Have a written plan.
- Discuss objectives with the students.
- Provide for varied learning styles and rates.
- Avoid lecturing.
- Maximize student involvement.
- Provide positive verbal and nonverbal feedback.
- Evaluate class procedures and outcomes with the students.

The aim of proficiency-oriented instruction is not that students learn language lessons. Rather, the goal is to encourage and guide students to use what they have learned in new situations. Without this application phase in the instructional procedure, proficiency will not be achieved. Therein lies the challenge to the foreign language teacher. We wish you much success in this exciting undertaking.

Specific suggestions for teaching each unit appear in the blue-tabbed pages preceding the unit. Additional suggestions and answers to activities are provided in the annotated pupil pages.

Nuevos amigos

Foreign Language Programs

SPANISH

- **Nuevos amigos**
  Level 1

- **Nosotros, los jóvenes**
  Level 2

- **Nuestro mundo**
  Level 3

Nuevos amigos

HBJ HARCOURT BRACE JOVANOVICH, PUBLISHERS
Orlando   San Diego   Chicago   Dallas

Printed in the United States of America
ISBN 0-15-388300-6

PHOTO CREDITS   Key: (t) top, (b) bottom, (l) left, (r) right, (c) center
COVER: HBJ Photo/Peter Menzel
TABLE OF CONTENTS, page vi(t), HBJ Photo/Bob Daemmrich; vi(tc), HBJ Photo/David Phillips; vi(cl), HBJ Photo/Daniel Aubry; vi(c), HBJ Photo; vi(cr), HBJ Photo/David

Continued on page 392

iv

Writers

José B. Fernández
University of Central Florida
Orlando, FL

Nancy Ann Humbach
Finneytown High School
Cincinnatti, OH

María J. Cazabon
Florida International University
Miami, FL

Douglas Morgenstern
Massachusetts Institute of Technology
Cambridge, MA

Editorial Advisors

Robert L. Baker
Middlebury College
Middlebury, VT

Pat Barr-Harrison
Prince George's County Public
   Schools
Landover, MD

Ann Beusch
Hood College
Frederick, MD

Nunzio D. Cazzetta
Smithtown High School West
Smithtown, NY

Charles R. Hancock
Ohio State University
Columbus, OH

William Jassey
Norwalk Board of Education
Norwalk, CT

Dora Kennedy
Prince George's County
   Schools
Landover, MD

Ilonka Schmidt Mackey
Université Laval
Québec, Canada

Jack Thayer
Rolling Hills High School
Rolling Hills Estates, CA

Eduardo Zayas-Bazán
East Tennessee State
   University
Johnson City, TN

Consultants and Reviewers

Gladys Acosta Toia
Edison High School
Fairfax, VA

Nicholas Aversa
Great Neck Middle School
   South
Great Neck, NY

Larraine Gandolfi
Lincoln Sudbury Regional
   High School
Sudbury, MA

Carola Lago
Robert E. Lee High School
Springfield, VA

Adriana M. Mills
Klein High School
Klein, TX

Henry Shatz
Smithtown High School East
St. James, NY

Fern Weiland
Rockville, MD

Henry P. Ziegler
Princeton High School
Cincinnati, OH

Field Test Teachers

Phoebe Ruiz-Badeer
Accompsett Intermediate
   School
Smithtown, NY

Lynn Belardo
Roton Middle School
Norwalk, CT

William Miles
Good Counsel High School
Wheaton, MD

Jo-Ann Sbrizzi
Brian McMahon High School
South Norwalk, CT

Lorna K. Shapiro
Bartram Motivation Center
Philadelphia, PA

Greg Schepanski
Smithtown High School East
St. James, NY

Clifford Taggart
The Gilman School, Inc.
Baltimore, MD

Bonnie Walters
Frederick High School
Frederick, MD

Matilde Yorkshire
Staten Island Academy
Staten Island, NY

ACKNOWLEDGMENTS

We wish to express our thanks to the students pictured in this textbook and to the parents who allowed us to photograph these young people in their homes and in other places. We also thank the teachers and the families who helped us find these young people; the school administrators who allowed us to photograph the students in their schools; and the merchants who permitted us to photograph the students in their stores and other places of business.

YOUNG PEOPLE
María Aguila, Elizabeth Alejo, Samuel Fontaner, Domingo García, Mabel Greve, Manuel Hernández, Faby Herrera, Carla Herrera, Nathan Hughes, José Limón, Ernesto López, Gustavo Martínez, Germán Mastrángelo, José Luis Mayo, Alicia Mitterer, Julio Morales, Robin Schmidt, Elaine Vazquez, Peter Villa, Claudia Villegas, Gerardo Zendejas, Mauricio Zendejas, Xochitl Zendejas

TEACHERS AND FAMILIES
Nilsa Acevedo, Consuelo Bonilla, María Evelyn Borrero, Clara Fontaner, Erika Hampton, Nancy Limón, María Morales, Juanita Velázquez, Norma Villegas, Marta y Javier Zendejas

CONTENTS

INTRODUCTION
Spanish and You 1

PRIMERA PARTE

UNIDAD 1
¡Hola, amigos! 30

COMMUNICATIVE FUNCTIONS	GRAMMAR	CULTURE
Socializing • Asking how someone is • Saying how you are • Saying hello and goodbye	Spanish equivalents for the word you **(tú, usted)**	Greeting and meeting people
Exchanging information • Asking and giving names • Asking and giving someone else's name	Gender of nouns and the definite article	Common Spanish first names Spanish nicknames
Exchanging information • Asking and saying where people are from	Subject pronouns and the verb **ser** Interrogative sentences	Map of the Spanish-speaking world Spanish-speaking population
Recombining communicative functions, vocabulary, and grammar		Writing postcards in Spanish to a pen pal
Reading for practice and pleasure		Places throughout the world where Spanish is spoken

COMMUNICATIVE FUNCTIONS	GRAMMAR	CULTURE
Exchanging information • Asking for and giving an explanation	The verb **venir** Two uses of **no**	How students get to school in Spanish-speaking countries
Expressing attitudes and points of view • Asking about classes and giving your opinion	Numbers from 0 to 20 The days of the week The verb **tener** Telling time	The school system in the Spanish-speaking countries Grading system in the Spanish-speaking world
Exchanging information • Asking how much something costs and giving the price	Forming plurals Definite and indefinite articles Numbers from 21 to 100	Classroom practices in the Spanish-speaking world
Recombining communicative functions, vocabulary, and grammar		A Spanish-speaking student's appointment book A report card from Venezuela
Reading for practice and pleasure		Textbooks in Spanish What young people like to read

 VIÑETA CULTURAL 1: Pueblos y ciudades 125

COMMUNICATIVE FUNCTIONS	GRAMMAR	CULTURE
Expressing feelings and emotion • Talking about what you and others like and don't like	The verb **gustar**	Popular sports in Spanish-speaking countries
Exchanging information • Expressing what you need in order to do something	The present tense of **-ar** verbs The verb **jugar**	World Cup soccer championships
Exchanging information • Saying when and how often you play • Talking about the seasons and the weather	Word order The verb **hacer** in weather expressions	Seasons in the world's two hemispheres
Recombining communicative functions, vocabulary, and grammar		Students talk about their likes and dislikes concerning sports and pastimes
Reading for practice and pleasure		A Spanish television broadcast of a New York marathon
Reviewing communicative functions, vocabulary, and grammar		Leisure activities in Colombia

SEGUNDA PARTE

BASIC MATERIAL

COMMUNICATIVE FUNCTIONS	GRAMMAR	CULTURE
Exchanging information • Asking and saying where something is • Asking and giving directions	Possessive adjectives The verb **estar** The contraction **del**	Airports in Spanish-speaking countries
Exchanging information • Asking and saying where people are going **Socializing** • Answering the telephone, calling someone	The verb **ir** The contraction **al**	Notes on Spanish history Tourism in Spain Talking on the telephone
Exchanging information • Asking and saying the purpose of an action **Persuading** • Making suggestions	Verb endings in **-er** and **-ir**	Barajas Airport in Madrid The city of León
Recombining communicative functions, vocabulary, and grammar		A visit from Mexican friends
Reading for practice and pleasure		Six major cities in Spain

COMMUNICATIVE FUNCTIONS	GRAMMAR	CULTURE
Socializing • Making someone feel at home • Graciously accepting hospitality	The verb **querer**	Being a guest in a Spanish-speaking home Family life in Spanish-speaking homes
Exchanging information • Talking about age • Describing people and family relationships • Asking what someone or something is like **Expressing feelings and emotion** • Exclaiming	Descriptive adjectives: position and agreement	Spanish surnames The family in the Spanish-speaking world
Expressing attitudes and points of view • Asking for opinions and paying compliments	More possessive adjectives	Inside a Spanish-speaking home Houses in Spanish-speaking countries
Recombining communicative functions, vocabulary, and grammar		A family gathering in Mexico
Reading for practice and pleasure		Real estate ads in Spanish

COMMUNICATIVE FUNCTIONS	GRAMMAR	CULTURE
Socializing • Accepting and turning down invitations • Expressing regret **Expressing obligation** • Using **tener que**	The verb **poder** The verbs **salir** and **decir**	Where Spanish-speaking students go and what they do when going out
Expressing attitudes and points of view • Expressing intention • Expressing opinions **Persuading** • Making suggestions	Expressing future time Adjectives, adjective phrases, and deletion of nouns The verbs **pensar** and **empezar**	Going to the movies Film festival in Mar del Plata
Socializing • Getting someone's attention; interrupting politely • Asking information	The verb **saber** Direct objects and the personal **a** The verb **conocer**	Pop music concerts in Buenos Aires
Recombining communicative functions, vocabulary, and grammar		Writing an article for a Spanish magazine
Reading for practice and pleasure		Movie ads in a Spanish newspaper
Reviewing communicative functions, vocabulary, and grammar		A visitor from Costa Rica A letter from Costa Rica

TERCERA PARTE

BASIC MATERIAL

COMMUNICATIVE FUNCTIONS	GRAMMAR	CULTURE
Expressing attitudes and points of view • Saying what you like and don't like	The verb **gustar**	Eating at a restaurant Getting together at a cafe Different dishes served in Spanish-speaking countries
Expressing attitudes and points of view • Talking about food • Selecting what you like	The verb **hacer** Demonstrative adjectives	The metric system Two dishes with the same name
Expressing attitudes and points of view • Talking about whether people are hungry or thirsty • Expressing your enjoyment of food	The verb **poner**	The history of chocolate
Recombining communicative functions, vocabulary, and grammar		Where to go with your friends before the movies
Reading for practice and pleasure		A recipe for a Spanish dish

COMMUNICATIVE FUNCTIONS	GRAMMAR	CULTURE
Exchanging information • Saying what you usually do • Saying what you did at a specified time in the past • Expressing how long ago something happened	The preterit of regular **-ar** verbs	Spain's capital city Spain's second largest city
Exchanging information • Asking for information about something that happened in the past	The preterit of **hacer** The preterit of **ir**	Madrid's attractions
Exchanging information • Discussing whether or not something has already been done	Direct-object pronouns	A trip to Granada The Moorish legacy Two famous landmarks in Madrid
Recombining communicative functions, vocabulary, and grammar		Postcards from Madrid
Reading for practice and pleasure		A Spanish travel brochure

	BASIC MATERIAL

COMMUNICATIVE FUNCTIONS	GRAMMAR	CULTURE
Exchanging information • Talking about differences in quality and price • Asking and saying what something is made of **Expressing attitudes and points of view** • Asking and expressing opinions	Comparisons with **más** and **menos** Demonstrative pronouns	Shopping in Mexico City Conversion table of clothing sizes
Exchanging information • Discussing prices; striking a bargain	Indirect objects Numbers from 100 to 1,000	Street vendors in Spanish-speaking cities Where to find a bargain in Mexico City
Exchanging information • Saying what you did and what you are going to do	The preterit of **-er** and **-ir** verbs	Customer service in a store
Recombining communicative functions, vocabulary, and grammar		Shopping in Spanish
Reading for practice and pleasure		Finding a bargain in Mexico City
Reviewing communicative functions, vocabulary, and grammar		The Museum of Anthropology in Mexico City Chapultepec Park in Mexico City

FOR REFERENCE

MAPS

¡BIENVENIDOS!

Some of us are fortunate to be able to learn a new language by living in another country, but most of us are not. We begin learning the language and getting acquainted with a foreign culture in a classroom with the help of a teacher and a book. Your book can be a reliable guide if you know how to use it effectively. The following pages will help you get to know this book, **Nuevos amigos** (New Friends), and its various features.

Who speaks Spanish? Where is Spanish spoken? Where did the language come from? Why should I learn it? How can I learn it well? You'll find the answers to these questions in English, illustrated with colorful photographs, in the Introduction, which begins on page 1.

INTRODUCTION

Spanish and You

Welcome to the Spanish-speaking world! Today you are embarking on a new journey—the exploration and learning of Spanish. This trip will take you to many lands, where you will meet different people. The route you will take is the Spanish language; the destination is an understanding of how speakers of Spanish think, behave, and interact with others. You will discover their values, history, and traditions. Are you ready to start your trip?

Let's go!   ¡Vamos!

In this introduction you will learn:

 where Spanish is spoken around the world

 how Spanish and English are related

 about Spanish-speaking areas in the United States

 about Spanish and your leisure time activities—hobbies, sports, travel

 about the knowledge of Spanish and your future career

 suggestions for studying Spanish

1

PRIMERA PARTE

PART OPENER

There are twelve units in Nuevos amigos, which are grouped in three parts. Each part contains three units and a review unit based on them. At the beginning of each part, you'll see an illustrated table of contents like the one shown here. It will give you the number, title, and opening page of each unit (Unidad), as well as a brief preview in English of each unit's theme and content.

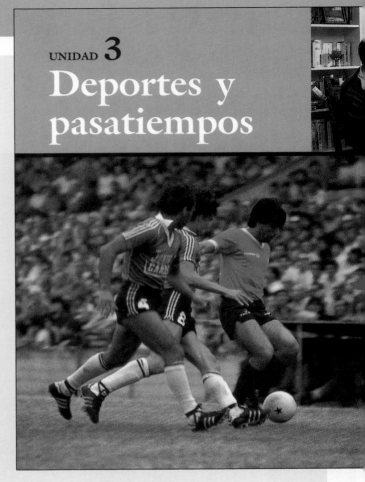

UNIDAD **3**

Deportes y pasatiempos

UNIT OPENER

There are nine units that present new material in your textbook. Each of these units opens the same way. Before you begin a unit, examine its opening pages. First scan the photos—they'll give you an idea what the unit is about. Next read the introductory paragraph—it sets the theme and provides information about the life and customs of Spanish-speaking people. Finally, look at the outline of the unit. Read the objectives of each section carefully—they'll tell you how you'll use Spanish to communicate with others.

REVIEW UNIT OPENER

Review is essential to learning a second language. It's good to stop now and then to ask yourself what you've learned and, more importantly, to practice your new skills in different situations. That's just what each review unit (Unidad de repaso) will help you do. There's one at the end of each part—three in the book. In the review unit you'll be introduced to a new theme and setting, but you won't have to

Fútbol—called *soccer* in the United States— is the national passion in most Spanish-speaking countries. Children learn to kick a ball almost as soon as they can walk. Some of the world's great soccer players come from South America. Other popular sports include *tenis, golf, béisbol, polo, vólibol, básquetbol.* As you can see, many sports names are similar in Spanish and English.

Pastimes like dancing, singing, playing the guitar, taking pictures, and playing dominos add fun to life.

In this unit you will:

SECTION A	talk about sports and pastimes . . . say which you like and which you don't like
SECTION B	talk about the seasons in which you play certain sports, and the equipment you need
SECTION C	say when and how often you play . . . talk about the seasons and the weather
TRY YOUR SKILLS	use what you've learned
VAMOS A LEER	read for practice and pleasure

91

UNIDAD **4**

¡Playa, sol y deportes!

Repaso

learn any new vocabulary, grammar, or communicative functions (language uses). Just concentrate on using what you've already studied in new and interesting ways.

With the exception of the three review units, each unit is made up of three sections. The beginning of each section will remind you of your objective and introduce you briefly, in English, to the theme of the section. Read these introductions carefully—they'll give you bits of information about Spanish-speaking people and their way of life.

SECTION B · describing people and family relationships . . . talking about age

Like nearly everyone else in the world, Hispanic people love to collect and show off family snapshots. You may need to know how to comment and ask questions about them.

B1 Fotos de la familia

Ana María, la hermana de Antonio, y su amiga Gloria, hablan de las fotos que Ana María tiene en su cuarto. Tiene fotos de todos los miembros de la familia.

GLORIA Tienes muchas fotografías. ¿Quién es la chica alta y morena? ¿Tu hermana?
ANA MARÍA No, mi hermana Consuelo es baja y rubia. Ella es Luisa, mi prima.
GLORIA ¿Cuántos años tiene?
ANA MARÍA Quince. ¡Es un genio! Es muy inteligente.
GLORIA ¡Qué fotografía tan bonita! ¿Quién es? ¿Tu padre?
ANA MARÍA Sí, es una foto de mi papá.
GLORIA ¡Qué guapo!
ANA MARÍA Mira, aquí está de nuevo, con mi mamá y toda la familia.
GLORIA La señora delgada y rubia, ¿quién es? ¡Qué linda!
ANA MARÍA Es mi tía Dolores, la madre de Luisa. Al lado está el esposo, mi tío José.

GLORIA Y aquí están tus abuelos, ¿no?
ANA MARÍA Sí, los padres de mamá. Los dos son bien simpáticos y cariñosos.
GLORIA ¿Cuántos hijos tienen? ¿Cinco?
ANA MARÍA No, una hija, mi mamá, y un hijo, mi tío José. El señor pelirrojo es un amigo de ellos. Los otros cuatro son amigos también.

168   Unidad 6

C6 ESTRUCTURAS ESENCIALES
The verb saber, to know

saber *to know*			
Sé	cuánto cuesta.	**Sabemos**	cuándo viene.
¿Sabes	dónde está?	**¿Sabéis**	si viene?
¿Sabe	cuál es?	**¿Saben**	qué hora es?

Saber means *to have information about something* or *to know a fact* such as a date or an address. When followed by an infinitive, **saber** means *to know how to do something:*

Yo **sé** nadar.   *I know how to (can) swim.*

GRAMMAR

In order to communicate effectively, you'll need to understand and use some grammatical forms. Look for these forms in the boxes with the heading **Estructuras esenciales** (*Essential Structures*). Once again, the color blue cues the importance of the material in the box.

C7 Actividad · Combinación

Form five sentences by choosing matching elements from the two groups.

Sí, yo	**sabes español.**
Nosotros no	**saben cuánto cuesta.**
Tú	**sabe bailar bien.**
Usted	**sé quien viene.**
Raúl y Pepa	**sabemos a qué hora es.**

C8 SE DICE ASÍ
Asking information

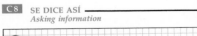

¿Sabes ¿Sabe	si hay entradas? dónde está la fila? si mi hermana está? cuándo viene mi hermana?	Do you know	if there are tickets? where the line is? if my sister is here? when my sister is coming?

COMMUNICATIVE FUNCTIONS

The material labeled **Se dice así** (*This is the way you say it*) in blue summarizes the phrases or sentences you'll need in order to accomplish your purpose—that is, to express and react to emotions, wishes, and opinions. Mastery of this material is the key to meeting the objective of the section.

C9 Conversación · Al teatro

One of your classmates is going to a concert. You want to go, too. You need to know where it is, on what day, at what time, and how much it costs. Ask your friend. Use a form of **saber** in your questions.

¡Vamos a salir!   211

BASIC MATERIAL

The material in each section is numbered in sequence together with the letter of the section: A1, A2, A3, and so on. The first presentation is always new or basic material, signaled by a number and title in blue. In some sections new material may be introduced in two or three other places. Wherever you see the color blue, you'll know that there's something new to learn. The new material is a model of what to say in a situation. Its authentic language and pictures will help you appreciate the different attitudes and surroundings of Spanish-speaking people.

ACTIVITIES

The headings of all the activities in the section begin with the word **Actividad** in orange. It's your signal to practice, either orally or in writing. Many of the activities are designed so that you may work together with your classmates in pairs or in small groups.

LISTENING

Listening is an essential skill that requires practice to develop. Whenever you see this cassette symbol ▥ after a heading, you'll know that the material is recorded, with pauses provided for your repetition or responses. A special listening comprehension exercise in each section is headed **Comprensión.** In order to respond, you will need to listen as your teacher plays the cassette or reads the Spanish to you.

CULTURE NOTES

The heading **¿Sabes que . . . ?** (*Do you know that . . . ?*) in green invites you to find out more about the life of Spanish-speaking people. These culture notes in English provide additional information about the theme of the section to help you increase your cultural awareness.

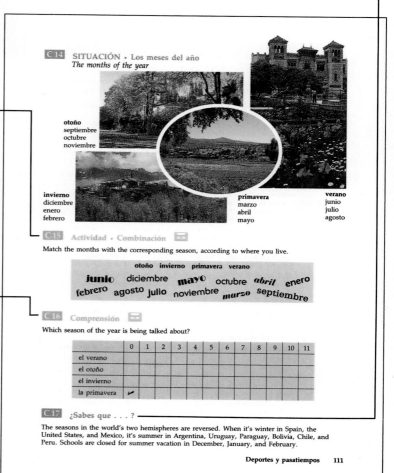

C14 SITUACIÓN · Los meses del año
The months of the year

otoño
septiembre
octubre
noviembre

invierno
diciembre
enero
febrero

primavera
marzo
abril
mayo

verano
junio
julio
agosto

C15 Actividad · Combinación ▥

Match the months with the corresponding season, according to where you live.

otoño invierno primavera verano

junio   diciembre   mayo   octubre   abril   enero
febrero   agosto   julio   noviembre   marzo   septiembre

C16 Comprensión ▥

Which season of the year is being talked about?

	0	1	2	3	4	5	6	7	8	9	10	11
el verano												
el otoño												
el invierno												
la primavera	✔											

C17 ¿Sabes que . . . ?

The seasons in the world's two hemispheres are reversed. When it's winter in Spain, the United States, and Mexico, it's summer in Argentina, Uruguay, Paraguay, Bolivia, Chile, and Peru. Schools are closed for summer vacation in December, January, and February.

Deportes y pasatiempos   111

TRY YOUR SKILLS

This section will let you experiment with the skills and knowledge you've gathered in the previous sections of the unit. Its variety of activities will give you many opportunities to practice communicating with others.

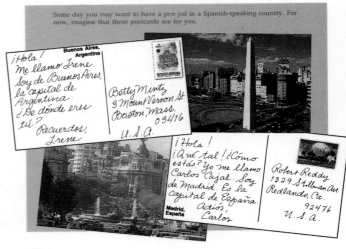

You've learned how to greet people, give some information about yourself, and ask others about themselves. Here are some further opportunities to use your new skills!

1 Tarjetas postales

Some day you may want to have a pen pal in a Spanish-speaking country. For now, imagine that these postcards are for you.

2 Actividad • ¿Quién es la chica? ¿Quién es el chico?

Tell about your new pen pals. What are their names? Where are they from?

3 Actividad • ¡A escribir!

Write a postcard introducing yourself to a pen pal in a Spanish-speaking country. Use the postcards above as a model.

¡Hola, amigos!   49

¿LO SABES?

Let's review some important points you have learned in this unit.

 SECTION A

When you are in a Spanish restaurant, can you order food at different tir of the day?
Order in Spanish something you might want for breakfast, something for lunch, and something for dinner.

Do you know how to talk about the foods you like and dislike?
Using **A mí me gusta(n)** and **A mí no me gusta(n)**, mention five types of food you like and five you don't.

Can you say what you would like to have for breakfast, lunch, and dinn and what your friends and family would like (or don't like) to have for each meal if you were in a Spanish country?
First, make a list of the different types of food you have for each meal, th say who likes them and who doesn't.

 SECTION B

Can you talk to a friend who is organizing a picnic and find out information about it?
Write down five questions you might ask.

When organizing a picnic, can you say how you're going to contribute?
Make five sentences talking about what you are bringing and the steps that you'll follow to get it.

Can you choose items at the food store, fruit stand, or pastry shop?
Write down five of your selections, using forms of **este** or **ese**.

Are you able to tell the store clerk what you really want?
Answer these suggestions with **no**, and indicate what you want instead.

¿Esas peras?	¿Esta piña?	¿Esas uvas?
¿Estos melocotones?	¿Esta tarta?	¿Ese bizcocho?

 SECTION C

When you are in a Spanish-speaking environment and you want a glass of water and something to eat, what would you say?
Make up four sentences.

Do you know how to ask in Spanish for something you need at the table?
Ask for:

a cup	a knife	a napkin	a glass	a fork
a small plate	a dish	a spoon	a small spoon	

Can you complain in Spanish about the food or the service?
Write down five complaints you might have.

Do you know different ways to say how much you like the food?
You are having a meal with a Spanish-speaking family. What would you say about . . .

la sopa	el arroz	el flan	la carne	las verduras	la tarta

262   Unidad 9

SELF-CHECK

Each of the nine basic units ends with a one-page self-check called **¿Lo sabes?** (*Do you know it?*). It includes a series of questions in English that you should ask yourself. Following the questions are short activities that will check your knowledge and skills. The questions are grouped by section, so, if you can't answer yes to a question or if the exercise shows you need to review, you'll know which section to turn to.

VOCABULARIO

SECTION A
- **amable** *kind*
- **bienvenido, -a** *welcome*
- **la casa** *house*
- **con permiso** *excuse me*
- **la cosa** *thing*
- **el cuarto** *room*
- **es un placer . . .** *it's a pleasure . . .*
- **estás en tu casa** *make yourself at home*
- **igualmente** *likewise*
- **un momento** *just a moment*
- **norteamericano, -a** *American*
- **pasa** *come in*
- **pasar** *to spend (time); come in*
- **el placer** *pleasure*
- **querer (ie)** *to want*
- **el refresco** *soda*
- **la sala** *living room*
- **la vacación** *vacation*
- **ver** *to see*
- **la visita** *visit*

SECTION B
- **alto, -a** *tall*
- **antipático, -a** *not nice*
- **bajo, -a** *short*
- **bien** *very*
- **bonito, -a** *pretty*
- **cariñoso, -a** *affectionate*
- **casado, -a** *married*
- **¿cómo es?** *what's he, (she, it) like?*
- **¿Cuántos cuartos hay?** *How many rooms are there?*
- **¿cuántos años tiene?** *how old are you (is he/she?)*
- **de ellos** *their*
- **de nuevo** *again*
- **delgado, -a** *thin*

- **los dos, las dos** *the two*
- **egoísta** *selfish*
- **el esposo** *husband*
- **la esposa** *wife*
- **estar casado, -a** *to be married*
- **la familia** *family*
- **feo, -a** *ugly*
- **la foto** *photo*
- **la fotografía** *photograph*
- **generoso** *generous*
- **gordo, -a** *fat*
- **guapo, -a** *handsome*
- **el hijo** *son*
- **la hija** *daughter*
- **los hijos** *children, sons and daughters*
- **lindo, -a** *pretty*
- **la madrastra** *stepmother*
- **la madre** *mother*
- **los miembros de la familia** *family members (see p. 171)*
- **moreno, -a** *dark (hair, complexion)*
- **murió** *(he) died*
- **¿no?** *right?*
- **el padrastro** *stepfather*
- **el padre** *father*
- **los padres** *parents*
- **papá** *dad*
- **pelirrojo, -a** *redheaded*
- **¡qué cuarto tan bonito!** *what a pretty room!*
- **¡qué guapo!** *how handsome!*
- **rubio, -a** *fair, blonde*
- **el señor** *man*
- **la señora** *woman*
- **simpático, -a** *nice*
- **tan** *so*
- **tener . . . años** *to be . . . years old*
- **todo, -a, -os, -as** *all*

- **tonto, -a** *dumb*
- **la visita** *visitor*

SECTION C
- **el apartamento** *apartment*
- **la cocina** *kitchen*
- **el comedor** *dining room*
- **cómodo, -a** *comfortable*
- **cuando** *when*
- **de él** *his*
- **de ella** *her*
- **de ellas** *their*
- **de usted** *your*
- **de ustedes** *your*
- **empezar (ie)** *to start*
- **la entrada** *entrance*
- **este, -a** *this*
- **frente a** *across from*
- **el garaje** *garage*
- **grande** *large*
- **importante** *important*
- **el jardín** *garden*
- **más** *most*
- **mis** *my (pl.)*
- **nuestro, -a, -os, -as** *our*
- **el pasillo** *hall*
- **pequeño, -a** *small, little*
- **¡por supuesto!** *of course!*
- **prohibido, -a** *off limits*
- **la puerta** *door, gate*
- **la sala de estar** *family room*
- **sus** *her, his, their (pl.)*
- **el tiempo** *time*
- **el tiempo libre** *free time*
- **tus** *your (pl.)*
- **usar** *to use*
- **¡vamos!** *let's go!*
- **vivir** *to live*
- **vuestro, -a, -os, -as** *(fam. pl.)*
- **¡ya sé!** *I know it!*

ESTUDIO DE PALABRAS

1. Write a list of the polite expressions you can use when you meet new friends and visit their home.

2. Make a list of the words you can use to describe a house or an apartment.

La familia

VOCABULARY

The Spanish-English vocabulary list, **Vocabulario,** after the self-check, contains the words and phrases you'll need to know. They're grouped according to the sections of the unit. A word-study exercise, **Estudio de palabras,** below the list, will focus your attention on the vocabulary and provide helpful ways to work with and learn the new words and phrases.

READING

A reading section, **Vamos a leer** (*Let's read*) concludes the unit. Here you'll find one or more reading selections related to the unit's theme. They include postcards, movie ads, recipes, character sketches, and factual selections. In each reading section, you'll also find an episode of the adventure story, **El regalo** (*The gift*). Most reading selections are followed by questions and activities designed to help you practice and develop your reading skills.

VAMOS A LEER°

Antes de leer *Before reading*

Before you begin to read in Spanish, here are a few suggestions. Read each new selection through for general meaning without looking up any words. Cognates— words that look alike in Spanish and English and have a similar meaning—will help you. Try to pronounce them the Spanish way, and write them down.

El mundo hispánico

España es un país° de Europa°, al suroeste° de Francia. Sus vecinos° son Francia y Portugal. La capital de España es Madrid. María Bernal es de Madrid.

Luisa Cano es de California y Pedro Gómez es de Texas. Los dos° son de los Estados Unidos. Ellos son mexicano americanos°.

vamos a leer *let's read* **un país** *a country* **de Europa** *of Europe* **al suroeste** *to the southwest*
sus vecinos *its neighbors* **los dos** *both* **mexicano americanos** *Mexican Americans*

PHOTO ESSAYS

Following each review unit in the book, you'll find a cultural photo essay called **Viñeta cultural.** The three essays will allow you to look into the life and surroundings of people who speak Spanish. The text in English provides interesting information on each theme. The photo captions are in Spanish.

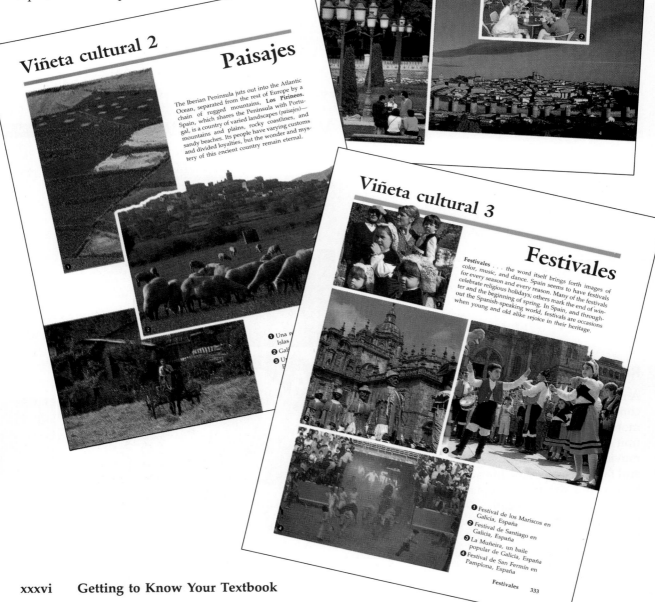

Viñeta cultural 1

Pueblos y ciudades

In the large, bustling cities of the Spanish-speaking world, and the many small villages that dot the countryside, visitors can find great contrasts and a wide variety of cultures. In Spain, medieval castles, Gothic cathedrals, and ancient aqueducts are dramatic reminders of the past amidst the modern life of today.

❶ Iglesia de la Sagrada Familia en Barcelona, España
❷ Un café al aire libre en Barcelona, España
❸ El parque del Retiro en Madrid, España
❹ La hermosa ciudad de Ávila, España

Viñeta cultural 2   Paisajes

The Iberian Peninsula juts out into the Atlantic Ocean, separated from the rest of Europe by a chain of rugged mountains, **Los Pirineos.** Spain, which shares the Peninsula with Portugal, is a country of varied landscapes *(paisajes)*—mountains and plains, rocky coastlines, and sandy beaches. Its people have varying customs and divided loyalties, but the wonder and mystery of this ancient country remain eternal.

❶ Una r...
Islas...
❷ Gal...
❸ U...
E...

Viñeta cultural 3

Festivales

Festivales . . . the word itself brings forth images of color, music, and dance. Spain seems to have festivals for every season and every reason. Many of the festivals celebrate religious holidays; others mark the end of winter and the beginning of spring. In Spain, and throughout the Spanish-speaking world, festivals are occasions when young and old alike rejoice in their heritage.

❶ Festival de los Mariscos en Galicia, España
❷ Festival de Santiago en Galicia, España
❸ La Muñeira, un baile popular de Galicia, España
❹ Festival de San Fermín en Pamplona, España

Festivales   333

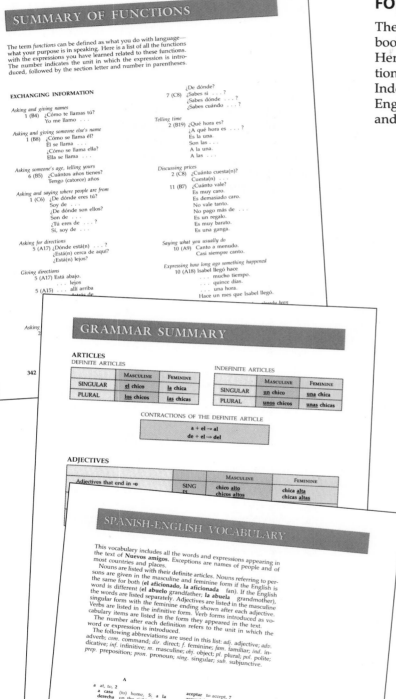

FOR REFERENCE

The reference section at the end of the textbook provides you with valuable aids. Here you may consult a Summary of Functions, Grammar Summary, Numbers, Verb Index, English Equivalents, Spanish-English and English-Spanish Vocabularies, and Grammar Index.

SUMMARY OF FUNCTIONS

The Summary of Functions sums up the communicative functions you have learned and practiced in a variety of situations throughout this textbook. If you want to ask for directions, invite someone to a party, pay a compliment, or respond to a friend's good fortune, for example, you will find the appropriate phrases and sentences listed here, as well as the unit in which the particular function was introduced.

GRAMMAR SUMMARY

The grammar points that have been presented in the book are organized in tables for easy reference and review in the Grammar Summary.

SPANISH-ENGLISH VOCABULARY

The Spanish-English Vocabulary contains all the words you will come across in this textbook. Besides the English meanings of the words, you can check on the gender of the nouns and identify the adjectives. The number you see after each entry tells you in which unit the word first appeared.

¡A COMENZAR!

There it is, a special textbook that will help you enlarge your view of the world and enable you to contribute to better understanding and communication among people. Now you're ready to begin an exciting, rewarding experience—learning another language and meeting new friends, **Nuevos amigos.**

INTRODUCTION
Spanish and You

What is Spanish like? Where do Spanish-speaking people live? How is Spanish related to English? Why should I learn Spanish? How should I go about doing it? The Introduction, which has been designed with such questions in mind, provides information about Spanish-speaking countries, the Spanish language, and careers that require a knowledge of Spanish, as well as hints on how to learn a second language. You may present the Introduction before or concurrently with Unit 1. A list of materials that you may need while teaching the Introduction appears on page T23.

OBJECTIVE To develop an understanding of the importance of Spanish language and culture throughout the world

Pages
1–3

1 **WHERE SPANISH IS SPOKEN**

Examine the maps on pages 2 and 3 with the students. Ask the students which countries and cities they know or have visited. As the students answer, repeat the name of the country or city in Spanish and have them say it after you. Next, divide the class into cooperative learning groups and assign one of the following regions of the Hispanic world to each group: Spain, North America, Central America, the Caribbean, and South America. Have the members of each group locate the countries in their assigned region. Then ask a volunteer from each group to point out the countries on a map of the world, naming them in Spanish.

Pages
4–15

The photo essay, a visual description of the Hispanic world, should appeal to the curiosity and imagination of the students. Discuss the photos with the students and encourage them to begin looking for similarities and differences between the Hispanic world and the United States.

Pages 4 and 5 Preserving, adapting, and changing help maintain the contrasts between the old and the new. The photographs on these pages show how the Spanish heritage in the United States is being preserved.

Pages 6 and 7 Mexico is one of the world's most attractive tourist centers. Ask the students which cities or regions of the United States are tourist centers.

Pages 8 and 9 Central America is a mixture of both Indian and Spanish culture. The Mayan civilization was one of the greatest civilizations of the Western Hemisphere. Ask the students what they know about the Mayan culture. For homework, have the students list the contributions of the Mayas, the Aztecs, and the Incas.

Discuss with the students the contrasts between the old and the new represented by the photographs and captions. To what extent are such contrasts evident in the region in which the students live?

Pages 11 and 13 Naturally, Spanish-speaking people prefer having a meal at a restaurant, or one prepared at home, made with fresh ingredients purchased at the **mercado** earlier in the day. They also enjoy bargaining with the salespeople.

Page 12 The students may have been introduced to **El Cid** and Miguel de Cervantes Saavedra in their social studies or literature classes. Ask them what they know about these two men. Then identify for the class King Juan Carlos, Pablo Picasso, Plácido Domingo, and Sor Juana Inés de la Cruz. For

homework, have the students list five famous Spanish-speaking people and their contributions to the world.

Pages 14 and 15 The Hispanic world is a most exciting and interesting place, and the Spanish language is the passport to this world.

Activities

1. With the class, brainstorm places in the Americas named after Spanish people, cities, or towns. For homework, assign a place to each student. The students should find out the origin of the names.
2. Distribute to the students world maps that include the names of capitals and other cities, or have them locate such maps themselves in encyclopedias or atlases.
3. Divide the class into cooperative learning groups of three students each. Assign an area of Spanish America to each group. For homework, the members should research when and why the Spanish influence began there. The next day the group members should compare their findings. One member should write two or three paragraphs summarizing the information, another should revise the paragraphs, and the third should report the group's conclusions to the class.

2 HOW SPANISH AND ENGLISH ARE RELATED

Have the students read the first paragraph. Then, on the board or on an overhead transparency, write the following words: **colegio, fábrica,** and **lectura.** Say the words aloud and have the students repeat them. Ask what the words might mean. After the students have answered, identify and explain these false cognates.

The students might assume that Spanish borrows as many words from English today as English has borrowed from Spanish. This, of course, is something that Spanish-speakers would not allow to happen. The **Real Academia Española** polices the purity of the Spanish language, officially allowing a limited number of words of foreign origin into the Spanish language each year.

Point out the list of Spanish words used in the English language at the top of page 17. Ask the students to provide a list of five additional Spanish words that are used in English.

Activities

After the students have noted their Spanish contacts, call on individuals to report their findings to the class. Also, ask them to identify the "borrowed" words they taught to a friend or a family member.

3 SPANISH IN THE UNITED STATES

Have the students look at the map. Ask them what they know about San Antonio, San Francisco, and Santa Fe. For homework, have the students write two or three paragraphs about a Spanish city in the United States.

Activities

1. Have the students use a Spanish-English dictionary to complete the activity. Call on volunteers to supply the name and their meanings.

2. Ask the students to work with a partner. They should use the map of the United States to locate the cities listed. Then assign at least five cities to each pair and ask the students to find out the English meaning. Have the students report to the class.

4   SPANISH FOR LEISURE

Have the students read the text and captions about sports. Again, to illustrate the similarities between Spanish and English, list **el beísbol, el fútbol, el vólibol, el esquí,** and **el básquetbol** on the board or a transparency. Have the students say the names of the sports after you. Students who are interested in baseball, football, or basketball might research **El Mundial, La serie del Caribe,** or the life of Spanish-speaking sports stars and share their findings with the class.

After students have read these captions, have them look at the captions of musical groups and at the television schedule. As they examine these items, the popularity of Spanish culture in the United States should become evident. You might ask the students if they ever listen to Spanish music or view Spanish movies or television programs.

Activity

Use the items that the students bring to class to make a bulletin-board display. You might entitle the display **Nuestro mundo hispánico.**

5   SPANISH AND YOUR FUTURE CAREER

Before the students read the text, have them brainstorm careers for which they think Spanish might be useful. List these on the board; have the students compare the list to what they learn from reading the text.

Bring in issues of newspapers from large metropolitan areas. Have the students look through the ads to find jobs that require a knowledge of Spanish. They should report their findings to the rest of the class.

Activities

1. If the students do not have access to people in the community who use Spanish in their work, ask several advanced Spanish students to role-play such people for the class.
2. Before dividing the class into small groups, ask several students what careers interest them. Have classmates use their imaginations to suggest how Spanish would be useful for those individuals. Then have the students complete the activity in groups, as instructed.

6   SUGGESTIONS FOR STUDYING SPANISH

Ask several artistic students to prepare signs of the words that summarize how to study Spanish. Display the signs in the classroom and refer to them periodically to remind the students of the techniques that will help them learn Spanish.

The Spanish alphabet

Use letter flashcards to teach the students the alphabet in Spanish. Practice five or six letters at a time; then go on to the next five or six letters.

Continue in this way until the class is able to identify most of the letters.

For listening practice, distribute to the students in Spanish a "secret message" similar to the following one:

| C | D | Y | F | G | O | I | H | J | A | K | LL | M | Q | N | O | R | E | RR | S | T | U | P | V | W | A | X | Ñ | Y | O | Z | L |

They should cross out the letters that they hear you say in order to find the message. When you have finished, have volunteers say in Spanish which letters remain. Their answers should reveal the message **Yo amo español.** Act out the meaning of the phrase for the class.

Some classroom "survival" phrases

You might construct a language "ladder" in the classroom. Write each expression on a narrow strip of colored paper. As you say and act out the expression, show this "rung" to the class; then attach the "rung" to the vertical bars of the "ladder" (also to be made of strips of colored paper) on the wall in the classroom. As the language "ladder" grows, it will serve as a handy reminder.

Activity

You might wish to do an activity called **buscando un tesoro** (scavenger hunt). Form small groups of four students. Tell the groups that they have one week to complete the activity and that they must do so by discussing the questions with their group members or with advanced Spanish students (who have previously prepared answers to the questions). When the groups have decided which questions need to be discussed with advanced students, those questions should be assigned to group members. Each group member must then find an advanced Spanish student who knows the answer to his or her question. At the end of a week, see how many of the groups have successfully completed the activity.

TEACHER-PREPARED MATERIALS
Introduction   Map of the world, letter flashcards, newspapers, language ladder

UNIT RESOURCES
Transparencies 1–4

INTRODUCTION

Spanish and You

Welcome to the Spanish-speaking world! Today you are embarking on a new journey—the exploration and learning of Spanish. This trip will take you to many lands, where you will meet different people. The route you will take is the Spanish language; the destination is an understanding of how speakers of Spanish think, behave, and interact with others. You will discover their values, history, and traditions. Are you ready to start your trip?

Let's go!   *¡Vamos!*

In this introduction you will learn:

 1   where Spanish is spoken around the world

 2   how Spanish and English are related

 3   about Spanish-speaking areas in the United States

 4   about Spanish and your leisure time activities—hobbies, sports, travel

 5   about the knowledge of Spanish and your future career

 6   suggestions for studying Spanish

CALIFORNIA

Chicago

New York City

ESPAÑA

Madrid

Los Angeles
ARIZONA
NEW MEXICO
Ciudad de México

TEXAS

MÉXICO

St. Augustine
FLORIDA
Miami
La Habana

CUBA

ISLAS
CANARIAS

PUERTO RICO
REPÚBLICA DOMINICANA

Caracas

VENEZUELA

GUATEMALA
EL SALVADOR
HONDURAS
NICARAGUA
COSTA RICA
PANAMÁ
ECUADOR
COLOMBIA

Bogotá

Lima

PERÚ

BOLIVIA

PARAGUAY

Santiago

CHILE

Buenos Aires

ARGENTINA

URUGUAY

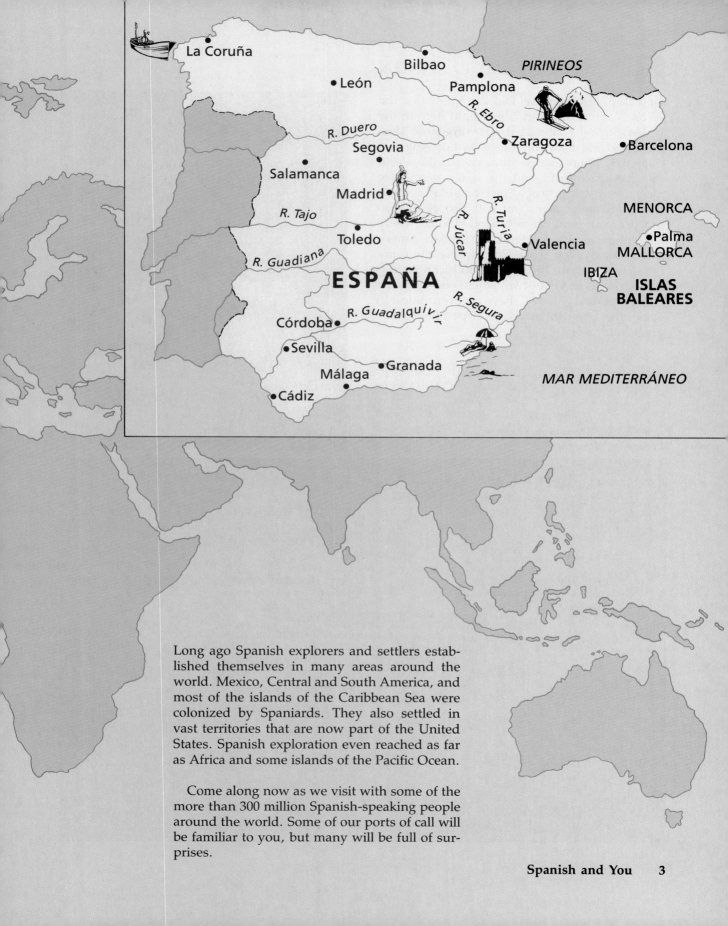

Long ago Spanish explorers and settlers established themselves in many areas around the world. Mexico, Central and South America, and most of the islands of the Caribbean Sea were colonized by Spaniards. They also settled in vast territories that are now part of the United States. Spanish exploration even reached as far as Africa and some islands of the Pacific Ocean.

Come along now as we visit with some of the more than 300 million Spanish-speaking people around the world. Some of our ports of call will be familiar to you, but many will be full of surprises.

Spanish and You   3

1 WHERE SPANISH IS SPOKEN

First stop, first surprise! Did you know that the second largest Mexican city is right here in the United States? That's right, there are more Mexicans and Mexican Americans in Los Angeles, California, than in any other city in the world except Mexico City! And the sign you will see most often will probably be **Se habla español,** *Spanish is spoken here.* You will also be able to practice your Spanish in Miami, Florida, where about half of the residents are Cuban Americans, and in New York City, where there are hundreds of thousands of Puerto Rican Americans. In fact, just about anywhere you go in the United States you will have opportunities to speak the Spanish language, especially in our great Southwest!

Celebration at Calle Ocho in Miami, Florida

Old Spanish Mission in Santa Barbara, California

Color and music combine to create
excitement in a Hispanic American
Day Parade.

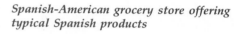

Portrait of a girl in
Mexican costume

Spanish-American grocery store offering
typical Spanish products

The Riverwalk in San Antonio offers a
breathtaking view of its river.

Moving southward across the Rio Grande we come to Mexico, a land of surprising contrasts. Probably a country many of you will visit at least once, it is a breathtaking land of beautiful mountains and white, sandy beaches. Or you can climb the pyramids of the Sun and the Moon at Teotihuacán, parasail over Acapulco Bay, or bargain with artisans in the market-places of Toluca. Everywhere you will see the unique Mexican blend of Spanish and Indian cultures.

Steps leading to El Castillo in Chichén Itzá, one of the most important of the ancient Mayan cities

Vacation resort in Puerto Vallarta, Mexico, where romance and adventure go hand in hand

*In the **Plaza de las Tres Culturas** you can see examples of Aztec and Colonial architecture as well as modern high-rises.*

Mexico is one of the world's leading producers of silver. Pictured here is a silver shop in Taxco, Mexico.

The world-renowned **Ballet Folklórico** *on stage in Mexico City*

Parasailing in Acapulco, Mexico

A moment in time . . . fine food and good conversation in a restaurant in Mexico

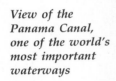

Central America covers a smaller area than Texas, but its population is greater by more than three million. Each country of Central America has its own unique character. Guatemala and Honduras were inhabited by the Mayans, who could predict eclipses of the sun and moon with far greater accuracy than the Europeans of their time. El Salvador is a land of volcanoes, some still very active indeed. Nicaragua has the largest lake in the region, complete with fresh-water sharks! Costa Rica has no army, and has the most democratic form of government in Central America. And Panama, of course, is the home of the Panama Canal and the San Blas Indians, who live on artificial islands off the Atlantic coast.

Young Costa Rican

View of the Panama Canal, one of the world's most important waterways

The Spanish conquerors were astonished by the splendors of the gold found in Peru.

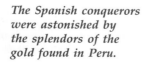

Native Indian girl in costume, Guatemala

View of Lake Atitlán, with surrounding volcanoes, in Guatemala

Fishing in Lake Atitlán, Guatemala

Traces of Mayan civilization are everywhere in the mountainous land of Guatemala. Pictured here is a Mayan-Tikal site in Petán.

Mayan Ball Court in Copán, Honduras

Most South Americans speak the same Spanish that you will learn. Whether they are descendants of the Incas of Peru, or of the cowboys of the Argentine plains, the gauchos, they all speak the same language. In fact, the only countries of South America where Spanish is not spoken are Brazil, Guyana, French Guiana, and Surinam. And so, in Cuzco you can stroll among buildings constructed on ancient Incan foundations, catch the sun on a Caribbean beach in Venezuela, or dance the night away in a disco in Buenos Aires, all without having to buy additional phrasebooks!

Machu Picchu, the famous "lost city" of the Incas of Peru, located high in the Andes. It was not rediscovered until 1911.

*The twin towers of the **Centro Simón Bolívar** in Caracas, Venezuela, serve as a gateway to the downtown area of the city.*

View of church by the sea in Cartagena, Colombia

Reed boats on Lake Titicaca, Uros Island, Peru

Family barbecue in Buenos Aires, Argentina

No description of the Spanish-speaking world would be complete without the country where it all started. Spain is the homeland, and although the Spanish-speaking countries around the world all have unique identities, they share the cultural bond of language and heritage. Spain is the land of great thinkers—the Muslim mathematicians and scientists of the Middle Ages and Maimonides, the great Jewish philosopher and judge. It is the country of warriors like Rodrigo Díaz de Vivar, a Spanish hero so respected by his enemies, the Moors, that they called him El Cid (a term of respect meaning *sir*), and of Don Quixote, hero of Cervantes' seventeenth-century novel. It was from Spain that Christopher Columbus sailed in search of Asia and found a new world. And now you can return to explore castles where medieval knights planned battles and crusades, and spoke *Castilian*, the language which later became modern-day Spanish. Or perhaps you would rather shout **olé** at the bullring in Madrid and later that evening applaud flamenco dancers!

A view of Poniente Beach, Costa Blanca, Spain

The Alhambra, a palace complex of ancient Moorish architecture surrounded by woodlands, gardens, fountains, and buildings.

The Pyrenees, a chain of mountains that spreads across France and Spain

12   **Introduction**

A flamenco dancer
in Seville, Spain

The City of Ávila in Spain sits on a hill surrounded by massive walls.

Buying and selling at an outdoor market
in Barcelona, Spain

Young people in the gardens of a palace
in Málaga, Spain

Spanish and You 13

Whatever your interests, the Spanish language will be your passport to excitement throughout the world!

Playing in the snow on the slopes of Cotopaxi, in Ecuador

View of a parish church in the town of San Miguel de Allende, Mexico

Three Spanish-American boys from San Antonio, Texas

View of the Peruvian altiplano, a high plateau in the Andes

Built by the Spaniards, El Morro overlooks the Atlantic Ocean in San Juan, Puerto Rico.

The Alcázar in Segovia, Spain, is one of the architectural treasures of the region.

View of Isla Grande on the Atlantic Coast of Panama

Group of teenaged tourists in the Aragón region of Spain

Children wearing traditional folk dance costumes in Tenerife, Canary Islands

¡SUPERIOR! ¡ESPECTACULAR! ¡MAGNÍFICO!

¡EXTRAORDINARIO! ¡ESTUPENDO! ¡FABULOSO!

¡MARAVILLOSO! ¡INCREÍBLE! ¡FANTÁSTICO!

All of the words above are adjectives that describe Spanish. Can you guess their meaning? Write your answers on a slip of paper and then check them with the help of your teacher. You will probably notice that the Spanish and English spellings are similar. In fact, some words are spelled exactly the same! These Spanish/English look-alikes will be of help to you as you learn Spanish. They are called *cognates*. But please beware! Some look-alikes may fool you; they are known as false cognates. Here is an example: the Spanish word **pan** means *bread* in English—not *pan*.

Why do Spanish and English have so many words which are similar? One reason is that Spanish is a *Romance* language, which means that it came from the language of the ancient Romans—Latin. In its early history Spain was called *Hispania*, and was part of the Roman Empire. Britain was part of that same empire, so the English language also shows the influence of Latin. Another reason is that many Spanish words have come into English because much of our country was first settled by Spaniards, and their descendants are now Americans.

Here are some Spanish words that are used in English. Do you recognize them?

alpaca	chile	taco	taxi
fiesta	piano	sombrero	mosquito

Some students who are studying Spanish like to use Spanish names. Most Spanish names and their English versions are cognates. If you want to be called by a Spanish name, you can choose one from the following list.

For girls		**For boys**	
Alma	*Alma*	Alberto	*Albert*
Alicia	*Alice*	Alfredo	*Alfred*
Ana	*Ann*	Andrés	*Andrew*
Bárbara	*Barbara*	Carlos	*Charles, Carl*
Beatriz	*Beatrice*	Eduardo	*Edward*
Carolina	*Caroline*	Jorge	*George*
Elena	*Ellen, Helen*	Enrique	*Henry*
Juana	*Jane, Jean*	Juan	*John*
Lucía	*Lucy*	José	*Joseph*
Margarita	*Margaret*	Pablo	*Paul*
María	*Mary, Marie*	Ricardo	*Richard*
Teresa	*Theresa*	Roberto	*Robert*

Activities

For a two-day period, keep a log on your contacts with Spanish. Include the following:

- Names of foods found in the supermarket
- References to Spanish-speaking countries on radio, TV, and in newspapers and magazines
- Spanish songs on radio or TV
- Call letters of local Spanish radio or TV stations
- Uses of borrowed Spanish words

Share your findings with your class. As a follow-up, teach a friend or family member two Spanish ''borrowed'' words.

3 SPANISH IN THE UNITED STATES

As you recall, the ancient Romans called Spain *Hispania*. That is why the term *Hispanic* is used to refer to people from all of the Spanish-speaking countries, as well as to people of Spanish background within the United States.

The Hispanics who live in Central America and South America are also called *Spanish Americans*, or *Latin Americans* (because Spanish is a Romance language derived from Latin).

Activities

Colorado	*High pole*
Florida	*Yellow*
Montana	*Mountain king*
Nevada	*Of mountains*
Amarillo	*Colored, reddish*
Palo Alto	*Snow-covered*
Monterey	*Full of flowers*

1. **A name game** See if you can match these names with their explanations or true meanings. Copy the two columns onto a sheet of paper and draw a line connecting each place and its meaning. Find additional Spanish place names and determine their original meanings. For example: Los Angeles/*the angels*. Are there any in your state? What do they mean?

2. **Spanish place names** Look at the names of the cities in the box. Spanish names like these can be found throughout the United States. Find out the English meaning of these Spanish names.

Aurora *(Colorado)*	Los Molinos *(California)*	Sacramento *(California)*	San Francisco *(California)*
El Dorado *(Kansas)*	Mesa *(Arizona)*	Salinas *(California)*	Rio Grande *(Ohio)*
El Paso *(Texas)*	Plano *(Texas)*	San Antonio *(Texas)*	Valparaiso *(Indiana)*
Las Cruces *(New Mexico)*	Pueblo *(Colorado)*	San Diego *(California)*	Ventana *(Arizona)*
Las Vegas *(Nevada)*	Reno *(Nevada)*	Santa Fe *(New Mexico)*	Zapata *(Texas)*

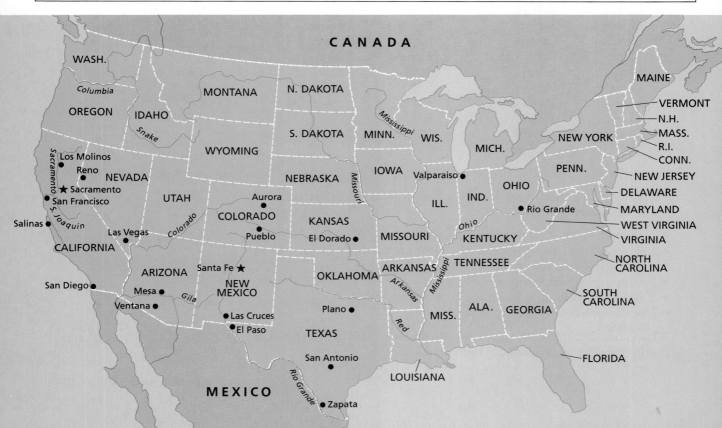

4 SPANISH FOR LEISURE

When people talk about studying Spanish, they usually mean learning and using it only in the classroom. But learning about the culture and language of Spanish-speaking countries can go beyond school into leisure activities that are interesting and fun. What are your hobbies and interests? Do you like sports? Most of the sports that are played in the United States are also found in Spanish America and Spain. See if you can guess the English equivalents of the names of these sports. Cover the answer key and then check your answers:

> football/soccer, tennis, golf, baseball, polo, volleyball, basketball

fútbol, tenis, golf, béisbol, polo, vólibol, básquetbol

Note that **fútbol** as played in Spain and Spanish America is called *soccer* here in the United States. American-style football is called **fútbol americano**.

Fútbol (soccer) is almost an obsession in Spanish America and in Europe. Thanks to satellite TV, you can follow international competitions in soccer and a number of other sports. If you are a soccer fan, you may even find yourself rooting for your favorite Spanish-speaking team and cheering in Spanish.

Béisbol is popular in Mexico, and the vocabulary in Spanish is easy—for example, **el filder, el cácher, el pícher,** and **el shorstop.**

Mountain-climbing as well as skiing are popular in the Andes Mountains. Because the seasons south of the equator are reversed, you would be skiing in July and August!

Spanish and You 19

Music is part of everyday life in Spain and Spanish America. Many famous singers and musicians come from Spanish-speaking countries. Latin music is also popular in the United States. You are probably already familiar with the "Latin beat" and with some of the popular Hispanic musical groups and singers. Because there are large Hispanic communities in the United States, cassettes and records are more readily available in Spanish than in other foreign languages. Make a list of your favorite Spanish songs, singers, groups, or records and cassettes and share it with the class or post it on the bulletin board.

Teenagers browsing in a Spanish-American record store

The Miami Sound Machine, a Spanish-American singing group that mixes a Latin rhythm with rock music

Menudo, a singing group from Puerto Rico

Again, because there are large Hispanic communities in the United States, newspapers, magazines, and books in Spanish are easy to get. There are even comic books in Spanish! Young people in Spain and Spanish America like to watch TV and go to the movies. If there is a Spanish television station in your area, you will be able to watch a soap opera or two in Spanish. The TV schedule will give you some idea of the programs that are available.

Don Quijote is a classic of Spanish literature, which has been translated into many languages, including English. Millions of people have enjoyed the adventures of Don Quixote. The book has even been turned into a musical called *Man of La Mancha*. Here you can see a painting of Don Quixote and his servant, Sancho Panza, by Pablo Picasso.

Don Quijote, *a classic tale of a man in search of the impossible dream*

Tourists arriving in Peru

Although you may not be going to a Spanish-speaking country or area right away, eventually you might. You might even live there for a while with a family as an exchange student. In the meantime, reading books or watching travel films about these countries can be interesting and fun. So is having a pen pal from Spain, Mexico, or Peru with whom you can exchange letters or cassettes. Your teacher can tell you where to write to get the name of a pen pal. Having a pen pal is one way of keeping up on the latest records, sports news, TV programs, and board and video games—not to mention exchanging stamps and comparing notes on life in general in both your countries. You may start out by writing mostly in English, but you will find yourself gradually using more and more Spanish. Many Hispanic teenagers study English, so your pen pal will welcome the opportunity to practice English.

Learning Spanish requires study and concentration. But the most important thing about studying any foreign language is discovering how people live in other parts of the world—what they value, what they like, and what is important to them. Learning Spanish can become more than schoolwork—it can become a hobby.

Prince Phillip, heir to the throne of Spain, appears here on the cover of **Hola,** *a popular Spanish magazine.*

Activity

Bring to class an item related to the Spanish language or Hispanic culture that you have found recently. It could be a recipe, a news item, information about travel to Spain or Latin America, a TV or radio program, or even a commercial. Share your findings with the class or with your learning group. Put the item in your Spanish notebook to start your collection. Be on the lookout for other items!

5 SPANISH AND YOUR FUTURE CAREER

Have you ever wondered what you will be doing ten . . . fifteen . . . or even twenty years from now? Where you will be working? What kind of job you will have? Because you are going to study Spanish, you may find it useful for the career that you will eventually choose. A career in almost any field that you name—from art to zoology—can be combined with a knowledge of Spanish.

For many jobs, knowing a foreign language is helpful, but for some it is essential. Teachers of Spanish must be fluent in the language and also know a great deal about the history, geography, and daily life of the countries or regions where Spanish is spoken. Teachers who can combine Spanish with science, mathematics, and social studies are needed to work with students who come to the United States from Spanish-speaking countries.

Translators and interpreters also must be very familiar with both Spanish and English. Most translators specialize in one field, such as medicine or commerce. Interpreters, who have to translate what people are saying in court or at meetings, must think very quickly in both Spanish and English. Interpreters also work in businesses and international organizations.

These interpreters translate a speech for the Spanish-speaking people at the United Nations.

This teacher is teaching people who need to know Spanish in their jobs.

Not only do American travelers go to Spain and to countries in Central and South America, but Spanish-speaking people from those countries come to the United States on business and vacation trips. Travel agents and tour guides therefore find Spanish very helpful in their work, as do flight attendants on airlines that serve Spanish America and Spain. Can you describe how a tour guide, travel agent, and flight attendant use Spanish in their jobs?

Spanish is an important international language, especially in agriculture, banking, business, and technology. Food importers travel regularly to Mexico and to countries in Central America, where they sample and buy fruits and vegetables. Spanish-American countries, such as Mexico and Venezuela, sell oil to the United States. Therefore, legal documents are printed in Spanish, and negotiations often are conducted in Spanish as well as English. In order to succeed, companies in the United States that sell their products to Spanish-speaking countries must have salespeople who are familiar with Hispanic culture and who know Spanish well.

People who work in international banking and trade find that speaking Spanish is extremely helpful. A bilingual secretary, for example, must be able to type and transcribe letters in both Spanish and English. An international corporate lawyer has to be fluent in Spanish as well as English and must know not only the laws in the United States but the laws of the countries with which he or she is dealing.

Would you like to live in a foreign country? Many companies have offices in Spanish-speaking countries and employ thousands of Americans. Jobs are available in manufacturing, engineering, banking, and many other areas.

This guide in a theme park helps visitors who come from Spanish-speaking countries.

An international banker consults with a Spanish-speaking client.

Knowing Spanish will help this corporate lawyer with the research of laws in other countries.

Because there are many Hispanic communities in the United States, opportunities to use Spanish in various types of jobs are increasing. In certain states, such as Texas, California, Florida, New York, and Colorado, salespeople in stores, personnel in hotels and restaurants, doctors and nurses in hospitals, as well as police, firefighters, librarians, school secretaries, and auto mechanics speak Spanish as well as English to serve the people in their communities. There are often Spanish newspapers in addition to radio and TV programs in Spanish. These states attract many visitors from Spanish America as well as from Spain and other parts of the United States.

It helps to speak the language of your customers when you are selling something! In the picture below, what kinds of questions might this visitor from Argentina be asking the salesperson and how might he answer? Fortunately, there is a sign in the store window that says **Se habla español** (*Spanish is spoken here*).

Police officers, firefighters, and paramedics in large cities like Chicago, New York, Los Angeles, San Antonio, or Miami need to know Spanish to help people in the Hispanic communities that they serve.

A police officer gives directions in Spanish to two visitors.

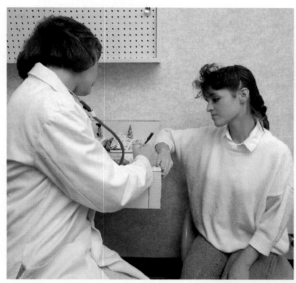

A doctor questions her patient in Spanish about her medical history.

Spanish-speaking salespeople can be helpful to our foreign visitors.

Activities

Before you make a career choice, it is wise to talk with as many people as you can about their jobs—what they do and what they like and don't like about their jobs.

1. **Interviews** If you know somebody in your family, school, or neighborhood who uses Spanish in his or her work, interview this person. Ask the following (you may add questions to the list if you wish):

   - Please describe your job.
   - How do you use Spanish in your work?
   - What types of Spanish courses did you take?
   - What do you like best about your job?
   - What do you like least about your job?
   - Do you travel as part of your job? Where?

   Write the interview or record it on a cassette to share with the class or your learning group.

2. **Spanish in action** Look at the jobs listed below. Who are all these people and why are they speaking Spanish? Work in a group of two or three students. Try to think of as many reasons as possible why Spanish would be useful to these people. Take notes on your ideas and report to the class or write them to post on the bulletin board. If you really want to be creative, write an imaginary interview with one of these people. Follow the questions in activity 1 if you wish.

   aerospace engineer   manager of gift shop   auto mechanic

   museum director   computer programmer

   real estate agent   cosmetologist   singer   dentist

   social worker   farmer

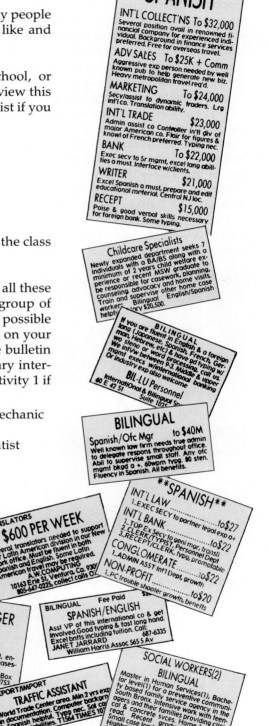

6 SUGGESTIONS FOR STUDYING SPANISH

LISTEN

Listening is particularly important in the beginning because you have to get used to a new set of sounds. You will have to listen carefully to what is being said so that you can answer in Spanish.

PRACTICE

Learning a foreign language is like learning to play a musical instrument. You have to practice a little every day. Daily short periods are more effective than one long, last-minute cramming session.

VISUALIZE

Remembering Spanish vocabulary is easy if you visualize what a sentence, phrase, or word means. For example, if you are practicing the sentence **Los chicos van a nadar** (*The boys are going swimming*), try to hold in your mind an image of children swimming in a lake while you say the sentence to yourself several times.

CONNECT

Make use of your English connections. When you read, find cognates (words which are very similar in different languages and have similar meanings) like these: **música,** *music;* **famoso,** *famous;* **ensalada,** *salad.* They will help you understand the meaning of the sentence or paragraph. Also, group Spanish words into word families—for example: **amigo,** *friend;* **amistad,** *friendship;* **amable,** *friendly.*

ORGANIZE

Look for ways to organize the material you are learning. Use memory devices. For example, make up a new word using the first letters of the words you are learning.

EXPAND

Use Spanish outside class. Speak Spanish with friends and classmates or find people who speak Spanish and practice with them. Talk into a cassette recorder in Spanish for practice; then after a few weeks listen to yourself. You will be surprised at your progress! Tune in to the Spanish-language radio and television stations in your area. You may not undestand much at first, but it will get easier as you learn more Spanish.

ENJOY

You may want to choose a new name in Spanish. Join the Spanish Club and make new friends. Above all—don't be afraid to make mistakes in Spanish. Concentrate on getting your message across and have fun doing it.

The Spanish alphabet

The Spanish alphabet has 30 letters. All words beginning with **k** and **w** are of foreign origin. There are no words in Spanish starting with **rr,** although **r** is pronounced as **erre** at the beginning of a word.

El alfabeto

a	a	**n**	ene
b	be	**ñ**	eñe
c	ce	**o**	o
ch	che	**p**	pe
d	de	**q**	ku
e	e	**r**	ere
f	efe	**rr**	erre
g	ge	**s**	ese
h	hache	**t**	te
i	i	**u**	u
j	jota	**v**	ve
k	ka	**w**	doble ve
l	ele	**x**	equis
ll	elle	**y**	i griega
m	eme	**z**	zeta

Some classroom "survival" phrases

These are some of the expressions your teacher will be using in the classroom. Learn to *recognize* them when you hear them.

- Escuche(n), por favor.   *Listen, please.*
- Repita(n) después de mí.   *Repeat after me.*
- Díga(n)lo otra vez.   *Say it again.*
- Pónga(n)se de pie, por favor.   *Stand up, please.*
- Siénte(n)se, por favor.   *Sit down, please.*
- Silencio, por favor.   *Quiet, please.*
- Saque(n) una hoja de papel.   *Take out a sheet of paper.*
- Preste(n) atención.   *Pay attention.*
- ¡Está bien! ¡Es correcto!   *That's right!*
- No está bien. No es correcto.   *That's wrong.*

¡Buena suerte!   *Good luck!*

PRIMERA PARTE

UNIDAD 1 ¡Hola, amigos!
Scope and Sequence

	BASIC MATERIAL	COMMUNICATIVE FUNCTIONS
SECTION A	**En el colegio** (A1) **Saludos** (A10) **María Luisa y la profesora** (A16)	**Socializing** • Asking how someone is • Saying how you are • Saying hello and goodbye
SECTION B	**En la escuela. En la clase** (B1) **Después de la clase** (B6)	**Exchanging information** • Asking and giving names • Asking and giving someone else's name
SECTION C	**¿De dónde son?** (C1) **Aquí se habla español** (C3)	**Exchanging information** • Asking and telling where people are from
TRY YOUR SKILLS	Pronunciation (rhythm) Sound-letter correspondences (letters **h, ñ**) Dictation	
VAMOS A LEER	**El mundo hispánico** (various cities and countries where people speak Spanish) **Un paseo por el parque** (greetings in Spanish-speaking countries) **El regalo** (The characters of this continuing mystery introduce themselves.)	

WRITING A variety of controlled and open-ended writing activities appear in the Pupil's Edition. The Teacher's Notes identify other activities suitable for writing practice.

COOPERATIVE LEARNING Many of the activities in the Pupil's Edition lend themselves to cooperative learning. The Teacher's Notes explain some of the many instances where this teaching strategy can be particularly effective. For guidelines on how to use cooperative learning, see page T13.

GRAMMAR	CULTURE	RE-ENTRY
Spanish equivalents for the word *you* (**tú, usted**) (A17)	Greeting and meeting people	
Gender of nouns and the definite article (B15)	Common Spanish first names Spanish nicknames	
Subject pronouns and the verb **ser** (C10) Interrogative sentences (C17)	Map of the Spanish-speaking world Spanish-speaking population	
Recombining communicative functions, grammar, and vocabulary		
Reading for practice and pleasure		

TEACHER-PREPARED MATERIALS
Section A Pictures of children, adults
Section B Cue cards for B6, pictures of famous people, name tags, 3 × 5 cards
Section C Pictures of famous people, boys, girls, mixed groups; flashcards of subject pronouns
Try Your Skills Name tags

UNIT RESOURCES
Manual de actividades, Unit 1
Manual de ejercicios, Unit 1
Unit 1 Cassettes
Transparencies 1–3
Quizzes 1–3
Unit 1 Test

SECTION A

OBJECTIVES **To socialize:** ask how someone is; say how you are; say hello and goodbye

CULTURAL BACKGROUND   In this unit, the students will learn the correct social use of the language in greetings and farewell situations. They will also discover how to ask and give basic introductory information in Spanish.

Spanish-speaking people are extremely careful to use the appropriate word or phrases in order to conform with the formality or informality of a given situation. For instance, one must choose between **tú** and **usted** when addressing someone, or use **Buenos días** instead of **Hola** when greeting a person formally.

Spanish speakers tend to stand closer than Americans when greeting or speaking with someone. They also shake hands when introduced. If a man is introduced to a woman, she usually waits until he extends his hand to shake it. Once they are good friends, men frequently embrace each other when they meet. Women usually greet each other with a kiss on the cheek.

MOTIVATING ACTIVITY   Ask volunteers to demonstrate the various ways in which they normally greet others, both in formal and informal situations. Then demonstrate the different ways of greeting that are customary among Spanish speakers. (By starting with the familiar, with what they are used to, students may be less reluctant to participate.) Have volunteers practice these greetings. Ask them how they feel in these situations.

A1

En el colegio

Have the students keep their books closed to present these brief dialogs. Begin the presentation by saying **¡Hola!** to the class and have the students repeat after you. Then greet several individuals in the class, using a handshake and saying **¡Hola!** Tell the students to greet two classmates.

Call on a few students to greet you. Respond with **¡Hola! ¿Cómo estás?** Have the students repeat after you. Then introduce **Muy bien** or **Muy mal.** Act out the meaning of these responses and have the students repeat these expressions after you.

Practice this introduction with several students until most students can greet each other without difficulty.

Introduce **¡Chao!** and **¡Adiós!** Have the students repeat these words after you and ask them when they would use these expressions. Have three or four students move around the class, greeting several classmates. Then call on three or four other students to do the same. Continue this until all the students have had the opportunity to practice the greetings and farewells.

Now play the cassette or read aloud the two dialogs in section A1. Have the students open their books and follow along as they listen. After most of the students are able to pronounce the words correctly, you may wish to divide the class into pairs to practice reading the dialogs aloud. Have one student read Ramón's role and the other student read Anita's role. Then have the students switch roles.

A2 ## Actividad • Reacciones

For cooperative learning, have the students work in pairs. One student should read the first expression from the left column, and the other should give the appropriate response from the column on the right. Each student should make sure that his or her partner can respond accurately. After students have finished the activity, they should reverse roles.

SLOWER-PACED LEARNING   After completing the activity orally, you may wish to assign it as a written activity in class or at home.

A3   Actividad • Y ahora tú

Since it is important to speak Spanish as often as possible in class, tell students that they will be selecting a Spanish name to create a culturally authentic environment. Refer to the list of Spanish names on page 38. Help the students pronounce the names correctly.

Have the students work in pairs, making sure they reverse roles. Have students select new partners often so the same students do not work together all the time.

SLOWER-PACED LEARNING   You may wish to scramble the exchanges on a felt board. Call on individuals to arrange them in order. Then have the students read aloud the exchanges to practice pronunciation.

A4   SE DICE ASÍ

Call the students' attention to A4. Explain that all sections named **SE DICE ASÍ** will contain essential information about communication skills for which they will be responsible.

Point out the expressions **¿Qué tal?** and **¿Cómo estás tú?** Explain to students that these are the expressions they will use to greet their friends. Later they will learn more formal greetings.

A5   Actividad • Charla

Tell the students about the importance of body language. They should try to mimic the expressions shown in the illustrations. Remind them that **¡Qué pena!** is often used when one wishes to express sympathy.

Circulate quickly around the class, asking students how they are and commenting before breaking into pairs.

CHALLENGE   You may wish to introduce the proverb **"Las penas con pan son buenas."** (If you have enough to eat, your troubles aren't quite so bad.) Explain that proverbs are an integral part of Spanish culture and Spanish-speaking people often quote them in conversation. You may wish to introduce a new proverb in each unit.

A6   Actividad • ¡A escribir!

Have several volunteers copy their unscrambled dialogs on the board or a transparency. You may also wish to elicit lines from students for more class participation. Direct students to exchange their papers for correction.

A7   Actividad • Para completar

Students should complete the activity orally and then in writing. Remind students to include the written accents, inverted question marks, and exclamation points when completing this activity. Point out that in Spanish the letter **h** is always silent.

CHALLENGE   You may wish to review the alphabet by requiring students to first spell their names and then spell their written responses in Spanish.

A8 Actividad • Me llamo . . .

Have the students use the Spanish names they selected in A3 to prepare the name tags.

A9 ¿Sabes que . . . ?

Tell students that Spanish-speaking people are generally extremely polite. First impressions are important, and so when they meet a person who speaks Spanish, they should convey a sincere attitude of pleasure. Remind students that Spanish-speaking people stand close and use gestures when greeting and speaking with others.

A10 SITUACIÓN • Saludos

This **situación** introduces new greetings, this time in a more formal setting. Point out how these exchanges indicate formality but are also used among good friends of different age groups.

Tell the students about the contrast in the greetings. The teacher is addressed as **señor, señora, señorita** or **señor Colón, señorita López,** or **señora Valdés.** Point out that they would address fellow students by their first names. You may wish to write the following on the board or a transparency:

Carmen y el señor Colón.
Buenos días, señor.
Buenos días, señor Colón.

Have the students repeat chorally. Stress linking and point out the use of **el** in the first example, when talking about **Sr. Colón.** Indicate that the article is not used when talking directly to someone, as seen in the last two examples.

Indicate that the symbol above the **ñ** is called a **tilde.** Explain that the sound of this letter is similar to the sound represented by *ny* in the English word *canyon.* Have students practice the sound both chorally and individually.

At this time you may want to spend some time stressing pronunciation:

Carmen y el señor Colón.
Buenos días, señor Colón.
Buenos días, señorita.

Indicate that the Spanish **c** before *a, o, u* has a sound similar to the English *c* in the word *care,* but without the puff of air: **Carmen, Colón.** Stress the linking as marked. In the first phrase, the letters are pronounced as one cluster. In the last two phrases, the double **s** is pronounced like one **s.** Point out that in many Spanish-speaking countries the final **s** in **Buenos** is not sounded.

Notice the pronunciation of **Jorge.** Explain that the sound of **j** and the sound of **g** before **e** and **i** are the same. Point out that in many Latin American countries the sound is similar to a strongly pronounced English *h,* as in the word *home.*

Finally, you may wish to practice the question intonation in **¿Cómo estás tú?** This pronunciation practice will help prepare the students for A11. As you play the cassette or read aloud, have the students listen carefully to the greetings. For cooperative learning, have students work in pairs to practice the short dialogs. Each member of the group should make sure that his or her partner understands and is able to produce the exchanges accurately. Call on each group to role-play the dialogs for the class.

A11 Actividad • Falta algo

Do this activity orally first so students will know what they are supposed to write later. They should complete this activity according to A10. You may ask students to complete the written activity in class or at home.

A12 SE DICE ASÍ

Review the formal and familiar greetings with students. Practice greetings and farewells with **Buenos días, Buenas tardes,** and **Buenas noches.**

A13 Comprensión 📼

You'll hear different people exchanging greetings. Decide whether the exchange is taking place in the morning (11 A.M.), in the afternoon (3 P.M.), or at night (9 P.M.). Then mark your answer in the corresponding box. For example, you hear: **Buenas tardes, señor Molina** and the reply **¿Cómo estás, Lupe?** The greeting is taking place in the afternoon **(Buenas tardes),** so you mark your answer in the row marked 3 P.M.

1. —Buenos días, Roberto.
    —¡Hola, Jorge! ¿Qué tal?   11 A.M.
2. —¡Hasta mañana, señora Martínez!
    —Adiós, Carlos. Buenas noches.   9 P.M.
3. —Buenas tardes, Carmen, ¿qué tal?
    —Bien, gracias, señora.   3 P.M.
4. —Buenas noches, señorita.
    —Adiós, señor López. ¡Hasta mañana!   9 P.M.
5. —¡Hola, Ramón! Buenas tardes.
    —¿Cómo estás, Pablo?   3 P.M.
6. —Buenos días, ¿cómo estás?
    —Regular, ¿y tú?   11 A.M.

Now check your answers. *Read each exchange again and give the correct answer.*

A14 Actividad • Y ahora tú . . .

For cooperative learning, have the students work in groups of three or four. Each student will represent one of the people portrayed in the activity. Then they will say hello and goodbye to every person in the group. One person can be responsible for making sure that varied responses are given and that each student in the group can accurately express the appropriate greetings. Remind students to include gestures when speaking.

A15 Actividad • ¿Buenos días, buenas tardes o buenas noches? 📼

Have students greet the people mentioned in the cues. Use the time of day and the person's name in parentheses as a guide to the appropriate expression.

SLOWER-PACED LEARNING Have several students play the role of the receptionist. The other students can select a name tag with the time of day written on it. Have the receptionists take turns greeting the people arriving at the office.

CHALLENGE   Turn this activity into a game by drawing lots. Half the class will be receptionists and the other half, clients. The clients are to make name tags with the names that appear in this activity. The time of day should also be included on the name tag. Then divide the class into two teams, including the same number of clients and receptionists on each team. Have members of each team face each other so that each client is facing a receptionist. Allow one point for each correct greeting and one point for correct pronunciation. The team with the most points wins.

A 16   SITUACIÓN • María Luisa y la profesora

Tell the students that they are going to listen to a dialog between a student and her teacher. As you play the cassette or read aloud, have the students listen carefully and practice their pronunciation by repeating the exchanges during the pauses.

A 17   ESTRUCTURAS ESENCIALES

You may want to stress the differences between the formal and the familiar. Tell students to use **tú** as the correct equivalent of *you* to address a close friend, a relative, or a child. Use **usted** in all other situations.

As a cultural point, you may indicate that in most Spanish-speaking countries, young people tend to call each other **tú** although they are meeting one another for the first time. Adults will use **tú** with all children. This usage is called **tutear**. The students should use **usted** when addressing a teacher and most adults. Point out that it is polite to allow the native speaker to suggest the use of **tú**.

Point out the difference between **¿Cómo estás tú?** and **¿Cómo está usted?** Explain that **estás** is the **tú** form of the verb *to be* **(estar)** and that **está** is the **usted** form of the verb. You may want to refer the students to English for the conjugation of the verb *to be*. Have them write this information in the grammar section of their notebook.

Indicate that Spanish, like English, has several question words that indicate the type of information we want to know. Two of them in Spanish are **¿Cómo . . . ?** *(How . . . ?)* and **¿Qué . . . ?** *(What . . . ?)* Point out that Spanish uses two question marks, one at the beginning of a question **(¿)** and the other at the end **(?)**.

A 18   Actividad • ¡A escoger!

Have students complete the activity orally first and then in writing. For cooperative learning, students may form groups of two or three, each having a name tag, for example: **profesor Colón, Elena, señora Martínez,** or **Ramón.** Have the students greet each other according to the name tags. Remind students that everyone in the group should make sure that all members can complete the activity accurately. You may wish to circulate among the students, greeting some by their first name and others by their last name and having them respond appropriately.

A 19   Actividad • Combinación

You may wish to tell the students to use this activity as a pattern to make up their own dialogs. Ask each student to prepare his or her own script, using expressions from the boxes.

After the students have finished the scripts at home or in class, have them act out the dialogs in class with the appropriate intonation and gestures.

A 20 Comprensión

Listen carefully as some people speak to you in Spanish. After each statement, decide which of the following you would say in reply.

1. —¿Cómo estás? *¡Muy bien, gracias!*
2. —Buenas noches, ¡hasta mañana! (woman's voice) *¡Adiós, señora!*
3. —¡Adiós! *¡Adiós!*
4. —Bien, gracias. ¡Chao! *¡Chao!*
5. —Regular, hasta luego. *¡Hasta luego!*
6. —Buenos días, ¿qué tal? (man's voice) *¡Buenos días, señor!*
7. —¡Hola! *¡Hola!*

Now check your answers. *Read each exchange again and give the correct answer.*

A 21 Actividad • Situaciones

Ask students to complete the caption for each illustration. Have students write the completed captions and check their answers.

Next have each student cover the captions and state them orally by looking only at the illustration. Call on several students to give the captions.

Point out that the sound of **qu** in the name **Quique** is similar to the sound of **c** in **Colón**. Both resemble the sound of the letter *c* in the word *care*.

SECTION B

OBJECTIVES **To exchange information:** ask and give names; ask and give someone else's name

CULTURAL BACKGROUND It is customary in many Spanish-speaking countries for a child to receive the name of his or her father or mother. Also, many families name their children after saints. There is at least one saint for every day of the year. The child receives the name of the saint corresponding to the day he or she was born. This is also the reason why many Spanish-speaking people celebrate not only their birthday but also their **santo.**

MOTIVATING ACTIVITY You may wish to play the music of the Spanish birthday song **"Feliz cumpleaños."** Write the words on the board or a transparency and have the students write them in their notebooks. They may sing the song for a classmate's birthday.

> Cumpleaños feliz,
> Te deseamos a ti.
> Cumpleaños *(name),*
> Cumpleaños feliz.

B 1 En la escuela. En la clase.

Introduce yourself to the class by saying: **¡Hola! Yo me llamo** *(your full name).* Say **Yo me llamo . . .** again and have the students repeat after you. Then ask several students **¿Cómo te llamas tú?** Students should be able to respond in Spanish with **Yo me llamo . . .** Continue this procedure until most of the students can respond accurately.

Now have the students ask the question. Make sure they are using the proper intonation. After students have practiced asking the question, they should continue the exchange, using a chain drill.

MAESTRO(A)	Yo me llamo . . . ¿Cómo te llamas tú?
ALICIA	Yo me llamo . . . ¿Cómo te llamas tú?
FERNANDO	Yo me llamo . . . ¿Cómo te llamas tú?

Next read aloud or play the cassette and have the students listen with their books closed. Ask them to discover the names of the girl and boy who speak. Can they find out the name of the last person who spoke? Then have students open their books to read the conversation aloud. Call on pairs of students to role-play the dialog.

SLOWER-PACED LEARNING Play the cassette or read aloud as the students follow along in their books. Read the conversation aloud and have the students repeat after you, first chorally, then in smaller groups, and finally individually.

B2 Actividad • Para completar

Have the students complete the sentences according to the dialog in B1. Do the exercise orally first; then, for extra writing practice, have the students write the sentences in class or at home.

SLOWER-PACED LEARNING Provide the students with choices. Write the scrambled answers on the board or a transparency and have the students select the appropriate word or words to complete the sentence.

B3 ¿Sabes que . . . ?

Read aloud the lists of Spanish names to the students. Tell them that this is just a short list, and ask if they know any other Spanish names. Have the students call out the new names as you or a volunteer writes them on the board or a transparency.

B4 SE DICE ASÍ

Have the students read the chart silently. Then explain that **¿Cómo te llamas tú?** is used for informal situations. They will use this exchange when speaking to people of the same age group or to children.

B5 Actividad • Presentaciones

Suggest that students model their introductions on B1. They should ask the names of four or five classmates.

B6 SITUACIÓN • Después de la clase

Begin this activity by introducing new vocabulary items. Ask a student the familiar line **¿Cómo te llamas?** and wait for his or her response. Now ask a student in Spanish about a girl in the class. Directing your question to one student, point out a girl as you say: **¿Cómo se llama la chica?** Point out a few more girls and have the students repeat after you: **¿Cómo se llama la chica?** Now answer by saying: **Ella se llama** (the girl's name). Point to a few girls and say **ella.** Follow the same procedure for: **¿Cómo se llama él?** and **Él**

se llama . . . Then alternately point out boys and girls to check comprehension.

Now read aloud or play the cassette as students follow along in their books. Then have the students read the dialog aloud.

SLOWER-PACED LEARNING Have the students prepare cue cards to role-play the dialog. The cue cards should contain the first two words of each line. Suggest to the students that they practice with a partner and use the cue cards when they role-play the dialog for the class.

CHALLENGE Assign the students the same work as above; however, the conversation will now be between two girls instead of two boys. They must change the name Lupe to José and substitute feminine names for Antonio and Ricardo. Students will have to make other adjustments as they prepare to role-play the dialog.

B7 Actividad • Para completar

Have the students complete the activity orally and then assign it as a written activity to complete in class or at home.

B8 SE DICE ASÍ

Have students read the chart silently. Then, for cooperative learning, have the students work in groups of three. Each group must have at least one boy or girl so that they will be able to practice **él** and **ella**. Ask them to practice the exchanges in B4 and B8. They should take turns asking and giving names. Students should make sure that the members of their group understand and are able to produce the statements and questions. Then ask the group members to identify each other for the class.

B9 Actividad • Nombres y más nombres

Have the students work in pairs. One student will ask the question and the other will give the appropriate response. Then have them switch roles.

CHALLENGE Provide only the words in parentheses as cues. Have the students work in pairs, asking the names of their classmates and answering as indicated by the cue.

> (Ana)—¿Cómo se llama la chica?
> —Ella se llama Ana.

B10 Actividad • ¿Cómo se llama?

As a variation, have each student bring a picture of a famous person to class. Request that the pictures be large enough to be seen from a distance. They may be used later in group or individual activities. Divide the class into two groups. Each group will select a picture at random and ask: **¿Cómo se llama ella/él?** The other group must respond: **Él/Ella se llama . . .**

SLOWER-PACED LEARNING Have the students bring photographs of friends and family from home. Working in pairs, each student should look at his or her partner's pictures and ask the names of the people in the photograph. Students might also prefer to use magazine pictures and to make up Spanish names.

B11 Actividad • ¡A escribir!

Do the activity orally first. You may ask the students to complete the written activity in class or at home. Write the answers on the board or a transparency and have the students check their work.

B12 ¿Sabes que . . . ?

Nicknames are popular in Spanish. While English speakers often shorten a name by cutting off the ending (Robert—Rob, Susan—Sue), Spanish names can be shortened by omitting the first, last, or even the middle part of the name (Guadalupe—Lupe, Alberto—Beto, María Isabel—Maribel).

In Spanish-speaking countries, people are fond of using nicknames, or **apodos** in Spanish, that refer to a person's physical appearance. This is not considered rude or offensive behavior; on the contrary, it demonstrates the true affection one has for the other.

BOYS	GIRLS
Alejandro: Alex, Xando	**Ana:** Anita, Nita
Antonio: Toño, Toñito	**Beatriz:** Betty, Betti
Carlos: Carlitos	**Carmen:** Carmencita, Carmela
Cristóbal: Tobal	**Catalina:** Cata, Cati, Catuca
Enrique: Quique, Quico	**Dolores:** Lola, Lolita
Federico: Fede, Federiquito, Lico	**Graciela:** Chela
Francisco: Paco, Pancho	**Guadalupe:** Lupe, Lupita
Guillermo: Guillermito, Memo	**Isabel:** Bela, Belita, Belica
Jaime: Jaimito	**Luisa:** Luisita
José: Pepe, Pepito,	**Lourdes:** Lulú
Juan: Juanito, Juancho, Juanillo	**María:** Mariquita, Mari
Ignacio: Nacho	**María Isabel:** Maribel, Marisel
Manuel: Manolo, Manolito	**María Luisa:** Marilú
Miguel: Miguelito	**Mercedes:** Mecha, Meche
Pablo: Pablito, Pablín	**Josefa:** Fina, Pepa, Pepita
Pedro: Perico, Periquito	**Roberta:** Berta
Roberto: Beto	**Rosario:** Chayo, Charito
Salvador: Chavo	**Teresa:** Tere

B13 Actividad • ¡A escribir!

Have students work in pairs to complete this activity. You may wish to have students role-play their dialogs.

SLOWER-PACED LEARNING Provide students with several key words to guide them as they write the dialog. The following words may be helpful.

▌ ¡Hola!/me llamo/gusto/estás/chao

B14 Actividad • Un juego

This game is appropriate in classes where the students do not know each other at the beginning of the school year.

As a variation, have the students put their name tags in a box and then pick tags out of the box at random. Students should wear the new name tags during the game. Members of one team should give the correct names of members of the other team.

B 15 ESTRUCTURAS ESENCIALES

Read the explanation about gender of nouns and the definite article with the students. Point out the use of **el** or **la** before **señor, señorita,** and **señora** when talking about a person. Note that **el** and **la** are not used when talking directly to the person: **Buenas noches, señora.**

B 16 Actividad • ¿El or la?

Call on individuals to give the appropriate article for each noun. You may also wish to write a list on the board or a transparency and review with the class for added practice.

SLOWER-PACED LEARNING   Write the vocabulary items that are nouns from Sections A and B on separate 3 × 5 cards. Place the cards in a box and have students select a card from the box. Have each student read aloud the word and give its definite article.

B 17 Actividad • ¿Qué crees?

Have students complete the activity and check their work. You or a volunteer may write on the board or transparency while students dictate the masculine and feminine nouns. Make sure the students use the Spanish pronunciation of these words.

B 18 Comprensión

You'll hear the voice of different teenagers greeting their friends. After listening to the names of the persons being greeted, decide for each whether the name of a boy **(Chico)** or a girl **(Chica)** is used, and mark your answer in the corresponding box. For example, you hear: **¿Qué tal, Inés?** Since **Inés** is a girl's name, the check mark is placed in the row labeled **Chica.**

1. —¡Hola, Tomás! *Chico*
2. —¿Cómo estás, Ana? *Chica*
3. —¡Adiós, Isabel! *Chica*
4. —Buenas tardes, Ramón. *Chico*
5. —Hasta mañana, Tere. *Chica*
6. —Buenas noches, Felipe. *Chico*
7. —¡Chao, Esteban! *Chico*
8. —Muchas gracias, Lupe. *Chica*
9. —Hasta luego, Víctor. *Chico*
10. —De nada, Pilar. *Chica*
11. —Yo, regular. ¿Y tú, Dolores? *Chica*
12. —Buenos días, Manuel. *Chico*

Now check your answers. *Read each sentence again and give the correct answer.*

B 19 SITUACIÓN • Una sorpresa

Have pairs of students read the captions aloud. Encourage students to use gestures (hand movement, shaking the head, moving the shoulders) when they speak. They might feel awkward at first, but as they practice, using gestures will seem more natural to them.

SECTION C

OBJECTIVES **To exchange information:** ask and say where people are from

CULTURAL BACKGROUND You may wish to point out that although there are many differences in pronunciation and sometimes in vocabulary in the Hispanic world, Spanish-speaking people can always communicate and understand one another. In Cuba, Puerto Rico, and other Caribbean countries, many people don't pronounce the *s* and also slice off word endings. People from Argentina pronounce **y** and **ll** as the *j* in the English word *Joe.*

Not only does the intonation vary from country to country, but sometimes vocabulary is different, too. For example, in Spain a car is **coche** and in other South American countries it is **carro** or **máquina.** A bus is **guagua** in Puerto Rico and Cuba, **camión** in Mexico, **autobús** in Spain, and **colectivo** in Argentina.

You may wish to point out that in the English-speaking world, pronunciation and vocabulary also vary, yet communication is not hampered. You may cite some examples of vocabulary differences, such as *lift* (elevator), *flat* (apartment), and *queue* (line), as well as pronunciation differences in England, Australia, Scotland, Ireland, and the United States.

MOTIVATING ACTIVITY Ask the students if they can identify words that vary in English-speaking countries. Then write on the board or a transparency a list of words that vary among Spanish-speaking countries.

C1   ¿De dónde son?

Begin the presentation by telling the students the origin of well-known Americans. For example, **Bruce Springsteen es de New Jersey.** Point out the cities you name on a map. Then ask the students if one of their classmates is from Spain. After they have responded **no,** model the answer **Él/Ella es de** *(name of your town or city)* for repetition. Use several similar examples. Now tell the students where you are from, using **Yo soy de** . . . Then ask a student: **¿De dónde eres tú?** If the student responds with only the name of the city or town, model the complete sentence **Yo soy de** . . . for repetition. You may wish to ask **¿De dónde es él/ella?** from time to time to make sure that the students are paying attention to their classmates' answers.

Read the captions aloud or play the cassette as the students follow along in the text. Then call for repetition. Next have individuals read the captions aloud as you point out the cities on a map showing Spanish-speaking countries.

C2   Actividad • ¿Cuál país?

For cooperative learning, have the students assume the identity of the young people in the photos, after they have listened to and read the captions. Divide the class into groups of three to four students and have them ask one another their names and where they are from. As they answer, the students should point to the country they mention on the maps on pages 2 and 3. Students should make sure that the members of their group understand and are able to produce the questions and statements.

C3   SITUACIÓN • Aquí se habla español

Have students follow along in their books as you read or as you play the cassette. Then the students may work in pairs. One student should ask

where a particular person in C3 is from. The other student should respond. Have students switch roles.

C4 Actividad • ¿Cómo se llama . . . ?

Students will have the opportunity to practice asking and giving the name of someone. Make sure they answer in complete sentences using **Él/Ella se llama . . .**

SLOWER-PACED LEARNING You may wish to use pictures of famous people for additional practice of ____ **de** ____ structures and also for a review of names.

Photographs of the following or similar Spanish-speaking celebrities may be found in newspapers or magazines: Dave Concepción, a talented baseball player from Venezuela; Miguel de la Madrid, the president of Mexico; Plácido Domingo, an opera singer born in Spain and raised in Mexico; and Norma Leandro, an outstanding Argentinian actress.

C5 Actividad • Combinación

For cooperative learning, have students form groups of five. Each student in a group is to form a sentence, choosing an element from each column. Students should be sure that every person in the group can accurately form the sentences.

C6 SE DICE ASÍ

Have the students read the chart silently. Point out the examples that show how to ask and say where people are from. Note the subject and verb agreement and explain to students that the verb **ser** is used to indicate origin.

C7 Actividad • Charla

Complete this activity as a chain drill. If students are all from the same area, you may write on slips of paper the names of Spanish-speaking cities or countries. Then have students select a slip of paper and reply accordingly.

CHALLENGE Show students pictures from magazines or give the name of a city and a person's name. Have them guess what country the person mentioned is from.

C8 Actividad • ¿De dónde es él? ¿De dónde es ella?

Call on individuals to identify each picture and say where the person is from. If a student gives the name of the country in English, say the Spanish name and have him or her repeat it. Make sure the students use the Spanish pronunciation for names such as California, Texas, and Mexico.

C9 Actividad • ¿Sí o no?

This game can be played by dividing the class into two groups. Each group will choose a person from C1. Students from each group may ask up to five questions, which must be answered with **Sí** or **No.** If the group cannot guess the identity of the mystery person, the other group receives one point.

Have students adopt a new identity. They must choose a name, city, and country. They will keep this identity throughout the year, as it may be incorporated in other activities. Have each student prepare an identity card with his or her new name, country, and city.

Unidad 1 Teacher's Notes T37

SLOWER-PACED LEARNING Prepare name cards from the list and put in parentheses the name of the country where each person is from. Distribute the cards to the students. Have the class ask individuals the **Sí** or **No** questions. When a student guesses the individual's origin and identity, the student holding the card must confirm by restating his or her name and origin: **Sí, me llamo . . . Soy de . . .**

C10 ESTRUCTURAS ESENCIALES

Prepare flashcards of the subject pronouns. As you follow the procedure described below, hold up the appropriate card when stating each pronoun.

Review the subject pronouns **yo, usted,** and **tú.** Remind students to use **tú** with friends and children, and use **usted** when addressing an adult.

Have three groups of students stand at the front of the room. One group should contain all boys, one group should have all girls, and the third group should be mixed. If this is not possible, have the students in each group hold magazine pictures to represent the groups.

Ask the group of boys **¿De dónde son ustedes?** Have the group reply **Nosotros somos de** . . . Turn to the rest of the class and ask a student **¿De dónde son los chicos?** Remind the students to include the subject pronoun when answering. After the student replies **Ellos son de** . . . , have the class repeat the phrase. Repeat this procedure with the mixed group.

Now turn to the group of girls. Follow the same procedure as above, using **nosotras, chicas,** and **ellas.**

Have the students copy the conjugation of the verb **ser** in their notebooks. Explain that this is an irregular verb and its forms must be learned. Compare it to the irregular verb *to be* in English. They will use the verb **ser** to indicate origin and to identify the subject. Have the students read the explanations in C10.

SLOWER-PACED LEARNING Have the students copy the chart in their notebooks. Then, on a separate sheet of paper, have the students write the following sentences and complete them with the correct word.

1. Yo _____ la chica nueva. (es, *soy*)
2. Diego, ¿ _____ tú de México? (es, *eres*)
3. Ustedes _____ de los Estados Unidos. (es, *son*)
4. Juan y Elena _____ de California. (somos, *son*)
5. Arturo y Carlos, ¿ _____ ustedes amigos? (soy, *son*)

C11 Actividad • ¿Quién? ¿Yo?

For cooperative learning, have the students work in pairs. They should take turns asking and answering the questions. Each student should make sure that his or her partner can answer accurately, using the correct subject pronoun. Then call on pairs randomly to provide the answers for the class.

C12 Actividad • ¡A escribir!

Have the students write the sentences using the correct subject pronoun. After they have completed the sentences, you or a volunteer may write the answers on a transparency or the board as students dictate.

SLOWER-PACED LEARNING Have the students do the activity orally before writing it. They can write the sentences in class or at home.

C13 Actividad • Una entrevista 📼

After the students have written the questions and corrected their work, have them role-play the interview with a partner.

C14 Actividad • Falta algo

Keep the verb **ser** in context by having the students read and write the complete sentence. To correct the work, you or a volunteer may write the sentences on the board or a transparency as the students dictate them.

CHALLENGE Dictate to the class five sentences similar to the ones in the activity. Call on volunteers to write their sentences on the board or a transparency for correction.

C15 Actividad • Combinación

Call on individuals to form a sentence by choosing an element from each column. You may also wish to have the students complete this activity orally and in pairs.

For writing practice, have students write the sentences in class or at home. Collect the papers and check their work.

C16 ¿Sabes que . . . ?

Refer to the photographs and information on pages 19–22 of the Introduction. Tell students they can watch television, listen to the radio, or even read the newspaper in Spanish right here in the United States. The Spanish cable television station, **Univisión,** offers news, entertainment, and sports to many areas around the country. You can buy Spanish magazines such as **Vanidades, Buen Hogar, Hola,** and **Time en Español** on newstands located in most international airports. In many states, such as Florida, Texas, California, and New Mexico, Spanish can be heard just about anywhere!

C17 ESTRUCTURAS ESENCIALES

Read aloud the first two sample questions while students listen with their books closed. Ask students to identify the sentences as statements or questions. Explain that they can form an interrogative sentence simply by changing the intonation and adding question marks. Write the first two questions on the board or a transparency. Point out the inverted question mark at the beginning of the sentence and the standard one at the end.

Now read aloud the last two sample questions. Tell students that they can also form a question by placing the verb at the beginning of a sentence and adding the question marks. Write the last two sample questions on the board or a transparency.

Write the sample answers on the board or a transparency.

C18 Actividad • Preguntas . . . 📼

Have students work in pairs. They should take turns asking the questions. Circulate among the students, making note of the most obvious errors and correcting intonation.

To review, repeat the exercise with the class, but with books closed. Call on individuals to ask the new questions.

C19 Comprensión

You'll hear eight different questions followed by a cue. After you hear each question and the cue, select an appropriate answer from your list.

1. —¿De dónde son ustedes? (pause) México   **C** *Somos de México.*
2. —¿Irene? (pause) De Argentina.   **F** *Irene es de Argentina.*
3. —¿De dónde es Pablo? (pause) Puerto Rico   **E** *Pablo es de Puerto Rico.*
4. —¿De dónde eres tú? (pause) Boston   **B** *Yo soy de Boston.*
5. —¿De dónde es María? (pause) España   **A** *María es de España.*
6. —¿Y Carlos? (pause) España   **D** *Carlos es de España.*
7. —Y Tomás y Luis, ¿de dónde son? (pause) San Antonio   **H** *Tomás y Luis son de San Antonio.*
8. —¿Es ella de Colorado? (pause) California   **G** *Ella es de California.*

Now check your answers. *Read each question again and give the correct answer.* (Answers will vary slightly.)

TRY YOUR SKILLS

OBJECTIVE   To recombine communicative functions, grammar, and vocabulary

CULTURAL BACKGROUND   Most Spanish speakers are informal when visiting other people. They may drop in on friends without telephoning beforehand, or they may call an hour or so before they arrive. This is especially true in the afternoons and among women. Spanish-speaking people always welcome a visit from close friends or family, and usually have extra food and refreshments on hand for the "visitas." **Mi casa es tu casa** is not just a saying but a way of life.

1   Tarjetas postales

Have the students look at the postcards. Identify the cities and countries pictured for the students. Tell them to close their books and listen as you read aloud or play the cassette. Then have them open their books and read the postcards.

2   Actividad • ¿Quién es la chica? ¿Quién es el chico?

Have students work in pairs. Each one must select a postcard from Skills 1 and give information about his or her new pen pal.

CHALLENGE   Have students ask questions about their partner's pen pal, such as **¿De dónde es? ¿Cómo se llama? ¿Es de España?**

3   Actividad • ¡A escribir!

Ask the students to bring in pictures from magazines or photos of their favorite Spanish-speaking city. Then have them write a postcard to an imaginary pen pal in that city. Have students use Skills 2 as a model. Display their postcards in the classroom.

4   Actividad • ¿Qué falta?

Have pairs of students complete the activity orally, before they write the conversation.

SLOWER-PACED LEARNING   Have the students role-play the dialogs after they complete the oral and written activity.

5   Actividad • Diálogos

For cooperative learning, have students work in small groups of no more than four students to make up their dialog. Have everyone in the group participate in at least one of the dialogs. Students should make sure that every person in the group understands and can accurately produce the sentences.

6   Actividad • ¡Buenas noches!

Prepare name tags for all of the names listed. Place them at the front of the room. Divide the class into two groups. One student will select a name tag and the other will greet him or her. Remind students to use the appropriate greeting for adults and peers.

     As a variation, give each student a name tag. Let students move through the room, greeting each other, or have them form receiving lines. To make the role-play more realistic, you may wish to have the students greet the person while putting the name tag on him or her.

7   Actividad • Reacciones

Have the students work in pairs. Tell them to take turns reading the sentence and giving the response.

8   Actividad • ¡Bienvenidos!

For cooperative learning, have students compare and combine the conversations they have written and then role-play them. Everyone in the group should participate and have a speaking part.

9   Actividad • ¡A escoger!

Tell the students that they will listen as you play the cassette or read. They should select the correct response from those given.

SLOWER-PACED LEARNING   Have the students complete the activity orally. Then they should write the sentences and the appropriate responses in class or at home.

10   Pronunciación, lectura, dictado

As the students repeat in chorus during the pauses, monitor their participation by changing your position in the room and repeating with them. If some individuals stumble over the words, stop the cassette or stop reading and then repeat the word or words with which the students have difficulty. Then call for group repetition. Do not single out individuals for correction at this time.

> **1.** Listen carefully and repeat what you hear.
> The letter **h:** In Spanish, the letter **h** is always silent. The words **hola**

and **Oscar** both start with the same sound. Listen to the following words and repeat in the pauses provided.

      Héctor   hola   hamburguesa   Hernández

The sound of **ñ**: In Spanish the sound of **ñ** is similar to the sound of *ny* in the English word *canyon* but is somewhat shorter. Listen to these words with **ñ** and repeat.

      Muñoz   señora Núñez   español   mañana

2. Listen to the following words and repeat.

      hola   hasta   señora Henríquez   Honduras

Listen to the following words with **ñ** and repeat.

      señor   señorita   señora   España   español   mañana

3. Write the following sentences from dictation. First listen to the sentence as it is read to you. Then you will hear the sentence again in short segments, with a pause after each segment to allow you time to write. Finally you will hear the sentence a third time so that you may check your work. Let's begin.

      ¡Hola, *(pause)* Hilda!
      ¡Hasta mañana, *(pause)* señor Núñez!
      Horacio es *(pause)* de Honduras.

¿LO SABES?

SECTION A

Call on individuals to say hello and goodbye to the people listed in Section A. Remind the students to use formal expressions when speaking to adults.

    For further practice with greetings, have the students work with a partner. They should create a dialog, using **¿Qué tal? ¿Cómo estás?** and **¿Cómo está?**

SECTION B

Have the students work in pairs. First they are to introduce themselves and say hello. Each student should complete the sentences by asking the name of his or her partner and other classmates.

    For writing practice, have the students write the sentences on a separate sheet of paper, adding the missing words. Students may exchange papers to correct their work.

SECTION C

For the first part of this activity, ask the students to supply the missing word or words to complete the questions and answers about where someone is from.

    When completing the second part of the activity, have the students write the correct form of the verb **ser.** They should provide the missing elements to form a complete sentence.

VOCABULARIO

Have the students review these words and expressions by using them in sentences. Some will suggest sentences they have used often in class, while others may try to combine as many of the words and expressions as they can in one sentence.

ESTUDIO DE PALABRAS

The students should have a **vocabulario** section in their notebooks where they can keep vocabulary notes and also record information from the **Estudio de palabras.**

Begin this study by telling students that all nouns in Spanish are masculine or feminine, and that they have a corresponding article **el** or **la.** Explain that although most nouns can be easily identified as masculine or feminine by their endings **-o** or **-a,** there are many that can be misleading. Point out **el día, el profesor,** and **la clase.**

Continue by having the students make two lists of the nouns, one for masculine words and one for the feminine. Remind them to include the article. To check their work, you or a volunteer can write the lists on the board as the students dictate the words.

VAMOS A LEER

OBJECTIVE   To read for practice and pleasure

EL MUNDO HISPÁNICO

The following steps will assist the students to become more proficient readers:

    a. Motivate the students to read by giving an exciting preview or stimulating their interest and ability.
    b. Relate the reading to the students' background.
    c. Clarify unfamiliar words.
    d. Set the purpose for the selection.
    e. Have them read silently.
    f. Check their comprehension after they have completed the reading.

You may wish to use all the reading selections, or select one or two. For cooperative learning, you may assign a different selection to each group. Have them discuss the content and then give a short summary of the selection to the class.

Encourage the students to use context clues and cognates to help them comprehend new words. With their books closed, give them a list of cognates to guess meanings before they open their books. Show flash cards or write on the board or a transparency words such as **libertad, independencia, América, computadora, Europa,** and **béisbol.** Ask students to guess the word in English. Explain that sometimes the pronunciation of a word is the only difference. Ask the students to change one letter in the words **norte, papel,** and **plato** to translate them into English.

Now, write the following sentence on the board and ask the students to supply the missing word: *David, write on the . . . , not on the wall.* Explain to the students that they can find the meaning of an unknown word if they understand the surrounding words.

Write this sentence on the board or a transparency: **Gracias a la escuela técnica, la compañía de computadoras gana mucho.** Ask the students for a general translation. Did they figure out what **gana** meant? If they saw the word **isla**-- and the last two letters were blurred, what do they think the word would be in English?

Before reading the first article, explain the meaning of **mundo** in **El mundo hispánico.** Next have the students read the article silent. Ask the students to summarize the article—in English—or to give the main point. Then read the article aloud or play the cassette once or twice as students follow along in their books.

As a follow-up assignment, have each student (or pairs of students) choose a Spanish-speaking country or city to research. They should look for specific information, such as location, historical background, other languages spoken, and population. Students should report the results of their research to the class in English. They may illustrate their project with posters, post-cards, maps, and travel brochures of the countries and cities.

Actividad • ¡Faltan palabras!

Have students complete the activity orally and then write the sentences in class or at home.

Actividad • Proyecto

Some students may wish to share their postcard with the class. Have them exchange postcards and read the messages. Make any necessary corrections and display the postcards in the classroom.

UN PASEO POR EL PARQUE

Have the students read aloud the exchanges between these people at the park. Then read aloud or play the cassette as the students follow along in their books. They may practice the greetings with a classmate.

Taking an afternoon walk is an old custom in Spanish-speaking countries, especially in small towns. On Sundays, in **el parque,** the girls would walk in one direction while the boys walked in the other, thus meeting each other and having the chance to say hello. Now the modern **paseo** is done by car. The young people slowly circle the main square or central park in their cars, stopping to greet friends. They call this **una vuelta.**

Actividad

Role-play a stroll through the park. Ask students to practice their greetings as they act out the reading. Encourage them to use gestures as they speak.

EL REGALO

Tell the students that they are going to read the first episode of a continuing story. There is a new and exciting adventure in every unit.

Have the students quickly scan the article and find the cognates. Some examples are **familia, tragedia, inteligente, perfecto,** and **fantástico.**

You may wish to explain to the students that the word **colonia** is used primarily in Mexico. The major cities are divided into many small areas, **colonias,** and given names. In other parts of the Spanish-speaking world the students may hear *neighborhood* as **vecindario, barrio, vecindad, reparto,** or **urbanización.**

Now have the students read the story **El regalo** silently. Then play the cassette or read aloud as students follow along in their books. For cooperative learning, divide the class into groups of five students and have them practice and role-play the dialogs.

Actividad • Para completar

Have the students supply the missing elements to complete the sentences. Have them refer to **El regalo** for the information.

¡Hola, amigos!

Making new friends is exciting, especially if they speak another language. When you meet a Spanish-speaking person for the first time, you will want to say hello. The two of you will want to find out a little bit about each other.

In this unit you will:

SECTION A	greet people . . . ask how someone is . . . say goodbye
SECTION B	give your name . . . ask someone's name . . . say what other people's names are
SECTION C	say where you are from and ask where others are from
TRY YOUR SKILLS	use what you've learned
VAMOS A LEER	read for practice and pleasure

31

SECTION A

greeting people . . . asking how someone is . . . saying goodbye

Vacation is over, and it's back to school! Students greet one another and their teachers before classes begin.

Point out the inverted question marks and exclamation points. You may wish to refer to C17 where they are introduced.

A1

En el colegio

Also, have the students notice the written accents on "Cómo", "Ramón", "tú", and "adiós".

RAMÓN ¡Hola, Anita! ¿Cómo estás?
ANITA Muy bien, Ramón. Gracias, ¿y tú?
RAMÓN ¿Yo? Regular. ¡Hasta luego!
ANITA ¡Chao!
RAMÓN ¡Adiós!

¿Qué tal?

¿Yo? ¡Muy mal!

¡Qué pena!

A2 Actividad *Activity* • Reacciones *Reactions*

Have the students refer to A1 to complete this activity. Possible answers are given.
Match each statement or question on the left with an appropriate response on the right.

¡Hola!   ¡Hasta luego!

¿Cómo estás?   Regular.

Muy bien, ¿y tú?   Muy bien, gracias.

¡Adiós!   ¡Muy mal!

¡Chao!   ¡Hola!

¿Qué tal?   ¡Adiós!

32 Unidad 1

Actividad • Y ahora tú . . .   *And now you . . .*   Point out that the <u>h</u> in Spanish is always silent.

Choose a Spanish first name either from the list on page 17 or from another source. With a classmate, practice reading this dialog using your new names.

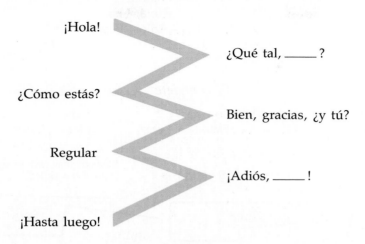

¡Hola!

¿Qué tal, _____ ?

¿Cómo estás?

Bien, gracias, ¿y tú?

Regular

¡Adiós, _____ !

¡Hasta luego!

A4   SE DICE ASÍ   *This is how you say it*
     Asking how someone is and saying how you are

You may wish to point out that <u>qu</u> represents one sound in Spanish, similar to the English <u>k</u> sound.

PREGUNTA	QUESTION	RESPUESTA	ANSWER
¿Qué tal?	How are things?	Bien, gracias.	Fine, thanks.
¿Cómo estás tú?	How are you?		

A5   Actividad • Charla   *Small talk*   Answers will vary.

With your classmate, create your own dialog. Take turns asking how the other person is and then replying.

Muy bien

Bien

Regular

Mal

Muy mal

Actividad • ¡A escribir! *Let's write!* Possible answers are given.

Unscramble the following conversation. Then write it out correctly.

—¡Hasta luego, Inés!
—Muy bien, gracias.
—¡Hola, Inés!
—¿Cómo estás?

—Regular, ¿y tú?
—¡Hola, Pepe!
—¡Adiós, Pepe!

—¡Hola, Inés!
—¡Hola, Pepe!
—¿Cómo estás?
—Regular, ¿y tú?
—Muy bien, gracias.
—¡Hasta luego, Inés!
—¡Adiós, Pepe!

A 7 **Actividad • Para completar** *To complete* Possible answers are given.

Luis—¡Hola, _____! Elsa
Elsa— . . . ¡Hola, Luis!

Luis—¿Cómo estás?
Elsa— . . . Muy bien, ¿y tú?

Luis— . . . Regular, gracias.
Elsa—¡Adiós!

A 8 **Actividad • Me llamo . . .** *My name is . . .* Students may wish to select a nickname from those listed in B12.

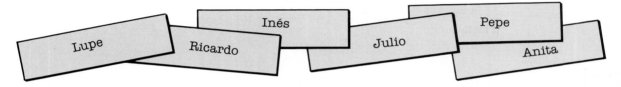

Lupe   Ricardo   Inés   Julio   Pepe   Anita

Choose a Spanish name either from the list in B3 (page 38) or from another source. Make a name tag showing your new Spanish name. Wearing your tag, turn to your right or left, greeting each of your classmates and saying goodbye.

A 9 **¿Sabes que . . . ?** *Do you know that . . . ?*

Spanish-speaking boys and girls often shake hands upon meeting. Girls usually kiss each other on the cheek.

You may wish to point out the Spanish consonant ñ. It is similar to the English sound ny as in "canyon".

A 10 **SITUACIÓN • Saludos** *Greetings*

Carmen y el señor Colón   Jorge y la señorita López   Alicia y la señora Valdés

—Buenos días, señor.
—Buenos días, Carmen.

—Buenas tardes, señorita.
—¡Adiós! Hasta mañana, Jorge.

—Buenas noches, señora.
—Buenas noches, Alicia. ¿Cómo estás tú?

Actividad • Falta algo *Something's missing* Refer to dialogs in A10.

Supply the missing words.

1. Buenos _____ . días
2. _____ tardes. Buenas
3. _____ mañana, señorita López. Hasta
4. ¿Cómo _____ tú, Jorge? estás

5. _____ noches. Buenas
6. Alicia y la _____ Valdés. señora
7. Buenas noches, _____ Colón. señor
8. Buenos días, _____ López. señorita

A12 SE DICE ASÍ
Saying hello and goodbye
You may wish to explain that "adiós" comes from the expression "Vaya con Dios".

Formal, respectful	**Buenos días, señor.** Good morning (Hello), sir.	**Adiós, señorita.** Goodbye, miss.
Friendly, familiar	**¡Hola, Anita!** Hi, Anita!	**¡Chao, Eduardo!** 'Bye, Eduardo!

Buenos días is used until noon. **Buenas tardes** is used until nightfall. **Buenas noches** is used in the evening as both hello and goodbye.

When you say hello or goodbye to your teacher or any adult, it's polite to complete your hello or goodbye by adding **señor,** *sir, Mr.,* **señora,** *ma'am, Mrs.,* or **señorita,** *Miss.* The written abbreviations of these titles are **Sr., Sra.,** and **Srta.**

A13 Comprensión *Comprehension* For script and answers, see p. T29.

Greetings: Morning, afternoon, or night?

	0	1	2	3	4	5	6
11 A.M.		✔					✔
3 P.M.	✔			✔		✔	
9 P.M.			✔		✔		

A14 Actividad • Y ahora tú . . .

Greet each of the people pictured below. Then say goodbye to each one. Possible answers are given.

Roberto
Buenos días, Roberto.
Chao, Roberto.

Lupe
Buenas tardes, Lupe.
Chao, Lupe.

Srta. López
Buenas noches, Srta. López.
Buenas noches, Srta. López.

Sr. González
Buenos días, Sr. González.
Adiós, Sr. González.

Sra. Martínez
Buenas tardes, Sra. Martínez.
Adiós, Sra. Martínez.

¡Hola, amigos! 35

1. Buenas tardes, Srta. Ortiz. 2. Buenos días, Sr. González. 3. Buenas tardes, Sra. Martínez. 4. Buenos días, Sr. Soto.
5. Buenas noches, Srta. Portillo.

A 15 Actividad • ¿Buenos días, buenas tardes o buenas noches?

In your summer job as a bilingual receptionist, you must greet people in Spanish
as they arrive for appointments. Here are some entries from your appointment book.

> (9:00 P.M., Mr. Ruiz)   Buenas noches, señor Ruiz.

1. (4:00 P.M., Miss Ortiz)
2. (10:00 A.M., Mr. González)
3. (3:00 P.M., Mrs. Martínez)
4. (9:00 A.M., Mr. Soto)
5. (8:00 P.M., Miss Portillo)

6. (5:00 P.M., Mr. Rivera)
7. (11:00 A.M., Miss Alonso)
8. (9:00 P.M., Mrs. Henríquez)
9. (4:30 P.M., Mr. Silva)
10. (12:30 P.M., Mrs. Pérez)

6. Buenas tardes, Sr. Rivera. 7. Buenos días, Srta. Alonso. 8. Buenas noches, Sra. Henríquez. 9. Buenas tardes, Sr. Silva.
10. Buenas tardes, Sra. Pérez.

A 16 SITUACIÓN • María Luisa y la profesora

SRA. VALDÉS   Buenos días, María Luisa.
               ¿Cómo estás?
MARÍA LUISA   Muy bien, señora, gracias.
               ¿Y cómo está usted?
SRA. VALDÉS   Bien, gracias.

A 17 ESTRUCTURAS ESENCIALES *Essential Structures*
Spanish equivalents for the word you

Spanish has several words that are equivalents for the English word *you*. These words are called
pronouns. Use **tú** when you talk to a friend or relative. Use **usted** when you address an adult
you don't know well. A different verb form goes with each pronoun. Until now, you have used
them together in questions. You may wish to point out the accent on "tú".

Informal	*Formal*
¿Question word + **estás** + **tú?**	¿Question word + **está** + **usted?**
¡Hola, Jorge! ¿Cómo estás tú?	Buenas noches, señora. ¿Cómo está usted?

Words like **¿Cómo?** (*How*) and **¿Qué?** (*What*) are question words. They indicate the
type of information being requested.

A 18 Actividad • ¡A escoger! *Let's choose*

Using A16 as a model, choose the proper completion for each sentence.

1. Buenos días, profesor Colón. ¿Cómo / estás? / <u>está usted?</u>
2. ¡Hola, Elena! ¿Cómo / <u>estás?</u> / está usted?
3. Buenos días, señora Martínez. ¿Cómo / estás? / <u>está usted?</u>
4. ¿Qué tal, Ramón? ¿Cómo / <u>estás?</u> / está usted?

Stress the use of "Ud". A young person uses "Usted" in addressing an older person. The older person may use "tú" when
addressing the younger person. Students should address their teachers with "Ud."

Actividad • Combinación *Combination* Answers will vary.

Pair up with a classmate. Make your own dialogs using items from this table.
Take the parts of different characters in each dialog and include the names in
your dialog lines.

Buenas noches **Hola** **Buenos días** **Buenas tardes**	**¿Cómo estás?** **¿Qué tal?** **¿Cómo está?**	**Muy bien** **Regular** **Mal** **Bien, gracias.** **Muy mal**	**Hasta mañana** **Chao** **¡Qué pena!** **Adiós** **Hasta luego**

A 20 Comprensión   For script and answers, see page T31.

Some people will speak to you in Spanish. Which of the following would you say in reply?

¡Hola!   ¡Buenos días, señor!   ¡Hasta luego!   ¡Chao!
¡Adiós!   ¡Muy bien, gracias!   ¡Adiós, señora!

A 21 Actividad • Situaciones *Situations*

What are these people saying to each other? Copy and complete each caption.

1.
—¡Hola, Lola! ¿ _____ estás?
—¡ _____ , Pepe! ¿Qué _____ ?
1. Cómo/Hola/tal

2.
—¡Buenas _____ ! ¿Cómo _____ ?
—Muy _____ , gracias. ¿Y _____ ?
2. tardes/estás/bien/usted

3.
—¡ _____ , Sr. Ramos!
—¡Buenos _____ , Lola!
3. Hola/días

4.
—¡Hasta _____ , Quique!
—¡Adiós, _____ Soto!
4. luego/señor

¡Hola, amigos!   37

Introducing yourself is the most direct way to make new friends. Sometimes another friend can help. Point out that the initial r in "Ricardo" and "Roque" are strongly trilled.

B1   En la escuela. En la clase.

RICARDO   ¡Hola! Yo me llamo Ricardo.
              ¿Cómo te llamas tú?
LUPE   Me llamo Lupe.
              ¡Mucho gusto!
RICARDO   ¡Mucho gusto! Bueno . . .
              hasta luego, Lupe.
LUPE   Hasta luego, Ricardo.

Él se llama Ricardo.

Ella se llama Lupe.

B2   Actividad • Para completar

Complete the sentences according to the dialog.

1. ¿Cómo te . . . ?
2. Yo me llamo . . .
3. Me . . . Lupe.
4. ¡Mucho . . . !
5. Hasta . . . , Ricardo.

1. llamas   2. Ricardo   3. llamo   4. gusto   5. luego

B3   ¿Sabes que . . . ?

Many Spanish names are like English names: **Felipe** *Philip*, **Antonio**, *Anthony*, **Tomás**, *Thomas*. Other Spanish names are quite different: **Soledad, Javier, Pilar, Diego.** Here are some common Spanish first names. Do you know any others? Which ones?

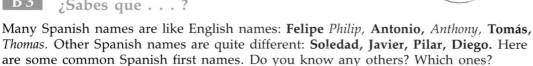

Nombres de chicos y chicas							
CHICOS				CHICAS			
Alberto	Esteban	Juan	Pedro	Alicia	Dolores	Inés	Pilar
Alfonso	Fernando	Julio	Ramón	Amalia	Elena	Luisa	Rosario
Carlos	Francisco	Manuel	Raúl	Ana	Elsa	Margarita	Sofía
Diego	Gonzalo	Miguel	Santiago	Blanca	Eva	María	Soledad
Enrique	Guillermo	Pablo	Víctor	Cristina	Guadalupe	Olga	Victoria

SE DICE ASÍ
Asking and giving names

¿Cómo te llamas tú?	Yo me llamo . . .
What's your name?	My name is . . .

B5   Actividad • Presentaciones   *Introductions*

Choose a Spanish name for yourself if you haven't done so before. Introduce yourself to your friends and ask them what their names are. You introduce yourself saying **Yo me llamo . . . ¿Cómo te llamas tú?** The second student answers: **Me llamo . . . Mucho gusto,** and continues to introduce himself, asking the next student's name.

B6   SITUACIÓN • Después de la clase   *After school*

En el patio de la escuela.

ANTONIO   ¡Ricardo!, ¡Ricardo!
RICARDO   ¿Sí?
ANTONIO   ¡Oye! Por favor, ¿cómo se llama la chica nueva?
RICARDO   ¿Quién, la chica de Arizona?
ANTONIO   No, la chica de México.
RICARDO   Ella se llama Lupe.
ANTONIO   ¿Lupe? Gracias, Ricardo.
RICARDO   De nada, Antonio.

Ricardo
y Antonio

B7   Actividad • Para completar

Complete the sentences according to B6.

1. Por favor, ¿cómo . . . ?   se llama la chica nueva
2. ¿Quién, la . . . de Arizona?   chica
3. No, la chica de . . .   México.
4. Ella se . . . Lupe.   llama
5. Gracias, . . .   Ricardo.
6. De . . .   nada, Antonio.

B8   SE DICE ASÍ
Asking and giving someone else's name

¿Cómo se llama él?	Él se llama Ricardo.
What's his name?	His name is Ricardo.
¿Cómo se llama ella?	Ella se llama Lupe.
What's her name?	Her name is Lupe.

B9 Actividad • Nombres y más nombres *Names and more names*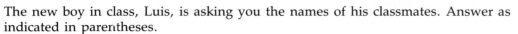

The new boy in class, Luis, is asking you the names of his classmates. Answer as indicated in parentheses.

> —¿Cómo se llama la chica? (Ana)
> —Ella se llama Ana.

1. ¿Cómo se llama el chico? (Paco)
2. ¿Cómo se llama ella? (Lupe)
3. ¿Cómo se llama el chico de California? (Pepe)
4. ¿Cómo se llama la chica de Nuevo México? (Ana)

5. ¿Cómo te llamas tú? Yo me llamo . . .
6. ¿Cómo se llama él? (Tomás) Él se llama Tomás.
7. ¿Cómo se llama el señor Ortega? (Esteban) Él se llama Esteban.
8. ¡Oye! ¿Cómo me llamo yo? (Luis) Tú te llamas Luis.

1. Él se llama Paco. 2. Ella se llama Lupe. 3. Él se llama Pepe. 4. Ella se llama Ana.

B10 Actividad • ¿Cómo se llama . . . ? Answers will vary.

Ask a friend the Spanish names of other students in the classroom. Ask: **¿Cómo se llama el chico?** or **¿Cómo se llama la chica?**

B11 Actividad • ¡A escribir!

Complete the answer to each question. Use subject pronouns often in the first few units. Elicit these from students so that they will become familiar with them.

1. ¿Cómo te llamas?
_____ Dolores. Yo me llamo
2. ¿Cómo se llama el chico?
_____ Diego. Él se llama
3. ¿Se llama ella María?
No, _____ Isabel. ella se llama
4. ¿Se llama él Francisco?
No, _____ Pablo. él se llama

5. ¿Cómo se llama la chica?
_____ Susana. Ella se llama
6. ¿Te llamas tú José?
No, _____ Enrique. yo me llamo
7. ¿Quién, la chica de Texas?
No, la _____ de Arizona. chica
8. ¿Se llama Irene?
No, se _____ Inés. llama

B12 ¿Sabes que . . . ?

Persons named **José** are likely to have the nickname **Pepe**. Other common Spanish nicknames are:

Lupe for Guadalupe
Paco for Francisco
Lola for Dolores
Mongo for Ramón
Fina for Josefina
Tere for Teresa
Quique for Enrique
Ale for Alejandro or Alejandra

B13 Actividad • ¡A escribir! Answers will vary. Have the students use the dialog in B1 as a guide.

Antonio finally meets the new girl, Lupe. Write their conversation. Use dashes at the beginning of each line to indicate a change of speaker. Ex: —¡Hola! Yo me llamo Antonio.
¿Cómo te llamas tú?
—Me llamo Lupe.
¡Mucho gusto!

40   Unidad 1

Actividad • Un juego *A game* Answers will vary.

The class divides into two teams. Students take turns trying to recall the Spanish names of players on the opposing team, asking ¿**Te llamas . . . ?** The student being questioned replies **Sí, me llamo . . .** or **No, me llamo . . .** Each correct guess is worth one point. After everybody has been questioned, volunteers may try to name all the students on the opposing team, saying **Él/ella se llama . . .**

B 15 ESTRUCTURAS ESENCIALES
Gender of nouns and the definite article

Definite article	Noun
el	chico
el	colegio
la	chica
la	escuela

1. A word that names a person **(chico, chica)** or a place or a thing **(colegio, escuela)** is called a *noun.* In Spanish, every noun has a gender: either masculine gender or feminine gender.

2. Most nouns ending in **-o** are masculine **(chico, colegio)**. Most nouns ending in **-a** are feminine **(chica, escuela)**.

3. The Spanish form of the definite article *(the)* depends on the gender of the noun it accompanies.
   el is used with a *masculine noun* **el chico, el colegio**
   la is used with a *feminine noun* **la chica, la escuela**

Note: Not all Spanish nouns end in **-o** or **-a**—for example, **señor** and **clase.** One good way to remember the gender of this type of noun is to learn the noun with its definite article: **el señor, la clase.**

B 16 Actividad • ¿El o la?

Say the following nouns with their definite articles.

escuela, clase, señorita, colegio, señora, chico, patio, señor
la escuela, la clase, la señorita, el colegio, la señora, el chico, el patio, el señor

B 17 Actividad • ¿Qué crees? *What do you think?*

Masculine
el director
el actor
el ángel
el café
el tigre
el ingeniero
el fotógrafo

The Spanish words in the following list have *cognates* in English. They are similar in form and meaning to English words, though pronounced very differently. Can you figure out the gender of each word? On a piece of paper, write two headings: masculine and feminine. Now write each word from the list under the appropriate heading. Include the articles.

el director	el actor	la televisión	la imaginación	el fotógrafo
la fotografía	la idea	el café	el ingeniero	la hamburguesa
la rosa	el ángel	el tigre	la directora	la doctora

Feminine: la fotografía, la rosa, la idea, la televisión, la imaginación, la directora, la hamburguesa, la doctora

¡Hola, amigos!   41

B 18 Comprensión — For script and answers, see p. T35.

B 18 Comprensión

Boy or girl? That is the question.

	0	1	2	3	4	5	6	7	8	9	10	11	12
Chico		✓			✓		✓	✓		✓			✓
Chica	✓		✓	✓		✓			✓		✓	✓	

B 19 SITUACIÓN · Una sorpresa *A surprise*

Spanish is spoken in many countries, including the United States. The Spanish-speaking young people in this section are from California, Texas, Puerto Rico, Mexico, Spain, and Argentina. You'll be meeting them again.

The trilled r is especially difficult for some students. You may wish to point out the proper pronunciation of "Puerto Rico".

C1

¿De dónde son?

Él se llama Pedro Gómez. Pedro es de Texas, Estados Unidos.

María Bernal y Carlos Cajal. Ellos son de España.

Nosotras somos de México. Yo me llamo Elena Llansó. Ella se llama Rosa. ¿De dónde son ustedes?

Yo me llamo Pablo Matos. Soy de Puerto Rico. ¿De dónde eres tú?

C2 Actividad • ¿Cuál país? *Which country?*

Look at the map on the following page. Find the countries where the young people in C1 are from.

You may wish to point out the accent in "país". Present it with the article "el": "el país", to clarify gender.

¡Hola, amigos!   43

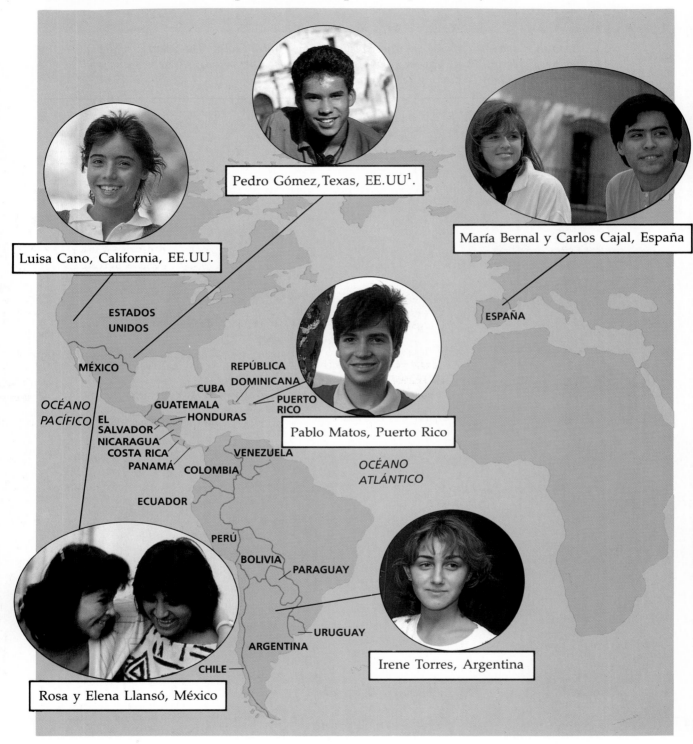

Pedro Gómez, Texas, EE.UU[1].

Luisa Cano, California, EE.UU.

María Bernal y Carlos Cajal, España

Pablo Matos, Puerto Rico

Irene Torres, Argentina

Rosa y Elena Llansó, México

ESTADOS
UNIDOS

MÉXICO

OCÉANO
PACÍFICO

REPÚBLICA
DOMINICANA
CUBA
GUATEMALA
HONDURAS
EL
SALVADOR
NICARAGUA
COSTA RICA
PANAMÁ
COLOMBIA
VENEZUELA
ECUADOR
PERÚ
BOLIVIA
PARAGUAY
URUGUAY
ARGENTINA
CHILE

PUERTO
RICO

OCÉANO
ATLÁNTICO

ESPAÑA

---

[1]**EE.UU.** is an abbreviation for **los Estados Unidos,** *The United States.*

Point out the Spanish pronunciation of "Texas", "California", "Puerto Rico", "México" and "Argentina".

Actividad • ¿Cómo se llama . . . ?

Do you remember their names?

1. ¿el chico de Texas? Se llama Pedro Gómez.
2. ¿la chica de España? Se llama María Bernal.
3. ¿el chico de Puerto Rico? Se llama Pablo Matos.

4. ¿el chico de España? Se llama Carlos Cajal.
5. ¿la chica de México? Se llama Rosa Elena Llansó.
6. ¿la chica de California? Se llama Luisa Cano.

C5 Actividad • Combinación Possible answers are given.

To say where these people are from, choose an item from each column to form
your answer. You will have to use some items more than once.

Pablo Matos es de Puerto Rico.   María y Carlos son de España.
Irene es de Argentina.   Nosotros somos de México.   Rosa y Elena son de México.

Pablo Matos Nosotros Rosa y Elena Irene María y Carlos	es de somos de son de	los Estados Unidos España México Puerto Rico Argentina

C6 SE DICE ASÍ
Asking and saying where people are from

¿De dónde eres tú?	Soy de Los Ángeles.
¿De dónde son ellos?	Son de España.
¿De dónde es ella?	Es de Argentina.
¿Tú eres de México?	Sí, soy de México.

The definite article can be used
with the names of some countries:
"la Argentina, el Perú, el Ecuador,
el Paraguay," and "el Uruguay."
However, it must be used with
"El Salvador."

C7 Actividad • Charla Free conversation

Ask your classmates where they are from and reply when they ask you.

—¿De dónde eres tú?
—Yo soy de Chicago. ¿Y tú?
—Yo soy de San Diego.

C8 Actividad • ¿De dónde es él? ¿De dónde es ella?

Look at the photos in C3. Identify each person
and say where he or she is from.
Él es Pedro Gomez.
Es de Texas.

Él es Pablo Matos.
Es de Puerto Rico.

Ellos son María Bernal y Carlos Cajal.
Son de España.

Ellas son Rosa y Elena Llansó.
Son de México.

Ella es Irene Torres.
Es de Argentina.

Ella es Luisa Cano.
Es de California.

¡Hola, amigos! 45

Actividad • **¿Sí o no?** Answers will vary.

Imagine that you are one of the people in C1. Your classmates will try to guess your identity by asking you questions. Reply **sí** or **no**. Here are some questions to try.

—¿Eres de España?　　　　—¿Te llamas . . . ?

Point out that "sí" (yes) always carries an accent.

C10 **ESTRUCTURAS ESENCIALES**
Subject pronouns and the verb **ser** *(to be)*

Again, contrast the use of "tú" and "Usted". Repeat that in this text "Ustedes" will be used as the plural of both "tú" and "Usted". Explain that this is the preferred usage in most of the Spanish-speaking world.

| Singular | | Plural | |
Subject Pronoun	Verb Form	Subject Pronoun	Verb Form
yo	soy	nosotros(as)	somos
tú	eres	vosotros(as)	sois
usted (Ud.) }\n él }\n ella }	es	ustedes (Uds.) }\n ellos }\n ellas }	son

1. Do not capitalize the pronoun **yo** (*I*) except at the beginning of the sentence.

2. In Spanish America, **ustedes** (abbreviated **Uds.**) is used as the plural form of both **tú** and **usted** (abbreviated **Ud.**). In Spain, however, the plural form of **tú** is **vosotros**. In this textbook, only the form **ustedes** (**Uds.**) will be used.

3. The masculine plural forms **nosotros** and **ellos** are used to refer to any group of males or to any mixed group of males and females. The feminine forms **nosotras** and **ellas** are used to refer to a group that includes females only.

4. The name of the verb, for example **ser** (*to be*), is called the infinitive. This is the form you will find in dictionaries and in vocabulary lists.

5. When you use a Spanish verb, you need to pick a form of the verb that agrees with the subject noun or pronoun:　**yo soy** *I am;*　**tú eres** *You are;*　**Elena es** *Elena is.*

6. Most native speakers of Spanish use a verb without a subject pronoun because the verb form alone indicates who the subject is.
　　¿De dónde **es** Pedro? **Es** de Texas.　　*Where is Pedro from? He's from Texas.*

7. The English verb *to be* has two Spanish equivalents, the verbs **ser** and **estar**. You will learn the verb **estar** in Unit 5. Use the verb **ser** to express *who* or *what the subject is*, and to indicate origin.
　　Soy María Bernal.　　　　　　*I am María Bernal.*
　　Pablo Matos **es** de Puerto Rico.　　*Pablo Matos is from Puerto Rico.*
　　María y Pablo **son** estudiantes.　　*María and Pablo are students.*

C11 **Actividad** • **¿Quién? ¿Yo?** *Who, me?*　📼

Sides are being chosen for a game. People are not sure who has been picked.
Answer affirmatively, using the correct subject pronoun.

　　—¿María y Carmen?　—Sí, ellas.　　—¿Pablo y yo?　—Sí, ustedes.

1. ¿Enrique? Sí, él.
2. ¿Yo? Sí, tú.
3. ¿Silvia y tú? Sí, nosotros.
4. ¿Juan y Carlos? Sí, ellos.
5. ¿Ustedes? Sí, nosotros.
6. ¿La chica y yo? Sí, ustedes.
7. ¿Inés y Anita? Sí, ellas.
8. ¿La señora Valdés? Sí, ella.
9. ¿Usted y Pablo? Sí, nosotros.

Actividad • ¡A escribir!

Suppose you are one of the editors of your school's newspaper. You find that your star reporter repeats names too often. Rewrite her sentences, changing the underlined words to a subject pronoun.

> La chica es María López. <u>María López</u> es de Puerto Rico.
>
> La chica es María López. <u>Ella</u> es de Puerto Rico.
>
> Jorge y yo somos de California. <u>Jorge y yo</u> somos de los Estados Unidos.
>
> Jorge y yo somos de California. <u>Nosotros</u> somos de los Estados Unidos.

1. El chico es Roberto Mercado. <u>Roberto Mercado</u> es de Argentina. Él es de Argentina.
2. ¿De dónde son Matilde y Carmen? <u>Matilde y Carmen</u> son de México. Ellas son de México.
3. La chica es Sofía. <u>Sofía</u> es de Madrid. Ella es de Madrid.
4. El chico es Miguel. <u>Miguel</u> es de Puerto Rico. Él es de Puerto Rico.
5. Dolores y yo somos de El Paso. <u>Dolores y yo</u> somos de Texas. Nosotros somos de Texas.
6. ¿De dónde son Marta y José? <u>Marta y José</u> son de Miami. Ellos son de Miami.
7. El señor Machado y Sara son de la Florida. Sí, <u>el señor Machado y Sara</u> son de Miami. Ellos son de Miami.
8. ¿De dónde es Lupe? <u>Lupe</u> es de Arizona. Ella es de Arizona.

C13 Actividad • Una entrevista *An interview*

Soledad is being interviewed for the school magazine. Here are her answers to the reporter's questions. Write the questions.

1. ¿Cómo te llamas?
1. Me llamo Soledad Muñoz.
2. Soy de San Agustín.
2. ¿De dónde eres?

¿Cómo se llama el chico?
3. El chico se llama Salvador.
4. La chica se llama Rosario.
¿Cómo se llama la chica?

¿De dónde son ellos?
5. Ellos son de Texas.
6. Somos de los Estados Unidos.
¿De dónde son ustedes?

C14 Actividad • Falta algo

Supply the correct form of **ser.**

1. Él _es_ de California.
2. Nosotras _somos_ de México.
3. ¿_Eres_ tú Miguel Soto?
4. Tú y yo _somos_ de los Estados Unidos.
5. ¿De dónde _son_ ustedes?
6. Ellas _son_ de España.
7. Lupe _es_ de Panamá.
8. Yo _soy_ de Chile.

C15 Actividad • Combinación Possible answers are given.

Form at least five sentences in Spanish by choosing the appropriate items from each column. You will have to use some verb forms more than once.

> Yo soy de España. Usted es de México. Tú eres de San Antonio. Nosotros somos de la Florida.

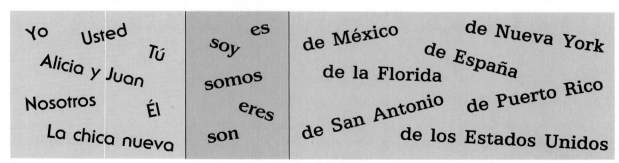

Yo Usted Tú Alicia y Juan Nosotros Él La chica nueva

es soy somos eres son

de México de Nueva York de España de la Florida de San Antonio de Puerto Rico de los Estados Unidos

Él es de los Estados Unidos. Alicia y Juan son de Nueva York.
La chica nueva es de Puerto Rico.

¡Hola, amigos! **47**

More than 285 million people speak Spanish. Many live in the United States (more than 20 million). Others live in Spain, Mexico, Central America, South America, and the islands of the Caribbean.

C17 ESTRUCTURAS ESENCIALES
Interrogative sentences

The following four questions elicit a *yes/no* answer.

¿Tú eres de México?	Sí, soy de México.
¿Tú eres Miguel Soto?	Sí, soy Miguel Soto.
¿Es Carmen de Texas?	Sí, Carmen es de Texas.
¿Es Ud. el señor Colón?	Sí, soy el señor Colón.

Two ways of asking questions to elicit *yes/no* answers:

1	¿subject + verb + rest of sentence?
2	¿verb + subject + rest of sentence?

1. As you have seen, Spanish uses two question marks, an inverted one at the beginning of the sentence and a standard one at the end.

2. In both examples of interrogative sentences there is a change of intonation. The voice rises at the end of the sentence.

3. Notice that in the first two examples above, a regular sentence is made interrogative by only changing the intonation and adding the question marks.

4. In the last two examples, the verb is placed at the beginning of the sentence and the question marks are added.

You may want to do a personalized question/ answer exercise using the students' real names:

Y_____ , ¿es ella de México?
Sí, _____ es . . .
¿Es Ud. _____ ?
Sí, yo soy _____ .

Encourage students to answer with complete sentences.

C18 Actividad • Preguntas *Questions*

Your friend's questions are based on incorrect guesses. Ask the question again using the correct information given in parentheses.

—¿Eres tú de España? (los Estados Unidos)
—¿Eres tú de los Estados Unidos?

1. ¿Son ellos de Argentina? (México)
2. ¿Son ustedes de Perú? (Venezuela)
3. ¿Es ella María López? (Blanca Nieves)
4. ¿Es él Pablo Matos? (Pedro Matos)

5. ¿Eres tú de Puerto Rico? (España)
6. ¿Son ellas María y Ana? (Teresa y Eva)
7. ¿Es ella de Nuevo México? (Nevada)
8. ¿Eres tú de Acapulco? (la Florida)

1. ¿Son ellos de México?   4. ¿Es él Pedro Matos?
2. ¿Son ustedes de Venezuela? 5. ¿Eres tú de España?
3. ¿Es ella Blanca Nieves?   6. ¿Son ellas Teresa y Eva?

7. ¿Es ella de Nevada?   8. ¿Eres tú de la Florida?

C19 Comprensión   For script and answers, see p. T40.

Where are they from? Select an appropriate answer from the list.

A. Ella es de España.
B. Yo soy de Boston.
C. Somos de México.

D. Carlos es de España.
E. De Puerto Rico.
F. Irene es de Argentina.

G. No, es de California.
H. Son de San Antonio.

You've learned how to greet people, give some information about yourself, and ask others about themselves. Here are some further opportunities to use your new skills!

1

Tarjetas postales 📼

Some day you may want to have a pen pal in a Spanish-speaking country. For now, imagine that these postcards are for you.

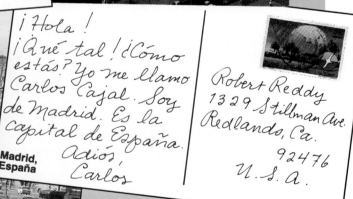

¡Hola!
Me llamo Irene.
Soy de Buenos Aires,
la capital de
Argentina.
¿De dónde eres
tú?
Recuerdos,
Irene

Buenos Aires, Argentina

Betty Mintz
3 Mount Vernon St.
Boston, Mass.
03416
U.S.A.

¡Hola!
¡Qué tal! ¿Cómo
estás? Yo me llamo
Carlos Cajal. Soy
de Madrid. Es la
capital de España.
Adiós,
Carlos

Madrid, España

Robert Reddy
1329 Stillman Ave.
Redlands, Ca.
92476
U.S.A.

2 Actividad • ¿Quién es la chica? ¿Quién es el chico?

Tell about your new pen pals. What are their names? Where are they from? Possible answers are given.
La chica se llama Irene. Es de Buenos Aires, Argentina.
El chico se llama Carlos Cajal. Es de Madrid, España.

3 Actividad • ¡A escribir!

Write a postcard introducing yourself to a pen pal in a Spanish-speaking country.
Use the postcards above as a model. Answers will vary.

4 Actividad • ¿Qué falta? *What's missing?*

Read the dialogs, supplying the missing words. Then, write the lines.

1. EVA ¿Cómo te _____ tú? llamas
ROSA Me _____ Rosa. llamo
EVA ¿Cómo _____ tú, Rosa? estás
ROSA Muy _____, gracias. bien

2. RICARDO ¿De dónde _____ tú? eres
ALBERTO Yo _____ México. soy de
RICARDO ¿Y Diego? ¿De _____ es él? dónde
ALBERTO Diego _____ de Argentina. es

5 Actividad • Diálogos *Dialogs* Answers will vary.

Ex: —Señor Colón, ¿cómo está usted?
—Yo estoy muy bien.
—¿De dónde es usted?
—Yo soy de Costa Rica, y ¿de dónde es usted, señorita?

Talk with a classmate. From each numbered group, use as many words and phrases as you can and add other words of your own.

1. Señor / señorita / ¿cómo . . . ? / muy / ¿de dónde . . . ? / Costa Rica
2. Buenos / llamas / Gabriel / Susana / gusto / adiós
3. ¿Qué tal? / llama / chico de México / Pablo / gracias

6 Actividad • ¡Buenas noches! Answers will vary.

It's 8:00 P.M. You are at the door, handing out printed name tags at a Spanish festival. As people arrive, greet them and find out where they're from.

Señor Alonso, Carmen, Señora Méndez, Señorita Colón, Luz, Tomás, and Señor García arrive.

Señor Alonso Buenas noches, señor.
(arrives) ¿Cómo se llama usted?
¿De dónde es usted?

Carmen ¡Hola!
(arrives) ¿Cómo te llamas tú?
¿De dónde eres tú?

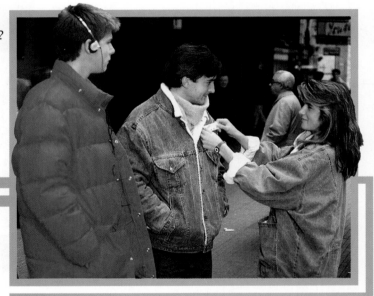

7 Actividad • Reacciones

Possible answers are given.
Give the correct reply to the following.

1. Buenos días. Buenos días.
2. ¿El chico se llama José? Sí, él se llama José.
3. Yo me llamo Gloria. Mucho gusto.
4. ¿Eres de España? No, soy de México.

5. Adiós. Adiós.
6. ¿Cómo estás? Muy bien, ¿y tú?
7. Buenas tardes. Buenas tardes.
8. Hasta mañana. Hasta mañana.

8 Actividad • ¡Bienvenidos! *Welcome!*

You are at the airport to meet exchange
students arriving from Spanish-speaking
countries. What do you say? Write one
possible conversation. Possible dialog is given.

—¡Hola! Me llamo José.
—¿Cómo se llaman ustedes?
—Yo me llamo Ana.
—Él se llama Jorge.
—Somos de España.
—Mucho gusto.

9 Actividad • ¡A escoger!

Choose the appropriate reply and say it.

¿Cómo estás?
• Soy de Argentina.   • Bien, gracias.   • José Gómez.   • De nada.
You would say: *Bien, gracias.*

1. ¿De dónde eres?
• Muy bien, gracias.   • <u>Soy de Puerto Rico.</u>   • Se llama Fabio.   • Buenas tardes.
2. ¿Cómo se llama ella?
• Buenas noches.   • Javier González.   • Mucho gusto.   • <u>Isabel Parra.</u>
3. ¿Qué tal?
• Adiós.   • <u>Bien. ¿Y tú?</u>   • Ella es de Texas.   • De Puerto Rico.
4. Me llamo Pilar.
• Muy bien.   • No, soy de Argentina.   • Hasta luego.   • <u>Mucho gusto.</u>
5. ¿Es usted de México?
• Muy bien.   • De nada.   • <u>No, soy de Nevada.</u>   • Hasta luego.
6. ¿Cómo está Lupe?
• Buenos días.   • <u>Muy bien, gracias.</u>   • Lupe López.   • De España.
7. Adiós.
• ¡Hola!   • Buenos días.   • <u>Hasta mañana.</u>   • Rosa Santos.
8. ¿Yo? ¡Muy mal!
• Bien, gracias.   • <u>¡Qué pena!</u>   • Muy bien.   • Hasta luego.
9. ¿Se llama Carlos?
• <u>No, Pepe.</u>   • De México.   • Regular.   • ¿Y tú?

10 Pronunciación, lectura, dictado For script, see p. T41–T42.

1. Listen carefully and repeat what you hear.

2. The Spanish consonants **h** (always silent) and **ñ.** Listen, then read aloud.
   hola   hasta   Sra. Henríquez   Honduras
   señor   señorita   señora   España   español   mañana

3. Copy the following sentences to prepare yourself to write them from dictation.
   ¡Hola, Hilda!   ¡Hasta mañana, señor Núñez!   Horacio es de Honduras.

¡Hola, amigos! 51

¿LO SABES?

Let's review some important points you have learned in this unit.

1. ¿Qué tal?/¡Chao!   2. ¡Hola!/Hasta luego.   3. Buenas noches, señor./Adiós.

SECTION A

Do you know different ways to say hello and goodbye to young people and adults in Spanish?

Say hello and goodbye to the following people in Spanish, using different expressions.   Possible answers are given.

1. Eva	**3.** Mr. González	**5.** Miss López
2. Pablo	**4.** Mrs. González	**6.** your teacher

4. Buenos días, señora./Adiós.   5. Buenas tardes, señorita./Hasta luego.   6. Buenas tardes, . . . /Hasta mañana.

SECTION B

Do you know how to introduce yourself, give your name, and say what other people's names are?

Say hello to your new classmates and give your name.

Find out what their names are. Start the questions using **¿Cómo . . .**

1. _____ tú?	**3.** _____ él? 3. ¿Cómo se llama él?
2. _____ ella?	**4.** _____ la chica? 4. ¿Cómo se llama la chica?

1. ¿Cómo te llamas tú?   2. ¿Cómo se llama ella?

Say what their names are.

Se llama **1.** _____ Lupe.   **3.** _____ Diego. Se llama

se llama **2.** Usted _____ Roberto.   **4.** Te _____ Carmen. llamas

---

SECTION C

Can you ask and say where people are from?

Complete the following questions and answers about where someone is from.

1. ¿ _____ tú?	_____ California.	¿De dónde eres . . . Soy de . . .
2. ¿ _____ él?	_____ Puerto Rico.	¿De dónde es . . . Es de . . .
3. ¿ _____ ella?	_____ Argentina.	¿De dónde es . . . Es de . . .

Do you know the forms of the verb *ser*?

Write the correct form of **ser** that goes with each subject.

1. Ustedes	**3.** Juan y Eva	**5.** Nosotras	**7.** El chico
2. Yo	**4.** Usted	**6.** Ellas	**8.** Tú

1. son 2. soy 3. son 4. es 5. somos 6. son 7. es 8. eres

VOCABULARIO

ESTUDIO DE PALABRAS

Look through the vocabulary list and pick out the nouns that identify persons, places, or things. Make two new lists, one for the masculine words and one for the feminine. Include the corresponding article.

Nouns: colegio, profesor(a), señor(a), señorita, clase, chico, chica, escuela, México, patio, España, los Estados Unidos.

¡Hola, amigos!   53

VAMOS A LEER°

Antes de leer   *Before reading*

Before you begin to read in Spanish, here are a few suggestions. Read each new selection through for general meaning without looking up any words. Cognates—words that look alike in Spanish and English and have a similar meaning—will help you. Try to pronounce them the Spanish way, and write them down.

El mundo hispánico

España es un país° de Europa°, al suroeste° de Francia. Sus vecinos° son Francia y Portugal. La capital de España es Madrid. María Bernal es de Madrid.

Luisa Cano es de California y Pedro Gómez es de Texas. Los dos° son de los Estados Unidos. Ellos son mexicano americanos°.

---

vamos a leer *let's read*   **un país** *a country*   **de Europa** *of Europe*   **al suroeste** *to the southwest*
sus vecinos *its neighbors*   **los dos** *both*   **mexicano americanos** *Mexican Americans*

Jorge Llansó es de México, un país al sur° de los Estados Unidos. La capital de México es la Ciudad° de México. Jorge es de la capital.

Pablo Matos es de San Juan, la capital de Puerto Rico. Puerto Rico es una° isla° en el Mar° Caribe. En Puerto Rico hablan° español.

¿De dónde es Irene Torres? Ella es de Argentina, un país de Suramérica°. Sus vecinos son: Uruguay al este°, Chile al oeste°, y Bolivia y Paraguay al norte°.

Actividad • ¡Faltan palabras!

Complete these statements, according to the reading **El mundo hispánico,** supplying the missing information.

1. Puerto Rico es una . . .   isla.
2. Madrid es . . . de España.   la capital.
3. Luisa Cano y Pedro Gómez son de . . .
4. Uruguay es un país de . . .   Suramérica.
5. México es un país . . . los Estados Unidos.

3. los EE.UU.   5. al sur de

6. En España y en Suramérica hablan . . .   español.
7. Chile es un . . .   país de Suramérica.
8. Un país al norte de Argentina es . . .
9. San Juan es la capital de . . .   Puerto Rico.

8.   Bolivia o Paraguay.

Actividad • Proyecto   *Project*

Make a postcard. On a piece of thin cardboard, tape a picture from a magazine showing one of the Spanish-speaking countries mentioned in the reading. On the other side of the card, write a message home in Spanish about the country.

---

al sur *to the south*   **ciudad** *city*   **una** *an*   **isla** *island*   **mar** *sea*   **hablan** *they speak*   **Suramérica** *South America*
al este *to the east*   **al oeste** *to the west*   **al norte** *to the north*

Un paseo por el parque°

Taking an afternoon walk is a cherished custom in Spanish-speaking countries.
Read what people say when they see each other in the park.

Actividad

Find replies for the greetings in the picture of the park, above. Then practice the
exchanges with a classmate. Answers may vary.

Un paseo por el parque *A stroll in the park*   **a todo el mundo** *to everybody*   **más o menos** *so-so*   **¿Qué hay?** *What's
up?*   **nada** *nothing*   **. . . están ustedes?** *are you?* (plural)

El regalo°

DANIEL	Me llamo Daniel Arias. Soy de México. Vivo° con mi° familia en una colonia° de la capital.
ADRIANA	Soy Adriana Arias. Daniel y yo somos hermanos°.
DANIEL	Sí, ella y yo somos hermanos. ¡Qué tragedia!
ADRIANA	Daniel es mi hermano menor°.
DANIEL	"¡Menor!" Sólo un año° menor.
ADRIANA	Mi hermano es inteligente. Es perfecto.
DANIEL	Gracias. Mi hermana es inteligente. Es simpática°.

Tocan a la puerta°.

SEÑOR	Buenas tardes. ¿Familia Arias?
ADRIANA	Sí, ¿es para mi mamá°?
SEÑOR	No. ¿Eres Adriana Arias? Y tú, ¿eres Daniel Arias?
DANIEL	Sí.
SEÑOR	Es un regalo para ustedes. Hasta luego.
DANIEL	Adiós, señor. Adriana, ¿qué es?
ADRIANA	Un regalo para nosotros, ¡tonto°!
DANIEL	¡Fantástico!

You may choose students to play the roles of *Adriana* and *Daniel* and role-play the dialog.

Actividad • Para completar

Complete the following sentences according to **El regalo.**

1. El chico se llama . . . Daniel Arias.
2. Él es de . . . México.
3. La chica se llama . . . Adriana Arias

4. Daniel y Adriana son . . . hermanos.
5. Ellos son de . . . México.
6. El regalo es para . . . ellos.

---

regalo *gift* **Vivo** *I live* **mi** *my* **colonia** *neighborhood* **hermanos** *brother and sister* **hermano menor** *younger brother* **Sólo un año** *Only one year* **simpática** *nice* **Tocan a la puerta.** *Someone knocks at the door.* **para mi mamá** *for my mom* **tonto** *fool*

UNIDAD 2 **En la escuela**
Scope and Sequence

	BASIC MATERIAL	COMMUNICATIVE FUNCTIONS
SECTION A	¿Cómo vienes a la escuela? (A1)	**Exchanging information** • Asking for and giving an explanation
SECTION B	¿Qué materias tienes hoy? (B1) El horario de Enrique (B8) Diferencia de opiniones (B25)	**Expressing attitudes and points of view** • Asking about classes and giving your opinion
SECTION C	¿Cuánto cuesta? (C1) Compras para la escuela (C7)	**Exchanging information** • Asking how much something costs and giving the price
TRY YOUR SKILLS	Pronunciation (letters **ch, ll**) Sound-letter correspondences (the letters **ch, ll**) Dictation	
VAMOS A LEER	**Libros para la escuela** (Spanish schoolbooks) **Y para los ratos libres** (Spanish books for leisure time) **¡Socorro!** (a nightmare) **El regalo** (The mystery gift arrives.)	

WRITING   A variety of controlled and open-ended writing activities appear in the Pupil's Edition. The Teacher's Notes identify other activities suitable for writing practice.

COOPERATIVE LEARNING   Many of the activities in the Pupil's Edition lend themselves to cooperative learning. The Teacher's Notes explain some of the many instances where this teaching strategy can be particularly effective. For guidelines on how to use cooperative learning, see page T13.

GRAMMAR	CULTURE	RE-ENTRY
The verb **venir** (A5) The uses of **no** (A12)	How students get to school in Spanish- speaking countries	Exchanging names
Numbers from 0 to 20 (B4) The days of the week (B10) The verb **tener** (B13) Telling time (B19)	The school system in Spanish-speaking countries The grading system in the Spanish-speaking world	Interrogative sentences The verb **ser**
Forming plurals (C3) Definite and indefinite articles (C11) Numbers from 21 to 100 (C16)	Classroom practices in the Spanish-speaking world	

Recombining communicative functions, grammar, and vocabulary

Reading for practice and pleasure

TEACHER-PREPARED MATERIALS

Section A Flashcards, magazine pictures
of school bus, students on foot, a car,
bicycle, subway; flashcards of question
words, name cards

Section B Flashcards, toy clock,
cardboard, fasteners, television or
movie schedule

Section C Paper money, index cards

UNIT RESOURCES

Manual de actividades, Unit 2
Manual de ejercicios, Unit 2
Unit 2 Cassettes
Transparencies 4–6
Quizzes 4–6
Unit 2 Test

UNIDAD

2

A1–3

OBJECTIVES **To exchange information:** ask for and give an explanation

CULTURAL BACKGROUND In most Spanish-speaking countries, public education is free from elementary school through high school. However, the demand for education is greater in most cases than the facilities can meet.

Most public colleges and universities offer free tuition or charge a minimum registration fee. The Spanish equivalent of both *college* and *university* is **universidad. Colegio** in many Spanish-speaking countries is a secondary institution; in others it is a primary institution. The word **colegio** is commonly used as a synonym for **escuela** *(school).*

Most private schools are operated by religious organizations and are usually less crowded than public schools. Many of them are not co-educational. Boys and girls from these schools will go to school together for the first time when they enter the university.

MOTIVATING ACTIVITY Have the students do a survey on how students come to school. They should write a questionnaire and ask as many students as possible. After completing Section A of Unit 1, the students may enjoy providing the information in Spanish.

A1   ¿Cómo vienes a la escuela?

Prepare flashcards or clip pictures from magazines of a school bus, students walking, a car, a bicycle, and the subway.

Introduce the new vocabulary by using the flashcards or pictures and the verb **venir.** Hold up the illustration of the bus and say **Yo vengo en autobús.** Have students repeat chorally. Hand the picture of the bus to a student and have him say **Yo vengo en autobús.**

Repeat this procedure for all the forms of transportation. Then ask several students **¿Cómo vienes tú?** Students should be able to respond in Spanish: **Yo vengo en/a . . .**

Tell students they will now listen carefully with their books closed as you read aloud or play the cassette. Have them try to identify how Carlos and José get to school. **(Carlos viene en auto. José viene a pie.)**

A2   Actividad • ¿Es cierto o no?

Have an individual read the first statement. Call on another student to respond with **Es cierto** or **No es cierto.** If the response is **No es cierto,** ask a student to restate the sentence to make it agree with A1.

ANSWERS:
1. Es cierto.
2. No es cierto. Algunos vienen tarde.
3. No es cierto. El autobús número ocho viene tarde.
4. No es cierto. Andrés viene en auto.
5. No es cierto. Vienen en metro.
6. No es cierto. Raúl viene en metro con Marta.
7. Es cierto.
8. No es cierto. José viene hoy a pie.
9. No es cierto. Carlos viene en autobús.
10. No es cierto. Vienen en autobús.

A3   Actividad • ¿Qué es?

Have the students look at the pictures and say **Es un/una.** Ask students what they think **un** and **una** represent in English. If necessary, explain that

un and una are the Spanish equivalent of *a* or *an*. The **-o** for **uno** is dropped before masculine nouns, but **una** remains intact for the feminine nouns.

Point to objects or pictures of singular nouns around the room and practice **Es un/una . . .** Make sure to use objects whose Spanish name is familiar to the students. You may wish to add classroom vocabulary for enrichment.

Es una silla.	Es una pizarra.
Es un escritorio.	Es un borrador.
Es un librero.	Es una pluma.

A4 Comprensión

SLOWER-PACED LEARNING Before presenting the comprehension activity, review the dialog in A1. Have the students identify how each student in A1 gets to school.

You'll hear nine sentences. After listening to each sentence, decide whether it is true or false according to the information in **¿Cómo vienes a la escuela?** Check the row labeled **Sí** if the sentence is true. If the sentence is false, use the row labeled **No.** For example, you hear: **La escuela se llama Alfredo Gutiérrez.** Your check mark goes in the row marked **No,** since the name of the school is **Benito Juárez,** not **Alfredo Gutiérrez.**

1. —Los estudiantes vienen de muchas partes. *Sí*
2. —Todos vienen tarde hoy. *No*
3. —Algunos vienen tarde. *Sí*
4. —El autobús número 8 viene temprano. *No*
5. —Andrés viene en autobús. *No*
6. —Raúl y Marta vienen en bicicleta. *No*
7. —José viene a pie hoy. *Sí*
8. —Andrés viene con Carlos. *No*
9. —Carlos viene en autobús. *Sí*

Now check your answers. *Read each sentence again and give the correct answer.*

A5 ESTRUCTURAS ESENCIALES

Write several sentences with the forms of **venir** on the board or a transparency. Have the students point out the verb forms that go with each pronoun. Ask them to identify the preposition **en** in each sentence and to guess the rule.

To confirm their reasoning, have the students open their books and follow along as you read the explanation.

A6 Actividad • ¿Tarde o temprano?

Have the students work in pairs. One will be the bus driver who will read the list. The other should respond that the person will be arriving late. Have the students switch roles.

CHALLENGE Have the students imagine that they are giving a party. They are checking to see how their friends are coming and if they are coming early or late.

¿Cómo viene Jorge?
¿Cuándo viene?

A7 Actividad • A la escuela . . . ¡rápido!

Call on the students to say how the people in the illustrations come to school. Remind them to use **a pie** (on foot) when someone is walking and **en** plus the means of transportation to express other ways of arriving.

A8 Actividad • ¡A escribir!

After completing the activity orally, have the students write sentences in class or at home. To check their work, have students exchange papers.

A9 ¿Sabes que . . . ?

Discuss with the students the advantages and disadvantages of having to wait until age 18 to receive a driver's license.

A10 SE DICE ASÍ

Point out that in Spanish one does not use an auxiliary verb, such as the English *do* or *does,* in a negative sentence. Write the question words on flashcards. Hold up a card and give a sample sentence using the question word indicated. Call on volunteers to make up other sentences using the question words.

A11 Actividad • Charla

Have the students work in pairs. Explain that each student must ask the other questions about how he or she comes to school. When they have completed the exercise, the students must report the information to the class.

As a variation, write a list on the board or a transparency of places in the area, such as **el supermercado, la biblioteca,** or **la casa de tu amigo.** Students should say how they go to each of these places. You may also wish to use names of local places, particularly those of interest to students.

SLOWER-PACED LEARNING Allow the students to refer to their notes or books as they work with a classmate. They may use the vocabulary listed below Section A at the end of the unit to help them in their conversations.

A12 ESTRUCTURAS ESENCIALES

To present the use of **no** in Spanish, draw an X through an illustration of a car. Say **Yo no vengo en auto** and have the students repeat after you. Show other pictures of various means of transportation and ask students to make up a negative sentence for each picture.

Now give to a student the picture of the car with an X. Ask a classmate ¿*(student's name)* **viene en auto?** and respond **No,** *(student's name)* **no viene en auto.** Using the various illustrations, ask questions and have the students respond negatively.

Point out to the students that they may add **señor, señora,** or **señorita** to the first **no** to be more polite. **No, señor, Carlos no viene en bicicleta.**

At this time you may wish to introduce the Spanish gesture for the word **no.** Hold the index finger of the right hand about two inches from the face in front of the mouth and wave it from right to left several times. Encourage students to use this and the other gesture of moving the head from side to side when giving a negative response.

A 13   Actividad • ¿Un autobús nuevo?

Have the students respond as indicated to each question. For writing practice, have the students write the questions and answers.

A 14   Actividad • Comprensión

You'll hear different people talking about how they get to school. Put a check mark in the row labeled **No** if the second person makes an inappropriate reply, and in the row marked **Sí** if the reply is appropriate. For example, you hear: **¡Hola! ¿Qué tal? No, vengo a pie.** The check mark for 0 is in the **No** row, since the answer does not correspond to the greeting.

     1. —¿Cómo vienen ustedes?
        —Venimos en metro. *Sí*
     2. —¿Vienes con José?
        —No, vengo a pie. *No*
     3. —¿Vienes en bicicleta?
        —Sí, vengo en bicicleta ¿y tú? *Sí*
     4. —Ahí viene Carlos.
        —No, venimos en auto. *No*
     5. —¿Por qué vienen tarde?
        —Yo no sé. *Sí*
     6. —¿Todos vienen temprano?
        —Andrés viene en auto. *No*
     7. —¿Quién viene a pie?
        —No, yo vengo en autobús. *No*
     8. —¿Tú vienes con la chica nueva?
        —Sí, vengo con la chica nueva. ¿Por qué? *Sí*

Now check your answers. *Read each exchange again and give the correct answer.*

A 15   Actividad • ¿Sí o no? ¿Por qué?

The students should work in pairs. Since **¡No!** and **¡Sí!** require little imagination, encourage students to give an explanation as often as possible.

A 16   Actividad • ¡A escribir!

Before assigning the written work, have the students complete the activity orally.

     You may wish to explain that these statements are often followed by the word **¿verdad?** The students can add it to their sentences as a variation. **Ellos son de Texas, ¿verdad?**

CHALLENGE   Have the students answer each sentence negatively and then supply the correct information.

> —Tú te llamas Raquel, ¿verdad?
> —No, no me llamo Raquel. Me llamo Rosa.

OBJECTIVES   **To express attitudes and points of view:** ask about classes and give your opinion

CULTURAL BACKGROUND   Since the students in many Hispanic countries

study more subjects in one semester than the students in the United States, it can be noted that they do not have every subject each day. Their schedule more clearly resembles our conception of a college schedule. In many Spanish-speaking countries, school subjects are also called **asignaturas.**

It is also common for students to attend classes on Saturday. Many students work in the morning or afternoons, so most schools offer evening and morning classes. They are called **turno matutino** and **turno vespertino.** In some countries, half a day of classes, either morning or afternoon, is called **media sesión** or **medio turno.** Evening classes are also commonly called **clases nocturnas.**

MOTIVATING ACTIVITY   Have the students discuss whether they would prefer to attend evening or morning classes. How would they like going to school on Saturday?

B1   ¿Qué materias tienes hoy?

Write the word **materias** on the board or a transparency and say the names of the subjects which are cognates, such as **inglés, matemáticas,** and **ciencia.** Explain to the students that these words all belong to the category of **materias.**

Introduce the verb **tener** by providing students with examples. Point to your book on the desk and say **Yo tengo un libro.** Point to an object on a student's desk and say *(Student's name)* **tiene un** *(object's name).* Continue with this procedure until most of the students are able to make up a sentence with the verb **tener.**

With books closed, have the students listen to the dialog as you read aloud or play the cassette. Tell students that the dialog is about two boys who are discussing the classes they have for the day.

Now have the students open their books and read silently. Tell them to use context clues and cognates to help them understand the new vocabulary.

B2   Actividad • ¿Es cierto o no?

Have the students use the dialog in B1 to complete the activity. When a statement is false, they should reply **No es cierto** and correct the sentence to agree with the dialog.

B3   ¿Sabes que . . . ?

In many Spanish-speaking countries, students may combine the academic courses offered in the **secundaria** with secretarial or vocational courses. When they graduate from the **secundaria,** students may enter the **bachillerato** or begin a career as secretaries or technicians. Students from most Spanish-speaking countries are required by law to complete only the **escuela primaria,** although students from the middle class who live in cities generally continue their education through high school.

B4   ESTRUCTURAS ESENCIALES

Introduce the numbers using flashcards with numerals on them. On the other side of the cards, write the words for the numbers so the students may practice reading them.

B5   Actividad • La clase de matemáticas

Pairs of students may practice the numbers before completing the exercise.

SLOWER-PACED LEARNING   Read aloud pairs of numbers. Tell the students to write the smaller (or the larger) number in each pair.

B6   Actividad • ¡A escribir!

Use this as a class activity by dictating, with books closed, the number word and have the students write the numerals. Do it fairly rapidly, as numbers are usually said quickly.

CHALLENGE   Have pairs of students challenge others to see how many different numbers they can identify in one minute. The numbers must be cued at random.

B7   Actividad • Un juego

Tell students to copy the game board as shown, using different numbers. They should mark the number cued. You or a volunteer should call out the numbers in random order.

B8   SITUACIÓN • El horario de Enrique

Point out the word **horario** and remind the students that the **h** is silent in Spanish.

Have the students identify the cognates and explain that the *f* sound (as in *far*) is always represented by the letter **f.** There is no consonant blend *ph* in Spanish.

B9   Actividad • ¿Qué clase es?

Divide students into groups and ask them to give the name of the subject that is being studied. Then have each group report its findings to the class.

B10   ESTRUCTURAS ESENCIALES

Write **Hoy es** _____ on the board or a transparency. Fill in the day of the week each day before classes begin. You also may wish to leave the blank and ask at the start of class: **¿Qué día es hoy?** A volunteer may then fill in the appropriate day of the week.

Ask the students to repeat the days of the week after you. Then practice a quick drill with individuals, having one student begin with **domingo.** The next student should give the name of the following day until all students have responded. Mention to the students that **lunes** is considered by many Spanish speakers to be the first day of the week.

CHALLENGE   The students may wish to research the origin of the naming of the days of the week. Have them report their findings to the class.

B11   Actividad • El pobre Enrique

Have the students refer to Enrique's schedule in B8, on page 67, to complete the activity. First ask **¿Tiene Enrique clases el sábado? ¿el domingo?** Then call on individuals to tell what courses he has each day.

B 12 Actividad • ¿Qué tiene Enrique hoy?

After the students have completed the activity orally, have them write the questions and answers.

B 13 ESTRUCTURAS ESENCIALES

Read the chart with students. Review the forms of **tener** as a dialog. One example of a classroom dialog is as follows:

TEACHER	Yo tengo cinco clases. ¿Y tú, José?
JOSÉ	Yo tengo cuatro clases.
TEACHER	María, ¿tiene José cinco clases?
MARÍA	No, José tiene cuatro clases.
TEACHER	Marta, ¿tienen ustedes *(point to another student)* cinco clases?
MARTA	No, tenemos cuatro clases.

Have the students include **tener** in the grammar section of their notebooks.

B 14 Actividad • ¿Tienes clase?

Call on individuals to supply the missing forms of **tener**.

CHALLENGE   Have a group of students practice the forms of **tener** in conversation. They should choose a topic, such as a class schedule, and include the days of the week.

B 15 Actividad • Combinación

Have students form at least ten sentences with the items from each column. This may be done orally or in writing. Give the meaning of **deportes** and **pintura** if necessary.

To re-enter interrogative sentences, have the students form five questions using the items from each column. The students may work with a partner and answer each question.

¿Tiene Alicia español los lunes?
No, ella tiene español los martes.

B 16 Actividad • Un momento, por favor

For cooperative learning, have the students work in pairs. Each student should make sure that his or her partner understands and is able to complete the sentences.

SLOWER-PACED LEARNING   Ask two students to demonstrate this exercise. Tell them to pretend that one is working in the guidance office and the other is a counselor requesting information. Encourage students to preface the answer occasionally by first saying **Un momento, por favor.**

B 17 Actividad • ¡A escribir!

Tell students to write their weekly schedule. Have them complete the activity in class or at home.

B 18 Actividad • ¡Los horarios!

Have students work in pairs to compare their schedules. They should take turns asking or answering questions about the schedules.

SLOWER-PACED LEARNING   Write possible questions on the board or a transparency. Have the students refer to the questions for help with the conversations.

B 19

ESTRUCTURAS ESENCIALES

Use a toy clock with movable hands to teach time. Show one o'clock on the clock and say **Es la una.** Have the students repeat. Now show two o'clock on the clock and say **Son las dos.** Repeat this procedure, demonstrating and saying the time. Explain to students that they should use the singular form of the verb **ser (es)** to express **Es la una** because **una** is one. With all other hours, they should use the plural form of the verb **ser (son).**

Show various hours on the clock and ask the students **¿Qué hora es?** Next have the students turn to a classmate and ask the time.

Have each student make a toy clock. Provide the students with cardboard and fasteners. Then have them quiz each other on the time.

Tell students that when they want to ask at what time something takes place, they should use **a: ¿A qué hora son las clases (es la clase)?** Point out that they should use **son** because they are asking about *the classes.* They would use **es** if they were talking about *the class.* They should also respond with **a** when stating at what time something occurs: **A las dos.**

B 20

Actividad • ¿Qué hora es?

Have the students complete the activity in pairs. They should take turns giving the time and saying what class they have.

B 21

Comprensión 📼

You'll hear ten sentences. Each one makes reference to a specific time of day. On a separate piece of paper, write down the time you hear. For example, you hear: **Yo tengo biología a las dos.** You write *2:00.*

  1. —Andrés tiene inglés a las doce.   *12:00*
  2. —Nosotros tenemos clase a la una.   *1:00*
  3. —¿Tienes tú clase a las nueve?   *9:00*
  4. —Ana tiene clase de química a las tres.   *3:00*
  5. —No, él tiene computadoras a las once.   *11:00*
  6. —Yo tengo historia a las ocho.   *8:00*
  7. —Sí, la clase es a las doce.   *12:00*
  8. —¿Tiene ella clase de matemáticas a la una?   *1:00*
  9. —No, tiene clase a las dos.   *2:00*
  10. —Tenemos clase a las diez.   *10:00*

Now check your answers. *Read each sentence again and give the correct answer.*

B 22

Actividad • ¿A qué hora?

Pairs of students should complete this activity orally. Have them follow the model and switch roles.

As a variation, bring in a television or movie schedule and have the students question each other about what time the various programs or movies are being shown.

B 23 Actividad • ¿Qué hora es en la Ciudad de México?

You may wish to practice the activity with the class before breaking into pairs. Tell the students to give the time as listed for a specific city, then ask what the time is in another city from the box.

For writing practice, have the students write ten questions and answers using the information in the box and following the model. Collect the papers and correct the sentences.

B 24 Actividad • Charla

Have the students practice telling time as they talk about their schedules. Call on several volunteers to present their exchanges to the class.

SLOWER-PACED LEARNING Write on the board or a transparency the days of the week and the names of school subjects. Tell students to use these words as a guide.

B 25 SITUACIÓN • Diferencia de opiniones

Write the following pairs on the board or a transparency: **aburrida, interesante; difícil, fácil;** and **poca, mucha.** Then tell students that these words are opposites and ask if they can identify the words in each pair. You may also wish to point out that **preferida** is a synonym for **favorita,** and **bastante** is synonymous with **mucho.**

Play the cassette or read the dialog aloud as students follow along in their books. Remind them that receiving a grade of ten in many Spanish-speaking countries is equivalent to 100 in the United States.

B 26 Actividad • ¿Andrés o Clara?

Have the students close their books. Say each sentence and call on individuals to say what Andrés and Clara like or dislike, using the vocabulary given in B25.

B 27 Actividad • ¡A escoger!

Students should write the completed sentences on a separate sheet of paper. You or a volunteer may write the sentences on the board or a transparency as the students dictate them.

B 28 SE DICE ASÍ

Read the chart with students. Explain that **¿Cómo es . . . ?** is used when asking what something or someone is like. When they want to ask which is their favorite class or subject, students should use **¿Cuál es . . . ?**

B 29 Actividad • Charla

While the students are working in pairs, advise them not to use their books. Explain that this is the time to practice what they have learned and to express themselves so they are understood and can understand their partners. You should circulate and correct or suggest when necessary.

SLOWER-PACED LEARNING Have the students use their notes or the book as a guide in their conversation. Tell them to use gestures when speaking to help their partners understand what they are trying to say.

B30 Actividad • Encuesta

For cooperative learning, divide the students into groups. Everyone in the group should be interviewed, and each group should report the results to the class. Combine the results to find out which subject is the favorite. Have the students take turns asking the questions so everyone gets the opportunity to practice **¿Cómo es . . . ?** and **¿Cuál es . . . ?**

B31 Actividad • ¿Español? ¡Cinco estrellas!

Suggest that students choose subjects that were not included in the survey in B30. They may wish to prepare a chart to record the information.

SLOWER-PACED LEARNING Write some questions on the board or a transparency for students to use as a model. A few suggestions are **¿Cómo es la clase de ciencias? ¿Cómo se llama tu profesor/a de música?**

B32 ¿Sabes que . . . ?

You may wish to discuss the various differences between going to school in the United States and attending school in a Spanish-speaking country. Tell students that most schools in Spanish-speaking countries require that the students wear uniforms. Ask them if they would prefer wearing uniforms or regular clothes to school. Would they like to go to an all-girl, all-boy, or co-ed school?

B33 Comprensión

You'll hear six pairs of students talking about their classes. After listening to their exchanges, decide whether or not they are taking the same courses on the same day and at the same time. If they are, place your check mark in the row labeled **Sí;** if they are not, you should place your mark in the **No** row. For example, you hear: **Tengo biología los jueves, ¿y tú?** and the response: **Los martes.** You place your mark in the **No** row, since these students are not taking biology on the same day.

1. —Tengo historia a las nueve.
   —Yo, a las diez. *No*
2. —¿Tenemos matemáticas ahora?
   —Sí, ¿vienes? *Sí*
3. —Yo tengo inglés ahora.
   —Yo, geografía. *No*
4. —¿Con quién tenemos ciencias?
   —Con el señor González. *Sí*
5. —¿Tenemos química los viernes?
   —No, los jueves. *Sí*
6. —Tengo computadoras los lunes, ¿y tú?
   —Los miércoles. *No*

Now check your answers. *Read each exchange again and give the correct answer.*

B34 Actividad • ¿Qué tienen?

Have students read the expressions, supplying the missing words according

to the pictures. Then ask them to cover the pictures and complete the sentences with other words or expressions that make sense in the framework given.

SLOWER-PACED LEARNING Write the missing words on the board or a transparency. Tell the students to select the appropriate word to complete each sentence.

B 35 Actividad • ¡A escribir!

You may wish to let students practice this activity orally in class so they know what to write later at home.

SECTION C

OBJECTIVES **To exchange information:** ask how much something costs and give the price

CULTURAL BACKGROUND Shopping for school supplies in Spanish-speaking countries is very similar to shopping in the United States, except that Hispanic students generally must buy their textbooks. For a geography class in Mexico, students might be asked to purchase maps for different projects. Students may go to a school supply store called a **papelería** and buy them. The maps are simple line drawings containing little or no information. Students fill in the maps with labels, colors, or symbols.

MOTIVATING ACTIVITY Discuss the slang words used for *money*. In some Spanish-speaking countries it is **plata**. In Guatemala **pisto** is used and in other places, **moneda**. **Lana** is used in Mexico, and **pelo** is used in Spain.

C1 ¿Cuánto cuesta?

Before presenting this conversation, set up the classroom as a store with a big sign posted **LA TIENDA**. Display the objects mentioned in the dialog: **regla, calculadora, bolígrafos, cartera.** You may add a few more: **lápiz, goma, libro, papel.** You might want to mention that **mochila** is also commonly used for *school bag* in many Spanish-speaking countries. Have a price tag in view for each item. Use pesos or improvise with photocopies or pictures of pesos. First hold up an item and identify it in Spanish, **calculadora.** Then ask **¿Cuánto cuesta?** Hold up the price tag and state the amount: **El precio es catorce pesos.** Do this for each object displayed.

Play the cassette or read aloud the dialog, showing the items mentioned as the class listens. Then have students role-play the dialog in the same way. They may use their books or cue cards if necessary. Call on different students for each section.

C2 Actividad • No es así

Have the students complete the activity orally. Then for writing practice, tell the students to write the sentences so that they are true according to the dialog.

C3 ESTRUCTURAS ESENCIALES

To demonstrate the plural of nouns, hold up a pen and say **Tengo un bolígrafo.** Now hold up two pens and say **Tengo dos bolígrafos.** Practice this procedure with the students, providing the plural of the various objects

you hold up. Point out to the students that the accent is omitted when you form the plural of **autobús.**

C4 Actividad • En la tienda

Have the class do this activity as a chain drill at a quick pace until all the students have had the opportunity to respond. Then add a few more items that were not mentioned, such as **papel, reloj,** or **revista.**

C5 Comprensión

If the people talking mention only one person or item, place a check mark in the row labeled *One.* If you hear more than one article or person being mentioned, place your check mark in the row labeled *More than one.* For example, you hear: **¿Cuánto cuestan las calculadoras?** The check mark is placed in the row labeled *More than one,* since the question refers to **las calculadoras.**

1. —Señorita, el libro no tiene precio. *One*
2. —Muchos estudiantes vienen tarde. *More than one*
3. —¿El autobús número cinco, por favor? *One*
4. —¿Los bolígrafos? Dos dólares. *More than one*
5. —¿Tienes bicicleta? *One*
6. —Una regla, por favor. *One*
7. —No, no tenemos calculadoras. *More than one*
8. —¿Necesitas quince pesos? *More than one*
9. —Tengo diez materias. *More than one*
10. —¿Hay un autobús ahí? *One*

Now check your answers. *Read each sentence again and give the correct answer.*

C6 Actividad • ¡A escribir!

SLOWER-PACED LEARNING   Have the students complete the activity orally before they write the two lists. Have them exchange papers to correct their work.

CHALLENGE   After the students make the two lists, have them use each word in a sentence. Call on volunteers to read their sentences aloud.

C7 SITUACIÓN • Compras para la escuela

Explain that **Compras** is shopping. Tell the students to follow along in their books, paying close attention to the illustrations. Point out that the plural of **lápiz** is **lápices** and explain that words ending in **z** in the singular change the **z** to **c** in the plural.

C8 SE DICE ASÍ

Read the chart aloud to the students. Demonstrate the models by using the objects with a price tag mentioned in C1. As you hold up an item, say **¿Cuánto cuesta?** Have the students repeat. Now ask a student **¿Cuánto cuesta?** and have him or her respond with **Cuesta . . .**

To demonstrate the plural form, **¿Cuánto cuestan?,** hold up two or more items and repeat the same procedure as above.

C9 Actividad • ¿Cuánto cuestan?

Have the students choose a partner to complete the activity. They should take turns asking how much the items cost. You may wish to check comprehension by adding items not listed.

ANSWERS:
1. ¿Cuánto cuestan las calculadoras? Cuestan ocho dólares.
2. ¿Cuánto cuestan las reglas? Cuestan dos dólares.
3. ¿Cuánto cuestan los bolígrafos? Cuestan cuatro dólares por seis.
4. ¿Cuánto cuesta una regla con calculadora? Cuesta catorce dólares.
5. ¿Cuánto cuesta un libro de inglés? Cuesta trece dólares.
6. ¿Cuánto cuestan los libros de historia? Cuestan nueve dólares.

C10 ESTRUCTURAS ESENCIALES

With books closed, write these phrases on the board or a transparency: **el chico, los chicos—la chica, las chicas.** Ask the students to formulate the rules. Then have them open their books and follow along as you read the explanation about definite and indefinite articles.

Remind students that most words which end in **-o** are masculine and most which end in **-a** are feminine. They should use a dictionary to look up the gender if they are unsure.

C11 Actividad • ¿Cuál artículo?

Remind students that **un, una** are equivalent to *a, any* and **unos, unas** to *some*.

SLOWERED-PACED LEARNING Have students first supply singular and plural definite articles for four nouns on the board or a transparency. Have them do the same with indefinite articles. In each case, give them one noun that does not end in **-a** or **-o**, such as **señor, ciudad,** and **clase.**

C12 Actividad • En venta

Have pairs of students complete this activity orally. They should switch roles. Use the store scene in the classroom from C1 to role-play the dialog between a client and salesclerk.

For writing practice, after the students have completed the activity orally, have them write the exchanges in class or at home. Then have volunteers read their exchanges to the class.

ANSWERS:
1. ¡Buenos días! Necesito un cuaderno.
   ¡ No hay problema! Tenemos cuadernos en venta.
2. ¡Buenos días! Necesito una goma.
   ¡No hay problema! Tenemos gomas en venta.
3. ¡Buenos días! Necesito un compás.
   ¡No hay problema! Tenemos compases en venta.
4. ¡Buenos días! Necesito un lápiz.
   ¡No hay problema! Tenemos lápices en venta.
5. ¡Buenos días! Necesito un marcador.
   ¡No hay problema! Tenemos marcadores en venta.

6. ¡Buenos días! Necesito un bolígrafo.
¡No hay problema! Tenemos bolígrafos en venta.
7. ¡Buenos días! Necesito una revista.
¡No hay problema! Tenemos revistas en venta.
8. ¡Buenos días! Necesito una pluma.
¡No hay problema! Tenemos plumas en venta.

C13 ¿Sabes que . . . ?

At the end of the school year if a student receives a failing grade, he or she has the opportunity to take a comprehensive exam called **examen extraordinario.** If the student passes this test, he or she receives credit for the course. If the student fails on the second try, the entire year must be repeated. This evaluation usually is given during summer vacation before the next school year begins.

C14 ESTRUCTURAS ESENCIALES

Read the numbers aloud and have the students repeat.

Explain that it is possible to write *21* as **veinte y uno,** but time has eroded the two sounds of **e** and **i** and the most common spelling is as written in the book.

Ask the students to point out which numbers have accents. Write them on the board or a transparency. Tell the students that if a word ends in any consonant except **n** or **s,** it is stressed on the last syllable. If it ends in any vowel or **n** or **s,** the stress falls on the next-to-last syllable. Accent marks negate these two rules. When any other syllable is stressed, a written accent must be displayed.

C15 Actividad • Los ganadores

SLOWER-PACED LEARNING Suggest to the students that they make their own flash cards using 3 × 5 index cards. They should write the numeral on one side of the card and the Spanish word for the number on the other. Circulate through the classroom to check for spelling and accent marks.

CHALLENGE Students may enjoy playing the game called **Caracoles** (Snails). A student begins by saying **uno,** the next student should say **dos,** and the next. **tres,** and so on. When the number 7 **(siete),** any derivative (17, 27, 37 . . .), or any multiple (14, 21, . . .) is stated, the student must say **caracoles** instead of the number. If the student fails to say this, he or she no longer plays. Play to 100 and repeat until there is a winner, **un ganador.**

As a variation, give each student ten chips. When a student makes a mistake, he or she must give up a chip. At the end of the game, the student with the most chips is the **ganador.**

ANSWERS:
(*First line*) ochenta y siete; noventa y nueve; veintitrés; cuarenta y seis; sesenta y cinco; setenta y ocho; noventa; treinta y cinco; veintinueve; cuarenta y ocho; cien; cincuenta y seis; sesenta y siete; veinticuatro; noventa y ocho; (*Second line*) ochenta y tres; setenta y cinco; treinta y tres; setenta y seis; cuarenta y ocho; sesenta y tres; treinta y nueve; setenta y nueve; treinta; cincuenta; cuarenta y tres; ochenta; veinticinco; sesenta y nueve; cuarenta y dos

C16 ESTRUCTURAS ESENCIALES

Read the explanation about numbers with the students. Explain that the numbers are placed before the noun and they do not change, except for the number **uno. Uno** drops the **-o** when used with masculine nouns. With feminine nouns, **uno** is changed to **una.**

Point out that compound numbers greater than 29 are written separately and linked by **y.**

C17 Actividad • Hora de inventario

Before selecting pairs, present the model to the students. Then call on several individuals to do the first two items. Tell students to switch roles when working with a classmate.

C18 Actividad • Varios precios

For cooperative learning, divide the class into groups of three or four to complete the activity. Each student should make sure that each member of the group can ask the prices and answer the questions appropriately.

C19 Conversación • ¿Cuánto cuesta?

Suggest to the students that they practice the conversation with a classmate with whom they have not practiced before.

SLOWER-PACED LEARNING Tell students to follow the model as a guide and to replace the items and the numbers in the dialog with their own.

C20 Actividad • ¡A escribir!

Have the students write the numerals and numbers in words used in their dialogs. Have them exchange papers to correct their spelling.

C21 Actividad • Una confusión

SLOWER-PACED LEARNING Students may have difficulty choosing the beginning sentence. Tell them to select an expression a vendor would use when a customer walks into a store.

CHALLENGE Have the students write similar dialogs and then scramble them. They should exchange the scrambled dialogs with one another and try to unscramble the dialogs they receive.

C22 Comprensión

Different people are discussing prices at the store. After listening to their exchanges, look in rows A, B, C, or D to find the corresponding price given in numerals. Then circle the correct amount. For example, you hear: **¿Cuánto cuestan?** and the response: **Cuestan diez cincuenta.** *$10.50* circled in row C is the correct amount.

1. —¿El precio de la calculadora?
   —Diez noventa y nueve. *D. $10.99*
2. —Por favor, ¿cuánto cuestan?
   —Cinco setenta y cinco. *A. $5.75*
3. —¿Y los marcadores?

—Dos por un dólar.   *A. $1.00*
4. —¿Tiene carteras?
   —Sí, cuestan treinta y tres treinta.   *B. $33.30*
5. —Cuestan cincuenta y seis dólares.
   —Gracias, pero no tengo tanto.   *C. $56.00*

Now check your answers. *Read each exchange again and give the correct answer.*

C23   Actividad • Anuncios

Tell students they may use props and music for their presentations. Provide the students with words such as **rebaja, gratis, en venta,** and **precio.**

CHALLENGE   Have the students work in pairs to make up a television commercial to advertise the items on sale. Have them present their commercials to the class.

TRY YOUR SKILLS

OBJECTIVE   To recombine communicative functions, grammar, and vocabulary

CULTURAL BACKGROUND   Home computers are just beginning to be very popular in Spanish-speaking countries. Students who do not have one at home and have a computer class need to spend a lot of time practicing at school. Most public high schools do not offer computer classes because of the enormous expense, but in the larger cities there are a few private high schools that offer computer classes. There are also many technical schools that specialize in computer education throughout Spanish America and Spain.

1   Agenda

For cooperative learning, have the students form groups of two. After listening to the cassette, each individual may prepare some questions to ask the other member of the group. He or she should make sure that the group members understand the questions and are able to answer them.

Have students make a weekly schedule at home or in class. They may read their appointments aloud in groups formed for Skills 2.

2   Actividad • Dolor de cabeza

After the students have finished making their schedules, divide the class into groups of four students. Each member of the group must make up a schedule by asking other members if they can make the appointment.

3   Actividad • No es así

Practice this activity with the class before the students form groups of three. For writing practice, have the students write the sentences and their responses.

UNIDAD
2

4 **Actividad • El boletín de Patricia**

Discuss Patricia's report card with the students. You or a volunteer may wish to write the differences and similarities on the board or a transparency.

5 **Actividad • ¿Y en los Estados Unidos?**

After students complete the activity orally in pairs, you may wish to have them use the questions as a guide to write a short paragraph in class or at home. Then ask several students to read their paragraphs aloud.

As a variation, have the students interview an imaginary exchange student who volunteers. They should keep lists of questions to ask visitors. Have them practice interviewing you or other students.

6 **Pronunciación, lectura, dictado**

1. Listen carefully and repeat what you hear.
   The sound of **ll**: The Spanish **ll** has a sound similar to the English *y* in the words *yes* and *yellow*. Listen to the following words with **ll** and repeat in the pauses provided.

   Llansó   ellas   llama   llamas

   SLOWER-PACED LEARNING [Tell the students that **ll** is a letter (double "ell"). It affects alphabetization in vocabulary lists. It follows the letter **l** ("ell").]

   The sound of **ch**: In Spanish the sound of **ch** is very similar to the English *ch* in the words *choose* and *church*. Listen to the following words with **ch** and repeat.

   chicos   ocho   mucho   chao

   Like **ll** (double "ell"), **ch** is a letter in the Spanish alphabet and does affect order in vocabulary lists. It's alphabetized after the letter **c**.

2. Listen, and read aloud.
   Listen to the sounds of **ll** and **ch** in the following Spanish words. Then, as you look at your book, read them aloud.

llamo	llamas	llamamos	ellos	ella
chicos	chao	muchos	ocho	Chávez

3. Write the following sentences from dictation. First listen to the sentence as it is read to you. Then you will hear the sentence again in short segments, with a pause after each segment to allow you time to write. Finally you will hear the sentence a third time so that you may check your work. Let's begin.

   Ella se llama *(pause)* Estrella Llorens.
   Guillermo es *(pause)* de Chicago.
   Chela es *(pause)* la chica *(pause)* de Chile.

SECTION A

Write the questions with **venir** on a transparency or the board so students may correct their work. To practice the position of **no,** ask the students to answer each question negatively. Then state an alternative means of transportation.

SECTION B

Include some numbers from 21 through 100.
Have the students dictate the sentences with the verb **tener** as you write them.

SECTION C

For further practice, you may wish to give each student $40 of play money in **pesos.** Tell them they must purchase at least three items from the school supply store.

ANSWERS:
1. Un lápiz cuesta un dólar. Dos lápices cuestan dos dólares.
2. Un diccionario cuesta veinticuatro dólares. Dos diccionarios cuestan cuarenta y ocho dólares.
3. Una pluma cuesta cuarenta y cinco dólares. Dos plumas cuestan noventa dólares.
4. Un libro de matemáticas cuesta catorce dólares. Dos libros de matemáticas cuestan veintiocho dólares.
5. Una calculadora cuesta tres noventa y cinco. Dos calculadoras cuestan siete noventa.
6. Una cartera cuesta treinta y cinco dólares. Dos carteras cuestan setenta dólares.
7. Un cuaderno cuesta dos noventa y cinco. Dos cuadernos cuestan cinco noventa.
8. Una goma cuesta dos dólares. Dos gomas cuestan cuatro dólares.

VOCABULARIO

Begin the vocabulary review by asking students to write a sentence using a noun from the list. Then play the "Wheel of Fortune" game using the sentences. Write the sentence on a transparency and cover each letter with a paper square. The letters are uncovered as the students correctly identify them. You may wish to use single words from the vocabulary lists instead of the sentences.

ESTUDIO DE PALABRAS

Tell the students to locate all the words with a written accent and write them in a list to be added to the **Vocabulario** section of their notebooks.

VAMOS A LEER

OBJECTIVE   To read for practice and pleasure

LIBROS PARA LA ESCUELA Y PARA LOS RATOS LIBRES

Ask the students about the types of books they like to read. Have them look at the various book titles and tell which one they would choose.

Sin mirar

Ask the students to cover the page or close their books and see what they can remember. You may wish to give the subject areas to help students remember.

¡SOCORRO!

Have the students read the selection once without consulting the vocabulary. Then tell them to reread using the footnotes. Read aloud or play the cassette and have the students answer the questions in **Preguntas y respuestas.**

Actividad • Combinación

Have the students do the activity in class or at home. For writing practice, have them write the complete sentences.

EL REGALO

Review the events of the first episode of **El regalo** with the students. Tell them that they are now going to read the second episode to find out what the surprise gift is.

Have the students read the selection silently. Then call on volunteers to read aloud or role-play the dialog.

Preguntas y respuestas

For cooperative learning, have the students form groups to review the dialog and answer the questions.

ANSWERS:
1. Es un regalo anónimo. Es un regalo misterioso.
2. No, el paquete no tiene remitente.
3. No, los chicos no tienen televisor.
4. Es portátil, pero no tiene pilas.
5. Tiene tres canales.
6. No, no necesita pilas para funcionar.
7. Son las cinco y es jueves.
8. Es viernes y son las seis.
9. Hay una superventa.
10. No, el presidente no se llama Manuel Roldán.

Actividad • ¿Es cierto o no?

Direct the students to write a short summary of **El regalo** by using the corrected statements from this activity. They may add their own sentences if they wish.

ANSWERS:

1. No es cierto. La etiqueta dice Daniel y Adriana Arias.
2. Es cierto.
3. No es cierto. El televisor es para Daniel y Adriana.
4. No es cierto. La revista "Hoy" tiene una entrevista con el presidente de la república.
5. Es cierto.
6. Es cierto.
7. No es cierto. Miran las noticias en el Canal Uno.
8. No es cierto. En la tienda Díaz hay bolígrafos a treinta pesos.
9. No es cierto. El televisor no necesita pilas.
10. Es cierto.

UNIDAD 2
En la escuela

Schools in Spain and Latin America are not very different from your own. Many students attend private schools, usually called *colegios*. Others go to public schools, called *escuelas públicas*.

As in the United States, schools are often named after famous people. In this unit you will see one school named for Benito Juárez (1806–1872), president of Mexico around the time of Abraham Lincoln. Another school is named for Simón Bolívar, the Liberator (1783–1830), who was a hero of the Spanish American independence movement.

In this unit, you will:

SECTION A	talk about how you get to school
SECTION B	talk about your school schedule and subjects
SECTION C	learn to shop for school supplies
TRY YOUR SKILLS	use what you've learned
VAMOS A LEER	read for practice and pleasure

SECTION A

talking about how to get to school

With a population of about 20 million, Mexico City may be the most densely populated city in the world. Students who live there travel through heavy traffic on their way to school. Some walk while others ride a bike, come by car, or take a bus or subway.

A1

¿Cómo vienes a la escuela?

Los estudiantes de la Escuela Secundaria Benito Juárez vienen de muchas partes de la ciudad. Muchos vienen temprano, pero no todos. Algunos vienen tarde hoy. ¿Por qué? Porque el autobús escolar número ocho tiene un problema. Pero, ¡mira!, ahí viene el autobús.

ISABEL	Andrés, ¿vienes tú en autobús con Carlos?
ANDRÉS	No, yo no vengo en autobús, vengo en auto.
ISABEL	Y ustedes, ¿cómo vienen?
RAÚL Y MARTA	Nosotros venimos en metro.
ISABEL	¿Y José? ¿Cuándo viene? ¿Viene él con Carlos?
MARTA	Yo no sé.
ANDRÉS	Mira, ahí viene José.
ISABEL	¿No viene en bicicleta?
RAÚL	No, hoy viene a pie.
ISABEL	¡Ah, por fin viene el autobús! ¡Carlos, mi libro de inglés, por favor!

You may wish to point out the correct pronunciation of <u>v</u> in "venir."

A2 Actividad • ¿Es cierto o no? For answers, see p. T48.

Say whether the following statements are correct **(Es cierto)** or not **(No es cierto)** according to the information in A1. Correct the statements that aren't true.

1. Los estudiantes vienen de muchas partes de la ciudad.
2. Todos vienen temprano.
3. El autobús número ocho viene temprano.
4. Andrés viene en bicicleta.
5. Raúl y Marta vienen a pie.

6. Raúl viene en metro con Carlos.
7. José viene a pie.
8. José viene hoy en autobús.
9. Carlos viene en bicicleta.
10. Isabel y Carlos vienen en auto.

A3 Actividad • ¿Qué es? *What is it?* You may wish to mention that "autobús" is also called "camión" in Mexico and "guagua" in the Canary Islands, Cuba, and Puerto Rico.

Es

un . . . autobús

un . . . auto

una . . . bicicleta

un . . . metro

A4 Comprensión For script and answers, see p. T49.

Are they all coming to school?

	0	1	2	3	4	5	6	7	8	9
Sí		✔		✔				✔		✔
No	✔		✔		✔	✔	✔		✔	

ESTRUCTURAS ESENCIALES
The verb venir

venir *to come*					
Yo	**vengo**	a pie.	Nosotros(as)	**venimos**	en bicicleta.
Tú	**vienes**	en auto.	Vosotros(as)	**venís**	en metro.
Usted, él, ella	**viene**	en metro	Ustedes, ellos(as)	**vienen**	en autobús.

1. The pronouns **usted, él,** and **ella** go with the same form, **viene.**

2. The pronouns **ustedes, ellos,** and **ellas** go with the same form, **vienen.**

3. Use **a pie** when somebody walks somewhere. With a means of transportation use the formula:
en + means of transportation.

Actividad • ¿Tarde o temprano?   *Late or early?*

The school bus has had some trouble this morning. Report that the following
people are coming to school late.

—¿Enrique?　　　　　　 —¿Yo?
—Enrique viene tarde.　　 —Tú vienes tarde.
　　　　　　　　　　　　　　vienen
1. ¿Carmen? viene　**2.** ¿Jorge y Antonio?　　**3.** ¿La chica nueva? viene　**4.** ¿Usted? viene
5. ¿Nosotros? venimos　**6.** ¿Tú? vengo　　　　 **7.** ¿Ustedes? vienen　　　　**8.** ¿Raúl y yo? venimos

Actividad • A la escuela . . . ¡rápido!

Look at the drawings and say how you think these people come to school.

Él viene en auto.

Ellos vienen en bicicleta.

1.　　　　　　　　　　　　**2.**

3.　　　　　　　　　　　**4.**　　　　　　　　　**5.**

Ellos vienen en autobús.　　　Ella viene a pie.　　　Él viene en metro.

Actividad • ¡A escribir!

Write the correct form of **venir**.

1. El autobús _____ tarde. *viene*
2. Nosotros _____ en metro. *venimos*
3. Yo _____ temprano. *vengo*
4. Ellos no _____ temprano. *vienen*
5. El profesor _____ en auto. *viene*
6. Ustedes _____ en bicicleta. *vienen*
7. ¿Cómo _____ Isabel? *viene*
8. Ella _____ a pie. *viene*
9. Tú no _____ en autobús. *vienes*

A9 ¿Sabes que . . . ?

In Spanish-speaking countries, the minimum age for obtaining a driver's license is 18. Few high school students drive cars or motorcycles. Bicycles are fairly common in large cities but to travel anywhere, most students use public transportation. Private schools sometimes have their own buses. Students who attend public schools usually use public buses.

A10 SE DICE ASÍ
Asking for and giving an explanation

¿Cómo vienen a la escuela?	Vienen en autobús.
How do they come to school?	They come by bus.
¿Por qué vienen tarde?	Porque el autobús tiene un problema.
Why are they late?	Because the bus has a problem.
	(Because there's a problem with the bus.)

To find out something, you can ask a question beginning with a question word:

¿Cómo? *How?* **¿Quién?** *Who?* **¿Por qué?** *Why?*
¿Cuándo? *When?* **¿De dónde?** *From where?* **¿Qué?** *What?*

When used to ask why, **¿por qué?** is written as two words. The **qué** has a written accent. When used to tell why, **porque** (*because*) is a single word without any accent.

You may wish to remind the students to include accents on the question words.

A11 Actividad • Charla Free conversation

With a classmate, talk about how you come to school. Here are some questions you might use.

¿Cómo vienes a la escuela? ¿Vienes temprano? ¿tarde? ¿Por qué?

A12 ESTRUCTURAS ESENCIALES
Two uses of no

To say *no* in Spanish, simply place the word **no** in front of the verb.

Yo **no** vengo en autobús.   *I do not come by bus.*

If the answer to a question is in the negative, the word **no** will appear twice, at the beginning of the sentence, as in English, and in front of the verb, meaning *not*.

—¿Carlos viene en bicicleta?   *Does Carlos come by bike?*
—**No,** Carlos **no** viene en bicicleta.   *No, he does not come by bike.*

1. Sí, vengo temprano. 2. No, ellos no vienen temprano. 3. Sí, Alicia viene temprano. 4. Sí, Carlos y María vienen temprano. 5. No, tú no vienes temprano.

A 13 Actividad • ¿Un autobús nuevo?

Perhaps we need a larger bus? The minibus we have now has to make two trips, so half the students come to school early and half come to school late. A classmate is asking who comes early. Answer as indicated.

　　—¿Viene Ramón temprano? (No)
　　—No, Ramón no viene temprano.

1. ¿Vienes temprano? (Sí)
2. ¿Vienen ellos temprano? (No)
3. ¿Viene Alicia temprano? (Sí)
4. ¿Vienen Carlos y María temprano? (Sí)
5. ¿Vengo temprano? (No)

A 14 Comprensión

For script and answers, see p. T51.
Are you sure? Is that the answer?

	0	1	2	3	4	5	6	7	8
Sí		✔		✔		✔			✔
No	✔		✔		✔		✔	✔	

A 15 Actividad • ¿Sí o no? ¿Por qué? Students will create their own mini dialogs following the model.

Ask these questions. Your classmate will answer **sí** or **no.** When you ask "How come?" your classmate will explain or say **¡No sé!** *(I don't know!)*

　　—¿Vienes en autobús?　　　—¿Vienes en metro?
　　—No.　　　　　　　　　　 —Sí.
　　—¿Por qué?　　　　　　　 —¿Por qué?
　　—Vengo a pie.　　　　　　—Porque vengo con Soledad.

1. ¿Vienes temprano?
2. ¿Tienes un problema?
3. ¿Vienes de México?
4. ¿Vienes a pie?
5. ¿Viene tarde el autobús?
6. ¿Viene José con Carlos?
7. ¿Vienen Raúl y Marta en metro?
8. ¿No vienen Isabel y Andrés en bicicleta?

A 16 Actividad • ¡A escribir!

No es así. No, it's not so. Alfredo doesn't have his facts straight. Write answers to his remarks, telling him he's mistaken.

　　—Ellos son de Texas.
　　—No, ellos no son de Texas, Alfredo.

1. Tú te llamas Ramón. No, yo no me llamo Ramón.
2. Ella se llama Ramona. No, ella no se llama Ramona.
3. Tú eres de España. No, yo no soy de España.
4. Ellos son de España. No, ellos no son de España.
5. Tú vienes en auto. No, yo no vengo en auto.
6. Ellos vienen en autobús. No, ellos no vienen en autobús.
7. Isabel viene tarde. No, Isabel no viene tarde.
8. Ustedes vienen tarde. No, nosotros no venimos tarde.
9. Tú vienes tarde. No, yo no vengo tarde.
10. Tú estás muy mal. No, yo no estoy muy mal.

Students in Spanish-speaking countries usually take ten or more subjects. Keeping them straight at the beginning of a new school year isn't easy.

Point out the use of the definite articles with titles of respect: "La señora Suárez".

B1 ¿Qué materias tienes hoy?

En el recreo

ALBERTO	¡Hola, Enrique! ¿Tienes clase de matemáticas?
ENRIQUE	No, tengo inglés.
ALBERTO	¿A qué hora?
ENRIQUE	A las diez. ¿Y tú?, ¿qué tienes?
ALBERTO	Hoy tengo clase de computadoras.
ENRIQUE	¿Hay muchos estudiantes?
ALBERTO	Como veinte.
ENRIQUE	Y, el profesor, ¿quién es?
ALBERTO	Tenemos una profesora: la señora Suárez. ¿Cuántas materias tienes tú?

ENRIQUE	Diez, once . . . no sé. ¿Qué hora es?
ALBERTO	¡Oh! Son casi las diez. ¡Adiós!
ENRIQUE	¡Chao!

B2 Actividad • ¿Es cierto o no?

Say whether the statements are correct (**Es cierto**) or not (**No es cierto**) according to B1. Correct the statements that aren't true.

1. Es el recreo.
2. Enrique tiene clase de matemáticas.
3. Enrique no tiene clase de inglés.
4. Hay como diez estudiantes en la clase de Alberto.
5. Enrique tiene clase de inglés a las diez.
6. El profesor de la clase de computadoras es Benito Martínez.
7. ¿Qué hora es? Son casi las once.
8. Enrique tiene veinte materias.

1. Es cierto.   2. No es cierto. Enrique tiene clase de inglés.   3. No es cierto. Enrique tiene clase de inglés.   4. No es cierto. Hay como veinte.   5. Es cierto.   6. No es cierto. La profesora de la clase de computadoras es la Sra. Suárez.   7. No es cierto. Son casi las diez.   8. No es cierto. Alberto tiene diez u once materias.

En la escuela 65

In many Spanish-speaking countries, the first six years of school are called **escuela primaria.** Three years of **secundaria** follow, which are equivalent to junior high school and the first two years of high school. Many students then enter the **bachillerato** for three more years of studies concentrating on the arts or sciences.

B4   ESTRUCTURAS ESENCIALES
Numbers from 0 to 20

You may wish to point out the diphthongs in the numbers "veinte", "siete", "cuatro", "nueve" and the accent marks in "número" and "dieciséis."

0 cero	**1** uno	**2** dos	**3** tres	**4** cuatro	**5** cinco
6 seis	**7** siete	**8** ocho	**9** nueve	**10** diez
11 once	**12** doce	**13** trece	**14** catorce	**15** quince
16 dieciséis	**17** diecisiete	**18** dieciocho	**19** diecinueve	**20** veinte

When talking about numbers **(números),** **uno** changes to **un** before a masculine noun and to **una** before a feminine noun.

B5   Actividad • La clase de matemáticas

• Read these numbers aloud in Spanish.

  18, 11, 2, 14   5, 19, 12, 13   2, 3, 4, 5, 6, 17, 15, 13, 7, 8, 10, 9

• Go through the numbers again, subtracting one from each.

• Now go through them adding one.

B6   Actividad • ¡A escribir!

Write the following as numerals.

  doce, tres, quince, siete, dieciséis, dieciocho, veinte, seis, trece, uno, cuatro, nueve
  12   3   15   7   16   18   20   6   13   1   4   9

B7 Actividad · Un juego

Draw a rectangle and divide it into twenty-one squares as shown. Number the squares from 0 to 20 in any order you choose. Use each number only once. Someone will call numbers from 0 to 20 in random order. The first to fill in a horizontal line is the winner.

8	2	5	13	14	11	16
7	1	6	4	15	0	12
9	10	3	19	17	18	20

B8 SITUACIÓN · El horario de Enrique   *Enrique's Schedule*

Enrique es estudiante de la Escuela Secundaria Benito Juárez. Tiene un horario fuerte. Hay diez materias, pero no hay clases el sábado.

You may wish to point out that school subjects are not capitalized.

Horario	LUNES	MARTES	MIÉRCOLES	JUEVES	VIERNES	SÁBADO	DOMINGO
9:00 AM	historia	ciencias naturales	historia	ciencias naturales	español		
10:00 AM	mat.	mat.	comput.	mat.	ed. física		
11:00 AM	comput.	ed. física	español	comput.	historia		
12:00 PM	ALMUERZO						
1:00 PM	español	español	ed. física	español	comput.		
2:00 PM	física	física	mat.	física	mat.		
Actividades Extra Curriculares	música	fútbol	fútbol	música	pintura		

NO HAY CLASES

You may wish to tell the students that "manualidades" is equivalent to "arts and crafts."

Yo tengo otras materias—álgebra a las 4, biología a las 5, filosofía a las 6, francés a las 7, manualidades a las 8, química a las 9...

B9 Actividad • ¿Qué clase es?

As you walk past various classrooms, you hear a teacher or a student saying the following things. Try to guess what subject is being studied. You already saw some of the subjects in B8.

1. . . . un círculo, un triángulo y un rectángulo . . . geometría
2. . . . los ácidos, en combinación con oxígeno y nitrógeno . . . química
3. ¡Muy bien! Tienes mucho talento, los colores son muy artísticos . . . pintura
4. . . . la repetición de la melodía del compositor clásico . . . música
5. . . . y las partículas en el núcleo del átomo . . . física
6. . . . el Océano Pacífico, el Atlántico, el Mar Mediterráneo . . . geografía
7. . . . el "cursor" indica la posición del próximo carácter . . . computadoras
8. . . . las células nerviosas son entidades autónomas . . . biología
9. . . . anunciaron la independencia de la república . . . historia

B10 ESTRUCTURAS ESENCIALES
Los días de la semana   *The days of the week*

lunes	martes	miércoles	jueves	viernes	sábado	domingo

1. Notice that the days of the week are not capitalized in Spanish.

2. The days of the week are masculine in Spanish and take the definite article **el.** To say the plural form of a day, use the plural article **los.** Add **-s** to the day if it doesn't end in **-s** already **(sábado, domingo).**

    los lunes   *Mondays*   los sábados   *Saturdays*

3. To express *on* (any given day or days), use **el** or **los.**

    Tengo inglés el lunes.   *I have English on Monday (or next Monday).*
    Tengo inglés los lunes.   *I have English on Mondays.*

4. When telling what day it is, omit the article.

    Hoy es jueves.   *Today is Thursday.*

B11 Actividad • El pobre Enrique   *Poor Enrique*   See schedule in B8, p. 67, for answers.

Tell what courses Enrique has each day, according to his schedule in B8.

    El lunes Enrique tiene español, historia, física . . .

B12 Actividad • ¿Qué tiene Enrique hoy?

Answer the following questions about Enrique's schedule (see B8).

    —¿Cuándo tiene Enrique música?
    —Tiene música los lunes y los jueves.

1. La actividad extra-curricular de hoy es pintura. ¿Qué día es hoy? viernes
2. ¿Cuándo tiene Enrique educación física? viernes
3. ¿Tiene él historia los viernes? Sí, viernes
4. ¿Cuándo tiene ciencias naturales? martes/jueves
5. ¿Tiene él español los miércoles? ¿Y tú? Sí, tiene.

B13 ESTRUCTURAS ESENCIALES
The verb tener

tener *to have*					
Yo	**tengo**	clase hoy.	Nosotros(as)	**tenemos**	música.
Tú	**tienes**	inglés.	Vosotros(as)	**tenéis**	química.
Usted, él, ella	**tiene**	dibujo.	Ustedes, ellos(as)	**tienen**	historia.

B14 Actividad • ¿Tienes clase?

Supply the missing forms of **tener.**

1. ¿_____ tú ciencias ahora? Tienes
2. No, yo no _____ ciencias los martes. tengo
3. Nosotros _____ ciencias los martes. tenemos
4. ¿_____ ustedes clase con el profesor Suárez? Tienen
5. No, ellos _____ química hoy. tienen
6. ¿Qué día _____ nosotros clase de química? tenemos
7. Ustedes _____ clase los jueves, tienen nosotros _____ clase los miércoles. tenemos
8. Yo _____ clase ahora. tengo
9. ¿Qué clase _____ tú? tienes

B15 Actividad • Combinación

Answers will vary. Ex: Nosotros tenemos ciencias naturales los lunes.

Form sentences by choosing items from each column.

nosotros ellas Alicia tú ustedes Felipe y José él ella yo Rosario	*tiene* *tienen* *tenemos* *tengo* *tienes*	ciencias naturales educación física computadoras deportes español pintura ciencias sociales	los lunes los martes los miércoles los jueves los viernes

B16 Actividad • Un momento, por favor. *Just a moment, please.*

You have the class's schedule on file. Answer the supervisor's questions after first looking at your notes in parentheses.

—¿Tienes tú clases hoy? (No)
—No, hoy yo no tengo clases.

Remind students that English uses *do* and *don't* to ask a question, but Spanish does not.

1. ¿Qué materias tienes tú hoy? (historia y física) Hoy tengo historia y física.
2. ¿Tienen los chicos español hoy? (Sí)
3. ¿Tenemos física hoy? (No) No, hoy no tenemos física.
4. ¿Tienen ellas música los martes? (viernes) No, tienen música los viernes.
5. ¿Qué materias tiene Norma hoy? (inglés y ciencias) Hoy Norma tiene inglés y ciencias.
6. ¿Tiene Marisa clase de computadoras hoy? (Sí) Sí, Marisa tiene clase de computadoras.
7. ¿Tienes tú español hoy? (matemáticas)
8. ¿Tienen ustedes biología hoy? (No)

2. Sí, hoy tienen español.
7. No, yo tengo matemáticas hoy.
8. No, no tenemos biología hoy.

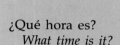 **B 17** Actividad • ¡A escribir! Answers will vary.

Haz tu horario. Make your own schedule. Write the names of the days of the week and fill in the subjects you're taking in school. **¡En español!** *In Spanish!*, of course.

B 18 Actividad • Los horarios Answers will vary.

Compare schedules with a classmate, like this.

¿Tienes matemáticas hoy? ¿Qué tienes el martes a las dos? ¿Tienes inglés a las nueve?

B 19 ESTRUCTURAS ESENCIALES
Telling time

¿Qué hora es? *What time is it?*	 Es la una. *It's one o'clock.*	 Son las dos. *It's two o'clock.*
¿A qué hora es el recreo? *(At) what time is recess?*	 A la una. *(At) one.*	 A las dos. *(At) two.*

1. **Es** and **la** are used with **una**: (1:00) **Es la una.** For other hours use **las** and **son**: (2:00) **Son las dos**; (5:00) **Son las cinco.**

2. The equivalent of *past* or *after* is **y**: (10:05) **Son las diez y cinco.** Note that the hour is given before the minutes.

3. The equivalent of *to* or *till* is **menos**: (7:50) **Son las ocho menos diez.**

4. To ask or say at what time something happens use **a**: **¿A qué hora son las clases?** In your answer, use **media** for the half hours and **cuarto** as the equivalent for the quarter hours: (8:15) **A las ocho y cuarto.** (12:30) **A las doce y media.** (8:45) **A las nueve menos cuarto.**

You may wish to emphasize the use of the definite article in time expressions: "la" with "una" and "las" with all other hours.

B 20 Actividad • ¿Qué hora es?

Pair up with a classmate and say the time as indicated. Your classmate will say what class he or she has, or say **No tengo clase** if he/she has no class.

11:00	—Son las once. —Tengo geografía.

1. Son las diez.
2. Son las ocho y media.
3. Son las diez menos cuarto.
4. Es la una.
5. Son las cuatro y quince.
6. Son las siete.
7. Son las tres.
8. Son las doce y cinco.

1. 10:00 **2.** 8:30 **3.** 9:45 **4.** 1:00 **5.** 4:15 **6.** 7:00 **7.** 3:00 **8.** 12:05

Comprensión 🔲 For script and answers, see p. T55.

Make sure the time is right.

0	1	2	3	4	5	6	7	8	9	10
2:00	12:00	1:00	9:00	3:00	11:00	8:00	12:00	1:00	2:00	10:00

B 22 Actividad • ¿A qué hora?

Your classmate asks what time various classes are. Answer as indicated; then switch roles.

1. ¿A qué hora tenemos inglés el lunes?
2. ¿A qué hora tenemos inglés los martes y miércoles?
3. ¿A qué hora tenemos física los lunes, miércoles y viernes?
4. ¿A qué hora tenemos matemáticas el miércoles?
5. ¿A qué hora tenemos ciencias naturales el martes?
6. ¿A qué hora tenemos música el jueves?
7. ¿A qué hora tenemos geografía el jueves?
8. ¿A qué hora tenemos educación física el viernes?

dibujo, viernes: 2:00
—¿A qué hora tenemos dibujo el viernes?
—A las dos.

1. inglés, lunes: 1:00   A la una.
2. inglés, martes y miércoles: 9:00   A las nueve.
3. física, lunes, miércoles y viernes: 11:30
4. matemáticas, miércoles: 10:45

5. ciencias naturales, martes: 11:20   A las once y veinte.
6. música, jueves: 2:00   A las dos.
7. geografía, jueves: 1:10   A la una y diez.
8. educación física, viernes: 11:00   A las once.

3. A las once y media.
4. A las once menos cuarto.

B 23 Actividad • ¿Qué hora es en la Ciudad de México? Answers will vary.

Long-distance callers need to think what time it is at the other end of the line. Team up with a classmate and test each other on figuring out the time in the cities listed.

—Son las cuatro en Lima. ¿Qué hora es en Madrid?
—Son las diez. ¿Qué hora es en Seattle?
—Es la una. ¿Qué . . . ?

Los Ángeles • Seattle	12:00
Denver • Albuquerque	1:00
San Antonio • México D.F.	2:00
Miami • Lima • Nueva York	3:00
Puerto Rico • Santiago de Chile	4:00
Buenos Aires • Montevideo	5:00
Madrid • Barcelona	9:00

B 24 Actividad • Charla Free conversation

With a partner, talk about your classes and schedule.

¿Qué días tienes clase de . . . ?

El . . . (los . . .), ¿y tú?

¿A qué hora tienes clase de . . . ?

A la . . . (A las . . .), ¿y tú?

En la escuela   71

ANDRÉS	¿Qué tienes tú ahora?
CLARA	Biología, ¿y tú?
ANDRÉS	Historia. Con el Sr. Galván. Es mi materia preferida.
CLARA	¿Tu materia preferida? ¡Es muy aburrida! Es difícil. Hay mucha tarea.
ANDRÉS	¡Al contrario! Es fácil. Es muy interesante. Y tu materia favorita, ¿cuál es?
CLARA	Química.
ANDRÉS	Tienes bastante tarea y no es interesante, ¿verdad?
CLARA	No, es muy interesante.
ANDRÉS	¿Cuántas materias tienes?
CLARA	Tengo diez.
ANDRÉS	¿Diez? ¡Eres un genio!

B 26 Actividad · ¿Andrés o Clara? You may wish to point out the definite article used for respect: "el señor Galv

Who might be saying each of the following lines, according to B25?

1. Mi materia preferida es química. Clara
2. El señor Galván es el profesor de historia. Andrés
3. ¡La historia es difícil! Clara

4. Tengo biología ahora. Clara
5. La historia es muy interesante. Andrés
6. Tienes bastante tarea en química. Andrés

B 27 Actividad · ¡A escoger!

Choose the proper completion for each sentence according to B25. Then write them down.

You may wish to tell students that nouns used in a general sense require the definite article. However, the article is not necessary with specific school subjects.
El español es fácil. Tengo clase de español. Tengo química hoy.

1. Clara tiene ahora
   • química.   • historia.   • <u>biología.</u>
2. Andrés tiene ahora
   • biología.   • <u>historia.</u>   • química.
3. Andrés tiene clase con
   • Benito Juárez.   • <u>el señor Galván.</u>   • Clara.
4. La materia preferida de Andrés es
   • biología.   • química.   • <u>historia.</u>
5. Pero, Andrés, la historia es
   • muy difícil.   • <u>difícil.</u>   • muy interesante.
6. La materia preferida de Clara es
   • biología.   • química.   • historia.
7. Pero, Clara, la química no es
   • <u>interesante.</u>   • bastante aburrida.   • difícil.
8. Andrés y Clara tienen . . .
   • muchas materias.   • <u>una diferencia de opiniones.</u>   • inglés ahora.

SE DICE ASÍ
Asking about classes and giving your opinion

¿Cómo es la clase? ¿Es interesante? How's the class? Is it interesting?	No, es aburrida. No, it's boring.
¿Cuál es tu materia preferida? What's (Which is) your favorite subject?	Dibujo. Drawing.

B 29 Actividad • Charla   Free conversation   Ex. ¿Tienes un diez? Al contrario, tengo un cinco.

Talk about classes with a partner. Use **¿verdad?** if you want to ask, and **al contrario** if you don't agree. Here are some hints to help you get started.

—¿Qué materias tienes?
—¿Cuál es tu materia preferida?
—¿Cómo es la clase?
—¿Qué días tienes clases?

—¿A qué hora?
—¿Tienes mucha tarea?
—¿Tienes un diez?

B 30 Actividad • Encuesta   *Survey*   Answers will vary.

You have to interview your classmates for an article that will appear in a Spanish newspaper. Ask them what they think of each class (**¿Cómo es la clase de inglés?**, etc.), find out which class is their favorite (**¿Cuál . . . ?**), and note their responses on a form like the one below. Report your results to the class.

Materia:	fácil	difícil	aburrida	interesante	preferida
inglés	3	6	5	4	5
español					
matemáticas					

B 31 Actividad • ¿Español? ¡Cinco estrellas!   *Spanish? Five stars!*   Answers will vary.

You are trying to decide what classes to take next semester. Ask a classmate about a few classes—who the teacher is, and how many stars each class rates according to the following scale:

muy interesante   bastante interesante   aburrida   muy aburrida

B 32 ¿Sabes que . . . ?

A student gets a ten in math, and is called a genius? **Sí, ¡por supuesto!** *(Yes, of course!)* The grading system in many high schools in Spanish-speaking countries goes from 0 to 10. A 9 is **notable** *(excellent)*, and a 10 is very rare indeed. Some schools grade with a scale of 0–20, others use a 0–100 scale. There are other differences. Many schools are not coed. Also, instead of a general high school, teenagers must choose among technical schools that prepare them to be office workers or technicians, normal schools that prepare them to be teachers, and **colegios** that lead to the university.

EVALUACIÓN

90 – 100	9–10	Sobresaliente
80 – 89	8	Notable
70 – 79	7	Aprovechado
60 – 69	6	Aprobado
0 – 59	0–5	Suspenso

B 33 Comprensión   For script and answers, see p. 157.

Who's taking the same courses?

	0	1	2	3	4	5	6
Sí					✔	✔	
No	✔	✔		✔			✔

B 34 Actividad • ¿Qué tienen?

Supply the missing words.

—Mañana tengo <u>música</u>.
¡Es <u>fácil</u> ! No <u>tengo</u> tarea.

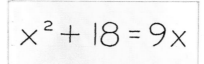

$$x^2 + 18 = 9x$$

—Yo tengo _____ . química
Tengo poca _____ . tarea

—¡Tengo un <u>diez</u> en _____ !
—¡Eres un genio!   matemáticas

—Yo tengo <u>biología</u>. Tengo <u>mucha</u> tarea. ¡Es difícil!

B 35 Actividad • ¡A escribir!

Write three sentences about three of your own classes. Tell about your grades (0 to 10!), your homework, and how you feel about each class. Answers will vary.

shopping for school supplies

Classes begin and it's time to buy school supplies. In Puerto Rico, everyone uses U.S. dollars, but they're called **pesos.**

C1 ¿Cuánto cuesta? 📼

En una tienda en San Juan, Puerto Rico.

ROSA   Miguel, ¡una regla con calculadora!
MIGUEL   ¿Sí? ¿Cuánto cuesta?
ROSA   Catorce noventa y nueve.

MIGUEL   Por favor, señor, ¿cuánto cuestan los bolígrafos? No tienen precio.
VENDEDOR   Tres por dos pesos.
MIGUEL   Gracias.

ROSA   Perdón, ¿tiene usted carteras?
VENDEDORA   Sí, cuestan quince pesos.
ROSA   ¡Uy!, no tengo tanto. Gracias, señora.

MIGUEL   ¿Qué más necesitas?
ROSA   ¡Dinero, por supuesto!

C2   Actividad • No es así   *It's not so*

Restate these sentences so that they are true according to the dialog.

—Rosa tiene quince pesos.
—No, no tiene quince pesos.
—El vendedor no tiene carteras.
—Sí, tiene carteras.

1. No hay regla con calculadora.
2. La regla cuesta veinte pesos.
3. No hay bolígrafos en la tienda.
4. Los bolígrafos tienen precio.

5. Dos bolígrafos cuestan tres pesos.
6. Las carteras cuestan diez pesos.
7. Rosa tiene dinero para una cartera.
8. Rosa no necesita más dinero.

1. Sí, hay regla con calculadora.
2. No, la regla cuesta catorce noventa y nueve.
3. Sí, hay bolígrafos.
4. No, los bolígrafos no tienen precio.

5. No, tres bolígrafos cuestan dos pesos.
6. No, las carteras cuestan quince pesos.
7. No, Rosa no tiene dinero para una cartera.
8. Sí, Rosa necesita más dinero.

En la escuela   75

Forming plurals

regla   reglas   libro   libros

If a noun ends in a vowel (**a, e, i, o,** or **u**), you form the plural by adding **-s.**

regla   reglas   libro   libros

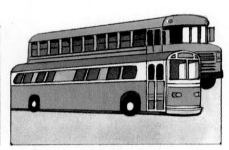

señor   señores   autobús   autobuses

If a word ends in a consonant (any letter except **a, e, i, o,** or **u**),
you form the plural by adding **-es.**

señor   señores   autobús   autobuses

Point out that "autobús" loses its accent in the plural: "autobuses".

C4 Actividad • En la tienda

You work in a store after school. When customers ask if you have certain items,
reply *yes*, you have them.

—¿Una regla?
—Sí, tenemos reglas.

1. ¿Una calculadora?   Sí, tenemos calculadoras.
2. ¿Un libro?   Sí, tenemos libros.
3. ¿Un bolígrafo?   Sí, tenemos bolígrafos.
4. ¿Una bicicleta?   Sí, tenemos bicicletas.
5. ¿Una computadora?   Sí, tenemos computadoras.
6. ¿Una pintura?   Sí, tenemos pinturas.
7. ¿Un dibujo?   Sí, tenemos dibujos.
8. ¿Una cartera?   Sí, tenemos carteras.

C5 Comprensión   For script and answers, see p. T59.

One or more?

	0	1	2	3	4	5	6	7	8	9	10
one		✔		✔		✔	✔				✔
more than one	✔		✔		✔			✔	✔	✔	

C6   Actividad • ¡A escribir!

Using the words below, make two lists; one with the singular words and one with the plurals.

    escuela clases bolígrafos chico autobús reglas profesores
    bicicletas cartera señoras dólares libro chicas

Plural: clases, bolígrafos, reglas, profesores, bicicletas, señoras, dólares, chicas Singular: escuela, chico, autobús, cartera, libro

C7   SITUACIÓN • Compras para la escuela

—Por favor, ¿cuánto cuesta . . .

Remind the students that the definite article must agree in number and gender with the noun.

    un cuaderno?   un lápiz?   una goma?   un marcador?   un compás?

—¡Hay rebajas! Tenemos . . .

    unos cuadernos,   unas revistas,   unas plumas,

    unos lápices[1]   y unos diccionarios en venta.

C8   SE DICE ASÍ
    Asking how much something costs and giving the price

	Singular	¿Cuánto cuesta?	Cuesta . . .
		How much does it cost?	It costs . . . (It's . . .)
	Plural	¿Cuánto cuestan?	Cuestan . . .
		How much do they cost?	They cost . . . (They are . . .)

---

[1]The plural of **lápiz** *(pencil)* is **lápices** *(pencils)*. Words ending in **z** in the singular change to **c** in the plural.

Actividad • ¿Cuánto cuestan?

Pair up with a classmate. Ask how much these items cost. Your classmate will answer as indicated. Then switch roles.

el bolígrafo, $3
—¿Cuánto cuesta el bolígrafo?
—Cuesta tres dólares.

las reglas, $4
—¿Cuánto cuestan las reglas?
—Cuestan cuatro dólares.

1. las calculadoras, $8
2. las reglas, $2

3. los bolígrafos, 6 por $4
4. una regla con calculadora, $14

5. un libro de inglés, $13
6. los libros de historia, $9

C10 ESTRUCTURAS ESENCIALES
Definite and indefinite articles

Both Spanish and English have two kinds of articles, definite and indefinite. As you have already learned, the definite article *(the)* has four forms in Spanish:

	Singular	Plural
Masculine	**el**	**los**
Feminine	**la**	**las**

The form you use depends on the gender (masculine or feminine) and number (singular or plural) of the noun you want to say.

el chico; **el** cuaderno
the boy; the notebook

los chicos; **los** cuadernos
the boys; the notebooks

la chica; **la** escuela
the girl; the school

las chicas; **las** escuelas
the girls; the schools

The Spanish indefinite article, which is equivalent to English *a* and *an* in the singular and *some* in the plural, also has four forms.

	Singular	Plural
Masculine	**un**	**unos**
Feminine	**una**	**unas**

un chico; **un** cuaderno
a boy; a notebook

unos chicos; **unos** cuadernos
some boys; some notebooks

una chica; **una** escuela
a girl; a school

unas chicas; **unas** escuelas
some girls; some schools

C11 Actividad • ¿Cuál artículo?

Fill in the blanks with the appropriate definite or indefinite article.

Tengo _unas_ clases que tienen _unos_ profesores muy interesantes. _Los_ martes a _la_ una hay biología. _La_ biología es muy interesante. A _las_ dos tengo español. _El_ español es fácil. Tengo _un_ profesor de Madrid.

C12 Actividad • En venta *For sale* For answers, see p. T60–T61.

Say you need the indicated items. Your classmate replies that they are for sale.

—¡Buenos días! Necesito un libro de inglés.
—¡No hay problema! Tenemos libros de inglés en venta.

1. cuaderno	3. compás	5. marcador	7. revista
2. goma	4. lápiz	6. bolígrafo	8. pluma

C13 ¿Sabes que . . . ?

Schools in the Spanish-speaking world usually don't provide lockers for students. Students carry their books and supplies to school and take them back home every day. In countries where the weather gets cold, students hang their coats in their classrooms. Students in the same grade usually take the same courses and stay in the same classroom; different teachers come to their classrooms to teach the different subjects.

C14 ESTRUCTURAS ESENCIALES
Numbers from 21 to 100

21 veintiuno	**22** veintidós	**23** veintitrés	**24** veinticuatro	**25** veinticinco
26 veintiséis	**27** veintisiete	**28** veintiocho	**29** veintinueve	**30** treinta
31 treinta y uno	**32** treinta y dos	**40** cuarenta	**41** cuarenta y uno	**50** cincuenta
60 sesenta	**70** setenta	**80** ochenta	**90** noventa	**100** cien

C15 Actividad • Los ganadores *The winners* For answers, see p. T61.

You've been chosen by a local store to read the student I.D. numbers of 30 winners in a contest. Read the numbers aloud.

87	99	23	46	65	78	90	35	29	48	100	56	67	24	98
83	75	33	76	48	63	39	79	30	50	43	80	25	69	42

ESTRUCTURAS ESENCIALES
Use of numbers with nouns

Numbers are placed before the noun: **veintiocho chicas, treinta chicos.**
Uno changes its ending, depending on the noun's gender and number.

> **uno, veintiuno, treinta y uno**
> **un** chico, **una** chica
> **veintiún** chicos, **veintiuna** chicas
> **treinta y un** chicos, **treinta y una** chicas

Compound numbers beyond 29 are written separately and linked by a **y: treinta y ocho, cuarenta y dos.**

C17 **Actividad • Hora de inventario** *Inventory time*

Your job after school in the school-supplies store is getting complicated. Now your boss wants to take inventory. Say you have the quantities indicated as he calls out the item.
1. ¡Cuadernos! Veintiún cuadernos 2. ¡Plumas! Treinta y ocho plumas. 3. ¡Reglas! Setenta y nueve reglas. 4. ¡Compases! Ochenta y cuatro compases. 5. ¡Diccionarios! Sesenta y un diccionarios. 6. ¡Revistas! Cincuenta y siete revistas. 7. ¡Bolígrafos! Treinta y un bolígrafos. 8. ¡Marcadores! Treinta y tres marcadores.

> gomas, 41
> —¡Gomas!
> —Cuarenta y una gomas.

1. cuadernos, 21   **3.** reglas, 79   **5.** diccionarios, 61   **7.** bolígrafos, 31
2. plumas, 38   **4.** compases, 84   **6.** revistas, 57   **8.** marcadores, 33

C18 **Actividad • Varios precios** *Different prices*

In a department store in San Juan, Puerto Rico, customers are asking the prices of many items. You, the salesperson, must answer their questions.
1. Veintitrés pesos. 2. No, nueve noventa y cinco. 3. Cien pesos. 4. No, cuesta setenta y cinco pesos. 5. Treinta y cuatro cuarenta y cinco.

> —¿Cuánto cuesta? ($15)   —¿Cuánto cuestan? ($15.99)
> —Quince pesos.   —Quince noventa y nueve.

1. ¿Cuánto cuestan? ($23)
2. ¿Cuestan 10 pesos? (No, $9.95)
3. ¿Cuánto cuesta? ($100)
4. ¿Cuesta 80 pesos? (No, $75)

5. ¿Cuánto cuesta la calculadora? ($34.45)
6. ¿Cuestan 2 pesos? (No, $20)   No, cuestan veinte.
7. ¿Cuánto cuesta el libro? ($14.65) Catorce sesenta y cinco.
8. ¿Cuesta 59 pesos? (No, $60)   No, cuesta sesenta pesos.

C19 **Conversación • ¿Cuánto cuesta?**

Pair up with a classmate. One of you is the customer, and the other one is the salesperson. Alternate roles. Choose six objects from C7. Ask about their prices. If the price seems high say, **¡Uy, no tengo tanto!** *(Wow! I don't have that much!)* If the price seems reasonable, buy the quantity you want.

> Tú   ¿Cuánto cuestan los cuadernos?
> VENDEDOR/A   Dos pesos.
> Tú   Bueno, dos por favor. ¿Y las reglas?
> VENDEDOR/A   Siete pesos.
> Tú   ¡Uy, no tengo tanto! Adiós.

C20 Actividad • ¡A escribir! Answers will vary.

Put down in writing all the prices used by the salesperson in C19.

($23) veintitrés pesos

C21 Actividad • Una confusión

Make sense out of the following conversation between two customers and the salesperson. Say the lines in their correct order and then write them.

—Cinco por diez dólares.
—Adiós.
—Por favor, ¿cuánto cuestan los cuadernos?
—Buenos días.
—¡Uy, no tengo tanto!

—Buenos días.
—Por favor, ¿cuánto cuestan los cuadernos?
—Cinco por diez dólares.
—¡Uy, no tengo tanto!
—Adiós.

C22 Comprensión For script and answers, see pp. T62–T63.

Finding the corresponding price

	ESPAÑOL	calculadora	CUADERNO	pen	case	DICCIONARIO
A	$50.00	$10.00	$ 5.75	$ 1.00	$33.00	$ 6.05
B	$10.00	$99.00	$75.00	$ 2.01	$33.30	$ 5.06
C	$10.50	$99.10	$70.05	$12.00	$30.33	$56.00
D	$15.50	$10.99	$ 5.00	$ 1.02	$30.00	$65.00

C23 Actividad • Anuncios *Ads*

You work as an announcer for a Spanish television station. The local store has the following items on sale. Name the articles. Give their prices. Try to make your ads sound as attractive as possible.

—carteras ($40.00)
—calculadoras ($25.00)
—libros de español ($15.00)
—diccionarios ($13.00)
—reglas ($3.15)

En la escuela 81

1   Agenda 🔲

Take a look at Elena's appointment book for next week.

AGENDA

AGENDA

19	lunes	10:00 Miguel y Susana : Inglés 3:00 Ricardo 5:30 Hilda
20	martes	4:00 música 5:00 computadoras
21	miércoles	4:00 cerámica 5:30 ballet
22	jueves	3:00 deportes
23	viernes	

Make a weekly schedule of your own, using imaginary people and events or real ones. Be ready to read your appointments to the class.

2   Actividad • Dolor de cabeza   *Headache*   Answers will vary.

You work for the photographer who's going to take every student's picture for the yearbook. Try to schedule everyone. Your classmates will look at their appointment books (1) to see if they can make it.

—¿Vienes el viernes a las tres?
—No, tengo deportes a las tres.

3 Actividad • **No es así** Answers will vary.

Choose a partner. One of you will read an entry. Deny what you hear; then repeat the information with a number that is 10 lower or 10 higher. Take turns responding.

> La calculadora cuesta $19.   Ex—No, hay 18.
> —No, cuesta $9.   No es así, hay 38.
> —No es así, cuesta $29.

1. Hay 28 estudiantes en la clase de historia.
2. Tenemos 40 dólares.
3. Luisa tiene diez clases hoy.
4. Hay 60 bicicletas aquí.
5. La profesora viene con treinta libros.

6. Hay dieciséis o diecisiete chicos en la clase.
7. El diccionario de español-inglés cuesta $15.99.
8. Ella tiene 18 dólares en la cartera.
9. Vienen quince estudiantes el martes.
10. Carlos viene a clase con doce plumas.

4 Actividad • **El boletín de Patricia** *Patricia's report card* Answers will vary.

Here's Patricia's report card. She's a high school student in Caracas, Venezuela. How many subjects does she take? Does she take more or fewer subjects than you? Do both of you have any of the same subjects? What subjects does she take that you don't have? What about the grading system? What is the highest mark in this grading system? Is the same grading system used for all her subjects?

MATERIAS	RENDIMIENTO ESCOLAR						PREVIA	FINAL
	1er. Lapso		2o. Lapso		3er. Lapso			
	Califi-cación	Ina-sis-ten-cia.	Califi-cación	Ina-sis-ten-cia.	Califi-cación	Ina-sis-ten-cia.		
Español	7	1	8	1	7	0	7	7
Matemáticas	8	1	8	0	8	0	8	8
Biología	9	2	9	0	10	1	9	9
Química	10	1	9	0	10	0	9	9
Física	9	1	10	1	10	0	10	10
Geografía	6	2	7	0	7	0	7	7
Historia	8	1	8	2	8	1	8	8
Inglés	7	2	8	0	8	0	6	7
Computadoras	10	3	10	1	10	1	10	10
Manualidades	9	1	10	0	9	0	9	9
Música	10	1	10	0	10	0	10	10
Educación Física	8	1	7	0	8	1	8	8

5 Actividad • **¿Y en los Estados Unidos?** Answers will vary.

An exchange student from Guadalajara, Mexico, is interviewing students in your area. She asks you the following questions. How would you answer?

1. ¿Cómo se llama la escuela?
2. ¿Cómo vienes a la escuela?
3. ¿Qué materias tienes?
4. ¿Qué días tienes clases de español?
5. ¿A qué hora?
6. ¿Tienes español hoy?

7. ¿Tienes mucha tarea?
8. ¿Es español una materia fácil o difícil? ¿Es interesante o aburrida?
9. ¿A qué hora tienes recreo?
10. ¿Vienes a la escuela los sábados?

6 Pronunciación, lectura, dictado   For script, see p. T64.

1. Listen carefully and repeat what you hear.

2. The sound of the Spanish consonants **ll** and **ch**. Listen, then read aloud.

llamo	llamas	llamamos	ellos	ellas
chicos	chao	muchos	ocho	Chávez

3. Copy the following sentences to prepare yourself to write them from dictation.
   Ella se llama Estrella Llorens.
   Guillermo es de Chicago.
   Chela es la chica de Chile.

¿LO SABES?

Let's review some important points you have learned in this unit.

SECTION A

Can you ask about the ways people get to school?
Use a form of **venir** each time.

—Lola, pie   ¿Viene Lola a pie?

1. Silvia, metro
2. Nosotros, autobús
3. Tú, pie
4. Magdalena, bicicleta
5. Alejandro, auto
6. Ustedes, autobús

1. ¿Viene Silvia en metro?
2. ¿Venimos nosotros en autobús?
3. ¿Vienes tú a pie? 4. ¿Viene Magdalena en bicicleta? 5. ¿Viene Alejandro en auto?
6. ¿Vienen ustedes en autobús?

SECTION B

Do you know the numbers from zero to twenty?
Complete these number sequences and write out the words. After you have finished writing, read them aloud.

2, 4, 6, __8__ dos, cuatro, seis, ocho

1. 4, 3, 2, __1__
2. 10, 13, 16, __19__
3. 20, 18, 15, __11__
4. 0, 6, 12, __18__
5. 15, 11, 7, __3__
6. 9, 10, 12, __15__

1. cuatro, tres, dos, uno
2. diez, trece, dieciséis, diecinueve
3. veinte, dieciocho, quince, once
4. cero, seis, doce, dieciocho
5. quince, once, siete, tres
6. nueve, diez, doce, quince

Can you talk about your class schedule with a partner?
Talk about all your classes for each day of the week. Be sure to include the names of the days of the week. Answers will vary.

Do you know the forms of the verb *tener*?
Write the correct form of **tener** that goes with each subject.

1. Él / dibujo.
2. Nosotros / español.
3. José y Marisa / álgebra.
4. Yo / química.
5. Usted / geografía.
6. Tú / música.

1. tiene 2. tenemos 3. tienen 4. tengo 5. tiene 6. tienes

Do you know how to ask and tell what time it is?
Say what time it is: 1:00, 3:15, 10:00, 5:30, 8:50, 12:00.
Using your weekly schedule from skills 1 on page 82, say at what time you have each class.

Es la una. Son las tres y cuarto/ quince. Son las diez. Son las cinco y media. Son las nueve menos diez. Son las doce.

Tengo inglés a las ocho.

Ask a classmate at what time his/her classes are. Answers will vary.

SECTION C

When you go into a store, can you ask the price of different school items?
Ask how much these items cost.

1. la calculadora
2. el bolígrafo
3. las carteras ¿Cuánto cuestan las carteras?
4. el diccionario ¿Cuánto cuesta el diccionario?

1. ¿Cuánto cuesta la calculadora? 2. ¿Cuánto cuesta el bolígrafo?

Can you say the price of each item? For answers, see p. T65.
Tell how much each item costs. Then tell how much two of them cost.

1. lápiz, $1
2. diccionario, $24
3. pluma, $45
4. libro de matemáticas, $14
5. calculadora, $3.95
6. cartera, $35
7. cuaderno, $2.95
8. goma, $2

VOCABULARIO

SECTION A

a *at, to*
a pie *on foot*
ahí *there*
algunos, -as *some*
el **auto** *car, automobile*
el **autobús** *bus*
el **autobús escolar** *school bus*
la **bicicleta** *bicycle*
la **ciudad** *city*
con *with*
¿cuándo? *when?*
de *of*
en *by*
la **escuela secundaria**
    secondary school
el **estudiante** *student (male)*
la **estudiante** *student (female)*
hoy *today*
el **inglés** *English (language)*
el **libro** *book*
los *the*
el **metro** *subway*
mi *my*
¡mira! *look!*
muchos, -as *many, a lot*
no *not*
el **número** *number*
pero *but*
por fin *finally*
¿por qué? *why?*
porque *because*
el **problema** *problem*
¿qué? *what?*
rápido *quickly*
tarde *late*
temprano *early*
tiene *it has*
todos *all*
un, una *a, an*
venir *to come*
yo no sé *I don't know*

SECTION B

a la una *at one o'clock*
¿a qué hora? *at what time?*
aburrido, -a *boring*
la **actividad** *activity*

ahora *now*
al (a + el) *to the, at the*
    (contraction)
al contrario *on the contrary*
el **álgebra** *algebra*
el **almuerzo** *lunch*
bastante *rather*
casi *almost*
la **ciencia** *science*
la **clase** *class*
como *about*
la **computadora** *computer*
¿cuál? *what? which?*
¿cuántos, -as? *how many?*
del (de + el) *of the, from*
    the (contraction)
los **deportes** *sports*
los **días de la semana** *days of*
    the week (see p. 68)
el **dibujo** *drawing*
difícil *difficult*
la **educación física** *physical*
    education
es la una *it's one o'clock*
el **español** *Spanish language*
fácil *easy*
la **física** *physics*
el **francés** *French language*
fuerte *heavy*
el **genio** *genius*
la **geografía** *geography*
la **geometría** *geometry*
hay *there is, there are*
la **historia** *history*
la **hora** *time, hour*
el **horario** *schedule*
interesante *interesting*
las *the (fem. pl.)*
las **materias** *subjects (see p. 67)*
mucha *a lot of*
o *or*
otras *other*
la **pintura** *painting*
poca *a little*
preferida *favorite*
¿qué hora es? *what time is it?*
la **química** *chemistry*
el **recreo** *recess*

la **semana** *week*
son las diez *it's ten o'clock*
la **tarea** *homework*
tener *to have*
tu *your*
¿verdad? *really?*

SECTION C

el **bolígrafo** *ballpoint pen*
bueno *well, all right*
la **calculadora** *calculator*
la **cartera** *schoolbag*
el **compás** *compass*
la **compra** *shopping*
el **cuaderno** *notebook*
¿cuánto cuesta? *how much*
    does it cost?
¿cuánto cuestan? *how much*
    do they cost?
cuesta *it costs*
cuestan *they cost*
el **diccionario** *dictionary*
el **dinero** *money*
en venta *for sale*
la **goma** *eraser*
el **hombre** *man*
el **lápiz (pl. lápices)** *pencil*
el **marcador** *felt-tip marker*
más *more; else*
los **números** *numbers (see p. 66*
    and p. 79)
el **peso** *peso*
perdón *excuse me*
la **pluma** *fountain pen*
por *for*
por favor *please*
el **precio** *price*
¿qué más necesitas? *what*
    else do you need?
la **rebaja** *discount*
la **regla** *ruler*
la **revista** *magazine*
tanto *so (as, that) much*
la **tienda** *store*
unos, unas *some*
el **vendedor, la vendedora**
    salesperson

ESTUDIO DE PALABRAS

Written accent marks
Some Spanish words have an accent mark written on the stressed vowel.
Accent marks tell the reader how to pronounce the words. Find all the words
in the vocabulary that have an accent mark, and write them in a new list.

ahí, autobús, ¿cuándo?, inglés, número, ¿por qué?, ¿qué?, rápido, sé, álgebra, ¿cuál?, geografía,
¿cuántos?, días, difícil, física, fácil, francés, química, bolígrafo, compás, lápiz, más, perdón

VAMOS A LEER

Antes de leer

Spanish-speaking students use books like these for their classes. Can you guess by their titles what subjects they deal with? Are they similar to your own books? Which ones would you like to read?

Libros para la escuela

Y para los ratos libres°. . . .

Tiras cómicas, ciencia ficción y aventuras.

Sin mirar   *Without looking*

How many of the book and magazine titles can you remember without looking at these pages?

Y para los ratos libres *And for your free time*

Socorro°

Read the selection once without consulting the vocabulary.
Then read it again, looking up the words you don't know.

Es lunes. Son las ocho de la mañana°. ¡Es tarde! Hoy es un día terrible. ¡Examen° de matemáticas! ¡A las nueve! No tengo el libro. No tengo los ejercicios°. Corro°. El autobús no viene ¡Viene un taxi! Lo tomo°. Cuesta diez dólares. ¡Es mucho! No tengo dinero.

Llego° a la escuela. Está desierta°, abandonada°. Entro a° la clase. La profesora espera°. El examen es muy difícil. Tiene cien preguntas. ¿Qué puedo hacer°? ¡SOCORRO!

Me despierto°. ¿Qué pasa?° ¡No hay° clases! No hay examen de matemáticas. No es lunes. Es domingo. ¡Qué suerte!°

Preguntas y respuestas

1. ¿Qué día es? Es lunes.
2. ¿Qué hora es? Son las ocho de la mañana.
3. ¿Viene el autobús? No, el autobús no viene.
4. ¿Cuánto cuesta el taxi? El taxi cuesta diez dólares.
5. ¿Cómo está la escuela?
5. La escuela está desierta, abandonada.

6. ¿Es fácil el examen? No, el examen es muy difícil.
7. ¿Cuántas preguntas tiene? Tiene cien preguntas.
8. ¿Es lunes? No es el lunes, es domingo.
9. ¿Hay clases? No, no hay clases.
10. ¿Hay examen de matemáticas?
10. No, no hay examen de matemáticas.

Actividad • Combinación

Choose the correct ending from the right column to complete the sentence in the left column.

Son las ocho . . .   espera.
Hoy es un día . . .   de la mañana.
No tengo los . . .   terrible.
Llego a la . . .   difícil.
La profesora . . .   ejercicios.
El examen es muy . . .   escuela.

Socorro *Help!*   **de la mañana** *in the morning*   **examen** *exam, test*   **ejercicios** *exercises*   **corro** *I run*   **lo tomo** *I take it*   **llego** *I arrive*   **desierta** *deserted*   **abandonada** *abandoned*   **entro a** *I go in (to)*   **espera** *waits*   **¿Qué puedo hacer?** *What can I do?*   **me despierto** *I wake up*   **¿Qué pasa?** *What's up?*   **hay** *there is (are)*   **¡Qué suerte!** *How lucky!*

El regalo

DANIEL   ¿De quién es el regalo? ¿De dónde viene? ¿Lo abrimos°?

ADRIANA   Un momento. Vamos a ver°. La etiqueta° dice°:

Daniel y Adriana Arias
Ciudad de México

     Sí, es para nosotros, pero no tiene remitente°. Es un regalo anónimo.

DANIEL   ¿Anónimo? ¿Cómo anónimo?

ADRIANA   Es un misterio. Es un regalo misterioso.

DANIEL   Pero, si abrimos el paquete°, el misterio termina°, ¿no? Estoy seguro°
     que hay una tarjeta° adentro° con el remitente.

Adriana abre° el paquete.

ADRIANA   No, no hay tarjeta. ¡Es un televisor° pequeño°!

DANIEL   ¡Bah! Ya° tenemos televisor.

ADRIANA   No, no tenemos. El televisor de casa° es de papá y mamá. Ahora
     nosotros tenemos televisor. Éste° es para nosotros y para nadie más.°

Los chicos miran el televisor.

DANIEL   ¡Mira Adriana! No tiene cable. ¿Tiene pilas°? ¿Vienen las pilas en el paquete?

ADRIANA   No. Es un televisor portátil°, pero no tiene pilas. Sólo° tiene tres
     canales°: 1, 17 y 99.

DANIEL   ¿Sólo tres canales? ¡Es muy poco! Seguro que no funciona°.

¿Lo abrimos? *Do we open it?*   **Vamos a ver** *Let's see*   **etiqueta** *label*   **dice** *it says*   **remitente** *sender*
paquete *parcel*   **termina** *it's over*   **Estoy seguro** *I'm sure*   **tarjeta** *card*   **adentro** *inside*   **abre** *opens*   **televisor** *TV*
set   **pequeño** *small*   **ya** *already*   **casa** *home*   **Éste** *This one*   **nadie más** *nobody else*   **pilas** *batteries*
portátil *portable*   **sólo** *only*   **canales** *channels*   **no funciona** *it doesn't work*

ADRIANA	¡Sí, funciona! ¡Funciona! Mira, el Canal Uno.
DANIEL	¿Funciona? ¿Funciona sin° pilas?
ADRIANA	Escucha°.

LOCUTOR° Después de los anuncios°, las noticias° de las 6, de hoy, viernes.

ADRIANA	¿Cómo? Hoy es jueves, no es viernes. Hay un error.
DANIEL	Y son las cinco, ¿no? ¿Qué hora es, Adriana?
ADRIANA	Las cinco. Son las cinco, y hoy es jueves.
LOCUTOR	¡Superventa! Sí, señores, superventa en la Tienda Díaz. Sólo hasta el martes. Bolígrafos "Maravilla" Treinta pesos Calculadoras "Uno más uno" Ochenta y cinco pesos Y en la revista "Hoy" una entrevista° especial con el presidente de la República, el señor Martín Roldán.
DANIEL	¿Martín Roldán? El presidente no se llama Martín Roldán. ¿Es una broma°?

Adriana apaga° el televisor.

Preguntas y respuestas   For answers, see p. T66.

Answer the following questions about **El regalo.**

1. ¿De quién es el regalo? ¿Cómo es?
2. ¿Tiene remitente el paquete?
3. ¿Tienen los chicos televisor?
4. ¿Cómo es el televisor nuevo?
5. ¿Cuántos canales tiene?
6. ¿Necesita pilas para funcionar?
7. ¿Qué hora y qué día es?
8. ¿Qué hora y qué día es en el Canal Uno?
9. ¿Qué hay en la Tienda Díaz?
10. ¿Se llama Martín Roldán el presidente?

Actividad • ¿Es cierto o no?   For answers, see p. T67.

Say whether the statements are correct or not. Correct the statements that aren't true.

1. La etiqueta dice Pedro y Rosa Arias.
2. El paquete no tiene remitente.
3. El televisor es para papá y mamá.
4. La revista "Hoy" tiene una entrevista con el locutor.
5. El presidente no se llama Martín Roldán.
6. El televisor funciona sin pilas.
7. Los chicos miran las noticias en el canal 17.
8. En la Tienda Díaz hay bolígrafos a ochenta y cinco pesos.
9. El televisor necesita cable y pilas.
10. El televisor sólo tiene tres canales.

---

sin *without*   **escucha** *listen!*   **locutor** *announcer*   **anuncios** *ads*   **noticias** *news*   **entrevista** *interview*   **broma** *joke*
apaga *turns off*

UNIDAD 3 **Deportes y pasatiempos**
Scope and Sequence

	BASIC MATERIAL	COMMUNICATIVE FUNCTIONS
SECTION A	¿Qué deporte te gusta? (A1) Pasatiempos (A9) El judo (A16)	**Expressing feelings and emotions** • Talking about what you and others like and don't like to do
SECTION B	¡Un fanfarrón! (B1) ¿Qué necesitamos para jugar? (B11)	**Exchanging information** • Saying what you need in order to do something
SECTION C	¿Juegas siempre? (C1) ¿Qué tiempo hace? (C9) Los meses del año (C14)	**Exchanging information** • Saying when and how often you play • Talking about the seasons and the weather
TRY YOUR SKILLS	Pronunciation (vowels **a, e, o**) Sound-letter correspondences (vowels **a, e, o**) Dictation	
VAMOS A LEER	**Un maratón** (A Spanish TV station is broadcasting a marathon from New York.) **El regalo** (Adriana and Daniel watch a program on the new and mysterious television.)	

WRITING   A variety of controlled and open-ended writing activities appear in the Pupil's Edition. The Teacher's Notes identify other activities suitable for writing practice.

COOPERATIVE LEARNING   Many of the activities in the Pupil's Edition lend themselves to cooperative learning. The Teacher's Notes explain some of the many instances where this teaching strategy can be particularly effective. For guidelines on how to use cooperative learning, see page T13.

GRAMMAR	CULTURE	RE-ENTRY
The verb **gustar** (A4)	Popular sports in Spanish-speaking countries	Days of the week
The present tense of **-ar** verbs (B3) The verb **jugar** (B16)	World Cup Soccer Championship	Numbers from 0 to 20
Word order (C4) The verb **hacer** in weather expressions (C11)	Seasons in the world's two hemispheres	The verb **ser**
Recombining communicative functions, grammar, and vocabulary		
Reading for practice and pleasure		

TEACHER-PREPARED MATERIALS

Section A Pictures of sports, sports personalities, person playing the guitar; construction paper in various colors

Section B Magazine pictures of sports, seasons, piano

Section C Toy clock, calendar, pictures or slides of weather scenes, globe

UNIT RESOURCES

Manual de actividades, Unit 3
Manual de ejercicios, Unit 3
Unit 3 Cassettes
Transparencies 7–9
Quizzes 7–9
Unit 3 Test

SECTION

A

OBJECTIVES **To express feelings and emotions:** talk about what you and others like and don't like to do

CULTURAL BACKGROUND When Mexico hosted the World Cup Soccer Championship in 1986, millions of people from different parts of the world attended or watched on television. Argentina won the games, and the Argentinians celebrated along with their Spanish-speaking neighbors in all of Spanish America.

Soccer, or **fútbol,** is the most popular sport in Spanish-speaking countries. Children can be seen playing **fútbol** at all hours of the day in the streets of Mexico, Spain, or Argentina. On weekends, parks are filled with amateur soccer teams. In Mexico City, the **Estadio Azteca** is one of the largest stadiums in the world, holding more than 100,000 people.

MOTIVATING ACTIVITY Have the students decorate the bulletin board with pictures illustrating popular sports in Spanish-speaking countries. As they learn the Spanish name for each sport, they may label each picture.

A1 ¿Qué deporte te gusta?

Display magazine pictures of the sports depicted in this section. Point to each picture illustrating a sport and name the sport with its article **(el tenis).** Have the students repeat. Then hold up the picture illustrating tennis and, while pointing to yourself, say **Me gusta el tenis.** Then ask the students **¿Qué deporte te gusta?**

To introduce **no me gusta . . . ,** you may wish to follow the same procedure, adding a gesture of thumbs down or shaking your head and saying **No me gusta . . .**

Now play the cassette or read aloud while the students listen. Have them practice the lines in groups of three. One student may be Miguel, and the other two may talk about Olga and Pedro. Have the students exchange roles so that everyone has the opportunity to practice each role.

A2 Actividad • ¡Para completar!

Have the students complete the sentences with a partner. Then, for writing practice, assign this activity as written homework.

CHALLENGE Have the students make up five original questions based on the dialog in A1. Then have them exchange papers and answer each other's questions.

A3 Actividad • Y ahora, tú

Call on individuals to say which sports they like and don't like. Point out to the students that the infinitives **nadar, correr,** and **montar** do not take an article.

To re-enter the days of the week, have the students say what sport or pastime they like or dislike on a particular day.

> Me gusta patinar el lunes.
> No me gusta estudiar el sábado.

SLOWER-PACED LEARNING Use magazine pictures illustrating the sports mentioned in the box. Write on the board or a transparency the names of the sports with their appropriate articles. Have the students choose a picture

illustrating a sport they like or don't like and form a sentence. They may use the names on the board or transparency as a reference.

A4 ESTRUCTURAS ESENCIALES

Read the explanations of the verb **gustar** with the class. You may wish to practice the forms of **gustar** with the students by following the model below.

TEACHER	Me gusta el béisbol. Raúl, ¿te gusta el béisbol?
RAÚL	Sí, me gusta el béisbol.
TEACHER	María, ¿le gusta a Raúl el béisbol?
MARÍA	Sí, le gusta el béisbol.
TEACHER	María y Raúl, ¿les gusta el béisbol?
MARÍA AND RAÚL	Sí, nos gusta el béisbol.

Remind students that nouns require a definite article when used with **gustar.** Tell the students that the infinitive in Spanish does not need a pre-position. Point out the comparison to English (**nadar,** *to swim*) for clarification.

To reinforce items 3 and 4 in A4, ask the students to name three class-mates and say what they like or don't like. Remind them to add **a** plus the name when using the verb **gustar.**

A María le gusta la gimnasia.
A David no le gusta el volibol.
A ellos no les gusta correr.

A5 Comprensión 📼

You'll hear different people talking about sports. Put a check mark in the row labeled **No** if the second person's reply is inappropriate, and in the row marked **Sí** if the reply is appropriate. For example, you hear: **¿Te gusta el fútbol?** and the response: **No, a ella le gusta correr.** The check mark goes in the **No** row, since the second person's reply is inappropriate.

1. —¿Le gusta a Olga nadar?
   —Sí, le gusta mucho. *Sí*
2. —¿Te gusta el básquetbol?
   —No, no te gusta. *No*
3. —Me gusta correr.
   —¿Te gusta? *Sí*
4. —¿Le gusta a Alberto montar en bicicleta?
   —No, a él le gusta correr. *Sí*
5. —¿Te gusta nadar?
   —Sí, le gusta la gimnasia. *No*
6. —¿Y el béisbol te gusta?
   —Sí, me gusta mucho. *Sí*
7. —¿Qué deporte le gusta?
   —No me gusta. *No*
8. —¿Te gusta el tenis?
   —Sí, a Pedro le gusta. *No*
9. —¿Y la gimnasia?
   —También me gusta. *Sí*
10. —¿Montar en bicicleta?
    —A Isabel le gusta el tenis. *No*

Now check your answers. *Read each exchange again and give the correct answer.*

A6 Actividad • Charla

Demonstrate the model with one of the students. Explain that **pero** means *but*. Have each student pair up with a partner that he or she have not worked with before. Tell them they are going to find out their classmate's likes and dislikes about sports. They should be prepared to report their findings to the class.

SLOWER-PACED LEARNING Review the names of the sports and activities with the students. Have them identify the sports and activities, using the appropriate article.

A7 ¿Sabes que . . . ?

You may wish to present this popular cheer to the students. They may enjoy practicing the cheer for the next school sports event.

> A la bim,
> A la bao,
> A la bim, bom, ba;
> (School's name), (School's name)
> ¡Ra, ra, ra!

SLOWER-PACED LEARNING Ask the students to bring magazine pictures of famous Hispanic sports personalities. You may wish to give points to the student who brings the most. Have them present these famous people to the class by using the following models.

> Él/Ella se llama . . .
> Es de . . .
> Le gusta . . .
> Él/Ella juega . . .

A8 Actividad • ¡A escribir!

Before assigning this writing activity, have the students do it orally. Ask the students to complete the first sentence after you have read the model with them. Be sure they understand the formation. You may have to give other examples. When the activity is completed, call on students to read aloud their sentences. You may wish to have several volunteers write their sentences on the board or a transparency for correction.

A9 SITUACIÓN • Pasatiempos

Prepare the students for listening and understanding these mini-interviews by introducing the new verbs. Pictures from magazines can be used to illustrate these verbs. You may also use TPR (total physical response) while saying the verb. Then have the students copy your actions and repeat the verb. Cup your hand over your ear and say **escuchar.** Have the class imitate and repeat. Then, as you hold up several records, say **escuchar discos.** To introduce the verb **cantar,** open your mouth as if to sing with a sheet of music. Play an imaginary piano or guitar to present **tocar.** Use similar demonstrations to introduce the following actions: **tomar fotografías, hablar por teléfono, trabajar y jugar con la computadora,** and **mirar televisión.**

Now play the cassette or read aloud as the students listen with books closed. Ask them to try to find out what each teenager likes and doesn't like to do. Ask a few questions to see how much the students are able to understand with books closed. Then have the students follow along in their books

as they listen again. You may wish to repeat the questions that the students were unable to answer before.

Begin a conversation with the students by asking questions such as **¿Qué le gusta a Bruce Springsteen?** or **¿Qué le gusta a Marta?**

A 10 Actividad • ¡A escribir!

Students may complete this activity at home or in class. You or a volunteer may write the corrected sentences on the board or a transparency, as the students dictate them.

SLOWER-PACED LEARNING   Do the activity orally in class. Then assign it for written homework to be corrected in class the following day.

A 11 Actividad • Reacciones

Have the students repeat the exclamations after you model them to assure correct pronunciation. Point out the **rr** in the word **horrible.** Tell the students that it is similar to the sound a child makes when he or she is imitating the noise of an airplane. Then ask pairs of students to complete the activity orally.

A 12 SE DICE ASÍ

Reinforce the information in the chart with a chain drill using **¿Qué te gusta?** and **¿Te gusta . . . ?** Then ask randomly what others like and don't like to do by saying **¿Qué (no) le gusta a . . . ?** Finally, read the chart aloud as students follow along in their books.

A 13 Conversación • ¿Qué te gusta? ¿Qué no te gusta?

Before beginning the activity, select two students to present the model to the class. Then have the other students each choose a partner and make up a dialog based on the model. Call on several volunteers to act out their dialog for the class.

A 14 Comprensión 📼

You will hear a short description of what Pepe likes and what he doesn't like. Put a check mark in the box labeled **Sí** if he likes the item and in the box labeled **No** if he doesn't like it. For example, you hear: **A Pepe no le gusta escuchar discos.** You mark the box labeled **No** next to the words **escuchar discos,** because Pepe does not like to listen to records.

A Pepe no le gusta escuchar discos, a él le gusta tomar fotografías. Y ¿tocar la guitarra? A Pepe le gusta tocar la guitarra y bailar también. Pero no le gusta patinar o mirar televisión.

1. —¿escuchar discos? *No*
2. —¿tomar fotografías? *Sí*
3. —¿tocar la guitarra? *Sí*
4. —¿bailar? *Sí*
5. —¿patinar? *No*
6. —¿mirar televisión? *No*

Now check your answers. *Read the paragraph and questions again and give the correct answer.*

A15 Actividad • ¡A escribir!

Have the students identify the mood of each person in the illustrations and write at least two sentences for each caption.

SLOWER-PACED LEARNING To give the students a model to follow, show a picture of a person smiling and playing the guitar and say **Le gusta tocar la guitarra. ¡Es fantástico!** You may wish to call on volunteers to provide other captions for the picture. Then tell the students to write their own captions for each picture in the activity.

CHALLENGE Tell the students to bring pictures from magazines depicting people doing different activities and to write a caption for each picture. Ask them to try to find people with different facial expressions in order to vary their captions. Students may prefer to draw their own cartoon-type pictures and write the captions. Have them show the pictures and read aloud their captions to the class.

A16 SITUACIÓN • El judo

Before you read aloud or play the cassette, teach the colors. Prepare pieces of colored construction paper and use them as flashcards to elicit the names of the colors. Give the cards to individuals who show the correct color, as their classmates say the Spanish word. You might also use flags from different Spanish-speaking countries or other objects to illustrate the different colors. Another quick and easy way to present the colors is to select several students to stand before the class. Use their clothing colors to teach the vocabulary.

Encourage students to listen carefully as you read aloud or play the cassette. Tell them that the passage is about a boy named Esteban and his favorite pastime, **judo.**

A17 Actividad • ¡A escoger!

Have the students write the sentences so that they may practice writing the colors. Call on individuals to dictate as you or a volunteer writes the sentences on the board or a transparency.

A18 Actividad • Rompecabezas

For cooperative learning, have the students solve the puzzle in groups of two. Find out which group finishes first and have the rest of the class use the cheer from the Teacher's Notes on A7 to congratulate them.

CHALLENGE Students may enjoy making up similar word puzzles from the vocabulary listed below Section A on page 115. Then have them exchange puzzles and solve the one they receive.

OBJECTIVE **To exchange information:** say what you need in order to do something

CULTURAL BACKGROUND Although soccer may be the favorite sport in the majority of Spanish-speaking countries, there are many other popular sports. Baseball, volleyball, swimming, tennis, and a variety of other sports are enjoyed by fans and participants alike. The concern with physical fitness is

apparent in many parts of Latin America and Spain. Women can be seen jogging and running marathons, which they would not have done several years ago. Health spas and sports clubs are also becoming very popular.

Many famous baseball players from Spanish America play for the major leagues in the United States. **Guillermo Vilas** from Argentina and **Raúl Ramírez** from Mexico at one time were among the top ten tennis players in the world. Athletes from Mexico and Spain currently hold world records in **caminata** (race walking).

MOTIVATING ACTIVITY   Ask baseball fans in the class to bring in baseball cards of famous players from Spanish-speaking countries. You may also have the students research Spanish-speaking athletes and report their findings to the class.

B1   ¡Un fanfarrón!

Before presenting the interview, teach the seasons of the year. Display magazine pictures or drawings as you name the seasons, and ask the students to repeat. Also have available pictures illustrating skiing, ice skating, tennis, swimming, and soccer. Relate the various sports with the appropriate season. You may wish to ask the students **¿Qué te gusta practicar en verano?** and have them name the sport as they respond **Me gusta nadar en verano.**

Point out the title to the students and explain that **un fanfarrón** is a braggart. Have them follow along in the book as you read aloud or play the cassette.

Then ask the students to identify the cognates (**honor, atleta, campeón, practico, medalla, trofeo**). Help them identify unknown words by using context clues. Finally, play the cassette or read aloud again and have the students repeat.

B2   Actividad • Combinación

Have the class complete these sentences orally by calling on various students at random. Then assign the activity for homework. Instruct the students to complete the activity without looking at the original selection. You may wish to have the students reread the original selection before they do the activity.

For cooperative learning, have the students work in pairs to complete the activity. They should make sure their partner is able to match the items correctly.

B3   ESTRUCTURAS ESENCIALES

Introduce the forms of the **-ar** verbs by using the following or similar presentation.

TEACHER	Yo hablo inglés. ¿Y tú?
DIANA	Yo hablo inglés.
TEACHER	¿Hablas inglés?
SERGIO	Sí, yo hablo inglés.
TEACHER	Sergio habla inglés.

Continue this procedure until all forms have been practiced.

Explain that Spanish verbs are grouped according to their infinitive ending into three conjugations: **-ar, -er,** and **-ir.** The verbs **hablar** and **ganar** belong to the category of **-ar** verbs.

Tell the students that since **-ar** is an infinitive ending, the stem is the part of the verb that remains when the infinitive ending is removed. Write

Unidad 3   Teacher's Notes   T75

on the board or a transparency some of the verbs found in item 4 in B3. Have the students identify their stems.

Now write on the board or a transparency the forms of **hablar** and **ganar**. Explain the stem and how the endings are used to indicate who or what is doing the action. Have the students write the forms of the present tense **-ar** verbs in the verb section of their notebooks. Next to each infinitive form, they should write the stem. Be sure they write the stem of **estudiar** correctly. Many students may tend to drop the *i*. Also, point out that **montar** is *to ride astride*, as on a horse or a bicycle.

Tell the students that they should now be able to identify the forms of any **-ar** verb, given the infinitive. Using the same verbs from item 4 in B3, do a quick drill with the students. Give the subject and elicit the verb form. Students should say the subject pronoun and verb form together, but remind the students that the subject pronoun is not always stated.

For writing practice in class or at home, prepare sentences in which the students supply the correct form of the verb or the missing verb ending.

B4 Comprensión

You'll hear ten short exchanges between different people. Put a check mark in the corresponding box only when the second person's reply is appropriate to what the first one asks. For example, you hear: **¿Hablan ellos español?** and the response: **No, hablan francés.** Since the reply is appropriate, there is a check mark in the box under *0*.

1. —¿Estudias inglés?
   —No, a las tres.
2. —¿Necesitas dinero?
   —No, gracias. (✔)
3. —¿Practican mucho?
   —Sí, de Argentina.
4. —¿Patinamos el domingo?
   —¡Fantástico! (✔)
5. —¿A qué hora practicas?
   —A las cuatro. (✔)
6. —¿Quién canta?
   —No, el lunes.
7. —¿Toman fotografías?
   —Sí, le gusta el tenis.
8. —¿Habla Pepe inglés?
   —No, con Alicia.
9. —¿Escuchas un disco?
   —Sí, pero no me gusta. (✔)
10. —¿Esquiamos el sábado?
    —No, el domingo. (✔)

Now check your answers. *Read each exchange again and give the correct answer.*

B5 Actividad • Sí, me gusta bailar

Have pairs of students respond orally to the questions. You may wish to do the first three sentences with the class so the students will be able to follow a model. Remind the students to use **a** plus a proper name when forming sentences with the verb **gustar. (A Eduardo le gusta patinar.)**

As a variation, have the students answer the questions negatively and then give a true statement.

> ¿Escuchas música?
> No. No escucho música.
> Monto en bicicleta.

B6 Actividad • Combinación

For cooperative learning, form groups of two or three to complete the activity. Tell the students that they must make sure that all the members of the group can form the sentences correctly. For writing practice, you may wish to have the students write as many sentences as possible in a limited time.

Point out to the students that the verb **tocar** is used for playing an instrument and the verb **jugar** for playing a game. You may wish to explain that **tocar** also means to touch, and tell the following joke. You will need a picture or drawing of a piano.

> —¿Tocas el piano?
> —Sí, toco el piano. (Go to the piano and touch it.)

B7 Actividad • ¡A escribir!

You may wish to have the students do this activity orally in class and then, at home, write five original sentences telling things they do.

SLOWER-PACED LEARNING Prepare sentences similar to those in the activity. Tell the students to provide the correct forms of the verb **estudiar.**

B8 Actividad • Periodista

Tell the students to look at the pictures. Explain that they will be describing the activities depicted in the pictures, using different subject pronouns. Ask **¿Qué pasa en la foto número uno?** Have the class respond in unison. Now ask the students to change the subject to **José,** and request a response. Continue with the other pictures. Have the class repeat after an individual has given the appropriate response.

SLOWER-PACED LEARNING Write the infinitive forms of the verbs needed to complete the activity on the board or a transparency. Have the students tell what is going on in each picture, using the correct form of the verb that best describes the action taking place. You may also wish to mime the actions to review the vocabulary.

CHALLENGE When the students have described the action in all six pictures, have them look at the pictures again. Encourage the students to provide more information, forming sentences such as **Les gusta cantar** or **Pepe y Ramón estudian mucho.**

B9 Actividad • Charla

Have the students talk to their partners about the activities in B8. Tell them to use the questions as a guide and to be prepared to tell the class at least two things they learned about their partners.

B10 ¿Sabes que . . . ?

Appealing mascots, such as pandas or other animals, represent most interna-

tional sports events. In 1986 at the World Cup Soccer Championship in Mexico, the mascot was called **Pique,** a green pepper with a large **sombrero** and a mustache. He was dressed in the national colors green, white, and red. The very first mascot, called World Cup Willie, was from England, then came the Mexican **Juanito,** followed by the German Tip and Tap. Argentina's mascot was called **Gauchito,** and Spain called its mascot **Naranjito.**

B 11 SITUACIÓN • ¿Qué necesitamos para jugar?

Begin the activity by asking the students **¿Qué necesitamos para estudiar? (libros, papel) ¿para bailar? (música).** Have pictures available or bring the objects to class. Teach the names of equipment used to participate in different sports by demonstrating each object and saying **Para practicar** *(sport)* **necesitamos . . .**

Have the students look at the illustrations and repeat **Para practicar béisbol necesitamos una pelota, un bate y un guante.** You may wish to ask students to identify the false cognate, **red.** Have them write it in the false cognates section of their notebooks. Also point out the nouns that do not end in **-o** or **-a** and tell the students to make note of the article that each takes (feminine or masculine).

Then call on individuals to follow the model and say what is needed to play each sport. Now with books closed, elicit from each student an item that is needed for one of the sports.

B 12 Actividad • ¡A escoger!

Have the students complete this activity without referring to the pictures in B11. Make sure students use the Spanish pronunciation when referring to names of sports such as **tenis, béisbol,** and **volibol.**

B 13 Actividad • No es así

For cooperative learning, have the students work in pairs. Have each student correct the statements by naming a different item needed to play the sport. Tell students that they should make sure their partners can understand and correct the sentences appropriately.

B 14 SE DICE ASÍ

Have the students read the explanation silently. Remind students that the infinitive is the name of the verb. To check comprehension, call on individuals to form questions and others to respond using **para** plus a verb in the infinitive.

As a variation, after oral practice, prepare a transparency with blanks for **para.** Have the students decide why **para** is used in each situation.

Re–enter the numbers by having the students make a list of the school supplies they need to complete an imaginary project. Ask students to name the items and list the quantities; then call on individuals to read their lists following the model: **Para** *(subject)* **necesito . . .**

B 15 Actividad • Charla

Have the students take turns asking the questions and giving the information. Encourage them to include sports that are not on the list. If the students ask, provide the Spanish names of equipment or sports not listed. Have them write the new vocabulary in their notebooks.

B 16 ESTRUCTURAS ESENCIALES

To teach the verb **jugar**, follow the same procedure as mentioned in B3. Use sports pictures to elicit responses.

Read the explanation aloud with the students. Then read aloud the chart and have the students repeat.

Provide the subject pronoun or a proper noun and ask the students to make up a sentence using the correct form of the verb **jugar**. Remind them that the first-person plural form does not change to **-ue**.

B 17 Actividad • ¿Juegan?

Have the students do this activity with a partner. Circulate among the students to verify that they are responding with the appropriate subject pronoun and verb form. Tell the students to exchange roles.

B 18 Actividad • Falta algo

Call on individuals to complete the sentences with the correct form of the verb **jugar.** Try to go from one student to the next as quickly as possible. Each student should be able to complete at least one sentence.

SLOWER-PACED LEARNING   After completing the activity orally, have the students write the sentences in class or at home. Have them exchange papers to correct each other's work.

CHALLENGE   Have the students form five sentences using **jugar** and **tocar.** Call on volunteers to read their sentences aloud.

B 19 Actividad • ¡A actuar!

Have the students work with a partner to form a new dialog by changing the italicized word. Encourage students to use gestures when they practice and when they present their dialog to the class.

CHALLENGE   Tell the students to make up their own dialog. They should include the names of sports or activities and their equipment in the dialogs. Correct the students' work and have them act out their dialogs for the class.

B 20 Actividad • ¿Y ustedes, amigos?

Have the students make a chart like the one in the book, or provide students with a copy of the chart. Have them list at least five activities or sports.

Tell the students to ask their classmates in Spanish if they enjoy the same sports or activities as they themselves do. They should note the information in their chart.

Then call on students to report their findings. They should give the names of the students who do or do not have interests similar to theirs. They may also give the numbers of students and the name of the activity or sport. For example, **Seis estudiantes (no) patinan.**

B 21 Actividad • ¡A adivinar!

After the students have chosen a new partner, tell them to play the guessing game. One should try to challenge the other by mentioning only two pieces of equipment needed to play the sport, while the partner tries to guess what sport is played. They should switch roles at least five times, selecting five different activities or sports.

SECTION C

OBJECTIVE **To exchange information:** say when and how often you play; talk about the seasons and the weather

CULTURAL BACKGROUND Football, **fútbol americano,** is becoming very popular in many countries in Spanish America. Fans can watch Monday Night Football and Sunday games on television. In Mexico, **fútbol americano** is played at the major universities. The big game of the year is between **UNAM (Universidad Nacional Autónoma de México)** and **El Politécnico (Instituto Politécnico Nacional).** More than 40,000 young fans flock to this game every year. Students might also be interested to learn that Spanish-speaking fans whistle to show disgust during a game. Most Americans whistle to cheer and encourage their team.

MOTIVATING ACTIVITY Hispanic countries do not have as many organized sports in school as the United States. Many schools in Spanish-speaking countries compete in team sports such as soccer, volleyball, and basketball. Have the students discuss the pros and cons of contact sports in high school.

C1

¿Juegas siempre?

Before presenting the activity, teach the adverbs that appear in the dialog. You may wish to use a toy clock to present the adverb phrases **por la mañana, por la tarde,** and **por la noche.** Place the hands of the clock at 7:00 A.M. and say **Juego tenis por la mañana.** Have the students repeat. Now set the clock for 4:00 P.M. and ask the students to repeat, as you say **Juego tenis por la tarde.** Finally, set the clock at 7:00 P.M. and say **Juego tenis por la noche.** Practice these adverbs with the students by changing the time on the clock and having the students form their own sentences.

Use a calendar to demonstrate **a veces, a menudo,** and **todos los días.** Point out that **siempre** and **nunca** are opposites. Call on students to provide sentences using these adverbs.

With books closed, have the students listen as you read aloud or play the cassette. Tell the students that they will hear a conversation between a girl, Sara, and a boy, Felipe. They should try to find out what sport they are discussing and how often each character plays.

For cooperative learning, have the students practice the dialog in pairs. Then they should role-play the dialog for the class, using the appropriate gestures and intonations.

C2

Actividad • ¡A escoger!

Have the students cover the dialog while they do this activity. Call on individuals to complete the sentences orally by selecting the best option.

SLOWER-PACED LEARNING Have the students work in pairs. They should first complete the activity orally, then in writing. Call on individuals to select the option that best completes each sentence. They may refer to the dialog as they do the activity.

C3

Actividad • ¡No, al contrario!

Tell the students to select a partner. One student should select a word or phrase, and the other should respond with its opposite. Then they should make up sentences, using the words in the box and telling what they do.

Before selecting the pairs, ask one student to go to the front of the room and demonstrate the model with you. You may wish to do two or three exchanges so that the students understand what they are supposed to do.

CHALLENGE   Tell the pairs of students to include a verb in their exchanges. They may use some of the verbs listed in B3. Provide the model **¿Bailas siempre? No, nunca bailo.**

C4   ESTRUCTURAS ESENCIALES

Ask the students to read the chart and the explanation silently. Explain that in Spanish, it is correct to use two negatives in a sentence. Point out how the sentence changes when **nunca** is placed after the verb. Remind the students that they must add **no** before the verb.

SLOWER-PACED LEARNING   Have the students work in groups of three to practice using the adverbs in a complete sentence. Write the following verbs on the board or a transparency and ask the students to select a verb from the list.

> jugar
> bailar
> practicar
> tocar
> cantar
> nadar

C5   Conversación • Los deportes y los pasatiempos

Select a student to discuss with you what sports or pastimes each of you enjoys. Tell the students to listen as you present the model.

Then have the students select partners to complete the activity. They should find out what their classmates like to do and how often, on which days, and at what time of day they normally practice.

When the students have found out the information, ask each pair to share with the class what they have learned about their partner. If they have many different activities, you may suggest that the students select only two of the sports or pastimes to report to the class.

C6   Actividad • ¡A escribir!

You may wish to ask the students to respond affirmatively to the questions. They can then select an appropriate adverb to explain how often or when they do what is stated.

SLOWER-PACED LEARNING   Have the students complete the activity orally before they write the sentences at home or in class. If the students are to write the sentences at home, they should begin the writing in class so that they are able to relate the oral and written work.

CHALLENGE   Tell the students that if they give a negative response, they should follow up by stating an activity they enjoy.

> —¿Juegas tenis?
> —No, no juego tenis nunca. Juego básquetbol a menudo.
>   or
> —No, nunca juego tenis. Juego básquetbol a menudo.

Unidad 3   Teacher's Notes   T81

C7 Actividad • Una entrevista

Explain to students that they must use all eight questions in their interview. Suggest that they choose a classmate they have not worked with before. The students may wish to take notes during the interview. This will help them later as they complete the next activity.

As a variation, the students may wish to pretend they are a famous or an imaginary person. They may complete the interview as a **fanfarrón** or as Julio Iglesias, a romantic singer from Spain.

C8 Actividad • ¡A escribir!

Have the students write the dialog in class or at home. Collect the papers and correct their work. Then call on several volunteers to present their dialogs to the class.

C9 SITUACIÓN • ¿Qué tiempo hace?

Have available magazine pictures or illustrations of various weather scenes. Show a picture of a cool day on the lake and say, **Hace fresco,** and then have the class repeat. Do the same for **Hace sol** and **Hace calor.** Show a beach scene and say **Es la playa; hace buen tiempo para la playa.** Continue the same procedure with **hace frío, nieva, llueve, hace viento,** and **hace mal tiempo.**

Play the cassette or read aloud as the students follow along in their books. Have the students practice the dialog in small groups. Then call on individuals to role-play each dialog.

You may wish to reinforce the weather expressions by asking the students to give a weather report each time the class meets. As a variation, the students may report the weather conditions of a particular city from a Spanish-speaking country of their choice.

C10 Actividad • Reacciones

For cooperative learning, divide the class into groups of three. Each group must write three dialogs using the elements in the boxes. Explain to the students that they must make sure that everyone in the group understands the content and is able to contribute in writing the dialogs. Call on the groups to present their dialogs to the class.

C11 ESTRUCTURAS ESENCIALES

Pointing to the weather pictures from C9, ask the students to repeat the expressions in the box. Ask them what all the expressions have in common. (the verb **hacer**). Have the students repeat the expressions using **muy** and **mucho,** and then read the explanation aloud. Be sure that the students understand and correctly pronounce the words **llueve** and **nieva.** You may also wish to show slides or magazine photos illustrating the seasons of the year.

SLOWER-PACED LEARNING   Call on students to use the correct weather expression from the box as you point to the magazine pictures or illustrations. Remind students not to use **hace** with **nieva** and **llueve.**

CHALLENGE   You may wish to have the students practice the verb **hacer** in weather expressions by reporting their feelings in terms of a weather report. Ask how they feel under various circumstances: **el lunes por la mañana**

(hace mal tiempo); **el viernes por la tarde (hace sol); cuando juegan deportes (hace calor); antes de un examen (hace frío); después de la escuela (hace buen tiempo).** The students may wish to make posters illustrating their weather/emotions and writing the appropriate caption for each illustration.

C12 ## Actividad • ¡Al contrario!

Call on students or have them volunteer to read the expression and state the opposite. Then ask the students to close their books and turn to the person closest to them. Each student should comment on the weather and respond by stating the opposite.

C13 ## Actividad • Charla

Explain that discussing the weather is a universal pastime. In countries in the tropics, weather reports are seldom given because the weather does not change as in the extreme Northern Hemisphere or Southern Hemisphere. Have the students comment, with a partner, about the weather, following the model.

C14 ## SITUACIÓN • Los meses del año

Display the illustrations of the seasons from B1. Quickly review the names of the seasons with the students. Point to the appropriate illustration as you give the names of the months that belong with the season depicted in the illustration. Have the students repeat after you. Then point to the illustration and ask the students to provide the months of the year that correspond to the season.

You may wish to introduce the following well-known refrain: **Febrero es loco, y marzo no poco.** This expression refers to the unpredictable weather pattern in the months of February and March. It can be hot one day and cold the next.

Discuss typical weather patterns in your area for each month. Then have the students open their books. Point out that the months of the year are not capitalized in Spanish.

C15 ## Actividad • Combinación

Have pairs of students complete this activity with books closed. One student should name a season of the year and the other should identify the months that correspond to that season. Then they should switch roles. Each pair should continue the activity until they can both correctly identify the months and seasons of the year.

As an extension activity, you may wish to teach the following rhyme to the students:

Primavera . . .	¡Él la espera!
Verano . . .	¡Pide la mano!
Otoño . . .	¡Llega un retoño!
Invierno . . .	¡Es un infierno!
¡Esto es el amor! . . .	¡Sí señor!

SLOWER-PACED LEARNING Write on the board or a transparency the names of the seasons and months of the year. Tell the students to refer to these as they complete the oral activity.

C16 **Comprensión** 🔲

Each comment that you'll hear refers to either the weather, months of the year, sports, or pastimes. Listen very carefully, and decide what season of the year is being talked about. Put your check mark in the corresponding row. For example, you hear: **No me gusta abril. En la primavera llueve mucho.** You put a check mark in the row labeled **primavera.**

1. Pero ahora es octubre y en el otoño hace fresco. *otoño*
2. Es verano y hace calor. No tenemos clases. *verano*
3. Nieva siempre en el invierno. ¿Esquiamos? *invierno*
4. Hace buen tiempo para la playa en el verano, ¿no? *verano*
5. Me gusta mayo, porque me gusta la primavera. Siempre hace buen tiempo. *primavera*
6. ¡El invierno es estupendo para patinar en hielo! *invierno*
7. No, en abril no nieva. En la primavera llueve. *primavera*
8. ¿Quién esquía en julio en el verano? Nosotros no. *verano*
9. Hace mucho frío en el invierno. ¡Ideal para mirar televisión! *invierno*
10. En noviembre cuando es el otoño, yo siempre juego fútbol, ¿y tú? *otoño*
11. Hace sol y hace calor en el verano. ¿Ustedes nadan? *verano*

Now check your answers. *Read each sentence again and give the correct answer.*

C17 **¿Sabes que . . . ?**

Use a globe and discuss with the students the weather and seasons in the two hemispheres.

To re-enter the verb **ser,** have the students make up sentences telling where a person is from and what he or she does in a particular month.

> Carolina es de Argentina.
> Ella nada en diciembre.
> Mario es de Honduras.
> Él nada en agosto.

Explain to the students how to give the date in Spanish. Tell them that when the date is expressed in numbers, the day is given first, then the month, and finally the year. Therefore December 9, 1990, would be expressed in Spanish as: **9/12/90 el 9 de diciembre de 1990.** Call on volunteers to read the date aloud and write it on the board at the beginning of each class.

TRY
YOUR
SKILLS

OBJECTIVE To recombine communicative functions, grammar, and vocabulary

CULTURAL BACKGROUND In Argentina there are many large race tracks and stadiums because Argentinians are great fans of horseracing, auto-racing, polo, and a game called **pato. Pato** is a sport similar to polo, played by riders on horseback who carry a ball with six handles. The object of the game is to get the ball, which is also called **el pato,** into the opposing net. You may wish to refer students to the photograph on page 132 of the student's book.

1   El equipo

Play the cassette or read aloud as the students follow along in their books. Then have the students select a partner and decide what sport they would like to coach. Tell them they must choose at least three players for their team. The students may wish to give their new team a Spanish name.

Then call on each pair of coaches to identify their sport and name their new players. They must state their reasons for choosing each person.

2   Actividad • ¡Que hable! ¡Que hable!

Tell the students to prepare the description without mentioning the name of the sport. Have a volunteer read aloud the description and have the class try to guess what sport the student described.

As a variation, you may wish to play a game of ten questions. Divide the class into two teams. One student from team A thinks of a sport. The members of team B take turns asking questions that can be answered **Sí** or **No.** The team that guesses the most sports with the least amount of questions wins. Examples of questions: **¿Juegas todos los días? ¿Tienes una red? ¿Es un deporte de invierno?**

3   Actividad • Composición

Have the students include at least eight sentences in the composition, describing their favorite sport. They should give the composition a title, such as **Mi deporte favorito.** Remind the students to include the accents where needed and to check their spelling.

Collect the papers and correct the errors. Call on individuals to read their compositions aloud. Have the students find pictures to display on the bulletin board with their compositions.

SLOWER-PACED LEARNING   Write on the board or a transparency a list of vocabulary the students may use to write their compositions. The following or similar words may be used.

> béisbol
> fútbol
> tenis
> raqueta
> pelota
> guante
> siempre
> nunca
> a menudo
> verano
> primavera
> otoño

4   Actividad • Una encuesta

In order to minimize confusion, you may wish to divide the class into groups. Have each group report its findings to the class. You may combine the information from each group in order to find out which sports are practiced the most. Copy the chart on the board or a transparency and have each group report its findings as you or a volunteer writes the information.

Pronunciación, lectura, dictado

1. Listen carefully and repeat what you hear.

The five vowels in Spanish are **a, e, i, o,** and **u.** The sounds of these vowels do not change from one word to another as they do in English. English speakers tend to draw out their vowel sounds, changing the position of their tongue and lips while saying them. This change in position is called a glide. There is no glide in the Spanish vowel sounds. Make sure you pronounce Spanish vowels cleanly without trailing off into other sounds.

SLOWER-PACED LEARNING The sound of **a:** The sound of Spanish **a** is similar to the sound of *a* in the English word *father.* Listen to the sound of **a** in the following words and repeat.

> hasta   nadar   mañana   Panamá

The sound of **e:** In Spanish, the sound of **e** is similar to the sound of *e* in the English words *met* and *less.* Now, listen and repeat in the pauses provided.

> Elena   tenis   tener   en

The sound of **o:** The Spanish **o** is a short, pure vowel. It is similar to the sound of *o* in the English word *so,* but without any glide. Listen to the following words with the sound of **o** and repeat.

> ocho   otoño   agosto   todo

2. Listen, and then read aloud.

Listen to the following words containing the sounds of **a, e,** and **o** and then repeat.

> hay   correr   montar   once   voy   hoy   básquetbol

3. Write the following sentences from dictation. First listen to the sentence as it is read to you. Then you will hear the sentence again in short segments, with a pause after each segment to allow you time to write. Finally, you will hear the sentence a third time so that you may check your work. Let's begin.

> La amiga *(pause)* de Marta *(pause)* nada.
> Nosotros tenemos clases *(pause)* a las tres.
> La profesora *(pause)* practica deportes *(pause)* todos los martes.
> Tú hablas mucho *(pause)* con Ana.

¿LO SABES?

SECTION A

For further practice with expressing likes and dislikes in sports, have the students make believe they are champions in a sport of their choice. Have them talk with a partner about their likes and dislikes, how often they practice, and why they like the sport.

You may wish to do this section orally. Then have the students write the sentences at home or in class. If the students need additional practice with the seasons and months of the year, you may wish to ask the following or similar questions.

¿Qué deporte practicas en el verano?
¿Cuándo nadas?
¿Qué te gusta jugar en el otoño?
¿Practicas el tenis en el invierno?
¿Cuál es tu pasatiempo favorito en la primavera?
¿Cuál mes es mejor para esquiar?

Encourage students to include in their sentences different adverbs that explain how often and when they practice sports and pastimes. Have volunteers read the sentences aloud. Also, for oral practice, have the students select a partner to talk about the weather. Tell them to include the months and seasons and discuss the weather at a particular time of year.

VOCABULARIO

ESTUDIO DE PALABRAS

Have the students find items in the vocabulary list that belong to the following categories and write them down.

1. names of sports
2. sports equipment
3. action verbs
4. names of pastimes
5. seasons
6. weather expressions

To practice the vocabulary in context, you may wish to play a game called **béisbol.** Draw a baseball diamond on the board or a transparency. Write the numbers 1, 2, and 3 to indicate the bases and the word **jonrón** for home plate. Write the vocabulary items on slips of paper or small cards and shuffle them. If you are using the board, you will need four magnetic markers to indicate players on bases. If you are using a transparency, you may use paper clips.

The first player "at bat" decides if he or she is going for a single, a double, a triple, or a home run. Then "the pitcher" from the opposing team selects a slip of paper or card and reads the vocabulary item. The student "at bat" must then use the word in a sentence. The batter will be given a word for each base he or she chooses. For example, if the "batter" has selected a home run, then he or she must correctly use four different words in separate sentences. If any sentence is incorrect, he or she will be "out." Each team is allowed three outs. If the student answers correctly, the marker is placed on the base he or she chose previously, and the next player has a turn "at bat."

V
O
C
A
B
U
L
A
R
I
O

VAMOS A LEER

UN MARATÓN

Allow sufficient time for the students to read the entire story silently. Next have the students read the story one section at a time.

Before reading the selection, you may wish to have the students look at the illustrations and lead a short discussion on marathons to arouse interest.

Preguntas y respuestas

Call on students to answer the questions after reading one section at a time. Accept short answers, since the main object is to read with fluency and comprehension.

SLOWER-PACED LEARNING Have the students tell briefly in English what happens in each section. For example, after reading the first section, they might say, "They are running in New York City. Someone has won the race." Do not ask the students to translate. You should, however, explain the meaning of a word or expression that hinders comprehension.

Actividad • ¿Es cierto o no?

You may wish to have the students complete this activity without referring to the selection or with books closed. Call on individuals to correct the statements so that they agree with the reading.

For writing practice, have the students write the corrected statements. Then call on the students to read the sentences aloud.

Actividad • Una entrevista

After the students have written their interviews, have them role-play the dialog with a partner. Suggest that they bring props from home. You may wish to have them refer to **Un maratón** as a guide.

EL REGALO

Call on individuals to summarize the story line of the previous two episodes. Explain that in this episode they will find out what is so unusual about the television.

Ask the students to read the selection silently. Then you may call on volunteers to read aloud each section and select two students to read aloud Daniel and Adriana's lines.

Preguntas y respuestas

Students may work with a partner. Have them take turns asking and answering the questions. Then you may wish to call on volunteers to provide the answers for the class.

Actividad • Asociaciones

Tell the students to review the selection and list the expressions and sentences associated with each topic listed. Have them write at least one sentence for each topic.

CHALLENGE Ask groups of students to write a paragraph using as many of the expressions as possible. They may make the paragraph as humorous or imaginative as they like. The groups should be small so that each student may participate.

UNIDAD **3**
Deportes y pasatiempos

Fútbol—called *soccer* in the United States—is the national passion in most Spanish-speaking countries. Children learn to kick a ball almost as soon as they can walk. Some of the world's great soccer players come from South America. Other popular sports include *tenis, golf, béisbol, polo, vólibol, básquetbol.* As you can see, many sports names are similar in Spanish and English.

Pastimes like dancing, singing, playing the guitar, taking pictures, and playing dominos add fun to life.

In this unit you will:

SECTION A	talk about sports and pastimes . . . say which you like and which you don't like
SECTION B	talk about the seasons in which you play certain sports, and the equipment you need
SECTION C	say when and how often you play . . . talk about the seasons and the weather
TRY YOUR SKILLS	use what you've learned
VAMOS A LEER	read for practice and pleasure

SECTION A

talking about which sports and pastimes you like and which you don't like

In Spanish-speaking countries, nearly everybody you meet talks about sports and leisure-time activities. Join in the conversation.

A1 ¿Qué deporte te gusta? 🔊

¿Qué deporte te gusta, Miguel?

Me gusta el béisbol.
¡No me gusta la gimnasia!

También me gusta mucho el tenis.
¡Y no me gusta correr!
Pero sí me gusta montar en bicicleta.

¿Qué deporte le gusta a Pedro?

A Pedro le gusta nadar.
Pero no le gusta el fútbol.

¿Qué deporte le gusta a Olga?

A Olga le gusta el volibol.
Pero no le gusta el básquetbol.

A2 Actividad • Para completar

Complete these sentences for Miguel.

1. Me gusta el . . .   el béisbol.
2. También me gusta mucho . . .   el tenis.
3. Pero no me gusta la . . .   gimnasia.
4. Y no me gusta . . .   correr.
5. Pero sí me gusta . . .   montar en bicicleta.
6. ¿Qué deporte te . . . ?   gusta

92   Unidad 3

Complete these sentences about Pedro, Olga, and yourself.

7. A Pedro le gusta . . . nadar.
8. A Olga le gusta . . . el volibol.
9. A Pedro no le gusta . . . el fútbol.

10. A Olga no le gusta . . . el básquetbol.
11. Me gusta . . .
12. No me gusta . . .

A3 Actividad • Y ahora, tú Answers will vary.

Say what you like to practice and what you don't like. Ex: Me gusta la gimnasia.
No me gusta correr.

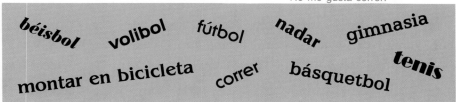

béisbol   volibol   fútbol   nadar   gimnasia
montar en bicicleta   correr   básquetbol   tenis

A4 ESTRUCTURAS ESENCIALES
The verb gustar

To say you like something, use the verb **gustar,** *to like.*

Me gusta el tenis.	*I like tennis.*	*(Tennis is pleasing to me.)*
Te gusta el béisbol.	*You* **(tú)** *like baseball.*	*(Baseball is pleasing to you.)*
Le gusta nadar.	*He/She likes* ⎫ *to swim.* *You* **(usted)** *like* ⎭	*(Swimming is pleasing to him/her/you.)*
No le gusta el volibol.	*He/She doesn't like* ⎫ *volleyball.* *You* **(usted)** *don't like* ⎭	*(Volleyball is not pleasing to him/her/you.)*

Stress the use of the verb "gustar" using classroom situations.
1. Use **me, te,** and **le** to say who does the liking. ¿Qué te gusta? Me gusta _____ . Te gustan los libros? Sí, me
. . . No, no me . . . ¿Qué le gusta a *(student's name)*? A _____ le gusta _____.

Me gusta el tenis.   *I like tennis.*
Te gusta el béisbol.   *You* **(tú)** *like baseball.*
Le gusta nadar.   *He/She/You* **(usted)** *like to swim.*

2. a. Put a definite article before any noun you use to mention what you like.

Me gusta **el** béisbol.   Te gusta **el** volibol.   Le gusta **la** gimnasia.
I like baseball.   *You like volleyball.*   *She likes gymnastics.*

b. But don't use a definite article when you use an infinitive **(correr, nadar)** to express what you like.

Me gusta **correr.**   ¿Te gusta **nadar?**
I like to run.   *Do you like to swim?*

3. For clarification, you may want to name the person who does the liking by adding at the beginning of the sentence the preposition **a** + the name of the person.

A Olga le gusta el volibol. **A Pedro** le gusta nadar.

4. To say somebody doesn't like something, put **no** right before **me, te,** or **le.**

No me gusta correr.   ¿**No** te gusta nadar?   A Pedro **no** le gusta el tenis.

A5 Comprensión — For script and answers, see p. T71.

A5 Comprensión

Are you sure? Is that the answer?

	0	1	2	3	4	5	6	7	8	9	10
Sí		✓		✓	✓		✓			✓	
No	✓		✓			✓		✓	✓		✓

A6 Actividad • Charla   Free conversation.

¿Te gusta o no? With a partner, talk about which sports you like and which you don't like.

¿Te gusta . . . ?

Ex. ¿Te gusta el tenis?
Sí, me gusta el tenis.
¿Te gusta nadar? No, no
me gusta nadar, pero sí
me gusta correr.

• Sí, me gusta . . .
• No, no me gusta . . .
  pero sí . . .

volibol   nadar   gimnasia
correr
tenis   montar en bicicleta
básquetbol   fútbol   béisbol

A7 ¿Sabes que . . . ?

Indicate that "fútbol" refers to soccer. American football is called "fútbol americano" in Spanish-speaking countries.

Fútbol (*soccer* in the U.S.) is the most popular sport in Spain and most of Spanish America. Professional teams play before tremendous crowds in the stadiums while the rest of the nation watches on TV. The popularity of any one sport varies from country to country. Baseball is more important than soccer in Cuba, the Dominican Republic, Puerto Rico, and Venezuela. Many players from these countries as well as from Mexico and Central America have made their way to the major leagues in the United States and achieved stardom. Skiing attracts many to the mountains of Spain, Chile, and Argentina. Bicycle racing is especially important in Colombia. **La corrida,** *bullfighting,* attracts large audiences in Spain and Mexico. Many regard it as a form of art, not a sport.

1. A Raúl le gusta el volibol.
   A Olga no le gusta el volibol.

2. A Antonia le gusta correr.
   A Carlos no le gusta correr.

3. A Roberto no le gusta el fútbol.
   A Pablo le gusta el fútbol.

A8   Actividad • ¡A escribir!

¿Qué le gusta? Everyone has different likes and dislikes.
Complete the sentences and write them out.

Luisa / sí   A Luisa le gusta el tenis.
Carlos / no   A Carlos no le gusta.

1. Raúl / sí
    Olga / no

2. Antonia / sí
    Carlos / no

3. Roberto / no
    Pablo / sí

4. José / sí
    Cora / no

5. Marta / no
    Diego / sí

6. Pablo / no
    Anita / sí

7. Carmen / sí
    Pedro / sí

8. Lola / no
    María / sí

4. A José le gusta montar en bicicleta.
   A Cora no le gusta.

5. A Marta no le gusta nadar.
   A Diego le gusta.

6. A Pablo no le gusta el básquetbol.
   A Anita le gusta.

A9   SITUACIÓN • Pasatiempos 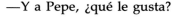

7. A Carmen le gusta el béisbol./A Pedro le gusta el béisbol.
8. A Lola no le gusta la gimnasia./A María le gusta.

Luisa and Pedro, star reporters of the newspaper **El tiempo,** are comparing notes for a
feature article about favorite pastimes of teenagers.

—¿Qué pasatiempo le gusta a
  Alberto?

—¿A Ofelia le gusta estudiar
  música y cantar?

—Y a Pepe, ¿qué le gusta?

—A Alberto le gusta
  escuchar discos.
  Dice que es divertido.

—No, no le gusta.
  Dice que es muy aburrido.
  Le gusta patinar.

—A Pepe, le gusta tocar
  la guitarra y bailar.
—¿Por qué?
—Dice que es ¡estupendo!

Deportes y pasatiempos   **95**

—¿Y a Tato y a Lola?

—¿Qué te gusta, Luisa?

—Pedro, ¿te gusta mirar televisión también?

—A Tato le gusta tomar fotografías, pero a Lola le gusta hablar por teléfono.

—Me gusta trabajar y jugar con la computadora. ¡Es fantástico! Y también me gusta mirar televisión.

—¡No! Odio mirar televisión.
—¿Por qué?
—¡Es horrible!

You may wish to mention that "fotografía" is more commonly expressed as "la foto" and "televisión" as "la tele".

A 10 Actividad • ¡A escribir!

No es así. The editor's report is confused. Correct the statements that are not based on information in A9.   1. A Alberto le gusta escuchar discos.   2. A Ofelia le gusta patinar.

1. A Alberto le gusta patinar.
2. A Ofelia le gusta mucho tocar música.
3. A Pepe le gusta escuchar discos.
4. A Tato no le gusta tomar fotografías.

5. A Luisa no le gusta trabajar con la computadora.
6. A Pedro no le gusta mirar televisión.

3. A Pepe le gusta tocar la guitarra y bailar.   4. A Tato le gusta tomar fotografías.   5. A Luisa le gusta trabajar y jugar con la computadora.   6. Es cierto.

A 11 Actividad • Reacciones   Answers will vary.

Your partner asks what you think of various activities. You should answer with a sentence that appropriately expresses your opinion. Then, switch roles.

—¿Patinar?   —¡Es estupendo!

¿Escuchar música?
¿Cantar? ¿Bailar?
¿Patinar?
¿Tocar la guitarra?
¿Estudiar?

¿Mirar televisión?
¿Hablar por teléfono?
¿Tomar fotografías?
¿Trabajar con la computadora?
¿Montar en bicicleta?

¡Es estupendo!
¡Es aburrido!
¡Es horrible!
¡Es fantástico!
¡Es divertido!

SE DICE ASÍ
Talking about what you and others like and don't like to do

¿Qué te gusta? What do you like?	Me gusta patinar. I like to skate.
¿Qué no le gusta a Ofelia? What doesn't Ofelia like?	No le gusta tocar música. She doesn't like to play music.
¿Te gusta correr? Do you like to jog?	Sí, me gusta (mucho) correr. Es estupendo. Yes, I like to jog (very much). It's great. No, no me gusta. Odio correr. Es aburrido. No, I don't like it. I hate to jog. It's boring.

A 13 **Conversación • ¿Qué te gusta? ¿Qué no te gusta?** Free conversation.

With a partner, create a dialog about what you like or don't like to do. Perform it for the class. This model may help.

ANA ¿Te gusta mirar televisión?
PEDRO No, no me gusta.
ANA ¿Por qué?
PEDRO ¡Es horrible!
ANA ¿Qué te gusta?
PEDRO ¡Me gusta tocar la guitarra!

¿Te gusta . . . ?

¡Me gusta mucho! ¿Por qué? ¡Es . . . divertido, estupendo, fantástico! **No, no me gusta. ¿Por qué? Es** . . . aburrido, horrible. **¡Odio!** . . .

A 14 **Comprensión** For script and answers, see p. T73.

¿Le gusta a Pepe . . . ?

	Sí	No		Sí	No
1. ¿escuchar discos?		✔	4. ¿bailar?	✔	
2. ¿tomar fotografías?	✔		5. ¿patinar?		✔
3. ¿tocar la guitarra?	✔		6. ¿mirar televisión?		✔

A 15 **Actividad • ¡A escribir!** Possible answers are given.

Write comments about each picture. Use the expressions in A13.

1. A Carolina no le gusta tomar fotografías. Es aburrido.

2. A la profesora le gusta escuchar la música. ¡Es fantástico!

3. A Manuel no le gusta mirar televisión.

Deportes y pasatiempos   97

Es horrible.

Point out the pronunciation of "j" in "judo".

A 16 SITUACIÓN • El judo

Me llamo Esteban Rodríguez. Mi pasatiempo
favorito es el judo. Me gusta practicar judo.
Soy cinturón azul. Después del azul vienen el
cinturón marrón y el cinturón negro. En el
judo hay un cinturón de color diferente para
cada categoría. El blanco es para los
principiantes y el negro para los más
avanzados. No hay cinturón rojo. Hay siete
colores en total:

blanco   amarillo   anaranjado

negro

verde   azul   marrón

A 17 Actividad • ¡A escoger!

Choose the option that best fits A16.

1. El pasatiempo favorito de Esteban es
   • practicar. • el judo. • los colores.
2. Esteban es
   • cinturón blanco. • cinturón azul. • cinturón negro.
3. Después del cinturón azul vienen
   • el blanco y el negro. • el marrón y el negro. • el azul y el negro.
4. En el judo hay un cinturón de color diferente para
   • cada estudiante. • cada principiante. • cada categoría.
5. El blanco es
   • para los más avanzados. • para los principiantes. • para Esteban.
6. El negro es
   • para los principiantes. • para Esteban. • para los más avanzados.

A 18 Actividad • Rompecabezas
Colores escondidos   Hidden colors

The seven colors of judo belts are hidden in the squares.
Find them!

blanco
amarillo
anaranjado
verde
azul
marrón
negro

A	Ver	Blan	na
llo	co	zul	de
ja	ri	do	Ne
Ma	gro	rrón	ran

98   **Unidad 3**

*Are you a sports fanatic? Do you wait for winter and think about snow? Does spring mean baseball for you and not flowers? Spanish-speaking fans (**aficionados**) and athletes are among the most enthusiastic in the world.*

B1 ¡Un fanfarrón! 📼

Una entrevista imaginaria

Gracias por todo, amigos. Es un honor ser el atleta del año. Pero sí, ¡es verdad! Practico todos los deportes y juego en todas las estaciones. Como todo campeón, gano muchos premios.

Me gusta el invierno. ¡Soy estupendo en el hielo! Patino muy bien y . . . ¡esquiar es fantástico!

¡Ah, la primavera! ¡Soy campeón en la cancha de tenis! Ivan Lendl y yo somos amigos. Pero ahora no hablamos de Ivan.

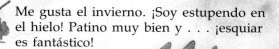

En el verano, participo en los Juegos Olímpicos. Tengo medalla de oro en natación.

¿Preguntas, por favor? ¿Me gusta el fútbol? Sí, pero en el otoño. ¿Con quién practico? Diego Maradona y yo practicamos mucho.

¿Mi deporte favorito? ¡Ganar en todo momento! Y, ¡muchas gracias por el trofeo, amigos!

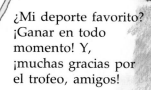

Deportes y pasatiempos   99

Actividad • Combinación Answers will vary. Ex: Es un honor ser el atleta del año.

Otro fanfarrón. Match the activities on the left with the corresponding items in the box at the right.

Es un honor ser . . .
Practico . . .
Juego . . .
Gano . . .
Soy estupendo . . .
Patino . . .
Soy campeón . . .
Participo . . .
Tengo . . .
Muchas gracias . . .

muchos premios   una medalla de oro   muy bien
en todas las estaciones   en la cancha de tenis
el atleta del año   por el trofeo   todos los deportes
en los Juegos Olímpicos   en el hielo

B3 ESTRUCTURAS ESENCIALES
The present tense of -ar *verbs*

	hablar *to talk*		**ganar** *to win*	
Yo	**hablo**	español.	**Gano**	premios.
Tú	**hablas**	español.	**Ganas**	premios.
Usted, él, ella	**habla**	español.	**Gana**	premios.
Nosotros(as)	**hablamos**	español.	**Ganamos**	premios.
Vosotros(as)	**habláis**	español.	**Ganáis**	premios.
Ustedes, ellos(as)	**hablan**	español.	**Ganan**	premios.

Have the students repeat the subject pronoun with the verb form. Indicate that the "vosotros" form is included only for recognition.

1. Spanish verbs are grouped according to their infinitive ending into three conjugations: **-ar, -er,** and **-ir.**

2. As you learned in Unit 1, the infinitive is the name of the verb, thus **hablar** *to talk,* and **ganar** *to win* are infinitives. Remove the **-ar** ending for these two infinitives and you have their stems: **habl-,** and **gan-.**

3. You can produce the present tense forms for **hablar** and **ganar** and most other regular **-ar** verbs by adding the following endings to the stem:

> **-o, -as, -a, -amos, -áis, -an**

The endings indicate who is doing the action. When you add **-o** to the stem **habl-,** you get **hablo,** *I speak.* When you add **-as** to the stem **habl-,** you get **hablas,** *you speak.* And so on.

4. Here are some other regular **-ar** verbs you have seen.

bailar	*to dance*	**montar**	*to ride*	**practicar**	*to practice*
cantar	*to sing*	**nadar**	*to swim*	**tocar**	*to play* (an instrument)
escuchar	*to listen to*	**necesitar**	*to need*	**trabajar**	*to work*
estudiar	*to study*	**patinar**	*to skate*		
mirar	*to look at*	**participar**	*to participate*		

You can produce the present-tense forms of these **-ar** verbs in the same way as the forms of **hablar** and **ganar** because these verbs are regular. That is, all their forms follow the basic pattern for **-ar** verbs.

B4 Comprensión   For script and answers, see p. T76.

Is the reply appropriate?

0	1	2	3	4	5	6	7	8	9	10
✔		✔		✔	✔				✔	✔

B5 Actividad • Sí, me gusta bailar

Answer the following questions affirmatively.

—¿Escuchas música?
—Sí, me gusta escuchar música.

1. Sí, le gusta patinar.
2. Sí, me gusta nadar.
3. Sí, me gusta hablar español.
4. Sí, le gusta mirar televisión.
5. Sí, le gusta tocar la guitarra.
6. Sí, me gusta bailar.

1. ¿Patina bien Eduardo?
2. ¿Nadas?
3. ¿Hablas español?

4. ¿Mira Alicia televisión?
5. ¿Toca él la guitarra?
6. ¿Bailas?

7. ¿Montas en bicicleta?
8. ¿Practicas béisbol?
9. ¿Cantan bien?

7. Sí, me gusta montar en bicicleta.   8. Sí, me gusta practicar béisbol.   9. Sí, le gusta cantar.

B6 Actividad • Combinación

Choose elements from each group to form five complete sentences.

Yo	patinamos	un premio
Los chicos	toco	televisión
Felipe y yo	montan	en el hielo
Olga	miras	en bicicleta
Tú	gana	la guitarra

Yo toco la guitarra.
Los chicos montan en bicicleta.
Felipe y yo patinamos en el hielo.
Olga gana un premio.
Tú miras televisión.

B7 Actividad • ¡A escribir!

Falta algo. Write the following sentences, providing the correct forms of the verb **practicar**.

1. Tú ____ volibol, ¿no?   practicas
2. ¿ ____ tú y yo?   Practicamos
3. No, yo ____ con ella.   practico
4. Ella ____ tenis los sábados.   practica

5. ¿ ____ ellas básquetbol?   Practican
6. No, ____ béisbol.   practican
7. Nosotros ____ básquetbol.   practicamos
8. ¿Cuándo ____ ustedes?   practican

Deportes y pasatiempos   101

Actividad • Periodista *Journalist*

Tell what is going on in each picture. Use the subject that is given.

1. Ellos   tocan la guitarra.

2. María y yo   bailamos.

3. El chico   juega básquetbol.

4. Yo   monto en bicicleta.

5. Pepe y Ramón
escuchan discos.

6. Tú   hablas por teléfono.

B9 Actividad • Charla   Free conversation.

Talk to your partner about the activities in B8. Do you
practice any of them? Do you like or dislike them? You
might want to use statements and questions like these:

—Yo (no) toco la guitarra.
—¿Tocas tú la guitarra? Sí, toco la guitarra.
—¿Te gusta tocar la guitarra? No, no me gusta tocar
la guitarra.

B10 ¿Sabes que . . . ?

When Argentina defeated West Germany in the final game of
the 1986 **Campeonato mundial de fútbol** (*World Cup Soccer
Championships*), several billion people around the world
were watching on TV. No other sports event attracts as
much attention as these games, which are held every four
years. Since 1930, when Uruguay won the title in the first
Campeonato mundial de fútbol, half the championships
have been won by European teams and the rest by teams
from Latin America. The 1982 series was held in Spain;
Mexico hosted the series in 1970 and again in 1986. Italy
will be the host in 1990.

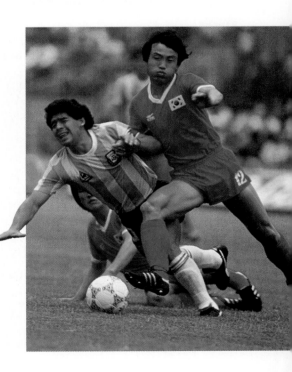

B 11 SITUACIÓN • ¿Qué necesitamos para jugar?

What equipment do we need to play various sports? **Para practicar un deporte necesitamos muchas cosas . . .** Para practicar tenis necesitamos una pelota, una raqueta, unos zapatos de tenis, y una red.

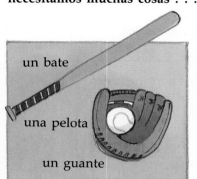

un bate

una pelota

un guante

una red

zapatos de tenis

pelota

una raqueta

una canasta

un balón

Para practicar básquetbol necesitamos un balón y una canasta. Para practicar béisbol necesitamos un bate, una pelota y un guante,

Para practicar esquí necesitamos . . . botas, bastones de esquiar y esquís.

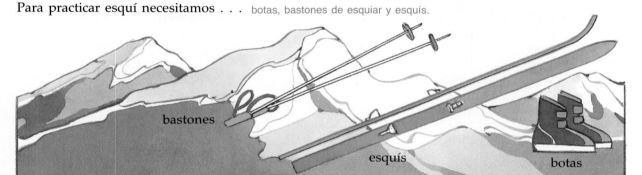

bastones

esquís

botas

B 12 Actividad • ¡A escoger!

Choose the appropriate equipment for each of the sports mentioned.

1. Para jugar béisbol necesitamos . . .
   • unas botas • una pelota • una raqueta
2. Para jugar tenis necesitamos . . .
   • un guante • una red • una canasta
3. Para practicar esquí necesitamos . . .
   • un bate • unos zapatos • unas botas
4. Para jugar volibol necesitamos . . .
   • un cinturón • una red • una canasta

B 13 Actividad • No es así

The equipment is all wrong! Correct the statements below, using the name of the right equipment needed. Possible answers are given.

1. Me gusta el béisbol. Tengo *una red*. un bate
2. ¿Practicamos tenis? ¿Necesitas *un bate?* una raqueta
3. Venimos a jugar volibol, pero no tenemos *raqueta*. una red
4. En la cancha de tenis hay *una canasta*. una red
5. ¡No practico esquí! No tengo *guante*. botas
6. A él le gusta el tenis, pero no tiene *bastones*. pelota
7. ¿Practicas béisbol? ¿Tienes *un esquí?* un bate
8. ¿Vienen a jugar básquetbol? Necesitan *guantes*. un balón

SE DICE ASÍ
Saying what you need in order to do something

	¿Qué necesitas para bailar?	Para bailar necesito música.

To express for which purpose you need something, use **para** plus a verb in the infinitive at the beginning or at the end of the sentence.

B 15 Actividad • Charla   Answers may vary.

With a partner, talk about what you need to practice different sports.

¿Qué necesitas para practicar . . .?

béisbol

tenis

básquetbol

esquí

raqueta
zapatos de tenis
canasta
esquís
bate
pelota
bastones
guantes
botas de esquí

Para practicar . . . necesito . . .

1. Para practicar béisbol necesito un bate, una pelota y un guante.
2. Para practicar tenis necesito una raqueta, pelotas y zapatos de tenis.
3. Para practicar básquetbol, necesito una canasta.   4. Para practicar esquí necesito botas, esquís y bastones.

B 16 ESTRUCTURAS ESENCIALES
The verb jugar

In the present indicative tense, the verb **jugar** changes the stem-vowel **u** to **ue** in all forms except the first and second person plural. The endings are regular **-ar** endings.

jugar *to play*					
Yo	**juego**	fútbol.	Nosotros(as)	**jugamos**	básquetbol.
Tú	**juegas**	tenis.	Vosotros(as)	**jugáis**	tenis.
Usted, él, ella	**juega**	volibol.	Ustedes, ellos(as)	**juegan**	béisbol.

B 17 Actividad • ¿Juegan?

Who's playing? Answer as indicated, using a form of **jugar**.   You may wish to mention that a common alternate form is "jugar a (al)"; i.e. "jugar a la pelota; jugar al tenis".

¿Juega usted? (no)—No, yo no juego.
¿Alicia y usted? (sí)—Sí, nosotros jugamos.

Yo juego volibol, y ¿tú? (no); ¿Ustedes? (no); ¿Los chicos? (sí); ¿Pablo? (sí); ¿Pablo y yo? (sí); ¿Elvira? (sí); ¿Clara y tú? (no); ¿Yo? (sí); ¿Nora y Raúl? (sí); ¿El fanfarrón? (¡No, señor!).

No, yo no juego. No, nosotros no jugamos. Sí, los chicos juegan. Sí, Pablo juega. Sí, Pablo y tú juegan. Sí, Elvira juega. No, Clara y yo no jugamos. Sí, tú juegas. Sí, Nora y Raúl juegan. ¡No, señor! El fanfarrón no juega.

Actividad • Falta algo

Complete using the corresponding form of **jugar.**

—¿_ ustedes tenis?
—¿Juegan ustedes tenis?
—¿_ tú tenis? Sí, yo _ . Alicia _ y Pedro _ también. Ellos _ los sábados.
Juegas *juego* *juega* *juega* *juegan*
jugamos Nosotros _ volibol en la escuela. ¿_ ustedes en la escuela? *Juegan*
—Sí, pero nosotros _ béisbol. Pedro y Carmen _ básquetbol. ¿ _ ustedes
básquetbol? *jugamos* *juegan* *Juegan*
—No, nosotros no _ . Yo no _ . ¿_ tú?
jugamos *juego* *Juegas*

B 19 **Actividad • ¡A actuar!** *Let's act!* Answers will vary.

With a partner, create your own dialog by changing the italicized words in the following script. You can use the words from B15 to talk about your favorite sport. Then act out your new dialog for the class.

A. Me gusta *el béisbol.*
B. ¿Tienes *un bate?*
A. No.
B. ¿Tienes *un guante?*

A. No. Necesito *un guante.*
B. ¿Tienes *una pelota?*
A. No. Necesito *una pelota* también.
B. ¡Pero tú necesitas todo!

B 20 **Actividad • ¿Y ustedes, amigos?** Answers will vary.

You want to find classmates with interests similar to yours. List your activities in a chart, like the one below. Leave a space on the right where you can write the names of classmates who enjoy the same activities, and those who don't. Ask questions if necessary. **¿Patinas? ¿Cantas? ¿Bailas?** Once you've filled in your chart, report who does what.

Yo	Amigos	
	Sí	No
Patino	*María, Silvia*	*Olga*
Canto	*Jorge*	*Elena, Julia*
Bailo	*Olga*	

Yo patino. María y Silvia patinan también. María, Silvia y yo patinamos, pero Olga no patina.

B 21 **Actividad • ¡A adivinar!** *Guess!* Answers will vary.

A classmate will tell you what equipment he or she has and you have to guess what sport is played. Then, switch roles.

—Tengo un bate y una pelota. Ex: —Tengo una raqueta y unas pelotas.
—Juegas béisbol. —Juegas tenis.

saying when and how often you play . . . talking about the months, the seasons, and the weather

Why do you think so many major league baseball stars come from countries in the Caribbean? How often do you play sports? Does it depend on the weather? The seasons? Do you practice a lot?

C1 ¿Juegas siempre?

FELIPE	¿Te gusta jugar tenis, Sara?
SARA	Sí, a veces juego. No juego a menudo.
FELIPE	Yo juego siempre. Juego todos los días.
SARA	Necesito practicar más. ¿Jugamos un partido hoy por la tarde?

FELIPE	Por la tarde, no. ¿Por la noche?
SARA	No, nunca juego por la noche.
FELIPE	¿Y mañana por la mañana?
SARA	Bueno, ¡de acuerdo! ¡Hasta mañana!

C2 Actividad • ¡A escoger!

Select the option that best completes the sentence according to the dialog.

1. El diálogo se llama
   • ¿No juegas nunca? • ¿Juegas todos los días? • <u>¿Juegas siempre?</u>
2. A Sara
   • no le gusta el tenis. • <u>le gusta el tenis.</u> • no le gusta jugar.
3. Sara juega
   • siempre. • a menudo. • <u>a veces.</u>
4. Felipe juega tenis
   • <u>todos los días.</u> • a veces. • nunca.

5. Sara necesita
   • practicar por la mañana.   • <u>practicar más.</u>   • jugar por la noche.
6. Ella no juega
   • <u>por la noche.</u>   • nunca.   • mañana.
7. <u>Ellos no juegan</u>
   • nunca.   • <u>hoy.</u>   • mañana.
8. Felipe y Sara juegan
   • hoy por la noche.   • mañana por la tarde.   • <u>mañana por la mañana.</u>

C3   Actividad • ¡No, al contrario! *No, on the contrary!*

Pair up with a classmate, and be difficult! No matter which phrase your classmate chooses, reply with the opposite. Exchange roles.

   —¿Juegas béisbol hoy?
   —No, mañana.

siempre   sí
por la mañana
hoy
a menudo
   a veces
mañana
no
   nunca
por la noche

¡Soy perfecto! ¡Nunca necesito practicar!

Ex: ¿Juegas siempre?
No, nunca.
¿Practicas por la mañana?
No, por la noche.
¿Juegas volibol a menudo?
No, a veces.

C4   ESTRUCTURAS ESENCIALES
   Word order

Siempre juego. Juego **siempre.**	*I always play.*
A veces juego. Juego **a veces.**	*Sometimes I play.*
Nunca juego. **No** juego **nunca.**	*I never play.*

You can place expressions that say *how often* either before or after your verb.
When you place **nunca** after a verb, put **no** before the verb.

Ex. ¿Qué deportes practicas? Practico los jueves y domingos. ¿Qué pasatiempo te gusta?
Practico tenis. ¿Cuándo? Me gusta escuchar discos.
¿Qué días? Por la tarde. ¿Escuchas discos por la tarde?
No siempre, a veces por la noche.

C5 Conversación • Los deportes y los pasatiempos

Work with a partner. Find out what sports and pastimes each of you enjoy, and when and
how often you practice. Ask at least ten questions.

—¿Qué deportes practicas? ¿Qué pasatiempo te gusta?

¿Todos los días?

¿Siempre,
a veces,
nunca?

¿Qué días?

¿los lunes,
martes,
miércoles, . . . ?

¿Cuándo?

¿por la mañana,
por la tarde,
por la noche?

¿béisbol? ¿bailar? ¿básquetbol? ¿discos?
¿tenis? ¿volibol? ¿fútbol?
¿guitarra? ¿cantar? ¿patinar? ¿bicicleta? ¿televisión?

C6 Actividad • ¡A escribir! Answers will vary.

Write sentences saying how often or when you do the following things, using C5
as a guide.

—¿Juegas tenis? —Sí, juego todos los días. Juego por la tarde.

Ex: Sí, miro televisión los miércoles por la mañana.

1. ¿Miras televisión?
2. ¿Tocas la guitarra?
3. ¿Escuchas discos?
4. ¿Bailas?
5. ¿Cantas?
6. ¿Hablas mucho por teléfono?
7. ¿Nadas?
8. ¿Patinas?
9. ¿Montas en bicicleta?
10. ¿Trabajas con la computadora?
11. ¿Practicas deportes?

2. ¿Cuándo juegas? Juego los martes por la tarde. 3. ¿Dónde juegas? Juego en el parque. 4. Juego a las tres de la tarde.
5. Juego jueves y viernes. 6. Juego con Sara y Miguel. 7. ¿Cómo juegas? Juego muy bien. 8. Necesito una raqueta, zapatos
de tenis y pelotas.

C7 Actividad • Una entrevista Possible answers are given.

Interview a classmate about his or her favorite sport or pastime. Ask the
questions below. Use **jugar** and **practicar** in your questions. Exchange roles.

1. ¿Qué deporte (pasatiempo) te gusta? **2.** ¿Cuándo . . . ? **3.** ¿Dónde . . . ? **4.** ¿A qué hora?
5. ¿Qué días? **6.** ¿Con quién? **7.** ¿Cómo . . . ?, ¿bien o mal? **8.** ¿Qué necesitas para practicar?

C8 Actividad • ¡A escribir!

Write the interview from exercise C7 in dialog form. You may wish to bring several pictures to class
that illustrate different weather conditions, and ask
students to react to them. i.e. ¿"Hace frío"?
(pointing to the picture)

C9 SITUACIÓN • ¿Qué tiempo hace? *How's the weather?*

ANITA ¡Otro día horrible! Hace mal
tiempo. Llueve y hace mucho viento.
CONSUELO Ideal para mirar televisión
y escuchar discos.

LUISA ¡Hace frío!
CARMEN Sí, pero no nieva. ¡Estupendo
para patinar en hielo!

FELIPE ¿Hace fresco?
JULIÁN No, hace sol y hace calor.
¡Es un día magnífico!
FELIPE Por fin hace buen tiempo
para la playa.

C10 Actividad • Reacciones Answers will vary.

Create three short dialogs by combining elements from the three groups. Be ready
to read them in class. Ex. Hace sol y hace calor. ¡Es un día magnífico! Hace buen tiempo para la playa.

Hace sol y hace calor. Hace frío. Llueve y hace viento.	Estupendo para patinar en hielo. Ideal para mirar televisión. Hace buen tiempo para la playa.	¡Otro día horrible! ¡Es un día magnífico! Pero no nieva.

ESTRUCTURAS ESENCIALES
The verb hacer *in weather expressions*

Hace (muy) buen tiempo. Hace (mucho) calor. Hace (mucho) sol.	It's (very) nice out. It's (very) hot. It's (very) sunny.
Hace (muy) mal tiempo. Hace fresco. Hace (mucho) frío. Hace (mucho) viento.	The weather is (very) bad. It's cool. It's (very) cold. It's (very) windy.

1. To talk about the weather, you need to know several expressions with **hace. Hace** is a form of the verb **hacer,** *to make, to do.*

2. To express the idea *very.*
   a. Use **mucho,** an adjective, to describe a noun.
   > Hace **mucho** calor. *It's very hot.* (Literally, *it makes much heat.*)

   b. Use **muy,** an adverb, to describe an adjective.
   > Hace **muy** mal tiempo. *It's very bad out.*
   > (Literally, *it makes very bad weather.*)

3. **Hace** does not appear in every weather expression. Since **nieva,** *it's snowing,* and **llueve,** *it's raining*, are verbs, the verb **hacer** is not used.

C12 Actividad • ¡Al contrario!

The weather report is often dead wrong. React to the forecast by stating the opposite.

—Hace buen tiempo.
—Al contrario, hace mal tiempo.

1. Al contrario, hace calor. 2. Al contrario, hace muy mal tiempo para nadar. 3. Al contrario, llueve. 4. Al contrario, hace (muy) buen tiempo. 5. Al contrario, hace frío. 6. Al contrario, hace sol.

1. Hace frío.
2. Hace buen tiempo para nadar.
3. Hace sol.
4. Hace mal tiempo.
5. Hace calor.
6. Llueve.

C13 Actividad • Charla

Work with a partner, talk about the weather using different expressions and activities.

¡Hace buen tiempo!

Ex. Hace buen tiempo.
¡Ideal! ¿Jugamos tenis?

Hoy nieva.
¡Magnífico! Mañana esquiamos.

hace viento llueve
mal tiempo nieva
frío buen tiempo calor

¡magnífico!
¡horrible!
¡estupendo!
¡ideal!

¡Ideal para jugar béisbol!

You may wish to use the definite article with the seasons to indicate gender: "el otoño", "el verano".

C14 SITUACIÓN • Los meses del año
The months of the year

otoño
septiembre
octubre
noviembre

invierno
diciembre
enero
febrero

primavera
marzo
abril
mayo

verano
junio
julio
agosto

C15 Actividad • Combinación

Match the months with the corresponding season, according to where you live.

otoño   invierno   primavera   verano

junio   diciembre   mayo   octubre   abril   enero
febrero   agosto   julio   noviembre   marzo   septiembre

Otoño
septiembre
octubre
noviembre

Invierno
diciembre
enero
febrero

Primavera
marzo
abril
mayo

Verano
junio
julio
agosto

C16 Comprensión   For script and answers, see p. T84.

Which season of the year is being talked about?

	0	1	2	3	4	5	6	7	8	9	10	11
el verano		✓			✓				✓			✓
el otoño		✓									✓	
el invierno			✓				✓		✓			
la primavera	✓					✓		✓				

C17 ¿Sabes que . . . ?

The seasons in the world's two hemispheres are reversed. When it's winter in Spain, the United States, and Mexico, it's summer in Argentina, Uruguay, Paraguay, Bolivia, Chile, and Peru. Schools are closed for summer vacation in December, January, and February.

1

El equipo° 📼

It's your job as coach to form a top-notch team to practice your favorite sport. You have to get a few good players together to form the nucleus of the team. The list below includes a brief description of the students who might be interested in playing the sport. Work with a partner. Study the list, decide on the sport you will coach, and pick the most promising players.

—Juego fútbol muy bien. Soy un campeón. Pero estudio mucho los lunes y martes.

CARLOS

—Juego fútbol bastante bien. Soy experta en volibol. También patino.

MARÍA

—Me gusta el tenis y también el fútbol. Mi deporte favorito es el béisbol.

ROBERTO

—Juego un poco° de tenis. Patino muy bien. No practico otro deporte.

MARIO

—Me gusta el tenis y el fútbol. Pero no me gusta jugar fútbol con chicos.

CAROLINA

—Juego béisbol todos los días. El béisbol es fantástico.

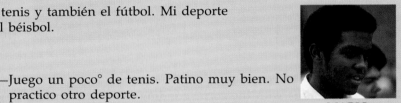

ALBERTO

—Me gusta jugar cuando° hace calor. El verano° es ideal para jugar fútbol o béisbol.

LUPE

—Mi prima° es campeona regional de básquetbol, pero a mí me gusta patinar. También me gusta practicar deportes. Tengo mucho talento atlético.

TERESA

—Toco la guitarra eléctrica. Pero también me gusta jugar tenis y béisbol.

EDUARDO

—Me gusta estudiar y me gusta jugar básquetbol y béisbol.

DAVID

el equipo *team*   un poco *a little*   cuando *when*   verano *summer*   prima *cousin*

2 Actividad • ¡Que hable! ¡Que hable! *Speech! Speech!* Answers will vary.

Prepare in Spanish a description of your favorite sport and read it in class. What equipment is needed to play? When is it played? In what season? In what kind of weather? How often? What days? Do you play it also? Be ready to answer questions from your classmates.

3 Actividad • Composición Answers will vary.

Mi deporte (pasatiempo) favorito. Write in Spanish all you know about your favorite sport or hobby. Use Skills 2 above as a guideline.

4 Actividad • Una encuesta Answers will vary.

Ask your classmates how often they practice a sport or pastime and in what season. Record their responses in a chart like the one below, using a similar code.

¿Deporte o pasatiempo?	¿Cuándo practicas?		¿En qué estación?	
béisbol	nunca	0	otoño	o
tenis				
mirar televisión	a veces	1	invierno	i
computadoras	a menudo	2	primavera	p
básquetbol . . .	todos los días	3	verano	v

For each sport or activity, add the numbers and note the season when it is usually practiced. Then report to the class which sports and pastimes are practiced the most, and in which season.

5 Pronunciación, lectura, dictado For script, see p. T86.

1. Listen and repeat what you hear.

2. The sound of the Spanish vowels **a, e** and **o.** Listen, then read aloud.
   hay   correr   montar   once   voy   hoy   básquetbol   Orlando

3. Copy the following sentences to prepare yourself to write them from dictation.
   La amiga de Marta nada.
   Nosotros tenemos clases a las tres.
   La profesora practica deportes todos los martes.
   Tú hablas mucho con Ana.

¿LO SABES?

Let's review some important points you have learned in this unit.

SECTION A

When talking about sports and pastimes in Spanish, can you name a few?
Name five. Add the definite article if necessary or use an infinitive. Answers will vary.
Ex. 1. jugar tenis 2. jugar fútbol 3. mirar televisión 4. jugar béisbol 5. escuchar discos
Can you talk about your likes, dislikes, or preferences in sports?
Answer the following questions, expressing your preferences and say why
you feel that way. Possible answers are given.

¿Qué deporte te gusta? ¿Por qué? Me gusta el volibol porque juego con mis amigos.
¿Cuál es tu pasatiempo favorito? ¿Por qué? Me gusta ver televisión porque es divertido.
¿Qué deporte practican en tu escuela? En mi escuela practican volibol.
¿Te gusta? ¿Por qué? Me gusta jugar con mis amigos.

SECTION B

Can you tell in which seasons you play different sports?
Make up four sentences. Possible answers are given below.

En (name of season) jugamos / practicamos (name of sport).

Do you know what equipment is needed for different sports?
Say what sport needs the following equipment. Start your sentences with
Necesitamos . . .

una raqueta	un bate	bastones
esquís	botas	unas pelotas
un balón	una canasta	un guante

For answers to Section B, see below.

SECTION C

**Can you say how often you practice a sport or pastime, and whether you
practice in the morning, in the afternoon, or at night?**
Write four sentences. Say how often and when you practice two sports and
two pastimes. Possible answers are given.

Siempre juego tenis por la tarde. Veo televisión todas las noches a las ocho.
Siempre nado en el verano. Juego fútbol siempre
en el otoño.

Can you talk about the weather?
Answer these questions. Answers will vary. Ex. Hoy llueve y hace frío.
El tiempo está bueno para ir al cine.

¿Qué tiempo hace hoy?
¿Llueve?
¿Nieva?
¿Para qué está bueno el tiempo?

B. 1. En verano jugamos/practicamos béisbol. 2. En invierno jugamos/practicamos esquí. 3. En otoño
jugamos/practicamos fútbol. 4. En primavera jugamos/practicamos tenis.

Necesitamos una raqueta para jugar tenis. Necesitamos esquís para esquiar. Necesitamos un balón para jugar
básquetbol/volibol/fútbol. Necesitamos un bate para jugar béisbol. Necesitamos botas para esquiar.
Necesitamos una canasta para jugar básquetbol. Necesitamos bastones para esquiar. Necesitamos pelotas
para jugar tenis. Necesitamos un guante para jugar béisbol.

VOCABULARIO

SECTION A

amarillo, -a *yellow*
anaranjado, -a *orange*
avanzado, -a *advanced*
azul *blue*
bailar *to dance*
blanco, -a *white*
cada *each*
cantar *to sing*
la **categoría** *category*
el **cinturón (pl. cinturones)** *belt*
el **color** *color*
correr *to run, to jog*
dice que . . . *he (she) says (that) . . .*
el **disco** *record*
divertido, -a *fun*
escuchar *to listen (to)*
estudiar *to study*
estupendo, -a *great*
fantástico, -a *fantastic*
el **fútbol** *soccer*
la **gimnasia** *gymnastics*
la **guitarra** *guitar*
gustar *to like, to be pleasing to*
  me gusta *I like*
  le gusta *you like, he/she likes*
  te gusta *you like*
hablar *to speak, talk*
jugar (ue) *to play*
marrón *brown*
mirar *to look at, watch*
montar *to ride*
mucho *a lot*
nadar *to swim*
negro, -a *black*
odio *I hate*
el **pasatiempo** *pastime*
para *for*
patinar *to skate*
practicar *to practice, play*
el **principiante** *beginner (m.)*
la **principiante** *beginner (f.)*
rojo *red*
también *also, too*
el **teléfono** *telephone*
  por teléfono *on the telephone*
el **tenis** *tennis*
tocar *to play (a musical instrument)*
tomar *to take*

tomar fotografías *to take photographs*
trabajar *to work*
verde *green*
el **volibol** *volleyball*

SECTION B

el **amigo, la amiga** *friend*
el **año** *year*
el **atleta** *athlete (m.)*
la **atleta** *athlete (f.)*
el **balón** *ball (basketball, volleyball, soccer ball)*
el **bastón (pl. bastones)** *ski pole*
el **bate** *bat*
la **bota** *ski boot*
el **campeón, la campeona** *champion*
la **canasta** *basketball hoop*
la **cancha de tenis** *tennis court*
como *as, like*
en todo momento *every time*
la **entrevista** *interview*
es verdad *it's true*
esquiar *to ski, skiing*
los **esquís** *skis*
la **estación** *season*
el **fanfarrón** *braggart*
favorito, -a *favorite*
ganar *to win*
el **guante** *glove, mitt*
el **hielo** *ice*
imaginario, -a *imaginary*
el **invierno** *winter*
el **juego** *game*
los **Juegos Olímpicos** *Olympic Games*
la **medalla de oro** *gold medal*
muchas gracias *thank you very much*
la **natación** *swimming*
necesitar *to need*
el **otoño** *fall, autumn*
para *to, in order to*
la **pelota** *ball (baseball, tennis ball)*
la **pregunta** *question*
el **premio** *prize*
la **primavera** *spring*
la **raqueta** *racquet*
la **red** *net*

todo *everything*
todo, -a, -os, -as *all, every*
el **trofeo** *trophy*
el **verano** *summer*
el **zapato** *shoe*
los **zapatos de tenis** *tennis shoes*

SECTION C

a menudo *often*
a veces *sometimes*
de acuerdo *all right*
hace (muy) buen tiempo *it's (very) nice out*
hace (mucho) calor *it's (very) hot out*
hace fresco *it's cool out*
hace (mucho) frío *it's (very) cold out*
hace (muy) mal tiempo *the weather is (very) bad*
hace (mucho) sol *it's (very) sunny*
hace (mucho) viento *it's (very) windy*
los **demás** *the rest*
llueve *it's raining*
magnífico, -a *excellent, very good*
mañana *tomorrow*
la **mañana** *morning*
  por la mañana *in the morning*
el **mes** *month*
los **meses del año** *months of the year (see p. 111)*
nieva *it's snowing*
la **noche** *night*
  por la noche *at night*
nunca *never*
otro, -a *other, another*
el **partido** *game, match*
patinar en hielo *to ice skate*
la **playa** *beach*
¿qué tiempo hace? *how's the weather?*
siempre *always*
la **tarde** *afternoon*
  por la tarde *in the afternoon*
todos los días *every day*

ESTUDIO DE PALABRAS

Rearrange the vocabulary of the unit in broad thematic categories like the following:
Names of sports/Sports equipment/Verbs that express sports actions/Names of pastimes/
The seasons/Weather expressions. Group the rest of the words in a category called "Others".

VAMOS A LEER

Antes de leer

Before reading, look at the illustrations and the title. You should have an idea of what the selection is about. This will help you guess the meanings of new words without having to look them up.

Un maratón

A Spanish TV station is broadcasting a marathon from New York.

Por° las calles° de Nueva York.

LOCUTORA°   Los corredores° pasan por° las calles de Nueva York. ¡Todos° corren a la meta°, en el Parque Central! Pero . . . ¡sí! ¡Uno llega° a la meta! ¡Gana la competencia!

LOCUTORA   ¡Estupendo! ¿Cómo se llama usted?

GANADOR   Me llamo Ángel. Ángel Dos Pasos°.

LOCUTORA   ¡Dos Pasos! ¡Qué buen nombre° para el ganador°! ¿Y de dónde es usted?

GANADOR   Soy de Madrid, España.

LOCUTORA   ¡De Madrid! ¿Y cómo corre° en Nueva York?

---

por *along*   **las calles** *streets*   **locutora** *newscaster*   **corredores** *runners*   **pasar por** *to pass through*   **todos** *all, everybody*   **la meta** *finish line*   **llegar** *to arrive*   **dos pasos** *two steps*   **nombre** *name*   **ganador** *winner*   **corre** *you (usted) run*

116   Unidad 3

GANADOR	Aquí° estoy. En la capital del mundo°. Con permiso°, un saludo a la familia y a los amigos en Madrid. ¡Juanita! ¿Me miras° en televisión? ¡Un saludo, chica!
LOCUTORA	¿Y quién es Juanita?
GANADOR	¡La novia°! Adiós, Juanita, ¡adiós!
LOCUTORA	Aquí, desde° el maratón de Nueva York. ¡Hasta luego!

1. Los corredores pasan por las calles de Nueva York. 2. Todos corren a la meta. 3. La meta está en el Parque Central. 4. El ganador se llama Ángel Dos Pasos. 5. Él es de Madrid. 6. Para él, Nueva York es la capital del mundo. 7. Juanita es su novia. 8. La locutora está en Nueva York.

Preguntas y respuestas

1. ¿Por dónde pasan los corredores?
2. ¿Adónde corren todos?
3. ¿Dónde está la meta?
4. ¿Cómo se llama el ganador?
5. ¿De dónde es él?
6. Para él, ¿qué es Nueva York?
7. ¿Quién es Juanita?
8. ¿Dónde está la locutora?

Actividad • ¿Es cierto o no?

Change the following statements so they agree with the reading.

1. Los corredores pasan por el maratón de Nueva York. Los corredores pasan por las calles de Nueva York.
2. Todos corren a la capital. Todos corren a la meta.
3. Dos corredores llegan a la meta. Un corredor llega a la meta.
4. El locutor se llama Ángel. El ganador se llama Ángel.
5. Ángel Dos Pasos es de Nueva York. Ángel Dos Pasos es de Madrid, España.
6. Juanita está en el Parque Central. Juanita está en Madrid.
7. El maratón es en España. El maratón es en Nueva York.

Actividad • Una entrevista Possible interview is given.

Imagine that you have to interview an athlete from your school. Using the marathon interview as a model, think how you would find out the information you need. When you've imagined your way through the interview and made some notes, write the interview.

—¿Cómo se llama usted?
—Me llamo Jorge Sánchez.
—¿De dónde es usted?
—Soy de Burke, Virginia.
—¿Cuántas veces practica tenis por semana?
—Practico todos los días durante la primavera, el verano y el otoño.
—¡Estupendo!

---

aquí *here* **mundo** *world* **con permiso** *with your permission* **¿me miras?** *are you watching me?* **la novia** *girlfriend*
desde *from*

El regalo 📼

Adriana y Daniel terminan° la tarea.
A Daniel le gusta la música; toca la guitarra
un poco, y después escucha el radio.

Hace sol. Adriana sale° y juega volibol con
unas amigas.

Pero los dos hermanos no dejan de pensar en° el regalo misterioso.

En su cuarto° Adriana prende° el televisor en el Canal 17.

Hay un partido de fútbol; juega el equipo° favorito de ellos. Los dos miran
como° hipnotizados. Hay un momento de confusión. Uno de los jugadores patea°
el balón, y el locutor grita° "¡Gol!"

De pronto°, ¡Adriana y Daniel están° en el estadio de fútbol! Daniel mira a
Adriana.

---

terminan *finish*   **sale** *goes out*   **dejan de pensar en** *stop thinking of*   **cuarto** *room*   **prende** *turns on*   **equipo** *team*
como *as if*   **patea** *kicks*   **grita** *shouts*   **de pronto** *suddenly*   **están** *they are*

DANIEL   ¡Estoy loco! ¡Es imposible!
ADRIANA   No, Daniel, no estás loco . . . Estamos° en el estadio, en el partido de
          fútbol del Canal 17.

(Hace frío y llueve. El público grita.)

ADRIANA   Vamos a casa° Daniel. Es tarde.

(Salen° del estadio y esperan° el autobús.)

ADRIANA   No me gusta el televisor, es muy
          peligroso°.
DANIEL   No es peligroso, pero debemos°
          controlarlo°.
ADRIANA   ¿Hablamos con papá y mamá?
DANIEL   No. El televisor es un secreto. El
          Canal 17 es fantástico. Mira, ahí
          viene el autobús.

Preguntas y respuestas   Possible answers are given.

Answer the following questions about what you have just read.

1. ¿A Daniel le gusta tocar la guitarra? ¿Qué le gusta jugar a Adriana?
   1. Sí, a Daniel le gusta tocar la guitarra. Adriana juega volibol.
2. ¿Dónde tienen los chicos el televisor?   2. El televisor está en el cuarto de Adriana.
3. ¿Qué miran en el Canal 17?   Miran un partido de fútbol.
4. ¿Qué equipo juega?   Juega el equipo favorito de Daniel y Adriana.
5. ¿Están Adriana y Daniel en el estadio?   Sí, están en el estadio.
6. ¿Qué tiempo hace?   Hace frío y llueve.
7. ¿Le gusta a Adriana el televisor? ¿Por qué?   No le gusta el televisor porque es muy peligroso.

Actividad • Asociaciones   Possible answers are given.

Give as many words, phrases, and sentences as you can that are associated with
these topics from the reading.

1. la música   A Daniel le gusta la música./Daniel toca la guitarra./Daniel escucha el radio.
2. "¡Gol!"   El locutor grita ¡Gol!
3. el estadio   Están en el estadio./Salen del estadio.
4. el Canal 17   Adriana prende el televisor en el Canal 17./Estamos en el partido de fútbol del Canal 17./El Canal 17 es fantástico.
5. vamos a casa   Vamos a casa, Daniel. Es tarde.
6. llueve   Hace frío y llueve.
7. el volibol   Adriana sale y juega volibol con sus amigas.

---

estamos *we are*   **vamos a casa** *let's go home*   **salen** *they leave*   **esperan** *they wait for*   **peligroso** *dangerous*
debemos *we ought to*   **controlarlo** *to control it*

UNIDAD 4 ¡Playa, sol y deportes!
Repaso

TEACHER-PREPARED MATERIALS	UNIT RESOURCES
Review 4 Map of Colombia, cue cards for 11, poster board or cardboard	**Manual de actividades** Unit 4 **Manual de ejercicios** Unit 4 Unit 4 Cassette Transparency 10 Review Test 1

Unit 4 reviews functions, grammar, and vocabulary that the students have studied in Units 1–3. No new material is included. This unit provides communicative and writing practice in different situations; that is, different applications and uses of the same material. If your students require further practice, you will find additional review exercises in Unit 4 of the **Manual de actividades** and the **Manual de ejercicios.** If, on the other hand, your students have successfully mastered the material in Units 1–3, you may wish to omit parts of Unit 4. Some of the activities in this unit lend themselves to cooperative learning.

OBJECTIVE To review communicative functions, grammar, and vocabulary from Units 1–3

CULTURAL BACKGROUND Because of the climate and location of most Spanish-speaking countries, tourists flock to their beaches and resorts. The world's most famous vacation spots are in Spain and Spanish America. They offer not only all types of sports and leisure-time activities but also interesting architecture, museums, and ancient ruins.

A popular vacation spot is Colombia, which is well known for its varied climate. Swimmers and sunbathers enjoy the beautiful beaches along the Caribbean coast. The snow-capped peaks of the Andes Mountains attract skiers. Most of the people live in the fertile valleys and basins of the Andes Mountains in western Colombia. Bogotá, Colombia's capital and largest city, lies in the basin of the Andes. You may wish to mention that Colombia was named after Christopher Columbus, whose name in Spanish is **Cristóbal Colón.**

MOTIVATING ACTIVITY Have the students look at a map of Colombia. Ask them to name the major cities. For extra credit, the students may wish to research information about Colombia's major cities, government, people and culture, or history.

1   Verano en Cartagena

CULTURAL BACKGROUND Point out Cartagena on a map of Colombia. It is the chief seaport on the northwestern coast of Colombia. Nearly 450,000 people live in Cartagena, which was founded in 1533. Cartagena has extensive colonial fortifications built by the Spaniards in the seventeenth and eighteenth centuries. They were built to protect the rich and thriving port from the pirates.

Most Colombians admire writers and poets. Many lawyers and teachers in Colombia write poetry in their spare time. Colombia's most outstanding

writer today, Gabriel José García Márquez, won the Nobel Prize for Literature in 1982. One of his most famous works is **Cien años de soledad** (*One Hundred Years of Solitude*).

Have the students read the postcards silently. You may wish to point out that the numbers on the address follow the street name. Then play the cassette or read aloud as students follow along in their books.

To check comprehension, you may wish to ask the following questions:

1. ¿Cómo se llama el amigo de Enrique?
2. ¿Qué le gusta a Enrique?
3. ¿De dónde es Carlos?
4. ¿Qué tiempo hace en Cartagena?
5. ¿Cómo se llama la amiga de Leticia?

2 Actividad • ¡A escoger!

Call on individuals to choose the option that best agrees with Enrique and Leticia's postcards. You may wish to discuss the postcards with the students by asking re-entry questions such as **¿Quién es la amiga de Susana? ¿De dónde es Susana? ¿Qué estación del año es?** or **¿Quién es Carlos? ¿Es de Colombia?**

3 Actividad • Para completar

Have the students complete the activity with a partner. Explain to each pair that they should provide the response marked **tú.** They should respond by listening carefully to the question and by looking at the next line. This will provide a cue as to what they should say. The students should exchange roles, so that each student has an opportunity to respond.

SLOWER-PACED LEARNING If students have difficulty supplying the response of **tú,** you may suggest they first write their responses. Then the students may choose a partner to correct and practice the conversation.

4 Actividad • Charla

Call on the pairs of students to role-play the conversation they had in Activity 3 for the class. Remind students to use gestures when speaking.

5 Actividad • Mi amigo Enrique

Ask the students to write a short description of Enrique. They should write about what he likes, where he is from, and what sport he likes to play. Collect the papers and correct the students' work.

SLOWER-PACED LEARNING Brainstorm with the class statements about Enrique. You or a volunteer may write them on the board or a transparency. Tell the students to use this information for their descriptions. You may also refer students to the postcards in 1 so that they know how to begin and end their notes.

6 Actividad • ¿Hablas español?

For cooperative learning, have the students work in pairs. Each student should take notes as he or she describes the Spanish class, other subjects,

and school in general. They should combine their notes and report to the class. The students may refer to Unit 2 (B28), page 73.

7 Actividad • Charla

Have the students work in pairs to discuss their likes and dislikes about school, sports, and seasons. Suggest that they incorporate expressions from Unit 3 (A12), page 97, to describe their feelings. Remind the students to be prepared to share with the class something they have learned about their partner.

SLOWER-PACED LEARNING   Review school subjects, time, sports, and seasons with the students. You may wish to provide a model, such as **Me llamo Luisa. Soy una chica nueva en la escuela. La clase de historia es horrible. No me gusta estudiar las fechas.**

As a variation, you may wish to have students play a game called **La gira del mundo** as a way of reviewing. List the following categories on the board or a transparency: **las materias, los deportes, la hora, los días, las estaciones, los meses.** If your classroom is arranged in rows, have a student stand beside the last desk in each row. Say a word from the list. The student who calls out the correct category advances to stand beside the next desk. Continue in the same manner until one student reaches the first desk in the row, winning the game. This game can be adapted to various room arrangements.

8 SITUACIÓN • ¿Quién juega tenis?

Since the students are familiar with the grammar, functions, and vocabulary found in this cartoon, have them read it silently. Then you may play the cassette or read the cartoon aloud. You may wish to have the students role-play the cartoon.

CHALLENGE   Ask the students to write and illustrate their own cartoons. Display the cartoons in the classroom.

9 Actividad • Preguntas y respuestas

Have the students answer the questions orally. Then call on volunteers to retell the cartoon in Spanish. Re-enter the negative by asking the students to name each character and explain why he or she can't play tennis.

For writing practice, tell the students to write the answers in complete sentences. Have them exchange papers and correct their work.

10 Actividad • No es así

You may wish to assign this activity as written work to complete at home or in class. Then call on volunteers to read aloud their corrected sentences as you or a student writes them on the board or a transparency.

11 Actividad • Charla

Tell the students to choose a partner to complete the activity. The classmate who is playing the role of Manuel should suggest at least four activities. The other student should give an excuse for why he or she does not want to do what Manuel suggests. Have the student use **¿Quién juega tenis?** as a guide. Each pair of students should present their dialog to the class.

SLOWER-PACED LEARNING   The students may need to prepare cue cards to role-play their dialog. They may write the name of each sport or pastime that Manuel suggests and the subject of each excuse.

> Cue card 1: Tenis
> Cue card 2: Clase a las tres
> Cue card 3: Escuchar música
> Cue card 4: Tarea

12   **Actividad • ¿De dónde son?**

Have the students work in pairs to discover where the people are from in the activity. To verify their answers, call on volunteers to read aloud the rhymes. Students may also enjoy writing original rhymes.

13   **Actividad • ¡A escribir!**

Have the students make a postcard from poster board or cardboard. They may illustrate it themselves or cut a picture from a magazine and paste it on one side of the postcard. On the other side, they should write a note which includes the name of the city they are visiting, something about the weather, and what they like or dislike about the place.

As a variation, you may wish to have the students write the postcard to a member of the class. Write the name of each student on a slip of paper and have the students pick names. The next day you or a volunteer may deliver the mail. Each student should read his or her postcard and comment to the class something about the friend's trip, such as **A Elena no le gusta el calor de Puerto Rico.**

Viñeta cultural 1
Pueblos y ciudades

OBJECTIVES

1. To familiarize the student with the great variety of towns and cities that exist in the Hispanic world
2. To make the student aware of the differences among the towns and cities of the Hispanic world
3. To make the student cognizant of how towns and cities in the Hispanic world are generally planned and built
4. To make the student aware of how people live in towns and cities of the Hispanic world

MOTIVATING ACTIVITIES

1. Request students to write key points on the board about this **Viñeta cultural.**
2. Ask the students to tell, in general, what they think about towns and cities of the Hispanic world.
3. Ask those students who have visited towns and cities in the Hispanic world about their impressions.
4. Ask the students to compare and contrast towns and cities in the Hispanic world with those in the United States.
5. Ask each student to prepare an oral report about a town or city of the Hispanic world or an American city where Spanish influence is visible.

CULTURAL BACKGROUND   The Hispanic world is very extensive. Spanish is spoken in Spain, in many parts of the United States, Mexico, Central America, Cuba, the Dominican Republic, Puerto Rico, and in nine republics of South America. Since the Spanish language is spoken in so many regions around the world, it is not exactly uniform and the customs are not exactly the same in many instances.

Towns and cities throughout the Hispanic world are like the Spanish language itself, unique and distinct. Moving from one end to the other of the Hispanic world, one is impressed by the multicolored variety of its towns and cities. There are towns the color of the very earth in which they are rooted, others whose streets are paved with cobblestones, and cities with balconies made of beautifully carved mahogany.

The towns in the Argentine **Pampas** are basically agricultural and distant from each other. Towns high in the Peruvian Andes or close to the warm waters of the Caribbean have a typically impressive beauty. The Spanish city of Avila, with the best-preserved walls in Europe, has a medieval touch. The city of Granada, with the palaces of the Alhambra and the Generalife, has a definite Arabic flavor, while the city of Sevilla, with its Arabic Giralda Tower and its massive Gothic Cathedral, is a combination of both Moorish and Christian Spain.

Just as each town and city is different, each has also developed its own particular crafts and skills. The towns of Camariñas and Almagro in Spain are famous for their embroidery and lace making. A number of little towns in the interior of Honduras are the wood-carving centers of Central America,

while the tiny villages around Cuenca, Ecuador are noted for the straw-weaving skills of their citizens. When it comes to **ponchos** and **ruanas,** few towns can rival Tunja in Colombia.

If one finds differences among towns and cities of the Hispanic world, there are also similarities. One common place of interest shared by cities and towns of all sizes is the **Plaza Mayor**—the central square. It is in the **Plaza Mayor** that the life of the people is centered. Since the Spaniards explored, conquered, and colonized the majority of the Western Hemisphere, it was natural that Spanish life and customs should be transplanted to the new lands, and the idea of the **Plaza Mayor** was no exception. The great majority of the towns and cities in Spanish America were originally built around a **plaza** with a church or cathedral on one side and a city hall on the other. Here, under the arcades of the buildings around the **Plaza Mayor,** is where each town or city celebrates its colorful festivals and where its vendors set up their stalls. It is here where some of the people shop, while others gather to socialize or take a stroll. Thus, the **Plaza Mayor** has helped to develop the daily life of the people and their character in general.

Another common characteristic of the towns and cities of the Hispanic world is the architecture of many of their houses. The houses, as in Spain, have **patios** *(courtyards)* and are built close to one another and close to the sidewalks. Many of them have balconies facing the streets and wrought-iron ornaments covering the windows.

The Hispanic world also has many large cities. Mexico City, built on the foundation of the ancient Aztec capital of Tenochtitlán, is the largest city in the world, with over 18,000,000 inhabitants. Buenos Aires, situated on the shore of the **Río de la Plata,** is the capital of Argentina. A city of nearly 10,000,000 people, it is the most important capital in South America and one of the most active and sophisticated cities in the world. There is also Lima, the capital of Peru. While Old Lima retains the charm and beauty of its Spanish Colonial past, the rest is a modern metropolis with tall buildings and wide boulevards. In Spain, there is the bustling capital of Madrid and beautiful Barcelona with its ample **ramblas** *(walks)* and the magnificent **Iglesia de la Sagrada Familia** *(Church of the Holy Family),* which the great Spanish architect Gaudí left unfinished.

In most of the cities of the Hispanic world one will find towering skyscrapers, beautiful parks, sidewalk cafés and, of course, soccer stadiums and traffic jams!

The Hispanic architectural and artistic presence in the United States is undoubtedly a strong one. Evidence of this can be found in the missions of San Antonio, the plaza of Santa Fe, the murals of Los Angeles, and the massive fortress of the Castillo de San Marcos in St. Augustine, Florida.

Today, Hispanics throughout the Hispanic world and in the United States preserve their history while they build a promising future.

¡Playa, sol y deportes!

Repaso

For additional background information on Cartagena, see p. T90.

1 Verano en Cartagena 📼

Cartagena is a resort city in Colombia. It's a port on the Caribbean Sea and has a tropical climate and fine beaches. The old fortifications, that were built by the Spaniards in the 17th century to protect the city from attacking pirates, are one of its tourist attractions.

CARTAGENA, PLAYA

¡Hola!
En Cartagena hace sol y muy buen tiempo.
Me gusta la playa
¡Hasta el jueves!
Tu amigo,
Enrique

Carlos Ramos
Calle Libertad 88
Bogotá

CARTAGENA, VISTA DE LA CIUDAD

¡Hola, Susana!
¿Qué tal? ¿Hace frío allí? En Cartagena hace calor, y me gusta la playa.
Chao,
Leticia

Susana Sánchez
Cantones 27-7 I
Quito
Ecuador

¡Playa, sol y deportes! 121

2   Actividad • ¡A escoger!

Choose the option that best agrees with Enrique's and Leticia's postcards.

1. **En Cartagena**   • hace frío y llueve   • hace muy buen tiempo   • no hace sol
2. **A Enrique**   • le gusta la playa   • le gusta el tiempo   • no le gusta el sol
3. **¡Hasta**   • mañana!   • el jueves!   • luego!
4. **Enrique es amigo de**   • Susana   • Leticia   • Carlos
5. **¿Hace frío en**   • Bogotá?   • Cartagena?   • Quito?
6. **En Cartagena**   • hace calor   • hace frío   • hace mal tiempo
7. **La tarjeta de Leticia es para**   • Carlos   • Enrique   • Susana
8. **Las tarjetas vienen de**   • Quito   • Colombia   • Bogotá

3   Actividad • Para completar   Some answers will vary.

You are spending a week in Cartagena with your family. You meet Enrique on the beach. Supply your part of the conversation.

ENRIQUE: ¡Hola! Me llamo Enrique. ¿Cómo te llamas tú?   ¡Hola! Yo me llamo . . . . or
TÚ: _____   Mucho gusto. Yo me llamo . . .
ENRIQUE: Yo soy de Bogotá. Y tú, ¿de dónde eres?
TÚ: _____   Soy de . . . .
ENRIQUE: ¿Por qué no juegas volibol con nosotros?
TÚ: _____   No, gracias. Yo no juego volibol. ¿Te gusta la playa?
ENRIQUE: Bueno. Me gusta la playa, pero me gusta más el tenis. ¿Juegas tú?
TÚ: _____   Sí, yo juego.
ENRIQUE: ¿Por qué no jugamos mañana?
TÚ: _____   Fantástico. ¿A qué hora?
ENRIQUE: ¿A las diez?
TÚ: _____   Sí, mañana a las diez.
ENRIQUE: Bueno, ¡hasta mañana!

4   Actividad • Charla   Free conversation

Pair off with a classmate. One of you is Enrique. You meet on the beach. Act out the conversation in Skills 3. Switch roles.

5   Actividad • Mi amigo Enrique
Ex. Mi amigo Enrique es de Bogotá. No le gusta jugar volibol.
Le gusta la playa, pero le gusta más jugar tenis. (Student's versions may var

Write a short note to a friend. Tell your friend about Enrique, where he is from, what he likes, and what sport he likes to play.

6   Actividad • ¿Hablas español?   Each conversation will vary.

Enrique is very impressed with your Spanish. He wants to know about your Spanish classes, about school in general and the subjects you are taking. Make some notes of what you are planning to tell your new friend. Report it to the class.

7   Actividad • Charla   Free conversation

With a partner talk about your likes and dislikes in school, sports, and seasons. Tell why you like or dislike them. Listen to what your partner has to say; then report your partner's likes and dislikes to the class.

9 Actividad • Preguntas y respuestas

1. Es martes. 2. Porque mañana tiene clase de física y mucha tarea. 3. Anita tiene clase de música a las cuatro. 4. No, Jorge tiene raqueta. 5. No, Luis y Pepe vienen para practicar básquetbol. 6. Carmela está muy mal. 7. No, ella nunca juega lo martes. 8. No, el profesor de tenis no viene hoy. El profesor no viene los martes.

Answer in complete sentences according to **¿Quién juega tenis?**

1. ¿Qué día es?
2. ¿Por qué no juega Raúl?
3. ¿Qué clase tiene Anita? ¿A qué hora?
4. ¿Tiene Jorge raqueta?

5. ¿Vienen Luis y Pepe a jugar tenis?
6. ¿Cómo está Carmela?
7. ¿Juega ella los martes?
8. ¿Viene hoy el profesor de tenis? ¿Por qué?

10 Actividad • No es así

1. A Manuel le gusta el tenis. 2. Raúl tiene clase de física mañana. 3. Raúl tiene mucha tarea mañana. 4. Anita tiene clase de música a las cuatro. 5. Jorge no tiene raqueta. 6. Luis y Pepe vienen para practicar básquetbol. 7. Luis practica básquetbol con Pepe. 8. Carmen está muy mal. 9. Carmen nunca juega tenis los martes. 10. El profesor de tenis no tiene clases hoy. 11. El profesor de tenis no viene hoy. 12. Los chicos no juegan tenis con Manuel.

Change the following statements to make them agree with **¿Quién juega tenis?**

1. A Manuel no le gusta el tenis.
2. Raúl tiene clase de música mañana.
3. Raúl tiene poca tarea para mañana.
4. Anita tiene clase de química a las cinco.
5. Jorge tiene dos raquetas para jugar tenis.
6. Luis y Pepe vienen para practicar tenis.

7. Luis practica tenis con Pepe.
8. Carmen está muy bien.
9. Carmen siempre juega tenis los martes.
10. El profesor de tenis tiene clases hoy.
11. El profesor de física no viene hoy.
12. Los chicos juegan tenis con Manuel.

11 Actividad • Charla

Each student will create his or her version. Ex. No puedo jugar tenis. Mañana tengo un examen de química.

Excusas. Pair off with a classmate. One of you is Manuel. The other one doesn't want to do what Manuel suggests. Think up good excuses based on what Raúl, Anita, Jorge, Luis, and Carmela say in the cartoon. Present your dialog to the class.

12 Actividad • ¿De dónde son?

Discover where all these people are from. The clue is that their names rhyme with the places where they live! Read your answers aloud to see if you are correct.

Fredo es de Laredo.

1. Olivia es de ___c___ .
2. Ramón es de ___f___ .
3. Alicia es de ___h___ .
4. Cristina es de ___g___ .
5. Federico es de ___a___ .
6. María es de ___e___ .
7. Manuela es de ___b___ .
8. Ramona es de ___d___ .

a. Puerto Rico
b. Venezuela
c. Bolivia
d. Pamplona
e. Andalucía
f. Aragón
g. Argentina
h. Galicia

13 Actividad • ¡A escribir!

Write a postcard to a friend from a place you have visited or that you'd like to visit. Tell your friend what you like and what you don't like about the place where you are. You can also write about new friends you've met and sports you practice there.

Each student will create his or her own version.

  Ex. Me gusta mucho Cancún. La playa es muy bonita. Tengo un amigo nuevo, Jorge. A Jorge le gusta el tenis.

Viñeta cultural 1

Pueblos y ciudades

In the large, bustling cities of the Spanish-speaking world, and the many small villages that dot the countryside, visitors can find great contrasts and a wide variety of cultures. In Spain, medieval castles, Gothic cathedrals, and ancient aqueducts are dramatic reminders of the past amidst the modern life of today.

❶ Iglesia de la Sagrada Familia en Barcelona, España

❷ Un café al aire libre en Barcelona, España

❸ El parque del Retiro en Madrid, España

❹ La hermosa ciudad de Ávila, España

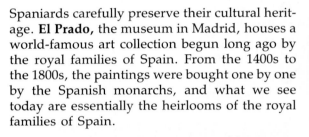

Spaniards carefully preserve their cultural heritage. **El Prado,** the museum in Madrid, houses a world-famous art collection begun long ago by the royal families of Spain. From the 1400s to the 1800s, the paintings were bought one by one by the Spanish monarchs, and what we see today are essentially the heirlooms of the royal families of Spain.

❶ La plaza España en Madrid, España
❷ El Palacio Real en Madrid, España
❸ Plaza de España en Sevilla, España
❹ La Fiesta Brava en Sevilla, España
❺ Museo del Prado en Madrid, España

In many cities and towns of the United States, the Hispanic presence can be seen and heard. Walk along any street and you can hear Spanish words that have become part of the English language—**mosquito, fiesta, taxi, patio.** Architectural styles reflect the Spanish influence with its red-tiled roofs, arched doorways, and brightly painted walls. Even in our food we enjoy a special Hispanic **sabor** (*flavor*).

❶ Un café cubano en Miami, Florida

❷ El Morro de Puerto Rico

❸ Los hermosos y coloridos murales hispanos en Sacramento, California

❹ La Misión de San Gabriel en San Gabriel, California

127

1. El centro de Guadalajara, México

2. El parque Chapultepec en la Ciudad de México

3. Tejedoras indias de Oaxaca, México

4. Una máscara antigua de jade hecha por los mayas en Palenque, México

5. Fiesta típica en Guanajuato, México

6. Mercado de frutas en el Yucatán, México

In many parts of Mexico, especially in rural areas, traditional ways of life continue in the present. Even Mexico City, the capital, is a mixture of the ancient and the modern. There, tall skyscrapers stand beside buildings that are many centuries old. Indians dressed in traditional garb, woven by hand, walk by elegant shops offering the latest in European fashions.

128   Viñeta cultural 1

1. Día de mercado en el pueblo de Chichicastenango, Guatemala

2. Las ruinas de Antigua, Guatemala

3. Una ciudad moderna de Guatemala

4. Un puesto de frutas en San José, Costa Rica

While the cities of Central America are the centers of economic and political life, the rural areas are characterized by farming. It is unfortunate that today the region is torn by unrest. One exception is Costa Rica. This small country, which boasts of not having an army, was honored in 1987 when its president, Oscar Arias, was presented with the Nobel Prize for Peace.

In addition to its many picturesque towns, such as Cuzco in Peru, South America has many large cities, among them Caracas, Bogotá, Lima, and Buenos Aires. Caracas is the birthplace of Simón Bolívar, the man most honored and loved in South America. Born of wealthy parents, he grew up determined to free his people of Spanish rule. In 1821, after ten years of war, he finally defeated the Spaniards. He brought independence to four South American countries and was given the title of **El Libertador.**

❶ La playa de Boca Grande en Cartagena, Colombia

❷ La Plaza de Bolívar en Tunja, Colombia

❸ El hermoso puerto de Caraballeda, Venezuela

1. La Catedral de Cuzco, Perú
2. La Plaza de Armas en Lima, Perú
3. Estatua de Francisco Pizarro en Lima, Perú
4. Paredes construidas por los incas en Cuzco, Perú

1. El puerto de Valparaíso, Chile
2. Un jardín hermoso en Viña del Mar, Chile
3. El juego del pato en Buenos Aires, Argentina
4. La Plaza de Mayo y la Casa Rosada en Buenos Aires, Argentina

Argentina and Chile are progressive countries with beautiful modern cities and extensive areas of open land. Both countries have thriving cattle industries, and agriculture plays an important role in their economies. In Chile, the fishing industry is a key source of income. Both countries also have famous resorts, where people from all over the continent come to enjoy vacations and watch traditional sports such as "El pato" and polo.

SEGUNDA PARTE

UNIDAD 5 **En el aeropuerto**
Scope and Sequence

	BASIC MATERIAL	COMMUNICATIVE FUNCTIONS
SECTION A	**¿Dónde está?** (A1) **En información** (A15)	**Exchanging information** • Asking and saying where something is • Asking and giving directions
SECTION B	**¿Adónde van?** (B1) **Conversación por teléfono** (B11) **¡Hay problemas con el teléfono!** (B16)	**Exchanging information** • Asking and saying where people are going **Socializing** • Answering the telephone • Calling someone
SECTION C	**En la sala de espera** (C1)	**Exchanging information** • Asking and saying the purpose of an action **Persuading** • Making suggestions
TRY YOUR SKILLS	Pronunciation (vowels **u** and **i**) Sound-letter correspondences (vowels **u** and **i**) Dictation	
VAMOS A LEER	**En España** (various cities to visit while in Spain) **El regalo** (The secret television tells the future.)	

WRITING   A variety of controlled and open-ended writing activities appear in the Pupil's Edition. The Teacher's Notes identify other activities suitable for writing practice.

COOPERATIVE LEARNING   Many of the activities in the Pupil's Edition lend themselves to cooperative learning. The Teacher's Notes explain some of the many instances where this teaching strategy can be particularly effective. For guidelines on how to use cooperative learning, see page T13.

GRAMMAR	CULTURE	RE-ENTRY
Possessive adjectives (A4) The verb **estar** (A10) The contraction **del** (A19)	The airport in Spanish- speaking countries	Greetings
The verb **ir** (B3) The contraction **al** (B6)	Notes on Spanish history Tourism in Spain Talking on the telephone	Telling time Numbers from 1 to 100
Verbs ending in **-er** and **-ir** (C8)	Barajas Airport in Madrid The city of León	Days of the week Irregular verbs **ir** and **tener**

Recombining communicative functions, grammar, and vocabulary

Reading for practice and pleasure

TEACHER-PREPARED MATERIALS
Section A Travel items, pictures of people
at the airport, school, post office,
cafeteria; list of major Spanish-speaking
cities, world atlas or globe
Section B Toy telephone, pictures of
cities, cutouts of teenagers
Section C Post cards, traveler's check,
stamps, letter, newspaper
Try Your Skills Toy telephone

UNIT RESOURCES
Manual de actividades, Unit 5
Manual de ejercicios, Unit 5
Unit 5 Cassettes
Transparencies 11–13
Quizzes 10–12
Unit 5 Test

5

A1

A

OBJECTIVES **To exchange information:** ask and say where something is, ask and give directions

CULTURAL BACKGROUND Iberia Airline is the largest international airline in Spain. Another airline, Aviaco, provides domestic flights to different cities within the country. One can also travel through Spain by train. The national railway is called **RENFE.** In Spanish, a stewardess is called an **azafata.** This word, which means the queen's lady-in-waiting, comes from the Moors. Another word used in Mexico and other Spanish-speaking countries for a stewardess is **aeromoza.**

Barajas Airport is Spain's largest airport located about twenty miles from Madrid. The next largest airport, Prat, is in Barcelona.

MOTIVATING ACTIVITY Ask the students to research the current rate of exchange in Spain. If Spanish money, **pesetas,** is available, display it in the classroom. The students might also choose a city of interest in Spain and find out information about it. They should report their findings to the class.

A1 ¿Dónde está?

Before presenting the dialog, you may wish to illustrate the use of the possessive adjectives by acting out situations: display a pencil that belongs to you and say **Es mi lápiz.** Then pick up a notebook from a student's desk and say **Es tu cuaderno.** Finally point to a book on another student's desk and say **Es su libro.** Continue this procedure using other objects and have the students repeat after you. You may wish to ask the students questions and have them respond.

TEACHER ¿Es tu libro?
CARLOTA Sí, es mi libro.
TEACHER ¿Es tu cuaderno?
EDMUNDO No, no es mi cuaderno. Es su cuaderno.

To present the new vocabulary, bring to class travel items, such as a suitcase, camera, map, dictionary, and passport. Identify each item and ask the students to repeat.

You may wish to prepare signs designating different sections of an airport, such as **Aduana, Sección de equipaje,** or **Inmigración,** and, if possible, to get pictures of Barajas airport. Now play the cassette or read aloud the dialog. Then have the students role-play parts of the dialog at designated places in the classroom.

To check comprehension, prepare a series of guiding questions to be answered briefly as the students listen to the dialog. Have them write the answers as they listen. You may repeat the dialog for the students who were unable to answer the questions the first time.

¿Quiénes llegan a Madrid? *un grupo (unos) estudiantes*
¿De dónde son los estudiantes? *(de) Boston*
¿Cómo se llama el aeropuerto? *Barajas*
¿Cuál es el número del vuelo? *321*
¿A cuál sección van primero? *a la sección de equipaje*
¿Qué necesitan para las maletas? *(un) carro*
¿Dónde está la cámara de Alicia? *en la cartera*
¿Dónde está el diccionario? *en el asiento del avión*
¿Dónde está el pasaporte de Alicia? *en el bolsillo*

SLOWER-PACED LEARNING Have the students role-play two or three lines of the dialog at a time.

A2 Actividad • ¿Es cierto o no?

Prior to the activity, have the students make up their own true or false statements to challenge their classmates: **Los estudiantes entran por la puerta 23. Necesitan un avión para las maletas.**

A3 Actividad • Combinación

For cooperative learning, have pairs of students complete the activity. Each pair must see how many sentences they can form by using an element from each column. They will have five minutes. Then call on each pair to dictate the sentences as you or a volunteer write them on the board or a transparency. This may also be used as a homework assignment.

A4 ESTRUCTURAS ESENCIALES

Write the following or similar examples on the board or a transparency.

> Tú y él van a la playa el domingo.
> ¿Dónde está tu amigo?

Stress the difference between **tú** and **tu.** Point out that the possessive adjective **tu** does not have a written accent like the subject pronoun. Have the students read and study the explanation about possessive adjectives. Call on individuals to form a sentence, using one of the possessive adjectives listed in the chart.

For further practice, you may wish to collect items that belong to various students. Ask a student: **¿Es tu cuaderno?** He or she should reply **No, no es mi cuaderno** or **Sí, es mi cuaderno.**

A5 Actividad • Maletas, maletas . . .

Have the students choose a partner to complete this oral activity. They should each take turns forming sentences with the correct possessive adjective.

A6 SE DICE ASÍ

Read aloud the information in the chart as the students follow along in their books. Explain that **¿Dónde está?** is used to ask where something is and **está** is used in the response.

A7 Actividad • Y ahora tú

Have the students find a partner and choose at least five personal or classroom objects. Tell them to try to include at least three items from those mentioned in the dialog. They may also use pictures from magazines if the items are too large or not available. Assign areas of the classroom to each pair of students. One student should place an object within the assigned area and ask his or her partner where it is located. The other student must answer using possessive adjectives. Have them take turns asking the questions and giving the location of each object.

A8 Actividad • ¡A escribir!

Have the students complete this activity in class or at home. Call on volunteers to dictate their sentences as you write them on the board or a transparency. Have the students exchange papers and correct each other's work.

UNIDAD 5

A9–12

A9 ¿Sabes que . . . ?

You may wish to explain to the students that passports are required when traveling overseas. Also, a visa is needed to enter most countries; it is stamped inside the passport. To obtain a visa, many people must go to the nearest embassy or consulate of the particular country they wish to visit. In many countries, citizens of the United States are given a visa upon arrival in the country. No previous paperwork or documentation is needed, unless the person wishes to remain in the country for a long period of time to study or work. You may wish to mention that a visa is **un visado** in Spanish.

A10 ESTRUCTURAS ESENCIALES

Use pictures to introduce the verb **estar.** Show each picture and say where the person is: **Ella está en la escuela.** Then read the explanation aloud of the verb **estar** as the students follow along in their books.

Re-enter the expression **¿Cómo está?** and the various responses learned in Unit 2. Do a brief individualized question/answer drill: **Yo estoy muy bien. ¿Cómo está Ud.? ¿Y Uds.? ¿Y ella?** and so on. Reinforce the use of the verb **estar** to express location by showing the pictures of people at the airport, cafeteria, school, and so on. Now ask the students to say where each person is located. **Él está en el aeropuerto.**

A11 Comprensión

You will hear five short conversations. For each one, decide which of the words or expressions listed best describes what is being discussed. For example, you hear: **No está en la puerta ocho** and the response: **No, está en la puerta nueve.** The expression that best describes what they're talking about is **el vuelo 321.** That is why the check mark is placed in the row next to **el vuelo 321.**

1. —¿Están aquí?
   —No, no están en la tienda.
   —Están allí.   *los teléfonos*
2. —Ya estoy aquí.
   —¿Aquí? ¿Dónde?
   —Estoy en el aeropuerto.   *yo*
3. —¿No está en tu cartera?
   —¿Y en tu bolsillo?
   —No, ¡está en el asiento del avión!   *tu pasaporte*
4. —¡Alberto! ¿Dónde estás?
   —En Madrid.
   —¡Estás en Madrid!   *tú*
5. —Sí, en el aeropuerto.
   —¿En qué aeropuerto?
   —Estamos en Barajas.   *nosotros*

Now check your answers. *Read each exchange again and give the correct answer.*

A12 Actividad • Falta algo

SLOWER-PACED LEARNING Have the students write the conversation and fill in the blanks with the correct form of the verb **estar.** After you have cor-

rected their work and the students have read the conversation aloud, call on pairs of students to role-play the dialog.

CHALLENGE Ask the students to complete the activity orally. Then call on pairs of students to role-play the telephone conversation.

A 13 Conversación

Have the students complete this activity with a partner. Each student should take turns asking for the information and providing the location of each object or person.

CHALLENGE You may wish to provide a list of major cities in Spanish-speaking countries. Have the students work with a partner, using the model in A13 and one of the transparency maps or a world atlas or globe as a guide. They should identify the country where each city is located. After the students have completed the activity, call on individuals to report their findings to the class.

A 14 Actividad • ¡A escribir!

As a variation, after correcting the writing assignment, you may ask the students to get together in pairs and take turns enacting their exchanges.

A 15 SITUACIÓN • En información

Before presenting the dialog, you may wish to teach the directional expressions using real-life classroom situations. Point to different students and objects while you use TPR (Total Physical Response) to illustrate the meaning of the following words. Have the students repeat each word after you.

aquí	arriba
allí	a la izquierda (de)
cerca (de)	a la derecha (de)
lejos (de)	al lado (de)
detrás (de)	abajo
delante (de)	entre

You may follow up with a personalized question/answer drill, while pointing to another student or a classroom object. Call on a volunteer to answer, using the correct directional expression.

—¿Dónde está la puerta?
— Está al lado de la pizarra.

Play the cassette or read the dialog aloud. Have the students follow along in their books as they listen. Then call on volunteers to role-play the dialog.

You may wish to set up an information booth in the classroom where students can practice asking and giving directions.

A 16 Actividad • ¡A escoger!

Supplement this activity by adding questions based on the dialogs. Also, students might make up their own questions and work in pairs, asking their partner the questions.

CHALLENGE The students may wish to make up some true or false statements about the dialogs to be used in a contest between opposing teams: **La cafetería está detrás de la casa de cambio** or **El correo está allá arriba.**

A 17 SE DICE ASÍ

Hide a number of objects in different locations throughout the classroom. Prepare a handout that gives the location of each object without mentioning the name of the object. Pairs of students should use the information on the handout to locate and identify each item. The students who identify the most objects in seven minutes win the game. You may wish to include some sentences such as the following:

1. ____ está detrás de la puerta.
2. ____ están delante de la ventana.
3. ____ está arriba, cerca del libro de matemáticas.

You may wish to teach this well-known toast (**brindis**). Students may use imaginary glasses or bring in juice or water and paper cups to practice the toast. Tell the students: **Vamos a hacer un brindis.** (*Let's make a toast.*)

Arriba, abajo
Al centro, (*touch glasses*)
Adentro (*drink*).

A 18 Actividad • ¡No, está allí!

SLOWER-PACED LEARNING Ask the students to tell where they or others are seated in the classroom in relation to other classmates: **Yo estoy a la derecha de Carolina. David está detrás de Carolina.**

CHALLENGE Begin a chain conversation. The person who starts has lost his or her suitcase and is looking for the baggage claim area.

STUDENT 1   ¿Dónde está mi maleta?
STUDENT 2   Está en la sección de equipaje.
STUDENT 3   ¿Dónde está la sección de equipaje?
STUDENT 4   Está detrás de la aduana.
STUDENT 5   ¿Dónde está la aduana?

A 19 ESTRUCTURAS ESENCIALES

Present the contraction **del** with examples illustrating its use. Write the following models on the board or a transparency.

el teléfono   La maleta está lejos del teléfono.
el libro   El cuaderno está cerca del libro.
la cartera   El dinero está dentro de la cartera.
la cafetería   El correo está detrás de la cafetería.

Ask the students to explain what happens in a sentence when the preposition **de** is followed by the definite article **el**. Confirm their hypothesis by reading the explanation in A19.

A 20 Actividad • ¿Está aquí?

You may wish to have the students complete this activity with a partner. Then call on individuals to read their answers aloud.

A 21 Actividad • ¡Información, por favor!

Have the students work in pairs. They should use the illustration in the book as a guide. Have them reverse roles once.

Then call on a few students to work at the information booth in the classroom. Ask the other students to go to the booth and ask for directions of places located in the airport. Have the students take turns asking and giving directions.

OBJECTIVES   **To exchange information:** ask and say where people are going; **to socialize:** answer the telephone, call someone

CULTURAL BACKGROUND   The way that Spanish-speaking people answer the telephone varies from country to country. In Mexico, they pick up the receiver and say **Bueno.** In Spain and other places, they answer by saying **Diga** or **Dígame.** A Venezuelan might say ¡**Aló!** In Argentina, people simply say ¡**Hola!** In other Spanish-speaking countries, they may say **Pronto.**

MOTIVATING ACTIVITY   Have the students practice the different ways of answering the telephone, using toy telephones. They may also have a short conversation using **estar,** as in A12, page 139.

B1

¿Adónde van?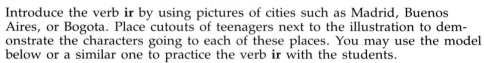

Introduce the verb **ir** by using pictures of cities such as Madrid, Buenos Aires, or Bogota. Place cutouts of teenagers next to the illustration to demonstrate the characters going to each of these places. You may use the model below or a similar one to practice the verb **ir** with the students.

| TEACHER | ¿Adónde va Marta? | TEACHER | ¿Va Marta a Bogotá? |
| JULIA | Marta va a Madrid. | DAVID | No, ella va a Madrid. |

Play the cassette or read aloud as the students follow along in their books. Have them listen carefully and find out where each student in the picture is going.

B2

Preguntas y respuestas

Have the students answer the questions with a partner. Then call on individuals to provide the correct answers. If the students have difficulty answering any of the questions, repeat the dialog and ask them to listen carefully for the correct response.

B3

ESTRUCTURAS ESENCIALES

Write several sentences containing forms of the verb **ir** on the board or a transparency. Call on volunteers to name the irregular forms. Also, ask the students to identify the similarity found in each example. After the students have recognized the preposition **a** in each sentence, point out that this preposition follows the verb **ir** and its usage resembles that of the English preposition *to.* Explain that when the verb **ir** is used in a question, the preposition **a** combines with the interrogative word **dónde** to become **adónde.** Now have the students verify their observations by asking them to open their books and read the information in the chart.

B4

Actividad • Para completar

Have the students choose a partner. They should each take turns reading and supplying the missing forms of the verb **ir.**

SLOWER-PACED LEARNING   Write the sentences on the board or a transparency. Call on volunteers to fill in the blanks with the correct forms of the verb **ir.**

B 5   Actividad • ¿Dónde estamos? ¿Adónde vamos?

Before the students select a classmate to work with, review the prepositions **en** and **a** with the class. Remind the students to use the preposition **a** with the verb **ir** and the preposition **en** with the verb **estar.**

At this point, you may wish to do an individualized question and answer drill:

(*Pointing to a student:*) _____ va a la tienda.
¿Adónde vas tú?
¿y ella? ¿y (*name of a student*)?

You may wish to re-enter the preposition **de** and practice the prepositions **en** and **a.** Ask the students to complete an oral or written drill as follows:

> Él es de México.
> _____ Argentina.
> _____ Caracas.
> _____ Madrid.
> _____ Perú.
> _____ Costa Rica.

SLOWER-PACED LEARNING   Repeat the previous drill with the verb **estar** and the preposition **en: Ellos están en México.** Then repeat the drill again, using the verb **ir** and the preposition **a: Vamos a México.**

B 6   ## ESTRUCTURAS ESENCIALES

Follow the same procedure as mentioned in the Teacher's Notes for A19 to present the contraction **al.** Use examples such as these to illustrate the preposition **a** and its contraction.

> el correo   Vamos al correo.
> la playa   Mario va a la playa.
> el parque   Nicolás va al parque.
> la tienda   Voy a la tienda.

B 7   Actividad • ¡No, no van allí!

Have the students complete the activity with a partner. They should switch roles. Remind them to use the contraction **al** when referring to a masculine noun.

B 8   Actividad • Charla

To re-enter previous vocabulary, have the students give the time of day when asking where their classmates are going.

> ¿Adónde vas a las dos?
> ¿Adónde van por la tarde?

B 9   Actividad • ¿Adónde vas?

For cooperative learning, have the students work in groups of three. They

should talk about where they are going after class, tomorrow, and on Saturday. Have the students ask each other questions about their plans. Each member of the group should make sure that the other members are able to communicate their ideas accurately. Then they should report the information to the class.

B 10 Actividad • ¡A escribir!

Students should complete this activity in class and their paragraphs should consist of at least four sentences. Encourage them to explain why they are planning to do each activity.

SLOWER-PACED LEARNING You may wish to ask the students to write five sentences about places where they go to relax. They should include the time and the day they enjoy going to these places.

> Voy al parque el sábado por la tarde.
> Los domingos siempre vamos a la playa por la mañana.

B 11 SITUACIÓN • Conversación por teléfono

Before presenting the dialog, introduce the regular verbs **llegar, tomar,** and **esperar.** Then ask the following or similar questions to further familiarize the students with the new verbs.

> ¿A qué hora llegas a la escuela?
> ¿Esperan a sus amigos después de las clases?
> ¿Tomas el autobús?

Have the students role-play the dialog using toy telephones. Then read aloud or play the cassette, while the students follow along in their books. Point out that Sr. González uses the informal command form when he tells Brian to wait at the airport (**No, espera allí.**).

SLOWER-PACED LEARNING You may wish to provide the students with a worksheet, to complete as they listen to the dialog. Ask the students to supply the information according to the conversation.
1. Brian llama al Sr. ____.
2. El ____ llega a las diez de la ____.
3. Brian ya ____ en Madrid.
4. Ya son las ____.
5. El Sr. González va por Brian en su ____.

B 12 Preguntas y respuestas

Have the students refer to the dialog in B11 to answer the questions. You may wish to have the students complete the activity with a partner.

ANSWERS:
1. Brian llama por teléfono.
2. Él llama al señor González.
3. El vuelo llega a las diez.
4. Brian ya está en Madrid.
5. Son las once.
6. Brian está en el aeropuerto.
7. Brian no debe tomar un taxi porque el señor González va en su coche al aeropuerto.
8. Va en su coche.

B 13 **Actividad • No es así**

After the students have completed the activity orally in class, for writing practice you may wish to have the students write the corrected statements. Correct the sentences with the entire class.

ANSWERS:
1. Brian llega a Madrid.
2. Brian llega por la mañana.
3. Brian está en el aeropuerto.
4. Él habla con el señor González.
5. El vuelo llega a las diez de la mañana.
6. El señor González está en Madrid.
7. Son las once.
8. El señor González va al aeropuerto dentro de una hora.
9. El señor González va al aeropuerto en coche.
10. El señor González tiene su coche.

B 14 **Actividad • Para completar**

Have the students complete the dialog with a classmate. Then call on volunteers to role-play the telephone conversation for the class.

B 15 **¿Sabes que . . . ?**

You may wish to discuss briefly with the class some of the contributions made to Spanish culture from different groups that populated the peninsula. Spain is a melting pot of different peoples and cultures. Each group left its own imprint on the peninsula. For instance, the Romans constructed roads, public buildings, and aqueducts, such as the one in Segovia. From the Visigoth Kingdoms came magnificent Gothic architecture. The Moors created wonderful gardens and palaces such as **La Alhambra** in Granada. The Spanish language contains many words of Arabic origin, such as **azúcar, algodón, fulano,** and **ojalá.** The Jews also contributed to Spanish culture through outstanding scholars and philosophers, such as **Maimónides.**

B 16 **SITUACIÓN • ¡Hay problemas con el teléfono!**

Before presenting the dialog, introduce the telephone expressions with a toy telephone. Have the students guess the meaning of the new expressions. Then ask the students to follow along in their books as you play the cassette or read aloud.

B 17 **Actividad • Combinación**

Have pairs of students use an element from each column to complete the expression so that it makes sense. Then ask them to make up a short dialog, using at least three expressions from B17. Call on volunteers to present their dialogs to the class.

B 18 **Comprensión**

All these people are making phone calls. After listening to what they say, decide whether the call they are trying to make goes through or not. Put a check mark below the corresponding number only when the words you hear indicate that the call is completed. For example, you hear: **Está ocupado.** You do not place a check mark because the call did not go through.

1. ¿Familia Pérez? (✔)
2. ¡No contestan!
3. ¡Diga! (✔)
4. ¡La comunicación se cortó!
5. Buenas tardes. Habla Carlos. (✔)
6. El señor Rodríguez, por favor. (✔)
7. Habla Carmen, ¿está Pepe? (✔)
8. No contestan.
9. Número equivocado.
10. ¡Hola! ¡Hola! Diga . . .

Now check your answers. *Read each phrase again and give the correct answer.*

B19 SE DICE ASÍ

Generally, in Spanish-speaking countries, the telephone number is given in double-digit numbers rather than in separate digits as in English. For example, if the number is 651–6415, one would say **seis cincuenta y uno, sesenta y cuatro, quince.**

Re-enter the numbers 1 to 100 by having the students practice the following or similar exchanges. Tell them to use the expressions in B19.

—Buenas tardes. Familia González.
—Buenas tardes. ¿Qué número es, por favor?
—525–6980.
—Perdón, número equivocado.

B20 Actividad • Conversaciones por teléfono

Using toy telephones, have pairs of students role-play one of the three situations for the class. Tell the students to use as many expressions as possible.

SECTION
C

OBJECTIVES **To exchange information:** ask and say the purpose of an action; **To persuade:** make suggestions

CULTURAL BACKGROUND You may wish to introduce some gestures commonly used in Spanish-speaking countries. To demonstrate **tener hambre,** rub your stomach with the palm of your hand in a circular motion several times. **Comer** or **comida** is represented by clumping the fingers together lengthwise and bringing them to the mouth. The wrist and forearm are kept still. The gesture used for **beber** is done by pointing the thumb in the direction of one's mouth. The fingers are folded into the palm, except for the smallest finger, which remains straight. Move the arm in an up-and-down motion towards the mouth.

Make students aware that these gestures should not be used in a formal social context.

MOTIVATING ACTIVITY Ask the students to demonstrate common gestures used in the United States. Have them practice the Spanish gestures with a partner. Then tell the students to use the gestures in conversation.

C1 En la sala de espera

Introduce the expressions **tener hambre** and **tener sed** in conjunction with

the verbs **comer** and **beber.** Use actions and gestures to teach the verbs **vender, escribir, subir, comer,** and **beber.**

Use the following sentences to introduce the verb **deber.** Have the students try to guess its meaning from the context clues.

Tengo hambre. Debo comer algo.
No tenemos pesetas. Debemos ir a la casa de cambio.

Also, bring a traveler's check, a post card, stamps, a letter, and a newspaper to class. As the students listen to the dialog, hold up the item as it is mentioned.

For cooperative learning, have the students form groups of four. Each student will play the part of a character in the dialog. Have the students role-play the dialog for the class.

C2 Actividad • Combinación

SLOWER-PACED LEARNING Before completing the activity, ask the following questions to check comprehension of the dialog in C1.

¿Dónde está Brian?
¿Quién tiene hambre?
¿Para qué va a la casa de cambio?
¿Qué venden en la tienda?
¿Dónde venden sellos?
¿Quién tiene el periódico en español?

C3 Actividad • ¡A escoger!

Ask the students to choose a partner and complete the activity. They should complete each sentence according to the dialog in C1.

C4 ¿Sabes que . . . ?

In the southern province of León stands the beautiful city of Salamanca. Its population is about 350,000. **La Universidad de Salamanca** was founded in 1220 and is one of the most famous universities in Spain.

Students may be interested in learning more about the province of León. You may wish to have volunteers research the cities of León and Salamanca. Have them report their findings to the class for extra credit.

C5 SE DICE ASÍ

Using familiar place names, ask the students **¿Va(n) a la cafetería? ¿Para qué?** Students should respond using the preposition **para** and an infinitive: **Para comer.**

Repeat this procedure with various place names. Then read the information found in the chart with the students.

C6 Actividad • Charla

Have the students select a partner and ask each other where they are going and why. They should use each of the places listed in the box at least once.

To re-enter the days of the week, suggest to the students that they include a day of the week with their questions. They may wish to make up their own responses.

> —¿Adónde vas el sábado?
> —Voy a la discoteca.
> —¿Para qué?
> —Para bailar.

For oral practice, you may wish to play a game similar to Jeopardy. Have a student say why he or she is going somewhere, without mentioning the name of the place: **Voy a estudiar.** Another student must name the place: **Vas a la escuela.**

C7 Actividad • ¡A escribir!

After the students complete the writing activity, have them exchange papers. Then call on students to dictate as you or a volunteer writes the sentences on the board or a transparency.

C8 ESTRUCTURAS ESENCIALES

Introduce the **-ir** and **-er** verbs by starting a conversation such as the following:

> TEACHER Yo siempre como en la cafetería.
> ¿Dónde comes tú?
> DIEGO Yo como en casa.
> TEACHER ¿Come él en la cafetería?
> BEATRIZ No, él come en casa.

Copy the chart onto the board or a transparency. Then call on students to point out the similarities and differences of the verbs **comer** and **escribir.** Now write several sentences with other **-er** and **-ir** verbs. Ask the students to find the similarities among these verbs and the verbs in the chart.

> Ellos venden periódicos.
> Carolina come en la cafetería.
> Nosotros debemos escribir cartas.
> Yo bebo algo.

Point out the verb **vender.** Ask the students to identify a word in English that resembles **vender.** Explain that its cognate in English is *vendor.* Tell them that there are similarities in spelling between cognates, but that they are pronounced differently.

C9 Actividad • ¿Qué deciden hacer?

CHALLENGE Tell the students to choose a partner. One student should ask a question, using the cues. Their partner should respond negatively and then correctly state what the person is selling.

> usted / revistas
> —¿Vende usted revistas?
> —No. Vendo periódicos.

C10 · Actividad • ¿Venden o no?

Have pairs of students ask each other the questions in C9. They should answer **Sí** to four questions and **No** to four questions.

C11 · Actividad • ¡A escribir!

After the students have completed the writing activity, collect the papers and correct their work.

As a variation, have the students write eight original sentences with the verbs **comer, escribir,** or **vender.** Call on volunteers to read aloud their sentences.

C12 · Actividad • Combinación

For cooperative learning, have the students form groups of two or three. Give each group five minutes to write as many complete sentences as possible. The group with the most sentences will receive an extra point.

SLOWER-PACED LEARNING   Begin this activity by reviewing with the students the verbs and vocabulary in the box. Make sure they know the meaning of the words before they do the activity.

C13 · Actividad • ¡A escribir!

After completing the writing activity, call on volunteers to read their sentences aloud. Have the students exchange papers to correct their work.

C14 · Actividad • Falta algo

You may wish to review the meanings of these verbs before students complete the activity. Have the students supply the appropriate verb in its correct form for each sentence.

C15 · SE DICE ASÍ

Present a model to the class: **¿Por qué no vamos a la tienda?** Then give possible responses, such as **Sí, buena idea; Gracias, pero tengo que estudiar.** Ask the students to suggest three activities to a classmate. Then read the chart aloud and have the students copy the information in their notebooks.

C16 · Conversación • ¿Por qué no . . . ?

SLOWER-PACED LEARNING   Review with the students the irregular verbs **ir** and **tener.** Use the following or similar sentences and have the students provide the correct form of the verb.

> Yo _____ una pelota.
> Los niños _____ al aeropuerto.
> Nosotros _____ una clase a las ocho.
> ¿ _____ tú a la cafetería?
> Miguel _____ el número de teléfono.

C17 **Comprensión**

You will hear ten short conversations between different people. Put a check mark under the appropriate number only if the second person's reply is appropriate to what the first person is saying. For example, you hear the question: **¿Escribes a casa?** and the response: **Sí, escribo a mi familia.** You write a check mark because the second person's reply is appropriate.

1. —¿Comen algo?
   —Sí, a la tienda.
2. —¿Debes llamar?
   —Sí, aquí tengo el número. (✔)
3. —¿Por qué no subimos?
   —No, ahora no. (✔)
4. —¿Venden postales aquí?
   —A cambiar un cheque.
5. —¿Está en la tienda?
   —Sí, tengo hambre.
6. —¿Tú esperas aquí?
   —A cambiar un cheque.
7. —¿Crees que debemos ir? (✔)
   —Sí, por supuesto. ¡Vamos!
8. —¿Subes a la cafetería?
   —Número equivocado.
9. —¿Por qué no comemos?
   —¿Tú tienes hambre? (✔)
10. —¿Deciden ir o no?
    —No, no vamos. (✔)

Now check your answers. *Read each exchange again and give the correct answer.*

TRY YOUR SKILLS

OBJECTIVE To recombine communicative functions, grammar, and vocabulary

CULTURAL BACKGROUND Mexico City Airport is located near the heart of the city. As you land at the international airport, you feel as if you are landing downtown. There is a variety of shops inside the airport where you can buy souvenirs, books, and food. Transportation to and from the airport includes public buses, the subway, taxis, collective taxis, tour buses, and private bus services provided by major hotels. The price of a taxi may vary greatly, so you must establish the fare with the driver before getting in the car.

MOTIVATING ACTIVITY Have the students role-play in Spanish a situation between a taxi driver in Mexico City and a tourist. The tourist must bargain with the driver for the best price. Model the following or a similar conversation with the class.

—Voy a la Zona Rosa. ¿Cuánto cuesta?
—Doscientos pesos.
—Es mucho dinero. ¿Por qué no cien pesos?
—Ciento cincuenta.
—Muy bien.

Unidad 5 Teacher's Notes T111

1   Pedro espera

Play the cassette or read aloud as the students follow along in their books. For writing practice, as a spot dictation, use a paragraph in which selected words are omitted and ask the students to listen for the missing words.

2   Actividad • Charla

Before beginning the activity, re-enter the following question words: **¿qué?, ¿cuándo?, ¿dónde?, ¿cómo?, ¿por qué?,** and **¿quién?.** Call out one question word at a time and elicit as many answers as possible for each. Then suggest a question word for students to use in a question to a classmate.

3   Actividad • ¡A escribir!

SLOWER-PACED LEARNING   You may wish to write a short conversation on the board or a transparency. Omit several words and have the students supply the missing text. Then call on volunteers to role-play the conversation for the class.

4   Actividad • Conversación telefónica

Have the students work with a partner to complete the telephone conversation. You may wish to refer the students to B14, which they may follow as a model.

5   Actividad • En la aduana

After the students have completed the writing activity, have them read their answers aloud. Collect the papers and correct them.

6   Actividad • ¡Diga!

For cooperative learning, form groups of two. Have the students decide what to say in each situation. Then call on each group to provide the appropriate expressions for the class. Have them role-play the situations using toy telephones.

7   Pronunciación, lectura, dictado

1. Listen carefully and repeat what you hear.
   The sound of **i:** In Spanish, the sound of the vowel **i** is similar to the sound of *ee* in the English word *see,* but is much shorter. Listen and repeat the following words.

        cinco   aquí   información   Cristina   sí

   The sound of **u:** In Spanish the sound of the vowel **u** is similar to the sound of *o* in the English words *to* and *do.* Listen and repeat the following words.

        tú   uno   Lupe   su   azul

2. Listen, and then read aloud.
   Listen to the following and repeat to practice the Spanish sounds **u** and **i.**

escuchar   Perú   gustar   mucho
Allí está Isabel con mi equipaje.
Necesito dinero para ir a Madrid.

3. Write the following sentences from dictation. First listen to the sentence as it is read to you. Then you will hear the sentence again in short segments, with a pause after each segment to allow you time to write. Finally, you will hear the sentence a third time so that you may check your work. Let's begin.

No tengo (*pause*) el número de teléfono (*pause*) de Humberto.
Escribo unas postales (*pause*) a mis amigos americanos.
El día está ideal (*pause*) para jugar tenis (*pause*) con Lucía.

¿LO SABES?

If the students need additional practice giving directions, have them draw the floor plan of an imaginary airport and then write eight to ten sentences describing where things are: **La cafetería está a la derecha de los teléfonos.** They may show the floor plan to a classmate, who will ask where everything is: **¿Dónde están los teléfonos?** The student with the floor plan should then answer: **Los teléfonos están arriba. La cafetería está a la derecha.**

For further practice talking on the telephone, the students might call a friend to discuss where they are going on the weekend. The first time they try to call, the number is busy. The next time they get a wrong number. Finally they reach their friend and the phone is disconnected, so they must call again. Have pairs of students present this situation to the class with toy telephones.

POSSIBLE ANSWERS:
1. La chica va a comer.
2. Yo voy a cambiar pesetas.
3. Ellos van a buscar la maleta.
4. Nosotros vamos a comprar sellos.
5. Alice va a escribir postales.
6. Tú vas a Acapulco en avión.

Have the students complete the activities with a partner. They might practice the expressions **¿Para qué?** and **¿Por qué no . . . ?** by having a conversation discussing three places they are going to go after school. They might mention some of the sports and leisure activities introduced in Unit 3.

ANSWERS:
1. Tengo hambre. Voy a la cafetería.
2. Necesito sellos. Voy al correo.
3. Necesito un diccionario. Voy a la tienda.
4. Salgo para Madrid. Voy al aeropuerto.
5. Quiero ver a Carmen. Voy a la sala de espera.
6. Salgo para Sevilla. Voy a la puerta 8.
7. Mi maleta no está aquí. Voy a la sección de equipaje.

VOCABULARIO

To review vocabulary, you may wish to play a game called **fútbol.** Draw a football field on the board or a transparency. Cut out a football from cardboard, and tape a small magnet on the back. Divide the class into two teams. The first team will start on the twenty-yard line and each player answers in turn. Each time there is a correct answer, the football will be moved ten yards in the direction of the team's goal line until the team gets a touchdown. If a member of the team responds incorrectly, the opposing team gets the football.

Here are a few sample questions you may use to play **fútbol:**
1. The opposite of **arriba** is ____ . *abajo*
2. Voy a comer. Tengo mucha ____ . *hambre*
3. Tengo una carta. Necesito ir al ____ . *correo*
4. El ____ 321 llega en una hora. *vuelo*
5. Madrid está muy ____ . *lejos*

ESTUDIO DE PALABRAS

Have the students work individually and write down their findings. Then correct the papers with the entire class. You may also have the students find items in the vocabulary list that belong to the category of direction words.

VAMOS A LEER

OBJECTIVE   To read for practice and pleasure

EN ESPAÑA

Introduce the reading by pointing out cities on a map of Spain. Allow sufficient time for the students to read the entire selection silently and then play the cassette or read aloud. Next, have the students read one caption at a time. Pause after each caption to check comprehension. Ask questions in Spanish about the content. Accept short answers, since the main object is to read with fluency and comprehension.

Actividad • Combinación

Have the students work with a partner to form sentences from the items in each column. For writing practice, have them write the sentences and exchange papers to check their work.

Actividades

For cooperative learning, have the students form groups of two or three to complete the second activity. Have the groups present the travel brochures to the class and report their findings.

EL REGALO

Before allowing the students to read, make up a matching activity with words from the story. This will help sensitize them to the fact that they can read cognates. Then call on volunteers to review quickly the previous epi-

sodes of **El regalo.** Next have the students read the story silently. You may wish to have the students form cooperative learning groups and present the dialog to the class.

Actividad • Asociaciones

CHALLENGE   Have pairs of students ask at least fourteen questions using the clues. If necessary, write the question words on the board or a transparency for the students to use as a guide. Each student should take turns asking and answering the questions.

SLOWER-PACED LEARNING   Have the students write the questions and exchange papers with another pair of students. Then they should answer one another's questions.

UNIDAD 5
En el aeropuerto

The Hispanic world is immense. Madrid is 3,593 miles from New York and 6,050 miles from Buenos Aires; Buenos Aires is 6,170 miles from Los Angeles! Rugged mountain chains, enormous deserts, and tropical forests in some countries make long trips by land impractical. Travel by air is the solution!

Airports are busy places. People come and go, in a hurry to get to their destination, but how? Where's flight 321? our luggage? the customs office? How do you find where you are supposed to go? You ask!

In this unit you will:

SECTION A	ask where something or someone is, and learn how to give directions
SECTION B	discuss where you and others are going . . . make a telephone call
SECTION C	make suggestions . . . say what people are doing
TRY YOUR SKILLS	use what you've learned
VAMOS A LEER	read for practice and pleasure

SECTION A
asking where something or someone is . . . giving directions

Many American students go to Spain each summer to study Spanish. Most arrive at Barajas, the country's largest airport, just outside Madrid. International airports can seem a bit confusing at first. But once you find your luggage, show your passport, and go through customs, you're on your way to an exciting adventure.

A1 ¿Dónde está?

Un grupo de estudiantes llega a Madrid. Vienen en el vuelo 321 de Boston. Entran por la puerta 9. Están en Barajas, el aeropuerto internacional. Van primero a la sección de equipaje. Necesitan un carro para las maletas. Después, a la aduana. ¡Ya está todo! ¿Y ahora? ¡A cambiar de avión o a buscar un taxi!

ADUANA
CUSTOMS
DOUANE

BRIAN   ¡Oh! Mi maleta no está. ¿Dónde está mi maleta?
ALICE   ¿Tu maleta? Allí está.
BRIAN   ¡Qué suerte! ¿Tienes tu cámara?
ALICE   Sí, está en mi cartera. Pero, ¿dónde está mi diccionario de español? ¿Y mi mapa?
BRIAN   ¿Tu diccionario? No sé. ¿No está aquí?
ALICE   No. ¡Está con el mapa en el asiento del avión!

ADUANERO   Su pasaporte, por favor.
ALICE   Está en el bolsillo. Aquí tiene, señor.
ADUANERO   Muchas gracias.
ALICE   De nada.

1. Un grupo de estudiantes llega a Madrid. 2. Vienen en el vuelo 321 de Boston. 3. Es cierto. 4. Van primero a la sección de equipaje. 5. Necesitan

A2 Actividad • ¿Es cierto o no?

Correct these sentences to make them agree with the dialog. Some of them are correct already.

1. Un grupo de profesores llega a Madrid.
2. Vienen en el vuelo 321 de San Francisco.
3. Están en Barajas, el aeropuerto de Madrid.
4. Van primero a la aduana.
5. Necesitan un taxi para las maletas.
6. Después, van a la sección de equipaje.
7. La maleta está allí. ¡Qué pena!
8. La cartera de Alice está en la cámara.
9. El diccionario está en el asiento del avión.
10. El pasaporte de Alice está en el avión.

un carro para las maletas. 6. Después, van a la aduana. 7. La maleta está allí. ¡Qué suerte! 8. La cámara está en la cartera de Alice. 9. Es cierto. 10. El pasaporte está en el bolsillo de Alice.

Actividad • Combinación Answers will vary. Ex: La maleta de Brian está aquí.

Let's see how many sentences you can form in five minutes, using an element from each column.

La maleta de Brian La cámara El diccionario El pasaporte El mapa	está no está	aquí. en el bolsillo. en la cartera. en el asiento. allí.

A4 ESTRUCTURAS ESENCIALES You may wish to indicate that "su" may be ambiguous, and that
Possessive adjectives special phrases to clarify it will be presented later.

Possessive adjectives (*my, your, his, her, its . . .*) always precede the nouns they introduce, and are never given vocal emphasis like in English. They agree in number with the noun they modify.

yo → mi	tú → tu	usted, él, ella → su
Mi maleta está aquí. *My suitcase is here.*	**Tu** maleta está aquí. *Your suitcase is here.*	**Su** maleta está aquí. *Your (His, Her) suitcase is here.*

Note that the possessive **tu** does not have a written accent like the subject pronoun **tú**. You will learn the plural forms of possessive adjectives in Unit 6.

A5 Actividad • Maletas, maletas . . .   6. Yo tengo una maleta. Mi maleta está allí.
7. Brian tiene una maleta. Su maleta está allí.

Help the group leader find out how many suitcases the group has and where they are. Say that each person has one and that it's there.

> Eduardo ——Eduardo tiene una maleta.
> Su maleta está allí.

él Ana usted ella tú yo Brian

1. Él tiene una maleta. Su maleta está allí. 2. Ana tiene una maleta. Su maleta está allí. 3. Usted tiene una maleta. Su maleta está allí. 4. Ella tiene una maleta. Su maleta está allí. 5. Tú tienes una maleta. Tu maleta está allí.

A6 SE DICE ASÍ
Asking and saying where something is

¿Dónde está mi pasaporte? Where's my passport?	Está en tu bolsillo. It's in your pocket.

En el aeropuerto 137

Each student will create his or her own dialog.

You can't find anything that belongs to you! A friend helps you find what you're looking for. Prepare a list of the items you can't find. (Take turns with a partner.)

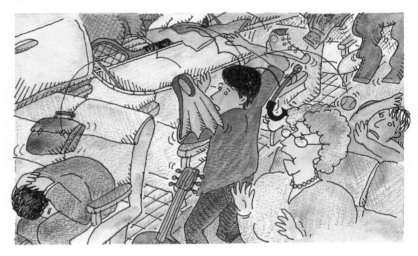

—¿Dónde está mi cartera?
—¿Tu cartera? Está aquí.

Ex:—¿Dónde está tu maleta?
　　—¿Mi maleta? Está en el asiento.

¿mi . . . ?
¿tu . . . ?

está . . .

maleta　**cámara**
diccionario　**mapa**
pasaporte　**equipaje**

allí　**bolsillo**　**maleta**
asiento　**aquí**　**cartera**

1. ¿Tiene Ud. una maleta?
   ¿Donde está su maleta?

2. ¿Tiene Brian una cámara?
   ¿Dónde está su cámara?

3. ¿Tienes tú un mapa?
   ¿Dónde está tu mapa?
4. ¿Tiene Ud. el equipaje?
   ¿Dónde está su equipaje?

A8   Actividad • ¡A escribir!

The group of students is at Barajas airport in Madrid, Spain. Ask them in writing where their belongings are. Follow the model.

Alicia / pasaporte
—¿Tiene Alicia el pasaporte?
—¿Dónde está su pasaporte?

5. ¿Tengo yo un diccionario?
   ¿Dónde está mi diccionario?

6. ¿Tiene Alicia una cartera?
   ¿Dónde está su cartera?
7. ¿Tiene Brian un carro?
   ¿Dónde está su carro?
8. ¿Tengo yo una revista?
   ¿Dónde está mi revista?

1. usted / maleta
2. Brian / cámara
3. tú / mapa
4. el señor / equipaje

5. yo / diccionario
6. Alicia / cartera
7. Brian / carro
8. yo / revista

A9   ¿Sabes que . . . ?

After your plane has landed in a Spanish-speaking country, you first go to the **Control de pasaportes.** An officer checks your passport to see if everything is in order. Then you proceed to **la aduana,** *customs.* There you find your baggage and stand by it while a customs officer examines what you have. If you are bringing in new articles not for your own use, you may have to pay import duties.

A 10 ESTRUCTURAS ESENCIALES
The verb estar

Here are the present-tense forms of **estar,** a second Spanish equivalent for the English verb *to be.* (You saw the present tense forms of **ser,** another equivalent, in Unit 1.)

estar *to be*					
Yo	**estoy**	aquí.	Nosotros (as)	**estamos**	en el avión.
Tú	**estás**	en el aeropuerto.	Vosotros (as)	**estáis**	en Madrid.
Usted/él/ella	**está**	en España.	Ustedes/ellos (as)	**están**	en la tienda.

1. Estar is used to express location.

   Estoy en el aeropuerto.

2. Estar is also used to indicate how someone is feeling.

   —¿Cómo **estás?** —**Estoy** bien, gracias.

For script and answers, see p. T100.

A 11 Comprensión

Which is the best description?

	0	1	2	3	4	5
Nosotros						✓
Tu pasaporte				✓		
Los teléfonos		✓				
Tú					✓	
El vuelo 321	✓					
Yo			✓			

INFORMACION
AEROPUERTO DE MADRID

Conexión Vuelos Nacionales
Domestic Connecting Flights

Teléfono
Phone

A 12 Actividad • Falta algo

Complete this phone conversation using **estar.**

   —¿Cómo estás tú?
   —Muy bien, ¿y tú?
   —Yo estoy bien también pero, ¿dónde estás tú, en Madrid?
   —Sí, aquí estoy . Alice está aquí también.
   —¡Alice está aquí! ¿Cómo está ella?
estamos —Bien. Nosotros ____ en España por el verano.
   —¿Están los chicos allí?
   —No, están en los EE.UU.
   —¡Qué suerte! ¿Están ellos bien? ¿Dónde están ?
   —Carlos está en Texas, y Luisa está en California. Ellos están allí hasta septiembre.

En el aeropuerto 139

Conversación Answers will vary.

¿Dónde están? Ask a classmate where the persons, places, and things included in the box at the left are. Possible answers are listed in the box at the right. Then switch roles.

—¿Dónde está Madrid?
—Está en España.

la maleta	ella
tú	el equipaje
el aduanero	los chicos
el pasaporte	la aduana
yo	el avión
Madrid	nosotros
ustedes	

en mi cartera	en la aduana
aquí	en el taxi
en la puerta	en el aeropuerto
en España	en Madrid
en el avión	en los Estados Unidos
en el bolsillo	

A 14 **Actividad • ¡A escribir!** Each student will create his or her own project.

Make a phone call. The person you called wants to know where you and your friends are and how you are feeling. Write down three questions and your answers using a form of **estar** in all of them.

Ex. 1. —¿Dónde están ustedes?
—Estamos en el aeropuerto
—¿Cómo están?
—Estamos muy bien.
—¿Dónde está Alicia?
—Alicia está en Texas.

A 15 **SITUACIÓN • En información**

Brian y Alice están en información. Tienen muchas preguntas.

aquí allí
cerca (de)
entre
lejos (de)
detrás (de)
delante (de)

BRIAN	Señorita, por favor, ¿dónde está la cafetería?
EMPLEADA	La cafetería está allí arriba. ¿Tienen ustedes pesetas?
ALICE	No, señorita. Tenemos cheques de viajero.
EMPLEADA	La casa de cambio está detrás de ustedes, a la izquierda.

BRIAN	¿Y el correo?
EMPLEADA	Abajo, al lado de los teléfonos y los baños.
ALICE	¿Hay una tienda cerca de aquí?
EMPLEADA	Sí, señorita, la tienda del aeropuerto está a la derecha.
ALICE	Muchas gracias, señorita.

A 16 Actividad • ¡A escoger!

Choose the best option to complete each sentence according to the information given in A15.

1. Brian y Alice están en
   • la sección de equipaje.   • la aduana.   • información.
2. Ellos tienen muchas
   • preguntas.   • pesetas.   • maletas.
3. La cafetería está
   • allí abajo.   • allí arriba.   • a la izquierda.
4. La casa de cambio está
   • a la derecha.   • a la izquierda.   • allí arriba.
5. El correo está
   • abajo.   • arriba.   • detrás.
6. El correo está
   • al lado de la tienda.   • al lado de la cafetería.   • al lado de los teléfonos.
7. ¿Hay una tienda
   • cerca de aquí?   • aquí detrás?   • al lado?
8. La tienda del aeropuerto está
   • a la izquierda.   • a la derecha.   • detrás de ustedes.

A 17 SE DICE ASÍ
Asking and giving directions

	¿Dónde está(n) . . . ?	Abajo.
	¿Está(n) cerca de aquí?	No, está(n) lejos.

You can use a form of **estar** and a location expression such as **lejos,** *far,* to ask or give directions.

A 18 Actividad • ¡No, está allí!

Help these confused passengers find the places they are looking for. Things are just the opposite of what they thought. Work with a partner.

—La aduana, ¿está aquí?
—No, está allí.

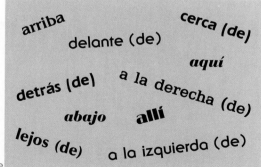

arriba   cerca (de)   delante (de)   aquí   detrás (de)   a la derecha (de)   abajo   allí   lejos (de)   a la izquierda (de)

1. La casa de cambio, ¿está arriba?   No, está abajo.
2. La tienda del aeropuerto, ¿está detrás?   No, está delante.
3. El teléfono, ¿está allí?   No, está aquí.
4. La cafetería, ¿está a la izquierda?   No, está a la derecha.
5. El correo, ¿está cerca?   No, está lejos.
6. El baño, ¿está abajo?   No, está arriba.
7. La sección de equipaje, ¿está delante de la aduana?   No, está detrás de la aduana.
8. Madrid, ¿está lejos?   No, está cerca.
9. Mi maleta, ¿está aquí?   No, está allí.
10. La puerta 11, ¿está a la derecha?
11. Los carros, ¿están detrás de nosotros?
12. Los taxis, ¿están cerca?

10. No, está a la izquierda.
11. No, están delante.   **En el aeropuerto**   **141**
12. No, están lejos.

ESTRUCTURAS ESENCIALES
The contraction **del**

When the preposition **de** is followed by the definite article **el,** the two contract to form the word **del.**

de	+	el	→	del
delante **de**	+	**el** teléfono	→	delante **del** teléfono *in front of the telephone*

1. **De** does not contract with the articles **la, los, las,** or with the pronoun **él.**

2. If **el** is part of a name, pronounce the contraction but don't write it.

Elena es **de El** Salvador.

A 20   Actividad • ¿Está aquí?

It's landing time. The passengers are gathering their belongings. Answer using the cues.

—¿Mi pasaporte?   Al lado / diccionario
—¿Mi pasaporte?—Está al lado del diccionario.

5. Están al lado del mapa.   6. Está cerca de las revistas.
7. Está lejos del asiento.   8. Está detrás del asiento.

1. —¿La maleta?   en / asiento
2. —¿Mi cámara?   detrás / maleta
3. —¿Tu cartera?   a la derecha / cámara
4. —¿El diccionario?   al lado / pasaporte

5. —¿Las revistas?   al lado / mapa
6. —¿El mapa?   cerca de / revistas
7. —¿El equipaje?   lejos de / asiento
8. —¿Tu guitarra?   detrás / asiento

1. Está en el asiento.   2. Está detrás de la maleta.   3. Está a la derecha de la cámara.   4. Está al lado del pasaporte.

A 21   Actividad • ¡Información, por favor!   Answers will vary.

You work at the information booth of a Spanish airport. A passenger asks you for directions. Basing your answers on the floor plan, explain where everything is.

tienda   —Señor (Señorita), ¿la tienda, por favor?
            —La tienda está arriba, a la derecha, al lado de la cafetería.

asking and saying where people are going . . . making a
telephone call

Spain, a country with 38 million citizens, received more than 38 million visitors in 1983—tourists, students, business people, and others. Many travel in large groups. The group's guide has to keep track of everyone, or the group won't ever be ready to proceed with its visit.

B1

¿Adónde van?

El profesor quiere saber adónde van los estudiantes.
¡Es muy difícil! Todos van a lugares diferentes.

B2 Preguntas y respuestas   *Questions and answers*

1. ¿Dónde están el profesor y los estudiantes?
2. ¿Adónde va Alicia?
3. ¿Quién va a la casa de cambio?
4. ¿Quién va a la cafetería?

5. ¿Adónde van George y Mary?
6. ¿Adónde va Brian?
7. ¿Quién va al baño?
8. ¿Va el profesor con los estudiantes?

1. Están en el aeropuerto. 2. Alice va a la casa de cambio. 3. Alice va a la casa de cambio.
4. Brian va a la cafetería. 5. Van a la tienda a comprar algo. 6. Brian va a la cafetería.
7. Gloria va al baño. 8. Sí, el profesor va con los estudiantes.   **En el aeropuerto**   **143**

The verb ir

This is one of the most useful verbs in Spanish. Its present-tense forms are irregular.

ir	*to go*				
Yo	**voy**	a la tienda.	Nosotros(as)	**vamos**	al aeropuerto.
Tú	**vas**	al correo.	Vosotros(as)	**váis**	a Barcelona.
Usted, él, ella	**va**	allí.	Ustedes, ellos(as)	**van**	a la aduana.

B4 Actividad • Para completar

Supply the missing forms of **ir.**

El profesor y los siete estudiantes no __van__ a
Madrid ahora. ¡No, señor! Están en el
aeropuerto en Boston. El profesor __va__
primero a la cafetería. Después __va__ a la
tienda a comprar algo. Brian __va__ a la tienda
también. Jennifer y yo __vamos__ a la sección de
equipaje.

—Tú __vas__ a la casa de cambio, ¿no?
—¿Ustedes __van__ a la cafetería primero?
—¡Estupendo!
—Pero, ¿por qué no __van__ ustedes a la casa
   de cambio después?

After B4, you may want to do a personalized question/answer drill, addressing a student. "¿Dónde vas a comer?" "Voy a comer en
la cafetería".

B5 Actividad • ¿Dónde estamos? ¿Adónde vamos?

Your classmate is impatient. Reply that the people mentioned will go there later.

     ¿Estamos en Madrid?
     —No, vamos a Madrid después.

1. ¿Está el avión en España?
2. ¿Está Alice en la cafetería?
3. ¿Están Brian y Jennifer en la tienda?
4. ¿Está el aduanero en la aduana?

5. ¿Están ustedes en la sección de equipaje?
6. ¿Estás tú en el correo?
7. ¿Estamos en la casa de cambio?
8. ¿Están ellos allí?

1. No, va a España después. 2. No, Alice va después. 3. No, van a la tienda después. 4. No, va a la
aduana después. 5. No, vamos a la sección de equipaje después. 6. No, voy al correo después. 7. No,
vamos a la casa de cambio después. 8. No, van allí después.

ESTRUCTURAS ESENCIALES
The contraction al

The preposition **a** contracts with the definite article **el** to form the word **al**.

a	+	el	→	al	
a	+	**el** aeropuerto	→	**al** aeropuerto	*to the airport*

1. The preposition **a** does not contract with **la, las, los**, or with the pronoun **él**.

2. If the **el** is part of a name, pronounce the contraction but don't write it.

      Elena va **a El** Salvador.

B 7   Actividad • ¡No, no van allí!

Say that the people mentioned don't go to the places suggested but to the places indicated in parentheses.

    ¿Vas a la tienda? (baño)
    —No, voy al baño.

1. No, van al aeropuerto.
2. No, van primero a la cafetería.
3. No, va al baño.
4. No, va a la puerta 7.
No, vamos a la aduana.

1. ¿Van los chicos a la escuela? (aeropuerto)
2. ¿Van primero a la casa de cambio? (cafetería)
3. ¿Va Gloria a la tienda? (baño)
4. ¿Va el profesor a la puerta 9? (puerta 7)
5. ¿Van ustedes al baño? (aduana)
6. ¿Va el profesor al avión? (sección de equipaje) No, va a la sección de equipaje.
7. ¿Vas a la aduana? (casa de cambio)
8. ¿Vamos a México? (Madrid)

7. No, voy a la casa de cambio. 8. No, vamos a Madrid.

B 8   Actividad • Charla

1. ¿Adónde va Pedro? 2. ¿Adónde vamos?
Va a Madrid.   Vamos a la casa de cambio.

Ask a classmate where these people are going. Your classmate should respond as indicated.

    ustedes / cafetería
    —¿Adónde van?
    —Vamos a la cafetería.

    tú / tienda
    —¿Adónde vas?
    —Voy a la tienda.

3. ¿Adónde van los chicos?
Van al baño.

4. ¿Adónde va el taxi?
Va al aeropuerto.

1. Pedro / Madrid
2. nosotros / casa de cambio
3. los chicos / baño
4. taxi / aeropuerto
5. Alice y Brian / sección de equipaje
6. tú / cafetería
7. ustedes / avión
8. usted / puerta cinco

5. ¿Adónde van Alice y Brian?
Van a la sección de equipaje.
6. ¿Adónde vas?
Voy a la cafetería.
7. ¿Adónde van?
Vamos al avión.
8. ¿Adónde va?
Voy a la puerta cinco.

B 9   Actividad • ¿Adónde vas?

Talk to your classmates about where you are going after class, tomorrow, and on Saturday . . . Answers will vary. Ex: —¿Adónde vas mañana?
—Voy al aeropuerto.

B 10   Actividad • ¡A escribir! Answers will vary.

Write a brief paragraph about what you are going to do next Saturday.

Brian llama por teléfono al señor González. ¡Hay un problema!

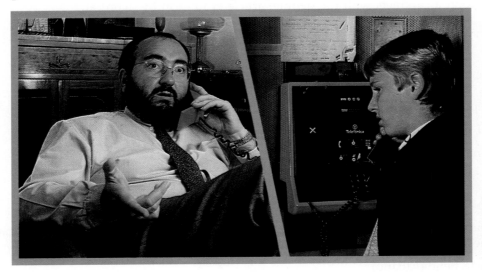

Sr. González	¡Diga!
Brian	Hola. ¿El señor González, por favor?
Sr. González	Sí, soy yo. ¿Quién habla?
Brian	Brian Conally.
Sr. González	¡Brian! ¿Dónde estás? Tu vuelo llega a las diez de la noche, ¿verdad?
Brian	Bueno, sí y no. El vuelo llega a las diez, pero de la mañana, no de la noche.
Sr. González	¿Entonces llegas mañana?
Brian	No, ya estoy en Madrid.
Sr. González	¡Qué confusión! ¡Y son las once!
Brian	¿Debo tomar un taxi?
Sr. González	No, espera allí. Yo voy en mi coche al aeropuerto. Estoy allí dentro de una hora.
Brian	Gracias, señor. Hasta luego.
Sr. González	Adiós, Brian.

B12 Preguntas y respuestas   For answers, see p. T105.

Answer the questions according to **Conversación por teléfono.**

1. ¿Quién llama por teléfono?
2. ¿A quién llama él?
3. ¿A qué hora llega el vuelo?
4. ¿Llega Brian mañana?
5. ¿Qué hora es?
6. ¿Dónde está Brian?
7. ¿Debe Brian tomar un taxi? ¿Por qué?
8. ¿Cómo va el señor González al aeropuerto?

B13 Actividad • No es así   For answers, see p. T106.

Correct the following statements to make them true according to B11.

1. Brian llega a Boston.
2. Brian llega mañana.
3. Brian está en la cafetería.
4. Él habla con Jennifer.
5. El vuelo llega a las diez de la noche.
6. El señor González no está en Madrid.
7. Son las doce.
8. El señor González va al aeropuerto dentro de dos horas.
9. El señor González va al aeropuerto en metro.
10. El señor González no tiene coche.

Actividad • Para completar

George is in Madrid, and he phones Gloria. Complete their conversation using B11 as a model.

GLORIA   ¡Diga!
GEORGE   Buenas tardes. ¿La señorita González, _____ ? por favor
GLORIA   Sí, ella está . ¿ Quién es?
GEORGE   George Ojeda, tu amigo de Boston.
GLORIA   ¡George! ¿ Dónde estás? ¿En Madrid?
GEORGE   Sí, estoy en el aeropuerto. ¿Debo tomar el autobús para tu casa?
GLORIA   No, voy en mi bicicleta. Estoy allí en tres horas.
GEORGE   ¿Tres horas? ¿Con tu _____ ? bicicleta
GLORIA   Sí. Es una bicicleta para dos. ¿Tienes muchas _____ ? maletas
GEORGE   Debo tomar el vuelo 322 para Boston, Gloria. ¡Adiós!

B 15   ¿Sabes que . . . ?

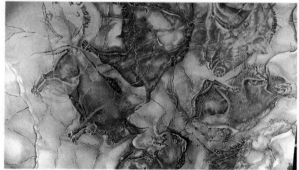

Spain has a very long history. Cave paintings in the north date from 25,000 B.C. The Romans arrived in 218 B.C. and ruled for seven centuries. In A.D. 409, Germanic tribes invaded the country from the north and conquered Spain from the Romans. In 711, Moslem invaders from North Africa entered the south and occupied almost all of Spain. Wars between northern Catholic and southern Moslem kingdoms continued off and on until 1492. In that year—the same year that Columbus discovered the New World—the troops of King Ferdinand and Queen Isabella drove the last Moslem forces from the Peninsula. The modern period of Spanish history had begun.

B 16   SITUACIÓN • ¡Hay problemas con el teléfono!

Join the elements in the two columns so that they make sense.

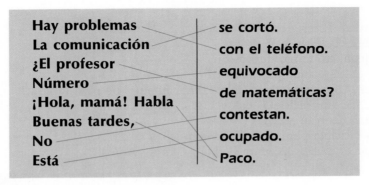

Hay problemas	**se cortó.**
La comunicación	**con el teléfono.**
¿El profesor	**equivocado**
Número	**de matemáticas?**
¡Hola, mamá! Habla	**contestan.**
Buenas tardes,	**ocupado.**
No	**Paco.**
Está	

B 18   **Comprensión**   For script and answers, see pp. T106–107.

Does the call go through?

0	1	2	3	4	5	6	7	8	9	10
	✔		✔		✔	✔	✔			

B 19   **SE DICE ASÍ**
Answering the telephone, calling someone

The person answering says	¡Diga! ¡Hola! ¡Aló! Buenas tardes, familia González.
The person calling responds	Buenas tardes. ¿El señor González, por favor?

Many short phrases may be used to begin telephone conversations. **Adiós** or **chao** is often used to say goodbye. In Mexico, persons answering often say **¿Bueno?**

B 20   **Actividad • Conversaciones por teléfono**
Each student will create his or her own dialog.
You're talking to a friend on the phone. Use as many expressions as you can. Work with a partner.

1. You call your friend and ask for another friend's telephone number.
2. Your friend calls you from a pay phone. You want to know if he/she is near where you are or far away.
3. You call a friend after arriving in Madrid. You'll wait at the airport in the cafeteria that is to the left of customs.

¡Hola!   Buenas noches,   ¡Diga!   Buenos días,   ¡Aló!   Buenas tardes   ¿Bueno?   ¿Sí?

making suggestions . . . saying what people are doing

At the Barajas airport, in Madrid, Chicago's O'Hare airport, or any other international airport, if you're not rushing to catch a plane, chances are you're waiting for a connecting flight. Can you suggest something to do while you wait?

En la sala de espera 📼

Brian está en el aeropuerto de Barajas en Madrid. Alice y otros estudiantes del grupo esperan la llegada del vuelo para ir a León. Deben esperar una hora. ¿Qué deciden hacer?

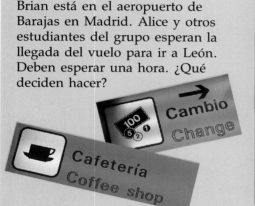

BRIAN	¡Tengo mucha hambre! ¿Por qué no subimos a la cafetería a comer y beber algo?
ALICE	¡Estupendo! Pero primero, creo que debemos ir a la casa de cambio.
BRIAN	¿Para qué?
ALICE	Para cambiar un cheque de viajero. ¿Tú vienes, Jennifer?
JENNIFER	No, yo ya tengo pesetas.
MARK	¿Por qué no escribes a casa? Venden postales en la tienda y sellos en el correo.
JENNIFER	¿Una carta a mi familia? Ahora, no. Yo espero aquí. Tengo el periódico de hoy en español.
MARK	Yo no tengo el periódico. ¡Chao!

Actividad • Combinación

Let's see how many sentences you can form by matching the items on the left with those on the right so that they make sense according to the dialog.

Los chicos esperan	un cheque de viajero.
Brian y Alice suben	una carta a su familia.
Primero deben ir	de hoy en español.
Deben cambiar	en el correo.
Jennifer ya	a la cafetería.
Venden sellos	la llegada del vuelo.
Jennifer no escribe	a la casa de cambio.
Ella tiene el periódico	tiene pesetas.

Actividad • ¡A escoger!

Choose the best option to complete each sentence according to the dialog in C1.

1. Brian, Alice y cuatro estudiantes más están en
   • <u>la sala de espera.</u> • la cafetería. • la tienda.
2. Los chicos esperan
   • un cheque de viajero. • <u>el vuelo para ir a León.</u> • postales de su familia.
3. Ellos deben esperar
   • a cuatro estudiantes más. • <u>una hora.</u> • el periódico de hoy.
4. Alice necesita cambiar
   • <u>un cheque de viajero.</u> • sellos en el correo. • pesetas.
5. Brian tiene
   • un cheque de viajero. • sellos. • <u>mucha hambre.</u>
6. Jennifer decide
   • <u>esperar allí.</u> • subir a la cafetería. • ir a la tienda.
7. Ella tiene
   • mucha hambre. • <u>el periódico.</u> • postales.
8. Mark no tiene
   • postales. • sellos. • <u>el periódico en español.</u>

C4 ¿Sabes que . . . ?

The city of León, founded by the Romans, is now an industrial and scientific center in northern Spain. Its gothic cathedral is one of the glories of European architecture. Besides its beautiful cities, churches, and museums, Spain has spectacular mountains, rich agricultural lands, and some of the finest beaches in Europe.

C5 SE DICE ASÍ
Asking and saying the purpose of an action

| ¿Vas a la tienda? ¿Para qué? | Para comprar algo. |
| You're going to the store? What for? | In order to buy something. |

When you want to ask the purpose of an action, use **¿Para qué?**
To answer, you can use **para** plus an infinitive.

Actividad • Charla Answers will vary.

Ask your partner where he or she is going and why he
or she is going there. Switch roles.

¿Adónde vas?

> Voy a . . . , al . . . , a la . . .

¿Para qué?

> Para . . .

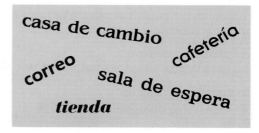

Each student will write his or her own sentences. Example:
Brian va al correo para comprar sellos.
Los estudiantes van a la casa de cambio para cambiar cheques.

C7 Actividad • ¡A escribir!

¿Adónde van? ¿Para qué? Choosing elements from each group of words, write
ten sentences explaining why various people are going to different places.

Brian **Alice** **Jennifer** **Mark y George** **Los estudiantes**	*va* *van*	**a la cafetería** **al correo** **a la tienda** **a la casa de cambio** **a la sala de espera**	*para*	**comer** **comprar** **esperar** **beber** **cambiar**	**sellos** **algo** **postales** **cheques** **a su familia**

C8 ESTRUCTURAS ESENCIALES
Verbs ending in -er *and* -ir

Spanish verbs are classified according to the ending of their infinitives into three conjugations:
-ar, -er, and **-ir.**

You learned the present-tense pattern for regular **-ar** verbs like **hablar** in Unit 3,
B3. The patterns for regular **-er** and **-ir** verbs follow.

	comer *to eat*	**escribir** *to write*
yo	com**o**	escrib**o**
tú	com**es**	escrib**es**
usted, él, ella	com**e**	escrib**e**
nosotros(as)	com**emos***	escrib**imos***
vosotros(as)	com**éis***	escrib**ís***
ustedes, ellos(as)	com**en**	escrib**en**

In the present tense, the **-er** and **-ir** verb endings are identical except for the
forms marked with an asterisk.

The regular **-er** verb **deber,** *should, ought to,* can be followed by the infinitive
of another verb.

Yo debo **esperar.**   Ellos deben **llamar** por teléfono.

Actividad • ¿Qué deciden hacer? 📼

You're at a Spanish airport. Find out if the stores sell what you need. Ask questions using **vender**.

usted / revistas
—¿Vende usted revistas?

1. ¿Venden.ustedes postales?
2. ¿Vende el señor diccionarios?
3. ¿Vendes tú sellos?
4. ¿Venden ellos cheques de viajero?

1. ustedes / postales
2. el señor / diccionarios
3. tú / sellos
4. ellos / cheques de viajero

5. la señora / periódicos   ¿Vende la señora periódicos?
6. los chicos / mapas   ¿Venden los chicos mapas?
7. ellos / cámaras   ¿Venden ellos cámaras?
8. ustedes / casetes   ¿Venden ustedes casetes?

C10 Actividad • ¿Venden o no?   Each student will create his or her own dialog.

Pair up with a partner. Ask each other the questions in C9. Alternate roles.
Answer four of the questions saying yes, you do; and four saying that you don't.

—¿Venden ellos cámaras?

—Sí, venden cámaras.
—No, no venden cámaras.

C11 Actividad • ¡A escribir!   Each student will write his or her own dialog.

Write the conversation you had with your partner in C10.   Ex. ¿Venden ustedes postales?
Sí, vendemos postales.

C12 Actividad • Combinación   Possible answers are given.

Describe what the people in the left column are doing or thinking by using an element from the column on the right. (Make sure that they agree.)

Peter	**deben cambiar un cheque.**
Nosotros	**escribe una postal.**
Los chicos	**come mucho.**
Tú	**venden postales, ¿no?**
Yo	**creo que el correo está a la izquierda.**
Usted	**bebo algo.**
Ustedes	**debemos llamar a Eduardo.**
Ellos	**vendemos sellos.**
Cynthia	**como en la cafetería.**
El empleado	**escribes a casa.**
	deciden ir a la tienda.

C13 Actividad • ¡A escribir!

Write as many logical sentences as you can, combining the people and the activities in C12.

C14 Actividad • Falta algo

These students are in the airport's cafeteria. Complete the sentences with the appropriate verb from the list below in its correct form. You may use a word more than once.

beber	creer	decidir	subir
comer	deber	escribir	vender

1. Nosotros _____ a la cafetería. *subimos*
2. ¿_____ tú algo? *Comes/Bebes*
3. ¿No _____ tú que tú y yo _____ comer algo? *crees/debemos*
4. Ellos _____ a las diez de la noche. *comen*
5. Los chicos _____ subir. *deciden/deben*
6. Ustedes _____ llamar a Enrique ahora. *deben/deciden*
7. Yo _____ a casa. *escribo*
8. Alice _____ que es una buena idea. *cree*
9. Rafael _____ una postal. *escribe*
10. Señor, por favor, ¿_____ usted sellos? *vende*

C15 SE DICE ASÍ
Making suggestions

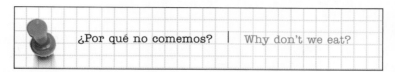

| ¿Por qué no comemos? | Why don't we eat? |

One way to make a suggestion is to ask **¿Por qué no . . .** (verb in plural) *Why don't we . . . ?*

C16 Conversación • ¿Por qué no . . . ? Answers will vary.

Suggest that a classmate do the following things with you. Your classmate will respond using the words given. Ex: —¿Por qué no subimos a la tienda?
—Bueno, yo necesito postales.

comer / hambre
—¿Por qué no comemos?
—Bueno. Yo tengo hambre. (*or:* Ahora no, yo no tengo hambre.)

1. subir a la tienda / necesitar postales
2. escribir a casa / tener sellos
3. esperar / ir sala de espera
4. cambiar un cheque / ir casa de cambio
5. llamar / tener número de teléfono
6. comer / ir cafetería

C17 Comprensión

For script and answers, see p. T111.

Is the reply appropriate?

0	1	2	3	4	5	6	7	8	9	10
✓		✓	✓				✓		✓	✓

En el aeropuerto 153

1 Pedro espera

¡Hoy es el día! Ramón y Rosario llegan de México. Pedro va al aeropuerto para esperar a los chicos. Primero va a información.

—Señor, por favor, ¿el vuelo No. 423 de México?
—Puerta No. 8. Llega a las siete.
—Gracias.

Son las seis. Pedro tiene una hora. Debe esperar, pero, ¿dónde? Va a la cafetería. Come y bebe algo. Veinte minutos después está en la tienda. Mira los periódicos, los libros, las revistas . . .

—¡Mmmmm! Hay unos casetes en venta . . . Cuestan mucho. ¡Oh! Tienen mapas . . . ¿Un mapa de la ciudad para Ramón y Rosario? No . . . , creo que ya tienen un mapa. ¿Y un diccionario en español? No, ellos hablan inglés y español. En la tienda venden postales también . . . postales . . . ¿para qué? Y . . . ¿qué hora es? ¡Es tarde! ¡El vuelo de los chicos!

Pedro corre a la puerta 8. Ramón y Rosario no están. ¿Dónde están los chicos? Pedro va a la sala de espera. ¡Qué suerte! ¡Ahí están Ramón y Rosario!
—¡Hola! ¡Hola! ¿Qué tal? ¡Aquí estoy!

2 Actividad • Charla Free conversation.

Pair off with a classmate. Ask each other questions about **Pedro espera** so that your answers retell the story.

—¿Quiénes vienen de México? ¿Adónde va Pedro? ¿Para qué?
Ramón y Rosario vienen de México. Pedro va al aeropuerto. Él espera a sus amigos.

3 Actividad • ¡A escribir! Answers will vary.

Finish the conversation between Pedro and his friends at the airport. How do they greet each other? What do they say?

4 Actividad • Conversación telefónica   Free conversation.

Pedro is calling home to let his family know their friends have arrived.
Play the role of Pedro. Work with a partner. Switch roles.

5 Actividad • En la aduana   Possible answers are given.

You're going through customs—without your luggage! A customs officer will ask you a series of
questions and will enter your answers into a computer. While you are waiting for your suitcase
to show up, write answers to the questions on a separate piece of paper.

1. ¿Habla usted español?   Sí, hablo español.
2. ¿Cómo se llama usted?   Me llamo . . .
3. ¿De dónde es usted?   Soy de . . .
4. ¿Tiene su pasaporte?   Sí, tengo pasaporte.
5. ¿Dónde está?   Estoy en . . .
6. ¿Adónde va?   Voy a . . .
7. ¿Para qué va allí?   Voy de vacaciones.
8. ¿Cómo va?   Voy en avión.
9. ¿Con quién va?   Voy con mi amigo.
10. ¿A qué hora va?   Voy a las once.

6 Actividad • ¡Diga!

6. Muchas gracias. Llamo mañana.
7. Se cortó la comunicación.
8. Lo siento. Número equivocado.

You're trying to reach Mr. González on the phone. No luck!
What would you say in the following situations?
Some answers may be repeated.

1. You asked for Mr. González but there was nobody
   there with that name.   1. Número equivocado.
2. You tried to reach Mr. González but you were cut off.   2. Se cortó la comunicación.
3. You dialed 5678 and you got 6578.   3. Número equivocado.
4. The line is busy.   Está ocupado.
5. Nobody answers.   Nadie contesta.
6. Mr. González is out today—he's coming in tomorrow.
7. The telephone went dead after a minute or two.
8. The person who answered your call said **familia Fernández.**

7 Pronunciación, lectura, dictado   For script, see pp. T112–113.

1. Listen carefully and repeat what you hear.

2. The sound of the Spanish vowels **u** and **i**. Listen and then read aloud.

> escuchar   Perú   gustar   mucho
> Allí está Isabel con mi equipaje.
> Necesito dinero para ir a Madrid.

3. Copy the following sentences to prepare yourself to write them from dictation.

> No tengo el número de teléfono de Humberto.
> Escribo unas postales a mis amigos americanos.
> El día está ideal para jugar tenis con Lucía.

En el aeropuerto   155

¿LO SABES?

Let's review some important points you have learned in this unit.

 SECTION A

Can you name in Spanish some of the things you need to take along when going on a trip? Answers will vary.
Name six.   pasaporte   mapas   dinero
            cámara   ropa   diccionarios

Do you know how to say where some of your things are and ask others about theirs?   Answers will vary.
Write five statements and ask five questions.

When somebody asks you for directions, how do you answer? Answers will vary.
You're standing at the entrance to your school. Give directions to go to:

   cafetería   baño   clase de música   teléfonos

 SECTION B

When you want to know where somebody is going, how do you ask?

   1. los chicos   **2.** tú   **3.** nosotros   **4.** Carlos   **5.** usted
   1. ¿Adónde van los chicos? 2. ¿Adónde vas tú? 3. ¿Adónde vamos nosotros?
   4. ¿Adónde va Carlos? 5. ¿Adónde va usted?

Do you know how to say where someone is going? For answers, see p. T113.
Tell where the following people are going, using the second word as a clue.

   1. la chica—comer   **4.** nosotros—sellos
   2. yo—pesetas   **5.** Alice—postales
   3. ellos—maleta   **6.** tú—avión

Are you able to answer the phone and to have a short conversation in Spanish?
The phone is ringing. You answer in Spanish. Use five different expressions.

You've tried to telephone Sr. González. Answers will vary.
A woman answers. What do you say now? Answers will vary.
—Hola. ¿Está el señor González, por favor?
You're trying to reach three different people on the phone. No luck!
Give three reasons why the calls can't go through.
La comunicación se cortó.   Número equivocado.   Hay problemas con el teléfono.

 SECTION C

Do you know how to say why you are doing something and to ask others for an explanation?
Explain why you are going to these places: For answers, see p. T113.

   cafetería   correo   tienda   aeropuerto
   sala de espera   puerta 8   sección de equipaje

Now ask three different people where they are going and why.

Are you able to suggest what to do or recommend a place to go?
You are at the airport with five friends. Respond to their statements or questions with helpful suggestions. Answers will vary.

   1. ¡Tengo hambre!   **2.** No tengo sellos.   **3.** ¿Esperamos aquí o arriba?
   4. La familia González llega dentro de una hora.   **5.** ¡No tenemos pesetas!

VOCABULARIO

SECTION A

a la derecha *on the right*
a la izquierda *on the left*
abajo *below*
la **aduana** *customs*
el **aduanero** *customs agent*
el **aeropuerto** *airport*
al lado de *beside*
allí *there*
aquí *here*
arriba *up (there)*
el **asiento** *seat*
el **avión** *airplane*
el **baño** *bathroom*
el **bolsillo** *pocket*
buscar *to look for*
la **cafetería** *cafeteria*
la **cámara** *camera*
cambiar (de) *to change*
la **cartera** *purse*
el **carro** *cart*
la **casa de cambio** *money exchange office*
cerca (de) *near*
el **correo, correos** *post office*
el **cheque de viajero** *traveler's check*
delante (de) *in front (of)*
después *then*
detrás (de) *behind*
el **empleado, la empleada** *employee*
en *at, on*
entrar *to enter*
entre *between*
el **equipaje** *baggage*
estar *to be*
el **grupo** *group*
la **información** *information*

lejos (de) *far (from)*
llegar *to arrive*
la **maleta** *suitcase*
el **mapa** *map*
el **pasaporte** *passport*
la **peseta** *monetary unit of Spain*
por *through*
primero *first*
la **puerta** *gate*
¡qué suerte! *what luck!*
la **sección de equipaje** *baggage claim*
su *your, his, her, its*
van *they go*
el **vuelo** *flight*
ya está todo *everything's finished*

SECTION B

¿adónde? *(to) where?*
algo *something*
¡aló! *hello?*
¿bueno? *hello?*
el **coche** *car*
comprar *to buy*
contestar *to answer*
de la mañana *in the morning, A.M.*
de la noche *at night, P.M.*
¿debo . . . ? *should I . . . ?*
dentro de *in, within*
¡diga! *hello?*
entonces *then*
esperar *to wait (for)*
está ocupado *its' busy*
¡hola! *hello?*
ir *to go*
¡la comunicación se cortó! *we were cut off!*

el **lugar** *place*
llamar *to call*
la **mamá** *mom*
no contestan *there's no answer*
número equivocado *wrong number*
¡qué confusión! *what a mixup!*
quiere *he wants*
saber *to know*
¿verdad? *right?*
ya *already*

SECTION C

a casa *(to) home*
beber *to drink*
cambiar *to cash*
la **carta** *letter*
el **casete** *cassette*
comer *to eat*
creer *to think*
deber *should*
decidir *to decide*
escribir *to write*
la **familia** *family*
hacer *to do*
la **llegada** *arrival*
más *other*
¿para qué? *for what?*
el **periódico** *newspaper*
¿por qué no . . . ? *why don't we . . . ?*
la **postal** *postcard*
que *that*
la **sala de espera** *waiting area*
el **sello** *stamp*
subir *to go up*
tener (mucha) hambre *to be (very) hungry*
vender *to sell*
yo no *not me*

ESTUDIO DE PALABRAS

Most nouns that end in **-o** are masculine; in **-a**, feminine. Be alert to the gender of the nouns. Look through the word lists for this unit and find the nouns that don't end in **-o** or **-a**. Write them in one of two lists, *masculine* or *feminine*.

Masculine: el avión, el coche, el lugar, el cheque, el equipaje, el pasaporte, el casete.
Feminine: la postal, la información, la sección, la noche, la comunicación, la confusión.

VAMOS A LEER

Antes de leer

If you're getting ready for a trip to a Spanish-speaking country, it will be useful to read some information about the place you're going to visit. You will notice that distances are expressed in meters and kilometers. One kilometer equals 5/8 of a mile. To convert kilometers into miles, divide by 1.6.

En España

¿Qué ciudad visitamos?

Once you are in Spain you might want to travel around the country. Here are some of the cities you might want to visit.

San Sebastián, en el norte° de España, es una ciudad ideal para el turismo. Tiene playas muy bonitas°.

Toledo, una ciudad medieval a orillas° del río Tajo°, es famosa por su arte y arquitectura, testimonios de su gran° pasado° histórico.

Segovia está cerca de Madrid, a 88 kilómetros de la capital. Su famoso acueducto° romano,° tiene más de dos mil° años.

---

norte *north*   **bonitas** *pretty*   **orilla** *shore*   **río Tajo** *Tagus River*   **gran** *great*   **pasado** *past*
famoso acueducto *famous aqueduct*   **romano** *Roman*   **dos mil** *two thousand*

You may wish to mention that although Spanish is the official language of Spain, there are also several other languages and dialects spoken, such as: "gallego", "catalán", and "vasco".

Barcelona, la segunda° ciudad española después de Madrid, es uno de los puertos° más importantes del Mediterráneo.

Valencia, en la costa mediterránea, es un importante centro industrial y agrícola°. Es famosa por sus flores° y huertas°.

Sevilla es la cuarta° ciudad de España. Sus calles° estrechas° y los patios en el interior de sus casas° son muy pintorescos.

Actividad • Combinación

Match the items in the two columns to form sentences that agree with what you have just read.

En Segovia hay   en San Sebastián.
Barcelona es   un puerto muy importante.
Hay playas muy bonitas   un famoso acueducto.
San Sebastián es   está a orillas del río Tajo.
Valencia es   calles muy pintorescas.
Barcelona   ideal para el turismo.
Sevilla tiene   es la segunda ciudad de España.
Toledo   famosa por sus flores y huertas.

Actividades   Each student will create his or her own version.

1. Pair up with a classmate. Pick out one of the cities described above and make up questions in Spanish about it. Be ready to answer in return.
2. Go to the library and find out more about one of the cities described. Use reference, geography, and travel books. Prepare an illustrated travel brochure for your class.

Example:
—¿Cómo se llama la cuarta ciudad española?
—Sevilla.
—¿Cómo son sus calles?
—Son estrechas y muy pintorescas.

---

segunda *second*   **puertos** *ports*   **agrícola** *agricultural*   **flores** *flowers*   **huertas** *orchards*   **cuarta** *fourth*
calles *streets*   **estrechas** *narrow*   **casas** *homes*

El regalo

Es viernes. Otra vez° delante del televisor, Adriana y Daniel
miran las noticias° en el Canal Uno.

Locutora	Y ahora, una información urgente. Madrid: Hoy, sábado once . . .
Daniel	¿Cómo? ¿Hoy sábado 11? Hoy es viernes diez.
Adriana	¡Ya sé, Daniel! ¡El Canal Uno trasmite° las noticias del futuro!
Daniel	¿Del futuro? ¡No! ¡Imposible!
Adriana	Sí, también es imposible mirar un partido por televisión, y de pronto°, estar en el estadio.
Daniel	Es verdad. Tienes razón°.
Adriana	Siempre tengo razón. Soy muy inteligente.
Daniel	Sí, porque eres mi hermana.
Adriana	¡Mira, el aeropuerto de Barajas!
Daniel	¿Y ese° avión? Es un avión enorme° . . .
Locutora	El vuelo 28 detenido° en Barajas. Los 219 pasajeros° a bordo son rehenes°. Todo indica° que el piloto, el señor Héctor Ríos, es el responsable del secuestro°.
Daniel	¿Llamamos a la policía?
Adriana	¡Pero, Daniel, por favor . . . ! La policía no va a creer que podemos ver° el futuro en el Canal Uno. Además°, el televisor es un secreto absoluto entre nosotros dos.
Daniel	Está bien. Entonces, ¿por qué no llamamos al aeropuerto? Ellos deben tener la información. Hoy es viernes. Tenemos tiempo° hasta mañana.

---

otra vez *again*   **noticias** *news*   **trasmite** *broadcasts*   **de pronto** *suddenly*   **tienes razón** *you are right*   **ese** *that*
enorme *huge*   **detenido** *detained*   **pasajeros** *passengers*   **rehenes** *hostages*   **indica** *suggests*   **el secuestro** *hijacking*
podemos ver *we can see*   **además** *besides*   **tiempo** *time*

Los chicos llaman al aeropuerto por teléfono. Los sábados, el vuelo 28, con destino a Madrid, hace escala° en México de una a dos de la tarde. Los sábados el piloto es siempre Héctor Ramos. ¿Ríos, y no Ramos? ¿Hay un error?

DANIEL   ¡Escucha°, Adriana! Tengo una idea sensacional.
ADRIANA   ¿Tú, una idea sensacional? No creo. Bueno, ¿cuál es?
DANIEL   En Madrid, el piloto se llama Héctor Ríos, ¿no? En México, el piloto es Héctor Ramos. Mañana en México, entre la una y las dos, Héctor Ríos sube al° avión, y toma control del vuelo.
ADRIANA   ¡Eres un genio! Mañana, a la una, estamos en el aeropuerto, y esperamos la llegada del vuelo.
DANIEL   ¡Fantástico!

El sábado los chicos van al aeropuerto. El vuelo 28 llega a la puerta número 8. Los chicos esperan. El vuelo llega. Primero, bajan° los pasajeros, después el piloto y el copiloto. Un pasajero y una aeromoza° siguen° al piloto. El piloto entra en la cafetería, detrás de él, el pasajero y la aeromoza. Daniel y Adriana deciden entrar también.

Actividad • Asociaciones   Answers will vary.

Work with a partner. Ask as many questions as you can about this chapter of **El regalo,** adding your own ideas to the clues below. You also have to answer your partner's questions.

1. el Canal Uno
2. el viernes 10
3. el sábado 11
4. en Barajas
5. el responsable del secuestro
6. el vuelo 28
7. Héctor Ríos
8. a la policía
9. un secreto
10. Héctor Ramos
11. hace escala
12. la puerta 8
13. un pasajero y una aeromoza
14. la cafetería

---

hace escala *makes a stopover*   **¡Escucha!** *Listen!*   **sube al** *gets on*   **bajan** *get off*   **aeromoza** *stewardess*
siguen *follow*

UNIDAD 6 La familia
Scope and Sequence

	BASIC MATERIAL	COMMUNICATIVE FUNCTIONS
SECTION A	La visita de Roberto (A1)	**Socializing** • Making someone feel at home • Graciously accepting hospitality
SECTION B	Fotos de la familia (B1) Una foto más (B8) Los miembros de la familia (B10) ¿Cómo eres tú? (B16)	**Exchanging information** • Talking about age • Describing people and family relationships • Asking what someone or something is like **Expressing feelings and emotions** • Exclaiming
SECTION C	La casa de Antonio (C1)	**Expressing attitudes and points of view** • Asking opinions and paying compliments
TRY YOUR SKILLS	Pronunciation (letters **c** and **qu**) Sound-letter correspondences (the letters **c** and **qu**) Dictation	
VAMOS A LEER	**¡Hogar, dulce hogar!** (finding the home of your dreams) **El regalo** (A mystery unravels at the airport.)	

WRITING   A variety of controlled and open-ended writing activities appear in the Pupil's Edition. The Teacher's Notes identify other activities suitable for writing practice.

COOPERATIVE LEARNING   Many of the activities in the Pupil's Edition lend themselves to cooperative learning. The Teacher's Notes explain some of the many instances where this teaching strategy can be particularly effective. For guidelines on how to use cooperative learning, see page T13.

GRAMMAR	CULTURE	RE-ENTRY
The verb **querer** (A6)	Being a guest in a Spanish-speaking home Family life in Spanish-speaking homes	Stem-changing verbs **tener** and **venir** Greetings
Descriptive adjectives: position and agreement (B13)	Spanish surnames The family in the Spanish-speaking world	The verb **ser**
More possessive adjectives (C10)	Inside a Spanish-speaking home Houses in Spanish-speaking countries	Prepositions of location Possessive adjectives **mi, tu,** and **su** Definite articles Verbs **parecer** and **gustar**

Recombining communicative functions, grammar, and vocabulary

Reading for practice and pleasure

TEACHER-PREPARED MATERIALS
Section A Flash cards of subject pronouns and the verb **querer**
Section B Pictures of people and families
Section C Pictures of houses
Try Your Skills Family pictures

UNIT RESOURCES
Manual de actividades, Unit 6
Manual de ejercicios, Unit 6
Unit 6 Cassettes
Transparencies 14–16
Quizzes 13–15
Unit 6 Test
Midterm Test
Proficiency Test 1

SECTION

A

OBJECTIVES **To socialize:** make someone feel at home, graciously accept hospitality

CULTURAL BACKGROUND Spanish-speaking people are generally warm and polite, and they expect the same courtesy in return. For example, when leaving a group or leaving the table after dinner, you always say **Con permiso** and wait a few seconds for a reply, usually **Sí, cómo no** or **por supuesto.** As they encounter a familiar group of people, Spanish speakers greet each person individually. Upon leaving, they say good-bye to everyone present by shaking hands or kissing the cheek of a good friend (women). When teenagers bring friends home, they usually spend a few moments with their parents before it is considered proper to leave the room.

Spanish-speaking people love to socialize. There is usually a family gathering or social event at least once a month. During the holidays, such as Christmas, there may be a family meal, party, or formal gathering every weekend. Children are also invited to most social events. They learn the proper social graces at a very young age.

It is important to know that Spanish speakers tend to stand close together when socializing, and many times make body contact.

MOTIVATING ACTIVITY Ask the students to cite instances when they are expected to use formal behavior in the United States. What happens when a friend comes to their house to visit? Do they speak to their parents using *Sir* and *Ma'am?* How would they feel about addressing their parents or other adults using the formal **usted**? Discuss relative distance from people in American groups as contrasted to Hispanic groups.

A1 La visita de Roberto

Show pictures illustrating **sala, cuarto,** and other rooms of the house, and also **refresco.** Say the words aloud and have the students repeat. Next have the students read the dialog and guess the meanings of the following expressions: **bienvenido, mucho gusto, igualmente, estás en tu casa, usted es muy amable, es un placer estar aquí,** and **con permiso.** You might also want to point out the new verb **querer.** Use the verb in several examples and have the students guess its meaning. Then read aloud or play the cassette as the students follow along in their books.

For cooperative learning, have the students form groups of three. Each student should make sure that everyone in the group understands the dialog. Have the groups role-play the dialog in class.

A2 Actividad • Para completar

For writing practice, have the students write the sentences. They should fill in the blanks with the correct word or phrase. Call on a volunteer to write on the board or on a transparency as the students dictate the sentences. Have them exchange papers to check their work.

SLOWER-PACED LEARNING You may wish to have the students fill in the missing words as you dictate the sentences. Have them copy the sentences in their notebooks. Read the complete sentences as the students listen and follow along in their books. Then repeat the sentences as the students fill in the blanks. Finally read the sentences again and have the students correct their work. You may also ask the students to repeat phrases for pronunciation practice, this time with books closed.

A3 Actividad • ¡No es así!

Have the students work in pairs to correct the sentences. Then call on individuals to read the true statements aloud.

A4 Actividad • ¡A escoger!

For writing practice, you may wish to assign this activity for homework after the students have completed it orally.

A5 ¿Sabes que . . . ?

The family unit in most Spanish-speaking countries is numerous, often including the grandparents, "in-laws," aunts, and uncles. Members of the extended family often live together or nearby (if not all of the members, at least some) and are included in all celebrations. You can get a sense of this family unity when you consider that the word for *first cousin* is **primo hermano.** To emphasize to the students the importance of the family, you may wish to introduce the following proverb: **"A los tuyos, con razón o sin ella."** *(Stick to your own whether they are right or wrong.)*

A6 ESTRUCTURAS ESENCIALES

Before introducing the forms of the verb **querer,** re-enter the stem-changing verbs **tener** and **venir** by having the students ask one another questions.

¿Tienes hambre?	Sí, necesito comer algo.
¿Cómo vienes a la escuela?	Vengo en autobús.
¿Por qué no vienes al cine?	Porque necesito estudiar.

To practice the verb **querer,** write the forms on separate cards. Do the same for the subject pronouns. Provide enough cards to involve everyone in the class. Shuffle all the cards and distribute them to the class. Have the students find a classmate with the subject card or the verb card that agrees with their own.

A7 Actividad • ¿Qué quieren hacer?

You may wish to assign this as a writing activity after completing it orally. Have the students exchange papers to correct their work.

A8 Actividad • ¡A escribir!

Have the students write the questions at home or in class. Then call on volunteers to read their questions aloud. Write the questions on the board or a transparency and have the students correct their work. Remind students that the inverted question mark should be placed at the point where the question begins in the sentence. Point out the example in the book and write the following or similar examples on the board or a transparency.

Y tú, ¿cómo estás?	¿Quieren ir al cine?
Sergio, ¿quieres un refresco?	¿Tenemos que ir a pie?

A9 Conversación • ¿Qué quieren?

Have the students complete this activity with a partner. They should take turns asking one another the questions and responding.

A 10 **SE DICE ASÍ**

Demonstrate the expressions to the students. Then have the students practice in small groups to prepare for the activity in A11.

A 11 **Actividad • Y ahora tú . . .**

Have pairs of students practice welcoming one another to their home. They should use the phrases in A10. Call on volunteers to present their dialogs to the class. Encourage the students to include the greetings and gestures described in Unit 1 (A9), page 34, and in Cultural Background, page T107.

A 12 **Comprensión**

From the expressions listed, choose a logical follow-up for each sentence or expression you hear. You will hear each one twice. Write the appropriate number in the corresponding box. For example, you hear: **Tú hablas español muy bien.** The check mark is placed next to **Muchas gracias.**

1. —Eduardo, Eduardo, ¿dónde estás?   5. *¡Estoy aquí!*
2. —Ya estoy aquí.   4. *¿Quieres pasar, por favor?*
3. —Pasa, por favor.   3. *¡Es un placer estar aquí!*
4. —Mucho gusto, Marisa.   2. *Igualmente.*
5. —Estás en tu casa.   1. *¡Usted es muy amable!*

Now check your answers. *Read each item again and give the correct answer.*

A 13 **Actividad • Charla**

For cooperative learning, form groups of two. Have the students imagine that a friend from Ecuador is coming to visit. One should be the friend from Ecuador. The other should welcome the friend to his or her house. The dialog may be between a parent and the visitor from Ecuador, or between the teenager and the visitor. Tell the students to be sure to use the **usted** form when speaking to an adult. Then have each group role-play the dialog in class.

A 14 **Actividad • ¡A escribir!**

Tell the students to write the dialog from A13 at home or in class. Remind them to use opening and closing punctuation.

SECTION B

OBJECTIVES   **To exchange information:** talk about age, describe people and family relationships, ask what someone or something is like; **To express feelings and emotions:** exclaim

CULTURAL BACKGROUND   Families in Spanish-speaking countries are changing quite rapidly today, especially in large cities. More women are entering the business world and obtaining more recognition. In Mexico, for example, children of working mothers are being cared for outside the home in **guarderías,** government-sponsored child care centers. Although many women prefer to stay at home, they are becoming more involved with the responsibilities and problems in the home and the community.

Godparents, **padrinos,** play an important role in the family. They as-

sume responsibility if the parents are unable to care for the child. Grandparents are cared for by their children or grandchildren.

MOTIVATING ACTIVITY   Some students may be surprised that women in many Spanish-speaking countries were granted the right to vote about the same time American women were. Beginning with Argentina, women voted in municipal elections as early as 1921. In Mexico, women voted in state elections in 1923. In 1929, Ecuador became the first Latin American country to grant universal suffrage in national elections. Because many Hispanic women have entered predominantly male professions, there have been a few adjustments in the Spanish language. There is still confusion concerning the correct title to use, such as **el presidente, la presidenta** or **la presidente, la abogada, la piloto, la médico.** You may wish to ask the students to list similar changes in the English language, such as *police officers, fire fighters, salesperson,* and so on.

B1 Fotos de la familia

Make a transparency of Ana María's family tree as shown in B12. Project the transparency and give the relationship of each member to other members of the family in a narrative that begins like this:

> Aquí está la familia de Ana María. La hermana de Ana María se llama Consuelo. Su hermano es Antonio. Su prima se llama Luisa. Raúl es su papá y Luz es su mamá. El tío de Ana María se llama José. Su tía se llama Dolores. María es su abuela y Juan es su abuelo.

SLOWER-PACED LEARNING   As the students look at the transparency, call out the relationship of one member of the family to another: **el tío de Luisa.** The students should write the person's name: **Raúl.**

To present the descriptive adjectives, clip magazine pictures that illustrate the following: **alto, bajo; delgado, gordo; moreno, rubio, pelirrojo; guapo, feo.** Identify the people in the pictures, using the appropriate adjectives. Then call on students to identify famous people with a descriptive adjective.

> Sylvester Stallone es moreno.
> Madonna es rubia.

Play the cassette or read the dialog aloud. Then call on volunteers to role-play the dialog in class.

B2 Preguntas y respuestas

Have the students work with a partner to ask and answer the questions. You may wish to ask the students to write the answers for homework.

B3 Actividad • Y ahora tú . . .

Some students may not wish to discuss their family in class. Tell students they may talk about an imaginary family.

Ask the students to bring photos of their real or imaginary family. Have them choose a partner and discuss the pictures, using the conversation in B1 as a model.

B4 ¿Sabes que . . . ?

To reinforce the Spanish words for family relationships, ask the students to assume the role of Ana María. Call out the name of another family member and ask the students to say the word that expresses the relationship of that

person to Ana María. For example, you say Antonio and the students should answer **hermano**.

B5 SE DICE ASÍ

Have each student select a partner and have each ask the other's age. Then ask each student to tell the partner's age to the class.

As a variation, students might enjoy bringing a photo of their favorite singer, actor, or athlete. They should show the picture to the class and provide additional information such as the person's name, age, likes and dislikes, and perhaps nationality.

B6 Actividad • Charla

Have the students work in pairs to ask and answer the questions. Then have them relay the information to the class.

CHALLENGE   You may wish to include the following or similar questions for the students to ask and answer.

¿Eres un tío/tía?
¿Cuántos hijos tiene tu hermano/hermana?
¿Cómo se llaman?

B7 Actividad • ¡A escribir!

CHALLENGE   Have the students include a brief description of each person in their list, such as **Mi hermano Andrés. Tiene 19 años. Es muy guapo.**

B8 SITUACIÓN • Una foto más

Explain to the students that **murió** means *died*. Relate the verb **morir** to English by supplying examples such as *mortician, mortuary, mortal wound*. Then point out the word **casada** and give several examples. Have the students try to guess the meaning.

Now play the cassette or read the dialog aloud. Have the students use context clues to determine the meaning of **padrastro**. When they have correctly identified the word, ask the students to explain how they arrived at the meaning. You may follow the same procedure with the word **madrastra**.

B9 Actividad • ¡A escoger!

Have the students choose the ending that best fits the conversation in B8. For writing practice, you may wish to have the students write the complete sentences.

B10 SITUACIÓN • Los miembros de la familia

Review the words for family relationships with the students. Read aloud the list and have the students repeat. Then have the students notice the pattern of gender, such as **primo, prima; hermano, hermana; abuelo, abuela.** Explain that the masculine plural form of the names for family relationships consist of a group which includes at least one male.

B11 Actividad • Ana María habla de su familia

Have the students work in pairs to supply the correct word and complete the sentence. The answers may also be written for homework.

CHALLENGE   Ask the students to add a description or give the age of the people mentioned in each sentence.

B12 Comprensión 🔊

Listen carefully as some of Ana María's relatives talk to you. Looking at Ana María's family tree, identify each speaker.

1. —Yo soy el tío de Ana María. Mi esposa se llama Dolores. *José*
2. —No, nosotros no tenemos un hijo. Tenemos una hija. *Dolores*
3. —Mi esposo no se llama José. José es mi hermano. *Luz*
4. —Mi papá se llama José. Ana María es mi prima. *Luisa*
5. —Tenemos dos hijos, Luz y José. *Juan y María*
6. —Yo soy la mamá de Antonio y de Ana María. *Luz*
7. —Luisa es mi prima. Mis hermanas se llaman Ana María y Consuelo. *Antonio*
8. —No, Juan y María no son mis padres. Son los padres de mi esposa. *Raúl*
9. —Soy la tía de Ana María. José es mi esposo. *Dolores*
10. —Yo no soy el papá de Ana María. Ella es hija de mi hermana. *José*

Now check your answers. *Read each sentence again and give the correct answer.*

B13 ESTRUCTURAS ESENCIALES

Clip five pictures from a magazine of the following: a man, a woman, two men, two women, and a mixed group. Place the pictures on the board and give each person an imaginary name. Then ask the students **¿Cómo se llama el señor alto?** The students should respond with the person's name. Then write on the board **(Mario) es un señor alto.** Referring to the picture of the woman, ask **¿Cómo se llama la señora alta?** After the students give her name, write **(María) es una señora alta.** Continue this procedure for each picture.

When the pictures have been identified and the sentences completed, have the students explain the position and agreement of the adjectives. Write their explanations on the board or a transparency. Then tell the students to look at the chart in their books. Read aloud the information with the students to confirm their observations.

B14 Actividad • ¿Quiénes son?

As a variation, you may wish to play a game called "10 Questions." Divide the class into two teams. Team A selects a person from the class without telling Team B his or her identity. Team B must identify the person by asking questions that elicit a **sí** or **no** answer. If Team B is able to guess the person's identity in ten questions or less, it receives a point. Then Team B has a turn to choose a classmate. Use the following or similar questions as a model.

¿Es un chico?   ¿Le gustan los deportes?
¿Es una chica inteligente?   ¿Es alto?

B15 ¿Sabes que . . . ?

Some Spanish and Spanish-American families are very strict with their children. Many teenagers are not allowed to date without a chaperone until they are over sixteen years old. A chaperone may be an older sister or brother, a parent or a relative. Dating in a group or double-dating is also popular. Most

socializing among teenagers is done with the families or friends with an adult present. Young people usually do not leave home until they get married.

Have the students look at the picture and try to guess the relationship and age of everyone pictured.

B16 | SITUACIÓN • ¿Cómo eres tú?

Write the following exchanges on the board or a transparency.

> ¿Cómo es tú profesor? Es alto y rubio.
> ¿Cómo eres tú? Yo soy muy inteligente.

Ask the students to identify the meaning of the two exchanges. Explain that the verb **ser** is used to describe what someone is like: either physical features or personality.

Have the students point out the cognates **inteligente, modesto, generoso,** and **egoísta.** Tell the students to identify the antonyms **tonto** and **antipática.**

Now play the cassette or read the captions aloud. Then have the students identify the pictures using the correct descriptive adjective.

B17 | SE DICE ASÍ

Ask questions with the verb **ser** and elicit responses, using the adjectives from B16. Then read the chart aloud.

For further practice, have the students form groups of three. Each person in the group should ask and describe what the other person is like.

> | CAROLINA | ¿Cómo es Marta? |
> |---|---|
> | MARGARITA | Ella es rubia. Tiene quince años. Es inteligente. |
> | MARTA | ¿Cómo es Margarita? |
> | CAROLINA | Es alta y muy guapa. Tiene catorce años. |
> | MARGARITA | ¿Cómo es Carolina? |
> | MARTA | Es simpática y baja. Es pelirroja. |

B18 | Conversación • La familia

Tell the students to discuss their families—real or imaginary—with a classmate. They may use the questions as a guide or add their own.

B19 | Actividad • Y ahora tú . . .

Have the students work in groups of two. They should describe themselves and two imaginary characters. The students may refer to the adjectives in B18.

B20 | Actividad • ¡A escribir!

When talking about the family, be sure to safeguard the privacy of individuals—some students may not wish to discuss their family situation. Offer the choice of writing about one's real family or a fictitious one.

CHALLENGE You may suggest to students to make a collage of themselves or their real or imaginary families. They should include adjectives that describe each person. Display the collages in the classroom.

B21 | SE DICE ASÍ

Introduce several expressions with cognates, such as **¡Qué fantástico! ¡Qué inteligente! ¡Qué generoso!** Have the students practice the pronunciation and

intonation of the exclamations. Point out that the word **qué** is accented in exclamations. Reinforce by reading aloud the sentences in the box.

SLOWER-PACED LEARNING Clip pictures from magazines for the students to describe. Have the students work with a partner. They should take turns using an exclamation to describe each picture.

(picture of a movie star)	¡Qué guapa!
(picture of a house)	¡Qué linda!
(picture of a monster)	¡Qué feo!

B 22 Actividad • Reacciones

CHALLENGE When the students have finished the oral activity, have them write eight original statements. They should exchange statements and use an appropriate adjective to express their reactions.

B 23 Actividad • Exclamaciones

Have the students use the clues to form the exclamation. For writing practice, ask them to write the sentences at home or in class.

B 24 Comprensión

> You will hear a series of sentences in Spanish. Each will be repeated. Decide which English expression best describes the purpose of the Spanish sentence. Indicate your choices by putting check marks in the appropriate box. For example, you hear: **Mucho gusto, señor Ramos.** The check mark is placed in the row labeled *Making someone's acquaintance.*
>
> **1.** —¿Quieres ver tu cuarto, Rosa? *Extending an invitation*
> **2.** —Y tu casa, ¿cómo es? *Asking what something is like*
> **3.** —Gracias, señora. Usted es muy amable. *Paying a compliment*
> **4.** —¿Te gusta? ¿Qué te parece? *Asking for an opinion*
> **5.** —¡Bienvenida, Rosa! Estás en tu casa. *Welcoming someone*
> **6.** —¡Qué casa tan bonita! *Exclaiming*
>
> Now check your answers. *Read each sentence again and give the correct answer.*

SECTION C

OBJECTIVES **To express attitudes and points of view:** ask opinions and pay compliments

CULTURAL BACKGROUND Houses in Spain and Spanish America are often quite different from those in the United States. In Mexico and other Hispanic countries, for example, the front wall of many houses borders the sidewalk. The backyard is often surrounded by a high adobe wall. As a rule, houses in Hispanic countries are built to preserve the privacy of the family. That is why most rooms in a house face an inner courtyard instead of opening to a surrounding garden as in the United States.

In Madrid, Spain, most people live in apartments called **pisos**. They may be as high as fifteen stories. The children play on the sidewalk or in the parks. Private homes are being built in suburbs on the outskirts of Madrid. Of course, in the country and in some parts of the city there are many styles of houses, but the designs are different from those of typical family homes in the United States.

MOTIVATING ACTIVITY   Have the students sketch or clip pictures from magazines of typical homes in the United States and Spanish-speaking countries. They may wish to label each picture in Spanish, such as **Casa en la ciudad, Casa en el campo, Apartamento.** Display the pictures in the classroom.

C1   La casa de Antonio

Using the illustrations from the book and pictures from magazines, present the rooms of the house. As you identify each item in Spanish, have the students repeat after you. Then hold up the pictures at random and ask the students to identify the rooms.

Introduce the verb **vivir** by writing several sentences on the board or a transparency. Ask the students to guess the meaning and the pattern. Explain that it is a regular **-ir** verb.

> Yo vivo en una casa.
> El presidente de los Estados Unidos vive en Washington.
> Nosotros vivimos en *(city name)*.

Play the cassette or read the dialog aloud. For cooperative learning, have pairs of students role-play the dialog. Label the classroom with names and pictures of the rooms in Antonio's house. Ask each group to role-play the conversation by walking to the rooms as they are mentioned in the dialog.

C2   Actividad • ¡A escoger!

Have the students choose the ending that best fits the conversation in C1. For writing practice, have them write complete sentences at home or in class.

C3   Preguntas y respuestas

Have the students work in pairs. They should take turns asking and answering the questions.

CHALLENGE   A student may make a false statement about Antonio's house: **La familia de Antonio no usa mucho la sala de estar.** A classmate should correct it: **No, la familia de Antonio sí usa mucho la sala de estar. Es el cuarto más importante.**

C4   Actividad • ¿Y en tu casa? . . . ¿en tu apartamento?

Tell the students to choose a partner. They should answer the questions about their own family and homes—real or imaginary.

CHALLENGE   Ask the students to use the questions as a guide to write a composition about their house. They may enjoy writing about an imaginary house in space or on the ocean floor.

SLOWER-PACED LEARNING   Have the students find pictures of their ideal home. They should write a caption for each picture. Display the pictures and captions in the classroom.

C5   Actividad • Adivinanza

Re-enter the prepositions of location from Unit 5 (A15), page 140. Have the students practice the expressions by naming the location of various objects in the classroom. Then have the students play the guessing game with a partner.

C6 Actividad • El plano de tu casa

Assign the activity for homework. Remind students to make a copy of the floor plan before writing the labels in Spanish. They should have two copies—one with and one without labels.

C7 Actividad • Charla

Have each student describe in Spanish his or her real or imaginary house as a classmate labels the floor plan. Then ask the students to compare the floor plan that they labeled in class with the floor plan labeled at home.

CHALLENGE   Distribute the floor plans that were assigned as homework in C6 so that the students do not receive their own. Have each student prepare a narrative of the plan and present it orally to the class. The students must listen and identify their own plan as they hear it described, by saying ¡Es mi casa!

C8 ¿Sabes que . . . ?

Explain that houses in large cities have limited space, so there might not be a special room for watching television and relaxing. Often in Spanish-speaking countries, the dining room is the most important room in the house. After meals, family and friends will linger at the table for conversation.

You might ask the students which is the most important room in their house. They should name the room and explain why they think it is important.

C9 Actividad • ¡A escribir!

Have the students complete the composition at home or in class. You may wish to introduce the word **hogar.** Have the students title their composition **Mi hogar** or **Mi casa.**

C10 ESTRUCTURAS ESENCIALES

Use objects in the classroom to re-enter **mi, tu,** and **su,** and to present the new possessive adjectives **nuestro(a)** and **su** (*their* and *your*). For the following presentation, use several objects (of each gender) that belong to you: a pencil, an eraser, a book, and so on.

> Aquí está un lápiz. Es mi lápiz.
> Aquí está una goma. Es mi goma.
> Aquí están unos libros. Son mis libros.

Say the pair of sentences as you hold up each object. The first sentence in each pair uses the definite article to show the number and gender of each noun so the students can see the relationship between the definite article in the first sentence and the possessive adjective in the second. Next involve the students in the following exchange:

> TEACHER   ¿Tienes un lápiz?
> HÉCTOR   Sí, aquí está mi lápiz.
> TEACHER   ¿Tienes una goma?
> CAROLINA   Sí, aquí está mi goma.
> TEACHER   ¿Tienes unos libros?
> MIGUEL   Sí, aquí están mis libros.

Continue this procedure until all the possessive adjectives have been presented.

C11 Actividad • En la fiesta

Call on students to form the sentences using the appropriate possessive adjective.

SLOWER-PACED LEARNING   Prior to the writing practice, compare the subject pronouns and possessives. You may wish to write the comparisons on the board or a transparency.

Yo—mi	ella—su
Tú—tu	usted—su
él—su	nosotros—nuestro

Have the students write complete sentences in class or at home. Call on a volunteer to write the sentences on the board or a transparency so the students may check their work. Then complete the activity orally.

C12 Conversación • ¿Quiénes son?

CHALLENGE   Tell the students to answer five questions with **No.** Then they should state a different relationship, using the preposition **de.**

> —¿Es él amigo de ustedes?
> —No. Es amigo de Juan.

C13 SE DICE ASÍ

To practice asking opinions and paying compliments, have the students ask each other questions about school, classes, sports, and so on. You may begin a chain drill. Ask the students to begin their questions with **¿Qué te parece . . . ?** and **¿Te gusta . . . ?**

> —¿Qué te parece la escuela?
> —Me gusta mucho. ¡Qué escuela tan estupenda!
> —¿Te gusta la clase de química?
> —No, es un poco aburrida.

C14 Conversación • La visita

CHALLENGE   For further practice, have the students work with a partner. They should answer the questions using the opposite of the adjective in parentheses.

> la tía de Antonio (simpática)
> —¿Te gusta la tía de Antonio?
> —No, no me gusta, es antipática.

C15 Actividad • ¡A escribir!

CHALLENGE   Tell the students to imagine they are listening to a conversation between a real estate agent and a couple wishing to buy a house. The couple should ask the agent about the house, then ask each other their opinions. Have the students write the conversation. Call on volunteers to read their dialogs aloud to the class.

C16
¿Sabes que . . . ?

Write the description of a typical Spanish house on the board or a transparency. Have groups of students draw the floor plan based on your description. They should label each room. They might also enjoy drawing a picture of the outside of the house. Then have each group compare its drawings.

C17 Actividad • Combinación

Call on students to match the answers with the appropriate questions. You may also wish to use this activity as a quiz.

TRY
YOUR
SKILLS

OBJECTIVE To recombine communicative functions, grammar, and vocabulary

CULTURAL BACKGROUND In Spain and most countries in Spanish America, parties are an important part of life. There are parties to celebrate an engagement, baptism, holiday, birth, anniversary, and so on. When one goes to a party, there are a few rules to follow. It is not considered polite to bring food or wine to a dinner party. The hosts might feel you don't think there will be enough food to eat or you won't enjoy the beverages served. In Venezuela and in many other countries, guests send flowers. It is also not considered polite to arrive before the time mentioned in the invitation or even at the set hour. Actually, arriving late is much better than arriving early. When giving a party, hosts or hostesses allow for more people than they invite. Some of the guests may bring along a relative or a neighbor.

1

Fiesta de familia

Have the students follow along in their books as you play the cassette or read the dialog aloud. To check comprehension, read the following statements aloud and ask the students to identify each person by his or her description.

1. Ella es la tía de Lola.   *Tía Consuelo*
2. Es el hermano de Lola.   *Tato*
3. Ella es la madre del papá de Lola.   *Josefina*
4. Ellos son primos de Lola.   *Pedro y Pablo*
5. Él es el abuelo de Lola y el padre de su papá.   *Don Mario Ramírez*

For writing practice, have the students write a sentence about each person or couple that Lola mentions in the dialog. They may also use the pictures in Skills 2 for reference.

2 SITUACIÓN • El árbol genealógico

Call out the names of the people in Lola's family tree and have the students identify the relationship to Lola. You may also wish to assign ages to the people and ask the students to include the person's age in their response.

(Delia Arias de Ramírez) Es la mamá de Lola. Tiene cuarenta años.

CHALLENGE Call out the names of the people in Lola's family tree and ask the students to identify the relationship to other members of the family.

(Delia Arias de Ramírez) Es la tía de Pablo. Es la hija de José y Elena.

3 ### Actividad • ¿Quiénes son? ¿Cómo son?

Have the students select a partner and describe each person listed. They should also tell what the person is like. Call on a few volunteers to share their descriptions with the class.

4 ### Actividad • Proyecto: Mi familia

Form cooperative learning groups of three or four students each. With pictures of his or her real or imaginary family, each student should introduce the members of the family and include a brief description. Tell the students to include their pets if they wish. Provide added vocabulary as needed. Then call on individuals to tell the class something about a classmate's family.

SLOWER-PACED LEARNING You might limit the number of family pictures you require to two or three. Before assigning the activity, distribute copies of a magazine picture of a teenager to the class. Tell the students to imagine that the teenager is a family member. Call on volunteers to describe him or her. Write the suggestions on the board or a transparency. Then have the students agree on a brief description and write it below the picture.

5 ### Actividad • Charla

You might suggest that the students first ask where their partner lives and whether he or she lives in a house or an apartment. They may also include directional prepositions to describe where each room is located in the house.

6 ### Actividad • Una entrevista

Explain to the students that **S.A.** stands for **Sociedad Anónima** *(Incorporated)*. After the students have had the opportunity to practice with a partner, call on pairs to present their interview to the class. You may wish to record or videotape several presentations.

7 ### Actividad • Una carta

SLOWER-PACED LEARNING Assign the writing activity after the students have done it orally in class.

8 ### Pronunciación, lectura, dictado

1. Listen carefully and repeat what you hear.
   In Spanish, the letter **c** before **a, o, u** (**ca, co, cu**) is pronounced *k*. The sound is similar to the English *k*, but without any explosion of air. Listen, and repeat the following words.

   canasta   simpático   comedor   coche   escultura   ocupado

   The Spanish letter **q** is always followed by **u**. When **qu** precedes **e** or **i**, it is pronounced like the English *k* in *kept, keep.* Listen, and repeat the following words.

   que   Roque   equipaje   básquetbol   quieres

2. Listen, and then read aloud.
   Listen to the following words and repeat.

   calculadora   cuál   como   con   aquí   quince   querer   raqueta

3. Write the following sentences from dictation. First listen to the sentence as it is read to you. Then you will hear the sentence again in short segments, with a pause after each segment to allow you time to write. Finally, you will hear the sentence a third time so that you may check your work. Let's begin.

   Los discos cuestan *(pause)* quince dólares.
   Queremos esquiar *(pause)* con Carlos *(pause)* en Colorado.
   La hermana de Rebeca *(pause)* está casada *(pause)* con un chico *(pause)* de Cuba.

¿LO SABES?

Have the students work with a partner. One will be a Spanish-speaking guest and the other will welcome the guest to his or her home. The guest should respond appropriately. To review the verb **querer,** have students offer the guest refreshments. They may also suggest various activities such as playing a sport or listening to music. Then have the students switch roles.

To review family relationships, have the students form cooperative learning groups. Have each group choose a well-known family from a television series or the comics. Then have them prepare a description of the family members, including their names, relationship to one another, ages, likes, and dislikes. The group may also write out the description of its chosen family. Finally, each group should role-play the members of the family before the class, telling as much as they can about themselves without giving their names. The class must guess which family they are.

To practice the possessive adjectives and the verbs **parecer** and **gustar,** have the students ask a classmate's impression about something or someone. You may wish to begin a chain conversation by following the model below.

José	¿Qué te parece la casa de Margarita?
Carolina	Su casa es muy bonita. Mario, ¿te gustan los discos de Michael Jackson?
Mario	Sus discos son aburridos. No me gustan. Linda, ¿qué te parece tu clase de inglés?
Linda	Mi maestro es fabuloso.

Unidad 6   Teacher's Notes   T131

VOCABULARIO

Have the students look for and make a list of the words that contain the letters **c** and **q.** Then they should select ten words or phrases from the list and write a sentence for each to demonstrate its meaning.

You may wish to play a vocabulary game with the students. Provide scratch paper for each student. Have the students choose a partner. Student A will select a word from the list and draw a picture that illustrates the meaning of the word. He or she must not give any vocal clues. Also, numbers and letters are not allowed. Student B must guess the word in two minutes or less. Tell the students to take turns drawing and identifying the word. For each correct word, a student will receive a point. At the end of the game, the student with the most points wins.

ESTUDIO DE PALABRAS

As a variation, ask the students to list the pairs of words that are synonyms and antonyms. Have them write the pairs in their notebooks.

VAMOS A LEER

OBJECTIVE   To read for practice and pleasure

¡HOGAR, DULCE HOGAR!

Have the students read the questionnaire and answer the questions about their dream home. You might wish to tell the students that **alberca** is another word in Spanish for swimming pool. It is widely used in Mexico. Also, **recámara** is sometimes used for **dormitorio** or **cuarto.**

¿Piscina, jardín, estudio?

To add to their description, the students might enjoy drawing a picture of their dream house or clipping a picture from a magazine. Explain that illustrations of homes may be found in real estate books which are available in many real estate offices and often found in supermarkets.

Actividad • Un agente de propiedades

Have the students work with a partner to match the customers with the appropriate homes. They should be prepared to explain in Spanish why they selected the house for each person or family.

Actividad

As a variation, the students may write an advertisement for a house or an apartment. Then have them describe a person, couple, or family that the home would be suitable for.

EL REGALO

Review the previous episodes of **El regalo** with the students. Point out new vocabulary and have the students use each word in a sentence that illustrates its meaning. Then ask the students to read silently.

After small groups role-play the dialog, have the students listen as you play the cassette or read the dialog aloud. Then lead a discussion about **El regalo** in Spanish. Ask the students to give their opinion and comment on the characters and story line.

> ¿Qué te parece la serie? ¿Héctor? ¿la aeromoza?
> ¿Te gusta este cuento? ¿Por qué?
> ¿Quieren leer más?
> ¿Cómo es Adriana? ¿Daniel? ¿el piloto?

Actividad • ¿Quién habla?

Ask the students to identify the characters who might say each of the statements listed. They should explain their answers.

UNIDAD 6
La familia

For most speakers of Spanish, the family comes first. For example, before a family member makes a major decision, the issue is discussed by the entire family. To have a better understanding of Spanish-speaking people, you need to understand about family relationships and manners.

In this unit you will:

SECTION A	welcome people . . . extend invitations
SECTION B	describe people and family relationships . . . talk about age
SECTION C	ask someone's opinion . . . pay compliments
TRY YOUR SKILLS	use what you've learned
VAMOS A LEER	read for practice and pleasure

163

SECTION A

welcoming people . . . extending invitations

Living abroad with a Hispanic family is a thrilling experience. You are warmly greeted when you arrive, and you gain new insights about yourself and other people every day.

You may wish to show different slides or tourist brochures showing the "Ciudad de México" to create a mood, and motivate students.

A1

La visita de Roberto

Roberto, un estudiante norteamericano de Los Ángeles, llega a la casa de su amigo Antonio en la Ciudad de México. Va a pasar un mes de vacaciones con la familia de Antonio.

ANTONIO	¡Mamá! ¡Mamá! ¿Dónde estás?
MAMÁ	Aquí estoy, Antonio. En la sala. ¡Bienvenido, Roberto! Pasa, por favor. ¿Cómo estás? Mucho gusto.
ROBERTO	Igualmente, señora.
MAMÁ	Estás en tu casa, Roberto.
ROBERTO	Muchas gracias, señora. Usted es muy amable. ¡Es un placer estar aquí con ustedes!

ANTONIO	Con permiso, mamá. Queremos escuchar música. Vamos a mi cuarto.
MAMÁ	¡Un momento, Antonio! ¿Dónde están las cosas de Roberto? ¿Por qué no van a su cuarto primero? Y tú, Roberto, ¿no tienes hambre? ¿Quieres comer algo? ¿Quieres un refresco?
ROBERTO	No, señora, muchas gracias.
ANTONIO	¿Quieres ver tu cuarto, Roberto?

A2 Actividad • Para completar

What is Antonio's mother saying to Roberto? Complete the phrases.

—¡ _____ , Roberto! Pasa, _____ . ¿Cómo _____ ? Mucho _____ . Estás en _____ .
¿No _____ hambre? ¿Quieres _____ ? ¿Quieres un _____ ?

(word bank: Bienvenido · por favor · estás · gusto · tu casa. · tienes · comer algo · refresco)

164 **Unidad 6**

Actividad • ¡No es así!

Correct these statements to make them true according to A1.

1. Roberto es de la Ciudad de México. Antonio es de la Ciudad de México.
2. Antonio llega de Los Ángeles. Roberto llega de Los Ángeles.
3. Antonio va a pasar un mes con la familia de Roberto. Roberto va a pasar un mes con la familia de Antonio.
4. La mamá de Antonio está en el cuarto de Roberto. La mamá de Antonio está en la sala.
5. La señora: "Estás en mi casa, Roberto". La señora: "Estás en tu casa, Roberto".
6. Roberto contesta: "Muchas gracias, señora. Tú eres muy amable".
7. Antonio y Roberto quieren mirar televisión. Antonio y Roberto quieren escuchar música.
8. La mamá pregunta dónde está la casa de Roberto. La mamá pregunta dónde están las cosas de Roberto.

6. Roberto contesta: "Muchas gracias, señora. Usted es muy amable."

A4 Actividad • ¡A escoger!

For each numbered sentence choose an ending that best fits **La visita de Roberto.**

1. Roberto llega a
   • Los Ángeles.   • la casa de un amigo.   • su cuarto.
2. Va a pasar un mes de vacaciones
   • con la familia.   • con su mamá.   • con los chicos.
3. La mamá de Antonio está en
   • Los Ángeles.   • su cuarto.   • la sala.
4. Es un placer estar
   • aquí.   • en Los Ángeles.   • en mi cuarto.
5. Antonio quiere
   • mirar televisión.   • comer algo.   • escuchar música.
6. Roberto no quiere
   • escuchar música.   • ver su cuarto.   • comer.

A5 ¿Sabes que . . . ?

Family life is very important in Spanish-speaking countries, and a great deal of socializing is done around the home. In many instances, grandparents live together with their married sons and daughters, and other relatives are frequent visitors, or live nearby. Even though much entertaining is done at home, only people within the family circle and close friends are invited. If you are a guest at a Spanish home, be sure to be polite and express your gratitude—you have been specially honored!

ESTRUCTURAS ESENCIALES
The verb **querer**

In Spanish, some verbs like **querer** have a change in the stem in the present tense. When the stem vowel **e** is stressed or emphasized, it changes to **ie.**

querer (ie) *to want*			
Quiero	comer ahora.	**Queremos**	un refresco.
¿Quieres	beber algo?	**¿Queréis**	ir?
¿Quiere	pasar?	**¿Quieren**	ver el cuarto?

Stem-changing verbs have regular endings like other **-ar, -er,** and **ir** verbs. They can be found in vocabulary lists with an indicator in parentheses such as: **querer (ie),** *to want.*

Querer can be followed by a noun or an infinitive.

Quiero un refresco. *I want a soda.*
Quiero nadar. *I want to swim.*

Stress the use of "querer" followed by an infinitive. After A9, you may wish to do a personalized question and answer drill, such as: "Y tú, ¿quieres algo?

A7   Actividad • ¿Qué quieren hacer? *What do they want to do?*

Complete the following sentences with the correct form of the verb **querer.**

1. ¿ _____ ustedes venir? Quieren
2. ¿Adónde _____ ir ustedes? quieren
3. Nosotros _____ ir a la ciudad. queremos
4. Yo, no. Yo _____ escuchar música. quiero

5. Antonio _____ ir a su cuarto. quiere
6. Los chicos _____ mirar televisión. quieren
7. Y tú, Roberto, ¿ _____ venir? quieres
8. No, yo _____ comer algo. quiero

A8   Actividad • ¡A escribir!   1. Ana ¿quieres ver la casa?
2. Susana y Pablo, ¿quieren escuchar discos?

Tienes invitados. You have guests—many of them—in your house. You ask what they want to do. Use the verb **querer.** Write down your questions.

3. Señora López, ¿quiere comer algo?   4. Antonio, ¿quieres subir a mi cuarto?   5. Ustedes, ¿quieren mirar televisión?

Roberto / ver mi cuarto
—Roberto, ¿quieres ver mi cuarto?

1. Ana / ver la casa
2. Susana y Pablo / escuchar discos
3. señora López / comer algo
4. Antonio / subir a mi cuarto

5. ustedes / mirar televisión
6. chicos / jugar
7. Isabel / ir a la sala
8. usted / venir con nosotros

6. Chicos, ¿quieren jugar?   7. Isabel, ¿quieres ir a la sala?   8. Usted, ¿quiere venir con nosotros?

A9   Conversación • ¿Qué quieren?   1. —¿Quieren ustedes bailar?—No, queremos escuchar música.
2. —¿Quiere usted comer?—No, quiero beber algo.

Pair up with a classmate. You make many suggestions but they are not accepted. Everybody wants to do something else. Follow the clues and switch roles.

3. —¿Quieren los chicos estudiar?—No, los chicos quieren jugar.
4. —¿Quieres ver la computadora?—No, quiero ir a mi cuarto.
5. —¿Quieren ustedes mirar televisión?—No, queremos hablar por teléfono.
6. —¿Quiere hablar con mamá?—No, quiero ir a la sala.

tú / jugar tenis / mirar televisión
—¿Quieres jugar tenis?
—No, quiero mirar televisión.

1. ustedes / bailar / escuchar música
2. usted / comer / beber algo
3. los chicos / estudiar / jugar
4. tú / ver la computadora / ir a mi cuarto

5. ustedes / mirar televisión / hablar por teléfono
6. usted / hablar con mamá / ir a la sala
7. tú / pasar / montar en bicicleta
8. ustedes / estudiar / bailar

7. —¿Quieres pasar?—No, quiero montar en bicicleta.
8. —¿Quieren ustedes estudiar?—No, queremos bailar.

SE DICE ASÍ
Making somebody feel at home; graciously accepting hospitality

HOST, HOSTESS	GUEST
¡Bienvenido(a)! Welcome!	¡Gracias! ¡Es un placer estar aquí! Thanks! It's a pleasure to be here!
¡Pasa! Come in!	Sí, ¡gracias, señor(a)! Yes, thank you, sir (ma'am)!
¡Mucho gusto! Pleased to meet you!	¡Igualmente, señor(a)! Likewise, sir (ma'am)!
¡Estás en tu casa! Make yourself at home!	¡Usted es muy amable! You're very kind!

A 11 Actividad • Y ahora tú . . . Free conversation.

Welcome a classmate to your home. Use as many of the phrases in A10 as you can. Then switch roles.

A 12 Comprensión   For script and answers, see p. T120.

Check the correct answer.

0	✔	Muchas gracias.
1	5	¡Usted es muy amable!
2	4	Igualmente.
3	3	¡Es un placer estar aquí!
4	2	¿Quieres pasar, por favor?
5	1	¡Estoy aquí!

A 13 Actividad • Charla   Free conversation.

Make a guest feel at home. With a partner, create a dialog using as many expressions as you can from the box below.

Ex. Pasa, por favor.
Muchas gracias
Es un placer estar aquí.
¿Quiere un refresco?

Usted es muy amable   Pasa, por favor   ¿Un refresco?   ¡Bienvenido!   Estás en tu casa   ¡Bienvenida!   ¿Quieres . . . ?   Es un placer estar aquí   Igualmente   Vamos a . . .   Con permiso   Mucho gusto

A 14 Actividad • ¡A escribir! Answers will vary.

Write down the conversation you had with your classmate in A13 in dialog form.

Like nearly everyone else in the world, Hispanic people love to collect and show off family snapshots. You may need to know how to comment and ask questions about them.

B1

Fotos de la familia 📼

Ana María, la hermana de Antonio, y su amiga Gloria, hablan de las fotos que Ana María tiene en su cuarto. Tiene fotos de todos los miembros de la familia.

GLORIA　Tienes muchas fotografías. ¿Quién es la chica alta y morena? ¿Tu hermana?

ANA MARÍA　No, mi hermana Consuelo es baja y rubia. Ella es Luisa, mi prima.

GLORIA　¿Cuántos años tiene?

ANA MARÍA　Quince. ¡Es un genio! Es muy inteligente.

GLORIA　¡Qué fotografía tan bonita! ¿Quién es? ¿Tu padre?

ANA MARÍA　Sí, es una foto de mi papá.

GLORIA　¡Qué guapo!

ANA MARÍA　Mira, aquí está de nuevo, con mi mamá y toda la familia.

GLORIA　La señora delgada y rubia, ¿quién es? ¡Qué linda!

ANA MARÍA　Es mi tía Dolores, la madre de Luisa. Al lado está el esposo, mi tío José.

GLORIA　Y aquí están tus abuelos, ¿no?

ANA MARÍA　Sí, los padres de mamá. Los dos son bien simpáticos y cariñosos.

GLORIA　¿Cuántos hijos tienen? ¿Cinco?

ANA MARÍA　No, una hija, mi mamá, y un hijo, mi tío José. El señor pelirrojo es un amigo de ellos. Los otros cuatro son amigos también.

1. Es la prima de Ana María. 2. Luisa tiene quince años. 3. Luisa es un genio. 4. El padre de Ana María 5. Es la tía de Ana María y la madre de Luisa. 6. Los abuelos de Ana María son simpáticos y cariñosos. 7. No, tienen dos hijos. 8. Es un amigo de los abuelos de Ana María.

B2 Preguntas y respuestas

Identify the people mentioned by Ana María according to B1, **Fotos de la familia**.

¿Quién es la chica baja?
—Es la hermana de Ana María.

1. ¿Quién es la chica alta y morena?
2. ¿Quién tiene quince años?
3. ¿Quién es un genio?
4. ¿Quién es el señor guapo?

5. ¿Quién es la señora delgada y rubia?
6. ¿Quiénes son simpáticos y cariñosos?
7. ¿Cuántos hijos tienen ellos, cinco?
8. ¿Quién es el señor pelirrojo?

B3 Actividad • Y ahora tú . . .

¿Cómo es tu familia?

Each student will have his or her own version. Ex. Tengo dos hermanas, Ana y María. Ana es rubia y María es morena. Son altas y también inteligentes. Tengo cinco tías . . .

1. ¿Tienes hermanos(as)? ¿Cuántos(as)?
2. ¿Cómo se llaman tus hermanos(as)?
3. ¿Son rubios(as) o morenos(as)?
4. ¿Son altos(as) o bajos(as)?

5. ¿Son inteligentes?
6. ¿Tienes tíos y tías? ¿Cómo se llaman?
7. ¿Tienes primos(as)? ¿Cuántos(as)?
8. ¿Cómo se llaman tus primos(as)?

B4 ¿Sabes que . . . ?

Spanish speakers usually have a first name (or a compound first name like **Ana María**) plus two surnames, their father's and their mother's. To find someone in the phone book, look under their paternal surname. Here is Ana María's family tree. Notice how the surnames **González** and **Rivas** descend to her.

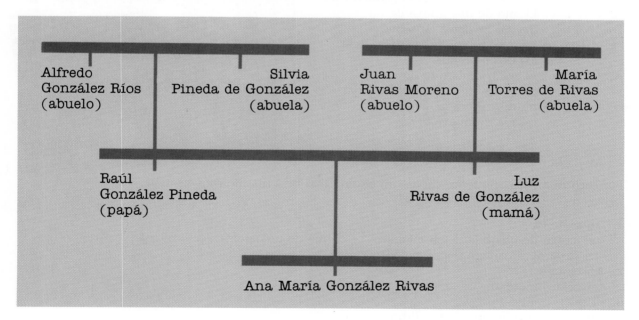

Alfredo
González Ríos
(abuelo)

Silvia
Pineda de González
(abuela)

Juan
Rivas Moreno
(abuelo)

María
Torres de Rivas
(abuela)

Raúl
González Pineda
(papá)

Luz
Rivas de González
(mamá)

Ana María González Rivas

When a woman marries, she usually drops her maternal surname and adds **de** plus her husband's paternal surname. Before her marriage, Ana María's mother was named **Luz Rivas Torres**. Now she is normally addressed as **Sra. Rivas de González**.

SE DICE ASÍ
Talking about age

	¿Cuántos años tienes?	Tengo catorce años.
	How old are you?	I am fourteen.

To ask or answer how old someone is, use the verb **tener.**

B 6   Actividad • Charla   Students will create their own dialogs following the model.

Ask a classmate. Be ready to answer yourself.

¿Cuantos años tienes? ¿Tienes hermanos(as)? ¿Cuántos años tienen? ¿Tienes primos(as)? ¿Cuántos años tienen?

B 7   Actividad • ¡A escribir!   Each student will have his or her own version.

Make a list of your brothers, sisters, cousins, and friends. (Use imaginary names if you'd prefer.) Then write their ages, like this:

Mi hermano Andrés tiene 19 años.

B 8   SITUACIÓN • Una foto más

GLORIA   ¡Qué chico tan guapo! ¿Quién es?
ANA MARÍA   El hijo de una amiga de mi
             mamá. Se llama Anselmo.
GLORIA   Es muy rubio. Sus padres, ¿son
             los dos morenos?
ANA MARÍA   El señor de la foto no es su
             papá. Es su padrastro. Su papá
             murió. Ahora la mamá está
             casada de nuevo.

B 9   Actividad • ¡A escoger!

For each numbered sentence choose an ending that best fits the conversation
between Gloria and Ana María.

1. Anselmo es
   • el amigo de una hija de su mamá.   • el hijo de una amiga de su mamá.
   • el papá de un amigo de su mamá.
2. Anselmo es
   • un chico moreno.   • muy guapo.   • un genio.
3. Él es
   • rubio.   • moreno.   • pelirrojo.
4. El señor de la foto es
   • su papá.   • su abuelo.   • su padrastro.
5. El papá de Anselmo
   • está casado.   • murió.   • es guapo.

el **esposo** *husband*	la **esposa** *wife*	los **esposos** *husband and wife*
el **abuelo** *grandfather*	la **abuela** *grandmother*	los **abuelos** *grandparents*
el **padre** *father*	la **madre** *mother*	los **padres** *parents*
el **hermano** *brother*	la **hermana** *sister*	los **hermanos** *brothers and sisters*
el **hijo** *son*	la **hija** *daughter*	los **hijos** *children*
el **tío** *uncle*	la **tía** *aunt*	los **tíos** *uncles and aunts*
el **primo** *cousin*	la **prima** *cousin (female)*	los **primos** *cousins*
el **padrastro** *stepfather*	la **madrastra** *stepmother*	los **padrastros** *stepparents*

The masculine plural nouns are used to refer to any group that includes at least one male:

los esposos *husband and wife*
los esposos *husbands and wives*
los esposos *husbands*

The context usually clarifies which meaning is intended.

B 11 Actividad • Ana María habla de su familia

Ana María is talking about her relatives. Complete her remarks with the correct word from the list.

Mi tío José es el ____ de mi mamá. hermano
Mi madre y tío José son los ____ de mis abuelos. hijos
Mi tío José y mi mamá son ____ . hermanos
Mi tía Dolores es la ____ de mi tío José. esposa
Luisa es la ____ de mis tíos José y Dolores. hija
Ella es mi ____ . prima
Mis ____ tienen tres hijos: mi hermano padres
Antonio, mi ____ Consuelo y yo. hermana

hermano hijos
hija hermanos
prima esposa
padres hermana

La familia de Ana María

```
                    Juan ——— María
                      |
         ┌────────────┴──────┐
    Raúl — Luz           José — Dolores
      |                       |
  ┌───┴────────┐              |
Consuelo  Antonio  Ana María  Luisa
```

B 13   ESTRUCTURAS ESENCIALES
Descriptive adjectives: position and agreement

Words that you use to describe a noun are called **adjectives.** If you say *The tall woman is smart,*
tall and *smart* are both **adjectives.** Some typical **adjectives** are shown in the following chart.

Masculine			*Feminine*		
Article	*Noun*	*Adjective*	*Article*	*Noun*	*Adjective*
el	señor	alt**o**	la	señora	alt**a**
los	señores	alt**os**	las	señoras	alt**as**
un	chico	inteligente	una	chica	inteligente
unos	chicos	inteligent**es**	unas	chicas	inteligent**es**
el	libro	difícil	la	clase	difícil
los	libros	difícil**es**	las	clases	difícil**es**

1. Spanish adjectives are usually placed after the noun they describe.

2. You need to be sure that the ending of your adjective reflects the number and gender of the noun it accompanies.

3. Many adjectives that end in **-o** in the masculine, like **alto,** end in **-a** in the feminine.
El señor **alto** es **aburrido.**   La señora **alta** es **aburrida.**

4. Adjectives that end in **-e,** like **inteligente,** stay the same with both masculine and feminine singular nouns. The same is true for many adjectives that end in a consonant, like **difícil.**

5. Adjectives form the plural the same way nouns do: words that end in a vowel add **-s** and words that end in a consonant add **-es.**

B 14   Actividad • ¿Quiénes son?

You invited your friend Consuelo to a family party. When she comes in, you tell her who the guests are. To complete the sentences, choose one of the adjectives in parentheses. Make changes to the ending of the adjective if necessary.

1. (rubio / alto) El chico _____ es mi hermano, la chica _____ es su amiga.
2. (pelirrojo / delgado) Los chicos _____ son los primos de la chica _____ .
3. (guapo / bajo) La señora _____ es la mamá del chico _____ .
4. (moreno / delgado) El señor _____ es el esposo de la señora _____ .

1. rubio (alto)/alta (rubia)   2. delgados (pelirrojos)/pelirroja (delgada)   3. baja (guapa)/guapo (bajo)   4. delgado/(moreno) morena (delgada)

B 15   ¿Sabes que . . . ?

Some Spanish and Spanish American families seem large because grandparents, cousins, uncles and aunts, and in-laws take part in every family activity. Most of the relatives, and close family friends, are likely to attend every family party and celebration. Given a choice, family members live as close together in a town as they possibly can, often in the same building.

¿alto o baja?

¿gordo o delgada?

¿feo o guapa?

¿moreno, rubia o pelirroja?

¿Cómo son ustedes?

¿tontos o inteligentes?

¿antipáticas o simpáticas?

¿Y cómo eres tú, Roque?

¿generosos o egoístas?

SE DICE ASÍ
Asking what someone or something is like

¿Cómo es?	What's (he, she, it) like?
¿Cómo es tu cuarto?	What's your room like?
¿Cómo son tus padres?	What are your parents like?
¿Cómo son tus clases?	What are your classes like?

B 18 Conversación • La familia

Get together with a classmate and ask each other the following questions about
your families.

modesto   *gordo*   alto   *delgado*   bajo   **guapo**
feo fantástico generoso antipático inteligente moreno *simpático*
rubio

1. ¿Cómo es tu papá? ¿tu mamá? ¿tu profesor(a)?
2. ¿Cómo son tus hermanos(as)? ¿primos(as)?
3. ¿Cómo son los chicos y las chicas de tu clase?
4. ¿Cómo son tus amigos(as)?
5. ¿Y cómo eres tú?

Students will create their own conversation. Ex. Mi papá es alto, inteligente y rubio.

B 19 Actividad • Y ahora tú . . . Students will have their own version.
Ex. Yo soy morena, delgada y simpática. . . .

Describe yourself. Then describe two imaginary characters: someone you like and
someone you don't like.

B 20 Actividad • ¡A escribir! Students will create their own version.
Ex. Soy simpático, moreno y gordo, pero guapo.

Write a brief description of yourself. Describe your family also.

B 21 SE DICE ASÍ
Exclaiming

¿Tu hermana? ¡Qué linda!	Your sister? How pretty!
¿Tu hermano? ¡Qué guapo!	Your brother? How handsome!
¿Tu cuarto? ¡Qué bonito!	Your room? How pretty!
¡Qué chica tan linda!	What a pretty girl!
¡Qué chico tan guapo!	What a handsome boy!
¡Qué cuarto tan bonito!	What a pretty room!

The adjective in an exclamation agrees in gender and number with the noun stated or
understood. The word **tan** in exclamations literally means *so*.

1. ¡Qué horrible! 2. ¡Qué divertido!/¡Qué aburrido! 3. ¡Qué guapo!/¡Qué feo!/¡Qué alto! 4. ¡Qué linda!/¡Qué bonita!/¡Qué fea! 5. ¡Qué bonita! 6. ¡Qué alto!/¡Qué guapo!/¡Qué feo! 7. ¡Qué divertido!/¡Qué aburrido! 8. ¡Qué divertido!/¡Qué aburrido!

B 22 Actividad • Reacciones

You and your friend are talking. One of you repeats a statement from the numbered list. The other expresses a reaction using an appropriate adjective from the box.

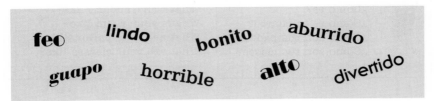

feo lindo bonito aburrido
guapo horrible alto divertido

—Es mi cuarto.
—¡Qué bonito!

1. Llueve y hace frío.
2. ¿Miramos fotos de mi familia?
3. Es una foto de mi tío Tomás.
4. Ella es mi prima Adela.

5. La sala de la casa.
6. Es mi primo. Juega básquetbol.
7. Le gusta practicar deportes.
8. ¿Por qué no escuchamos discos?

B 23 Actividad • Exclamaciones

React with an exclamation, using the clues. Remember that the adjectives should agree. Make the necessary changes.

casa/bonito
¡Qué casa tan bonita!

1. foto / feo ¡Qué foto tan fea!
2. familia / simpático ¡Qué familia tan simpática!
3. cuarto / grande ¡Qué cuarto tan grande!
4. chicos / guapo ¡Qué chicos tan guapos!
5. chicas / inteligente ¡Qué chicas tan inteligentes!
6. señora / amable ¡Qué señora tan amable!

7. chico / tonto ¡Qué chico tan tonto!
8. casa / lindo ¡Qué casa tan linda!
9. amigos / simpático
10. chica / antipático ¡Qué chica tan antipática!
11. fotos / bonito ¡Qué fotos tan bonitas!
12. chicos / divertido ¡Qué chicos tan divertidos!

B 24 Comprensión For script and answers, see p. T125.

Which is the best description?

	0	1	2	3	4	5	6
Paying a compliment				✔			
Welcoming someone						✔	
Making someone's acquaintance	✔						
Extending an invitation		✔					
Asking for an opinion					✔		
Exclaiming							✔
Asking what something is like			✔				

asking someone's opinion . . . paying compliments

When you visit the home of a Spanish-speaking family, be sure to compliment your hosts about how nice things are. It will also be very helpful for you to know the Spanish names of the rooms in the house.

C1 # La casa de Antonio

Antonio y Roberto están en la casa de Antonio.

la sala

el comedor

ROBERTO	Me gusta mucho tu cuarto, Antonio. Es muy cómodo.
ANTONIO	¿Quieres ver toda la casa?
ROBERTO	¡Por supuesto!
ANTONIO	Bueno, ¡vamos! Empezamos por la sala de estar.
ROBERTO	¡Qué linda!
ANTONIO	Aquí estamos en el comedor. Y, al lado por esta puerta, la cocina.
ROBERTO	¿Y el baño?
ANTONIO	Tenemos tres baños. Uno a la derecha de la entrada, otro en el pasillo, y otro en el cuarto de mis padres.
ROBERTO	¿Dónde estamos ahora?
ANTONIO	En la sala. No usamos mucho este cuarto. Es para cuando vienen visitas. Pasamos nuestro tiempo libre en la sala de estar. Es el cuarto más importante.
ROBERTO	¿Entramos aquí?

la cocina

ANTONIO	¡No, está prohibido! Es el cuarto de mis hermanas.
ROBERTO	¡Ya sé! Yo también tengo hermanas. Y vivimos en un apartamento pequeño. ¿Hay un garaje?
ANTONIO	Sí, en el jardín, detrás de la casa. ¿Qué te parece la casa, Roberto?
ROBERTO	Es grande y muy bonita. ¡Y mi cuarto es estupendo!

Actividad • ¡A escoger!

For each numbered sentence, choose the ending that best fits the conversation in C1.

1. Los chicos van primero
   • a la entrada y al pasillo. • al comedor y a la cocina. • al jardín y al garaje.
   • a la sala de estar.

2. La casa tiene
   • un baño en la cocina. • tres baños: uno a la izquierda de la entrada, otro
   en el cuarto de las hermanas y otro más en la cocina.
   • un baño en el cuarto de los padres de Antonio, otro a la derecha de la
   entrada y otro más en el pasillo. • dos baños.

3. La sala es para cuando
   • las hermanas están en la sala de estar. • los padres de Antonio quieren
   hablar. • vienen visitas. • quieren comer y estar en el comedor está prohibido.

4. No entran en el cuarto de las hermanas de Antonio porque
   • el cuarto está frente al garaje. • no usan mucho el cuarto.
   • está prohibido entrar. • es para cuando vienen visitas.

5. El garaje está
   • detrás del jardín. • frente a la entrada. • frente a la casa.
   • detrás de la casa y en el jardín.

1. Sí, le gusta. Es muy cómodo. 2. Van a la sala de estar, al comedor, a la cocina y a la sala. 3. Sí, le gusta. Es muy linda.
4. Tiene tres baños: Uno a la derecha de la entrada, el otro en el pasillo, y el otro en el cuarto de los padres de Antonio. 5. No,

C3 Preguntas y respuestas no usan mucho la sala. Usan la sala cuando vienen visitas. 6. Pasan el
tiempo libre en la sala de estar. 7. Está prohibido entrar en el cuarto de las
Answer the following questions according to **La casa de Antonio,** on p. 177. hermanas de Antonio.

1. ¿Le gusta a Roberto su cuarto? ¿Por qué?   6. ¿Dónde pasan el tiempo libre?
2. ¿A qué cuartos van Roberto y Antonio?   7. ¿Dónde está prohibido entrar?
3. ¿Le gusta a Roberto la sala de estar? ¿Por qué? 8. ¿Vive Roberto en una casa grande?
4. ¿Cuántos baños tiene la casa? ¿Dónde están? 9. ¿Dónde está el garaje en la casa de
5. ¿Usan mucho la sala en casa de Antonio?   Antonio?
   ¿Cuándo usan la sala?   10. ¿Qué le parece la casa a Roberto?

8. No, Roberto vive en un apartamento pequeño. 9. El garaje está detrás de la casa en el jardín. 10. Es grande y muy bonita.

C4 Actividad • ¿Y en tu casa? . . . ¿en tu apartamento?

Do you live in a house or an apartment? What is it like? Answer these questions.
You can base your answers on an imaginary home and family. Students will create their own version.
Ex. Vivo en una casa grande. Tiene
1. ¿Vives en una casa grande o en un apartamento pequeño? cinco cuartos y tres baños, sala,
2. ¿Te gusta tu cuarto? ¿Cómo es? sala de estar, comedor y cocina.
3. ¿En qué cuarto comen ustedes? ¿En el comedor? ¿En la cocina?
4. ¿Usan un cuarto para las visitas? ¿Cuál?
5. ¿Cuántos baños tiene tu casa? ¿Dónde están?
6. ¿Dónde pasan ustedes el tiempo libre?
7. ¿Cuántos teléfonos hay? ¿Dónde están?
8. ¿Cuál es el cuarto más importante de tu casa? ¿La sala? ¿La cocina? ¿Tu
   cuarto? ¿Por qué?
9. ¿Dónde está el televisor? ¿Tienes televisor en tu cuarto?
10. ¿Qué cuarto usas tú más? ¿La sala? ¿La cocina? ¿El comedor? ¿Tu cuarto? ¿Por qué?

Actividad · Adivinanza *Guessing game* Answers will vary.

Look at the floor plan of Antonio's house. Imagine you are in one of its rooms.
Explain to a classmate where you are, without naming the room itself. Use
prepositions from the following list as needed.

a la derecha de   **cerca de**   **frente a**
a la izquierda de   **entre**   **lejos de**
al lado de

Your classmate has to guess where you are.

—Estoy al lado de la cocina, frente a la sala de estar.
—Estás en el comedor.

C6 Actividad · El plano de tu casa Answers will vary.

Draw the floor plan of a house or apartment—either your own, or one you would like to
have. Make a copy of your plan for use in C7 before you write any words on it. Then
write the names of the rooms and spaces (garden, entrance, garage . . .) in Spanish.

C7 Actividad · Charla Free conversation.

Exchange unlabeled floor plans with a classmate. By asking each other questions in Spanish,
each of you should figure out what the different rooms are on the other's plan. Then label them.

La familia 179

Usually the **sala** of a Hispanic house is a living room used only when special guests are visiting. The **sala de estar** is the family room with the TV set where family members read, knit, watch TV, talk, and relax.

C9 Actividad • ¡A escribir! Each student will create his or her own version.

Mi casa. Write all you can about your house, how many rooms it has, what's the most important room, where you spend your free time. You can follow the questions below as a guideline. Write about an imaginary house if you'd prefer.

¿Cuántos cuartos hay?
¿Cuál es el cuarto más importante?
¿Cómo es?
¿Dónde estudias?

¿Tiene tu casa comedor?
¿Dónde comes? ¿En la cocina? ¿En el comedor?
¿Dónde pasas más tiempo?
¿Dónde está tu cuarto? ¿Cómo es?

C10 ESTRUCTURAS ESENCIALES
More possessive adjectives

Remind the students that possessive adjectives agree with the object possessed, *not* with the possessor.

You have already learned three of the possessive adjectives: **mi,** *my,* **tu,** *your,* and **su,** *his, hers, its; your.* The following chart shows them all.

	singular	*plural*	
(yo)	**mi**	**mis**	*my*
(tú)	**tu**	**tus**	*your* (informal)
(él) (ella) (Ud.)	**su**	**sus**	*his* *her* *its* *your* (formal)
(nosotros)	**nuestro** **nuestra**	**nuestros** **nuestras**	*our*
(vosotros)	**vuestro** **vuestra**	**vuestros** **vuestras**	*your*
(ellos) (ellas) (Uds.)	**su**	**sus**	*their* *your*

1. The possessive adjectives **su** and **sus** have several possible meanings. You may replace them with the following construction for clarification.

$$\text{article} + \text{noun} + \textbf{de} + \begin{cases} \textbf{él} \\ \textbf{ella} \text{ or} \\ \textbf{Uds.} \end{cases} \begin{cases} \textbf{ellos} \\ \textbf{ellas} \text{ or noun} \\ \textbf{Uds.} \end{cases}$$

su cuarto → el cuarto **de ella**
su casa → la casa **de Ud.**
su familia → la familia **de Ana María**

2. Possessive adjectives show agreement with the noun that follows. **Nuestro** (-a, -os, -as) shows gender and number agreement. **Mi, tu,** and **su** show number agreement only.

1. Carmen habla con sus abuelos. 2. El tío Tomás habla con sus hijos. 3. Yo hablo con mi abuelo. 4. Los chicos hablan con su padre. 5. El señor Colón habla con su hermana. 6. Nosotros hablamos con nuestros amigos. 7. Tú hablas con tu primo. 8. Mi prima habla con su madre.

C11 Actividad • En la fiesta

There's a party at Antonio's home. All the guests are talking to their own relatives. Sum up the situations using an appropriate possessive adjective, depending on who is talking.

Pedro / la hermana
Pedro habla con *su* hermana.

1. Carmen / los abuelos
2. Tío Tomás / los hijos
3. Yo / el abuelo
4. Los chicos / el padre
5. El señor Colón / la hermana
6. Nosotros / los amigos
7. Tú / el primo
8. Mi prima / la madre

C12 Conversación • ¿Quiénes son?

There's a big family reunion. You don't know for sure who everyone is. Ask your classmate. Using appropriate possessive adjectives, your classmate will confirm that you are right. Then switch roles.

—¿Es él el amigo de ustedes?
—Sí, es nuestro amigo.
—¿La chica alta es la hermana de Luis?
—Sí, es su hermana.

1. Sí, es su padre.
2. Sí, son sus padres.
3. Sí, son sus hermanos.
4. Sí, son tus primos.
5. Sí, es su hija.
6. Sí, es tu prima.
7. Sí, es mi amiga.
8. Sí, es nuestro amigo.
9. Sí, son mis abuelos.
10. Sí, son nuestras primas.

1. ¿El señor es el padre de Carmen?
2. ¿Son los padres de Raúl?
3. ¿Son los hermanos de Gloria?
4. ¿Son mis primos?
5. ¿Es ella la hija de la señora?

6. ¿Es mi prima?
7. ¿La chica guapa es tu amiga?
8. ¿El chico alto es el amigo de ustedes?
9. ¿Los señores son tus abuelos?
10. ¿Son ellas las primas de ustedes?

C13 SE DICE ASÍ
Asking opinions and paying compliments

¿Qué te parece nuestra casa? What do you think of our house?	Tu casa es muy linda. Your house is very pretty. ¡Qué casa linda! What a pretty house!
¿Te gusta mi cuarto? Do you like my room?	Sí, tu cuarto es muy cómodo. Yes, your room is very comfortable.

Conversación • La visita Answers will vary.

Pair up with a classmate. Imagine that you are visiting your classmate. He/she will ask your opinion on different subjects. Answer the questions using the adjective in parentheses and the correct possessive adjective. (Be careful to phrase your answer to fit the type of question your classmate asks.) Take turns.

la tía de Antonio (simpático)

A: ¿Te gusta la tía de Antonio?
¿Qué te parece la tía de Antonio?
¿Cómo es la tía de Antonio?

B: Sí, su tía es muy simpática.
Su tía es muy simpática.

1. tu cuarto (cómodo)
2. nuestra casa (grande)
3. nuestra cocina (lindo)
4. el amigo de mi hermana (alto)

5. la casa de mi tía (feo)
6. mi familia (simpático)
7. mi prima (divertido)
8. su amigo (guapo)

C15 Actividad • ¡A escribir! Each student will have his or her own version.

Write the conversation you had with your classmate in C14. Include questions and answers.

C16 ¿Sabes que . . . ?

Many houses in Spanish cities are built in a row, with no space between each house and no front lawn, like town houses. The main door may open into a hall leading to a large courtyard which is surrounded by the various rooms of the house. The courtyard, or **patio**, is an uncovered open area usually paved with tile or flagstone and decorated with many varieties of colorful plants and flowers. It is a pleasure to sit in almost any room of a Spanish house, because you will have a wonderful view of the **patio**.

C17 Actividad • Combinación

Match the answers on the right with the appropriate questions on the left.

1. ¿Qué te parece mi cuarto?
2. ¿Te gusta tu cuarto?
3. ¿Es alta tu mamá?
4. ¿Cómo es tu hermana?
5. ¿Y tu hermano?
6. ¿Tienes tíos?
7. ¿Cómo son tus primos?
8. ¿Son amigas de ustedes?

No, es baja.
Muy simpática.
Son divertidos.
Sí, dos.
No, son sus amigas.
Muy alto.
Sí, es grande.
Es muy bonito.

182   Unidad 6

TRY YOUR SKILLS

using what you've learned

1

Fiesta de familia

While you are a guest at Lola's home, her parents, Jorge Ramírez Duarte and Delia Pentón de Ramírez give a party. As the family members arrive, Lola introduces you and tells you who they are.

LOLA   Mi tía Consuelo, la esposa del hermano de mi papá.
Tío Guillermo, el esposo de tía Consuelo.
Tía Adela, la hermana de mamá.
Son mis abuelos, los padres de mi madre, don José y doña Elena.
Es mi abuela Josefina, la madre de mi papá.
Los hijos de tío Guillermo y tía Consuelo: Pedro y Pablo.
La hermana de Pedro. Se llama Estrella.
Tato, mi hermano.
Don Mario Ramírez, el padre de mi papá.
Mis primos, los hermanos de Pilar.
Mis padres, Jorge y Delia.

Can you identify Consuelo and the other guests in the picture? Write a sentence about each person or couple that Lola mentioned.

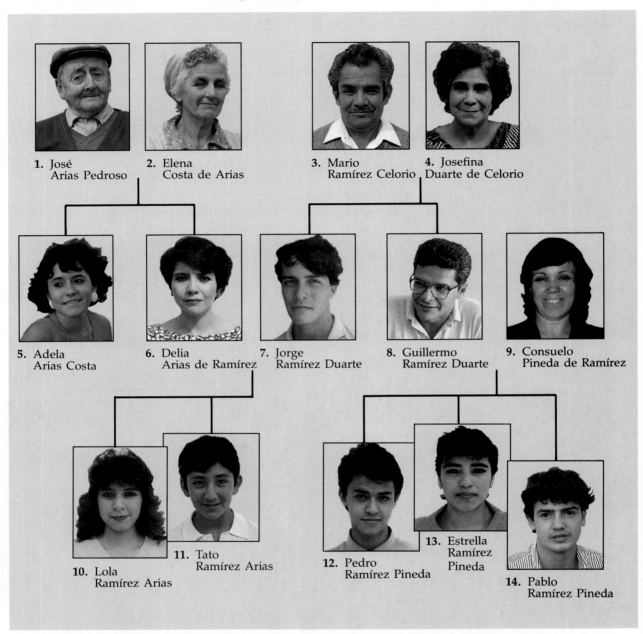

1. José
   Arias Pedroso

2. Elena
   Costa de Arias

3. Mario
   Ramírez Celorio

4. Josefina
   Duarte de Celorio

5. Adela
   Arias Costa

6. Delia
   Arias de Ramírez

7. Jorge
   Ramírez Duarte

8. Guillermo
   Ramírez Duarte

9. Consuelo
   Pineda de Ramírez

10. Lola
    Ramírez Arias

11. Tato
    Ramírez Arias

12. Pedro
    Ramírez Pineda

13. Estrella
    Ramírez
    Pineda

14. Pablo
    Ramírez Pineda

3 Actividad · ¿Quiénes son? ¿Cómo son? Free conversation.

Pair up with a classmate, who was also invited to Lola's party. It's three days later. Discuss the members of Lola's family one by one and compare your impressions—check the pictures in section 2 and your lists of names to refresh your memory of the party. For each person, one of you should give a physical description, and the other imagine what the person is like.

Consuelo   —La tía Consuelo es la esposa del hermano del papá de Lola.
           —Es alta y morena, ¿no?
           —Sí. Me parece muy simpática.

1. Tato	4. Doña Josefina	7. Delia	10. Estrella	13. Pedro
2. Doña Elena	5. Pablo	8. El abuelo Mario	11. Jorge	14. La tía Consuelo
3. Don José	6. La tía Adela	9. El tío Guillermo	12. Lola	

4   Actividad • **Proyecto: Mi familia**   Each student will create his or her own project.

Bring to class a few pictures of your family (or make up an imaginary family
using pictures from magazines). Be prepared to tell the class who they all are and
something about them. Be sure to make any adjectives you use agree in number
and gender with the noun.

5   Actividad • **Charla**   Free conversation. Ex. ¿Es grande el comedor de tu casa?

Pair up with a classmate. Ask each other about the house where you live, use
words from the box below.

sala   cuarto   televisor   garaje   baño
comedor   cocina   teléfono   jardín

6   Actividad • **Una entrevista**   Answers will vary.

Work with a partner. Your father has asked AMISTAD S.A. to place a Spanish-
speaking exchange student with your family. You have to tell the AMISTAD
representative about your (real or imagined) family and house. Describe the
house, tell how many rooms it has, and say what kind of student you would like
to have as a guest. Switch roles.

7   Actividad • **Una carta**   Each student will write his or her letter.

You want to participate in a student-exchange program yourself. To be placed
with a family in a Spanish-speaking country, you have to write a letter in
Spanish. Describe yourself and your likes and dislikes. Give some information
about the kind of family and type of house you would like.

8   Pronunciación, lectura, dictado   [cassette]   For script, see pp. T130–131.

1. Listen carefully and repeat what you hear.

2. The sound of Spanish **c** before **a, o, u** and the sound of **qu** are the same.
   Listen and then read aloud.

   calculadora   cuál   como   con   aquí   quince   querer   raqueta

3. Copy the following sentences to prepare yourself to write them from dictation.
   Los discos cuestan quince dólares.
   Queremos esquiar con Carlos en Colorado.
   La hermana de Rebeca está casada con un chico de Cuba.

¿LO SABES?

Let's review some important points you have learned in this unit.

Do you know how to make a Spanish-speaking guest feel at home and how to show your appreciation when visiting a Spanish-speaking home? Answers may vary.
Welcome a Spanish-speaking guest to your home. Bienvenido. Está en su casa.
Show your appreciation as a guest. Muchas gracias por el almuerzo.

Can you suggest different activities to friends, using the verb *querer*?
Invite the following people to do the suggested activities:

¿Quieren ustedes mirar televisión?/¿Quieren ustedes comer algo?

un amigo(a): escuchar música / ver mi cuarto
la Sra. González: pasar / beber un refresco
los chicos: mirar televisión / comer algo

¿Quieres escuchar música?/¿Quieres ver mi cuarto?/¿Quiere usted pasar?/¿Quiere beber un refresco?

Can you describe family members, other people, and things using:

| alto | inteligente | grande | guapo | Answers will vary. |
| divertido | bonito | rubio | simpático | Ex: El chico es muy alto. |

and changing their endings accordingly, describe:

un chico   una chica   tu casa   el colegio   tus hermanos
tus hermanas   un señor   una señora   tus primos   tus primas

When a friend is showing you something, can you react with an appropriate exclamatory remark?
Use the correct form of the adjective in parentheses.

1. ¡Qué lindo es tu cuarto!

2. ¡Qué bonita es tu casa!

1. Es mi cuarto. (lindo)
2. Es nuestra casa. (bonito)
3. Es mi hermana. (guapo) ¡Qué guapa es tu hermana!
4. Son las fotografías de mi familia. (lindo)
¡Qué familia tan linda!

Can you talk about family relationships?
Express as many relationships as you can for the people in the following family. Then talk about your own family. For answers, see below.

Esteban es el hijo de Tomás y María.
Ana es la esposa de Esteban, ellos tienen tres hijos: Julia, Juan y José.

Can you name five different rooms in a house or an apartment?
sala, sala de estar, comedor, cocina, baño, cuarto
Do you know how to express possession in Spanish?
For each item, compose a phrase with a possessive adjective.

1. nuestra familia
2. tus hermanos
3. mi cuarto
4. su hijo
5. su casa
6. sus fotos

1. familia / (nosotros)   2. hermanos / (tú)   3. cuarto / (yo)
4. hijo / (mi tío)   5. casa / (mis amigos)   6. fotos / (Antonio)

Are you able to ask someone's impression about something or somebody?
Rephrase each sentence using **parecer**.

1. ¿Qué te parece mi casa?

2. ¿Qué te parece mi primo?

1. ¿Te gusta la casa?   3. ¿Te gusta tu cuarto? 3. ¿Qué te parece tu cuarto?
2. ¿Te gusta mi primo?   4. ¿Te gusta la foto? 4. ¿Qué te parece la foto?
Answers will vary.

Compliment the following people on their possessions or relatives, as indicated. Use the correct form of an appropriate adjective. Ex. ¡Qué fotos tan lindas, María!

1. María: sus fotos.   2. Nosotros: nuestros discos.   3. Ellos: su hermana.

B. Esteban y Ana son esposos. Tomás y María son los padres de Esteban y los abuelos de Julia, Juan, y José. Ana y Esteban son los padres de Julia, Juan y José. Julia, Juan y José son hermanos.

VOCABULARIO

(see p. 171)

SECTION A

amable *kind*
bienvenido, -a *welcome*
la casa *house*
con permiso *excuse me*
la cosa *thing*
el cuarto *room*
es un placer . . . *it's a pleasure . . .*
estás en tu casa *make yourself at home*
igualmente *likewise*
un momento *just a moment*
norteamericano, -a *American*
pasa *come in*
pasar *to spend (time); come in*
el placer *pleasure*
querer (ie) *to want*
el refresco *soda*
la sala *living room*
la vacación *vacation*
ver *to see*
la visita *visit*

SECTION B

alto, -a *tall*
antipático, -a *not nice*
bajo, -a *short*
bien *very*
bonito, -a *pretty*
cariñoso, -a *affectionate*
casado, -a *married*
¿cómo es? *what's he, (she, it) like?*
¿Cuántos cuartos hay? *How many rooms are there?*
¿cuántos años tiene? *how old are you (is he/she?)*
de ellos *their*
de nuevo *again*
delgado, -a *thin*

los dos, las dos *the two*
egoísta *selfish*
el esposo *husband*
la esposa *wife*
estar casado, -a *to be married*
la familia *family*
feo, -a *ugly*
la foto *photo*
la fotografía *photograph*
generoso *generous*
gordo, -a *fat*
guapo, -a *handsome*
el hijo *son*
la hija *daughter*
los hijos *children, sons and daughters*
lindo, -a *pretty*
la madrastra *stepmother*
la madre *mother*
los miembros de la familia *family members (see p. 171)*
moreno, -a *dark (hair, complexion)*
murió *(he) died*
¿no? *right?*
el padrastro *stepfather*
el padre *father*
los padres *parents*
papá *dad*
pelirrojo, -a *redheaded*
el primo *cousin*
la prima *cousin*
¡qué cuarto tan bonito! *what a pretty room!*
¡qué guapo! *how handsome!*
rubio, -a *fair, blonde*
el señor *man*
la señora *woman*
simpático, -a *nice*
tan *so*
tener . . . años *to be . . . years old*
todo, -a, -os, -as *all*

tonto, -a *dumb*
la visita *visitor*

SECTION C

el apartamento *apartment*
la cocina *kitchen*
el comedor *dining room*
cómodo, -a *comfortable*
cuando *when*
de él *his*
de ella *her*
de ellas *their*
de usted *your*
de ustedes *your*
empezar (ie) *to start*
la entrada *entrance*
este, -a *this*
frente a *across from*
el garaje *garage*
grande *large*
importante *important*
el jardín *garden*
más *most*
mis *my (pl.)*
nuestro, -a, -os, -as *our*
el pasillo *hall*
pequeño, -a *small, little*
¡por supuesto! *of course!*
prohibido, -a *forbidden*
la puerta *door, gate*
la sala de estar *family room*
sus *her, his, their (pl.)*
el tiempo *time*
el tiempo libre *free time*
tus *your (pl.)*
usar *to use*
¡vamos! *let's go!*
vivir *to live*
vuestro, -a, -os, -as *your (fam. pl.)*
¡ya sé! *I know it!*

You may wish to have the students read the vocabulary at home before each section is introduced.

ESTUDIO DE PALABRAS

1. Write a list of the polite expressions you can use when you meet new friends and visit their home.

2. Make a list of the words you can use to describe a house or an apartment.

1. con permiso, es un placer, ¡qué cuarto tan bonito! 2. bonito(a), feo(a), lindo(a), cómodo(a), pequeño(a).

VAMOS A LEER

Antes de leer

Don't be slowed down in your reading by looking up all unknown words. Let the context help you guess the meaning. For example, in the sentence **Usted X las preguntas,** can you guess that **X** must be the Spanish word for *answer* **(contesta).** Sometimes you must read further before the meaning becomes clear to you.

¡HOGAR, DULCE HOGAR!

Home sweet home! Will this real estate agency help you find the home of your dreams?

AGENCIA BRAVO | CASAS APARTAMENTOS CONDOMINIOS | Teléfono: 32.78.21 Av. Quinta

Contesta° estas preguntas. ¡Escríbenos°! ¡Tú puedes° conseguir° la casa de tus sueños!

¿Es una casa grande? ( )
¿Pequeña? ( )
¿Un apartamento? ( )
¿Qué tiene?
    Una sala grande ( )
    Baños (1) (2) (3) (4)
    Sala de estar ( )
    Cocina ( )
    Comedor ( )
    Dormitorios (1) (2) (3) (4) (?)
    Estudio ( )
    Jardín ( )
    Piscina ( )
¿Dónde está?
    En los suburbios ( )
    En el campo° ( )
    En la ciudad ( )

¡Tenemos la casa de tus sueños°!

¿Piscina, jardín, estudio?

Write a description of what you want in your dream house. Take a poll of your classmates. Ask them: **¿Qué quieres en la casa de tus sueños?** Make a list of their answers and share your findings with the class.

---

contesta *answer* **escríbenos** *write us* **puedes** *you can* **conseguir** *to get* **campo** *country* **sueños** *dreams*

Point out that "e" replaces "y" before words beginning with "i" or "h": "madre e hija".

Actividad • Un agente de propiedades *A real estate agent*

You are a real estate agent. Below are descriptions of some of your customers as well as some ads for properties. Match the customers with the appropriate dwellings.

1. A young working woman is looking for an apartment to share.
2. A mother and her daughter need a house.
3. A young family is looking for a one-family house.
4. A professional man is looking for a room. He doesn't have a car.
5. A family whose elderly grandmother lives with them is seeking a house with a small apartment for her.

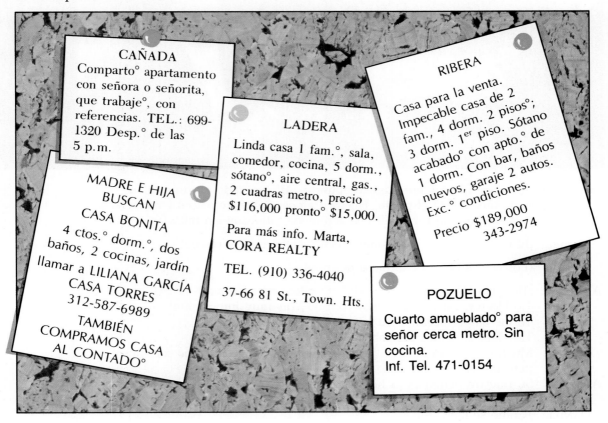

CAÑADA
Comparto° apartamento con señora o señorita, que trabaje°, con referencias. TEL.: 699-1320 Desp.° de las 5 p.m.

MADRE E HIJA BUSCAN CASA BONITA
4 ctos.° dorm.°, dos baños, 2 cocinas, jardín llamar a LILIANA GARCÍA CASA TORRES 312-587-6989
TAMBIÉN COMPRAMOS CASA AL CONTADO°

LADERA
Linda casa 1 fam.°, sala, comedor, cocina, 5 dorm., sótano°, aire central, gas., 2 cuadras metro, precio $116,000 pronto° $15,000.
Para más info. Marta, CORA REALTY
TEL. (910) 336-4040
37-66 81 St., Town. Hts.

RIBERA
Casa para la venta. Impecable casa de 2 fam., 4 dorm. 2 pisos°; 3 dorm. 1er piso. Sótano acabado° con apto.° de 1 dorm. Con bar, baños nuevos, garaje 2 autos. Exc.° condiciones.
Precio $189,000
343-2974

POZUELO
Cuarto amueblado° para señor cerca metro. Sin cocina.
Inf. Tel. 471-0154

Actividad

Pair up with a classmate. One is a real estate agent. The other plays the client. The client is looking for a house or an apartment. The agent has to offer what he or she has available. Make it sound attractive. Switch roles.

---

comparto *I share*   **que trabaje** *who works*   **desp.** *después*   **ctos.** *cuartos*   **dorm.** *dormitorio*   **al contado** *cash*
fam. *familia*   **sótano** *basement*   **pronto** *down payment*   **pisos** *stories*   **acabado** *finished*   **apto.** *apartamento*
exc. *excelentes*   **amueblado** *furnished*

El regalo

Adriana y Daniel van a la cafetería del aeropuerto. Allí, sentado en° una de las mesas° con la aeromoza, está el piloto, Héctor Ramos. Beben refrescos y conversan. En otra mesa está el hombre rubio. Él y la aeromoza intercambian miradas°.

DANIEL	¡El refresco! . . . , la aeromoza echó° algo en el refresco.
	(Los chicos corren a la mesa del piloto.)
ADRIANA	¡Tío! ¡Tío Héctor! ¿Cómo estás? (El piloto no contesta.)
DANIEL	Tío Héctor, queremos hablar contigo°. ¡Es muy importante!
HÉCTOR	Yo me llamo Héctor pero . . . ¿quiénes son ustedes?
DANIEL	Tío Héctor, somos tus sobrinos°.
HÉCTOR	Mucho gusto. Pero, . . . ¿mis sobrinos? Yo tengo muchos sobrinos, pero no . . .
ADRIANA	Sí, nuestra mamá es tu hermana.
HÉCTOR	¿Mi hermana? Mi hermana no tiene hijos.
DANIEL	¿Cómo se llama ella?
HÉCTOR	Sara. Es baja, un poco gorda y tiene cuarenta años . . .
DANIEL	Sí, Sara Ramos, nuestra mamá, tu hermana. Es alta y baja, digo°, baja y gorda.
AEROMOZA	¿Qué quieren ustedes? ¡Váyanse°!, o . . .
ADRIANA	O, ¿qué? ¿Va a llamar a la policía, señorita?

---

sentado en *seated at*   **mesas** *tables*   **intercambian miradas** *(They) exchange glances*   **echó** *poured*   **contigo** *with you*
sobrinos *nephew and niece*   **digo** *I mean*   **váyanse** *go away*

La aeromoza no contesta. Héctor comienza a sentir° los efectos del refresco. El señor rubio se levanta° de la mesa. Muchas personas se acercan°. El piloto se desmaya°. En la confusión la aeromoza y el señor rubio desaparecen°. Daniel y Adriana escapan. Ya en casa, ellos prenden° el televisor. La locutora entrevista° a una mujer bonita. Es la aeromoza.

LOCUTORA	La policía busca a dos chicos que trataron de° asesinar° a Héctor Ramos, un piloto de Mexicana de Aviación. Aquí con nosotros la aeromoza del vuelo 28.
AEROMOZA	Creo que son hermanos. El chico es alto y moreno, y tiene 14 ó 15 años. La hermana es mayor°, es flaca° y fea.
DANIEL	¡Hablan de nosotros°!
ADRIANA	¿Yo? ¿Flaca? ¿Fea? ¡Imposible!

Actividad • ¿Quién habla?

Which of the characters from **El regalo** might say or think each of the following?

1. Bueno, tengo unos minutos. Voy a tomar un refresco con ella. el piloto
2. ¿Quiénes son estos chicos? ¿Por qué quieren hablar con Héctor? la aeromoza
3. ¿Por qué están esos chicos en la mesa de mi amiga y el piloto? el hombre rubio
4. No es mi hermana Sara. Mi hermana Sara no tiene hijos. el piloto
5. Mi hermana es inteligente. Tenemos un plan muy bueno. Daniel
6. Yo soy delgada, no flaca. Y soy muy bonita. Adriana

---

comienza a sentir *starts to feel*   **se levanta** *gets up*   **se acercan** *(they) come close*   **se desmaya** *faints*
desaparecen *disappear*   **prenden** *(they) turn on*   **entrevista** *(she) interviews*   **que trataron de** *who tried to*   **asesinar** *to murder*   **mayor** *older*   **flaca** *skinny*   **de nosotros** *about us*

UNIDAD 7 **¡Vamos a salir!**
Scope and Sequence

	BASIC MATERIAL	COMMUNICATIVE FUNCTIONS
SECTION A	**¡A pasear!** (A1) **¿Adónde vamos hoy?** (A6) **¿Sales mucho?** (A17)	**Socializing** · Accepting and turning down invitations · Expressing regret · Giving an excuse **Expressing obligation** · Using **tener que**
SECTION B	**¿Qué vamos a ver?** (B1) **Mejor una policial** (B8)	**Expressing attitudes and points of view** · Expressing intention · Expressing opinions **Persuading** · Making suggestions
SECTION C	**¡Tito Ortega canta hoy!** (C1)	**Socializing** · Getting someone's attention · Interrupting politely · Asking for information
TRY YOUR SKILLS	Pronunciation (rhythm) Sound-letter correspondences (the letter **g** before **a, o, u**) Dictation	
VAMOS A LEER	**¿Qué dan hoy?** (movie ads in Spanish to choose from) **Guía de espectáculos** (a guide of movies in Spanish) **El regalo** (The police are looking for Daniel and Adriana.)	

WRITING   A variety of controlled and open-ended writing activities appear in the Pupil's Edition. The Teacher's Notes identify other activities suitable for writing practice.

COOPERATIVE LEARNING   Many of the activities in the Pupil's Edition lend themselves to cooperative learning. The Teacher's Notes explain some of the many instances where this teaching strategy can be particularly effective. For guidelines on how to use cooperative learning, see page T13.

GRAMMAR	CULTURE	RE–ENTRY
The verb **poder** (A3) The verbs **salir** and **decir** (A21)	Where Spanish-speaking students go and what they do when they go out	The verbs **querer, tener, venir**
Expressing future time (B3) Adjectives, adjective phrases, and deletion of nouns (B11) The verbs **pensar** and **empezar** (B18)	Going to the movies Film festival in Mar del Plata	Descriptive adjectives The verb **ir** Present tense of **-ar** verbs
The verb **saber** (C6) Direct objects and the personal **a** (C10) The verb **conocer** (C13)	Pop music concerts in Buenos Aires	Weather expressions Possessive adjectives
Recombining communicative functions, grammar, and vocabulary		
Reading for practice and pleasure		

TEACHER-PREPARED MATERIALS

Section A   Pictures of an ice-cream cone and a party, magazine pictures

Section B   Movie section of newspaper

UNIT RESOURCES

Manual de actividades, Unit 7
Manual de ejercicios, Unit 7
Unit 7 Cassettes
Transparencies 17–19
Quizzes 16–18
Unit 7 Test

OBJECTIVES **To socialize:** accept and turn down invitations; express regret, give an excuse; **to express obligation:** use **tener que.**

CULTURAL BACKGROUND Buenos Aires is the capital and largest city of Argentina. The name *Buenos Aires* literally means *"fair winds"*. Early Spanish sailors named the harbor at the site for the patron saint of fair winds, **Nuestra Señora Santa María del Buen Aire.** The city was founded twice, once in 1536 and again in 1580, after being destroyed by the Indians. Today it is one of the world's most modern cities. About a third of Argentina's people live in the Buenos Aires metropolitan area. They call themselves **porteños** (port dwellers). The widest street in the world, **Avenida 9 de Julio,** is located in the central business district of Buenos Aires. It is 425 feet (130 meters) wide.

There are many museums and libraries in Buenos Aires. The city is the cultural center of Latin America. The **Teatro Colón,** located in downtown Buenos Aires, is one of the most famous opera houses in the world.

MOTIVATING ACTIVITY Ask the students what places of interest—both historic and modern—in their region they would want to show a Hispanic visitor in the United States.

A1 ¡A pasear!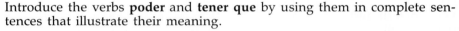

Introduce the verbs **poder** and **tener que** by using them in complete sentences that illustrate their meaning.

> Tengo un examen. Tengo que estudiar.
> Necesito dinero. Tengo que trabajar.
> Quiero ir al cine, pero no puedo.
> No podemos nadar en el invierno.

Next, teach expressions the students may use to show whether they are interested in going somewhere. Write the following expressions on the board or a transparency.

> ¿Quieres ir a jugar tenis?
> Sí, fantástico. ¡Vamos!

> ¿Vas a la fiesta el sábado?
> No, no puedo. Tengo que estudiar.

Have the students suggest other situations in which these expressions may be used, such as **¿Quieres salir?** and **¿Puedes ir al juego de fútbol?**

To present the new vocabulary, show pictures of an ice-cream cone and a party. Have the students repeat the new words after you. Ask questions that will require them to demonstrate understanding of the new words.

> ¿Cuándo toman helado?
> ¿Van a una fiesta este mes?

Play the cassette or read the dialog aloud. Then have the students work in groups of three to read and role-play the dialog.

A2 Combinación

As a variation, you may wish to write the items from each box on flash cards or on a transparency and play the game "Concentration". For writing practice, have the students write the complete sentences.

A3 ESTRUCTURAS ESENCIALES

Point out that the verb **poder,** like the verb **querer** that the students learned in Unit 6, is a stem-changing verb. Explain that **poder,** like its English equivalent, is usually followed by an infinitive. The **o** changes to **ue,** except in the **nosotros** form. Ask the students to write the forms of the verb **poder,** using the information they have about stem-changing verbs. Then have them check their verb forms by using the chart and making any necessary corrections.

To practice **poder** and re-enter the verb **querer,** write the following sentences on the board or a transparency. Have the students change the sentences, using forms of the verb **poder.**

> ¿Quieres dar una vuelta?
> José y Daniel quieren tomar un helado.
> Sergio quiere ir a la fiesta.
> Queremos estudiar el sábado.
> Quiero jugar fútbol con mis amigos.

A4 Actividad • ¡Nadie puede ir!

Have the students supply the correct form of the verb **poder.** Call on students to dictate the sentences as you or a volunteer write them on the board or a transparency.

A5 Actividad • ¿Quieres ir?

Ask each student to work with a partner. Have them take turns asking and answering questions with the verbs **querer** and **poder.**

A6 SITUACIÓN • ¿Adónde vamos hoy?

Play the cassette or read the captions aloud. Then tell the students to cover the captions. Have the students identify each picture as you ask: **En la foto arriba a la izquierda, ¿dónde están los muchachos?** The students should respond: **Están en la piscina.**

After the students have identified each photograph, ask questions such as, **¿Qué hacemos en la piscina?** and **¿Qué haces en una discoteca?**

A7 Actividad • Adivinanza

For cooperative learning, have the students work in pairs. They should take turns identifying the location of each person mentioned. Each student should make sure his or her partner can state the correct location of each person. Then call on individuals from each group to provide the answers for the class.

A8 Conversación • ¿Puedes ir . . . ?

Have each student work with a partner to ask and answer the questions. Then each student should tell the class where his or her partner is going and why.

A9 SE DICE ASÍ

To practice accepting and turning down invitations, have the students use the questions in A8, but this time they should provide a response from the chart. Divide the class into two groups. Have each group stand in two cir-

cles with the inner circle facing the outer circle. Then tell each student to ask the student facing him or her a question. After each question, the students in the inner circle should move to the right and ask their new partner another question.

A 10 Conversación • Vamos a . . .

Remind the students to use the contraction **al** when necessary. Also, you might have the students include the day or time in their questions.

> Vamos a la playa el sábado, ¿puedes venir?
> Vamos al cine mañana a las diez, ¿puedes venir?

A 11 SE DICE ASÍ

To practice **tener que,** call on students to list the things they have to do in order to accomplish each of the following:

> Sacar buenas notas
> Tener a sus papás contentos
> Ser atleta del año
> Ganar dinero
> Comprar un coche
> Ir al cine

A 12 Actividad • Instrucciones

For writing practice, have the students write complete sentences. They should supply the correct form of **tener que.**

A 13 Conversación • ¿Qué tienes que hacer?

Encourage the students to continue the conversation with their own questions. They might discuss what each person in their family has to do every day.

> Mi padre tiene que trabajar.
> Mi hermana tiene que ir a la escuela.
> Yo tengo que lavar los platos.

A 14 SE DICE ASÍ

Read the chart aloud to the students and have them repeat the expressions. You might introduce the exclamation **¡Ay!** for the students to use when expressing regret. **¡Ay! ¡Qué lástima!**

A 15 Actividad • Charla

Have each student team up with a partner. Using the list of places to go or one of his or her own, each student should extend an invitation to his or her partner. Then the partner must express regret and give an excuse. Have the students take turns.

A 16 Actividad • ¡A escribir!

CHALLENGE   Ask the students to write a dialog about the following situation. Explain that they want to go for a walk in the park because it is a warm, sunny day in spring. They call two friends and they both say no, each making an excuse. Finally, the third person they call accepts the invitation.

A17 SITUACIÓN • ¿Sales mucho?

Before presenting the interviews, explain the meaning of **¿Sales mucho?** and **¿Cuántas veces?** Introduce the verb **salir,** using the following dialog.

TEACHER	Yo salgo los domingos. ¿Cuándo sales tú?
MIGUEL	Yo salgo los viernes por la noche.
TEACHER	¿Sale Miguel los viernes por la mañana?
SANDRA	No, Miguel sale los viernes por la noche.

Continue the dialog until all forms of the verb **salir** have been presented and everyone has had the opportunity to respond. Then play the cassette or read aloud the interviews.

A18 Actividad • No es así

For writing practice, have the students write the corrected statements. Then call on volunteers to read their sentences aloud.

A19 Actividad • Preguntas y respuestas

Have the students work in pairs to supply the correct answers. Encourage them to refer to the interviews before answering. They may also write the answers in class or at home.

ANSWERS:
1. Entrevista a cuatro estudiantes.
2. ¿Sales mucho? ¿Cuántas veces por semana sales? ¿Qué te gusta hacer cuando sales?
3. Cristina va al cine, a conciertos, o a casa de sus amigos.
4. Sí, le gusta porque ¡bailar es fantástico!
5. Le gusta ir a las discotecas y a los bailes.
6. Le gusta salir a pasear.
7. Sale con otros chicos.
8. Marta sale los sábados por la noche y los domingos.
9. Porque puede volver a casa tarde.
10. A veces va al cine.

A20 Actividad • Entrevistas

SLOWER-PACED LEARNING Write the following questions on the board or a transparency for the students to use in their interviews. Suggest that they also add original questions.

1. ¿Cuándo te gusta salir?
2. ¿Sales a menudo?
3. ¿Adónde te gusta ir?
4. ¿Con quién sales?

A21 ESTRUCTURAS ESENCIALES

You may wish to ask the students to name other verbs that are similar in the **yo** form of the present tense, such as **vengo** and **tengo.**

To practice the verb **decir,** you may use a similar presentation as introduced for the verb **salir** in A17 above.

A22   Actividad • ¡A escribir!

Have the students write the complete sentences at home or in class. Then call on individuals to read their sentences aloud as you or a volunteer write them on the board or a transparency.

A23   Actividad • ¿Con quién salen?

Have each student work with a partner to form sentences with the verb **salir.** They may also include the names of their classmates as a variation.

A24   SE DICE ASÍ

To supplement the chart, you may wish to include **a menudo** and **bastante.** This will clarify the expressions used in the interviews and give the students additional vocabulary to use in A25.

A25   Conversación • De paseo

SLOWER-PACED LEARNING   After the students have answered the questions, have them write five sentences. Each student should state where and how often he or she goes out. Then ask the students to use magazine pictures to illustrate each sentence. Have them use the following words and phrases in their sentences:

> Bailar
> Nadar
> Ir a una fiesta
> Dar una vuelta
> Montar en bicicleta
> Muchas veces
> Nunca
> Los sábados
> Todos los días
> Siempre

A26   Conversación • ¿Sales mucho?

Have each student ask and answer the questions with a partner. Then the students should report their findings to the class.

A27   Actividad • ¿Qué preguntan?

As a variation, divide the class into groups of four. Choose one of the answers at random from the box and have the students write the question. Call on an individual from each group to read his or her question. Each team will receive a point for every member's question that matches. You may wish to point out the correct questions if more than one is acceptable. Continue the activity until all the answers have questions. The team with the most points wins.

A28   Actividad • ¡A escribir!

If the students have completed the activity as in A27, you may wish to assign a question and answer activity that will lead to free conversation.

A29 Comprensión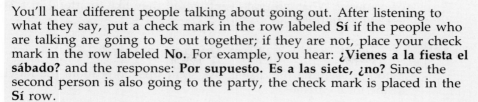

You'll hear different people talking about going out. After listening to what they say, put a check mark in the row labeled **Sí** if the people who are talking are going to be out together; if they are not, place your check mark in the row labeled **No**. For example, you hear: **¿Vienes a la fiesta el sábado?** and the response: **Por supuesto. Es a las siete, ¿no?** Since the second person is also going to the party, the check mark is placed in the **Sí** row.

1. —¿Vamos a la piscina?
   —No, no hace buen tiempo. *no*
2. —¿Quieren ir a la playa?
   —Bueno, ¿a qué hora? *sí*
3. —¿Por qué no damos una vuelta?
   —No, yo tengo que estudiar. *no*
4. —¿Tú no vienes? ¡Qué pena!
   —Lo siento, voy a casa de mis tíos. *no*
5. —¿A qué hora salimos?
   —A las cuatro, ¿qué te parece? *sí*
6. —¿Puedes estar en la cafetería a la una?
   —Sí, a la una estoy allí. *sí*
7. —¿Vienes con nosotros o no?
   —No, no puedo, tengo que estudiar. *no*
8. —¿Cuándo vamos al club? ¿el sábado?
   —Sí, el sábado. Mi hermana viene tambien. *sí*

Now check your answers. *Read each exchange again and give the correct answer.*

A30 Actividad • Una encuesta

Have the students combine their information to produce a general survey. They should find out how many students enjoy doing the same things, what days are the most popular for going out, when is the best time for going out, and how often teenagers go out each week.

A31 Actividad • Informe

After the interviews are completed and a general consensus has been made, have the students discuss what the teenagers in their town like to do with their free time. How does this differ from Spanish-speaking teenagers?

 SECTION B

OBJECTIVES   **To express attitudes and points of view:** express opinions; express intentions; **to persuade:** make suggestions

CULTURAL BACKGROUND   Mar del Plata is a coastal city in the southeastern part of Argentina, approximately 400 kilometers south of Buenos Aires. Argentines refer to it as the "Pearl of the Atlantic." Mar del Plata was declared a city in 1907 and has developed as Argentina's foremost summer resort. It is the home of one of the world's largest casinos, has many luxury hotels, and cultural events such as the annual international film festival.

MOTIVATING ACTIVITY Ask the students to name the annual cultural events in their area. Have they attended cultural events in another state or country? What cultural event would they like to attend in a Spanish-speaking country?

B1 ¿Qué vamos a ver?

Before presenting the dialog, ask some questions about the movies playing at the local cinemas.

> ¿Qué dan en el cine hoy?
> ¿Les gusta?
> ¿Quiénes son los actores y las actrices?
> ¿Cuál es tu película favorita?
> ¿Cuándo van al cine? ¿Por la noche? ¿Por la tarde?

Introduce the new vocabulary: **el periódico, la película, el cine,** and the verb **empezar.** Have the students role-play before you play the cassette or read the dialog aloud.

To check comprehension, you may wish to ask the following or similar questions.

> **1.** ¿Cómo se llama la película de ciencia-ficción?
> **2.** ¿Qué dan en el Savoy?
> **3.** *¿Basta de ruido* es una musical?
> **4.** ¿Qué película van a ver Paula y Miguel?

B2 Actividad • ¡A escoger!

Have the students choose the option that best completes each sentence, according to B1. For writing practice, have the students write out the sentences.

B3 ESTRUCTURAS ESENCIALES

Re-enter the verb **ir** and then write the following or similar examples on the board or a transparency.

> Voy a ir al cine mañana.
> Sergio va a dar una fiesta el sábado.
> Vamos a dar una vuelta por la tarde.

Call on students to identify what tense is expressed in the examples. Then ask them to identify the verbs in each sentence and how the future is expressed using this verb form.

To verify their predictions, have the students read the explanation in B3 on expressing future time.

SLOWER-PACED LEARNING Read aloud each expression in the box and have the students repeat it after you. You may also wish to give the English equivalent to clarify the structure for the students. Write the sentences on the board, omitting the verb **ir** or the infinitive. With books closed, have the students supply the missing word or words. Then they should open their books, check their work, and make any necessary corrections.

B4 Actividad • Combinación

Have each student work with a partner. They should match the items from each column to form five sentences.

B5 ## Actividad • ¿Qué van a hacer?

For writing practice, have the students write the sentences in class or at home. Ask them to exchange papers to correct the work.

B6 ## Conversación • El fin de semana

Have each student work with a partner to ask and answer the questions. Then have each student tell the class what his or her partner has planned for the weekend.

B7 ## Actividad • ¡A escribir!

Have the students make plans for a weekend in a city or town other than their own. They could imagine that they are going to Buenos Aires, Madrid, Caracas, or a small town in any Spanish-speaking country. Remind the students that they might do something different than what they are accustomed to doing in the United States, such as attend a bullfight **(una corrida),** go to **El Parque del Retiro,** or go to a soccer game **(un partido de fútbol).**

B8 ## SITUACIÓN • Mejor una policial

Before presenting the dialog, introduce the expression **tener ganas de.** Explain the term **dibujos animados** by giving examples such as *Snow White* **(Blanca Nieves),** *Pinocchio* **(Pinocho),** and so on. Then play the cassette or read aloud the dialog.

For cooperative learning, have the students work in pairs to role-play the dialog. Each student should make sure his or her partner understands and is able to present the dialog. Call on each pair to role-play the dialog for the class.

B9 ## Actividad • Combinación

Refer the students to the dialog in B8 to match each movie title with its correct description.

CHALLENGE Have the students bring in the movie section of a newspaper. Each student should work with a partner and describe each movie in Spanish.

The Princess Bride	aventura/amor
Robocop	ciencia-ficción/policial

B10 ## Actividad • Y ahora tú . . .

Have each student pair up with a classmate. They should take turns asking and answering the questions. Ask them to report their findings to the class or to a third person.

B11 ## ESTRUCTURAS ESENCIALES

Write the following examples on the board or a transparency:

Un libro cómico	Uno cómico
Un libro de terror	Uno de terror
Una película policial	Una policial

Ask the students to identify what occurs in the second column. Write their responses on the board or a transparency. To reinforce the students' observations, read aloud the explanation of adjectives, adjective phrases, and the deletion of nouns.

B12 Actividad • ¡Al cine!

Have the students rewrite the sentences, omitting the nouns that are not necessary. Remind the students to delete only the nouns that are repeated too often. They should reread the sentences after they edit them to make sure the dialog makes sense. Then call on volunteers to read their sentences aloud.

B13 Actividad • Charla

After the students have read the script aloud with their partners, call on volunteers to role-play their original scripts.

B14 Actividad • ¡A escribir!

To re-enter the descriptive adjectives from Unit 6, have the students write advertisements about two movies that are showing at a local cinema. The students should include a description of the movies , the names of the actors, and in what theater the movies are showing. Remind the students to use several adjectives in their advertisements.

B15 SE DICE ASÍ

Read aloud the expressions in the box to the students. Then have each student choose a partner to practice the expressions. They should replace the names of the movies with their own. They may also replace **al cine** and **al parque** with places they would like to go.

—¿Tienes ganas de ir a la casa de David?	—No, mejor vamos a tomar un helado.
—¿Vamos a ver *El cuento americano*?	—¿Y si vemos *Police Academy*?

B16 Conversación • ¿Qué quieres ver?

Tell the students to use the information in the box as a guide for their conversation. They should discuss where to go, what movie to see, and at what time to see it.

To re-enter the prepositions of location, have the students draw a map and give directions on how to get to the cinema.

B17 Actividad • ¡A escribir!

Collect and correct the dialogs. Then call on pairs to role-play the dialog for the class.

B18 ESTRUCTURAS ESENCIALES

Re-enter the **-ar** verbs with the students. Then write the verbs **pensar** and **empezar** on the board or a transparency. Explain that these verbs are stem-changing verbs. The stressed **e** changes to **ie.** Review the forms of **cerrar** to remind the students of the pattern. Then provide the subject pronouns and

call on individuals to provide the correct forms of **pensar** and **empezar.** Write them on the board or a transparency. Then have the students compare their responses with the forms on the chart in the book.

SLOWER-PACED LEARNING Write the structure of the verbs **empezar** and **pensar** on the board or a transparency, omitting the stems. Ask the students to provide the missing stem: **e** or **ie.**

Yo p_____nso.
Tú p_____zas.
Nosotros p_____nsamos.
Ustedes emp_____zan.

B 19 Actividad • ¿Qué piensan hacer?

For writing practice, have the students write the sentences with the correct form of **pensar.** Have them exchange papers to correct their work.

B 20 Actividad • ¿Piensan ir?

After the students have completed the activity, write the following or similar sentences on the board or a transparency. Have the students provide the correct form of the verb **empezar.**

1. ¿A qué hora _____ la película?
2. Las clases _____ a las ocho.
3. Nosotros _____ la tarea después de comer.
4. ¿Cuándo _____ tú a estudiar?

B 21 SE DICE ASÍ

Read aloud the expressions on the chart. Ask the students to identify the pattern that appears in the responses. Confirm students' observations by stating that the word **que** follows each verb and that in a negative response the word **no** is placed before the predicate.

Practice expressing opinions by starting a conversation such as **¿Creen que va a llover?, ¿Crees que el equipo de fútbol va a ganar el juego?,** and so on.

B 22 Actividad • ¿Qué crees?

Have the students complete the activity. They may discuss what movie they would like to see, using the completed questions as a guide.

B 23 Conversación • Opiniones

For cooperative learning, form groups of three. One student should read the sentence and the other two should express their opinions, using the words in parentheses as a guide. Each member of the group should make sure that everyone else understands and can respond appropriately.

B 24 Comprensión

Two friends are planning to go to the movies. Listen carefully as they discuss what movies they might see and where the movies are playing. After

listening to what they say, put a check mark in your list next to the names of the movies, cinemas, and types of movies mentioned in their conversation.

SOFÍA   ¿Por qué no vamos al cine?
MIGUEL   ¿Qué quieres ver?
SOFÍA   No sé, ¿qué te parece una película policial?
MIGUEL   Mejor una cómica.
SOFÍA   ¡Buena idea! ¿Sabes que dan *Genio de bolsillo* en el cine Parque?
MIGUEL   Pero no tengo ganas de ir al Parque. ¡Es lejos!
SOFÍA   ¿Y si vamos al cine Metro?
MIGUEL   ¿Qué dan?
SOFÍA   Creo que dan una película de ciencia-ficción, *La hora de las computadoras.*
MIGUEL   ¡Estupendo! ¡Vamos!

Películas	Cines	Clases
1. Genio de las computadoras	✔1. Parque	1. del oeste
✔2. Genio de bolsillo	2. Real	2. musical
3. Música de bolsillo	3. Conde	✔3. cómica
✔4. La hora de las computadoras	✔4. Metro	4. de amor
5. Música en el parque	5. Genio	✔5. policial
6. Computadoras musicales	6. Plaza	✔6. de ciencia-ficción
7. Computadoras de bolsillo	7. Arte	7. de dibujos animados

Now check your answers. *Read each exchange again and give the correct answer.*

SECTION C

OBJECTIVES **To socialize:** get someone's attention; interrupt politely; **to exchange information:** ask for information

CULTURAL BACKGROUND In Argentina, there are nearly 1,500 cinemas. Teenagers in Buenos Aires enjoy going to the theater, movies, and attending concerts. There are over thirty theaters in Buenos Aires. The famous **Teatro Colón** presents concerts and ballets as well as operas, and attracts large audiences. Luna Park is the largest auditorium in Buenos Aires, hosting international celebrities such as Frank Sinatra, Julio Iglesias, and Alberto Cortéz. It seats approximately 10,000 people and is located downtown.

MOTIVATING ACTIVITY Explain to the students that many teenagers in Argentina go to cafés before or after they go to a concert or the movies. Then ask the students where they enjoy going.

C1   **¡Tito Ortega canta hoy!**

Introduce the new vocabulary by showing pictures or using each word in a sentence that illustrates its meaning. You may wish to add that **cola** is also used for *line.* Elicit the Spanish word for *window,* and then point out the word **ventanilla.** Have the students guess its meaning.

Present the irregular verb **saber** by using the following or similar dialog:

TEACHER	Yo sé dónde está el cine. Carlos, ¿sabes dónde está?
CARLOS	Sí, yo sé dónde está.
TEACHER	Carlos y yo sabemos dónde está. ¿Ustedes saben?
MARIO AND CAROLINA	No, nosotros no sabemos.

Play the cassette or read aloud the dialog. Then have the students form cooperative learning groups to role-play the dialog.

SLOWER-PACED LEARNING   Distribute a series of true or false statements after the students listen to the dialog. As they listen, they may follow along in their books. Then allow the students time to read and consult the text as they indicate whether each statement is true or false.

C2 Actividad • Para completar

You may wish to have the students summarize the dialog before doing this activity. Have them exchange papers to correct their work.

As a variation, have the students make up four true and false statements and have a round-robin. False statements must be corrected. Student 1 reads a statement to student 2. Student 2 answers and reads a statement to student 3, and so on.

C3 SE DICE ASÍ

After reviewing the expressions in the box, read the following examples and have the students provide the correct responses.

Estás con tus amigos. Otro amigo viene.   *¡Mira! ¡Oye!*
En una cola del cine, quieres saber cuánto cuesta una entrada.
   ¡Perdón! ¡Por favor!
No quieres comer más. Tienes ganas de ir a tu cuarto.   *¡Permiso, por favor!*

C4 Actividad • Reacciones

For oral practice, have students work with a partner. Remind them to use appropriate expressions for each individual. They should not use **¡Oye!** or **¡Mira!** with someone they would address with **usted.**

C5 Actividad • ¡A escribir!

Call on volunteers to write on the board or a transparency as individuals read the statements aloud.

C6 ESTRUCTURAS ESENCIALES

Read aloud the examples and the explanation of the verb **saber.** Point out that the first-person singular of the verb **saber, sé,** requires an accent to differentiate it from the pronoun **se.**

C7 Actividad • Combinación

To practice the verbs learned in this unit, you may wish to write subject pronouns and sentence fragments (including the verb) on slips of paper. Divide the class into small groups. Each group member should have a slip with the

subject pronoun or the sentence fragment on it. Each member should find the other member in the group whose slip fits with his or her own slip to make a sentence.

C8 SE DICE ASÍ

Ask each student to practice asking for information with a partner. One student should play the role of a travel agent who provides information to a client who would like to go to Buenos Aires. The client should ask what the weather is like, where the airport is located, what the cost of a round-trip ticket (**billete de ida y vuelta**) is, and if tickets are available. Have the students switch roles.

C9 Conversación • Al teatro

CHALLENGE   Have the students expand the conversation and discuss the concert in detail. They should discuss who is playing at the concert, which of their friends are going, how they are going, and what time they will be returning. They might also have this conversation on the telephone, so ask them to include the expressions used while speaking on the phone.

C10 ESTRUCTURAS ESENCIALES

To introduce the direct objects and the personal **a,** write the following sentences on the board or a transparency.

> Veo la película.
> Buscamos el lápiz.
> Hector espera el avión.

Ask the students to identify the verb and the direct object in each sentence. Then have the students state whether each direct object names a person or a thing.
   Now write these sentences on the board or a transparency and ask the students to point out the difference.

> Veo a mi primo.
> Buscamos a la hermana de Carlos.
> Hector espera a su amigo.

   To confirm the students' observations, read aloud the explanation in the book. Then write the following paragraph on the board and ask the students to rewrite it on a sheet of paper, changing all the direct object items to persons and vice versa. They should also add or delete the personal **a** when necessary.

> Después de las clases, Consuelo espera <u>el autobús</u>. Ella mira a <u>sus amigos</u>. Tiene ganas de ver <u>una película</u> esta noche, pero sabe que es importante cuidar <u>los animales</u>.

C11 Actividad • ¿Qué dicen?

Have the students complete this activity in pairs. Remind the students to use the personal **a** when necessary.

C12 Actividad • ¡A escribir!

SLOWER-PACED LEARNING   Before the students complete the writing activity, you may wish to practice the use of direct objects and the personal **a.**

Read the following cues and call on individuals to form complete sentences, using the personal **a** when necessary.

> Mira/el periódico
> Mira/su hermano
> Ven/Juan
> Veo/el libro
> Lleva/su cartera
> Lleva/su amigo
> Tomamos/un helado
> Tomamos/el autobús

C13 ESTRUCTURAS ESENCIALES

To point out the difference between **conocer** and **saber,** write the following sentences on the board or a transparency and ask the students to identify the differences in meaning.

> Yo conozco a tu amigo.
> Él sabe llegar a la discoteca.
> Conocemos Acapulco.
> Ellos saben cuánto cuestan los boletos.

Confirm the students' observations by asking them to read the explanation in the book.

C14 Actividad • Una fiesta

For cooperative learning, form groups of three or four. The students in each group should ask and answer each of the questions to complete the dialog. As a variation, they should replace the names with their own and role-play the completed dialog for the class.

C15 Actividad • La familia de Tito Ortega

SLOWER-PACED LEARNING You may wish to write the dialog on the board or a transparency, including the blanks for **saber** and **conocer.** Then do the exercise orally with the students. For writing practice, the students may write the dialog at home.

After the students complete the dialog, re-enter the possessive adjectives introduced in Unit 6 and personalize the activity by asking about people and places within the students' own experience: **¿Conoces a mi hermana/o? ¿Sabes cómo es nuestra maestra de inglés?** They may respond with descriptive adjectives: **Sí, es alto y rubio. Sí, es muy simpática.**

TRY YOUR SKILLS

OBJECTIVE To recombine communicative functions, vocabulary, and grammar

CULTURAL BACKGROUND For Spanish-speaking teenagers, the most popular pastime is listening to and playing music. It is very common to see a group of young people singing together, as one person plays the guitar. They enjoy rock and folk music and admire the groups from the United States. In Spain, many musical groups imitate American rock musicians. They have evolved a new sound called **"flamenco rock"**. This type of music has a rock beat combined with a flamenco melody.

1

Para una revista

The students may work in pairs to prepare ten questions to ask their class-mates. To re-enter the seasons and the months of the year, tell the students that they may ask the questions referring to specific seasons or months of the year.

¿Qué te gusta hacer en el invierno?
¿Adónde vas en diciembre?

2

Actividad • Entrevistas

Have the students ask the ten questions they prepared in Skills 1 to five different classmates. Then they should report their findings to the class.

3

Actividad • ¡A escribir!

Brainstorm, with the class, titles that would be appropriate for their articles. Write them on the board or a transparency and tell the students to choose their favorite one. You might also prepare a brief article and read it to the students so that they know what they are to write.

4

Actividad • ¿Adónde vamos?

Before the students form groups, review with them how to accept or turn down invitations as presented in A9, on page 197. After everyone in the group has agreed on the arrangements, they should report their plans to the class. As a variation, the students may wish to write an invitation in Spanish to the other classmates, instead of reporting their plans.

5

Actividad • ¿Qué o a quién?

Each student may work with a partner to ask and answer the questions. Remind them to use the personal **a** when the direct object is a person.

When the students have completed the activity, suggest that each student write two additional sets of questions using other verbs such as **conocer, tomar,** or **ir a.** Then each student should select a new partner and answer one another's questions.

6

Conversación • Al teléfono

As a variation, have the students role-play the telephone conversation in class.

SLOWER-PACED LEARNING   The students should make cue cards to use when presenting their conversations to the class. They should not write the entire conversation on the cards; the question words should be sufficient.

7

Actividad • ¡A escribir!

CHALLENGE   You may wish to have the students write an imaginative telephone conversation based on a fictional character such as ET. They could entitle their conversation: **ET llama a casa.** Ask the students to describe what ET would arrange for entertainment, or have ET describe the world of fun on Earth to a fellow extraterrestrial.

8 **Pronunciación, lectura, dictado**

1. Listen carefully and repeat what you hear.
   The sound of **g**: When followed by the letters **a**, **o**, or **u**, Spanish **g** is pronounced like the *g* in the English words *girl* and *garden*. Listen to the following words and repeat each word.

algunos	gusta	tengo	García
amiga	goma	hamburguesa	guía

   Note that the letter **u** in the syllables **gue** and **gui** is always silent; therefore, only the **e** or the **i** is pronounced right after the **g**.

2. Listen, and then read aloud.
   Listen to the following words to review the sound of **g.** Then, as you look at your book, read each word aloud.

regular	gusto	lugar	gordo
Miguel	Guillermo	ganas	alguno

3. Write the following sentences from dictation. First, listen to each sentence as it is read to you. Then you will hear the sentence again in short segments, with a pause after each segment to allow you time to write. Finally, you will hear the sentence a third time so that you may check your work. Let's begin.

   No tengo ganas *(pause)* de jugar golf *(pause)* hoy.
   Me gusta mucho *(pause)* ir al cine *(pause)* con mi amigo *(pause)* Gustavo.
   ¡Magnífico! *(pause)* El domingo *(pause)* salgo con Gregorio.
   ¡Qué guapo *(pause)* y delgado *(pause)* es Guillermo Rodríguez!

¿LO SABES?

SECTION A

Before the students complete the exercise, review the expressions used to accept and turn down invitations. Remind the students to use **tengo que** when explaining why they cannot go. You may also wish to review the possessive adjectives.

SECTION B

After the students have written the five questions they prepared for Section B, you might have them exchange papers with a classmate and answer each other's questions.

For additional practice naming different kinds of movies, write the following list of movie titles on the board or a transparency and have the students describe them.   ellas

> *El sueño de amor*
> *El monstruo amarillo ataca la Tierra*
> *Los policías de la ciudad*
> *Los tres locos mexicanos*
> *El criminal del invierno*

SECTION C

For the first activity, have the students choose the appropriate expression that fits each situation. Remind them not to use **¡Mira!** and **¡Oye!** in formal situations.

For additional practice of the verbs **saber** and **conocer,** have the students complete the following activity.

1. Yo _____ tu amigo Nicolás *conozco*
2. Él _____ cuánto cuesta la entrada. *sabe*
3. Nosotros _____ Honduras. *conocemos*
4. Ustedes _____ nadar bien. *saben*
5. Mi hermano no _____ llegar al teatro. *sabe*

VOCABULARIO

Cadena de palabras   A student starts a sentence with one word. Successive students add one word to the partial sentence. Any student who cannot add a word, or who adds a word to which other words cannot be added, must drop out of the game. As the sentence grows in length, it should be written on the board as a memory aid. Have the students repeat all the words in the sentence each time a word is added.

ESTUDIO DE PALABRAS

After the students have listed the places where people go to enjoy themselves, have them classify the nouns as masculine or feminine. Ask the students to include the words in the **Vocabulario** section of their notebooks.

VAMOS A LEER

OBJECTIVE   To read for practice and pleasure

Antes de leer

You may wish to have the students practice expressing time in Spanish with a 24-hour clock before they read the selection. Write the following times on the board or a transparency and ask the students to convert each given time to standard time.

17:30	20:20
14:00	15:30
21:00	13:20
18:10	19:50

¿QUÉ DAN HOY?

Have the students read the title of each movie and look at the posters. Ask them to describe in Spanish what they see in the posters and name the type of film each poster represents. Read the posters aloud as the students follow along in their books.

GUÍA DE ESPECTÁCULOS

Have the students follow along in their books as you read aloud the movie schedule.

Actividad • Charla

Have pairs of students decide on a movie they both want to see. Have them report their plans to the class.

EL REGALO

After summarizing the previous episodes, have the students silently read this episode of **El regalo.** Then play the cassette or read aloud the dialog. Form cooperative learning groups to role-play the dialog for the class.

Actividad • Decisiones

Form groups of three students and have them decide what is best for Adriana and Daniel. They should be prepared to defend their decisions.

UNIDAD 7
¡Vamos a salir!

Spanish-speaking teenagers generally like to go out together in mixed groups. They may go to a movie or a concert. More often, they just go for a walk. In small cities, they may walk to the main square, where they meet their friends and chat. In a modern metropolis like Buenos Aires, Argentina's capital, they may go to a club or a shopping mall. Like teenagers everywhere, they have to plan, discuss, and agree on where they are going to go for a walk or what kind of movie or concert they will attend.

In this unit you will:

SECTION A	accept and turn down invitations
SECTION B	say what you are going to do . . . express opinions
SECTION C	get someone's attention . . . ask for information
TRY YOUR SKILLS	use what you've learned
VAMOS A LEER	read for practice and pleasure

SECTION A

Accepting and turning down invitations

What do Spanish-speaking students do when they go out? Where do they go? The answer depends partly on where you live. If they were living in Buenos Aires, they would have a lot of choices!

For additional information on Buenos Aires, see p. T136.

A1

¡A pasear!

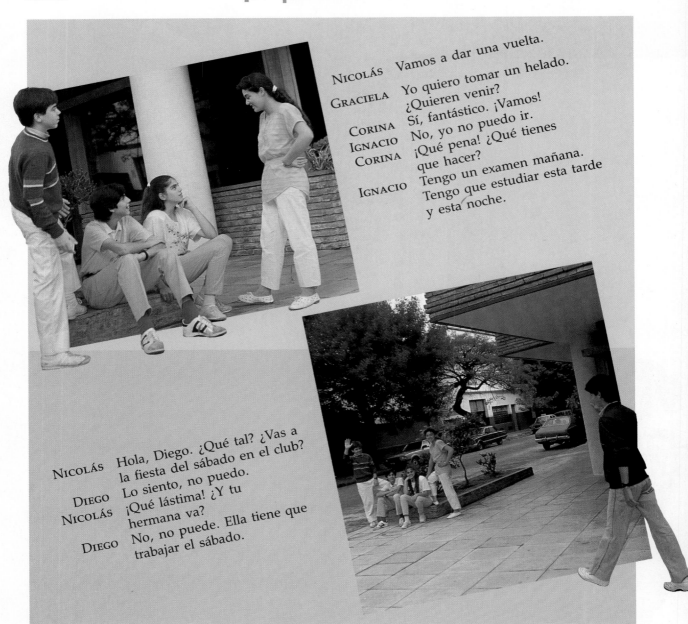

NICOLÁS Vamos a dar una vuelta.

GRACIELA Yo quiero tomar un helado. ¿Quieren venir?

CORINA Sí, fantástico. ¡Vamos!

IGNACIO No, yo no puedo ir.

CORINA ¡Qué pena! ¿Qué tienes que hacer?

IGNACIO Tengo un examen mañana. Tengo que estudiar esta tarde y esta noche.

NICOLÁS Hola, Diego. ¿Qué tal? ¿Vas a la fiesta del sábado en el club?

DIEGO Lo siento, no puedo.

NICOLÁS ¡Qué lástima! ¿Y tu hermana va?

DIEGO No, no puede. Ella tiene que trabajar el sábado.

Point out that young people in Spanish America go to places and do activities in groups, as portrayed in the dialog.

Yo no puedo ir. ¿Vas a la fiesta del sábado? Ella tiene que trabajar el sábado. Tengo que estudiar. Tengo un examen mañana. Quiero tomar un helado. Vamos a dar una vuelta. ¿Qué tienes que hacer?

A2 Combinación

Match the items in the two boxes to agree with the conversations in A1.

Vamos a	Tengo	puedo ir.	examen mañana.
Yo quiero	¿Qué tienes	fiesta del sábado?	tomar un helado.
Yo no	¿Vas a la	trabajar el sábado.	dar una vuelta.
Tengo un	Ella tiene que	que estudiar.	que hacer?

Stress that "poder" is usually followed by an infinitive, and rarely used alone, except for a short answer: "Sí, puedo. No, no puedo."

A3 ESTRUCTURAS ESENCIALES
The verb poder

poder (ue) *to be able, can*			
Puedo	ir a la fiesta.	**Podemos**	dar una vuelta.
¿Puedes	venir?	**Podéis**	estudiar.
Puede	esperar.	**Pueden**	tomar un helado.

You saw the stem-changing verb **querer** in Unit 6. **Poder** is also a stem-changing verb. In the four present-tense forms that are stressed on the stem, the stem vowel changes from **o** to **ue**. The stem of the **nosotros(as)** form does not change: **podemos**.

Poder has the same endings in the present tense as regular **-er** verbs. In sentences, **poder** is often followed by an infinitive.

No **puedo ir.**   *I can't go.*
Diego y Luisa no **pueden ir** a la fiesta.   *Diego and Luisa can't go to the party.*

A4 Actividad • ¡Nadie puede ir!

Complete the following using **poder.**

¡Vamos a la fiesta! ¿<u>Puede</u> ir tu hermana? No, no <u>puede</u> . ¿Y los chicos, <u>pueden</u>?
No, ellos no <u>pueden</u>. Ustedes, ¿<u>pueden</u>? No, nosotros no <u>podemos</u>
Y tú, ¿<u>puedes</u>? No, yo no <u>puedo</u> . Pero, ¿quién <u>puede</u> ir?

A5 Actividad • ¿Quieres ir?

Answer the following sentences using **querer** and **poder.**

—¿Quieres tú venir el sábado?
—Sí, quiero pero no puedo.

1. ¿Quieren ustedes dar una vuelta?
2. ¿Quiere usted venir?
3. ¿Quieres tú venir mañana?
4. ¿Quieren ustedes tomar un helado?
5. ¿Quieres tú esperar aquí?
6. ¿Quieren ir los chicos?

1. Sí, queremos pero no podemos. 2. Sí, quiero pero no puedo. 3. Sí, quiero pero no puedo. 4. Sí, queremos pero no podemos. 5. Sí, quiero pero no puedo. 6. Sí, quieren pero no pueden.

A6 SITUACIÓN · ¿Adónde vamos hoy?

¿a la piscina?

¿a una discoteca?

¿al cine?

¿al parque?

¿a la playa?

A7 Actividad · Adivinanza You may wish to point out that when *ir a* is followed by the masculine article *el*, *a* and *el* contract: *ir al cine.*

You have to guess where these people are according to what they're saying. Refer to the places mentioned in A6.

— ¿Quieres bailar?
  Están en la discoteca.

1. ¿Montamos en bicicleta? Están en el parque.
2. Hace mucho calor. Están en la playa/piscina.
3. Ella baila muy bien Están en la discoteca.
4. ¿Puedes ver bien? Están en el cine.
5. ¿Jugamos fútbol ahora? Están en el parque.

6. Siempre corren aquí. Están en el parque.
7. No quiero nadar, quiero comer. Están en la piscina.
8. ¿Corremos o montamos en bicicleta? Están en el parqu
9. Hace frío para nadar. Están en la piscina/parque.
10. Sí, me gusta mucho bailar. Están en la discoteca.

A8 Conversación · ¿Puedes ir . . . ? Answers will vary.

Pair-up with another student. Ask your partner the following questions. Exchange roles.

¿Quieres ir a . . . la piscina.
¿Puedes ir hoy a . . . la playa.
¿Por qué? Porque no tengo clase.
¿Puedes ir el sábado a . . . el cine.
¿Por qué? Porque quiero ir.

la piscina   el parque
la playa
la discoteca   el cine

196   Unidad 7

SE DICE ASÍ
Accepting or turning down invitations

	¿Quieres venir? Do you want to come?	Sí, fantástico. ¡Vamos! Yes, great! Let's go!
	¿Puedes venir? Can you come?	Lo siento, no puedo. I'm sorry, I can't.

A 10 Conversación • Vamos a . . . Answers will vary.

Tell your partner where you and your friends are going and ask him or her to join in.

—Vamos a la playa,
   ¿puedes venir?

• Sí, fantástico, vamos.
• Lo siento, no puedo.

el parque la piscina el cine la discoteca
el club   dar una vuelta   la playa

A 11 SE DICE ASÍ
Expressing obligation with **tener que**

Point out that in "tener que" + infinitive, only the verb "tener" is conjugated. The infinitive always remains unchanged.

	Tengo que estudiar. **Tienes que** venir a las ocho. **Tiene que** esperar.	**Tenemos que** trabajar. **Tenéis que** comer. **Tienen que** decidir.

When you want to say that *you have to do something,* you can use a form of **tener** followed by **que** and the infinitive of the verb that tells what has to be done.

A 12 Actividad • Instrucciones

Your musical group is playing for a party. The bandleader is giving instructions. Complete each instruction using the expression **tener que.**

tiene que/tiene que
1. Ustedes _____ venir temprano. tienen que
2. Todos _____ estar aquí a las nueve. tienen que
3. Tú _____ llamar a Ignacio. tienes que

4. Él también _____ venir. Él _____ cantar.
5. Su hermana _____ tocar la guitarra. tiene que
6. Nosotros _____ practicar. tenemos que

A 13 Conversación • ¿Qué tienes que hacer? Answers will vary.

Ask your partner what he/she has to do. Exchange roles.

1. ¿Qué tienes que hacer hoy después de la escuela?
2. ¿Tienes que ir a tu casa?
3. ¿Qué tienes que hacer en tu casa?
4. ¿Qué tienes que hacer mañana a las 8 de la mañana?

5. ¿Y a las 3 de la tarde?
6. ¿Tienes algo que hacer el fin de semana?
7. ¿Y el sábado?
8. ¿Qué tenemos que hacer para la clase de . . . ?

SE DICE ASÍ
Giving an excuse, expressing regret

The excuse—a reason why you can't.	Regret that the invitation can't be accepted.
No puedo, tengo que estudiar.	¡Qué lástima! ¡Qué pena!

A 15   Actividad • Charla   Free conversation

Extend an invitation to your partner. Your partner turns it down, giving a reason why. You express regret.

¿Vienes al club?

piscina cine
discoteca
parque
playa

Lo siento, no puedo, tengo que trabajar.

• ¡Qué lástima!
• ¡Qué pena!

esperar . . .
estar en . . .
estudiar . . .
ir a . . .
jugar . . .
practicar . . .

A 16   Actividad • ¡A escribir!

Write the conversation you had with your partner in A15.

A 17   SITUACIÓN • ¿Sales mucho?

La revista *Juventud de hoy* entrevista a cuatro estudiantes. Ellos contestan nuestras preguntas: ¿Sales mucho? ¿Cuántas veces por semana sales? ¿Qué te gusta hacer cuando sales?
You may wish to point out the spelling of "juventud" and "joven".

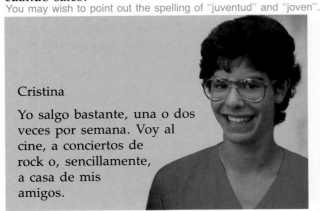

Cristina

Yo salgo bastante, una o dos veces por semana. Voy al cine, a conciertos de rock o, sencillamente, a casa de mis amigos.

Roberto

Lo que más me gusta es bailar. Yo voy a bailes y discotecas todo el tiempo. ¡Bailar es fantástico!

Ricardo

Me gusta mucho salir a pasear con otros chicos. Salimos a menudo. Damos una vuelta, si tenemos ganas, vamos a un café, tomamos algo y hablamos mucho.

Marta

Yo salgo todos los domingos. También los sábados por la noche. Me gusta salir los fines de semana porque puedo volver a casa tarde. A veces voy al cine.

A18 Actividad • No es así

1. Cristina va bastante al cine.
2. Sale una o dos veces por semana.

Correct these sentences so they are true according to the interviews in A17.

1. Cristina va bastante a casa de sus tíos.
2. Ella sale tres o cuatro veces por semana.
3. Roberto va mucho a casa de sus amigos.
4. Ricardo siempre va a pasear con sus hermanas.
5. Si tienen ganas, ellos van a la discoteca.
6. Marta tiene que volver temprano los sábados.

3. Roberto va mucho a bailar. 4. Ricardo siempre va a pasear con otros chicos.
5. Si tienen ganas, van a un café. 6. Marta puede volver tarde los sábados.

A19 Actividad • Preguntas y respuestas   For answers, see p. T139.

Answer the following questions according to the interviews in A17.

1. ¿A quiénes entrevista *Juventud de hoy?*
2. ¿Qué preguntas contestan ellos?
3. ¿Adónde va Cristina?
4. ¿Le gusta a Roberto bailar? ¿Por qué?
5. ¿Adónde le gusta ir a él?
6. ¿Qué le gusta a Ricardo?
7. ¿Con quién sale él?
8. ¿Qué días sale Marta?
9. ¿Por qué le gusta a ella salir los sábados?
10. ¿Adónde va ella a veces?

A20 Actividad • Entrevistas

Interview a classmate using A17 as a model.

A21 ESTRUCTURAS ESENCIALES
The verbs salir *and* decir (e → i)

salir *to go out*		decir *to say*	
salgo	salimos	digo	decimos
sales	salís	dices	decís
sale	salen	dice	dicen

1. The verbs **salir** and **decir** add a **-g-** in the **yo** form of the present tense.
2. In Spanish, some verbs like **decir** change the **e** to an **i** in the stem of all singular forms and the **ellos** plural form.
3. The endings of **salir** and **decir** are regular.

Actividad • ¡A escribir!

¿Cuándo salen? Write full sentences using **salir**.

los chicos / ahora   Los chicos salen ahora.

1. yo / por la tarde
2. nosotros / el sábado

3. ¿(tú) / mañana?
4. Marta y yo / esta noche

5. ¿(usted) / a menudo?
6. Ricardo / en dos minutos

1. Yo salgo por la tarde. 2. Nosotros salimos el sábado. 3. ¿Tú sales mañana? 4. Marta y yo salimos esta noche.
5. ¿Usted sale a menudo? 6. Ricardo sale en dos minutos.

A23 **Actividad • ¿Con quién salen?** Answers will vary. Ex: Isabel sale con sus padres.

Say who goes out with whom.

—Ella sale con su hermana.

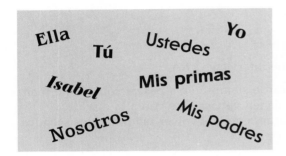

A24 **SE DICE ASÍ**
Asking how often people go out

¿Cuántas veces por semana sales?	¿Una vez? ¿Dos veces? ¿Tres o más?	• Yo salgo tres veces por semana. • Yo salgo una vez por semana.

A25 **Conversación • De paseo** Answers will vary.

Answer the following personal questions.

1. ¿Sales los fines de semana?
2. ¿Qué días sales? ¿Los sábados, los domingos?
3. ¿Qué te gusta hacer cuando sales?

4. ¿Con quién sales?
5. ¿Cómo vas? ¿En auto? ¿A pie?
6. ¿Cuántas veces por semana sales?

A26 **Conversación • ¿Sales mucho?** Answers will vary.

Once again explore the subject of going out, this time with a classmate.
Ask your partner:

1. ¿Dices que sales mucho?
2. ¿Cuántas veces por semana sales?
3. ¿Vas mucho al cine?
4. ¿Y a la discoteca?

5. Y tus amigos. ¿Van ellos al parque?
6. ¿A la playa?
7. ¿A discotecas?
8. ¿A bailes o a fiestas?

Actividad • ¿Qué preguntan? Answers will vary. Ex: —¿Sales mucho?
—Sí, salgo bastante.

State appropriate questions for each of the following answers.

Tengo un examen
Por la tarde
Sí, salgo bastante
Los fines de semana
Lo siento, no puedo
Con otros chicos
Al cine
A las diez
Tengo que estudiar
Matemáticas

A veces bailamos
A casa de nuestros amigos
Escuchar discos
Dos veces por semana
Con mi hermano

A 28 Actividad • ¡A escribir! Answers will vary.

Write your questions for A27, and their corresponding answers.

A 29 Comprensión [cassette icon] For script and answers, see p. T141.

Are we all going?

	0	1	2	3	4	5	6	7	8
Sí	✔		✔			✔	✔		✔
No		✔		✔	✔			✔	

A 30 Actividad • Una encuesta Each student will create his or her own data sheet.

Make a data sheet like the one shown below. Interview six of your classmates about how often they go out, on what days, and where they go. Write the answers on your sheet. Fill in all the spaces.

¿Quién?	¿Adónde?	¿Qué días?	¿Cuándo?	¿Cuántas veces por semana?
David	discoteca	sábados	por la noche	una
Paula	...	jueves y domingos	....	dos
....	cine	....	por la tarde	....

A 31 Actividad • Informe *Report* Guide the students on how to tabulate their findings and the ratio, according to the number of responses.

Report the results of your interview to the class. Indicate what form of entertainment is most popular among the classmates you interviewed. Prepare a written version of your report.

Saying what you are going to do . . . expressing opinions

Most Argentines love to go to the movies. The annual film festival in Mar del Plata is the country's most important showcase for new movies. To decide what movie to see, you need to be able to understand the ads in the newspaper.

For additional background on Mar del Plata, see p. T141.

You may wish to point out that *"el programa"* is a masculine word.

B1 ## ¿Qué vamos a ver?

Paula y Miguel están en el Café Suárez, en Buenos Aires. Dicen que piensan ir al cine, pero, ¿qué van a ver? Miguel mira el periódico.

MIGUEL   Mmm . . . Aquí está el programa de mañana. Van a dar *Bodas de plata.* ¿Hoy? . . . Hoy dan *Basta de ruido.*

MIGUEL   ¿Qué vamos a hacer? ¿Vamos al cine? ¿Qué clase de película quieres ver?

PAULA   ¿Qué dan en el cine Belgrano?

MIGUEL   *Detenidos en el tiempo.* ¡Premio de oro, Mar del Plata! Creo que es una película de ciencia-ficción.

PAULA   ¿Y si vamos al Savoy? ¿Qué te parece? ¿Qué dan ahí?

PAULA   *¿Basta de ruido?* Me parece que es una musical. Mejor vamos al Belgrano.

MIGUEL   Bueno, entonces, vamos a ver *Detenidos en el tiempo.* ¡Vamos! La película va a empezar. Son casi las seis.

Actividad • ¡A escoger!

Choose the option that better reflects the conversation in B1.

1. Paula y Miguel están en
   • el cine Savoy.   • Mar del Plata.   • <u>el Café Suárez</u>.
2. Miguel mira
   • a Paula.   • <u>el periódico</u>.   • la película *Basta de ruido*.
3. En el cine Belgrano dan
   • <u>*Detenidos en el tiempo*</u>.   • *Bodas de plata*.   • *Basta de ruido*.
4. Parece que *Basta de ruido* es
   • una película de ciencia-ficción.   • <u>una musical</u>.   • ¡Premio de oro!
5. En el cine Savoy van a dar *Bodas de plata*
   • hoy.   • <u>mañana</u>.   • el jueves.
6. Paula y Miguel van
   • <u>al cine Belgrano</u>.   • al Savoy.   • al Café Suárez.

B3 ESTRUCTURAS ESENCIALES
Expressing future time

To say what someone will do or is going to do, you can use:

1. A present-tense form of the verb.

   Paula **va** al cine.   *Paula goes to the movies.*

   Often other words, usually time expressions, are added to more clearly indicate the future time.

   ¿Qué película **dan mañana?**   *What movie is playing tomorrow?*
   ¿Qué película **dan a las nueve?** *What movie is playing at nine?*

2. A present-tense form of **ir** + **a** + the infinitive of the main verb.

Voy a ver la película.	**Vamos a ir** al cine.
¿Qué **vas a hacer?**	**Vais a dar** una vuelta.
Va a mirar el periódico.	**Van a tomar** algo.

To make a negative statement with **ir**, put **no** before the form of **ir**.

   Paula **no va a mirar** el periódico.   *Paula is not going to look at the paper.*
   ¿Tú **no vas a mirar** el periódico?   *Aren't you going to look at the paper?*

B4 Actividad • Combinación

¿Adónde van a ir? Match the three columns.

Cristina	**vamos a ir**	**con mis padres.**
Irene y yo	**van a bailar**	**un helado.**
Yo	**va a escuchar**	**a dar una vuelta.**
Tú	**voy a salir**	**un concierto de rock.**
Mario y ella	**vas a tomar**	**a una discoteca.**

1. Cristina va a escuchar un concierto de rock. 2. Irene y yo vamos a ir con mis padres. 3. Yo voy a salir a dar una vuelta. 4. Tú vas a tomar un helado. 5. Mario y ella van a bailar a una discoteca.

Actividad • ¿Qué van a hacer?

Complete the answers using the verb in parentheses in an **ir** + **a** + infinitive construction.

1. (hacer) ¿Qué _____ tú?   vas a hacer
2. (salir) Yo _____ .   voy a salir
3. (dar) ¿Y Paula? Ella _____ una vuelta.   va a dar
4. (tomar) Nosotros _____ un helado.
5. (salir) ¿Y Raúl y Mario? Ellos _____ con sus padres.
   4. vamos a tomar   5. van a salir

6. (estudiar) ¿Y tú? Yo _____ .   voy a estudiar.
7. (trabajar) ¿Y tu hermano? Él _____ con la computadora.   va a trabajar
8. (salir) ¿Y ustedes _____ ?   van a salir
9. (mirar) No, nosotros _____ televisión.   vamos a mirar
10. (ir) ¿Quién _____ al cine?   va a ir

B6 Conversación • El fin de semana   Answers will vary.

Make plans with a classmate to go out on the weekend.

¿Qué día van a salir? ¿Adónde van a ir? ¿Con quién? ¿A qué hora? ¿Cómo van a ir? ¿En auto, tren, autobús? ¿Cuánto dinero van a necesitar?

B7 Actividad • ¡A escribir!

Write down the plans for the weekend that you made with your partner.

B8 SITUACIÓN • Mejor una policial

TERESA	¿Vamos a ver *Sueño de amor?*
RAQUEL	No, hoy no tengo ganas de ver una película de amor.
TERESA	¿Y si vemos *El amigo de Frankenstein?*
RAQUEL	¿Una de terror? ¡No! Mejor vemos *Fantasía*.
TERESA	*Fantasía* es de dibujos animados. En el Rex dan una del oeste. ¿Qué te parece?
RAQUEL	Si quieres ver una de aventuras, aquí hay una: *Vuelo fantástico*.
TERESA	¿*Vuelo fantástico?* ¡No! Es de ciencia-ficción. Vamos a ver una cómica: *Líos locos*.

RAQUEL   *Crimen en el hielo*, ¡la mejor policial del año!
TERESA   ¿Una policial? ¡Fantástico! ¡Vamos!

B9 Actividad • Combinación   El amigo de Frankenstein es una película de terror.

Match each movie title with its correct description.

—*Sueño de amor* es una película de amor.

Sueño de amor es una película de amor.
Fantasía es una película de dibujos animados.
Vuelo fantástico es una película de ciencia ficción.

Sueño de amor	**cómica**
El amigo de Frankenstein	**policial**
Fantasía	**ciencia-ficción**
Vuelo fantástico	**dibujos animados**
Líos locos	**terror**
Crimen en el hielo	**amor**

Líos locos es una película cómica.
Crimen en el hielo es una película policial.

Actividad • Y ahora tú . . . Answers will vary.

Pair up with another student. Ask each other the questions. Take notes on what your partner answers and compare notes.

1. ¿Te gusta ir al cine? ¿Por qué?
2. ¿Vas al cine a menudo o ves películas por televisión?
3. ¿Qué clase de películas te gusta? ¿De amor, de aventuras . . . ?
4. ¿Vas a ir al cine hoy? ¿Y el fin de semana?
5. ¿Qué película tienes ganas de ver?
6. ¿Qué clase de película es?
7. ¿Tiene premios? ¿Cuáles?

B 11   ESTRUCTURAS ESENCIALES
Adjectives, adjective phrases, and the deletion of nouns

Point out that the adjective is used as a noun and that it will take the gender and number of the noun it replaces: "El chico mexicano. El mexicano."

1. You can describe a noun with an adjective. You can also use an adjective phrase with **de.**

   adjective
   Vemos una película **policial.**   *We're seeing a detective movie.*

   adjective phrase
   Vemos una película **de terror.**   *We're seeing a horror movie.*

2. It is common, unless confusion would result, to delete a noun that is modified by an adjective or adjective phrase.

   No, mejor vemos una policial.   *No, better to see a detective one.*

3. **Un** becomes **uno** if the noun is deleted. (Notice that while in Spanish you just delete the noun, in English you sometimes have to replace it with the word *one* or *ones.*)

   Él tiene tres coches, uno rojo   *He has three cars, a red one*
   y dos azules.   *and two blue ones.*

B 12   Actividad • ¡Al cine!   Possible answers are given.

Edit the following script for a movie commercial. The writers repeat nouns too often. Delete some of them.   Point out that *película* has been omitted in the model answer.

   —¿Vamos a ver una película musical?
   —No, mejor vemos una policial.

1. ¿Quieres ir al cine Rex?
2. ¿Y si vamos al cine Metropolitan?
3. En el cine Metropolitan dan una película de terror.
4. ¡No!, no quiero ver una película de terror.
5. Mejor vemos una película de ciencia-ficción.
6. ¡Buena idea! Vamos al cine Plata.

1. No, mejor vamos al Metropolitan.   2. No, mejor vamos al Rex.   3. No, mejor vemos una policial.   4. No, mejor vemos una de amor.   5. No, mejor vemos una de terror.   6. No, mejor vamos al Rex.

Actividad • Charla   Answers will vary.

Read the following script aloud with a partner. Then create a script of your own, replacing the underlined words.

A —¿Vamos al cine <u>Real</u>?
B —¿Al <u>Real</u>? ¿Qué película dan?
A —Una <u>de terror</u>, *La hermana de Drácula*.
B —No, no quiero ver una <u>de terror</u>.
    Quiero ver una <u>cómica</u>.

A —¿Una <u>cómica</u>? Entonces, podemos ver
    Líos locos.
B —¿Y si vemos una <u>musical</u>?
A —¡Fantástico! Vamos al Rex a ver
    Basta de ruido.

B 14   Actividad • ¡A escribir!

Prepare a written version of the script you created with your partner in B13.

B 15   SE DICE ASÍ
Different ways of making suggestions

¿Tienes ganas de ir al cine?	No, mejor vamos al parque.
¿Vamos a ver *Premio de honor*?	¿Por qué no vemos *Detenidos en el tiempo*?
¿Quieres ver *Detenidos en el tiempo*?	¿Y si vemos *Premio de honor*?

When people make suggestions, you sometimes want to respond with a better idea. One way is to begin with **No, mejor . . .** *(No, it would be better to . . .).* Another way is just to suggest something else, in the form of a question.

B 16   Conversación • ¿Qué quieres ver?   Answers will vary.

You and your friends want to go out. Discuss with a classmate what movie house to go to, what movie to see, and at what time. Here are some possibilities.   Ex: Vamos al nuevo a ver una policial a las cuatro.

Cines	Películas	Hora
Nuevo	policial	4 p.m.
Real	de ciencia-ficción	5 p.m.
Palace	de amor	6 p.m.
Plaza	cómica	7 p.m.

¿Vemos una película de misterio?

No, mejor una de ciencia-ficción.

B 17   Actividad • ¡A escribir!

Write a dialog based on the conversation you had in B16. Prepare to act out the dialog with your partner.

ESTRUCTURAS ESENCIALES
The verbs pensar *and* empezar (e → ie)

pensar	*to think*	empezar	*to begin*
pienso	pensamos	empiezo	empezamos
piensas	pensáis	empiezas	empezáis
piensa	piensan	empieza	empiezan

The verbs **pensar,** *to think, to plan,* and **empezar,** *to begin,* change the stressed **e** in the stem to **ie.** The **nosotros(as)** form does not change.

B 19 Actividad • ¿Qué piensan hacer?

Complete each of the following using the corresponding form of **pensar.**

¿Tú ____ ir al cine? —¿Tú piensas ir al cine?

piensas **1.** ¿Tú ____ salir el fin de semana?
piensas **2.** ¿Qué ____ hacer tú?
pensamos **3.** ¿Vas al cine? Nosotros también ____ ir.
piensan **4.** ¿Qué película ____ ustedes ver?
pensamos **5.** Nosotros ____ ver una cómica.
piensan **6.** ¿A qué cine ____ ustedes ir?
pensamos **7.** Nosotros ____ ir al Rex.
pienso **8.** ¡Fantástico! Yo ____ ir al Rex también.
piensa **9.** ¿Y Julia? Julia ____ ir al teatro.
pienso **10.** Yo ____ que ella no va a venir.

B 20 Actividad • ¿Piensan ir?

Substitute the underlined words with the appropriate form of **pensar.**

—<u>Voy a</u> salir temprano. —Pienso salir temprano.

Pienso **1.** <u>Voy a</u> ir al cine con Alberto.
Piensas **2.** ¿<u>Vas a</u> venir con nosotros?
pensamos **3.** Nosotros <u>vamos a</u> ver una película policial.

4. ¿Qué <u>quieres</u> ver tú? piensas
5. ¿<u>Quieres</u> ver una película cómica? Piensas
6. Nosotros <u>vamos a</u> ir temprano. pensamos

B 21 SE DICE ASÍ
Expressing opinions

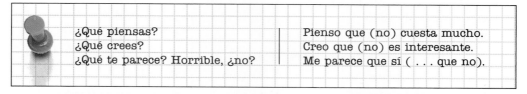

¿Qué piensas?	Pienso que (no) cuesta mucho.
¿Qué crees?	Creo que (no) es interesante.
¿Qué te parece? Horrible, ¿no?	Me parece que sí (. . . que no).

To ask what somebody thinks or to give your own opinion, you can use a form of **pensar** or **creer.** You can also use a construction with **parece.**

B 22 Actividad • ¿Qué crees? Possible answers are given.

Discuss a movie you want to see with a partner.
The following questions will give you a guideline.
Fill in the blanks with the appropriate information.
Then answer these questions using **pienso, creo,**
and **me parece.**

1. ¿Cuánto <u>cuesta</u> el cine? (costar)
2. ¿A qué hora <u>empieza</u> la película? (empezar)
3. ¿Cómo se <u>llama</u> la película? (llamar)
4. ¿Dónde <u>está</u> el cine Metro? (estar)
5. ¿ <u>Es</u> una película policial o cómica? (Ser)

1. Me parece que cuesta cinco pesos.
2. Creo que empieza a las diez de la noche.
3. Pienso que se llama *Hijos de un dios menor.*
4. Pienso que está lejos.
5. Me parece que es de amor.

B 23 Conversación • Opiniones Answers will vary.

Talk to two classmates. Say each sentence. Your classmates will express their
opinions, each using one of the words given in parentheses. Switch roles.

—Vamos a ver *Verano en la playa.*
  (estupenda / horrible)
• Creo que es estupenda.
• Me parece que es horrible.

1. Quiero ver *Premio de honor.*
   (interesante / aburrida)
2. El cine cuesta 10 dólares.
   (mucho / poco)
3. Dan la película en el Real.
   (lejos / cerca)
4. La película empieza a las doce.
   (tarde / temprano)
5. Es una película policial.
   (amor / oeste)

B 24 Comprensión For script and answers, see pp. T145–146.

Which one is it?

Películas	Cines	Clases
1. Genio de las computadoras	1. Parque	1. del oeste
2. Genio de bolsillo	2. Real	2. musical
3. Música de bolsillo	3. Conde	3. cómica
4. La hora de las computadoras	4. Metro	4. de amor
5. Música en el parque	5. Genio	5. policial
6. Computadoras musicales	6. Plaza	6. de ciencia-ficción
7. Computadoras de bolsillo	7. Arte	7. de dibujos animados

208   **Unidad 7**

Concerts of popular music in Buenos Aires often take place at Luna Park, a giant downtown auditorium. To hear a concert, you have to find out how to get there, arrange to meet your friends, find the line for tickets, and find out if any tickets are left.

C1 ¡Tito Ortega canta hoy!

En el autobús.

NICOLÁS	¡Mira, Paula! Ahí está Diego. ¡Hola, Diego! ¿Qué tal? ¿Conoces a Paula?
DIEGO	No. ¡Hola! ¿Cómo estás? ¿Adónde van?
PAULA	Al teatro, a escuchar a Tito Ortega.
DIEGO	¿Sí?, yo también.
NICOLÁS	¡Fantástico! Oye, Diego, ¿sabes dónde tenemos que bajar?
DIEGO	Sí, en la próxima parada, en la calle Sarmiento.

Frente al Luna Park.

DIEGO	¡Cuánta gente! ¡Permiso, por favor!
NICOLÁS	Perdón, señor. ¿Sabe si hay entradas?
SEÑOR	No, nosotros esperamos el autobús.
PAULA	Por favor, señora, ¿sabe cuál es la fila para comprar entradas?
SEÑORA	Hay entradas en la ventanilla, a la derecha, señorita.

Unos minutos más tarde.

PAULA	¿Vienes con nosotros, Diego?
DIEGO	No, espero a mi hermana. Ella busca a su amiga Susana.
NICOLÁS	¡Ahí están! Vamos, el concierto va a empezar.

Complete the sentences so they agree with C1.

1. Paula y Nicolás van al <u>al teatro</u> , a <u>escuchar</u>a Tito Ortega.
2. Ellos van en <u>autobús</u>. Tienen que <u>bajar</u> en la calle Sarmiento.
3. Diego, ¿ <u>conoces</u> tú a Paula?
4. ¡Cuánta <u>gente!</u> ! ¡<u>Permiso</u>, por favor!
5. ¿Cuál es la <u>fila</u> para comprar entradas?
6. Hay _____ en la _____, a la derecha.   entradas   ventanilla
7. Diego espera a su _____ . Ella busca a _____ .   su hermana   Susana
8. El concierto va a <u>empezar</u>.

C3   **SE DICE ASÍ**
Getting someone's attention, interrupting politely

	To get a friend's attention	¡Mira! ¡Oye!
	To get a stranger's attention	¡Por favor, señora! (señorita, señor) ¡Perdón!
	Interrupting politely or excusing an action you wish to take	¡Perdón! ¡Permiso, por favor!

C4   Actividad • Reacciones   Possible answers are given.

For each statement or question, select an appropriate lead-in from the expressions
in the box below.

—¡Aquí viene Roque!
—¡Mira! ¡Aquí viene Roque!

1. ¿Bajamos aquí?   ¡Oye!
2. Es mi parada.   Permiso, por favor.
3. ¿Puedo salir?   Perdón.

4. ¡Dan una película musical!   ¡Mira!
5. ¿Cuál es la fila para las entradas?   ¡Por favor, señor!
6. ¿Tienes dinero?   ¡Oye!

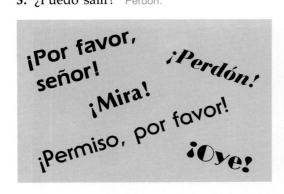

C5   Actividad • ¡A escribir!   Answers will vary.

Write down your reactions to the statements or questions in C4.

ESTRUCTURAS ESENCIÁLES
The verb **saber**, *to know*

saber *to know*			
Sé	cuánto cuesta.	**Sabemos**	cuándo viene.
¿Sabes	dónde está?	**¿Sabéis**	si viene?
¿Sabe	cuál es?	**¿Saben**	qué hora es?

Saber means *to have information about something* or *to know a fact* such as a date or an address. When followed by an infinitive, **saber** means *to know how to do something:*

Yo **sé** nadar.   *I know how to (can) swim.*

C7 Actividad • Combinación

Form five sentences by choosing matching elements from the two groups.

Sí, yo	**sabes español.**
Nosotros no	**saben cuánto cuesta.**
Tú	**sabe bailar bien.**
Usted	**sé quien viene.**
Raúl y Pepa	**sabemos a qué hora es.**

C8 SE DICE ASÍ
Asking information

	¿Sabes ¿Sabe	si hay entradas? dónde está la fila? si mi hermana está? cuándo viene mi hermana?	Do you know	if there are tickets? where the line is? if my sister is here? when my sister is coming?

C9 Conversación • Al teatro

One of your classmates is going to a concert. You want to go, too. You need to know where it is, on what day, at what time, and how much it costs. Ask your friend. Use a form of **saber** in your questions.

ESTRUCTURAS ESENCIALES
Direct objects and the personal a

| Ella espera **el autobús**. | Los chicos escuchan **un concierto**. |
| Mario espera **a su hermana**. | Los chicos escuchan **a Tito Ortega**. |

1. A *direct object* is the word or words you use to indicate who or what gets acted upon by the verb. In the example sentences, **autobús** and **hermana** tell us who or what gets waited for. **Concierto** and **Tito Ortega** tell us who or what gets listened to. They are direct objects.

2. You can identify the direct object as the word or words that answer the question *what* or *whom* about the subject.
    Ella espera **el autobús**. *(What is she waiting for?)*
    Mario espera **a su amiga**. *(Whom is Mario waiting for?)*

3. When a direct-object noun refers to a *person,* use the preposition **a** before the noun and its modifiers.
    Ella busca **a** su amiga Susana.   Diego espera **a** sus hermanas.

4. When the direct object is **quién** or some other pronoun that refers to a *person,* use the personal **a** before it.
    ¿A quién espera Diego?   Espera **a** su hermana.

5. Don't use the personal **a** after the verb **tener**.
    Paula **tiene** muchos hermanos.   Yo **tengo** muchos amigos.

6. Do not use the personal **a** when the direct object is not a person.
    Ella espera el autobús.

C11   Actividad • ¿Qué dicen?

There's too much noise—you can't hear what these people are saying. Ask for clarification. Use **¿Qué . . . ?** or **¿A quién . . . ?** in your question.

    —¿Los chicos? Van a escuchar un concierto.
    —¿Qué van a escuchar?
    —¿Los chicos? Van a escuchar a Tito Ortega.
    —¿A quién van a escuchar?

1. ¿Nosotros? Esperamos el autobús.
2. ¿Ellos? Esperan a sus amigos.
3. ¿Nosotros? Vamos a escuchar a Tito Ortega.
4. ¿Diego? Compra las entradas.
5. ¿Yo? Busco el dinero.
6. ¿Susana? Busca a su hermana.
7. ¿Él? Mira el periódico.
8. ¿Ellos? Miran a Tito Ortega.

1. ¿Qué esperan? 2. ¿A quiénes esperan? 3. ¿A quién van a escuchar? 4. ¿Qué compra Diego? 5. ¿Qué buscas tú? 6. ¿A quién busca Susana? 7. ¿Qué mira él? 8. ¿A quién miran ellos?

C12   Actividad • ¡A escribir!

All your friend's guesses are wrong. Say no and give the correct information as suggested in parentheses.

    —¿Esperas el autobús? (mi mamá)
    —No, espero a mi mamá.

1. ¿Buscas entradas? (mis amigos)
2. ¿Esperas a Gloria? (su prima)
3. ¿Esperan ustedes a José? (sus amigos)
4. ¿Buscas a tus amigos? (entradas)
5. ¿Miran ustedes el periódico? (Tito Ortega)

1. No, busco a mis amigos. 2. No, espero a su prima. 3. No, esperamos a sus amigos. 4. No, buscamos entradas. 5. No, miramos a Tito Ortega.

ESTRUCTURAS ESENCIALES
The verb conocer

The meaning of the English verb *to know*, is divided between two Spanish verbs, **conocer** and **saber.**

conocer *to know, to meet, to be familiar with*			
Conozco	a tu primo.	**Conocemos**	el lugar.
¿Conoces	a mi amiga?	**Conocéis**	Buenos Aires.
¿Conoce	mi casa?	**¿Conocen**	a Diego?

1. In the present tense, **conocer** is irregular in the **yo** form: **Conozco.** All other forms are regular.

2. Use **conocer** when you mean *to be acquainted with* or *to be familiar with a place or a person.*
   ¿Conoces a Paula?   *Do you know Paula?*
   Conocemos Argentina.   *We have been to (know) Argentina.*
   Remember to use the personal **a** whenever the direct object is a person.

3. Earlier in this unit you learned the verb **saber.** Use **saber** when you mean *to know a fact* or *to have information about something.*
   Él **sabe** dónde está el teatro.   *He knows where the theater is.*
   Ellos **saben** cuánto cuestan las entradas.   *They know how much the tickets cost.*

Actividad • Una fiesta

Nicolás is having a party at home. He's introducing his friends to his family.
Complete the following using **conocer.** Use the personal **a** also.

¿Usted _____ mi primo Raúl?
¿Usted conoce a mi primo Raúl?

1. ¿ _____ mi prima Corina?   Conoces a
2. Pablo, ¿tú _____ Corina?   conoces a
3. No, yo no _____ tu prima.   conozco a
4. ¿Y ustedes? Sí, nosotros _____ Corina, pero Miguel y Paula no _____ su hermana.   conocemos a   conocen a
5. ¿Ustedes _____ mis padres? Yo, sí.   conocen a
6. Yo no _____ tus padres.   conozco a
7. Señora, ¿usted _____ mi tío Julián?—No, ¡mucho gusto!   conoce a

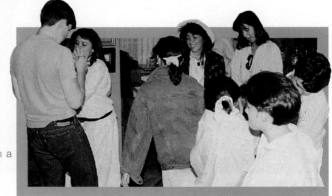

Actividad • La familia de Tito Ortega

Complete the dialog using appropriate forms of **saber** and **conocer.**

Luz   Quiero ir al concierto, pero no _____ sé dónde está el teatro. ¿Tú sabes dónde está?

Ale   No, pero yo _____ a Tito Ortega.   conozco

Luz   ¿Tú _____ a Tito Ortega?   conoces

Ale   Sí, yo _____ a toda su familia.   conozco

Luz   ¿Tú _____ a sus padres?   conoces

Ale   Y _____ a sus hermanos también.   conozco

Luz   ¿Tú _____ cuántos hermanos tiene?   sabes

Ale   Sí, pero yo no _____ cómo ir al teatro.   sé

1 Para una revista

You are a reporter for a Spanish magazine. You are preparing an article about what teenagers do when they go out. Prepare ten questions to ask your classmates about what they like to do when they go out, where, when, and how often they go out.

2 Actividad • Entrevistas Answers will vary.

Write down your questions for 1. Interview your classmates, and report the results to the class.

3 Actividad • ¡A escribir!

Write the article for your magazine based on your interviews. Choose a title for your article. Add pictures and illustrations to your article if you want.

4 Actividad • ¿Adónde vamos? Answers will vary.

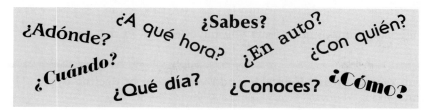

¿Adónde? ¿A qué hora? ¿Sabes? ¿En auto? ¿Con quién?
¿Cuándo? ¿Qué día? ¿Conoces? ¿Cómo?

Work with three or four classmates. You are going out together. Decide where you are going, what you are going to do there, and on what day and at what time you are meeting. Make sure that your arrangements are convenient for everybody in the group. Report your plans to the class and ask other classmates to join your group.

5 Actividad • ¿Qué o a quién?

Answer each question with one of the words in parentheses. Don't forget to use the personal **a** when necessary.

—¿Qué miras? ¿A quién miras? (un periódico / los chicos)
—Miro un periódico. Miro a los chicos.

1. ¿Qué buscan ellos? ¿A quién buscan? (Pablo / entradas) Buscan las entradas. Buscan a Pablo.
2. ¿Qué esperas? ¿A quién esperas? (el autobús / mis primos) Espero el autobús. Espero a mis primos.
3. ¿Qué quiere ver usted? ¿A quién quiere ver? (señor Ortega / una película) Quiero ver una película. Quiero ver al señor Ortega.
4. ¿Qué escuchas? ¿A quién escuchas? (mis amigos / música) Escucho música. Escucho a mis amigos.
5. ¿Qué miran ustedes? ¿A quién miran? (el periódico / Pablo) Miramos el periódico. Miramos a Pablo.

6 Conversación • Al teléfono

Work with a partner. Over the telephone, you decide to go to the movies. Discuss what movie you are going to see, what kind of movie it is, where it's shown, and at what time you are going. Report your decision to the class.

7 Actividad • ¡A escribir!

Write a dialog based on your telephone conversation with your friend.

8 Pronunciación, lectura, dictado For script, see p. T151.

1. Listen carefully and repeat what you hear.

2. The sound of the Spanish consonant **g** before **a, o, u.** Listen, then read aloud.

regular   gusto   lugar   gordo   Miguel   Guillermo   ganas   alguno

3. Copy the following sentences to prepare yourself to write them from dictation.

No tengo ganas de jugar golf hoy.
Me gusta mucho ir al cine con mi amigo Gustavo.
¡Magnífico! El domingo salgo con Gregorio.
¡Qué guapo y delgado es Guillermo Rodríguez!

¿LO SABES?

Let's review some important points you have learned in this unit.

SECTION A

Answers will vary.

When you receive an invitation, how do you accept or decline the invitation? Ex: 1. —Sí, ¡vamos! Me gusta ir al parque.
First, accept two of the following, and then turn two down, explaining why.

1. Voy al parque. ¿Vienes?
2. ¿Quieres salir el sábado?
3. Hay una fiesta el viernes, ¿vas?
4. Vamos al cine. ¿Quieres ir?

How would you ask friends to go to a concert with you, to go out to eat, to go to a dance, or to take a walk? Ex. —¿Quieres ir al concierto? —No, no puedo. Lo siento mucho.
Each invitation is turned down. How do you express your regrets?

Can you talk about who goes out with whom, and how often?
Form as many phrases as you can with the elements below, using the verb **salir.** Ex: Los chicos salen bastante con sus amigos.

mi prima	bastante	tus	primos
los chicos	a veces	mis	chicos
tu hermana	mucho	sus	padres
yo / tú	todo el tiempo	nuestros	amigos

When a new friend asks you about going out, what do you say?
Answer the following. Possible answers are given.

1. ¿Sales mucho?
2. ¿Qué días sales?
3. ¿Cuántas veces por semana sales?
4. ¿Con quién sales?

1. Sí, salgo mucho. 2. Salgo los sábados. 3. Salgo tres veces por semana. 4. Salgo con mis amigos.

SECTION B

You want to know what your friends are going to do for the weekend.
Write down five questions you might ask them. Answers will vary.

Are you able to suggest seeing different kinds of movies?
Replace the words in italics with five alternatives.

—¿Y si vemos *una cómica?* policial, de ciencia-ficción, de amor, musical, del oeste

SECTION C

How would you interrupt politely or excuse an action you wish to take?
Choose the expression that best applies to the following situations.

Mira   Oye   Permiso, por favor   Perdón

1. The bus is crowded and you want to get off. Permiso, por favor
2. Ask a friend where to get off. Oye
3. You need to interrupt a conversation. Perdón
4. You're passing by the movie house with a friend.
   The movie that you want to see is announced. Mira

Do you know how to ask for information? See below for examples.
Using **saber** and **conocer,** write down five questions to find out the date, time, and place of a party, and how to get there.

1. ¿Sabes cuándo es la fiesta?
2. ¿Sabes a qué hora es la fiesta?
3. ¿Sabes dónde es la fiesta?
4. ¿Conoces la casa?
5. ¿Sabes cómo ir a la fiesta?

VOCABULARIO

SECTION A

el **baile** dance
bastante a lot
el **café** coffeeshop
el **cine** movies, movie theater
el **concierto** concert
¿cuántas veces? how many times?
dar una vuelta to go for a walk
decir to say
la **discoteca** disco
entrevistar to interview
esta noche tonight
esta tarde this afternoon
el **examen** exam
la **fiesta** party
el **fin de semana** weekend
el **helado** ice cream
la **juventud** youth
lo que what, that
lo siento I'm sorry
el **parque** park
pasear to go for a walk
la **piscina** pool
poder (ue) to be able, can
por semana per week
¡qué lástima! what a shame!
salir to go out
sencillamente simply
tener ganas de to feel like
tener que to have to
todo, -a all
todo el tiempo all the time

tomar to have (eat or drink)
la **vez (pl. veces)** time
dos veces twice
una vez once
volver (ue) to return

SECTION B

el **amor** love
la **aventura** adventure
¡basta de . . . ! enough . . . !
las **bodas de plata** silver wedding anniversary
la **ciencia-ficción** science fiction
la **clase** kind
cómico, -a comic, comical
el **crimen** crime
dar una película to show a movie
detenido, -a suspended
el **dibujo animado** animated cartoon
la **historia** story
el **lío** complication
loco, -a crazy
mejor better, best
mejor . . . it would be better to . . .
la **película** film, movie
la **película de terror** horror movie
la **película musical** musical
la **película del oeste** Western

la **película policial** detective movie
pensar (ie) to think, plan
la **plata** silver
el **programa** program
el **ruido** noise
si if
¿si vamos . . . ? what if we go . . . ?
el **sueño** the dream
uno, -a (de) one
voy a I am going to (to indicate intention)

SECTION C

bajar to get off
conocer to know, meet, be acquainted with
¡cuánta gente! what a lot of people!
la **entrada** admission ticket
la **fila** line
la **gente** people
más tarde later
el **minuto** minute
la **parada** stop
permiso excuse me
próximo, -a next
saber to know (a fact)
saber (+ inf) to know how (+ inf)
el **teatro** theater
la **ventanilla** ticket window

You may wish to have the students read the vocabulary before each section is introduced.

1. el cine, el concierto, la discoteca, la fiesta, el parque, la piscina, el baile, el café, el restaurante, el teatro.

ESTUDIO DE PALABRAS

1. Review the vocabulary list above and find all the places where people go when they go out to enjoy themselves. Make a list of the places.

2. List all the words and phrases you can use to describe the different types of movies you can see. de amor, de aventuras, de ciencia-ficción, cómica, musical, de dibujos animados, de terror, del oeste, policial.

VAMOS A LEER

Antes de leer

You're all set to go to the movies and want to know at what time the show starts. Before looking at the ads in today's newspaper, you should be aware that in Spain and South America the 24-hour clock is used to express time. The 24-hour system goes from 0:01 (for 12:01 A.M.) to 24:00 (for midnight). So, to find out any time in the afternoon, add 12 hours to your P.M. time or subtract 12 hours from theirs.

¿Qué dan hoy?

Read the movie ads and decide what film you would like to see.

---

aclamada *acclaimed* **amada** *loved* **púrpura** *purple* **estreno** *premiere* **ha empezado** *has begun* **invasores** *invaders*
vuelve *returns*

Guía de espectáculos°

Cervantes. Tejas 2
Teléfono: 37-2390
Estreno nacional
Rambito y Rambón, su primera misión
Divertida comedia.
A las 16:40, 19:50 y 23.

Ateneo. Cerros 23
Teléfono 31-1045
Para chicos y grandes°.
El cuento° del Mago° de Oz
A las 13:25, 16:10, 18:50.
Las aventuras de Mónica y sus amigos
A las 14:45 y 17:30.

Capitol 2. Lavalle 315
Tel. 22-4372. Un filme para toda la familia.
Ralph Macchio
Pat Morita
El Karate Kid II
A las 13:10, 15:35 y 17:50. Sábado 20:20.

Atlas Santa Cruz.
Santa Cruz 201.
Tel. 332-1836.
Miss Mary
Con Julie Christie, Nacha Guevara. Un filme de María L. Bemberg. A las 13:50, 15:25, 17:50 y 20:15.

Paramount.
Corrientes 98
El color púrpura
Basada° en la historia de Alice Walker. Ganadora° del premio Pulitzer. Noticiero°, a las 18:50 y 22 horas.

Coliseum. Tetuán 114.
Tel 91-3442. Película de emocionantes aventuras.
Indiana Jones y el templo de la perdición°
Lunes a viernes 13:30, 17:55, 20:15, 22:40.
Sábado y domingo 17:30, 20:00, 22:45.

Lavalle. Princesa 7
Teléfono: 84-8888
Admiradora secreta
A las 17:55, 20:10 y 22:23.
Sábados función a la 1:20.

Filmoteca 1. Corrientes 654 Tel. 44-6676. Un filme de Alan Parker.
Pink Floyd (*The Wall*)
Una mezcla° fascinante de música, rock futurista, juegos de luces°, sonidos° y dibujos. La película musical más sensacional de la historia del cine. A las 15, 17, 19:21, 23
Viernes y sábados 1:20.

Broadway. Narváez 478 Teléfono 99-1660.
Locademia de policía
Una vez más las extravagantes aventuras de los policías de esta singular academia.

Actividad • Charla

Work with a partner. You're reading the newspaper together and considering the ads above. Decide on a movie you both want to see. Explain why you want to see it. Make plans regarding the day and time you wish to go.

---

espectáculos *shows* **grandes** *adults* **cuento** *story* **mago** *wizard* **basada** *based* **ganadora** *winner*
noticiero *newsreel* **perdición** *doom* **mezcla** *mixture* **luces** *lights* **sonidos** *sounds*

El regalo

Daniel y Adriana están muy preocupados. La policía los busca°. ¿Quién va a creer que ellos son inocentes y que los verdaderos° criminales son el piloto y la aeromoza?

ADRIANA No debemos salir. Tenemos que esperar.
DANIEL Pero tenemos que ir a la escuela. No podemos faltar° a clase.
ADRIANA Y vamos directamente° a casa después del colegio.

En la clase de matemáticas dos amigos le preguntan a Daniel:

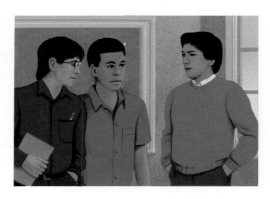

AMIGO Oye, ¿quieres ir con nosotros al cine esta noche? En uno de los cines del centro dan una película nueva. Es de aventuras.
DANIEL Lo siento. No puedo. Quiero, pero no puedo.
AMIGO ¿Y mañana? ¿O el sábado?
DANIEL No sé, estoy castigado°. Tal vez° dentro de dos o tres semanas.
AMIGO ¡Tanto tiempo! ¡Es como estar en la cárcel°! Tus padres son muy estrictos, ¿no?

Una amiga le habla a Adriana de sus planes para el fin de semana. Va a ir a una discoteca con unos amigos y después a una fiesta que va a estar estupenda.

---

los busca *is looking for them* **verdaderos** *true* **faltar** *miss* **directamente** *directly* **castigado** *punished*
tal vez *perhaps* **cárcel** *jail*

AMIGA	¿Pasamos por tu casa a las nueve?
ADRIANA	No, este fin de semana, mejor estudio.
AMIGA	¿En serio?° Estás muy cambiada°, Adriana.

Más tarde llega otra amiga.

AMIGA ¿Sabes? El viernes vamos a escuchar al grupo español. Uno de los músicos te quiere conocer. Se llama Esteban Arévalo. ¿Te compro una entrada?

Adriana no sabe qué hacer. Ella también quiere conocer a Esteban Arévalo . . . pero . . . no puede aceptar la invitación. Esa noche los chicos están aburridos.

ADRIANA	Yo quiero ir a ese concierto el viernes.
DANIEL	Yo sé por qué. Quieres conocer a "El Gato"°.
ADRIANA	¿Cómo? ¿A quién?
DANIEL	A Esteban Arévalo. Ese chico que tiene un ojo verde y otro azul, como los gatos exóticos.
ADRIANA	¡Estás loco! Es un muchacho muy guapo.
DANIEL	Sí, estoy loco. Es verdad. Los dos estamos locos porque queremos salir y no podemos. Hace ocho días que estamos en esta cárcel.
ADRIANA	Por lo menos° la comida de esta cárcel no es mala. Pero . . .

Los dos se miran°. Piensan en lo mismo°. Existe una diversión: el televisor. No pueden resistir la tentación. Allí está en un rincón°, esperando°.

Actividad • Decisiones   Answers will vary.

Adriana and Daniel are trying to decide what to do. What do you think is best and why? You can give them some other choices also.

1. ¿Debemos ir a la escuela?
2. ¿Podemos salir?
3. ¿Miramos televisión?
4. ¿Podemos invitar a nuestros amigos a ver el televisor secreto?
5. —Ustedes pueden . . .

¿en serio? *seriously?* **cambiada** *changed* **gato** *cat* **por lo menos** *at least* **se miran** *look at each other* **lo mismo** *the same thing* **rincón** *corner* **esperando** *waiting*

UNIDAD 8 **Bienvenida**

Repaso

TEACHER-PREPARED MATERIALS	UNIT RESOURCES
Review 8 passport, dictionary, airline ticket, suitcase, camera, television or movie schedule	**Manual de actividades,** Unit 8 **Manual de ejercicios,** Unit 8 Unit 8 cassette Transparency 20 Review Test 2

Unit 8 reviews functions, grammar, and vocabulary that the students have studied in Units 5–7. No new material is included. This unit provides communicative and writing practice in different situations; that is, it gives different applications and uses of the same material. If your students require further practice, you will find additional review exercises in Unit 8 of the **Manual de actividades** and the **Manual de ejercicios.** On the other hand, if your students have successfully mastered the material in Units 5–7, you may wish to omit parts of Unit 8. Some of the activities in this unit lend themselves to cooperative learning.

OBJECTIVE   To review communicative functions, grammar, and vocabulary from Units 5–7

CULTURAL BACKGROUND   Costa Rica may have received its name, which means "Rich Coast", as a result of Columbus's discovery of gold. Costa Ricans are called **Ticos** by their Central American neighbors because of their use of diminutives. A popular custom is called **Retreta.** Bands play music in the central squares of towns, while boys and men stroll around the square in twos and threes in one direction, the girls and women in the other.

1
La sala de espera

Before class, gather **un pasaporte, un diccionario, un billete de avión, una maleta,** and **una cámara** or pictures of these items. Ask the students to identify the items in Spanish. You may wish to explain that **plano** is a map of the city and **mapa** is a map of a country.

Play the cassette or have three students read the dialog aloud. You may ask about the things Elena does not have, such as **un libro** or **un mapa,** to verify the students' listening comprehension. Then have the students work in groups of three to read and role-play the dialog.

SLOWER-PACED LEARNING   Ask the following or similar questions to check comprehension.

> ¿De dónde es Elena?
> ¿Cuánto tiempo va a pasar en Nueva York?
> ¿Cómo se llama la tía de Elena?
> ¿Cómo es Miguel?

2
Actividad • No es así

Have the students do the activity with books closed. They should open their books to check their sentences with the dialog.

3 **Actividad • Charla**

Review adjectives and adjective agreement (Unit 6, page 172) with the class. Then have each student work with a partner to complete the oral activity. They may discuss a real or an imaginary family member.

4 **Actividad • ¡A escribir!**

As a variation, the students may write a description of a famous person. Collect the descriptions and correct them. Then have each student read aloud the description and have the other students try to guess the famous person's name.

5 **SITUACIÓN • Dos fiestas**

Review with the class family relationships (Unit 6, page 171), and the verb **ir** used with **a** plus an infinitive to express future time (Unit 7, page 203). Play the cassette or read the dialogs aloud. Have the students read the dialogs with a partner. Then form groups to role-play the dialog for the class.

6 **Preguntas y respuestas**

Have the students work with a partner to ask and answer the questions. For writing practice, ask the students to write five false statements. They should exchange statements with another classmate and correct each other's work. As a variation, you may wish to suggest playing a game in which one student chooses another to whom he or she reads a statement. Student 2 responds **Sí** or **No** and corrects the false statement. Then student 2 chooses student 3 and proceeds as above.

ANSWERS:
1. Los abuelos, los tíos de Nueva Jersey, los primos y todos los amigos van a la fiesta.
2. No necesita un diccionario porque habla un poco de inglés.
3. Quieren practicar español.
4. Dan una película de ciencia-ficción.
5. El domingo, Eric va a ir al cine con su primo.
6. Quiere ir a su casa a escuchar discos nuevos.
7. Están en casa de Karen.
8. La fiesta es para Elena.
9. Elena invita a sus amigos a ir a su casa en Costa Rica.
10. No, quiere bailar.

7 **Actividad • Charla**

Bring in copies of television and movie schedules. The students should classify all the movie and television titles in Spanish. For example, ***Batteries Not Included* es una película comica.** They might also create their own titles in Spanish and describe each movie.

8 **Actividad • ¡A escribir!**

Before the students begin the activity, review the expressions used for accepting and turning down invitations (Unit 7, page 197). The students may write the exchanges at home or in class. Then call on individuals to read the

sentences aloud as you or a volunteer writes them on the board or a transparency for correction.

CHALLENGE Write ten different situations on slips of paper and place in a hat or box. Call on two students at a time to select a situation and act it out.

9 Actividad • Fotos

Have the students look at the photos and describe what is happening in each one. Then have the students match Elena's comments to the appropriate photo. For writing practice, have the students write original captions for each photograph.

10 SITUACIÓN • Una carta de Elena a Miguel

Point out the salutation, **Querido Miguel,** and the complimentary closing, **Un abrazo.** Then play the cassette or read Elena's letter to Miguel aloud.

Have the students rewrite the letter in which Elena expresses her thanks for the visit and gives her opinions and impressions of New York. The students may also write a letter inviting a foreign student to their home. Tell the students to talk about what they plan to do when he or she comes to visit and discuss their real or imaginary families.

11 Actividad • Para completar

After the students complete all of the sentences, have them write a response to Elena's letter. They may accept her invitation or refuse and explain why. They might also include places they would like to visit and things they would like to do in Costa Rica.

Viñeta cultural 2

Paisajes

OBJECTIVES

1. To provide the student with a geographical background of the Hispanic world
2. To offer the student the opportunity to recognize that the Spanish-speaking world represents a great variety of landscapes
3. To make the student aware of the natural resources of the Hispanic world
4. To expand the students' knowledge of the Spanish-speaking world

MOTIVATING ACTIVITIES

1. Ask the students to provide commentaries about a geographic feature of a Spanish-speaking country.
2. Ask the students to provide information about some of the flora and fauna of the Hispanic world.
3. Ask the students to prepare a report concerning a particular product or natural resource of a Spanish-speaking country.
4. Ask the students to write a report about a Spanish-speaking country.
5. Ask the students to write to the consulates of the Spanish-speaking nations requesting brochures to prepare an exposition about the Hispanic world.

CULTURAL BACKGROUND Due to its green forests and cold regions, its rugged mountain ranges and vast plains, and its rocky coastlines and sunny beaches, Spain is often called "the miniature continent."

Spain, which shares the Iberian Peninsula with Portugal, covers an area of 224,325 square miles. Spain is the third-largest country in Europe after the Soviet Union and France.

Separated from the rest of Europe by the impressive mountain range of **Los Pirineos,** Spain's distinctive geographical features are its mountains. To the northeast there are the majestic **Pirineos,** which link with the **Cordillera Cantábrica** to the northwest. In the south, there are the mountain ranges of the Sierra Morena and the Sierra Nevada. The heart of Spain is the extensive central plateau known as the **Meseta,** covering an area of 120,000 square miles. The **Meseta,** in turn, is drained by four rivers: the Tajo, the Duero, the Guadalquivir, and the Guadiana. A fifth river, the Ebro, empties into the Mediterranean.

This pattern of rivers and mountains has divided the country into thirteen natural regions: **Galicia, Asturias, León, Extremadura, Andalucía, Murcia, Valencia, Cataluña, Aragón, Navarra, País Vasco, Castilla la Vieja,** and **Castilla la Nueva.** In addition, it has also contributed to forging the individualistic character of Spain's 39,000,000 inhabitants to the point that often it has been said that Spain is both one and many at the same time.

The Spanish landscape is as varied as its scenery. In humid northwestern Spain one finds the green **prados** (fields) of Asturias cultivated with corn, apples, and pears, as well as the breathtaking Galician **rías** (estuaries).

In the northeast, close to the **Pirineos,** one sees the stone houses huddled together as if to protect themselves from the cold.

Pages
229–31

Pages
232–33

Page
234

La Mancha, a countryside section of Castile with its many windmills and whitewashed houses, reminds us of **Don Quijote,** the famous character in Miguel de Cervantes Saavedra's novel.

The eastern and southern parts of Spain enjoy a delightful Mediterranean climate. Valencia, for example, known as the **huerta** *(orchard)* of Spain, yields rich harvests of rice, dates, citrus, and tropical fruits.

Seen from the sea, the Spanish coastline seems both treacherous and unfriendly, yet Spanish beaches, especially those around Andalucía's **Costa del Sol,** Alicante's **Costa Blanca,** and Cataluña's **Costa Brava,** are among the most frequented in the world.

Prior to the arrival of the Spaniards in the New World there were highly advanced Indian cultures in the Americas. Between 300 A.D. and 1,000 A.D., Mexico was an important cultural center where several highly developed Indian civilizations flourished. The remains of the ancient Mayan civilization can still be seen in places on the Yucatán Peninsula, such as the city of Chichén Itzá.

Other important centers of Mayan civilization were located in the Central American countries of Guatemala and Honduras. Central America is about 1,100 miles long. At its widest point, it is 300 miles from coast to coast. At its narrowest point, which is only 30 miles wide, lies the Panama Canal, known as the path between the oceans. There are six Spanish-speaking nations in Central America: Guatemala, Honduras, El Salvador, Nicaragua, Costa Rica, and Panama. Along the coast, the land is low and the climate is hot and humid. Rugged mountains, many of them volcanoes, crisscross these countries. Most Central Americans earn their living on farms, supplying the world with coffee, bananas, cacao, sugar cane, and tobacco.

The South American continent extends almost 5,000 miles from the jungles of Colombia to the icy Cape Horn in the South. There are nine Spanish-speaking republics in the continent: Venezuela, Colombia, Ecuador, Peru, Bolivia, Chile, Paraguay, Uruguay, and Argentina. Practically all of the countries of South America are mountainous. Along the western side of the continent lies the **Cordillera de los Andes,** the longest unbroken mountain range in the world. This mountain range is capped by glaciers with snow-covered peaks over 20,000 feet. Highest among these peaks is the 23,000 feet tall Aconcagua, the world's second highest, located on the Chilean-Argentine border. **Llamas, alpacas,** and **vicuñas** are found along the Andes. These animals were used as beasts of burden by the Incas prior to the arrival of the Spaniards. Today, we use the wool of these animals in some of our sweaters and coats. Another resident of these mountains is the **cóndor,** the world's largest bird.

The rivers of South America are great and useful. Among the important river systems of South America are the Magdalena-Cauca in Colombia, the Orinoco in Venezuela, the Paraná-Paraguay in Argentina and Paraguay, and the world's largest river, the Amazon.

South America is a continent of contrasts, where the climates vary from the "green hell" jungles of the Paraguayan Gran Chaco to the 1,800-mile Atacama desert in Chile. Most of the countries of South America are in a temperate zone opposite that of the United States. Therefore, their winter is in June, July, and August.

South America also has the equivalent of our Great Plains. The Argentine Pampas, an area about the size of Texas, is the grain and ranching capital of the continent.

Most of the nations of South America are still economically dependent on agriculture. Some of these agricultural products, including cacao, tomatoes, potatoes, tobacco, vanilla beans, and corn were cultivated by pre-Colombian inhabitants. Other products such as wheat, bananas, rice, grapes, oranges, and sugar cane were brought over by the Spaniards. While agriculture is the mainstay of most of the South American countries, there are rich deposits of copper, iron ore, tin, gold, silver, emeralds, and oil.

South America is a marvel of nature where one can find magnificent beaches, snow-covered mountains, beautiful lakes, unique forests and jungles, and majestic waterfalls. Today, South America holds as much enchantment as it once did for the Spanish **conquistadores.**

Bienvenida

Repaso

SHOPS	TIENDAS
RESTAURANTS	RESTAURANTES
BOARDING GATES	PUERTAS DE EMBARQUE

For additional background on Costa Rica, see p. T154.

1

La sala de espera 🎞

Aeropuerto Kennedy, Nueva York.

Miguel Hernández y su papá esperan a Elena, una prima de Costa Rica. Ella va a pasar un mes del verano con ellos en Nueva York.

MIGUEL ¿Dónde está la aduana? Elena tiene que pasar por la aduana, ¿no?

SEÑOR HERNÁNDEZ Sí, pero mira, allí está . . .

SEÑOR HERNÁNDEZ ¡Elena! ¡Elena! ¿Cómo estás? ¿Qué tal el vuelo? ¿Conoces a tu primo, Miguel?

ELENA Mucho gusto, Miguel. ¡Pero qué alto y guapo! Y, ¿cómo está tía Isabel?

MIGUEL Muy bien. Está en casa. ¿Tienes hambre? El almuerzo va a ser muy bueno. ¿Y tu equipaje?

ELENA Aquí está. Creo que tengo todo: mi diccionario—no hablo inglés muy bien—y el pasaporte en el bolsillo, la cámara. Y tú, Miguel, ¿tienes las maletas?

SEÑOR HERNÁNDEZ Sí, tenemos todo. Vamos al carro.

1. Miguel vive en Nueva York. 2. Elena viene en avión. 3. Elena es la prima de Miguel. 4. Es verano. 5. Elena es de Costa Rica. 6. Elena tiene que pasar por la aduana.

2 Actividad • No es así

Make these sentences true according to the conversation you have just read.

1. Miguel vive en Puerto Rico.
2. Elena viene en autobús.
3. Elena es la abuela de Miguel.
4. Es otoño.
5. Elena es de España.

6. Elena tiene que pasar por la cafetería.
7. La mamá de Miguel se llama Ana.
8. La tía está en el aeropuerto.
9. Elena habla inglés muy bien.
10. Van a casa en autobús.

7. La mamá de Miguel se llama Isabel. 8. La tía está en casa. 9. Elena no habla inglés muy bien. 10. Van a casa en carro.

3 Actividad • Charla Answers will vary.

Work with a classmate. Imagine that one of your favorite relatives is coming to visit. Describe the relative to your partner. Say how old he or she is, and tell where she or he lives. Then each of you should be prepared to describe the other's relative to the class.

—Mi prima Dolores tiene diecisiete años. Es alta y pelirroja. Es inteligente, bonita y muy simpática. Vive con su familia en Miami.

4 Actividad • ¡A escribir!

Write down the description of your classmate's relative and then describe your relative also.

5 SITUACIÓN • Dos fiestas

Miguel y Elena, su prima de Costa Rica, conversan.

MIGUEL Elena, ¿sabes que mañana es la fiesta, no? Viene toda la familia: los abuelos, los tíos de Nueva Jersey, los primos . . . y todos nuestros amigos.

ELENA ¡Qué divertido! Mira, ya no necesito el diccionario inglés/español. Hablo un poco de inglés y muchos de tus amigos quieren practicar español.

Con los amigos norteamericanos de Miguel.

BILL Dan una película de ciencia-ficción en el cine Roma. ¿Quieren ir?

BETH ¡Ay no! ¿Por qué no vamos a la película nueva de Matt Dillon?

ERIC Yo no puedo ir. El domingo voy con mi primo.

KAREN ¡Tengo una idea! ¿Por qué no vamos a casa? Tengo unos discos nuevos.

MIGUEL ¿Qué te parece, Elena?

ELENA ¡Estupendo!

Los chicos llegan a casa de Karen que le da a Elena una fiesta sorpresa.

KAREN A la derecha, por favor, vamos a la sala de estar.

ELENA ¡Oh! Una fiesta . . . y están todos nuestros amigos. ¡Qué sorpresa!

TODOS ¡Buena suerte, Elena!

ELENA ¡Qué emoción! Ustedes tienen que venir un día a casa en Costa Rica. *Thank you all* . . . mucho.

BILL ¿Elena, ahora quieres . . . *uh* . . . *uh* . . . *dance?*

ELENA ¿Bailar? Sí, con mucho gusto, Bill.

¡Y la fiesta empieza!

6 Preguntas y respuestas   For answers, see p. T155.

1. ¿Quiénes van a ir a la fiesta?
2. ¿Necesita Elena un diccionario? ¿Por qué?
3. ¿Qué quieren practicar los amigos de Miguel?
4. ¿Qué dan en el cine Roma?
5. ¿Adónde va a ir Eric el domingo? ¿Con quién?
6. ¿Adónde quiere ir Karen? ¿Por qué?
7. ¿Dónde están los amigos?
8. ¿Para quién es la fiesta?
9. ¿Adónde invita Elena a sus amigos?
10. ¿Bill quiere cantar?

7 Actividad • Charla Ex: —Hijos de un dios menor. —de amor

With a partner, try this quiz. One partner names a popular film, and the other tells in Spanish the film's category. Switch roles. Then try to do the same with **un programa de televisión.** Use these categories:

Película (o programa)

de aventuras   cómica   policial   de dibujos animados   de ciencia-ficción
musical   de amor   de terror

8 Actividad • ¡A escribir!

You receive five different invitations. Pick a suitable response from the column on the right and write it out. Use each response just once.

1. Voy a una fiesta en casa de Karen. ¿Quieres venir?
2. ¿Puedes salir esta tarde?
3. ¿Quieres ir a un concierto hoy?
4. ¿Vamos al cine esta noche?
5. Voy a comprar discos. ¿Quieres venir?

a. Sí, hay una película muy buena en el cine Roma.
b. No, no puedo. No tengo dinero.
c. Sí, me gusta mucho bailar. ¿A qué hora es?
d. No puedo. Tengo que estudiar.
e. No, gracias. No me gusta la música.

9 Actividad • Fotos Answers are numbered below pictures.

Back in Costa Rica, Elena shows her family some of the many photos she took on her vacation. What does she say about each one? Match her comments with the appropriate picture.

1. La fiesta es en la sala de estar.
2. Llego con dos maletas, la cámara, el pasaporte y mi diccionario.
3. Una fiesta fantástica en casa de Karen.
4. Miguel es alto y guapo.
5. El aeropuerto Kennedy es muy grande.
6. Están en fila para comprar entradas para un concierto.

Madison Square Garden

4,6

1,3

2,5

San José, 3 de octubre

Querido Miguel:

Tienes que venir a Costa Rica. ¿Por qué no vienes en las vacaciones de diciembre? Todos mis amigos te quieren conocer. Vamos a dar muchas fiestas en casa.

Aquí tienes fotos de casa. En la foto de la familia, mi hermano, Roberto, está al lado de mamá. Los chicos altos son los hijos de mis tíos. Ellos viven en Honduras.

Miguel, ¿sabes que en la clase de inglés soy la mejor?

Recuerdos a mis tíos.

Un abrazo,
Elena

11 Actividad • **Para completar**

Complete the following sentences according to Elena's letter.

1. Elena escribe a . . .
2. Ella invita a Miguel a . . .
3. Todos los amigos de Elena quieren . . .
4. Van a dar . . .
5. Con la carta van fotos de . . .
6. En la foto Roberto está . . .
7. Los chicos altos viven en . . .
8. En la clase de inglés Elena es . . .

1. Miguel 2. Costa Rica 3. conocer a Miguel. 4. muchas fiestas en casa. 5. casa. 6. al lado de mamá. 7. Honduras
8. la mejor.

Viñeta cultural 2

Paisajes

The Iberian Peninsula juts out into the Atlantic Ocean, separated from the rest of Europe by **Los Pirineos,** a chain of rugged mountains. Spain, which shares the Peninsula with Portugal, is a country of varied landscapes *(paisajes)*—mountains and plains, rocky coastlines, and sandy beaches. Its people have varying customs and divided loyalties, but the wonder and mystery of this ancient country remain unchanged.

❶ Una región agrícola en las Islas Canarias, España

❷ Galicia, al noroeste de España

❸ Una granja típica en los Pirineos, España

Paisajes   227

The countryside of Castile, with its many windmills, reminds us of Don Quixote, the famous character of Cervantes' novel. Castile consists of a huge, dry plateau called the **Meseta** that is broken by rolling hills and low mountains.

❶ Andorra, pequeño país en los Pirineos
❷ Provincias Vascongadas, España
❸ Un molino de viento en la tierra de Don Quijote, Castilla, España

When the Spaniards explored the Americas, they brought their language, their heritage, and their architectural skills. As far back as the 1400s, they built many towns, missions, and churches, some of which still stand today in Texas, California, New Mexico, Arizona, and Puerto Rico.

❶ Misión de Carmel en California, construida por los españoles alrededor de 1700

❷ Misión de San Javier del Bac en Tucson, Arizona

❸ El Álamo en San Antonio, Texas, fundado por los españoles alrededor de 1700

❹ El Yunque, Puerto Rico

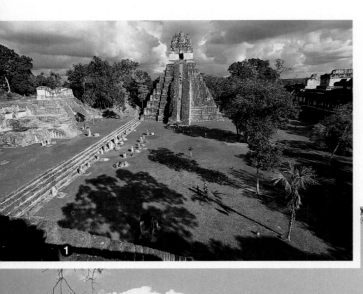

There were highly advanced Indian cultures in the Americas before Columbus. Between 300 and 1000 A.D., Mexico was an important cultural center where several highly developed Indian civilizations flourished. The remains of the ancient Mayan civilization can still be seen at places on the Yucatan Peninsula, such as the city of Chichén Itzá.

❶ Pirámide maya en Tikal, Guatemala, Centroamérica

❷ Ruinas de Chichén Itzá en Yucatán, México

❸ Pendiente de oro de la época precolombina, Costa Rica

Central America is about 1,100 miles long. At its widest point, it is 300 miles from coast to coast. At its narrowest point, which is only 30 miles wide, lies the Panama Canal. Rugged mountains crisscross all seven countries, and many of them are volcanoes. Most Central Americans earn their living on farms, supplying the world with coffee, bananas, cacao, sugar cane, and tobacco.

❶ Volcán Poás, Costa Rica

❷ Una hacienda ganadera en Costa Rica

❸ El canal de Panamá une el Atlántico con el Pacífico

❹ Una casa de campo en Costa Rica

The South American continent extends almost 5,000 miles from the jungles of Colombia in the north to the icy waters of Antarctica in the south. On this continent, you will find a great variety of landscapes and climates. Along the west coast lies the **Cordillera de los Andes,** which is strewn with volcanoes, torn into separate ranges by violent river torrents, and capped by glaciers. This cordillera is the longest unbroken mountain range in the world.

❶ Una vista de la playa de Macuto, Venezuela

❷ La cosecha de café, Colombia

❸ Niños trabajando en una granja de Colombia

❹ La Cordillera de los Andes en Colombia

❺ Valle del Cauca, Colombia

① Machu Picchu, la ciudad
perdida de los incas en Perú
② El río Amazonas de Suramérica
③ Puente colgante en el Perú
④ Lago Titicaca, Bolivia
⑤ Rebaño de ovejas en una
hacienda de Chile

Argentina, Chile, and Uruguay, the countries in the southern tip of South America, are in a temperate zone opposite that of the United States. Therefore, their winter is in June, July, and August. There you can find magnificent beaches, glaciers, mountains, and waterfalls such as Iguazú Falls.

❶ Vista de la Patagonia, Chile
❷ Territorio de la Tierra del Fuego, Argentina
❸ Viña del Mar, Chile
❹ Cataratas de Iguazú, Argentina

TERCERA PARTE

UNIDAD 9 ¡Buen provecho!
Scope and Sequence

	BASIC MATERIAL	COMMUNICATIVE FUNCTIONS
SECTION A	¿Qué comemos hoy? (A1) ¡A la mesa! (A6)	**Expressing attitudes and points of view** • Saying what you like and don't like
SECTION B	Un picnic (B1) La comida para el picnic (B3)	**Expressing attitudes and points of view** • Talking about food • Selecting what you like
SECTION C	Y por fin, ¡el picnic! (C1) Ponemos la mesa (C12)	**Expressing attitudes and points of view** • Talking about whether people are hungry or thirsty • Expressing your enjoyment of food • Asking for what you need at the table
TRY YOUR SKILLS	Pronunciation (the letter **r**) Sound-letter correspondence (the letter **r**) Dictation	
VAMOS A LEER	**Tortilla de patatas a la española** (a recipe for a Spanish tortilla) **De compras** (shopping for the ingredients) **El plátano** (writing a poem) **El regalo** (Where will the new button take Adriana and Daniel?)	

WRITING   A variety of controlled and open-ended writing activities appear in the Pupil's Edition. The Teacher's Notes identify other activities suitable for writing practice.

COOPERATIVE LEARNING   Many of the activities in the Pupil's Edition lend themselves to cooperative learning. The Teacher's Notes explain some of the many instances where this teaching strategy can be particularly effective. For guidelines on how to use cooperative learning, see page T13.

GRAMMAR	CULTURE	RE–ENTRY
The verb **gustar** (A11)	Eating at a restaurant Getting together at a café Different dishes served in Spanish-speaking countries	Telling time The verb **gustar** with **me, le,** and **te** Prepositional pronouns
The verb **hacer** (B5) Demonstrative adjectives (B10)	The metric system Two dishes with the same name	The verbs **venir, saber, tener, conocer,** and **estar** Expressions of location
The verb **poner** (C8)	The history of chocolate	The verb **tener** Adjectives (gender and number agreement)

Recombining communicative functions, grammar, and vocabulary

Reading for practice and pleasure

TEACHER-PREPARED MATERIALS
Section A Pictures of food items; cup and saucer, glass
Section B Pictures of fruit, various foods
Section C Pictures of food and beverages, plastic dishes and cutlery

UNIT RESOURCES
Manual de actividades, Unit 9
Manual de ejercicios, Unit 9
Unit 9 cassettes
Transparencies 21–23
Quizzes 19–21
Unit 9 Test

OBJECTIVES **To express attitudes and points of view:** say what you like and don't like

CULTURAL BACKGROUND   In most Spanish-speaking countries, mealtimes and meals differ from those in the United States. Breakfast is from 7:00 A.M. to 9:00 A.M., depending on when the work day begins. It usually consists of **café con leche** (boiled milk with strong espresso) or **chocolate y pan con mantequilla o mermelada, o pan dulce.** Lunch as we know it in the United States does not exist in Spain or Spanish America. The main meal, **el almuerzo,** also called **la comida,** is eaten between 1:00 P.M. and 4:00 P.M. in Spain and Mexico and in most of Spanish America between 12:30 P.M. and 1:30 P.M. It may consist of soup, beans, rice, meat, vegetables, salad, dessert, and coffee. This meal is sometimes followed by a **siesta.** The word **siesta** comes from Latin and means *la sexta hora* (a nap taken six hours after one arises in the morning). Often the entire family returns home for this meal and doesn't return to work or school until the late afternoon. Most stores are closed, but restaurants are busy for those who prefer to eat out. At about 5:00 P.M., many Spanish-speaking people have a snack, **una merienda,** consisting of a sandwich, fruit, and a beverage. A light supper, **la cena,** is usually eaten some time between 7:30 P.M. and 11:00 P.M.

MOTIVATING ACTIVITY   Ask the students if they have eaten in a Mexican, Latin American, or Spanish restaurant. Have them name foods from Spanish-speaking countries they have tasted or have heard of, and list them on the board. You may ask questions in Spanish, such as **¿Te gustan los tacos?** and **¿En qué restaurante comen ustedes?**

A1   **¿Qué comemos hoy?**

Gather pictures or drawings of the following items: **frijoles, arroz, arroz con pollo, pollo, cebollas, salsa de tomate, sopa, chile con carne, postre, helado de chocolate, leche, café, frutas, limón, enchiladas, carne, queso, agua mineral.** Introduce the new vocabulary by holding up the picture and saying: **Me gusta(n) la(s) . . .** Then ask the students to identify the foods in Spanish, asking: **¿Te gusta(n) . . . ?**

After the students are able to identify the different foods in Spanish, present the expression **El plato del día.** Explain that this is usually the special dish of the day, often served for the afternoon meal. Introduce the words **propina** and **cuenta.** Use the verbs **probar** and **dejar** in sentences which illustrate their meaning.

Play the cassette or read the dialog aloud. Then have the students role-play the dialog. They should bring props, such as a menu, plates, and so on.

SLOWER-PACED LEARNING   To check comprehension, ask the students the following or similar questions.

  1. ¿Cuál es el plato del día en el primer restaurante?
  2. ¿Qué quiere probar la señora Álvarez?
  3. ¿Quién quiere enchiladas?
  4. ¿Por qué el señor Álvarez quiere té con limón y fruta?
  5. ¿Quién va a pagar la cuenta?

A2   **Actividad • No es así**

Have the students change the sentences to make them agree with the dialog in A1. Have them exchange papers to correct their work.

T162   **Teacher's Notes   Unidad 9**

ANSWERS:
1. Los señores Álvarez escriben una guía turística sobre los restaurantes de San Antonio.
2. El plato del día es pollo con cebolla y salsa de tomate.
3. Al señor Álvarez no le gustan las cebollas.
4. Desean dos enchiladas de carne, una de queso y agua mineral.
5. De postre, la señora come helado de chocolate.
6. El señor está a dieta. Desea té con limón.
7. Sí, tiene la cuenta.
8. Los señores Álvarez no saben dónde dejar la propina.

A3 Actividad • Conversación

Have the students choose a partner to complete the activity. They should take turns asking each other the questions.

A4 Actividad • ¡A escribir!

As a variation, have each student write his or her composition in dialog form. They should use A1 as a guide.

A5 ¿Sabes que . . . ?

In Spain, groups of people assemble in the **Plaza Mayor** or in other town squares which are served by many different cafés. One of the typical drinks is called **horchata,** a milky drink made from almonds and other ingredients that are crushed and squeezed in water and sweetened with sugar. It can also be made with **chufas** (edible nut-like tubers). Cafés in Spain also serve **tapas** as a snack or at the beginning of a meal. These delicious hors d'oeuvres are becoming very popular in the United States.

A6 SITUACIÓN • ¡A la mesa!

Re-enter time expressions using a clock. Then introduce the expressions **por la mañana, al mediodía, por la tarde,** and **por la noche.** Bring to class a cup and saucer and a glass to present the words **una taza, un platillo,** and **un vaso.** Say the names of various drinks and ask the students to identify in Spanish what is used to serve each drink.

café con leche	taza y platillo
chocolate	taza y platillo
jugo	vaso
leche	vaso

Play the cassette or read the dialog aloud. Then have each student work with a partner and practice the dialog. Have them cover the captions and identify the foods pictured in each illustration.

For cooperative learning, ask the students to bring play food or pictures of food from home. They may work in small groups of three or four to create three main meals. Every member of the group should be able to correctly identify the names of the foods and the meals. Each group must present its menu and describe its foods to the class.

A7 Actividad • No es así

CHALLENGE Have the students form five false statements based on A6. Ask them to exchange their papers with another student and correct the statements.

A8 Actividad • ¡El menú está malo!

Remind the students about the differences in mealtimes in Spanish-speaking countries. Then tell the students to correct the menu by rearranging the items in each column.

ANSWERS:

Desayuno	de ocho a nueve de la mañana	café con leche chocolate
Almuerzo	una de la tarde	bistec postre refrescos
Merienda	cinco de la tarde	bocadillo jugo o leche
Cena	ocho de la noche	sopa ensalada

A9 Actividad • ¿A qué hora comes?

Before the students complete this activity, you may wish to bring magazine pictures of American food to class. This will provide additional vocabulary for the students to use when they discuss what they eat every day.

A10 Actividad • ¡A escribir!

The students may complete the activity at home or in class. Call on volunteers to read their compositions aloud to the class.

A11 ESTRUCTURAS ESENCIALES

Re-enter the verb **gustar** with **me, te,** and **le** by asking questions such as the following.

¿Te gusta la sopa de cebolla?   ¿A tu familia le gustan las verduras?
¿A quién le gusta?   ¿Te gustan los bocadillos?

To present **nos** and **les** with **gustar,** use the following or similar conversation.

TEACHER	Me gusta el helado. Juan, ¿te gusta el helado?
JUAN	Sí, me gusta el helado.
TEACHER	Nos gusta el helado. Tere, ¿te gusta el helado?
TERE	Sí, me gusta el helado.
TEACHER	¿Les gusta el helado?
JUAN AND TERE	Sí, nos gusta el helado.

Now read the explanation in the book with the students. Ask the students to practice the negative form with **gustar** and the form **a** plus *prepositional pronoun* for emphasis. You may also wish to re-enter **también** and **tampoco** and have the students practice the verb **gustar,** using these responses.

A mí no me gustan los tomates.   A mí tampoco.
A mi hermana le gusta la leche.   A mí también.

A12 Actividad • ¿Qué les gusta?

This activity may be completed at home or in class. You may call on volun-

teers to write the sentences on the board or a transparency. Have the students correct their work.

A 13 **Actividad • Combinación**

Call on students at random to form several sentences, combining an item from each column. For writing practice, have them write the sentences at home or in class.

A 14 **Actividad • ¡Están seguros!** 🔲

Remind the students that the prepositional pronouns are the same as the subject pronouns, except for **mí** and **ti**.

ANSWERS:
1. A él/ella/usted le gusta el jugo.
2. A mí me gusta comer.
3. A ellos/ellas/ustedes les gusta la ensalada.
4. A ti te gustan los postres.
5. A nosotros no nos gusta la cebolla.
6. A ellos/ellas/ustedes no les gustan las verduras.
7. A nosotros no nos gusta dejar propina.
8. A ti te gustan los helados.
9. A él/ella/usted le gusta el pan con mantequilla.
10. A mí me gustan los postres.
11. A mí no me gusta la cebolla.
12. A ellos/ellas/ustedes no les gusta el arroz.

A 15 **SE DICE ASÍ**

Read the expressions aloud to the students. Explain that **mole** is a spicy sauce commonly used over chicken in Mexico. It contains about thirty different spices and is made with chocolate and broth.

A 16 **Actividad • Charla**

For cooperative learning, divide the class into pairs. Have the students discuss the foods they like and dislike. Tell them to take notes and report their findings to the class.

A 17 **Actividad • ¡A escribir!**

Have the students include at least ten different items in their lists. They should ask several other students in the class about these foods and use **a** plus *a prepositional pronoun* to compare. Have them follow the model in their books. They may use **también** or **tampoco** in the sentences.

A 18 **Actividad • ¿Y en tu casa?**

Begin by asking students the questions at random. Then have them work in pairs and ask each other the questions.

A 19 **Actividad • ¡A escribir!**

Using the information they gathered from the conversation in A18, have the students write about what their partner's family likes and dislikes about food. When they have completed the writing activity, have them exchange papers with their partners and check each other's work.

Unidad 9   Teacher's Notes   T165

A 20 **¿Sabes que . . . ?**

If possible, have the students prepare a simple Spanish dish in class, such as **flan, tacos,** or **arroz con pollo.** You might also wish to have groups of students prepare several foods at home and bring them to class to eat at lunch.

Explain that hot chocolate in Spain is very strong and thick. It almost resembles pudding. Also, the tacos prepared in the United States differ from the tacos found in Mexico. Tacos in Mexico are made with steak, chicken, or pork. The **tortilla** is usually soft and made from cornmeal. The Mexicans do not use American cheese or lettuce, but prepare their tacos with a very hot and spicy sauce made with **chiles.**

A 21 **Comprensión**

You'll hear a series of short exchanges between people talking about food, meals, and restaurants. For each exchange, decide whether the type of food or restaurant suggested in the conversation meets with the speaker's approval or not. If it does, your check mark goes in the row labeled **Le(s) gusta(n);** if it does not, your check mark should be placed in the **No le(s) gusta(n)** row. For example, you hear: **¿Compro pizza para todos?** and the response: **No, a Clara y a Esteban la pizza no les gusta.** The check mark is placed in the **No le(s) gusta(n)** row, since Clara y Esteban don't like pizza.

1. —¡Camarero! Tacos, por favor.
   —No, yo no quiero tacos. Los tacos no me gustan.
   No le gusta(n).
2. —¿A ustedes les gustan las hamburguesas?
   —No, las hamburguesas no nos gustan. Nos gustan las papas fritas.   *No les gusta(n).*
3. —¿Compramos postres para los tíos?
   —Sí, creo que a ellos les gustan los postres.   *Les gusta(n).*
4. —¿Qué comemos? ¿Enchiladas de carne?
   —No, mejor de queso. Las de carne no me gustan.
   No le gusta(n).
5. —¿Toman sopa en tu casa? ¿Les gusta?
   —Sí, a mis hermanos les gusta mucho. Siempre toman sopa de verduras.   *les gusta(n).*
6. —¿Quiere papas fritas?
   —Por supuesto. ¿No sabes que es lo que más le gusta?
   Le gusta(n).
7. —¿Por qué no comen ensalada?
   —Porque no nos gusta.   *No les gusta(n).*
8. —¿Y ellos van a un restaurante español hoy?
   —Sí, a ellos les gusta mucho la comida española.   *Les gusta(n).*
9. —Hay pan y mantequilla, ¿quieren?
   —No, gracias. No nos gusta ni el pan ni la mantequilla.
   No les gusta(n).
10. —¿Van a comer helado?
    —No necesitas preguntar. Sabes que a todos les gustan los helados.   *Les gusta(n).*

Now check your answers. *Read each exchange again and give the correct answer.*

A 22 Actividad • ¡A escoger!

Have the students choose the most appropriate response to each of the waiter's statements.

CHALLENGE   After the students have completed the activity, have them write their own responses. Then call on individuals to read the original responses to the class.

A 23 Actividad • El restaurante

For cooperative learning, form groups of three. Two of the students will be customers, and the third will be the waiter or waitress. Have each group prepare a menu. They should use the suggestions in the book as a guide and add their own ideas. Then call on each group to role-play their restaurant scene for the class.

A 24 Actividad • ¡A escribir!

Have each group from A23 write the restaurant scene in dialog form. Collect the dialogs and correct them.

SECTION B

OBJECTIVES   **To express attitudes and points of view:** talk about food; select what you like

CULTURAL BACKGROUND   Music is an essential element for a picnic. In some Spanish-speaking countries, people will dance, play the guitar, and sing. Many picnics include wine. Freshly baked bread is eaten with every meal in Spain and Spanish America. In Mexico and Central America, except for Costa Rica, tortillas are preferred with meals.

MOTIVATING ACTIVITY   Write a list of the items commonly found at a picnic in Spain or Spanish America. Then have the students compare the items with the items they would take to an American picnic.

B 1   Un picnic

Before presenting the dialog, introduce the following verbs in the infinitive form and the third-person singular.

| freír | añadir | dorar | llorar |
| batir | cocinar | ayudar | cortar |

Have the students draw or cut out magazine pictures of a Spanish omelet, potatoes, eggs, onions, a bowl, a dish, a knife, a fork, and a frying pan. Then, using TPR (Total Physical Response), demonstrate each command as you ask the students to follow your instructions. They should use their pictures.

Toma el cuchillo.
Corta las patatas en trozos.

Corta las cebollas.
Llora.
Rompe los huevos en un plato hondo.

Bate los huevos.
Añade las patatas y las cebollas.
Fríe todo en una sartén.
Dora el otro lado.
Pon la tortilla en un plato.

Unidad 9   Teacher's Notes   T167

Now repeat the commands without demonstrating, and circulate among the students as you give each instruction.

Play the cassette or read the dialog aloud as the students follow along in their books. You may wish to explain the expression **A lo dicho, hecho** (*No sooner said than done*).

B2   Actividad • ¿Es cierto o no?

Have the students correct the false statements. They may exchange papers to correct their work.

B3   SITUACIÓN • La comida para el picnic

Ask the students: **¿Qué tenemos que hacer primero para un picnic?** They should respond: **Tenemos que ir a la tienda para comprar las cosas.** Explain that in many Spanish-speaking countries, grocery stores are not as popular as specialty stores or neighborhood general stores, called **bodegas, abastos,** or **colmados.** If people need fruit, they go to a fruit store, called **frutería;** if they need meat, they go to a butcher shop, called **carnicería,** and so on. Ask the students to name some of the items needed for a picnic. Then write on the board or a transparency the name of the store in Spanish where they could find the item.

fruta	frutería
carne	carnicería
pastel	pastelería

Ask the students what each of these names have in common. After they have correctly indicated that all the words end in **-ería,** explain that most names for stores are formed with **-ería** in Spanish. Using this information, call on individuals to make up names in Spanish for specialty stores.

Now play the cassette or read the captions aloud. Have the students identify the action in each illustration.

B4   Preguntas y respuestas

Have the students refer to B3 to answer each question. They should answer with complete sentences.

B5   ESTRUCTURAS ESENCIALES

Introduce the verb **hacer** using the following or similar conversation.

TEACHER	A mí me gusta hacer postres. Hago un postre cada semana. Margarita, ¿haces algo?
MARGARITA	Sí, hago la comida.
TEACHER	¡Qué bueno! Margarita hace la comida. ¿Quién más hace la comida?
PEPE	Yo hago la comida los sábados.
TEACHER	Pepe y Margarita hacen la comida.

Continue the dialog until all forms of the verb are presented. Then read the explanation aloud to the class. Point out that only the first-person singular is irregular; all other present indicative forms are regular.

CHALLENGE   To re-enter the verbs that have an irregular **yo** form, you may wish to have the students complete this crossword puzzle.

VERTICAL

1. Yo (hacer)
2. We
3. Sure
4. It (neuter)
5. __na (nombre de una chica)
6. Yo (venir)
9. Yo (saber)
11. Yo (conocer)

HORIZONTAL

3. Yo (salir)
7. Todo para mí: soy __ .
8. Yo (tener)
10. abbr. televisión
12. Yo (estar)

Crossword grid answers: SALGO, EGOISTA, TENGO, TELE, ESTOY, TENGO, VENGO, SEGURO, NOSOTROS, CONOZCO

B6 Actividad • ¿Qué hacen?

SLOWER-PACED LEARNING Have the students copy the sentences from their books, leaving spaces for the verbs. Then tell them to close their books. Read the sentences aloud with the correct verb forms in place. The students should write in the missing verb forms on their papers as they hear them.

B7 Actividad • ¿Quién lo hace?

Ask the students to work with a partner and say who makes what for the family picnic. They should take turns asking and answering the questions.

B8 Actividad • Charla

SLOWER-PACED LEARNING Brainstorm with the class the items they may take on the picnic. Write the list on the board or a transparency for the students to use as they plan their picnics.

For cooperative learning, form groups of two or three. Ask the students to assign duties for each member of the group, then report their plans to the class.

B9 Actividad • ¡A escribir!

As a variation, have the students write an invitation for their picnic. They should include the place, date, and time. They should also include as a reminder a list of what everyone is supposed to bring for the picnic.

B10 ESTRUCTURAS ESENCIALES

To present the demonstrative adjectives, point to a student near you and say: **Este chico es alto** or **Estos chicos son altos.** Then point to a girl and say: **Esta chica es rubia** or **Estas chicas son inteligentes.** Continue by pointing to someone farther away and saying: **Ese(a) chico(a) se llama** . . . or **Esos(as) chicos(as) son amigos(as).** Finally, point to the farthest student in the room and say: **Aquel/aquella chico(a) está lejos de la pizarra** or **Aquellos/aquellas chicas siempre hacen la tarea.**

Call on volunteers to explain the difference between each demonstrative adjective. Then ask the students to open their books and follow along as you read the chart and the explanation aloud.

You may wish to follow with a drill, using classroom objects and real-life situations:

> (Hold up your pen)—¿De quién es la pluma? ¿Es de la profesora?
> —Sí, esa pluma es de la profesora.
> (Point to an object) —¿De quién es ese lápiz? ¿Es de . . . ?
> —Sí (No), ese . . . es de . . .

B 11 **Actividad • En la frutería**

Before the students complete the activity, introduce the names of fruits by using magazine pictures. You may also ask each pair of students to bring magazine pictures or plastic fruit that they may use to complete the activity.

B 12 **Actividad • En el restaurante**

Re-enter the expressions of location such as **cerca de, al lado de** or **lejos de.** Then ask the students to complete the activity using these expressions.

B 13 **Comprensión**

> You'll hear ten short dialogs. Some of the people who are talking are getting ready for a picnic. After listening to each conversation, decide whether the persons who are talking are preparing a picnic or not, and place your check marks accordingly. For example, you hear: **¿Nosotros llevamos los refrescos?** and the response: **No, Ernesto lleva los refrescos. Nosotros compramos la fruta.** Under 0, the check mark is placed in the **Sí** row, since they're talking about what to bring to a picnic.
>
> 1. —¿Tú vas a cocinar ahora?
>   —No, hoy vamos a cenar en un restaurante. *No*
> 2. —¿Y las gaseosas?
>   —Tomás y Lucía. Ellos llevan las gaseosas y el jugo. *Sí*
> 3. —¿Te ayudo a cocinar?
>   —No, yo preparo la cena. Tú tienes que estudiar. *No*
> 4. —Por favor, ¿cuál es el plato del día?
>   —Arroz con pollo. Es muy bueno. *No*
> 5. —¿Sabes? Amalia va a hacer una tortilla.
>   —¡Qué bueno! Ella hace unas tortillas deliciosas. *Sí*
> 6. —¿Quieres hacer unos bocadillos?
>   —No, Ramón va a hacer los bocadillos. Yo llevo un pollo. *Sí*
> 7. —Vamos a ser como quince.
>   —Entonces vamos a comprar todos estos pasteles. *Sí*
> 8. —¿Haces una tarta?
>   —Sí, para Silvia. Ella da una fiesta hoy. *No*
> 9. —¿Desean postre los señores?
>   —No, gracias. La cuenta, por favor. *No*
> 10. —¡Qué bocadillos tan sabrosos!
>   —Pero, ¡no puedes comer esos bocadillos! Son para el picnic. *Sí*
>
> Now check your answers. *Read each exchange again and give the correct answer.*

B14 ¿Sabes que . . . ?

To practice **kilos** and **litros,** have the students set up a corner store in the classroom. The students should ask for kilos of certain items, such as **papas, cebollas, manzanas, uvas,** and so on. Then they should ask for **litros** of liquids, such as **leche, jugo, refresco,** and **agua.** To expand vocabulary, you may wish to introduce **medio kilo, medio litro,** and **cuarto kilo.**

B15 SE DICE ASÍ

Read the chart aloud with the students. Then have the students practice using the expressions with a partner.

B16 Actividad • Charla

The students should work with a partner. They should take turns role-playing the vendor and the customer. Encourage the students to use as many of the expressions and as much of the vocabulary as possible. If possible, to complete the activity, have each pair of students use pictures or clay images of the food mentioned in the activity.

B17 Actividad • ¡A escribir!

CHALLENGE   Have the students write a dialog called **En la pastelería.** They should describe a customer who cannot make a decision as to what he or she wants to buy. Explain that they may add a variety of different pastries by using **de** and the name of a fruit, such as **torta de manzana, pastel de fresas,** or **bizcocho de limón.** The students may also enjoy writing their dialog as a comic strip. Have them present their dialogs to the class.

B18 Actividad • La frutería

Ask the students to select a partner and take turns playing the roles of the vendor and customer.

SLOWER-PACED LEARNING   Before completing the activity, review the demonstrative adjectives with the students. Call on a few volunteers to complete the first examples. Then have the students work with a partner.

B19 Actividad • ¿Quieres frutas?

Have each student select a new partner to complete this activity.

B20 ¿Sabes que . . . ?

The Mexican corn tortilla is probably familiar to the students. You may wish to add that in Mexico, the tortilla is soft. Tortillas are served hot with every meal instead of bread. Since no preservatives are added, they must be made fresh every day. There are usually **tortillerías** in every neighborhood. They are open early every morning and close after the main meal at 4:00 P.M.

B21 Actividad • ¿Qué compramos?

After the students have decided what food they need for the picnic, have them tell the class. They may also wish to include other items that are necessary, such as **los platos de papel, hielo, música,** and so on.

OBJECTIVES **To express attitudes and points of view:** talk about whether people are hungry or thirsty; express your enjoyment of food; ask for what you need at the table

CULTURAL BACKGROUND Picnics are as popular in the Hispanic world as they are in the United States. The difference is what people eat and where they have the picnic. Because there are few national parks in Hispanic America and Spain, and even fewer picnic areas, people usually go to a ranch **(finca)** or a farm **(granja).** Beaches and coastal areas are also popular places for picnics.

Romerías, pilgrimages to a church for a celebration of a holy day, are very popular in Spain and in some Hispanic-American countries. A great many people usually attend the **Romerías.** They congregate around the church and eat whatever they brought from home. Most people usually take fresh bread, cold omelettes, ham, cheese, **empanadas** (meat pies), **croquetas,** and in Mexico **carnitas, tacos,** and **frijoles refritos.** There are always wine and beer for the adults and lemonade and fruit drinks for the children.

MOTIVATING ACTIVITY Ask the students to name events that are usually associated with picnics in the United States, such as the Fourth of July. Where do they go for a picnic? What foods do they take? What activities are planned for a picnic?

C1 Y por fin, ¡El picnic!

After you have introduced the new vocabulary, **la sal, la pimienta,** and the expression **No hay más remedio,** the students will be able to proceed directly with the dialog. Play the cassette or read the dialog aloud. Then form cooperative learning groups to role-play the picnic.

If possible, have a picnic with the students. You should discuss in Spanish the necessary preparations and decide when and where you can have the picnic. Divide the class into groups and assign responsibilities to each group.

C2 Actividad • ¿Es cierto o no?

When the students complete the activity, call on volunteers to read aloud the corrected statements. The students may exchange papers to correct their work.

C3 Preguntas y respuestas

As a variation, have the students make up original questions about the dialog in C1. They should choose a partner and answer one another's questions.

C4 SE DICE ASÍ

Write the following sentences on the board or a transparency and ask the students to identify the verb in each one.

> Tengo mucha hambre.
> Elsa tiene sed.

Then explain that the verb **tener** is used in Spanish to express hunger or thirst. For expansion, you may wish to add that **tener** is used in many idiomatic expressions referring to states or conditions, such as **tener frío,** to be cold, **tener calor,** to be hot, **tener miedo,** to be afraid, and so on.

C5   Actividad • Charla

Have the students choose a partner. Encourage them to make up statements that are different from those in the book. They should name local cafés or restaurants and food or refreshments they would like to order there.

C6   Actividad • ¡A escribir!

The students may work with the same partner from C5 to write their dialog. Then call on each pair to read the dialog aloud to the class.

C7   ¿Sabes que . . . ?

You may wish to tell the students that the beans of the cacao tree were so highly valued that they were used as a medium of exchange instead of money among the Aztecs and the Mayans. The students might enjoy finding out and discussing other discoveries the Spaniards made in the New World, such as the potato, the tomato, and the vanilla bean.

C8   ESTRUCTURAS ESENCIALES

Write the infinitive of **poner** and the subject pronouns on the board. Assign each team a subject pronoun. Have the members of each team go to the board one at a time in a relay race and fill in the correct form of the verb **poner.**

C9   Actividad • Combinación

Begin the activity orally. Then have the students write seven sentences. Call on students at random to read their sentences aloud.

C10   Actividad • ¿Quién pone la mesa?

SLOWER-PACED LEARNING   Have the students copy the sentences from their books, leaving spaces for the verbs. Then tell them to close their books. Read the sentences aloud with the correct verb forms in place. The students should write the missing verb forms on their papers as they hear them.

C11   Actividad • ¿Dónde ponemos la comida?

To complete this activity, ask the students to use pictures or drawings of the food and beverages presented in the activity. As student 1 asks the question, student 2 should respond by indicating where on the table his or her partner should place the food. Tell the students they may answer the questions beginning with **aquí** or **allí: Allí, al lado del tomate.** Finally, student 1 should place the picture in the correct place on the table.

C12   SITUACIÓN • Ponemos la mesa

Point out that most Spanish-speaking people place the teaspoon at the top of the plate instead of to the side as we do in the United States. Then bring in cutlery and a place setting of disposable or plastic dishes. Call on a student to set the table as suggested in the book. As you or a volunteer names each item used for a meal, the student should place the item in the correct position on the table.

Then read aloud or play the cassette. Have the students work with a partner and practice the new vocabulary by setting the table, following the instructions in the book.

C13 Actividad • Combinación

Give the students time to match the items in each box. Then ask individuals to read the completed sentences to the class.

C14 Actividad • ¡A escoger!

CHALLENGE Call on students to name other foods that could be eaten with the utensils listed in the book. Write their suggestions on the board or a transparency.

C15 Actividad • ¡Camarero, por favor!

Have the students complete the sentences, supplying the missing items. Then call on volunteers to read the sentences aloud.

C16 Actividad • Charla

SLOWER-PACED LEARNING Help students formulate the waiter or waitress's responses. Tell the students that if the customer complains of a missing item, the waiter or waitress should respond by stating: **Perdón, aquí está un/a** (the missing item).

CUSTOMER Tengo el cuchillo, pero no tengo un tenedor para comer el bistec.
WAITER Perdón, aquí está el tenedor.

C17 Actividad • ¡A escribir!

The students may work with their partner from C16 to compile a list of the complaints. Call on several pairs to read a few of the complaints aloud.

C18 Actividad • Falta algo

After completing the activity with the verb **poner,** you may wish to play a game called **Falta algo.** Remind students that the verb **faltar** follows the same pattern as the verb **gustar.** Divide the class into two teams. Set the table, omitting an item. The students must identify the missing item.

C19 Comprensión

You'll hear ten incomplete sentences. After listening to each one, decide which of the words in the box best completes what is being said, and place your check mark accordingly. For example, you hear: **¿Puedo cortar la naranja con este . . . ?** The check mark is placed next to **cuchillo** under 0, since the word **cuchillo** is the one that best completes the question.

1. Quiero cortar el bistec. ¿Puedo usar ese . . . ? *cuchillo*
2. Sí, voy a tomar sopa, por favor una . . . *cuchara*
3. ¿Dónde está el azúcar? ¿Y la . . . ? *cucharita*
4. Pero, no puedes comer el helado con un tenedor. Necesitas . . . *cucharita*

5. ¿Comes mantequilla con el pan? ¿Necesitas . . . ? *cuchillo*
6. Y ahora voy a comer la ensalada. ¡Oh!, no tengo . . . *tenedor*
7. Voy a cortar estas papas. ¿Dónde está el . . . ? *cuchillo*
8. Sí, yo puedo batir los huevos. ¿Tienes un . . . ? *tenedor*
9. Quiero comer flan. Por favor, una . . . *cucharita*
10. Para comer el arroz necesitas un . . . *tenedor*

Now check your answers. *Read each statement again and give the correct answer.*

C20 · SE DICE ASÍ

Re-enter adjectives and gender and number agreement. Then practice the expressions in the box by asking the students questions and having them respond, using an alternative expression.

> —¿Está sabrosa la sopa?
> —Sí, está rica.
> —¿Cómo es el almuerzo?
> —¡Qué buenos están los bocadillos!

C21 · Actividad • Reacciones

The students should complete this activity using the adjectives in parentheses as a guide. Explain that the word **buenísimo** is another way of saying **muy bueno**. It is not necessary to teach the **-ísimo** form at this time.

C22 · Actividad • ¡Vamos a comer!

This may be an opportune time to have different groups actually prepare some Spanish or Mexican dishes and have the class eat in the Spanish classroom during lunch or after school. Each food presented must be accompanied by an index card naming the food, giving the recipe in Spanish, and listing the names of the students responsible for preparing the dish.

C23 · Actividad • ¿A cuánto están?

The students may use the shopping list they prepared in C22 to complete the activity. Have the students substitute the underlined words with their own.

C24 · Actividad • La comida

For cooperative learning, divide the class into groups of three or four. Have the students discuss what they would bring to a class picnic. They should discuss their likes and dislikes and agree on a menu. Then call on a member of each group to read the menu to the class.

C25 · Actividad • ¡A escribir!

CHALLENGE Tell the students that they are the food editors for a local newspaper. They have to report on a new restaurant in town. They should give the name of the restaurant and its location, describe the food on the menu, and discuss the specialties of the house, saying whether they are good or not. Finally, the editor must give the readers an idea of the prices.

TRY
YOUR
SKILLS

OBJECTIVE   To recombine communicative functions, grammar, and vocabulary

CULTURAL BACKGROUND   Young people in Spanish-speaking countries do not eat out as often as American young people, but they do enjoy eating out. They may go to a special café, a traditional restaurant, or a sidewalk café. In Mexico and other Latin countries, there are special markets where people go to eat traditional food. The food is often inexpensive and is always delicious.

1   ¿Dónde comemos?

Have the students read the dialog silently as you read it aloud or play the cassette. Then have the students role-play the dialog.

2   Preguntas y respuestas

To check comprehension, have the students answer the questions about the dialog in Skills 1.

CHALLENGE   Have the students make up five false statements based on the dialog. They should exchange their papers with a partner and correct each other's statements.

3   Actividad • ¿Qué vamos a comer hoy?

Have students work in pairs to create their menu and shopping list. Then call on each pair to tell the class what it planned for each meal and what was on its shopping list.

4   Actividad • ¿Qué pedimos?

SLOWER-PACED LEARNING   Ask the students: **¿Qué va a comer Josefina?** As they suggest things, have them go to the board and list the items. They should list as many foods as possible. Then continue with the other people mentioned in the activity.

5   Actividad • Charla

Have the students team up with a partner and take turns asking and answering the questions.

6   Actividad • Una comida revuelta

Create cooperative learning groups of three. Have the students in each group work together to correct the conversation.

7   Actividad • Vamos a comer bien

Each cooperative learning group from Skills 6 should act out its new version of the dialog for the class.

8   Actividad • Una clase de cocina

After the students have read the opinions of the four students, begin the activity by asking questions about each student. **¿Qué le gusta a Alicia? ¿Qué sabe hacer? ¿Qué dice Ramón de una persona que no sabe hacer**

postres? ¿Cómo hace su postre favorito? ¿Qué le gusta a Concepción? ¿Qué no le gusta? ¿Qué le gusta a Félix, una cena ligera o una cena fuerte? ¿Qué come para la cena?

Then ask the students to identify which student attends the cooking class. They should give reasons why they chose that particular student and also explain why they think the other students don't attend the cooking class.

9 **Pronunciación, lectura, dictado**

1. Listen carefully and repeat what you hear.
The letter **r**: In Spanish the sound of **r** is very similar to the *d* sound in the English names *Betty* or *Teddy* when these words are pronounced very quickly. Listen to the following words and repeat in the pauses provided.

   ahora   divertido   horario   cuatro   ligero

   The trilled **r**: When the letter **r** begins a word or is part of the sequence **rr** between vowels, it is pronounced in Spanish with a strong trill. Listen and repeat.

   horrible   correr   aburrido   rápido   raqueta

2. Listen, and then read aloud.
Listen to the following words and sentences with the **r** and **rr** sounds and repeat.

   servilleta   tenedor   por favor   charlar   remedio
   propina   postre   fruta   pregunta   arriba

   Ricardo, vas a necesitar una sartén más grande para freír esos huevos. Vamos a preparar una tortilla para el almuerzo del martes.

3. Write the following sentences from dictation. First, listen to the sentence as it is read to you. Then, you will hear the sentence again in short segments, with a pause after each segment to allow you time to write. Finally, you will hear the sentence a third time so that you may check your work. Let's begin.

   Por favor, *(pause)* nos puede comprar *(pause)* tres refrescos de naranja.
   Creo que *(pause)* te va a gustar *(pause)* ese postre *(pause)* de frutas.
   El arroz *(pause)* en este restaurante *(pause)* es muy rico.
   Hace mucho calor *(pause)* para tomar *(pause)* chocolate con churros.

¿LO SABES?

 SECTION

A

For the first activity, you may wish to ask the students to work with a partner. One student should play the role of a waiter or waitress and the other should play the role of the customer; then they should switch roles.

To continue with the second activity, the waiter or waitress may suggest five typical dishes that are found in a Spanish-speaking country, and the customer should state whether he or she likes or dislikes them.

SECTION B

Have the students use question words such as **qué, cuándo, dónde, quién, a qué hora,** and **cómo.** For the second and third activities, have the students name five different items they are bringing to a picnic and tell where they must go to get each item.

SECTION C

Tell the students to include **Tengo hambre** and **Tengo sed** in their sentences. As the students ask for each of the items in the second activity, they may also include what they are going to do with each item.

Una taza para el chocolate, por favor.
Un cuchillo para cortar la carne.

VOCABULARIO

Since the majority of the words mentioned in the vocabulary list are foods, you may wish to ask the students to prepare a pocket picture dictionary. They may cut index cards in half and write the food word and either draw a picture or cut out a magazine picture to illustrate the food. The foods may be divided into categories and then alphabetized. The students may also include an English-Spanish list at the back of their pocket dictionary. Have the students punch holes in each card and fasten them together with a string or a ring. They may add new cards as they learn new foods.

VAMOS A LEER

OBJECTIVE To read for practice and pleasure

TORTILLA DE PATATAS A LA ESPAÑOLA

Play the cassette or read the recipe aloud. To check comprehension, you may wish to ask the following or similar questions.

1. ¿Cuántos kilos de patatas necesitas?
2. ¿Qué tienes que hacer primero?
3. ¿Cómo se cortan las cebollas?
4. ¿Cuántas cucharadas de aceite se ponen en la sartén?
5. ¿Por qué se mueve la sartén?
6. ¿Qué tienes que hacer cuando se dore bien?

Actividad • No es así

After the students have completed the activity, ask them to exchange papers and correct each other's statements.

Actividad • La tortilla de patatas

This is an optional activity. The students may enjoy preparing the tortilla for their family or classmates.

DE COMPRAS

Play the cassette or read the dialog aloud. Students should be able to read the dialog without any problem since no new vocabulary is introduced.

Actividad • Charla

Form two cooperative learning groups to present a dialog similar to **De compras.** Have the students bring to class the produce (or pictures of the items they plan to sell). The items or pictures should be marked with the price. One student will be the customer, and the other will be the owner of the produce stand.

EL PLÁTANO

After playing the cassette or reading the poem aloud, you may wish to present other poems to the class. The students might enjoy the following Quechuan poem.

El rocío
Las gotas de agua
que en las flores amanecen
son lágrimas de la luna
que de noche llora.

Actividad • ¡A escribir!

Have the students create their own diamond-shaped poem. Have them read their poems aloud in class. Then display the poems on the bulletin board.

EL REGALO

Before reading the episode of **El regalo,** explain that Adriana and Daniel will now be traveling to El Paso, Texas. Ask the students questions such as **¿Qué creen que van a hacer allí?, ¿Qué comen en Texas?** and **¿Dónde es El Paso?**

Play the cassette or read aloud the episode of **El regalo** as the students follow along in their books. Ask questions based on the story to check comprehension.

Actividad • ¿Quiénes hablan?

Ask the students to choose the character who might say the statements listed in the book. Remind students that they must justify their choices.

ANSWERS:
In the second part of each answer, students' replies could be different from those given below.

1. Adriana. Porque Adriana no quiere ir a Texas.
2. Daniel. Porque está en Texas y no conoce el lugar.
3. Adriana. Porque los chicos llegan a El Paso con el televisor y no tienen dinero.
4. El joven. Porque el joven escucha la conversación de los hermanos.
5. El joven. Porque el joven conoce un restaurante cerca de donde están los chicos.
6. Adriana. Porque Adriana piensa que los texanos son simpáticos y guapos.
7. Daniel. Porque tienen una billetera con mucho dinero.
8. Adriana. Porque Adriana tiene hambre.
9. Daniel. Porque Daniel quiere ir a Madrid inmediatamente.
10. Adriana. Porque Adriana no quiere ir a Madrid.

UNIDAD 9

¡Buen provecho!

¡Tacos! ¡Enchiladas! ¡Churros y chocolate!
¡Paella! ¡Arroz con pollo! Sampling the food
of other countries is an adventure you can
have without leaving home. If you like to
cook, read one of the recipes in this unit and
prepare a genuine *comida española* for your
friends. You can also visit one of the many
Spanish or Mexican restaurants in this
country. If you are able to visit other Spanish-
speaking nations, many more delights await
you. All you need is the willingness to try
new things and a readiness to understand the
customs of those around you.

In this unit you will:

SECTION A	say what foods you like and don't like
SECTION B	select the food you like . . . express your enjoyment of food
SECTION C	say you're hungry or thirsty . . . ask for what you need at the table
TRY YOUR SKILLS	use what you've learned
VAMOS A LEER	read for practice and pleasure

SECTION A

saying what foods you like and don't like

Service in the restaurants of Spain and of other Spanish-speaking countries is usually courteous and efficient, but not hurried. You'll be able to enjoy a new and delicious experience if you don't mind waiting.

A1

¿Qué comemos hoy?

Los señores Álvarez escriben sobre los restaurantes de San Antonio para una guía turística. ¿Qué van a comer hoy? ¿Comida española, tex-mex, del Caribe, pizza o hamburguesas?

CAMARERA	¿Desean ver el menú? El plato del día es pollo con cebolla y salsa de tomate.
SR. ÁLVAREZ	A mí no me gustan las cebollas. ¿Hay sopa?
SRA. ÁLVAREZ	Queremos probar algo típico tex-mex.
CAMARERA	¿Puede ser chile con carne?

CAMARERA	¿Y de postre, señores?
SRA. ÁLVAREZ	Un helado de chocolate, por favor, y café con leche.
SR. ÁLVAREZ	Fruta y té con limón para mí. Estoy a dieta.

CAMARERO	¿A ustedes les gustan las enchiladas? Es una especialidad de la casa.
SRA. ÁLVAREZ	Sí, me gustan mucho. Quiero dos de carne y una de queso.
SR. ÁLVAREZ	Y para beber, agua mineral.

SRA. ÁLVAREZ	¡Qué rápido cenamos aquí!
SR. ÁLVAREZ	Sí, voy a pagar la cuenta.
SRA. ÁLVAREZ	¿Cuánto dejamos de propina?
SR. ÁLVAREZ	¡No sé cuánto . . . ni dónde!

Actividad • No es así For answers, see p. T163.

Change the following sentences as necessary to make them true according to A1.

1. Los señores Álvarez escriben un diccionario de la comida del Caribe.
2. En **Sombrero Rosa** el plato del día es pizza con cebolla.
3. Al señor Álvarez le gustan las cebollas.
4. Desean tres enchiladas de queso y té con limón.
5. De postre, la señora come fruta.
6. La señora está a dieta. Desea agua mineral con limón.
7. El señor no tiene la cuenta.
8. Los señores Álvarez dejan la propina en la mesa.

A3 Actividad • Conversación Answers will vary.

Pair up with a partner and look over the pictures in A1. Then ask each other these questions.

1. ¿Vas tú a restaurantes a veces? ¿A qué restaurante vas?
2. ¿Tienes un restaurante favorito? ¿Cuál es?
3. De los restaurantes, ¿cuál te gusta más?
4. ¿Qué clase de comida te gusta?
5. ¿Cuál te gusta más: la sopa o el postre?

A4 Actividad • ¡A escribir!

Using the questions and answers to A3 as a guide, prepare a brief composition about the dinner you had at a restaurant.

A5 ¿Sabes que . . . ?

A **café** in Spanish-speaking countries is a place that serves sodas, coffee and tea, and other drinks; sandwiches and other light snacks, fruit, fruit juices, ice cream, and pastries. It usually has some tables and chairs on the sidewalk in front and others inside where there is also a small bar, a television set, a pay telephone, rest rooms, and in some countries, video game machines. In the evening, friends meet in their favorite **café,** play the video games or just chat and have a soda.

You may wish to mention that in Spain, they serve "tapas" in many cafe's. They are comparable to hors d'oeuvres and are becoming popular in the United States.

Comemos por la mañana, al mediodía, por la tarde y por la noche.
A la hora de la merienda, o entre comidas, lo mejor es un bocadillo y
un vaso de leche o de jugo.

Por la mañana, en el desayuno, nos gusta . . .

tomar café con leche o chocolate, comer pan con mantequilla, jalea o mermelada.

Al mediodía, en el almuerzo, nos gusta . . .   En el almuerzo, a mí me gusta . . .

un bistec o pescado, arroz, verduras y un
postre. Nuestro postre favorito es el flan.
A nosotros nos gusta una comida completa.

comer un bocadillo. Me gustan los bocadillos
de jamón y queso, con lechuga, tomate y
mayonesa. Las papas fritas me encantan.

Por la noche, para la cena, en casa les gusta . . .

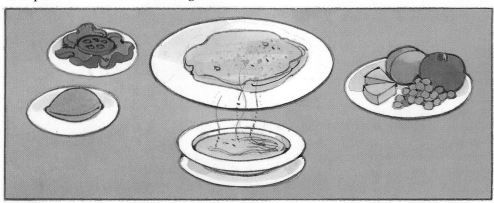

una comida ligera: tomar sopa, comer una tortilla con ensalada, pan, queso y fruta.

1. Como papas fritas en el almuerzo. 2. Nuestro postre favorito es el flan. 3. A mí me gusta un bocadillo de jamón y queso para el almuerzo. 4. A la hora de la merienda, lo mejor es un bocadillo y un vaso de leche.

A7 Actividad • No es así

Change the following sentences to make them true according to A6.

1. Como papas fritas en el desayuno.
2. Nuestro postre favorito es la sopa.
3. A mí me gusta un bocadillo de arroz en el almuerzo.
4. A la hora de la merienda lo mejor es un bistec.

For answers, see p. T164.

A8 Actividad • ¡El menú está malo!

The menu printer mixed up the meals, the hours, and the menu items.
Rearrange the three columns
as you think best.

RESTAURANTE ESTRELLA

Desayuno	cinco de la tarde	refrescos bistec postre
Almuerzo	ocho de la noche	chocolate café con leche
Cena	una de la tarde	bocadillo jugo o leche
Merienda	de ocho a nueve de la mañana	sopa ensalada

A9 Actividad • ¿A qué hora comes? Answers will vary.

Talk with a classmate about food and meals. Ask each other the following questions:

1. ¿A qué hora tomas el desayuno?
2. ¿Qué toman en tu casa en el desayuno? ¿Leche, jugo, café?
3. ¿Cuál es la hora del almuerzo en la escuela? ¿Y en tu casa?
4. ¿Tomas sopa en el almuerzo o en la cena?
5. ¿Comes ensalada en el almuerzo o en la cena?
6. ¿Cenas en tu casa? ¿Cuándo cenas en un restaurante?
7. ¿Tomas una merienda al volver de la escuela?
8. ¿A qué hora cenan en tu casa?
9. ¿Te gusta cenar tarde o temprano?
10. ¿Comes entre comidas? ¿Qué comes, un bocadillo?

A10 Actividad • ¡A escribir!

Using your answers to A9 as a guide, prepare a brief composition about meals at home. Start with **"En mi casa, tomamos el desayuno a las . . . "**

A11 ESTRUCTURAS ESENCIALES
The verb gustar

1. In Unit 3, you first used **gustar** to talk about liking something, and you learned to use **me, te,** and **le** to indicate the person who does the liking.

Me gusta comer.	*I like to eat.*
Te gusta el helado.	*You like ice cream.*
Le gusta la sopa.	$\left\{\begin{array}{l}\textit{She}\\\textit{He}\\\textit{You (Ud.)}\end{array}\right\}$ *likes soup.*

2. Use **nos** or **les** when more than one person likes something.

Nos gusta comer.	*We like to eat.*
Les gusta el helado.	$\left\{\begin{array}{l}\textit{They}\\\textit{You (Uds.)}\end{array}\right\}$ *like ice cream.*

3. Only two forms of the verb **gustar** are used. Use **gusta** if what is liked is singular. Use **gustan** if what is liked is plural.

A Luisa le gusta el helado.	*Luisa likes ice cream.*
Me gustan las enchiladas.	*I like enchiladas.*
Nos gustan los restaurantes españoles.	*We like Spanish restaurants.*
Te gustan las frutas.	*You like fruit.*

4. To say that people don't like something, place **no** before **me, te, le, nos, les.**

No me gusta el helado.	*I don't like ice cream.*
No nos gustan las enchiladas.	*We don't like enchiladas.*

5. For clarification or emphasis, you can add **a** + prepositional pronoun.

¿Yo? **A mí** me gusta el helado.
¿Tú? **A ti** no te gusta la cebolla.
A ella le gusta el helado.
A él le gustan las enchiladas.
A Ud. le gusta comer pescado.
A nosotros nos gusta estudiar.
A ellas les gustan los restaurantes mexicanos.
A Uds. les gusta la clase de español.
A Pepe le gusta comer.

Notice that the prepositional pronouns are the same as the subject pronouns, except that **mí** replaces **yo,** and **ti** replaces **tú.**

A12 Actividad • ¿Qué les gusta?

Say what the following people like to do. Follow the model.

—Anita (jugar tenis)
—A Anita le gusta jugar tenis.

1. A mi hermano le gusta bailar.
2. A Tomás y a Dora les gustan las enchiladas.
3. A ellos les gusta ir al cine.

1. Mi hermano (bailar)
2. Tomás y Dora (las enchiladas)
3. Ellos (ir al cine)
4. Nosotros (la ensalada)
5. Carolina (el postre)
6. Yo (los bocadillos de jamón y queso)

4. A nosotros nos gusta la ensalada.   5. A Carolina le gusta el postre.
6. A mí me gustan los bocadillos de jamón y queso.

Actividad • Combinación   Answers will vary. Ex: A mí no me gusta el pollo.
A él no le gusta la fruta.
A mis amigos no les gusta la carne.

Make up 10 sentences using items from each column.

—A ellos no les gusta la fruta.

A mí A ti				el pollo el café con leche
A él A ella		les		la cebolla la fruta el queso
A usted		te		el té con limón la carne
A nosotros	(no)	me	gusta(n) . . .	el pan con mantequilla comer
A ellos A ellas		le		la mayonesa las papas fritas
A ustedes		nos		el jugo el arroz
A mis amigos				los postres las verduras
				los helados la ensalada

¡Están seguros! *They're sure!*   For answers, see p. T165.

Make these sentences more emphatic by using a prepositional pronoun.

—No te gusta bailar.   —A ti no te gusta bailar.

1. Le gusta el jugo.
2. Me gusta comer.
3. Les gusta la ensalada.
4. Te gustan los postres.

5. No nos gusta la cebolla.
6. No les gustan las verduras.
7. No nos gusta dejar propina.
8. Te gustan los helados.

9. Le gusta el pan con mantequilla.
10. Me gustan los postres.
11. No me gusta la cebolla.
12. No les gusta el arroz.

SE DICE ASÍ
Saying what you like and don't like

¿Qué te gusta a ti y qué no?	A mí me gustan las enchiladas. A mí no me gusta el mole.
¿Qué les gusta a ustedes y qué no?	A nosotros nos gustan los postres. A nosotros no nos gusta la fruta.

Actividad • Charla

Get together with two or three classmates, talk about what foods you like and don't like. The list of foods in the last column of A13 may jog your memory. Report to the class who likes what, and who dislikes what.

—A mí me gusta la cebolla. ¿Y a ustedes?   —Sí, a nosotros nos gusta también.

Actividad • ¡A escribir!   Answers will vary.

Write two lists of the foods in A13—those you like and those you don't. Compare your likes and dislikes with those of your friends.

—A mí me gusta(n) . . . y a mis amigos les gusta(n) . . . también.
—A mí me gusta(n) . . . pero a mis amigos no les gusta(n) . . . .

Actividad • ¿Y en tu casa? Answers will vary.

Pair up with a partner and ask each other the following.

¿Qué comen en tu casa?
¿Qué comida(s) le(s) gusta(n) . .

 . . . a tu papá?
 . . . a tu mamá?
 . . . a tus hermanos?
 . . . a tus hermanas?
 . . . a ti?

sopa   hamburguesas   verduras   pollo
queso   helados   Postre
bocadillos   pan con mantequilla   arroz   carne

A 19   Actividad • ¡A escribir!

¿Les gusta o no? Write down the conversation you had with your partner. Talk about what you eat at home and your family's likes and dislikes about food.

A 20   ¿Sabes que . . . ?

Dishes like **arroz con pollo,** *chicken with rice,* are served in most Spanish-speaking countries. But many countries have a special dish. In Spain, for example, some people have **chocolate y churros** (doughnut-like pastries with no hole) for breakfast or snacks. **Paella,** associated with the city of Valencia, is another famous Spanish dish: it consists of a large platter of seafood, chicken, and saffron-colored (yellow) rice. **Tacos** (folded and filled corn tortillas) and **enchiladas** (rolled tortillas filled with meat or cheese, fried, and served with a chile sauce) are two of the scores of foods for which Mexico is famous. Sometimes foods are the same, but the names are different—potatoes, for example, are **patatas** in Spain and **papas** in the Americas. The vocabulary of food in Spanish is large. If you'd like to learn even half the words, get ready for a lifetime of good eating!

A 21   Comprensión   For script and answers, see p. T166.

Food, meals, and restaurants . . . do they like it or not?

	0	1	2	3	4	5	6	7	8	9	10
Le(s) gusta(n)				✔		✔	✔		✔		✔
No le(s) gusta(n)	✔	✔	✔		✔			✔		✔	

Actividad • ¡A escoger!

The waiter is talking to you. Choose the appropriate response.

1. ¿Qué desean ustedes?
   • No me gusta la cebolla.   • Chile con carne, por favor.
2. Hay enchiladas de queso y de carne.
   • Dos de queso.   • No me gustan las verduras.
3. El plato del día es pollo.
   • La sopa no me gusta.   • Bueno, y para beber un refresco.
4. ¿Y de postre?
   • Pollo con salsa.   • Helado de chocolate.
5. ¿Más café?
   • Un poco, por favor.   • Me gusta el café.
6. ¿Algo más?
   • No, gracias. La cuenta, por favor.   • La propina.
7. La cuenta, señores.
   • No me gusta.   • Gracias.
8. Gracias, buenas noches.
   • ¿Tienen chile con carne?   • Buenas noches.

A23 Actividad • El restaurante

To create the atmosphere of a restaurant, write out a menu in Spanish, make out
a bill, and bring props from home if you can. Work with two of your classmates.
Two of you will be the customers at a restaurant. The other one will be the waiter
or waitress. Add your own ideas to the following.

The customers:

• Enter the restaurant and ask for a table.
• Ask for the menu.

• Listen to the specials, decide what to have,
  and order their food.
• Eat. Make comments about the food. Call
  the waiter or waitress to order dessert. Ask
  for the bill.
• Look at the bill. Discuss how much tip to
  leave. Say good night and leave.

The waiter or waitress:

• Seats the customers.
• Brings the menu, and says what the specials
  of the day are.
• Takes their order. Asks what they want to
  drink.
• Brings dessert and the bill.

• Thanks the customers, and says good night.

A24 Actividad • ¡A escribir!

Write your restaurant
scene in dialog form.

¡Buen provecho!   245

talking about food . . . selecting the food you like

Picnics are great fun and are popular in Spanish-speaking countries. La tortilla, Spanish omelette, is a favorite dish since it is good hot or cold.

B1   Un picnic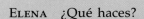

ELENA	¿Qué haces?
CARLOS	Preparo una tortilla para el picnic.
ELENA	¡Estupendo! A todos nos gusta la tortilla. Es muy rica. ¿Te ayudo?
CARLOS	¿Por qué no cortas estas patatas y esas cebollas en trozos pequeños? Después voy a freír todo.
ELENA	Bueno, a lo dicho, hecho. ¡Ay!
CARLOS	¿Por qué lloras, Elena?
ELENA	¡Son las cebollas por supuesto! Y ahora, ¿qué?

CARLOS   Ahora bato los huevos, añado las patatas y las cebollas y cocino todo en esta misma sartén. Tiene que dorarse de los dos lados. ¡Y aquí está nuestra tortilla!

ELENA   ¡Ay, qué hambre tengo!

1. Sí, es cierto 2. No, va a hacer una tortilla.
3. No, a Elena le gusta la tortilla.
4. No, Elena corta las patatas y las cebollas. 5. Sí, es cierto.

B2   Actividad • ¿Es cierto o no?

Say whether the following statements are correct or not according to B1.
Correct the statements that aren't true.

1. La tortilla es para un picnic.
2. Carlos va a hacer enchiladas.
3. A Elena no le gusta la tortilla.
4. Elena corta la fruta.
5. Carlos va a freír todo en una sartén.
6. Él bate las patatas y añade los huevos.
7. ¡Aquí está nuestra cocina!
8. Elena no tiene hambre.

6. No, él bate los huevos y añade las patatas. 7. ¡Aquí está nuestra tortilla! 8. Sí, Elena tiene hambre.

Miguel compra las frutas. Va a aquella frutería grande de la esquina.

Alicia hace bocadillos de jamón y queso, de pollo y de atún. ¡Qué sabrosos!

Sofía compra pasteles en una pastelería muy buena.

Manuel trae los refrescos.

¡Buen provecho! 247

1. Miguel compra las frutas en la frutería de la esquina.   2. Hay naranjas, uvas, manzanas y fresas.   3. Alicia prepara los bocadillos. Son de jamón y queso, de pollo y de atún. Son sabrosos.   4. Sofía compra pasteles en una pastelería muy buena.   5. Sofía lleva pasteles.   6. Manuel lleva los refrescos.   7. Él tiene todo en el coche.   8. El picnic va a ser estupendo.

B4   *Preguntas y respuestas*

Answer in complete sentences. Base your answers on B3.

1. ¿Qué compra Miguel? ¿Dónde?
2. ¿Qué más hay allí?
3. ¿Qué prepara Alicia? ¿De qué son? ¿Cómo son?
4. ¿Qué compra Sofía? ¿Dónde?

5. ¿Sabes qué lleva ella al picnic?
6. ¿Y Manuel, qué lleva?
7. ¿Dónde tiene él todo?
8. ¿Cómo va a ser el picnic?

B5   ## ESTRUCTURAS ESENCIALES
The verb **hacer,** *to do, to make*

hacer	*to do, to make*		
Hago	un postre.	**¿Hacemos**	un picnic?
¿Haces	bocadillos?	**¿Hacéis**	la comida?
Hace	un flan.	**Hacen**	la tortilla.

The present-tense forms of **hacer** are all regular except the **yo** form: **hago.**

The verb **hacer** is equivalent to two English verbs: *to do,* and *to make.*

—María, ¿qué **haces**?
—**Hago** la tarea.

—*María, what are you doing?*
—*I'm doing homework.*

—Enrique, ¿qué **haces**?
—**Hago** una tortilla de patatas.

—*Enrique, what are you making?*
—*I'm making a potato omelet.*

B6   *Actividad • ¿Qué hacen?*

Everybody has to make something for the picnic. Supply the missing forms of **hacer** to complete the conversation.

hacen 1. Carlos Y Elena ____ una tortilla.
hace 2. Alicia ____ bocadillos.
Hacen 3. ¿ ____ ustedes un pollo?

4. No, nosotros ____ una ensalada. hacemos
5. ¿Qué ____ tú? haces

6. Yo ____ un flan. hago
7. Y yo, ¿qué ____ ? hago
8. Tú puedes ____ una tarta. hacer

B7   *Actividad • ¿Quién lo hace?*

Using forms of **hacer,** say who makes what for the family picnic.

Mamá hace el pollo. Nosotros hacemos la tortilla. Tú haces los bocadillos. Yo hago la tarta. Ustedes hacen el flan. Ellos hacen la ensalada. Él hace el arroz. Nosotros hacemos los pasteles.

—¿La ensalada? —Celia y Raúl.
—Ellos hacen la ensalada.

—¿El pollo? —Mamá.
—¿La tortilla? —Carlos y yo.
—¿Los bocadillos? —Tú.

—¿La tarta? —Yo.
—¿El flan? —Alicia y tú.
—¿La ensalada? —Celia y Raúl.

—¿El arroz? —Pedro.
—¿Los pasteles? —Ramón y yo.

Pedro hace el arroz. Ramón y yo hacemos los pasteles.

B8   *Actividad • Charla*

Plan a picnic with two or three classmates. Discuss a good place, date, and time. Make up a shopping list and decide who should do what. Then report your plans to your classmates.

Actividad • ¡A escribir!

Nuestro picnic. Write down the plans that you and your classmates made for a picnic in B8.

B 10 ESTRUCTURAS ESENCIALES
Demonstrative adjectives

Practice the demonstrative adjectives using classroom objects. (Point to an object on a student's desk) Ask: "¿De quién es ese cuaderno? (este lápiz, aquella regla, ese libro)" Reverse roles and have the students ask the questions.

		Singular		Plural	
this/these	Masculine	**este**	chico	**estos**	chicos
	Feminine	**esta**	chica	**estas**	chicas
that/those	Masculine	**ese**	chico	**esos**	chicos
	Feminine	**esa**	chica	**esas**	chicas
	Masculine	**aquel**	chico	**aquellos**	chicos
	Feminine	**aquella**	chica	**aquellas**	chicas

1. Demonstrative adjectives are usually placed before the noun they modify. Like other adjectives in Spanish, they agree in gender and number with the noun.

2. Demonstrative adjectives point out people and things. The **este** forms correspond to the English *this, these*. The **ese** and **aquel** forms correspond to *that, those*. The difference is that **aquel** suggests greater distance from both speaker and listener than does **ese**.

B 11 Actividad • En la frutería

Work with a classmate. One of you is the customer; the other is the clerk at a fruit stand. Tell the clerk you want a kilo of the various fruits you point to. The clerk will show you the fruit to make sure it is what you want. Switch roles.

    las uvas   —Un kilo de esas uvas, por favor.
                —¿Estas uvas?

1. las manzanas   5. los plátanos
2. las fresas   6. los melocotones
3. los limones   7. las cerezas
4. los tomates   8. las naranjas

1. Un kilo de esas manzanas, por favor.
  —¿Estas manzanas?
2. Un kilo de esas fresas, por favor.
  —¿Estas fresas?
3. Un kilo de esos limones, por favor.
  —¿Estos limones?
4. Un kilo de esos tomates.
  —¿De estos tomates?
5. Un kilo de esos plátanos.
  —¿De estos plátanos?

6. Un kilo de esos melocotones
  ¿De estos melocotones?

7. Un kilo de esas cerezas
  —¿De estas cerezas?
8. Un kilo de esas naranjas
  —¿De estas naranjas?

B 12 Actividad • En el restaurante

Tell the waiter where you would like to sit. Use an appropriate form of **aquel**.

    entrada   —Cerca de aquella entrada, por favor.

1. puerta   3. señoritas   5. chicos
2. mesa   4. señor   6. chicas

1. Cerca de aquella puerta, por favor. 2. Cerca de aquella mesa, por favor.
3. Cerca de aquellas señoritas, por favor. 4. Cerca de aquel señor, por favor.
5. Cerca de aquellos chicos, por favor. 6. Cerca de aquellas chicas, por favor.

B 13 Comprensión 🖭 For script and answers, see p. T170.

Who is preparing a picnic?

	0	1	2	3	4	5	6	7	8	9	10
Sí	✔		✔			✔	✔	✔			✔
No		✔		✔	✔				✔	✔	

B 14 ¿Sabes que . . . ?

Kilos y litros. The metric system is used in Spanish-speaking countries to measure weight and volume. A 150-pound track star weighs 68 **kilos**—a kilo is 2.2 pounds. Potatoes, meat, and other items are bought by the kilo. Smaller amounts are measured in **gramos;** 1000 grams equal 1 kilo, and 28.3 grams equal 1 ounce.

Milk, water, wine, and other liquids, including gasoline, are all measured in **litros.** A liter is slightly larger than a quart. Cookbook recipes specify small amounts in **cucharadas y cucharaditas,** *tablespoons and teaspoons.*

B 15 SE DICE ASÍ
Selecting what you like

	—(Señor, quiero) Este bizcocho, por favor.
¿Quiere . . . ?	Sí, gracias Sí, y también . . . No, gracias. No, . . . esa No, mejor esos . . .

B 16 Actividad • Charla

Work with a partner. Take turns playing customer and vendor. Pick five of the items listed below. The vendor makes suggestions about what items to buy. The customer selects what he or she wants. Use as many of the expressions in B15 as possible.

—¿Quieres estas manzanas?

—Sí, y también . . .
—No, mejor esas naranjas.

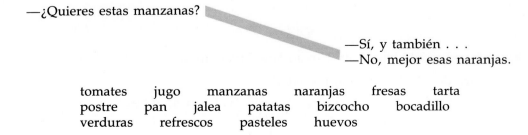

tomates	jugo	manzanas	naranjas	fresas	tarta
postre	pan	jalea	patatas	bizcocho	bocadillo
verduras	refrescos	pasteles	huevos

Actividad • ¡A escribir!

Write a dialog based on the suggestions from your classmate, and the selections you made in B16.

B 18   Actividad • La frutería

6. ¿Va a llevar estas peras? No, llevo esos melocotones, por favor.
7. ¿Lleva este pastel de fresa? No, voy a llevar ese bizcocho.

Work with a partner. One of you is the vendor, and the other is the customer. The vendor makes suggestions, using **este, estos, esta, estas.** The customer indicates another choice using **ese, esos, esa,** or **esas.** Then switch roles.

—¿Quiere / plátanos?   —No, quiero / melocotones.
—¿Quiere estos plátanos?   —No, quiero esos melocotones.

1. —¿Lleva / melón?   —No, / sandía, por favor.   ¿Lleva este melón? No, llevo esa sandía por favor.
2. —¿Le gustan / naranjas?   —No, quiero / plátanos.   ¿Le gustan estas naranjas? No, quiero esos plátanos.
3. —¿Compra / piña?   —No, mejor / cerezas.   ¿Compra esta piña? No, mejor compro esas cerezas.
4. —¿Le gustan / manzanas?   —No, llevo / plátanos.   ¿Le gustan estas manzanas? No, llevo esos plátanos.
5. —¿Quiere / uvas?   —No, quiero / melones.   ¿Quiere estas uvas? No, quiero esos melones.
6. —¿Va a llevar / peras?   —No, / melocotones, por favor.
7. —¿Lleva / pastel de fresa?   —No, voy a llevar / bizcocho.
8. —¿Quiere / tarta?   —No, mejor / pasteles.   ¿Quiere esta tarta? No, mejor esos pasteles.

B 19   Actividad • ¿Quieres frutas?

1. ¿Quiere ese melón? No, quiero aquella sandía.
2. ¿Le gustan esas naranjas? No, quiero aquellos plátanos.

Now the vendor asks the questions in B18 again, this time using **ese, esos, esa,** and **esas.** The customer answers using **aquel, aquella, aquellos,** and **aquellas.**

—¿Quiere / plátanos?   —No, quiero / melocotones.
—¿Quieres esos plátanos?   —No, quiero aquellos melocotones.

3. ¿Compra esa piña? No, mejor compro aquellas cerezas.
4. ¿Le gustan esas manzanas? No, llevo aquellos plátanos.
5. ¿Quiere esas uvas? No, quiero aquellos melones. 6. ¿Va a llevar esas peras? No, llevo aquellos melocotones, por favor. 7. ¿Lleva ese pastel de fresa? No, voy a llevar aquel bizcocho. 8. ¿Quiere esa tarta? No, mejor aquellos pasteles.

B 20   ¿Sabes que . . . ?

Mexican tortillas are flat corncakes used instead of bread. In Spain, a tortilla is an omelette. Potatoes and onions are thinly sliced and cooked in oil. When tender, the potatoes are drained and added to a bowl of beaten eggs, which are then cooked, completing the tortilla.

B 21   Actividad • ¿Qué compramos?   Answers will vary.

Work with one or two of your classmates. You are at the store getting food for a picnic. Discuss what to buy. Then report to the class what food you're buying.

—¿Compramos este melón o aquellos plátanos?
—Mejor, esas naranjas.
—¿Por qué no llevamos esos pasteles de manzana?
—Bueno, compramos los pasteles.

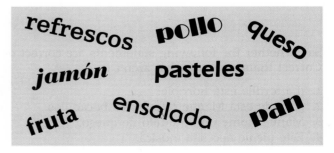

refrescos   pollo   queso
jamón   pasteles
fruta   ensalada   pan

SECTION C

saying you're hungry or thirsty . . . asking for what you need at the table . . . expressing your enjoyment of food.

Once you've shopped for the ingredients and made your picnic food, it's time to have the picnic. Is anybody hungry or thirsty?

C1

Y por fin, ¡el picnic!

MIGUEL La sal, por favor. ¡Esta tortilla está perfecta! Pero, ¿dónde está Manuel con los refrescos? Tengo mucha sed.

ELENA ¡Paciencia! Comes por tres, ¿sabes? ¡Ah, aquí viene!

MANUEL ¡Hola! ¡Cuánto tráfico! ¿Pongo la mesa? ¿Dónde van los refrescos?

ELENA La mesa ya está.

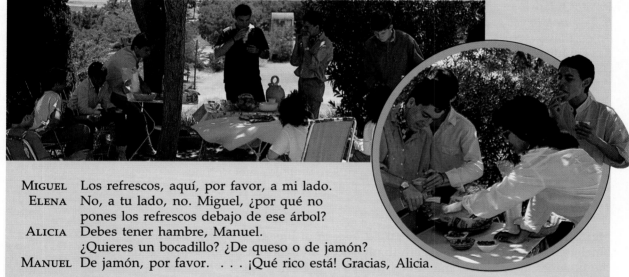

MIGUEL Los refrescos, aquí, por favor, a mi lado.

ELENA No, a tu lado, no. Miguel, ¿por qué no pones los refrescos debajo de ese árbol?

ALICIA Debes tener hambre, Manuel. ¿Quieres un bocadillo? ¿De queso o de jamón?

MANUEL De jamón, por favor. . . . ¡Qué rico está! Gracias, Alicia.

CARLOS Este picnic necesita música. Miguel, ¿por qué no pones este casete? ¿Quieres bailar, Alicia?

ALICIA ¡Cómo no! Es mi canción favorita.

MIGUEL Buena idea. Vamos, Elena. Si bailas conmigo, no como más.

ELENA ¡No hay más remedio! Vamos, Miguel.

C2 Actividad • ¿Es cierto o no?

1. ¡La tortilla está perfecta!
2. Manuel tiene los refrescos.
3. Manuel come un bocadillo de jamón.
4. Es cierto. 5. A Alicia le gusta la canción, es su favorita.

Say whether the following statements are correct or not according to C1.
Correct the statements that aren't true.

1. ¡La tortilla está horrible!
2. ¿Dónde está Manuel? Tiene los bocadillos.
3. Manuel come un bocadillo de queso.
4. Este picnic necesita música.

5. A Alicia no le gusta la canción.
6. A Miguel no le gusta bailar.
7. Miguel va a bailar con Alicia.

6. A Miguel le gusta bailar. 7. Miguel va a bailar con Elena.

C3   **Preguntas y respuestas**

Answer the following questions about C1.

1. ¿Le gusta a Miguel la tortilla? ¿Cómo sabes?
2. ¿Por qué espera Miguel a Manuel?
3. ¿Por qué llega tarde Manuel?
4. ¿Dónde ponen la comida? ¿Y los refrescos?

5. ¿Qué come Manuel? ¿Le gusta? ¿Cómo sabes?
6. ¿Qué necesita el picnic?
7. ¿Quiere bailar Alicia? ¿Por qué?
8. ¿Con quién baila Alicia? ¿Y Elena?

C4   **SE DICE ASÍ**
Talking about whether people are hungry or thirsty

¿Tienes sed, Miguel? Are you thirsty, Miguel?	Sí, tengo mucha sed. Yes, I'm very thirsty.
Elena no tiene hambre ahora. Elena is not hungry now.	Yo, sí. Tengo mucha hambre. I am. I'm very hungry.

C5   **Actividad • Charla**

With a classmate, discuss whether you are hungry or thirsty, where you want to go, and what you want to eat.

—¿Tienes hambre, Carmela?

Sí, tengo mucha hambre.

¿Comemos un bocadillo en este café?

No, mejor vamos al café Valencia. Tienen unas tartas deliciosas.

C6   **Actividad • ¡A escribir!**

Write a dialog of at least four exchanges based on the Charla in C5.

C7   **¿Sabes que . . . ?**

Chocolate is an extract from the seeds of the cacao tree. When Columbus discovered the New World in 1492, he also found cacao growing there, but the importance of the plant wasn't immediately recognized.

   In 1519, when Hernán Cortés began the Conquest of Mexico, he learned that the Aztec Emperor, Moctezuma, and the nobles of his court were very fond of drinking chocolate. These Spanish explorers brought the drink back to Spain, where it became very popular. It was so highly prized that Spanish officials kept the recipe a secret for a hundred years.

ESTRUCTURAS ESENCIALES
The verb **poner,** *to place, to put*

poner *to place, to put*			
¿Pongo	la comida allí?	**¿Ponemos**	los huevos en la sartén?
¿Pones	un casete?	**Ponéis**	todo debajo del árbol.
Pone	música.	**Ponen**	los refrescos en el coche.

The present-tense forms of **poner** are regular except the **yo** form: **pongo.** The expression **poner la mesa** means *to set the table.* However, when you put something on the table, you say: **poner en la mesa.**

C9 Actividad • Combinación Answers will vary. Ex: —Yo pongo la fruta en la mesa.

¿Qué ponen en la mesa? Form sentences using an item from each box. Add the appropriate form of **poner** and **en la mesa** to all your sentences.

—Ella pone las manzanas en la mesa.

Tú   Felipe y yo
Papá   Ella   Mamá
Manuel y Elena   Yo
Nosotros   Ustedes

los bocadillos   los pasteles
la fruta   el agua
los refrescos   las manzanas
la tortilla   la sal   el pan

C10 Actividad • ¿Quién pone la mesa?

Who's setting the table? Complete this conversation using appropriate forms of **poner.**

1. Yo no <u>pongo</u> la mesa. ¿<u>Pones</u> tú la mesa?
2. No, Julián y Elvira <u>ponen</u> la mesa.
3. ¿Nosotros? ¡No! Nosotros no ___ (ponemos) la mesa. Mejor, ustedes <u>ponen</u> la mesa.
4. ¿Por qué no <u>pones</u> tú la mesa?
5. ¿Y Daniel? No, él no <u>pone</u> la mesa. A él no le gusta <u>poner</u> la mesa.
6. ¿Quién? ¿Yo? ¡Nunca! Yo no voy a <u>poner</u> la mesa. Los chicos <u>ponen</u> la mesa.

C11 Actividad • ¿Dónde ponemos la comida? Answers will vary.

You are organizing a picnic. Help place the food everybody is bringing in the right place. Answer your friends' questions using as many expressions as you can from the list on the right.

¿Dónde pongo . . .

los refrescos	los bocadillos
el queso	el jamón
la lechuga	el tomate
el pan	la fruta
las tartas . . . ?	

delante de   arriba de   a la izquierda de
allí   a la derecha de
detrás de   debajo de   detrás de   aquí
entre   a la derecha de   al lado de

Ex: ¿Dónde pongo los refrescos? Pongo los refrescos aquí.

Para el desayuno pongo:

vaso para el jugo, platillo
para el pan y la mantequilla

plato hondo para el cereal,
cuchara y servilleta

taza con platillo, y cucharita
para el azúcar

Para el almuerzo ponemos:

plato hondo para la sopa

platillo para el bocadillo
y servilleta

sal, pimienta, mostaza
y catsup

Para la comida o para la cena ellos ponen:

platillo para la ensalada, plato
llano para la comida

tenedor, cuchillo, dos
cucharitas, servilleta

vaso para el agua y platillo
para el postre

¡Buen provecho! 255

Por favor, necesitamos un plato hondo para la sopa.
. . . un plato llano para la tortilla.
. . . una cuchara para el cereal.
. . . un platillo para el postre.
. . . una taza para el té.
. . . un vaso para la leche.
. . . un cuchillo para la carne.
. . . una cucharita para el azúcar.
. . . un tenedor para la ensalada.

C13 Actividad • Combinación

Match items in the two boxes.

—Por favor, necesitamos una taza para el té.

Por favor, necesitamos . . .	
un cuchillo	un plato llano
una cuchara	un vaso
un tenedor	un platillo
una taza	una cucharita
un plato hondo	

para . . .	
la sopa.	la leche.
la tortilla.	la carne.
el cereal.	el azúcar.
el postre.	la ensalada.
el té.	

C14 Actividad • ¡A escoger!

Choose the food for which the dish or flatware makes most sense.

1. **Plato hondo** • sopa • ensalada • bocadillo
2. **Vaso** • pollo • jugo • ensalada
3. **Tenedor** • sopa • helado • carne
4. **Cuchillo** • carne • cereal • huevos
5. **Platillo** • jugo • ensalada • agua
6. **Cucharita** • bocadillos • tortilla • postre
7. **Plato llano** • carne • cereal • sopa
8. **Taza** • pollo • tortilla • chocolate

C15 Actividad • ¡Camarero, por favor!

The service at the restaurant is absolutely terrible! All the customers are complaining. Complete the sentences with the names of the missing objects.

—Tengo el jugo, pero no tengo _____ . vaso.
—¿Cómo como la sopa? Necesito una _____ . cuchara.
—Aquí hay dos tenedores, pero no hay _____ para la carne. cuchillo
—Y mi _____ de leche, ¿dónde está? vaso
—¡Por favor! No puedo comer el pollo con una _____ de sopa. cuchara
—¿Cómo pongo el azúcar en el té? No tengo _____ . cucharita
—Sí, tengo la leche, pero, ¿dónde está el _____ para el cereal? plato hondo
—Me gusta la taza, es muy bonita. ¡Qué pena! No tiene _____ . platillo
—¿Con qué corto la carne? ¿Con la _____? cuchara

C16 Actividad • Charla

Work with a partner. One of you is a customer; the other is a waiter or waitress. Practice making some of your own complaints at the restaurant referred to in C15. Switch roles. Repeat your complaints for your classmates.

C17 Actividad • ¡A escribir!

Lista de quejas. Prepare a list of all the complaints you had in C16.

1. Ellos ponen la mesa. 2. Yo pongo el tenedor a la izquierda del plato. 3. Carlos quiere poner la mesa. 4. Tú pones los platos. 5. ¿Dónde pongo yo el vaso? 6. Ustedes no ponen las servilletas en la mesa. 7. Tú y yo ponemos los vasos.
8. ¿Pone usted la cucharita al lado del cuchillo?

C18 Actividad • Falta algo

Supply the missing forms of the verb **poner.**

1. Ellos / la mesa.
2. Yo / el tenedor a la izquierda del plato.
3. Carlos quiere / la mesa.
4. Tú / los platos.

5. ¿Dónde / yo el vaso?
6. Ustedes no / las servilletas en la mesa.
7. Tú y yo / los vasos.
8. ¿ / usted la cucharita al lado del cuchillo?

C19 Comprensión For script and answers, see p. T174.

What do they need?

	0	1	2	3	4	5	6	7	8	9	10
cuchillo	✔	✔				✔		✔			
cuchara			✔								
tenedor							✔		✔		✔
cucharita				✔	✔					✔	

C20 SE DICE ASÍ
Expressing your enjoyment of food

¡Esta sopa está muy sabrosa!
¡Estos bocadillos están muy buenos!
¡Estas uvas están muy ricas!
¡Este bizcocho está delicioso!
¡Estos pasteles están exquisitos!
¡Qué buenos están estos bocadillos!

Use adjectives like **sabroso** or **exquisito** to express how much you like particular dishes. Make sure your adjective agrees with the noun it modifies.

C21 Actividad • Reacciones

You are eating with some Spanish-speaking friends. Compliment the hostess when she asks your opinion about the food.

¿La sopa? (buenísimo)   —Esta sopa está buenísima.

1. ¿La sopa?   (delicioso)
2. ¿El pollo?   (rico)
3. ¿La salsa?   (buenísimo)
4. ¿La carne?   (sabroso)
5. ¿La ensalada?   (muy rico)
6. ¿Los helados?   (fantástico)
7. ¿La tortilla?   (sabroso)
8. ¿El flan?   (delicioso)
9. ¿El postre?   (muy bueno)
10. ¿Los plátanos? (muy rico)

1. Esta sopa está deliciosa. 2. Este pollo está rico. 3. Esta salsa está buenísima. 4. Esta carne está sabrosa. 5. Esta ensalada está muy rica. 6. Estos helados están fantásticos. 7. Esta tortilla está muy sabrosa. 8. Este flan está delicioso. 9. Este postre está muy bueno. 10. Estos plátanos están muy ricos.

¡Buen provecho!   257

Ex. Desayuno: A las ocho de
la mañana en mi casa.

1. leche
2. pan
3. mantequilla
4. azúcar
5. chocolate
6. frutas

C22 Actividad • ¡Vamos a comer! Answers will vary.

Work with a partner. You're going to have a meal together. Decide what meal
you're going to have (breakfast, lunch, or dinner), at what time, and where.
Make a shopping list for everything you need for your meal. You'll find some
suggestions below.

cereal frutas
pan flan
sopa carne
plátanos postre
salsa
queso helado
leche pollo
jugo jamón
huevos tortilla

C23 Actividad • ¿A cuánto están? *How much are they?* Answers will vary.

You and your classmate go shopping together. Prepare a shopping list using some
of the items in C22. Talk about what to buy. Follow the model replacing the
underlined words with items from your shopping list. Add your own ideas.

—¿A cuánto están <u>estos plátanos</u>?

—¿Llevamos <u>este queso o esa salsa</u>?

—<u>Ese pescado</u> parece muy bueno.

—¡Mira <u>aquellos postres</u>! Parecen <u>deliciosos.</u>

C24 Actividad • La comida Answers will vary.

Together with your partner, talk to your classmates about the meal you're
planning and the food you bought. Talk about how much you like the different
foods. If you don't like one of the foods, say what you think of it.

C25 Actividad • ¡A escribir!

Una comida buenísima. Write down the shopping list you made with your classmate in C22.
Then write the conversation you had when you went shopping together.
You can substitute items and include comments from the vendor at the food store also.

1   ¿Dónde comemos? 🎞️

Before going to the movies with a friend, you might want to eat something first.
Where would you like to go?

RICARDO   Alicia, la película no empieza hasta las nueve y yo tengo hambre ahora.

ALICIA   ¿Quieres ir a la cafetería a ver que tienen hoy?

RICARDO   Ya sabes, siempre el mismo menú: bocadillos, hamburguesas, ensaladas.

ALICIA   ¿Por qué no vamos mejor a un restaurante?

RICARDO   ¡Buena idea! A mí me gusta mucho la comida mexicana, ¿y a ti?

ALICIA   A mí también. Conozco un lugar donde hacen unas enchiladas deliciosas, y no está lejos de aquí.

RICARDO   ¡Fantástico! Pero no tengo mucho dinero.

ALICIA   Yo tengo bastante. Esta vez pago yo, tú pagas otro día.

RICARDO   De acuerdo. Vamos entonces.

1. Van al cine.   2. Porque tiene hambre.   3. Tienen bocadillos, hamburguesas y ensaladas.   4. Conoce un restaurante mexicano donde hacen enchiladas.   5. No está lejos.   6. Ricardo no tiene mucho dinero. 7. Alicia va a pagar porque Ricardo no tiene mucho dinero.   8. Sí, van a salir otro día porque Alicia dice que Ricardo paga otro día.

2   Preguntas y respuestas

Answer the questions according to **¿Dónde comemos?**

1. ¿Qué van a hacer Ricardo y Alicia a las nueve?
2. ¿Por qué quiere ir a comer Ricardo?
3. ¿Qué comida tienen en la cafetería?
4. ¿Qué lugar conoce Alicia?
   ¿Qué comida hacen allí?

5. ¿Está el restaurante lejos?
6. ¿Qué problema tiene Ricardo?
7. ¿Quién va a pagar? ¿Por qué?
8. ¿Van a salir los chicos otro día?
   ¿Cómo sabes?

¡Buen provecho!   259

3 Actividad • ¿Qué vamos a comer hoy? Answers will vary.

• Plan a breakfast and a supper, either just for yourself or for you and one friend or more. In Spanish, write out the menu for each meal. You can use some of the dishes from Skills 4 in your plan.
• Now make up a shopping list in Spanish of the things you need for the two meals.
• Tell the class what was on your shopping list and what you planned for each meal.

4 Actividad • ¿Qué pedimos? *What do we order?* Answers will vary. Ex: Para Josefina una enchilada. Para Blanca una ensalada. Para Rafael frijoles. Para Manuel una hamburguesa y papas fritas.

Four of your friends are going to have lunch in a restaurant. Josefina, who likes chicken, wants to try Mexican food. Blanca is dieting. Rafael, a vegetarian, won't eat meat, not even chicken. Manuel is hungry and likes everything. Order a meal for each of them.

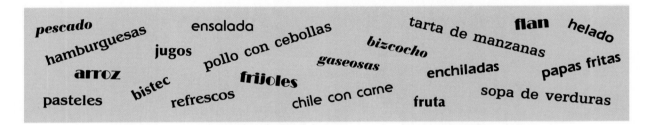

pescado
hamburguesas
ensalada
jugos
pollo con cebollas
arroz
bistec
frijoles
gaseosas
bizcocho
enchiladas
tarta de manzanas
flan
helado
papas fritas
pasteles
refrescos
chile con carne
fruta
sopa de verduras

5 Actividad • Charla Answers will vary.

With a classmate, ask and answer these questions.

1. ¿Te gusta comer en restaurantes o te gusta más comer en casa?
2. ¿Tienes un restaurante favorito? ¿Cuál es? ¿Por qué te gusta?
3. ¿Te gusta la comida mexicana?
4. ¿Cuál es tu comida favorita?
5. ¿Qué comes en el desayuno?
6. ¿Y en el almuerzo?

6 Actividad • Una comida revuelta *Scrambled meal*

Change words and expressions in the following dialog so that it makes sense.

CAMARERO   ¡Buenas noches, señores!
CLIENTE 1   Una cocina para tres, por favor.   Una mesa para tres, por favor.
CAMARERO   ¡Bien, aquí está la cuenta!   ¡Bien, aquí está el menú!
CLIENTE 2   ¿Cuál es la cuchara del día?   ¿Cuál es el plato del día?
CAMARERO   Arroz con tenedores.   Arroz con pollo.
CLIENTE 1   ¡Ay! No me gusta el arroz. Una sartén con cebolla, por favor.   ¡Ay! No me gusta el arroz. Un pollo con cebollas a la mexicana, por favor.
CAMARERO   ¿Y de beber, señora?
CLIENTE 2   Tengo sed. Tomates, por favor.   Tengo sed. Un refresco, por favor.
CLIENTE 3   No tengo servilleta para cortar la carne. Una servilleta, por favor.   No tengo cuchillo para cortar la carne. Un cuchillo, por favor.
CAMARERO   Bien, vuelvo enseguida.

(El camarero vuelve con la comida y los clientes bailan.)   El camarero vuelve con la comida y los clientes comen.

CAMARERO   ¡De postre tenemos una propina fantástica!   ¡De postre tenemos una tarta de manzana fantástica!
CLIENTE 1   No, gracias, para mí té con verduras.   No, gracias, para mí té con limón.
CLIENTE 2   Para mí, café.
CLIENTE 3   Es todo, ¡la mesa por favor!   Es todo, ¡la cuenta por favor!

7 Actividad • Vamos a comer bien *Let's eat right*

After correcting the dialog in Activity 6, practice with three classmates and then present it to the class.

8 Actividad • Una clase de cocina

The following are the responses given by four students. They were asked to talk briefly about their recipes and skills. One of them attends a cooking class. Can you tell which one?

Answer: Alicia Martínez

Me llamo Alicia Martínez. A mí me gustan las sopas. Creo que una buena sopa debe tener de todo. Yo sé hacer una sopa de carne y tomates buenísima. Saber cocinar bien es muy importante.

Soy Ramón Ballesteros. Una persona que no sabe hacer postres, no sabe cocinar. Para hacer mi postre favorito, pongo tres huevos y una taza de azúcar en un plato grande. Añado mostaza y una cebolla cortada.

Mucho gusto, Concepción Vázquez. A mí no me gusta cocinar. Me gusta poner la mesa. La presentación artística de la comida es muy importante. Siempre uso platos y vasos elegantes. Comer con servilletas feas es horrible.

Si a ustedes les gusta mucho comer, cenar tarde no es bueno. A mí me gusta una cena ligera: un trozo grande de carne con cuatro o cinco papas, un plato de arroz . . . postre. Tengo hambre. Me llamo Félix Villa. Gracias.

9 Pronunciación, lectura, dictado   For script, see p. T177.

1. Listen carefully and repeat what you hear.

2. The sound of the Spanish consonant **r**. Listen, and then read aloud.

servilleta   tenedor   por favor   charlar   remedio
propina   postre   fruta   pregunta   arriba

Ricardo, vas a necesitar una sartén más grande para freír esos huevos.
Vamos a preparar una tortilla para el almuerzo del martes.

3. Copy the following sentences to prepare yourself to write them from dictation.
Por favor, ¿nos puede comprar tres refrescos de naranja?
Creo que te va a gustar ese postre de frutas.
El arroz en este restaurante es muy rico.
Hace mucho calor para tomar chocolate con churros.

¿LO SABES?

Let's review some important points you have learned in this unit.

When you are in a Spanish restaurant, can you order food at different times of the day? Answers will vary. Ex: Para el desayuno me gusta una taza de té y pan.
Order in Spanish something you might want for breakfast, something for lunch, and something for dinner.

Do you know how to talk about the foods you like and dislike?
Using **A mí me gusta(n)** and **A mí no me gusta(n),** mention five types of food you like and five you don't. Answers will vary.
Ex: A mí me gusta el pollo. A mí no me gusta el flan.
Can you say what you would like to have for breakfast, lunch, and dinner and what your friends and family would like (or wouldn't like) to have for each meal if you were in a Spanish country? Answers will vary.
First, make a list of the different types of food you have for each meal, then say who likes them and who doesn't.

Can you talk to a friend who is organizing a picnic and find out information about it? Answers will vary.
Write down five questions you might ask. ¿Quiénes van a ir?/¿Preparan bocadillos? ¿Quién hace la tortilla? etc.
When organizing a picnic, can you say how you're going to contribute?
Make five sentences talking about what you are bringing and the steps that you'll follow to get it. Answers will vary.
Answers will vary.
Can you choose items at the food store, fruit stand, or pastry shop?
Write down five of your selections, using forms of **este** or **ese.** Ex. Quiero esa tarta.

Are you able to tell the store clerk what you really want? Answers will vary.
Answer these suggestions with **no,** and indicate what you want instead.

¿Esas peras?	¿Esta piña?	¿Esas uvas?
¿Estos melocotones?	¿Esta tarta?	¿Ese bizcocho?

Ex. No quiero esas peras, quiero aquella piña.

When you are in a Spanish-speaking environment and you want a glass of water and something to eat, what would you say? Answers will vary.
Make up four sentences. Ex. Quiero un vaso de agua y una hamburguesa, por favor.

Do you know how to ask in Spanish for something you need at the table?
Ask for: Ex. Una taza, por favor./Una servilleta y un cuchillo, por favor.

a cup   a knife   a napkin   a glass   a fork
a small plate   a dish   a spoon   a small spoon

Can you complain in Spanish about the food or the service? Answers will vary.
Write down five complaints you might have. Ex. El té no tiene limón.

Do you know different ways to say how much you like the food?
You are having a meal with a Spanish-speaking family. What would you say about . . . Answers will vary. Ex. La sopa está deliciosa.

la sopa   el arroz   el flan   la carne   las verduras   la tarta

VOCABULARIO

SECTION A

a dieta on a diet
el agua (f.) water
el arroz rice
el bistec beefsteak
el bocadillo snack; sandwich
¡Buen provecho! Enjoy it!
el café coffee
la camarera waitress
el camarero waiter
el Caribe Caribbean
la carne meat
la cebolla onion
la cena dinner, supper
cenar to have dinner
la cocina cooking, cuisine
la comida food; meal; dinner
completo, -a complete
¿cuánto? how much?
la cuenta bill, check
el chile con carne dish of beans, ground beef, and chilies
el chocolate chocolate
dejar to leave (behind)
desayuno breakfast
desear to like, want
encantar to delight
la enchilada rolled tortilla filled with meat or cheese
la ensalada salad
la especialidad specialty
el flan baked custard
los frijoles beans
la fruta fruit
la guía guidebook
gustar to like
les gusta(n) you (they) like
nos gusta(n) we like
la hamburguesa hamburger
la jalea jelly
el jamón ham
el jugo juice
la leche milk
la lechuga lettuce
les you (pl.), them
ligero, -a light (meal)
el limón lemon
la mantequilla butter
la mayonesa mayonnaise
el mediodía noon
lo mejor the best (thing)
el menú menu
la merienda snack, light meal in the afternoon
la mermelada marmalade
la mesa table
mí me

el mole spicy chocolate sauce
ni neither, nor
nos us
pagar to pay
el pan bread
las papas fritas french fries
el pescado fish
el peso monetary unit of Mexico, Bolivia, Chile
el plato del día specialty of the day
el pollo chicken
el postre dessert
de postre for dessert
principal main
probar to try
la propina tip
el queso cheese
el restaurante restaurant
rosa pink
la salsa sauce
sobre about
la sopa soup
te you
el té tea
ti you
típico, -a typical
el tomate tomato
la tortilla omelette
turístico, -a touristic
el vaso glass
la verdura green vegetable

SECTION B

a lo dicho, hecho no sooner said than done
añadir to add
aquel, aquella that
aquellos, -as those
el atún tuna
ayudar to help
batir to beat
el bizcocho cake
buenísimo, -a very good
la cereza cherry
cocinar to cook
cortar to cut
delicioso, -a delicious
dorarse to brown
ese, -a that
esos, -as those
la esquina corner (street)
este, -a this
estos, -as these
freír to fry
la fresa strawberry
la frutería fruit store

la gaseosa soda
hacer to do, make
el huevo egg
el kilo kilogram (2.2 pounds)
el lado side
llevar to take
llorar to cry
la manzana apple
el melocotón peach
el melón melon
mismo, -a same
la naranja orange
parecer to seem
el pastel pie; cake
la pastelería pastry; pastry shop
la patata potato (Spain)
la pera pear
la piña pineapple
el plátano banana; plantain
preparar to prepare
rico, -a tasty, delicious (food)
sabroso, -a tasty, delicious
la sandía watermelon
la sartén frying pan
la tarta tart, pastry
trae brings
el trozo piece
la uva grape

SECTION C

el árbol tree
el azúcar sugar
la canción song
cómo no of course
conmigo with me
la cuchara spoon
la cucharita teaspoon
el cuchillo knife
debajo (de) under
la mostaza mustard
no hay más remedio it can't be helped
la paciencia patience
la pimienta pepper
el platillo saucer, small plate
el plato dish, plate
el plato hondo soup dish
el plato llano dinner dish
poner to put
poner la mesa to set the table
la sal salt
la servilleta napkin
la taza cup
el tenedor fork
tener (mucha) sed to be (very) thirsty

You may wish to have the students read the vocabulary before each section is introduced.

VAMOS A LEER

Antes de leer

Try to read the recipe without looking at the glossary. Remember, many quick readings will improve your reading skills, vocabulary mastery, and enjoyment more than one painstaking reading during which you look up every word you are not sure of.

Tortilla de patatas a la española *(para 6 personas)*

8 huevos
2 cebollas
1 kg. de patatas

2 tazas de aceite°
(½ litro)
sal

Pelar° las patatas, lavarlas° y cortarlas fino°. Cortar las cebollas en trozos pequeños. Calentar° el aceite y freír las patatas y las cebollas; moverlas° y echarles° un poco de sal. Una vez fritas°, poner en un colador y quitar° el aceite de la sartén. Batir los huevos con un poco de sal, echar las patatas y las cebollas en el mismo plato de los huevos y moverlas con un tenedor. En una sartén grande poner 3 cucharadas de aceite. Calentar el aceite y añadir los huevos con las patatas y cebollas.

Mover la sartén para que no se pegue° la tortilla. Cuando se dore° bien, voltearla° en un plato y cocinar del otro lado. Servir° fría o caliente.

---

1. Poner el aceite en la sartén a calentar.
2. Echar un poco de sal a las patatas.
3. Echar las patatas y cebollas en el mismo plato de los huevos.

Actividad • No es así

Change the following statements so they agree with the **tortilla** recipe.

1. Poner el agua en la sartén a calentar.
2. Echar un poco de azúcar a las patatas.
3. Echar las patatas y cebollas en la misma taza de los huevos.
4. Batir los huevos con un cuchillo.

5. Añadir la sal al aceite cuando está frío.
6. Cuando la tortilla se dore, voltearla en una cuchara.

4. Batir los huevos con un tenedor. 5. Añadir los huevos con las patatas y cebollas al aceite cuando está caliente. 6. Cuando la tortilla se dore, voltearla en un plato.

Actividad • La tortilla de patatas

Are you a good cook? Do you want to follow the recipe and make your own **tortilla?** Make it and share it with your friends. Good luck!

---

aceite *oil* **pelar** *to peel* **lavarlas** *wash (them)* **cortarlas fino** *cut (them) into thin slices* **calentar** *to heat*
moverlas *stir (them)* **echarles** *add to them* **fritas** *fried* **quitar** *remove* **pegue** *stick* **se dore** *it turns brown*
voltearla *turn it over* **servir** *serve*

De compras°

Before making the **tortilla,** you have to shop
for the ingredients. Check the prices first,
so you don't pay more than you should.

SEÑORA	¿A cuánto están las cebollas hoy?
VENDEDOR	A cuarenta pesos la libra, señora.
SEÑORA	¿Cómo? En la Calle Ocho las venden a treinta y cinco la libra.
VENDEDOR	Entonces, señora, ¿por qué no las compra allí?
SEÑORA	Es que allí no tienen más cebollas hoy.
VENDEDOR	Pues, señora, cuando yo no tengo cebollas, también las vendo a treinta y cinco.

Actividad • Charla

With a partner, prepare a scene similar to **De compras.** Change produce, price,
and location. Then present it to your class.

El plátano

Notice the diamond-like shape of
this short poem. The words
don't rhyme, but the
poem follows
a pattern.

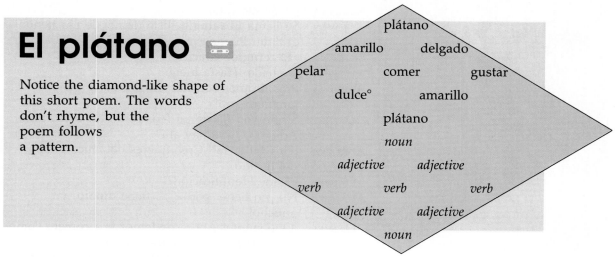

plátano
amarillo   delgado
pelar   comer   gustar
dulce°   amarillo
plátano
noun
adjective   *adjective*
verb   *verb*   *verb*
adjective   *adjective*
noun

Actividad • ¡A escribir!

Write your own diamond-shaped poem in Spanish. Follow the pattern of the
words above when preparing your poem.

---

de compras *shopping*   **dulce** *sweet*

El regalo

¡Hay otro botón° en el televisor! ¿Para qué es el nuevo botón? Los chicos no saben.
Daniel juega con el botón, lo aprieta°, y . . . ¡no pasa nada°!

DANIEL   Mira, Adriana, el Canal 17. Hay un programa sobre El Paso,
un programa de Texas.

ADRIANA   ¡Ah, sí! El Canal 17, ¿no? Pero, Daniel, ¡por favor! Después, tenemos que
ir a Texas, y, ¿cómo volvemos a casa? No, mejor miramos otro canal.

Pero, ¡ya es tarde! Los chicos llegan a El Paso con el televisor. Esta vez, el televisor
va con ellos. Ahora, ya saben para qué pueden usar el nuevo botón. Por suerte,
con el nuevo botón, no van a tener problemas para volver a México.

En El Paso

DANIEL   Tengo hambre y sed. ¿Dónde podemos comer?

ADRIANA   No sé. Además°, ¿a qué restaurante vamos a ir si no tenemos dinero?

Pasa un joven°. Él escucha la conversación de los dos hermanos. Es muy amable.

JOVEN   ¡Hola chicos! ¿Qué tal? ¿Ustedes buscan un
lugar para comer? Yo conozco un restaurante
mexicano muy cerca de aquí.

DANIEL   Muchas gracias. ¿Cómo se llama el restaurante?

ADRIANA   ¿Y dónde está?

JOVEN   Se llama **El refugio.** Está detrás de esa tienda
grande. Pueden ir por esa calle, a la derecha.

ADRIANA   **¿El refugio?** Gracias.

JOVEN   De nada. Hasta luego.

ADRIANA   ¡Los texanos son tan simpáticos! Y guapos
también, ¿no?

DANIEL   Sí, no son flacos° ni feos como tú. Pero, mira,
Adriana, ¿qué hay ahí?

ADRIANA   ¡Una billetera°! Creo que es del chico guapo,
del texano.

DANIEL   ¿Tiene identificación?

ADRIANA   No, no tiene, pero . . . tiene dinero, y . . .
¡mucho!

DANIEL   ¡Qué suerte! Ahora podemos ir a comer. Vamos
a **El refugio,** ¿no? ¿Qué te parece?

ADRIANA   Por supuesto. No conocemos otro restaurante.
¡Vamos!

---

botón *button*   **aprieta** *presses*   **no pasa nada** *nothing happens*   **además** *besides*   **pasa un joven** *a young man passes by*
flacos *skinny*   **billetera** *wallet*

En El refugio

En el restaurante, Daniel y Adriana esperan la comida. Unos mariachis° llegan a
El refugio. Van a tocar música y a cantar. Los músicos miran a los dos hermanos,
y empiezan a cantar:

> No pueden volver a casa,
> tienen que esperar.
> No pueden volver a casa,
> deben cruzar el mar°.
>
> Cerca de la Puerta del Sol°,
> para ustedes hay una flor°.
> Allí van, van muy rápido,
> con su televisor.

DANIEL   Adriana, esa canción° es para nosotros.
Debemos ir a Madrid inmediatamente.
¡Vamos rápido!

ADRIANA   Un momento, Daniel. Ahí viene el
camarero con la comida. ¿Por qué
no comemos primero? Yo tengo hambre.

DANIEL   Tú también escuchaste° la canción.
Es un mensaje° para nosotros. Con el
Canal 17, estamos en Madrid en un
minuto.

ADRIANA   Pero, ¿qué vamos a hacer en Madrid?
¿Vamos a buscar una flor en la
Puerta del Sol? ¡Es imposible, Daniel!

Actividad • ¿Quiénes hablan?   For possible answers, see p. T179.

Which of the characters from **El regalo** might say or think each of the following?
Why? Justify your choices in Spanish.

1. Yo no quiero mirar el Canal 17.
2. ¿Dónde hay un restaurante? Tengo hambre.
3. Yo también tengo hambre, pero no tenemos dinero.
4. Estos chicos buscan un restaurante.
5. Se llama **El refugio.** Pueden llegar por esa calle.
6. ¡Qué joven tan guapo!
7. ¡Qué suerte! ¡Vamos a comer!
8. Mejor, esperamos. Ahí viene el camarero.
9. Tú escuchaste la canción. Tiene un mensaje para nosotros.
10. ¿Una flor en la Puerta del Sol? ¡Imposible!

---

mariachis *Mexican band*   **cruzar el mar** *to cross the sea*   **Puerta del Sol** *famous plaza in Madrid*   **flor** *flower*
canción *song*   **escuchaste** *you heard*   **mensaje** *message*

UNIDAD 10 Un viaje estupendo
Scope and Sequence

	BASIC MATERIAL	COMMUNICATIVE FUNCTIONS
SECTION A	**El diario de Pilar** (A1) **Conversación de dos minutos** (A14)	**Exchanging information** • Saying what you usually do • Saying what you did at a specified time in the past
SECTION B	**Pilar llama desde Madrid** (B1)	**Exchanging information** • Asking for information about something that happened in the past
SECTION C	**Un viaje corto** (C1)	**Exchanging information** • Discussing whether or not something has already been done
TRY YOUR SKILLS	Pronunciation (the letters **z** and **s**) Sound-letter correspondences (the letters **z** and **s**) Dictation	
VAMOS A LEER	**¡A España!** (a tourist brochure of Spain) **Guía turística de nuestra galaxia** (a guided tour of our galaxy) **El regalo** (Adriana and Daniel travel to Spain.)	

WRITING A variety of controlled and open-ended writing activities appear in the Pupil's Edition. The Teacher's Notes identify other activities suitable for writing practice.

COOPERATIVE LEARNING Many of the activities in the Pupil's Edition lend themselves to cooperative learning. The Teacher's Notes explain some of the many instances where this teaching strategy can be particularly effective. For guidelines on how to use cooperative learning, see page T13.

GRAMMAR	CULTURE	RE–ENTRY
The preterit of regular **-ar** verbs (A6) Expressing how long ago something happened (A18)	Spain's capital city Spain's second-largest city	Expressing present and future time
The preterit of **hacer** (B5) The preterit of **ir** (B10)	Madrid's attractions	The present tense of **ir** The days of the week
Direct-object pronouns (C5)	A trip to Granada The Moorish legacy The famous landmarks in Madrid	Direct objects

Recombining communicative functions, grammar, and vocabulary

Reading for practice and pleasure

TEACHER-PREPARED MATERIALS
Section A Toy telephone
Section B Map of Madrid or Latin American city, travel brochures
Section C Airline tickets, suitcase, boxes

UNIT RESOURCES
Manual de actividades, Unit 10
Manual de ejercicios, Unit 10
Unit 10 Cassettes
Transparencies 24–26
Quizzes 22–24
Unit 10 Test

SECTION

A

OBJECTIVES **To exchange information:** say what you usually do, say what you did at a specified time in the past, express how long ago something happened.

CULTURAL BACKGROUND As you land at Barajas airport, an impressive view of the mountains and the terracotta-colored soil greets you. The first question you may ask yourself is, "Is this Madrid?"

As you enter the city, the mountains fade into a beautiful metropolis with a population of four million. There are many buildings that are centuries old, but there are also sections of the city that are as modern as New York City. You encounter road signs such as E with a slash mark going through it **(No estacionar)** and, surprisingly enough, a familiar road sign that has eight sides and reads *STOP*. Most shops close between the hours of two and five for **la comida** and the traditional **siesta.**

The pronunciation of Spanish in Spain differs somewhat from its pronunciation in Spanish America. One difference is that Spaniards pronounce the letter **c** as *th,* as in the word *thanks,* before **i** and **e.** The letter **z** is also pronounced as *th.*

MOTIVATING ACTIVITY Ask the students what they would take on a trip to Spain. What would they need to do before going on the trip?

A1   **El diario de Pilar**

Ask the students to read the title. Then ask them to guess what they think the activity will be about. Read the diary entry aloud as the students follow along in their books. Then read aloud the following false statements and ask the students to change them to make them true.

1. Llegó un regalo para Pilar.
2. Marisol es la hermana de Pilar.
3. Pilar va a ir a Barcelona.
4. Los padres de Pilar van a ir con ella.
5. Billy ya estudió la lección.

SLOWER-PACED LEARNING Have the students identify the verbs in the preterit. Write them on the board or a transparency. Give an example of the verb in a context that defines its meaning. Then read the dialog aloud. With books closed, ask the students to make at least three statements about what Pilar wrote in her diary.

A2 **Actividad • Para completar**

Assign this activity as written homework. The following day, have several students write their answers on the board or a transparency. Ask other students to correct any mistakes they find. Make any remaining corrections to the work on the board, and have the students correct their own work.

A3 **Actividad • Combinación**

Divide the class into pairs. Have each pair form as many sentences as possible in five minutes. When they have completed the activity, call on the students to read their sentences aloud. The pair with the most sentences wins.

A4 **Preguntas y respuestas**

This activity may be completed in class or at home. Have the students answer using complete sentences.

A5 **¿Sabes que . . . ?**

An impressive sight in Madrid is the **Palacio Real** (*Royal Palace*), built by the Bourbon Dynasty in the eighteenth century, which is now a museum. It is surrounded by guards and has an extraordinary collection of clocks. King Juan Carlos and his family live in the **Palacio Zarzuela,** which is part of **El Pardo** and is located on the outskirts of the city. King Juan Carlos became king when General Francisco Franco died in 1975. The king's wife, Sofia, is Greek, and is also of royal lineage. They have three children.

A6 **ESTRUCTURAS ESENCIALES**

Before presenting the preterit forms of the **-ar** verbs, demonstrate the difference between present, past, and future to the students. Have a student act out the activity as you say: (*Student's name*) **va a hablar por teléfono.** When the student is on the telephone, say: (*Student's name*) **habla por teléfono.** As the student returns to his or her desk, say: (*Student's name*) **habló por teléfono.** Call on several volunteers to use the telephone as you narrate what they are doing. Then have the students repeat the steps as they narrate aloud.

Once the students understand the difference between the tenses, introduce the preterit of regular **-ar** verbs by conducting the following or a similar conversation.

TEACHER Yo hablé con mi amigo por teléfono ayer. ¿Hablaste con tu amigo?
CLAUDIA Sí, yo hablé con Diego.
TEACHER Nosotros hablamos por teléfono. José y Alfredo, ¿hablaron ustedes por teléfono con alguien ayer?
JOSE No, no hablamos con nadie ayer.
TEACHER ¿Quiénes hablaron por teléfono ayer?

Now read the information aloud as the students follow along in their books. Have them copy the chart in the grammar section of their notebooks.

A7 **Actividad • ¿Qué planearon?**

Before assigning the activity, point out the stem of the verb **planear.** Make sure the students spell the first-person singular correctly, **planeé.**

A8 **Actividad • ¿Con quién hablaste?**

SLOWER-PACED LEARNING Write the dialog on the board or a transparency, including the blanks and the words in parentheses. Dictate the dialog and have the students fill in the blanks with the correct preterit form of the verb **hablar.**

A9 **SE DICE ASÍ**

Have the students repeat in unison the sentences in the chart. Then ask them to form similar sentences following the same pattern with the verbs **practicar, bailar,** and **estudiar.**

A10 **Actividad • Ayer también**

The students should complete this activity orally and in writing. You might also have them substitute a different verb to go with each sentence.

A 11 ## Actividad • Todos los días y ayer

Have the students choose a partner. They should take turns asking and answering the questions.

A 12 ## Actividad • ¡A escribir!

The students may complete this activity at home or in class. Ask them to write at least five different things they do every day. Then call on volunteers to read their sentences aloud to the class.

CHALLENGE Using the suggested model, have the students write a short paragraph about their routine every day. They may include their real or imaginary family members' activities as well.

A 13 ## Conversación • Ayer y hoy

After each student has had the opportunity to talk with their partners, call on individuals to explain to the class what his or her partner does every day and what he or she did yesterday. They should also include what their partners didn't do.

A 14 ## SITUACIÓN • Conversación de dos minutos

Before presenting the telephone conversation, introduce the expressions **apuradísima(o), está a punto de, dentro de, la semana pasada, hace una hora, hacer la maleta,** and **ya.**

Play the cassette or read the conversation aloud as the students follow along in their books. Have the students work with a partner to role-play the conversation.

CHALLENGE Play the cassette or read the conversation aloud. The students should listen with books closed. Ask the students either/or questions: **¿Salen para el aeropuerto dentro de dos minutos o en una hora?** If a question is answered incorrectly, have the students open their books and read the text silently until they find the correct answer.

A 15 ## Preguntas y respuestas

To check the answers, call on individuals to read their answers as you or a volunteer writes them on the board or a transparency.

A 16 ## Actividad • ¡A escoger!

After the students have become familiar with the material in A14, they should complete this activity by looking for the answers in the dialog. Have the students read the completed sentences aloud.

A 17 ## ¿Sabes que . . . ?

Barcelona, the oldest and second largest city in Spain, is a wonderful cultural center. It was founded by Amilcar Barca, the famous Cartagenian general who fought against Rome in the Punic War. From one corner to the next, one may see the cathedral built in the 1200s or the museum that contains Picasso's masterpieces painted in the nineteenth and twentieth centuries. Tradition says that Christopher Columbus announced his discovery of the New World in the **Plaza del Rey,** a courtyard surrounded by medieval tow-

ers. Barcelona has always been an important commercial center and has one of the busiest ports in Spain. It is the capital of the **Comunidad Autónomo de Cataluña.**

A 18 ESTRUCTURAS ESENCIALES

Write the following sentences on the board or a transparency.

> Marisol habló por teléfono hace una hora.
> Hace una hora que Marisol habló por teléfono.

Have the students identify the verb in each sentence and the sentence pattern. Then ask them to follow along in their books as you read aloud the information in the chart. Using the expressions in the box, ask the students to make up a few of their own and write them on the board or a transparency.

SLOWER-PACED LEARNING You may wish to introduce only one form of the verb **hacer** at a time. Once students are able to form sentences correctly, you may introduce the other form of **hace** + *time expressions* + **que.**

A 19 Actividad • ¡Cómo pasa el tiempo!

After students have formed the sentences with **hace** and **que,** you may wish to have them repeat the activity forming the sentence without **que.** For writing practice, have the students write the sentences at home or in class.

A 20 Comprensión

You'll hear ten short conversations. After listening to each one, decide whether the people talking are referring to present events *(present)*, or to something that took place in the past *(preterit)*. Then place your check mark in the appropriate box. For example, you hear: **¿Sales ahora?** and the response: **Sí, el taxi está aquí.** Under 0, the check mark is placed in the row labeled *Present.* Both verbs, **sales** and **está,** are in the present tense.

1. —¿Tienes permiso para ir?
   —No, tengo que hablar con mi papá. *Present*
2. —¿Planeaste el viaje con tu amiga?
   —Sí, Olga y yo planeamos todo. *Preterit*
3. —¿Viene tu amigo con nosotros?
   —No sé. Tiene que decidir qué hace. *Present*
4. —¿Cómo se llama él?
   —David. Es de Chile. *Present*
5. —¿Llamaste a David?
   —Sí, hablé con él. *Preterit*
6. —¿Cuándo regresa él a Chile?
   —No sabe. Cree que el mes próximo. *Present*
7. —¿Reservaste los billetes?
   —Sí, llamé ayer por la tarde. *Preterit*
8. —¿Preparaste las maletas?
   —Sí, ya preparé todo. *Preterit*
9. —¿Llegó la carta de tus primos?
   —No, no llegó. Tal vez mañana. *Preterit*
10. —¿Llevas tres maletas?
    —No, llevo una. Estas dos son de mi hermana. *Present*

Now check your answers. *Read each exchange again and give the correct answer.*

A 21   Conversación • El viaje

Tell the students to look at the pictures on page 277 of their books. Ask them to identify the pictures in Spanish. Then have the students use the pictures and the verbs in the book to tell their partners about the trip.

A 22   Actividad • ¡A escribir!

Assign this activity for homework. The next day, collect the reports and correct them.

A 23   Actividad • Una confusión

For cooperative learning, form groups of two. The students can assist each other in ascertaining the most sensible order. Once they have established the order, you can suggest they role-play the dialog. Call on volunteers to present the dialog to the class.

CHALLENGE   Ask the students to write a similar dialog and scramble the lines. Then they may exchange dialogs with another student to unscramble them.

SECTION B

OBJECTIVES   **To exchange information:** ask for information about something that happened in the past

CULTURAL BACKGROUND   **El Parque del Retiro** is a 350-acre park in Madrid. There is a zoo, several monuments, and a pond in the park. Not too far from the park is the **Prado** museum, which contains one of the world's finest art collections. Paintings by El Greco, Goya, Velázquez, Murillo, Zurbarán, and other foreign masters are enjoyed by thousands of people daily.

MOTIVATING ACTIVITY   Display a map of Madrid to the students. Have the students select a hotel and make an itinerary for a week. They can write in Spanish how to get from their hotel to the places they want to visit.

B 1   Pilar llama desde Madrid

Before presenting the dialog, you may wish to briefly introduce the preterit tense forms of the verbs **ir** and **hacer**. Two new verbs are introduced, **parar** and **remar**. Use these in a context that explains their meanings. You may also compare the words **parada** and **parar**. Finally, introduce the expression **¡Qué envidia!** Call on volunteers to guess its meaning.

Play the cassette or read the dialog aloud. Then form pairs to role-play the dialog for the class, using toy telephones.

SLOWER-PACED LEARNING   To check comprehension, you may wish to ask the following or similar questions.

> ¿Con quién habló Pilar?
> ¿Con quiénes hicieron planes los chicos?
> ¿Cómo fueron a la Puerta de Alcalá?
> ¿Dónde remaron?

B2 Actividad • ¡A escoger!

After the students have become familiar with the material in B1, they should complete this activity by looking for the answers in the dialog. Have the students read the completed sentences aloud.

B3 Actividad • ¿Es cierto o no? 🔲

The students should complete this activity orally and in writing. You might also have them make up their own false statements. Then the students may exchange papers with a partner.

CHALLENGE With books closed, dictate the sentences. Then have the students write **Es cierto** next to the correct statements and correct the false statements. Read the sentences again and ask the students to check their work. Finally, have them exchange papers and correct each other's sentences.

B4 ¿Sabes que . . . ?

When Spain became a great Colonial power in the 1500s, King Philip II made Madrid the capital of Spain. He also built the famous monastery of *San Lorenzo del Escorial* in 1563 to commemorate the battle of **San Quintón** against the French. He made the monastery his home. The **Puerta del Sol** marks the center of the city, from which extend main streets such as the **Calle de Alcalá** and the **Gran Vía.** The **Puerta del Sol** and the **Puerta de Alcalá** are ruins of the ancient wall that once surrounded the city. The **Plaza Mayor** is in the center of the city, where ceremonies, plays, and bullfights took place centuries ago. Most of the buildings that line these streets were built in the 1500s and 1600s.

B5 ESTRUCTURAS ESENCIALES

To present the irregular forms of the verb **hacer** in the preterit, you may wish to write the following conversation on the board or a transparency.

> JORGE Ayer hice toda la tarea.
> ELENA ¡Qué envidia! Elena hizo la tarea también. Yo no hice nada.
> JORGE ¿Qué hiciste tú, Paco?
> PACO Mis padres y yo hicimos planes para las vacaciones. Vamos a hacer lo mismo que el año pasado.
> ELENA ¿Qué hicieron el año pasado?
> PACO Visitamos a los abuelos en Madrid.

Call on students to identify the verb forms in each exchange. Read aloud the chart and information in the book. Then form cooperative learning groups of three. Have the students role-play the conversation for the class.

B6 Actividad • Una excursión 🔲

For writing practice, have the students write the complete sentences at home or in class. Then call on individuals to read the sentences aloud.

B7 Actividad • ¿Qué hicieron?

Do the activity orally with the class and then have several students write the sentences on the board or a transparency. Ask other students to correct any mistakes they find. Underline each of the verb forms for visual reinforcement of the spelling.

B 8 ### Actividad • Charla

SLOWER-PACED LEARNING After the students have had time to discuss what they did last weekend, ask the class to identify the person who did specified things: **¿Quién hizo una excursión? ¿Quién estudió?**

B 9 ### Actividad • ¡A escribir!

Assign this as homework. The next day, collect their work and correct it.

B 10 ## ESTRUCTURAS ESENCIALES

Before introducing the preterit tense of the verb **ir,** re-enter the present tense. Ask the students to state where they usually go on weekends. They may also include whether they go by bus, car, bicycle, and so on.

To present the preterit of the verb **ir,** you may wish to follow the same procedure as in A6, page T183. For further practice, you may wish to ask questions such as **¿Adónde fueron ayer? ¿Qué hicieron anoche? ¿Cómo fueron? ¿Hizo mal tiempo? ¿Con quién fueron?**

B 11 ### Actividad • Combinación

Call out the rejoinders and ask the students to identify the correct subjects. Then have the students write the sentences for writing practice.

B 12 ### Actividad • ¿Adónde fueron?

Ask the students to complete the dialog with a partner, supplying the correct forms of the verb **ir.** Then have the pairs role-play each dialog.

B 13 ### Actividad • Fuimos anoche

Students should respond negatively to each question. To re-enter the days of the week, the students may also reply stating a specific day of the week.

—¿Vas al cine?   —No, fui al cine el sábado.

B 14 ### Actividad • ¿Cómo fueron?

Before completing the activity, review the means of transportation with the students. Call on individuals to identify how each person or group is traveling: **Las muchachas van a pie. Ellos van en coche. El joven va en bicicleta. El señor va en moto.**

B 15 ### Actividad • ¡A escribir!

The list of people the students include may be real or imaginary. Explain that they should list at least ten different people.

B 16 ### Conversación • Ayer, anoche y la semana pasada

Allow the students at least five minutes with the first partner. Then signal the class to select another partner and ask and answer the questions. Do this until every student in the class has an opportunity to question and respond to five different students.

B 17 **Actividad • ¡A escribir!**

Ask the students to write a report on each of their conversations. Collect the reports and correct them. Then call on individuals to report their findings to the class.

B 18 **Comprensión**

Two friends are talking on the phone. First, you'll hear their entire conversation. Then segments of their conversation will be repeated. Decide whether each of the segments you hear is in the present tense or in the preterit, and place your check mark for each in the appropriate box. For example, you hear: **¿Fuiste a la fiesta?** and the response: **Sí, yo fui. Y tú, ¿por qué no fuiste?** Since the party they are talking about has already taken place (**fuiste, fui**), the check mark under 0 is placed in the row labeled *Preterit*.

DANIEL	Hola, Inés. Daniel habla. ¿Cómo estás?
INÉS	Bien, gracias, ¿y tú?
DANIEL	Bien también. *Present*

DANIEL	Necesito un favor.
INÉS	¿Cuál es? *Present*

DANIEL	¿Tú hiciste las tareas de inglés?
INÉS	Sí, pero no las terminé. *Preterit*

DANIEL	¡Ah! ¿No terminaste todavía?
INÉS	No, fui a dar una vuelta después de la escuela. *Preterit*

DANIEL	¿Quieres venir a casa? Podemos estudiar . . .
INÉS	No, no tengo ganas de salir ahora. Además, espero a mi prima. Viene en cinco minutos. *Present*

DANIEL	Bueno. ¿Tú preparaste el ejercicio de conversación?
INÉS	Sí, ¿y tú? *Preterit*

DANIEL	Yo también. ¿Quieres practicar?
INÉS	¿Por teléfono? No, no puedo.
DANIEL	¡Qué pena! ¿No te gusta hablar inglés por teléfono? *Present*

INÉS	Perdón, Daniel, pero llegó Mónica con las fotos.
DANIEL	¿Qué fotos?
INÉS	Las de México. Mónica fue a México y tomó unas fotos buenísimas. *Preterit*

DANIEL	¿Mónica fue a México? ¿Cuándo regresó?
INÉS	El lunes. Hace dos días. *Preterit*

DANIEL	¿Y Mónica tiene las fotos?
INÉS	Sí, aquí están.
DANIEL	¿Puedo ir a tu casa? Quiero ver las fotos.
INÉS	Por qué no vienes ahora?
DANIEL	¡Estupendo! Estoy allí en cinco minutos. ¡Hasta luego! *Present*

Now check your answers. *Read each exchange again and give the correct answer.*

B19 Actividad • ¿Adónde fueron?

Have the students work with a partner. They should form as many sentences as possible, using the verb **ir** and the elements in the boxes. Allow each pair ten minutes to complete the activity. Then see which pair formed the most correct sentences.

B20 Actividad • La ruta

CHALLENGE Bring to class several travel brochures or a map of a Spanish or Latin American city. Have the students select a point of interest on the map. Then ask them to describe how they go from the site to the airport. Remind the students to use the preterit tense of the verb forms.

B21 Actividad • ¡A escribir!

As a variation, have the students write the description of the route they took in B20. Then they should exchange papers with a partner. Using the partner's description, each student should draw a map.

SECTION C

OBJECTIVES **To exchange information:** discuss whether or not something has already been done

CULTURAL BACKGROUND The Moslems called Spain **"El Andaluz,"** from which the province **Andalucía** originated. In this province (whose major cities are Córdoba, Sevilla, and Granada) there are outstanding examples of Arabic architecture, such as **La Mezquita en Córdoba, La Giralda** and **El Alcázar en Sevilla,** and **La Alhambra** and **El Generalife en Granada.** In the eight centuries of Arabic rule, Spain flourished. The sciences, the arts, and commerce expanded as did the educational system. The Sephardic Jews contributed in great measure to the intellectual renaissance that occurred during this period. A great Jewish writer of this period was Avicebrón, a poet and philosopher, and Yehuda Haleui, one of the most famous poets of the time. Maimónides, the great philosopher, inspired Santo Tomás de Aquino and Alberto Magno.

MOTIVATING ACTIVITY Have the students look at a map of Spain to review the names and locations of the Spanish provinces. See what they can tell about each one.

C1 Un viaje corto

Bring to class airline tickets, a suitcase, and wrapped boxes that resemble gifts. Introduce the expressions **ya** and **estar listo(a).** Then ask the students: **¿Qué necesitamos antes de salir para un viaje?** Write their responses on the board or a transparency.

Play the cassette or read the dialog aloud as the students follow along in their books. Then have the students choose a partner and role-play the dialog. Volunteers may use the objects you brought to class to role-play the dialog for the other students.

CHALLENGE For further practice, have the students substitute the items mentioned in the dialog for a few of the items you have listed on the board. Then call on the students to role-play the new dialogs.

C2   ¿Es cierto o no?

Have the students refer to the dialog in C1 to correct the false statements.

C3   Actividad • ¡A escoger!

Have the students complete the activity with books closed. Then call on students to read aloud the complete sentences as you or a volunteer writes them on the board.

SLOWER-PACED LEARNING   Have the students refer back to the dialog in C1 to complete each statement.

C4   ¿Sabes que . . . ?

There is a saying in Spain which reads: **Es triste no poder ver, pero es espantoso ser ciego en Granada.** *(It is sad not being able to see, but it is horrible to be blind in Granada.)* The beauty of the **Alhambra** (the Red Palace) and its recreation hall, **El Generalife,** is breathtaking with its gardens, fountains, pools, waterfalls, orange groves, cypresses, and lemon trees. The Alhambra palace is so spread out with its intricate rooms and alcoves that tourists have gotten lost in its maze. It is said to be the most impressive monument of Moorish architecture in the world. It was the stronghold of the last Moorish king, Boabdil. It is not surprising that in the nineteenth century, Washington Irving, the author of *Rip Van Winkle,* decided to live in Granada and write his famous collection of short stories called *Tales of the Alhambra.*

C5   ESTRUCTURAS ESENCIALES

Cut out seven squares of cardboard and write a direct-object pronoun on each square. Attach a magnetic strip or tape to each piece of cardboard so that it will stick to the board. Cut out an additional seven squares to write the following sentence parts: **Pilar, llamó, el, taxi, a, su, hermana.**

Place the sentence parts on the board to read: **Pilar llamó el taxi.** Ask the students to identify the subject, verb, and direct object. Now ask the students how they would say the sentence in English, substituting the direct-object pronoun for **el taxi.** *(Pilar called it.)* Demonstrate how Spanish replaces the noun with a direct-object pronoun by removing the squares **el taxi** and placing the square **lo** before the verb. The sentence now reads **Pilar lo llamó.** Ask the students to identify the direct-object pronoun in Spanish. Remind them to use the personal **a** when the direct-object is a person or pet.

Continue with the example **Pilar llamó a su hermana.** Then read aloud the information and the chart.

C6   Actividad • ¿Me escuchaste?

Have the students complete the activity with another classmate. They should take turns asking and answering the questions.

C7   Actividad • ¿Hiciste todo?

SLOWER-PACED LEARNING   Before completing the activity, you might ask the students to identify the direct object in each sentence. Then call on another student to name its corresponding direct-object pronoun. Finally, have the students answer the questions, using direct-object pronouns.

C8 **Actividad • ¿Cuándo lo hiciste?**

Have the students pair off to do this activity. They should use direct-object pronouns and the expressions in the box in their answers.

C9 **Actividad • ¡A escribir!**

Provide the students with words such as **pero, y, entonces, también, primero, después,** and **luego** to include in their paragraphs.

C10 **Actividad • ¿Dónde lo compraste?**

You may wish to do this activity orally and in writing. Have the students exchange papers to correct their sentences.

C11 **¿Sabes que . . . ?**

You may wish to show pictures of the paintings by El Greco, Francisco Goya, Diego Velázquez, and Picasso to the students. Also, explain that **El Rastro** takes place on the street. It is blocked off from traffic and all the merchants bring their wares to sell. People wander from booth to booth making selections and bargaining for a good price.

C12 **Comprensión**

You'll hear different people talking. Put a check mark in the row labeled **No** if the second person makes an inappropriate reply, and in the row marked **Sí** if the reply is appropriate. For example, you hear: **¿Compraste el disco?** and the response: **Sí, lo compré ayer.** The check mark is placed in the **Sí** row since the answer is appropriate

1. —¿Miraste el periódico de hoy?
—Sí, lo escuché. *No*
2. —¿Tú tienes las revistas?
—No, no las tengo. *Sí*
3. —¿Lo compraste ayer?
—No, hoy por la mañana. *Sí*
4. —¿Escuchaste ese disco?
—Sí, llamé a Mario. *No*
5. —¿Llamó a los chicos?
—No, los llamé yo hace un momento. *Sí*
6. —¿Cuándo hacemos las maletas?
—Sí, Pepe las compró ayer. *No*
7. —¿Tienes la bicicleta?
—No, no la tengo aquí. *Sí*
8. —¿Preparamos la comida?
—Sí, la estudié, ¿y tú? *No*
9. —¿Reservaste los billetes?
—Sí, los reservo en un minuto. *No*
10. —¿Por qué no los miras?
—No, ahora no tengo tiempo. *Sí*

Now check your answers. *Read each exchange again and give the correct answer.*

C13 SE DICE ASÍ

Ask the students to think of three things they have already done; then restate the sentence saying they didn't do them after all. They should use complete sentences. **Ya escribí la carta. No, no la escribí. Ya limpié el cuarto. No, no lo limpié. Ya hice la tarea. No, no la hice.**

C14 Actividad • Sí, ya lo hice

Have one student ask the next student the first item. After responding, that student should turn to another and ask the next item, and so on, until all students have had the chance to ask and respond.

C15 Actividad • No, no lo hice

Follow the procedure as described in C14. Remind students that the direct-object pronoun precedes the verb, even in negative statements.

As a variation, have the students complete the activity as if their parents were planning the trip.

> ¿Ya planearon tus padres el viaje?
> No, no lo planearon todavía.

C16 Actividad • ¿Ya lo hiciste o no lo hiciste?

Have the students choose a partner to take turns asking and answering the questions. They should respond in complete sentences in either the affirmative or the negative.

C17 Actividad • ¡Ya lo hice todo!

Tell the students to imagine they are planning a trip. Based on where they plan to go, they should answer the questions.

CHALLENGE Have the students answer at least four of the questions negatively, following this model:

> No la contesté. La tengo que contestar mañana.

C18 Actividad • ¡A escribir!

Students may also use the questions and answers in C16 as a guide. They should include at least six items in their lists.

C19 Actividad • Una conversación telefónica

After the students have had time to complete the activity with their partners, call on random pairs to act out the telephone conversation for the class.

TRY YOUR SKILLS

OBJECTIVE To recombine communicative functions, grammar, and vocabulary

CULTURAL BACKGROUND The postcards shown are of Madrid, Spain. The postcard on the left shows the **Plaza de España,** located downtown. There you can see the main post office that was built at the beginning of this century. The other postcard shows the **Parque del Retiro,** a 350-acre park in the center of the city.

1

Recuerdos de Madrid

Brainstorm with the class names of places presented in this unit. List them on the board or on a transparency. Then ask the students where they would go if they were in Spain. Explain that they are going to read postcards written by students who are visiting Spain.

Have the students read the postcards silently. Then play the cassette or read each postcard aloud as students follow along in their books.

2 ## Actividad • ¿Es cierto o no?

Have the students refer to the postcards to correct the false statements.

3 ## Preguntas y respuestas

Have the students work with a partner and use the answers to the questions to summarize each postcard. Assign one student to record the answers and then report them to the rest of the class. Then each pair should work together to prepare an oral summary of Pilar and Billy's trip. Another student should attempt to restate the trips.

4 ## Actividad • Charla

SLOWER-PACED LEARNING Before having the students complete this activity, you may review the preterit tense of the irregular verbs **ir** and **hacer**.

5 ## Actividad • Postales

Have the students refer to Skills 1 when writing their original postcards.

6 ## Pronunciación, lectura, dictado

1. Listen carefully and repeat what you hear.
   The s sound: In Spanish the letter **c** before **e** and **i**, and the letters **s** and **z** are pronounced somewhat like the *s* in the English words *sit*, *say*, and *see*. Listen to and repeat the following words.

cinco	lápices	invitación	ciencia
señor	servilleta	delicioso	Isabel
lápiz	vez	zapato	manzana

   Only in Spain is the sound of these letters pronounced like the English *th* in the word *think*.

2. Listen, and then read aloud.
   Listen to the following words with the Spanish **s** sound and repeat.

cerámica	cine	gracias	cereza
enseguida	reservar	pesetas	clase
bolsillo	sol	Susana	sandía
azul	zanahoria	empezar	almorzar

3. Write the following sentences from dictation. First, listen to the sentence as it is read to you. Then, you will hear the sentence again in short segments, with a pause after each segment to allow you time to write. Finally, you will hear the sentence a third time so that you may check your work. Let's begin.

El señor González *(pause)* regresó de la oficina *(pause)* muy cansado.

La clase *(pause)* de educación física *(pause)* no es difícil.

La señorita *(pause)* de los zapatos azules *(pause)* es muy simpática.

La excursión *(pause)* sale el siete *(pause)* de marzo.

¿LO SABES?

When the students have had time to prepare, solicit their responses by asking: **¿Qué hiciste ayer? ¿Qué compraste? ¿Hablaste por teléfono?** Then have the students turn to the nearest classmate and ask if he or she did the same thing.

Remind the students to use the preterit tense when describing and asking questions about their trip. For the third activity, have the students talk about the route they took to school. Explain that landmarks may be a popular ice cream shop, the public library, or the corner gas station.

Have the students work with a partner to ask and answer the questions with **lo, la, los,** and **las.** Then call on volunteers to tell the class what they have already done.

VOCABULARIO

You may wish to play a word association game with the students. Divide the students into two teams, **equipo A** and **equipo B.** Have a student keep score on the board. As you give a word to a student on one team, he or she will have a few seconds to come up with another word that goes with it. For example, if you say **invitación,** an appropriate response would be **una invitación a la fiesta.** Students should not get help from teammates.

ESTUDIO DE PALABRAS

Expand this exercise and ask about other vocabulary. What words have they learned that come from English? What words do we use that come from Spanish?

VAMOS A LEER

OBJECTIVE To read for practice and pleasure

Antes de leer

Emphasize to the students that it is not necessary to understand every word in the selection. They should read to acquire a general understanding of the selection.

¡A ESPAÑA!

Introduce the selection by discussing **Las Fallas de Valencia.** (You can find more information on Valencia on page T222.) Then explain that the article is about a holiday in Valencia, Spain. Read the text aloud or play the cassette for the students.

Preguntas y respuestas

After the students have found the correct answers to these items, have them go back to the selection to find the exact sentence the phrase came from. They should ask about other vocabulary and phrases they didn't know. Ask the students to describe **Las Fallas** and **paella** in their own words.

ANSWERS:
1. Las Fallas de Valencia empiezan una semana antes de la fiesta de San José.
2. Va a empezar en la primavera.
3. Los valencianos saludan la primavera con hogueras.
4. En cada esquina hay una falla.
5. A la medianoche del día 19 se queman todas las fallas.
6. La paella valenciana tiene fama internacional.
7. Los ingredientes básicos son arroz amarillo, pollo, mariscos y legumbres.

Actividad • Un anuncio

Form cooperative learning groups of two or three students to complete this activity. They should create a tourist brochure of their city or town. Ask the students to illustrate it with original drawings or photographs. Display the brochures in the classroom.

GUÍA TURÍSTICA DE NUESTRA GALAXIA

Before reading the selection, you may wish to begin a brief discussion of science fiction. After playing the cassette or reading the brochure aloud to the students, ask the students what other tourist attractions they would include in this galaxy.

Actividad • Información, por favor

You may wish to set up an information booth in the classroom. Have the students take turns being the tour guide at the booth. They may ask the questions in the book and add their own.

ANSWERS

1. Puede estacionar su nave en la estación interplanetaria.
2. El restaurante está en la estación interplanetaria X32.
3. Los trajes espaciales están en el centro comercial galáctico.
4. Pueden mirar fotografías en el museo interplanetario.
5. Puede ir con sus hijos al museo interplanetario.
6. Pueden visitar la Casa-Museo "E.T." en el transbordador de la amistad.
7. La colección de animales está en el zoológico de la Vía Láctea.
8. Las píldoras alimenticias están en la estación interplanetaria.

Actividad • Charla

Encourage the students to use their imagination and expand their descriptions of their galactic trip.

EL REGALO

Before reading this episode of **El regalo,** ask the students: **¿Qué creen que va a pasar en este episodio? ¿Qué pasó en el episodio anterior? ¿Cómo son Adriana y Daniel?** Then play the cassette or read aloud the selection. Have the students role-play the dialogs.

SLOWER-PACED LEARNING   You may wish to divide the reading into four sections. Ask comprehensive questions after each section, making sure the students understand the content completely before continuing.

Actividad • No es así

Have the students correct each statement, according to **El regalo.** You may also check comprehension by asking the following or similar questions.

1. ¿Dónde deciden ir Daniel y Adriana?
2. ¿Qué deben buscar?
3. Desde El Paso, ¿por qué no van a España?
4. ¿A qué ciudad van en España primero? ¿Después?
5. ¿A quién ven en Madrid?
6. ¿Cómo se llama el cómplice de la aeromoza?
7. ¿Por qué chocaron los dos coches?
8. ¿Cómo se llama el chico de El Paso?
9. ¿Quién es su padre?
10. ¿Por qué dice que Daniel y Adriana le ayudaron al piloto muchísimo?

ANSWERS:

1. Daniel y Adriana deciden ir a Madrid para buscar la flor de la canción de los mariachis.
2. Los hermanos toman un autobús en Segovia para ir a Madrid.
3. Ellos encuentran un programa de España en México.
4. En México pueden ver un programa sobre Segovia.
5. En la parte antigua de Madrid, Adriana cree estar en el pasado.
6. Ellos toman el autobús para Madrid porque sale pronto.
7. La mujer que está parada frente al banco es la aeromoza del vuelo 28.
8. La aeromoza camina hasta la esquina y sube al coche.
9. El joven de El Paso es hijo del piloto.
10. Daniel y Adriana salvaron la vida del padre del joven de El Paso.

UNIDAD 10
Un viaje estupendo

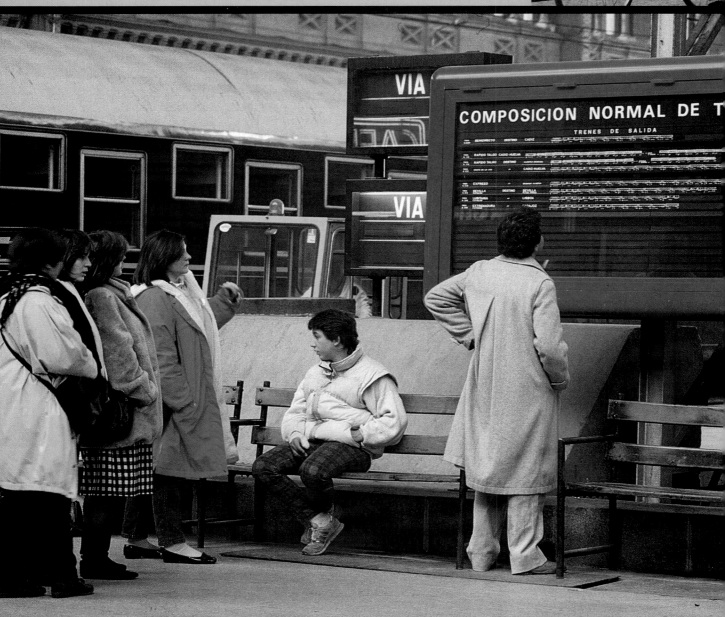

Isn't it time you started thinking about taking a trip yourself? For example, you might consider applying as an exchange student to Mexico, Spain, or some other Spanish-speaking countries. Ask your teacher what exchange programs may be open to you—if not for this year, then for the future. You might also consider traveling on your own, either with a group of friends or with your family. Making plans for a big trip is part of the excitement.

In this unit you will:

SECTION A	talk about what you did yesterday, the day before, and last summer
SECTION B	ask for information about something that happened in the past
SECTION C	ask whether or not someone did something
TRY YOUR SKILLS	use what you've learned
VAMOS A LEER	read for practice and pleasure

269

SECTION A

talking about what you did yesterday, the day before, and last summer

Traveling to a foreign city, seeing the landmarks—that's something to look forward to. When Madrid is the city you plan to visit, you're in for a special treat. Madrid is one of the great capital cities of the world, with fabulous avenues, palaces, parks, museums, stores, and a wonderful, fun loving population of over 3 million people. You'll have a great deal to tell your friends when you return!

A1

El diario de Pilar

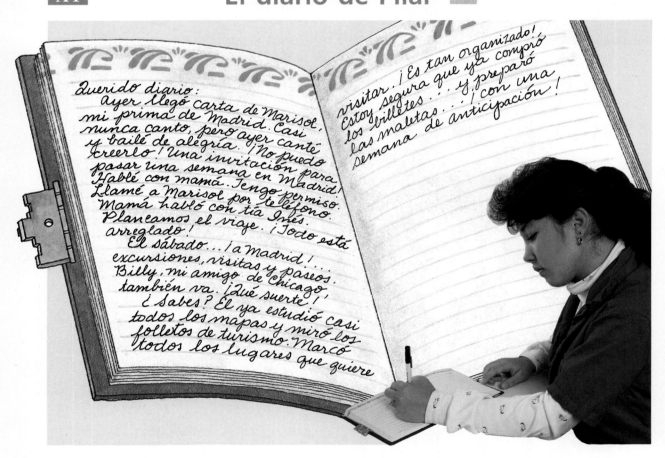

Querido diario:
Ayer llegó carta de Marisol, mi prima de Madrid. Casi nunca canto, pero ayer canté y bailé de alegría. ¡No puedo creerlo! Una invitación para pasar una semana en Madrid! Hablé con mamá. Tengo permiso. Llamé a Marisol por teléfono. Mamá habló con tía Inés. Planeamos el viaje. ¡Todo está arreglado!
El sábado... ¡a Madrid!... excursiones, visitas y paseos. Billy, mi amigo de Chicago también va. ¡Qué suerte! ¿Sabes? El ya estudió casi todos los mapas y miró los folletos de turismo. Marcó todos los lugares que quiere visitar. ¡Es tan organizado! Estoy segura que ya compró los billetes... y preparó las maletas... ¡con una semana de anticipación!

A2   Actividad • Para completar

Complete these sentences to make them agree with **El diario de Pilar.**

1. Ayer __llegó__ carta de Marisol, mi prima de __Madrid__.
2. Canté y __bailé__ de alegría.
3. __Hablé__ con mamá. Tengo __permiso__.
4. Llamé a __Marisol__ por __teléfono__.

5. Y __el sábado__. . ¡a Madrid!
6. Billy, mi __amigo__ de Chicago, también __va__.
7. ¿Sabes? Él ya __estudió__ casi todos los mapas.
8. Estoy segura que ya __compró__ los billetes.

270   Unidad 10

Ayer llegó la carta de Marisol. Canté y bailé de alegría. Llamé a Marisol por teléfono. Billy ya estudió todos los mapas. Él miró los folletos de turismo. Marcó todos los lugares que quiere visitar. Estoy segura que ya compró los billetes. También preparó las maletas.

A3 Actividad • Combinación

See how many logical sentences you can form by choosing items from both columns.

Ayer llegó	**los lugares que quiere visitar.**
Canté y bailé	**todos los mapas.**
Llamé a Marisol	**los folletos de turismo.**
Billy ya estudió	**de alegría.**
Él miró	**por teléfono.**
Marcó todos	**las maletas.**
Estoy segura que ya	**carta de Marisol.**
También preparó	**compró los billetes.**

A4 Preguntas y respuestas

4. La invitación es para pasar una semana en Madrid.
5. Sí, Pilar puede ir a Madrid, porque tiene permiso de su mamá.
6. Pilar va a Madrid el sábado.

Answer the following questions according to **El diario de Pilar.**

1. ¿Dónde escribe Pilar?   Pilar escribe en su diario.
2. ¿Quién es Marisol?   Marisol es la prima de Pilar.
3. ¿Dónde está Marisol?   Marisol está en Madrid.
4. ¿Para qué es la invitación?
5. ¿Puede ir Pilar a Madrid? ¿Por qué?

6. ¿Cuándo va a ir Pilar a Madrid?
7. ¿Con quién va a ir?   Va a ir con su amigo Billy.
8. ¿Qué va a hacer Pilar en Madrid?
9. ¿Cómo se llama el amigo de Pilar?
10. ¿Es él de Madrid?   No, él es de Chicago.

8. Pilar va a hacer excursiones, visitas y paseos.
9. El amigo de Pilar se llama Billy.

A5 ¿Sabes que . . . ?

Madrid, the capital of Spain, is a center of industry and communications, much like Chicago and New York. Primarily, however, it is Spain's administrative and governmental center, parallel to Washington, D.C. The Royal Palace, courts, ministries, and other governmental buildings are in Madrid. Spain's formal chief of state is the king: **el Rey** Juan Carlos. Spain's parliament, called **las Cortes,** elects a president of the government, whose responsibilities resemble those of the British prime minister.

Un viaje estupendo   271

ESTRUCTURAS ESENCIALES
The preterit (past tense) of regular -ar verbs

In order to express past actions you need to use a verb in the past tense: *I went to the movies yesterday.* In Spanish one such past tense is the preterit tense. It corresponds to the English simple past tense.

hablar *to talk*		
Yo	**hablé**	con Marisol.
¿Tú	**hablaste**	con tía Inés?
Usted, él, ella	**habló**	por teléfono.
Nosotros(as)	**hablamos**	ayer.
¿Vosotros(as)	**hablasteis**	con el aduanero?
Ustedes, ellos(as)	**hablaron**	anoche.

1. The verb forms in the chart are the preterit tense forms of the regular verb **hablar.** They express actions that took place and were completed in the past: **Hablé** con Marisol. *I talked with Marisol.*

2. You can produce the preterit forms of most other regular **-ar** verbs by adding the following endings to the stem:

-é, -aste, -ó, -amos, -asteis, -aron

When you add **-é** to the stem **habl-,** you get **hablé,** *I talked, I spoke.* The regular verb **planear** is conjugated like **hablar.** For example, when you add **-aste** to the stem **plane-,** you get **planeaste,** *you* **(tú)** *planned,* and so on.

3. Notice that the **yo** and the **usted, él, ella** forms have written accents.

Yo hablé.
Ella habló.

4. The **nosotros(as)** forms of **-ar** verbs are the same in the preterit and the present. Other words in the sentence usually make clear whether you are talking in the present or the past.

Hablamos con Billy ahora.   *We are talking to Billy now.*
Hablamos con Billy ayer.   *We talked to Billy yesterday.*

Actividad • ¿Qué planearon?

Using the preterit of **planear,** say who planned what.

1. Yo planeé el paseo. 2. Mamá planeó la comida. 3. Nosotros planeamos la excursión. 4. Los chicos planearon la visita. 5. Teresita planeó el menú. 6. Tú planeaste el viaje.

¿El viaje? Nosotros.
—Nosotros planeamos el viaje.

1. ¿El paseo? Yo.
2. ¿La comida? Mamá.
3. ¿La excursión? Nosotros.
4. ¿La visita? Los chicos.
5. ¿El menú? Teresita.

6. ¿El viaje? Tú.
7. ¿El baile? Ustedes.
8. ¿El concierto? La profesora.
9. ¿La fiesta? Mis primos.
10. ¿El horario? El señor Valdez.

7. Ustedes planearon el baile. 8. La profesora planeó el concierto. 9. Mis primos planearon la fiesta. 10. El señor Valdez planeó el horario.

A8 Actividad • ¿Con quién hablaste?

Complete the following, using the preterit tense of **hablar.**

—¿ ____ (tú) con Marisol? Hablaste
—No, yo no ____ con ella. hablé
—¿ ____ mamá con ella? Habló
—Sí, creo que mamá ____ con ella. habló
—¿Con quién ____ ustedes? hablaron

—(Nosotros) ____ con la tía Inés. hablamos
—Pero, ¿ ____ ustedes con Marisol también? hablaron
—Sí, (nosotros) ____ con Marisol, y hablamos
   Marisol ____ con Pilar. habló

A9 SE DICE ASÍ
*Saying what you usually do and then saying what
you did at specified times in the past*

Canto **a menudo** y **ayer también** canté.	*I often sing, and I also sang yesterday.*
Casi siempre canto, **pero ayer** no canté.	*I almost always sing, but I didn't sing yesterday.*
Casi nunca canto, **pero ayer** canté.	*I rarely sing, but I sang yesterday.*
Estudiamos **todos los días.**	*We study every day.*

A10 Actividad • Ayer también

Complete the following sentences using the preterit of the underlined verbs.

> <u>Hablo</u> a menudo en español y ayer también . . .
> Hablo a menudo en español y ayer también hablé.

1. Nosotros <u>estudiamos</u> a menudo. Ayer también . . . estudiamos
2. Marisol casi siempre <u>llama</u>, pero ayer no . . . llamó
3. Tú a menudo <u>compras</u> discos. Ayer también . . . compraste
4. Casi siempre <u>miro</u> televisión, pero ayer no . . . miré
5. <u>Cantan</u> casi siempre en español, pero ayer no . . . cantaron
6. Ella a menudo <u>espera</u> en la cafetería. Ayer también . . . esperó

A11 Actividad • Todos los días y ayer Answers will vary.

Team up with a partner. Using **siempre** or **todos los días,** ask whether the people
usually do what is mentioned. Your partner will answer negatively following the
model.

> Los chicos bailan.

> —¿Bailan los chicos siempre?
> —No, no bailan siempre,
>   pero ayer bailaron.

1. Pilar canta y baila.
2. Ella habla con su tía.
3. Pilar llama a su prima.
4. Ellos escuchan música.

5. Billy estudia con sus amigos.
6. Ellas miran televisión.
7. Marisol toma fotografías.
8. Los chicos montan en bicicleta.

Un viaje estupendo   273

Actividad • ¡A escribir! Answers will vary.

La rutina. Write down what you usually do every day and what you did or didn't
do yesterday. Use the expressions you learned in A9.

—Todos los días preparo las tareas, y ayer también preparé las tareas.
(pero ayer no preparé las tareas.)

A 13 Conversación • Ayer y hoy

Pair up with a classmate, talk about what you do every day
and what you did yesterday.

—¿Escuchas música
todos los días?

• Sí, escucho música siempre.
• No, no escucho música
todos los días.

—¿Y ayer escuchaste
música?

• Sí, ayer también escuché
música.
• Ayer no escuché música.
• No, ayer no escuché música.

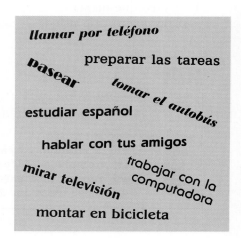

llamar por teléfono

preparar las tareas

pasear

tomar el autobús

estudiar español

hablar con tus amigos

mirar televisión

trabajar con la computadora

montar en bicicleta

A 14 SITUACIÓN • Conversación de dos minutos

Carlos llama por teléfono a Isabel en un mal momento. Isabel está a punto de
salir para el aeropuerto.

CARLOS   ¡Hola, Isabel! ¿Cómo estás?
ISABEL   ¡Apuradísima! No puedo hablar
ahora. Salimos para el aeropuerto
dentro de dos minutos. Vamos a
Barcelona.
CARLOS   ¿A Barcelona?

ISABEL   Sí. Vamos a visitar a la abuela.
Mamá reservó los billetes de avión
la semana pasada. Papá y mamá
llamaron a la abuela anoche. Papá
regresó de la oficina hace una hora.
El taxi ya llegó . . . y yo todavía
tengo que hacer mi maleta. ¡Adiós!

A 15   Preguntas y respuestas

Answer the following questions according to A14.

1. ¿Cómo está Isabel? ¿Por qué?
2. ¿Puede ella hablar mucho? ¿Por qué?
3. ¿Adónde va ella? Ella va a Barcelona.
4. ¿Qué va a hacer allí? Va a visitar a su abuela.
5. ¿Qué reservó la mamá de Isabel? ¿Cuándo?

6. ¿A quién llamaron? ¿Cuándo?
7. ¿Está el papá en la oficina todavía?
8. ¿Dónde está el papá? Está en su casa.
9. ¿Cuándo regresó? Regresó hace una hora.
10. ¿Cómo van al aeropuerto? Van al aeropuerto en taxi.

A 16   Actividad • ¡A escoger!

Choose the option that best completes each statement according to A14.

1. Isabel dice que está
   • muy bien.   • apuradísima.   • con su mamá.
2. Isabel y sus papás salen para
   • la oficina.   • la casa de Carlos.   • el aeropuerto.
3. Ellos salen para Barcelona
   • dentro de dos minutos.   • mañana.   • el sábado.
4. Van a Barcelona para
   • trabajar.   • visitar a la abuela.   • visitar a Carlos.
5. Mamá reservó los billetes
   • hace una hora.   • la semana pasada.   • hace dos minutos.
6. Llamaron a la abuela
   • la semana pasada.   • hace una hora.   • anoche.
7. Papá regresó de la oficina
   • anoche.   • hace cinco minutos.   • hace una hora.
8. Yo no terminé
   • de hacer mi maleta.   • de hablar por teléfono.   • de hablar con Carlos.

A 17   ¿Sabes que . . . ?

Barcelona, Spain's second-largest city, is a center of industry and a beautiful port on the Mediterranean Sea. Famous especially for its painters, architects, and sculptors, Barcelona is the capital of Cataluña, one of the 17 regions into which Spain is divided. The Catalan language is spoken along with Spanish throughout the region.

Un viaje estupendo   275

A 18 ESTRUCTURAS ESENCIALES
Expressing how long ago something happened

Isabel llegó **hace** { mucho tiempo. / quince días. / una hora. }   **Hace** { un mes / una semana / poco tiempo } **que** Isabel llegó.

subject +	verb in the preterit	+ **hace** +	expression of time	**Hace** +	expression of time	+ **que** + subject +	verb in the preterit

Use **hace** + time expression or **hace** + time expression + **que** to indicate how long ago an action took place. Notice that in both cases the verb of the sentence is in the preterit.

A 19 Actividad · ¡Cómo pasa el tiempo!

Form sentences with **hace** and **que** to indicate how long ago the events happened.

> Hoy es lunes 16. José llegó el lunes 2.
> **Hace** dos semanas **que** llegó.

1. Son las doce. El autobús llegó a las once. Hace una hora que llegó.
2. Hoy es miércoles. Isabel compró los billetes el miércoles pasado. Hace una semana que compró los billetes.
3. Hoy es el 5 de marzo. Marisol visitó a sus primos el 2 de marzo. Hace tres días que visitó a sus primos.
4. Hoy es el 4 de abril. Daniel llamó a su tía el 20 de marzo. Hace dieciséis días que llamó a su tía.
5. Es la una. Paco preparó las maletas a las doce. Hace una hora que preparó las maletas.
6. Hoy es sábado. Mis padres hablaron con los chicos el sábado pasado. Hace una semana que hablaron.
7. Son las cuatro. La excursión terminó a las tres. Hace una hora que terminó.
8. Hoy es el 8 de mayo. Los chicos estudiaron los mapas el 8 de abril. Hace un mes que estudiaron los mapas.

A 20 Comprensión   For script and answers, see p. T185.

Are they talking in the present or the preterit?

	0	1	2	3	4	5	6	7	8	9	10
Present	✔	✔		✔	✔		✔				✔
Preterit			✔			✔		✔	✔	✔	

A 21 Conversación · El viaje Possible conversation is given.

Work with a partner. Imagine that you are coming back from a trip to one of the places in the pictures on the next page—or to another place you have visited. In at least 10 sentences, tell your partner what you did there. Ask your classmate about his or her trip, using each of the verbs below.

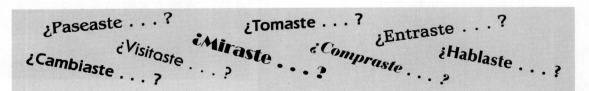

¿Paseaste . . . ?   ¿Tomaste . . . ?   ¿Entraste . . . ?
¿Visitaste . . . ?   ¿Miraste . . . ?   ¿Compraste . . . ?   ¿Hablaste . . . ?
¿Cambiaste . . . ?

276   Unidad 10

Paseamos mucho en Madrid. Tomé muchas fotos. Hablé con unos chicos de Barcelona. Visité el Parque del Retiro. Entré en muchas tiendas y compré muchas cosas.

¿Qué lugares visitaste?
¿Cambiaste de avión en Barcelona?
¿Tomaste fotos en el parque?
¿Qué compraste?
¿Paseaste por la ciudad?

Acapulco, México

Ask your partner:

¿Cuándo visitaste . . . ?
¿Cuánto tiempo pasaste allí?
¿Qué lugares visitaste?
¿Compraste algo?
¿Qué compraste?
¿Cuándo regresaste?

Barcelona, España

Madrid,
España

San Juan, Puerto Rico

San Francisco,
California

A 22 Actividad • ¡A escribir!

Prepare a written report about an imaginary trip to Mexico, Spain, or Puerto Rico.
Present your report orally in class.

A 23 Actividad • Una confusión

Make sense out of the following phone conversation, putting the lines in their correct order.

—Muy bien, ¿y tú?
—¿Te gustó?
—Diez días. Visitamos a la abuela, y a mis tíos también.
—Sí, ¿hablamos mañana? Tengo que salir ahora.
—¡Hola Carlota! ¿Cómo estás?
—Muy bien también. Regresamos ayer de Barcelona.
—Me gustó mucho. Visitamos la ciudad.
—¿Compraste muchas cosas?
—Bueno, hasta mañana.
—¿Cuánto tiempo pasaron en Barcelona?

1. ¡Hola, Carlota! ¿Cómo estás?
2. Muy bien, ¿y tú?
3. Muy bien también. Regresamos . . .
4. ¿Te gustó?
5. Me gustó mucho. Visitamos . . .
6. ¿Cuánto tiempo pasaron en . . .
7. Diez días. Visitamos . . .
8. ¿Compraste muchas cosas?
9. Sí, ¿hablamos mañana?...
10. Bueno, hasta mañana.

It's always exciting to receive long-distance calls from close friends or favorite relatives. If they're on a trip, we want to find out what places they've seen, where they went, and how everything is.

B1   # Pilar llama desde Madrid 📼

Pilar llama a su casa. Su hermana Socorro contesta el teléfono. Socorro quiere saber todo lo que pasa. Pregunta sin parar.

SOCORRO   ¡Hola, Pilar! ¿Cómo estás? ¿Y Billy? ¿Cómo llegaron? ¿Les gusta Madrid?

PILAR   Estamos muy bien, Socorro. ¿Está mamá?

SOCORRO   Sí, ya viene, pero, antes, ¿qué tal el viaje? ¿Adónde fueron hoy? ¿Qué hicieron?

PILAR   Fuimos primero a casa de los tíos. Dejamos nuestras cosas allí. Hablamos mucho. Hicimos planes también.

SOCORRO   Ya sé, ya sé . . . , pero, ¿qué más hicieron?

PILAR   Hicimos muchas cosas.

SOCORRO   ¿Fueron a la Gran Vía?

PILAR   No, fuimos en moto hasta la Puerta de Alcalá. Caminamos mucho. Después fuimos al Parque del Retiro. Remamos en el estanque. ¡Pasamos un día fantástico!

SOCORRO   ¡Qué envidia! Aquí viene mamá. ¡Hasta mañana!

PILAR   ¡Adiós, Socorro!

Actividad • ¡A escoger!

Choose the most appropriate option to complete each statement according to B1.

1. Pilar llama
  • a casa de sus tíos.   • <u>a su casa.</u>   • al Parque del Retiro.

2. Socorro es
  • <u>la hermana de Pilar.</u>   • su mamá.   • su tía de Madrid.

3. Socorro quiere
  • saber dónde está Pilar.   • hablar con su mamá.   • <u>saber todo lo que pasa.</u>

4. Pilar y Billy fueron a la Puerta de Alcalá
  • en autobús.   • en bicicleta.   • <u>en moto.</u>

5. Pilar y Billy remaron
  • en la Gran Vía.   • <u>en el estanque del parque.</u>   • en casa de los tíos.

6. Pilar está
  • <u>en Madrid.</u>   • en casa de Billy.   • en el estanque.

7. Pilar y Socorro van a hablar
  • <u>mañana.</u>   • después.   • dentro de cinco minutos.

8. Aquí viene
  • Socorro.   • Billy.   • <u>mamá.</u>

B3
1. Pilar llama desde Madrid.
2. Su hermana Socorro contesta el teléfono.
3. Es cierto.
4. Pilar quiere hablar con su mamá.
5. Pilar y Billy dejaron sus cosas en casa de los tíos.

B3 **Actividad • ¿Es cierto o no?**

Change the following sentences to make them true according to B1.

1. Pilar llama desde Sevilla.
2. Su mamá contesta el teléfono.
3. Pilar y Billy están en Madrid.
4. Pilar quiere hablar con su papá.
5. Pilar y Billy dejaron sus cosas en la Gran Vía.

6. Hoy fueron en moto hasta la Puerta de Alcalá. Es cierto.
7. Después fueron a la Gran Vía.
8. Más tarde remaron en el estanque. Es cierto.

7. Después fueron al Parque del Retiro.

B4 **¿Sabes que . . . ?**

European cities in the Middle Ages were surrounded by walls with large entrance gates, or **puertas.** As the cities' boundaries grew outward, the old walls eventually disappeared, but many of the old **puertas** remained. Madrid's oldest gate, **la Puerta del Sol,** is actually in the center of the city, where all subway lines and many bus routes originate. **La Puerta de Alcalá,** an 18th-century triumphal arch now surrounded by flowers, is another reference point. **La Gran Vía** is the central avenue in the heart of Madrid, lined with elegant shops, theaters, and cafés. Madrid also has many lovely parks: the biggest is **el Parque del Retiro,** with over 200 acres of lofty trees, flowers, secluded walks and gardens. It has a small lake where visitors may rent rowboats, and two buildings where art shows are held.

Un viaje estupendo 279

ESTRUCTURAS ESENCIALES
The preterit of hacer

hacer	*to do, to make*		
Hice	la comida.	**Hicimos**	unos bocadillos.
¿Hiciste	el viaje?	**¿Hicisteis**	muchas cosas?
Hizo	planes.	**Hicieron**	una excursión.

1. The preterit forms of **hacer** are irregular.

    Hizo muchas cosas ayer.   *He (She) did many things yesterday.*
    Hicimos unos bocadillos anoche.   *We made some sandwiches last night.*

2. The **usted, él, ella** form is **hizo.**

3. Notice that **hice** and **hizo** are stressed on the stem. Neither has a written accent.

B 6   Actividad • Una excursión

A group of friends and relatives are going on an excursion. Using the preterit of
hacer, say who went on the excursion.

    Ustedes—Ustedes hicieron la excursión.

1. Mamá	**4.** Los chicos	**7.** Yo
2. Usted	**5.** Tú	**8.** Mi hermano Javier
3. Pepe y yo	**6.** Ustedes	**9.** Mis tíos

Mamá hizo la excursión.
Usted hizo la excursión.
Pepe y yo hicimos la excursión.
Los chicos hicieron la excursión.
Tú hiciste la excursión.
Ustedes hicieron la excursión.
Yo hice la excursión.
Mi hermano Javier hizo la excursión
Mis tíos hicieron la excursión.

B 7   Actividad • ¿Qué hicieron?

Complete the following using the preterit of **hacer.**

    —¿Qué ____ ustedes el domingo? hicieron
hicimos —Nosotros ____ una excursión estupenda. Mi hermana _hizo_ todos los planes.
    Rosario _hizo_ la comida. Catalina y Julián ____ unos bocadillos. hicieron
    —¿Qué tiempo _hizo_ ?
    —_Hizo_ muy buen tiempo. Todos nosotros ____ algo. hicimos
    —Y tú, ¿qué _hiciste_ ? ¿ ____ tú la comida? Hiciste
    —No, yo _hice_ todos los planes para la excursión.

B 8   Actividad • Charla   Sample conversation is given.

¿Qué hiciste el fin de semana? Work with a partner. Talk about what
you did last weekend.

    —¿Qué hiciste? —¿Una excursión? —¿Adónde?
    —¿Con quién? —¿Visitaste a tus amigos? —¿Estudiaste?

—¿Qué hiciste el fin de
  semana?
—Hice una excursión a la
  playa.
—¿Con quién?
—Con Jorge y Ana.
—¿Nadaron?
—No, hizo mucho frío.
  Caminamos mucho y
  hablamos. Después
  comimos tacos.

B 9   Actividad • ¡A escribir!   Answers will vary.

Prepare a written report of the conversation you had with your partner in B8.

ESTRUCTURAS ESENCIALES
The preterit of **ir**

You may wish to point out that the verb "ser" has the same conjugation as the verb "ir" in the preterit. Point out that the context of the sentence clarifies the meaning.

ir *to go*			
Fui	a su casa.	**Fuimos**	en autobús.
Fuiste	en bicicleta.	**¿Fuisteis**	a pie?
Fue	al cine.	**Fueron**	a la Gran Vía.

The preterit forms of **ir** are irregular.

B 11   Actividad • Combinación

Let's see how many sentences you can prepare by matching the persons on the left with the activities on the right.

Marisol y yo fuimos a casa de Javier. Pilar fue a la Gran Vía. Los chicos fueron a dar una vuelta. Tú fuiste al cine. Yo fui al Parque del Retiro. Javier y tú fueron a dar una vuelta.

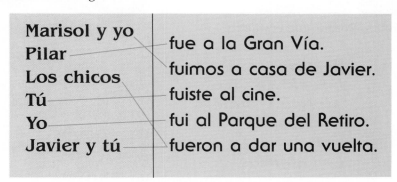

Marisol y yo
Pilar
Los chicos
Tú
Yo
Javier y tú

fue a la Gran Vía.
fuimos a casa de Javier.
fuiste al cine.
fui al Parque del Retiro.
fueron a dar una vuelta.

B 12   Actividad • ¿Adónde fueron?

It seems that everybody went somewhere last Sunday. With a partner, read the dialog, supplying the missing preterit forms of **ir.**

—¿Adónde ____ (tú) el domingo pasado? fuiste
—(Yo) ____ a casa de los tíos. fui
—¿Y Billy, adónde ____ ? fue
—Billy ____ a un concierto. fue
—¿ ____ ustedes al cine después? Fueron
—No, Billy ____ a la Gran Vía. fue

—Tía Inés y yo ____ a dar una vuelta. fuimos
—¿Y tú, adónde ____ ? fuiste
—Yo ____ al parque. fui
—¿Con quién ____ ? fuiste
—(Yo) ____ con mi amiga Carmen. fui

B 13   Actividad • Fuimos anoche 🔲

Work with a partner. Ask each other these questions. Answer using **No,** the preterit of **ir,** and **anoche.**

—¿Vas al cine?   —No, fui anoche.

1. ¿Van los chicos a casa de los tíos? No, fueron anoche.
2. ¿Va Pilar al cine? No, fue anoche.
3. ¿Vas tú al concierto? No, fui anoche.
4. ¿Van ustedes a la Gran Vía? No, fuimos anoche.
5. ¿Vamos al cine? No, fui anoche./No, fuimos anoche.
6. ¿Vas tú a la Puerta de Alcalá? No, fui anoche.
7. ¿Van Isabel y Julio? No, fueron anoche.
8. ¿Va tu hermana? No, fue anoche.

B 14   Actividad • ¿Cómo fueron?   Answers will vary.

Using items from both columns and the preterit of **ir,** say how everybody got to
the party last night in honor of tía Inés.

Rosario—en metro   —Rosario fue en metro.

Rosario	
Los chicos	
Alberto y Julián	**a pie**
Nosotros	**en coche**
Yo	**en autobús**
Los abuelos	**en metro**
Usted	**en bicicleta**
La señora Pérez	**en moto**
Tú	

B 15   Actividad • ¡A escribir!   Answers will vary.

Think of a party you went to recently. Write a list saying how everybody that you
remember got to the party.

B 16   Conversación • Ayer, anoche y la semana pasada   Sample conversation is given.

Find out from five friends what each one did yesterday, last night, and last week.
Report your findings to the class.

Ex.—¿Qué hiciste anoche?
  —Anoche fui al cine con Silvia.
  —¿Fueron en bicicleta?
  —No, fuimos a pie. Después
    comimos un helado.

Ayer El domingo
El fin de semana pasado   Anoche
      El sábado

B 17   Actividad • ¡A escribir!

Prepare a written report of your findings in B16.

Ex.—¿Qué hiciste anoche?
  —Anoche fui al cine con Silvia.
  —¿Fueron en bicicleta?
  —No, fuimos a pie. Después
    comimos un helado.

Which segments of the conversation are in the present or the preterit?

	0	1	2	3	4	5	6	7	8	9	10
Present		✔	✔		✔			✔			✔
Preterit	✔			✔	✔		✔		✔	✔	

B 19 Actividad • ¿Adónde fueron? Answers will vary. Ex. Mi prima fue al cine.

Say who went where using elements from the two boxes below. You can
also add how and when they went. Form as many sentences as you can.

¿Quién?

Yo   Mi prima   Nosotros
Mis amigos   Tu hermano
Consuelo   Los chicos   Tú

¿Adónde?

al cine   a la tienda   a la piscina
a una fiesta   a la discoteca
a un restaurante
a la playa   a casa de sus amigos

B 20 Actividad • La ruta Answers will vary.

Describe to a partner or the entire class how you got to a place and what you did
there. Use the map and the description as a model. Some possibilities: when you
went to a store, to a party, to the house of a friend or relative. . . .

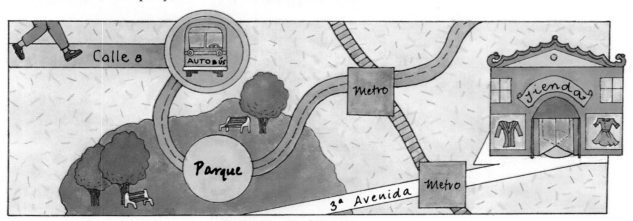

Fui a pie hasta la calle 8. Allí tomé el autobús y fui al parque. Después fui en
metro hasta la Tercera Avenida. Caminé por la Tercera Avenida hasta la tienda.
Compré muchas cosas.

B 21 Actividad • ¡A escribir!

Draw a map of the route in B20 and write a description of the trip, using at least
eight sentences.

SECTION C

asking whether or not someone did something

Getting ready for a weekend excursion sometimes seems to take as much energy and time as preparing for a much longer trip. It may be better to remain calm and do less planning—if we forget to pack something, we can live without it for two days.

You may wish to explain that in some Spanish-speaking countries "boleto" is used for "billete".

C1

Un viaje corto 📼

La mamá de Socorro quiere saber si está todo listo para el viaje a Granada.

MAMÁ	Socorro, ¿tienes los billetes?
SOCORRO	Sí, mamá, los tengo aquí.
MAMÁ	¿Hiciste las maletas?
SOCORRO	Sí, mamá, las preparé.
MAMÁ	¿Y los regalos?
SOCORRO	Están todos.
MAMÁ	¿Te llamó tu hermano?
SOCORRO	Sí, me llamó esta mañana.
MAMÁ	¿Llamaste al taxi?
SOCORRO	Sí, ya lo llamé.
MAMÁ	Bueno, ¿qué más? . . . ¿Tiene tu papá nuestro número de teléfono?
SOCORRO	Sí, lo tiene. Mamá, ¡por favor!, ¡sólo vamos a Granada por dos días!

C2 ¿Es cierto o no? 📼

Change the following statements to make them true according to the dialog in C1.

1. Socorro no tiene los regalos.
2. Ella hizo las maletas.
3. Socorro llamó a su hermano.
4. El hermano de Socorro llamó por teléfono.

5. Van a ir al aeropuerto en metro.
6. El papá de Socorro no va con ellas.
7. Socorro y su mamá van a Córdoba.
8. Socorro y su mamá van por una semana.

284 **Unidad 10**

1. Socorro tiene los regalos.
2. Es cierto.
3. Socorro no llamó por teléfono.
4. Es cierto.

5. Van a ir al aeropuerto en taxi.
6. Es cierto.
7. Socorro y su mamá van a Granada.
8. Socorro y su mamá van por dos días.

C3 Actividad • ¡A escoger!

Choose the most appropriate option to complete each statement according to C1.

1. Socorro tiene
   • <u>los billetes.</u>　　• los números.　　• los teléfonos.
2. Ella preparó
   • la comida.　　• <u>las maletas.</u>　　• las tareas.
3. El hermano de Socorro
   • llamó al taxi.　　• <u>llamó por teléfono.</u>　　• llamó ayer.
4. La mamá de Socorro _____ saber si no falta nada.
   • va a　　• puede　　• <u>quiere</u>
5. ¿Está todo listo para
   • el taxi?　　• <u>el viaje?</u>　　• tu hermano?
6. Socorro llamó
   • <u>al taxi.</u>　　• al papá.　　• al hermano.
7. ¿Tiene papá nuestro
   • billete?　　• asiento?　　• <u>número?</u>
8. Socorro y su mamá van de viaje
   • por dos semanas.　　• <u>por dos días.</u>　　• por tres días.

C4 ¿Sabes que . . . ?

In the eighth century, Moorish warriors from North Africa invaded Spain and eventually conquered nearly all of it. Spain's Moorish kingdoms became the richest states in Europe and centers of world learning. Granada, capital of the last Moorish state in Spain, was reconquered by the Christians in 1492, the year Colón discovered America. Every year tourists by the millions visit its surviving palaces and gardens, specifically the **Alhambra** and **Generalife,** situated in the foothills of the spectacular snowcapped Sierra Nevada mountains.

Un viaje estupendo　285

C5 ESTRUCTURAS ESENCIALES
Direct-object pronouns

In Unit 7, you began to use sentences that include direct objects. The verb in such sentences expresses an action, and the direct object indicates who or what gets acted upon.

Billy compra **el billete.**	*Billy buys the ticket.*
Pilar llamó **a su hermana.**	*Pilar called her sister.*

The *ticket* gets bought. The *sister* gets called. They are the direct objects. When the direct object refers to a person, you need to use the personal **a** before it.

You can also replace the direct object with a direct-object pronoun.

Singular		Plural	
me	me	**nos**	us
te	you (*fam.*)		
lo	him, you (*m.*), it (*m.*)	**los**	them, you (*m.*)
la	her, you (*f.*), it (*f.*)	**las**	them, you (*f.*)

1. The direct-object pronouns **me, te,** and **nos** are the same for both masculine or feminine nouns.

Sí, yo vengo.	Marisol **me** llamó.	*Marisol called me.*
Sí, tú vienes.	Marisol **te** llamó.	*Marisol called you.*
Sí, nosotros venimos. ⎫	Marisol **nos** llamó.	*Marisol called us.*
Sí, nosotras venimos. ⎭		

2. The pronouns **lo, la, los,** and **las** correspond to English *him, her, it, them,* and *you* (**usted, ustedes**). They reflect the gender and number of the direct-object persons or things.

Billy compra **el billete.** Billy **lo** compra.	*Billy buys it.*
Pilar llamó **a su hermana.** Pilar **la** llamó.	*Pilar called her.*
¿Conoces **a mis primos?** Sí **los** conozco.	*Yes, I know them.*
Marisol espera **a sus amigas.** Marisol **las** espera.	*Marisol is waiting for them.*

3. Place the direct-object pronoun right before the conjugated verb.

Yo llamé **a Carmen.**	*I called Carmen.*
Yo **la** llamé.	*I called her.*

4. In negative sentences **no** must precede the direct-object pronoun.

Yo **no** llamé **a Carmen.**	*I did not call Carmen.*
Yo **no la** llamé.	*I did not call her.*

C6 Actividad · ¿Me escuchaste?

While you were away on a trip, your family sent you a cassette recording. Everybody wants to know whether you heard what they had to say.

—¿A tía Inés?   —¿Escuchaste **a tía Inés?**   —Sí, **la** escuché.

1. ¿Al tío?	**3.** ¿A tus primos?	**5.** ¿A mí?	**7.** ¿A tu papá?
2. ¿A la abuela?	**4.** ¿A Susana?	**6.** ¿A nosotros?	**8.** ¿A tu hermano?

286   Unidad 10

1. ¿Escuchaste al tío?/Sí, lo escuché.   2. ¿Escuchaste a la abuela?/Sí, la escuché.   3. ¿Escuchaste a tus primos?/Sí, los escuché.   4. ¿Escuchaste a Susana?/Sí, la escuché.   5. ¿Me escuchaste?/Sí, te escuché.   6. ¿Nos escuchaste?/Sí, los escuché.   7. ¿Escuchaste a tu papá?/Sí, lo escuché.   8. ¿Escuchaste a tu hermano?/Sí, lo escuché.

C7   Actividad • ¿Hiciste todo?

Answer the following questions using the direct object pronouns, **lo, la, los,** or **las.**

> —¿Dejaste **las maletas?**
> —Sí, **las** dejé.

1. ¿Planeaste el viaje?
2. ¿Estudiaste los mapas?
3. ¿Miraste los folletos?
4. ¿Reservaste los billetes?
5. ¿Llamaste a tus amigos?
6. ¿Llamaste a tía Inés?
7. ¿Compraste los billetes?
8. ¿Hiciste las maletas?

1. Sí, lo planeé.   2. Sí, los estudié.
3. Sí, los miré.   4. Sí, los reservé.
5. Sí, los llamé.   6. Sí, la llamé.   7. Sí,
los compré.   8. Sí, las hice.

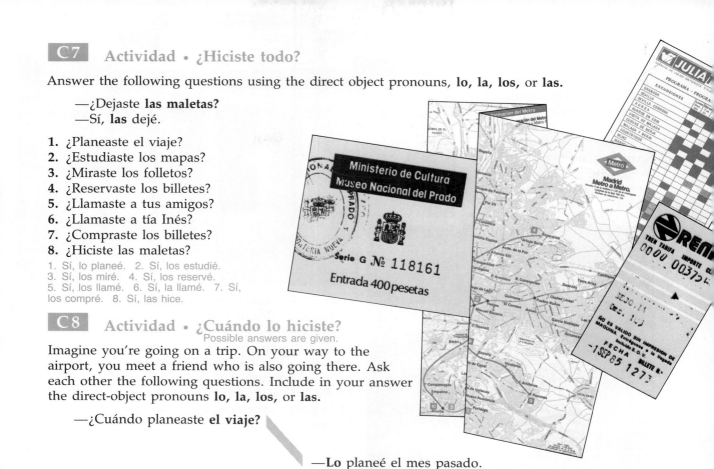

C8   Actividad • ¿Cuándo lo hiciste?

Possible answers are given.

Imagine you're going on a trip. On your way to the airport, you meet a friend who is also going there. Ask each other the following questions. Include in your answer the direct-object pronouns **lo, la, los,** or **las.**

> —¿Cuándo planeaste **el viaje?**

> —**Lo** planeé el mes pasado.

1. ¿Cuándo preparaste este viaje?
2. ¿Cuándo estudiaste los mapas?
3. ¿Cuándo miraste los folletos?
4. ¿Cuándo cambiaste el dinero?
5. ¿Cuándo reservaste los billetes?
6. ¿Cuándo compraste el diccionario?
7. ¿Cuándo hiciste las maletas?
8. ¿Cuándo llamaste al taxi?

hace un mes   *hace quince días*
el mes pasado   **ayer**   *anoche*
hace un año   *la semana pasada*
hace una semana

1. Lo preparé . . .   2. Los estudié . . .   3. Los miré . . .   4. Lo cambié . . .   5. Los reservé . . .   6. Lo compré . . .
7. Las hice . . .   8. Lo llamé . . .

C9   Actividad • ¡A escribir!   Answers will vary.

Using your answers to the questions in C8 as a base, prepare a brief paragraph about the trip.

1. ¿Los libros? Los compré en la Gran Vía.
2. ¿Los diccionarios? Los compré en una librería.
3. ¿Los casetes? Los compré en la calle.
4. ¿Los billetes? Los compré en el teatro.

C10   Actividad • ¿Dónde lo compraste?

You bought a lot of things during your trip. Say where you bought them.

> revistas / Madrid   —¿Las revistas?, **las** compré en Madrid.

1. libros / Gran Vía
2. diccionario / una librería
3. casetes / la calle
4. billetes / el teatro
5. mapa / Casa Suárez
6. cartera / una tienda
7. postales / el Prado
8. discos / el Rastro

5. ¿El mapa? Lo compré en la Casa Suárez.
6. ¿La cartera? La compré en una tienda.
7. ¿Las postales? Las compré en el Prado.
8. ¿Los discos? Los compré en el Rastro.

Un viaje estupendo   **287**

Madrid's **Museo del Prado** is one of the world's leading art museums. Great paintings by Diego Velázquez, El Greco, Francisco Goya, and other Spanish masters are displayed, along with major works of the Flemish and Italian schools.

Another famous attraction in Madrid is **El Rastro,** a flea market where each Sunday determined shoppers sift through an endless jumble of odds and ends. With luck, spending very little money, you may walk away with a rusty but working bicycle, a lovely antique brooch, or a fine group portrait of forgotten statesmen by an anonymous painter.

C12 Comprensión For script and answers, see p. T192.

Appropriate or inappropriate?

	0	1	2	3	4	5	6	7	8	9	10
Sí	✔		✔	✔		✔		✔			✔
No		✔			✔		✔		✔	✔	

C13 SE DICE ASÍ
Discussing whether or not something has already been done

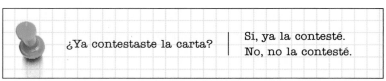

¿Ya contestaste la carta? | Sí, ya la contesté.
                          | No, no la contesté.

Use **ya** (*already*) in your questions and affirmative answers.

288   **Unidad 10**

Actividad • Sí, ya lo hice

1. Sí, ya la estudié. Y ellos la estudiaron también.
2. Sí, ya los miré. Y ellos los miraron también.

You and your friends are getting ready for a bicycle trip. Answer the following
questions about the trip saying yes, you've already done it, and your friends have
too. Use **lo, la, los,** or **las** in your answers.

3. Sí, ya lo llevé. Y ellos lo llevaron también.
4. Sí, ya los llamé. Y ellos los llamaron también.
5. Sí, ya la compré. Y ellos la compraron también.
6. Sí, ya los hice. Y ellos los hicieron también.

—¿Ya planeaste **el viaje?** ¿Y tus amigos?
—Sí, ya **lo** planeé. Y ellos **lo** planearon también.

1. ¿Ya estudiaste la ruta?
2. ¿Ya miraste los mapas?
3. ¿Ya llevaste el dinero?
4. ¿Ya llamaste a tus primos?
5. ¿Ya compraste la comida?
6. ¿Ya hiciste los bocadillos?

1. No, no la estudié.   2. No, no los miré.   3. No, no lo llevé.
4. No, no los llamé.

C15 Actividad • No, no lo hice

Now, answer the questions in C14, saying that you haven't done it.

—¿Ya planeaste **el viaje?**   —No, no **lo** planeé.

5. No, no la compré.
6. No, no los hice.

C16 Actividad • ¿Ya lo hiciste o no lo hiciste?   Answers will vary.

You and a classmate are getting ready for a trip. Ask each other:

1. ¿Preparaste las cosas?
2. ¿Compraste los billetes?
3. ¿Hiciste la maleta?
4. ¿Miraste los folletos?
5. ¿Estudiaste el mapa?
6. ¿Llamaste a tus amigos?
7. ¿Llamaste a tu papá?
8. ¿Escribiste los números de teléfono?

C17 Actividad • ¡Ya lo hice todo!

Before leaving, go over your checklist and say you already did each thing.

llamar / papá   —Ya lo llamé.

1. Ya la contesté.   2. Ya los compré.   3. Ya lo cambié.   4. Ya
la llamé.   5. Ya los compré.   6. Ya lo estudié.   7. Ya las
hice.   8. Ya lo llamé.

1. contestar / carta
2. comprar / billetes
3. cambiar / cheque
4. llamar / abuela
5. comprar / regalos
6. estudiar / mapa
7. hacer / maletas
8. llamar / taxi

C18 Actividad • ¡A escribir!

Write a list of all the things you did in preparation for a trip. Use your answers to
C17 as a guideline.

C19 Actividad • Una conversación telefónica   Free conversation.

Work with a partner. You are away on a trip and you call home. Your partner
answers the phone and asks you about your trip. Switch roles.

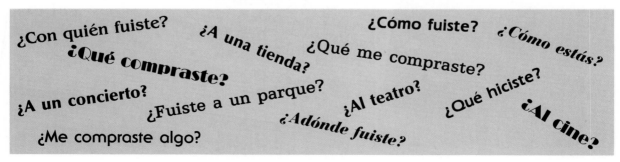

¿Con quién fuiste?   ¿A una tienda?   ¿Cómo fuiste?   ¿Cómo estás?
¿Qué compraste?   ¿Qué me compraste?
¿A un concierto?   ¿Fuiste a un parque?   ¿Al teatro?   ¿Qué hiciste?
¿Me compraste algo?   ¿Adónde fuiste?   ¿Al cine?

1 Recuerdos de Madrid

Desde Madrid, Pilar y Billy escriben postales.

Parque del Retiro, Madrid

Querida Isabel,
¿Cómo estás? Te escribo
desde Madrid. Me invitó
mi prima Marisol. ¡Es
una chica estupenda!
Mi amigo Billy también
está aquí. Llegamos ayer.
y vamos a estar una
semana en Madrid.
Hasta la próxima,
Pilar

Isabel Zaldívar
Calle Miranda
San Jua

Plaza de la Cibeles, Madrid

Queridos papá y mamá,
El sábado fui a un
partido de fútbol con
unos amigos de aquí. Tomé
muchas fotos. El domingo
fuimos al Rastro. Compré
cosas para todos. Por la
tarde fuimos al parque
del Retiro y tomamos
chocolate con churros.
Abrazos para toda la
familia, Billy

Familia Jones
88 Milan Circle
Chicago, Illinois
60665

U. S. A.

2 Actividad • ¿Es cierto o no?

Change the following sentences to make them true according to Pilar's and Billy's postcards.

1. Pilar escribe desde Sevilla.
2. Marisol es una chica estupenda.
3. Pilar y Billy llegaron la semana pasada.
4. Pilar escribe a una amiga.

5. El sábado Billy fue a un partido de fútbol.
6. Por la noche él fue al Rastro.
7. En el parque los chicos tomaron sopa.
8. Billy tomó muchas fotos.

3 Preguntas y respuestas.

Pair up with a partner. Ask each other the following questions.

1. ¿Desde dónde escribe Pilar?
2. ¿A quién escribe? Escribe a Isabel.
3. ¿Conoce Isabel a Pilar? Sí, Isabel conoce a Pilar.
4. ¿Adónde fue Billy el sábado? ¿Con quién fue?

5. ¿Adónde fue él el domingo?
6. ¿Qué compró él allí? Compró cosas para todos.
7. ¿Adónde fueron el domingo por la tarde?
8. ¿Qué tomaron después? Tomaron chocolate con churros.

Sample conversation is given.

—¿Adónde fuiste la semana pasada? —Fui a la playa.
—¿Con quién? —Con Jorge, su hermana y su prima.
—¿Qué hiciste allá? —Nadamos mucho y caminamos también.

4 Actividad • Charla

With a partner, talk about what you did last weekend, last week, and last summer.

—¿Adónde fuiste?
—¿Con quién?
—¿Qué hiciste allí?
—¿Compraste algo? ¿Qué?

el verano pasado
el fin de semana pasado
la semana pasada

5 Actividad • Postales

You're away on a trip. Write two postcards to different friends or to members of your family. Tell your friends what you did, what you saw, where you went and with whom, and what you bought during your trip.

6 Pronunciación, lectura, dictado   For script, see pp. T194–195.

1. Listen carefully and repeat what you hear.

2. The Spanish consonants **z** and **s** have the same sound. Listen, then read aloud.

cerámica   cine   gracias   cereza
enseguida   reservar   pesetas   clase
bolsillo   sol   Susana   sandía
azul   zanahoria   empezar   almorzar

3. Copy the following sentences to prepare yourself to write them from dictation.

El señor González regresó de la oficina muy cansado.
La clase de educación física no es difícil.
La señorita de los zapatos azules es muy simpática.
La excursión sale el siete de marzo.

¿LO SABES?

Let's review some important points you have learned in this unit.

SECTION A

Can you talk about what you did early this morning, yesterday, or last week? Possible answers are given.

Mention five things you did yesterday, using:

hablar   llamar   mirar   estudiar

comprar   preparar   planear   tomar

1. Ayer hablé con Ana.
2. Ayer llamé a Jorge.
3. Ayer miré televisión.
4. Ayer estudié con Rosa María.
5. Ayer compré un casete.
6. Ayer preparé tacos.

Are you able to find out if somebody did the same things you did yesterday?

Write down five questions you might ask.
Answers will vary. Ex: ¿Qué hiciste ayer?

7. Ayer planeé una excursión.
8. Ayer tomé un helado.

Using *también* and *pero*, can you talk about what you do every day and say whether you did or didn't do the same thing yesterday?

Form five sentences. Possible answers are given.

Casi siempre estudio después de comer. Hoy estudié en la escuela.
Hablo por teléfono a menudo y ayer también hablé.

SECTION B

What do you ask somebody who is just back from a trip? Answers will vary.
Ask five questions. Ex: ¿Qué tal el viaje?

Do you know how to talk about a trip you've just taken? Answers will vary.
Briefly describe to a friend what you did on your trip.
Ex: Fuimos a Segovia y vimos el museo y la catedral.

Are you able to talk about the route you took this morning going to school or this afternoon coming back home?

Did you walk? Did you take a train or a bus? What streets did you take? Did you go past any important landmarks? Possible answer is given.

Por la mañana fui a pie a la escuela. Por la tarde regresé en autobús.
Primero pasé por la Avenida Cinco de Mayo y después por la Zona Rosa. Visité el Palacio de Bellas Artes.

SECTION C

Do you know how to refer to people and things, using *lo, la, los,* and *las*?
Answer the following. Use **lo, la, los,** and **las.**

1. ¿Reservaste el billete?
2. ¿Tienes el pasaporte?
3. ¿Compraste los regalos?
4. ¿Estudiaste el mapa? Sí, lo estudié.
5. ¿Hiciste las maletas? Sí, las hice.
6. ¿Llamaste al taxi? Sí, lo llamé.

Sí, lo reservé.
Sí, lo tengo.
Sí, los compré.

Can you talk about what you've already done today?
Using **ya,** make up five sentences.

1. Ya estudié las matemáticas, pero todavía tengo que estudiar la física.
2. Ya compré la cámara para mi mamá, pero todavía tengo que comprar el regalo para papá.

VOCABULARIO

SECTION A

la **alegría** happiness
anoche last night
apuradísimo, -a in a big hurry
arreglado, -a arranged
ayer yesterday
el **billete** ticket
con una semana de anticipación a week ahead of time
creer to believe
creerlo to believe it
el **diario** diary
estar a punto de to be about to
la **excursión** excursion, pleasure trip
el **folleto** brochure
hace una hora an hour ago
hacer la maleta to pack a suitcase
la **invitación** invitation
lo it

marcar to mark
la **oficina** office
organizado, -a organized
pasado, -a last, past
la **semana pasada** last week
el **paseo** sightseeing trip
el **permiso** permission
planear to plan
querido, -a dear
regresar to return
reservar to reserve
seguro, -a sure
terminar to finish
todavía still
el **turismo** tourism
el **viaje** trip
ya already

SECTION B

antes before
caminar to walk
desde from
la **envidia** envy

¡qué envidia! what envy (I feel)! what luck!
el **estanque** pond
hasta as far as
la **moto** motorcycle
parar to stop
el **plan** plan
preguntar to ask
remar to row
sin without
sin parar without stopping
ya viene he(she) is coming

SECTION C

corto, -a short
la you (pol. sing.), her, it
las you (pl.), them
listo, -a ready
lo you (pol. sing.), him, it
los you (pl.), them
¿Qué más? What else?
el **regalo** present
la **ruta** route

You may wish to have the students read the vocabulary before each section is introduced.

ESTUDIO DE PALABRAS

1. Make a list of all the travel words in the unit vocabulary. Arrange them in meaningful groups to help you remember them—all the words about planning in one group, all the words about packing in another.
   folleto, hacer la maleta, paseo, turismo, viaje.

2. Then go through the unit list and collect all the new verbs. Verbs are the heart of your sentences—learn them well.
   creer, hacer la maleta, planear, reservar, regresar, remar, parar, terminar.

VAMOS A LEER

Antes de leer

As you read, do you say the words to yourself or move your lips? Put your finger on your lips while reading this travel brochure. If you're moving your lips, you are reading at a slower pace than you should.

¡A España!

ESPAÑA TE ESPERA SIEMPRE . . .

¡¡Viva° España!!
Valencia te brinda°
su imaginación°
con arte en una
explosión de luz,
flores y color.
Participa de° esta
imagen fascinante
y no olvides°
comer una
suculenta
PAELLA.

Las Fallas° de Valencia empiezan una semana antes de la fiesta de San José, el 19 de marzo. La primavera va a empezar y los valencianos° la saludan° con hogueras°. En cada esquina de la ciudad hay una falla y a la medianoche° del día 19, se queman° todas las fallas al mismo tiempo. Entonces la ciudad parece arder° por todas partes.

La paella, un delicioso plato original de Valencia, tiene hoy en día fama internacional. Los ingredientes básicos son arroz amarillo, pollo, mariscos° y legumbres°.

Preguntas y respuestas   For answers, see p. T196.

Answer the questions about what you have read.

1. ¿Cuándo empiezan las Fallas?
2. ¿Qué estación del año va a empezar?
3. ¿Cómo la saludan los valencianos?
4. ¿Qué hay en cada esquina de la ciudad?

5. ¿Cuándo se queman las fallas?
6. ¿Qué plato valenciano tiene fama internacional?
7. ¿Cuáles son sus ingredientes básicos?

Actividad • Un anuncio   *An ad*

Write a short ad about your city or town for a tourist brochure. Mention an important date or celebration in your town and say how it's celebrated. Talk about tourist attractions and places of interest in or near your town.

¡viva! *long live!*   **brinda** *offers*   **luz** *light*   **participa de** *share in*   **no olvides** *don't forget*   **fallas** *giant figures*
valencianos *natives of Valencia*   **la saludan** *greet it*   **hogueras** *bonfires*   **medianoche** *midnight*   **se queman** *are burned*
arder *to burn*   **mariscos** *seafood*   **legumbres** *vegetables*

294   Unidad 10

Guía turística de nuestra galaxia 📼

Folleto° imaginario para viajes del futuro.

**1. Estación interplanetaria
×32**—Amplio estacionamiento°
para su nave°—cómodos
restaurantes con la más amplia
variedad° de píldoras
alimenticias°

2. Centro comercial galáctico.
El último grito° de la moda
en trajes espaciales.

3. Museo interplanetario
—Reproducción de la primera
estación lunar—Amplio archivo°
fotográfico— Una experiencia
fascinante para toda la familia.

**4. Transbordador de la
amistad°**—Un robot
guía lo acompañará°
en una visita
inolvidable° a la
Casa-Museo "E.T."

**5. Zoológico de la Vía
Láctea°**—Una fascinante
colección de especies
animales, desde° un
monstruo de Hollywood
hasta° un elefante violeta
de Júpiter.

Actividad • Información, por favor For answers, see p. T197.

You are in charge of information at the intergalactic tourist center. Answer these
tourists' questions, giving all the information you can, according to **Guía turística.**

1. ¿Dónde puedo estacionar mi nave?
2. ¿El restaurante, por favor?
3. Necesito un traje espacial.
4. Queremos mirar fotografías.
5. ¿Dónde puedo ir con mis hijos?
6. ¿Podemos visitar la Casa-Museo "E.T."?
7. ¿La colección de animales?
8. ¡Píldoras alimenticias, por favor!

Actividad • Charla

You and your partner have just come back from a galactic trip. Talk to your
partner about the places you visited and what you saw there, and ask him or her
about the places he or she visited.

---

folleto *brochure*　**amplio estacionamiento** *ample parking*　**nave** *(space)ship*　**variedad** *variety*　**píldoras
alimenticias** *food capsules*　**el último grito** *the last word*　**archivo** *file*　**transbordador de la amistad** *friendship carrier*
lo acompañará *will accompany you*　**inolvidable** *unforgettable*　**Vía Láctea** *Milky Way*　**desde . . . hasta** *from . . . to*

El regalo

En El Paso, Daniel y su hermana deciden ir a Madrid. Deben buscar la flor° de la canción° de los mariachis°. Los chicos prenden° el televisor.

DANIEL Hoy no hay ningún° programa de España en el Canal 17. No podemos ir.

ADRIANA Pero, este programa es de México, Daniel. ¿Por qué no vamos a casa?

DANIEL ¿Crees que es una buena idea? . . . Bueno, está bien. Regresamos a México.

Al día siguiente, en México, los chicos encuentran° un programa sobre Segovia. Allí van los dos hermanos. Dan una vuelta por la ciudad, y llegan a la parte antigua°.

DANIEL ¡Qué ciudad tan bonita! ¿A ti te gusta, Adriana?

ADRIANA Me gusta mucho. Aquí, en la parte antigua, me parece estar en el pasado . . . ¡Oh, Daniel! Ahí hay un autobús para Madrid. Sale pronto°, ¿lo tomamos?

Los chicos llegan a Madrid y toman un taxi.

DANIEL A la Puerta del Sol, por favor.

TAXISTA Bien, llegamos pronto°. Ahora estamos en el centro de Madrid. Es como una rueda°, los números de las calles empiezan aquí.

Los chicos bajan° del taxi. Hay mucho tráfico y mucha gente en las calles. Pero, ¿cuál es la flor que deben encontrar, la flor de la canción de El Paso?

ADRIANA Ahora, ¿qué? ¿Por qué hicimos este viaje tan loco?

DANIEL Porque es nuestro destino y yo soy un genio.

ADRIANA Sí, sí, ya me convenciste°. ¡Daniel! ¡Mira a esa mujer!° La que está enfrente del° banco. Creo que la conozco, es . . .

DANIEL ¡Tienes razón! Es la aeromoza°, la mujer del secuestro° del vuelo 28. Debe estar en Madrid porque ese vuelo es de México a Madrid.

ADRIANA ¡Cuidado!° Si ella nos ve y nos reconoce°, puede hacer cualquier° cosa . . .

DANIEL Mira, ella va a cruzar° la calle. ¿La seguimos?°

---

flor *flower* **canción** *song* **mariachis** *Mexican band* **prenden** *they turn on* **no hay ningún** *there isn't any* **encuentran** *they find* **antigua** *old* **pronto** *soon* **rueda** *wheel* **bajan** *get out* **me convenciste** *convinced me* **mujer** *woman* **enfrente del** *in front of* **aeromoza** *flight attendant* **secuestro** *hijacking* **¡cuidado!** *be careful!* **nos reconoce** *recognizes us* **cualquier** *any* **cruzar** *to cross* **¿la seguimos?** *do we follow her?*

La aeromoza camina hasta la esquina y sube a° un coche. El chófer es un hombre°
rubio—el mismo del aeropuerto de México. ¡Es Héctor Ríos!, el cómplice° de la aeromoza.

De repente°, la aeromoza mira hacia° donde están Daniel y Adriana y grita° algo.
El coche va hacia los dos muchachos como una bala°. Un segundo° coche viene
por la derecha. Los dos vehículos chocan°.

Todo pasa tan rápido que Daniel y Adriana están paralizados. La gente se acerca°;
en pocos minutos llega la policía. El conductor del segundo coche habla con la
policía. Camina hacia Daniel y Adriana y los saluda con gran emoción. Adriana lo
reconoce inmediatamente: es el joven° guapo de El Paso.

ADRIANA	Daniel, ¡el joven de El Paso!
DANIEL	¿Qué hace él aquí?
JOVEN	¡Bienvenidos a Madrid!
DANIEL	Gracias . . . , pero, ¿quién eres tú?
JOVEN	Me llamo Omar Ramos.
ADRIANA	¿Ramos? ¿Como el piloto del vuelo 28?
JOVEN	Sí. El piloto Héctor Ramos Velázquez es mi padre. Ustedes lo ayudaron muchísimo.
DANIEL	¿Lo ayudamos? ¿Cómo?
JOVEN	Ustedes le salvaron la vida°. Salvaron la vida de mi padre.

Actividad • No es así

Correct the following statements, according to **El regalo.** For answers, see p. T197.

1. Daniel y Adriana deciden ir a Madrid para ver un programa sobre España.
2. Los hermanos toman un avión en El Paso para ir a Madrid.
3. Ellos encuentran un programa de España en El Paso.
4. En Segovia pueden ver un programa sobre México.
5. En la parte antigua de México, Adriana cree estar en el futuro.
6. Ellos no toman el tren para Madrid porque sale tarde.
7. La mujer que está enfrente del banco es la madre del piloto del vuelo 28.
8. La aeromoza camina hasta el banco y sube a un autobús.
9. El joven de El Paso es primo del piloto.
10. Daniel y Adriana salvaron la vida del tío de la aeromoza.

---

sube a *gets into* **hombre** *man* **cómplice** *accomplice* **de repente** *suddenly* **hacia** *towards* **grita** *yells* **bala** *bullet*
segundo *second* **chocan** *collide* **se acerca** *come near* **joven** *young man* **le salvaron la vida** *saved his life*

UNIDAD 11 ¡Vamos de compras!
Scope and Sequence

	BASIC MATERIAL	COMMUNICATIVE FUNCTIONS
SECTION A	¿Lo compramos? (A1) ¿Qué ropa compramos? (A8)	**Exchanging information** • Talking about differences in quality and price • Asking and saying what something is made of **Expressing attitudes and points of view** • Asking and expressing opinions
SECTION B	¡Es una ganga! (B1) El estéreo nuevo (B9)	**Exchanging information** • Discussing prices, making a bargain
SECTION C	Sección de quejas y reclamos (C1)	**Exchanging information** • Saying what you did and what you are going to do
TRY YOUR SKILLS	Pronunciation (the letters **b** and **v**) Sound-letter correspondences (the letters **b** and **v**) Dictation	
VAMOS A LEER	**Ropa para toda la familia** (naming articles of clothing in Spanish) **De compras** (what to buy in Mexico City) **El regalo** (Is the mystery solved?)	

WRITING A variety of controlled and open-ended writing activities appear in the Pupil's Edition. The Teacher's Notes identify other activities suitable for writing practice.

COOPERATIVE LEARNING Many of the activities in the Pupil's Edition lend themselves to cooperative learning. The Teacher's Notes explain some of the many instances where this teaching strategy can be particularly effective. For guidelines on how to use cooperative learning, see page T13.

GRAMMAR	CULTURE	RE-ENTRY
Comparisons with **más** and **menos** (A6) Demonstrative pronouns (A17)	Shopping in Mexico City Conversion table of clothing sizes	Demonstrative adjectives Colors The preterit of regular **-ar** verbs
Indirect objects (B5) Numbers from 100 to 1,000 (B11)	Street vendors in Spanish-speaking countries Where to find a bargain in Mexico City	Direct objects Indirect objects Numbers 0 to 100
The preterit of **-er** and **-ir** verbs (C4)	Customer service in a store	The preterit of regular **-ar** verbs The preterit of **hacer** Future expressed with **ir** + *infinitive* Direct-object pronouns

Recombining communicative functions, grammar, and vocabulary

Reading for practice and pleasure

TEACHER-PREPARED MATERIALS

Section A Magazine pictures of gift items, pictures of clothes, calculator

Section B Pictures of clothes, price tags

Try Your Skills Toy telephone

UNIT RESOURCES

Manual de actividades, Unit 11
Manual de ejercicios, Unit 11
Unit 11 Cassettes
Transparencies 27–29
Quizzes 24–27
Unit 11 Test

OBJECTIVES **To exchange information:** talk about differences in quality and price, ask and say what something is made of; **to express attitudes and points of view:** ask and express opinions

CULTURAL BACKGROUND The **Zona Rosa** in Mexico City is a charming area filled with boutiques, specialty shops, fine restaurants, and major hotels. Most stores there cater to tourists, and items are sold at fixed prices. Large department stores in Mexico City include Sears, Paris Londres, Liverpool, and Woolworth. The two largest shopping malls are **Plaza Satélite** (north of the city) and **Perisur** (south of the city).

MOTIVATING ACTIVITY Have the students list gift items from Mexico they would like to buy for real or imaginary family members and friends. Are some gifts more popular than others? Why?

A1 ¿Lo compramos?

You may wish to obtain a currency exchange table from a bank or a newspaper. The value of the **peso** in Mexico and in other countries fluctuates daily. Bring a calculator to class and, if possible, use the current rate of exchange for the **peso** when completing the activities. In cases where the numbers are very large, it may be advisable to use dollars.

Draw on the board two or three large store windows. In the "windows," tape magazine cutouts or draw pictures of the gift items mentioned in the text. Pretend to be window-shopping and tell the class: **Voy de compras.** Say the name of each item in Spanish and have the class repeat after you. Practice the words until the students can correctly identify the items.

Next, have the students assign prices in dollars to the gift items. As you write the prices on the board, comment on each by saying: **¡Es muy barato!** or **¡Es muy caro!** Continue until the students understand the adjectives **barato** and **caro.**

Then, ask the students what you should buy for your family or friends: **¿Qué puedo comprar para mi papá?** They should suggest different items. For each item suggested, respond with one of the comments from the dialog: **¡Es una preciosura! ¡No está mal! ¡Es bien lindo!** Convey the meaning of these comments by expression and gesture.

Have the students listen to the dialog as you read it aloud or play the cassette. Then have pairs of students read aloud and role-play the dialog.

A2 Actividad • ¿Es cierto o no?

Allow the students to refer to A1 as they correct the sentences. Then call on volunteers to read aloud the corrected statements.

A3 Actividad • ¡A escoger!

Ask the students to complete the activity orally and in writing. Collect the sentences and correct them.

A4 SE DICE ASÍ

To practice the expressions used to ask and express opinions, begin by pointing to an item in the "window" from A1. Say: **Me gusta el cinturón.** Then ask a student: **¿Qué te parece?** and have him or her respond using an

expression from the box. You may also wish to include the idiomatic expressions from the dialog, such as **¡Es una preciosura!** or **¡Es bien lindo!**

A5   Actividad • ¿Qué te parece?

Re-enter the demonstrative adjectives by having the students express their opinions about clothing items. **Me gustan estas botas. No me gustan aquellos guantes.**

Then have each student work with a partner and ask each other's opinion about the items in the box. Remind students that the verb **parecer** follows the same pattern as the verb **gustar.**

> ¿Qué te parecen los guantes?   ¿Te gustan los guantes?
> ¿Qué te parece esta cartera?   ¿Te gusta esta cartera?

A6   ESTRUCTURAS ESENCIALES

To introduce comparisons in Spanish, have a tall student stand up. Say: **Él/Ella es alto/a.** Now ask a taller student to stand next to the first student, and say: **Él/Ella es más alto/a que él/ella.** Then ask the students: **¿Es él/ella más o menos alto/a que él/ella?** Continue with other adjectives and examples.

> libro/grande   zapatos/nuevos   cartera/bonita

Point out that *than* is equivalent to **que** before a noun or a pronoun. Before a numeral it is equivalent to **de.** For example number 3, you may wish to ask the students to name several items in the classroom and use the construction: **cuesta/n más de** and **cuesta/n menos de.**

> El pizarrón cuesta más de veinte dólares.
> El libro de español cuesta menos de cincuenta pesos.

A7   Actividad • ¿Qué es más caro?

As a variation, have the students complete the activity, and then have them state which item costs more than fifty **pesos** and those that cost less than fifty **pesos.** Point out that **pesos** have different values in different countries.

> El cinturón cuesta menos de cincuenta pesos.
> La cartera cuesta más de cincuenta pesos.

A8   SITUACIÓN • ¿Qué ropa compramos?

Follow the same procedure as described in A1 to present the vocabulary. For additional practice, ask the students the following questions.

> 1. ¿Es tu camisa de algodón o de seda?
> 2. ¿De qué color es la falda de *(student's name)?*
> 3. ¿Tienes un abrigo de lana?
> 4. ¿Quién lleva chaqueta hoy?
> 5. ¿Es una chaqueta oscura o clara?
> 6. ¿Cuándo usas un traje de baño?

A9   Práctica • ¡A escoger!

Before completing the activity, re-enter the colors by asking the students to name the color of a classmate's clothes.

Elena tiene un suéter verde.
Los zapatos de Alicia son de color marrón.

A10 Actividad • Voy a comprar . . .

Have each student work with a partner to imagine they are going shopping. They should choose the clothes they want to buy from the list in A8. Have them discuss their opinions with their partners, using the expressions in A4.

A11 Actividad • ¡A escribir!

This activity may be completed at home or in class. Collect the conversations and correct them.

A12 ¿Sabes que . . . ?

Many countries in Spanish America such as Venezuela and Mexico, are well known for their leather shoes. When shopping for shoes in a Spanish-speaking country, it may be difficult to find your size if you need a narrow or extra-wide shoe. A great variety of shoe styles is available, but they do not offer shoes in varying widths. However, it is very easy to find shoes in small sizes that are sometimes difficult to find in the United States.

A13 Comprensión

At the store, two customers are shopping for clothes. First you'll hear their conversation with the salespeople; then you'll have to answer ten questions about what they said. Place your check mark in the row labeled **Sí** if your answer is affirmative. If it isn't, the check mark goes in the **No** row. For example, you hear: **¿Están en la tienda?** The answer is **Sí** since they're at the store. The check mark is placed in the **Sí** row.

SEÑORA	Señorita, la chaqueta verde, por favor.
VENDEDORA	Sí, señora. ¿Cuál quiere ver?
SEÑORA	La verde, a la izquierda. ¿Es de lana, no?
VENDEDORA	Sí. ¿Es para usted, señora? ¿Qué talla necesita?
SEÑORA	No, es para mi hija. Ella usa talla treinta y seis.
VENDEDORA	De lana, en talla treinta y seis, no tenemos más. ¿Quiere ver chaquetas de algodón?
SEÑORA	No, muchas gracias, señorita. Adiós.
SEÑOR	Señor, por favor.
VENDEDOR	Sí, ¿qué desea?
SEÑOR	¿Tienen camisas de seda?
VENDEDOR	Sí señor, blancas y azul claro. ¿Qué color y qué talla, por favor?
SEÑOR	Una blanca, talla treinta y nueve. ¿Cuánto cuestan?
VENDEDOR	Cien pesos.
SEÑOR	¡Cien pesos! ¡Ah, no! ¿No tienen camisas más baratas?
VENDEDOR	Sí, pero no de seda. Las de seda tienen todas el mismo precio.
SEÑOR	Son muy caras para mí. Gracias. Adiós.

1. ¿Quiere la señora una falda de lana? *no*
2. ¿Compra algo para ella? *no*

   3. ¿Necesita talla treinta y seis? *sí*
   4. ¿Quiere ella ver las chaquetas de algodón? *no*
   5. ¿Quiere el señor una camisa de seda? *sí*
   6. ¿Hay camisas de seda verdes en la tienda? *no*
   7. ¿Lleva el señor una camisa azul? *no*
   8. ¿Cuestan las camisas más de sesenta pesos? *sí*
   9. ¿Tienen todas las camisas de seda el mismo precio? *sí*
  10. ¿Compra el señor una camisa? *no*

Now check your answers. *Read each exchange again and give the correct answer.*

A14   Actividad • Charla

Have each student choose a partner to discuss their real or imaginary families, friends, sports figures, or other people. They should use **más que** and **menos que** in their conversations.

A15   SE DICE ASÍ

To practice the new structure, ask the students the following questions.

> ¿De qué es tu vestido?
> ¿De qué son tus zapatos?
> ¿Son tus pantalones de lana o de algodón?
> ¿De qué es tu camisa?

A16   Actividad • ¿Qué compraste?

Re-enter the use and the formation of the preterit of regular **-ar** verbs. Then have the students complete the activity orally and in writing.

A17   ESTRUCTURAS ESENCIALES

Before presenting the demonstrative pronouns, quickly review the demonstrative adjectives. Remind the students that they have already learned nominalization of adjectives. Point out that the demonstrative pronouns are nothing more than nominalized adjectives. Bring to class several clothing items or pictures of clothing. You will need two of each item: one should look old, worn, or outdated, the other, new and stylish.

    Have the students read the chart to themselves. Then have them repeat the demonstrative pronouns after you. Tell the students to pretend they are advising a friend what to wear to a party. Place the pair of clothing items on opposite sides of the classroom, and ask for students' advice: **¿Les gusta ese traje o aquél?** Model the response **¡Me gusta aquél!** and have the students repeat it while pointing to the item they feel is suitable. Do several examples in this manner, changing the position of the clothing items to practice the forms **éste, ése,** and **aquél.** Then go on but do not model the response—the question should be an adequate cue.

SLOWER-PACED LEARNING   As you prepare pictures or items for your presentation of the demonstrative pronouns, label them clearly with the names of the items and the correct articles **(la blusa).** Then proceed as suggested.

Unidad 11 Teacher's Notes   T203

A 18 **Actividad • No, quiero ésa**

Have each student work with a partner, to take turns playing the role of the customer and the clerk.

A 19 **Actividad • No, aquélla** 🔲

Follow the same procedure as in A18, this time having students substitute **aquél** for **ese**.

A 20 **Actividad • Conversación**

For cooperative learning, form groups of two. After each group has had a chance to ask and respond to the questions, call on groups at random to role-play the conversation.

A 21 **Comprensión** 🔲

Many customers are shopping at the store. After listening to each dialog, decide whether the form **este, ese,** and **aquel** being used are written with an accent mark or not. Then, place a check mark in the corresponding box. For example, you hear: **¿Lleva esos libros?** and the response: **No, quiero estas revistas.** The check mark is placed in the row labeled *No accent mark*, since in this conversation **esos** and **estos** are used as demonstrative adjectives, and the written accent is not needed.

1. —¿Quiere éstos?
   —Sí, compro éstos. *sí*
2. —¿Cuáles, aquéllos?
   —Sí, aquéllos a la derecha. *sí*
3. —¿Te gustan estos guantes?
   —Sí, son muy lindos. *no*
4. —¿Te parece bien éste?
   —No, ése me gusta más. *sí*
5. —¿Esta raqueta es más barata?
   —No señor, es más cara. *no*
6. —¿Y ésas?
   —Ésas están en venta. *sí*
7. —¿Le gusta a usted ése?
   —Sí, el azul. *sí*
8. —Aquellas botas son baratas, ¿no?
   —Sí, pero no me gustan. *no*
9. —¿Cuánto cuestan estas revistas?
   —¿Esas revistas? Cien pesos. *no*
10. —¿Por qué no compramos este disco?
    —Porque yo quiero este casete. *no*

Now check your answers. *Read each exchange again and give the correct answer.*

SECTION

B

OBJECTIVES **To exchange information:** discuss prices, strike a bargain

CULTURAL BACKGROUND There are many different types of stores in Mexico, each catering to a special clientele. The modern department stores

offer convenience and a wide variety of products. Specialty shops have a friendly atmosphere and frequently cater to people who live in the neighborhood. In these shops you may find some good bargains and unusual items. The markets are well known for the traditional way of shopping. Bargaining is the name of the game at the market. The Mexican government has sponsored a new style of market for tourists, many of whom are not familiar or comfortable with bargaining for souvenirs or fine jewelry. The government-sponsored markets offer Mexican goods labeled with fixed prices. Customers select the items they want and pay the amount stated.

MOTIVATING ACTIVITY After discussing the variety of shops in Mexico, ask the students to choose the kind of shopping they prefer. Do they like to bargain? At which shops do they think the best buys are found?

B1 ¡Es una ganga!

Tell the students that Marisa and her mother are in a **tienda de barrio.** Define this expression by giving examples of small shops in your area. Introduce the expression **¡Es una ganga!** by giving bargain prices of several items. **Este vestido de seda cuesta veinte dólares. ¡Es una ganga!** Explain that the verb **quedar** follows the same pattern as the verb **gustar,** and give several examples to define its meaning.

Play the cassette or read the dialog aloud as the students follow along in their books. After they have listened to the dialog, the students should tell what Marisa and her mother buy.

Next, have the students practice reading the dialog aloud. Ask them to identify the expressions used to discuss prices and bargains. Finally, have the students work in cooperative learning groups of three to role-play the dialog. Tell them they may vary the prices, the items, and so on.

B2 Preguntas y respuestas

Have the students refer to the dialog to answer the questions. Ask individuals to read the answers aloud.

B3 Actividad • Conversación

Have each student work with a partner to ask the questions and answer them. They should then report the partner's answers to the class.

B4 ¿Sabes que . . . ?

Explain to the students that when discussing a price with a salesclerk or street vendor, they must know how much they are willing to pay for an item before bargaining begins. Also, a shopper should not begin to bargain unless he or she has the intention of purchasing the item. It is considered very impolite for a customer to walk away after the price has been agreed upon.

B5 ESTRUCTURAS ESENCIALES

Have the students read the explanation to themselves about the parts of a sentence. Ask them how they might identify the indirect object of a sentence. Write several sentences on the board or a transparency, and have the students find the indirect objects. Then rewrite each sentence below the orig-

inal, replacing the indirect objects with **me, te, le, nos,** and **les.** Point out that **me, te,** and **nos** are identical to the direct-object pronouns. Point out that **le** is used for all third-person singular indirect-object pronouns and **les** for the plural. Ask the students to describe how the sentences have changed. As they answer, draw boxes for visual reinforcement as shown below.

> Marta mandó una carta a mi hermana.
> Marta le mandó una carta.
> Marta mandó una carta a sus abuelos.
> Marta les mandó una carta.

Have the students read the fourth and fifth parts of the explanation in B5. Then practice the indirect objects and indirect-object pronouns by dividing the class in half. Begin with a model sentence, and act out the situation **yo le compré un suéter.** Then cue a new indirect object: **a Natalia.** Half of the class should say the new sentence: **Yo compré un suéter para Natalia.** The other half of the class should use the indirect-object pronoun: **Yo le compré un suéter.** Continue in this manner; then have the groups switch roles so that both groups have the opportunity to use the indirect-object pronouns. Next, teach the class where the indirect-object pronouns should be positioned with the negative. Provide both oral and written examples.

SLOWER-PACED LEARNING Present the indirect-object pronouns over a period of several days. You might concentrate on the use of the pronouns one day and on their position the next.

B6   Actividad • ¿Qué les compras?

First, have the students identify the direct and indirect objects. Then have them identify the indirect-object pronouns that should be used to replace the indirect object. Finally, have them complete the activity, orally and in writing.

B7   Actividad • ¿Lo compraste?

Each student should work with a partner to complete this activity orally and in writing. Collect the papers and correct them.

ANSWERS:
1. —¿Le compraste el libro? —Sí, (No, no) le compré el libro.
2. —¿Les compraste los casetes? —Sí (No, no) les compré los casetes.
3. —¿Le compraste un regalo? —Sí, (No, no) le compré un regalo.
4. —¿Le compraste el disco? —Sí, (No, no) le compré el disco.
5. —¿Les compraste los casetes? —Sí, (No, no) les compré los casetes.
6. —¿Te compraste el suéter? —Sí, (No, no) me compré el suéter.
7. —¿Les compraste los pañuelos? —Sí, (No, no) les compré los pañuelos.
8. —¿Nos compraste los guantes? —Sí, (No, no) les compré los guantes.

B8   Comprensión

You'll hear different people talking. Put a check mark in the row labeled **no** if the second person makes an inappropriate reply, and in the row marked **sí** if the reply is appropriate. For example, you hear: **¿Qué les compraste?** and the response: **Te compré un suéter.** The check mark is

placed in the **no** row labeled 0, since the word **te,** used in the reply, doesn't correspond to the question, in which **les** is used.

1. —¿Nos vendes tu computadora?
   —Sí, le vendo la computadora a Pepe. *no*
2. —¿Me pagas el almuerzo, no?
   —¡No!, yo no te pago. Hoy pagas tú. *sí*
3. —¿Le llevas los discos a Elisa?
   —Sí, te llevo los discos ahora. *no*
4. —¿Les mandas las fotos por correo?
   —No, yo les llevo las fotos a su casa. *sí*
5. —¿Te espero en la cafetería?
   —No, mejor me esperas en la puerta. *sí*
6. —¿Rosario nos compró esas revistas?
   —Sí, me compró unos casetes. *no*
7. —¿A qué hora me esperas?
   —Te espero a las cuatro. *sí*
8. —¿Le mando esta postal a Ofelia?
   —Sí, les mando una. *no*
9. —¿Cuándo les escribes a tus primos?
   —Tus primos nunca nos escriben. *no*
10. —¿Por qué no me vendes esos discos?
    —Porque son mis discos y no los vendo. *sí*

Now check your answers. *Read each exchange again and give the correct answer.*

B9 SITUACIÓN • El estéreo nuevo

Introduce the verb **ahorrar** before presenting the situation. Have the students listen, as you play the cassette or read aloud Raúl's solution.
To check comprehension, you may wish to ask the following questions.

1. ¿Qué quiere comprar Raúl?
2. ¿Cuánto cuesta el estéreo?
3. ¿Por qué Raúl no quiere ahorrar veinticinco pesos por semana?
4. ¿Por cuánto tiempo tiene que ahorrar, si ahorra doscientos pesos por mes?

B10 Actividad • ¡A escoger!

Have the students refer to B9 to complete the activity. Ask volunteers to read aloud the completed sentences.

B11 ESTRUCTURAS ESENCIALES

Prepare flashcards to practice the numbers 100 to 1,000. Say the number aloud as you show the numeral; then ask the students to repeat. You or a volunteer may also dictate numbers for writing practice.
Read aloud the explanation to the students. Then ask questions that require the students to respond with a date. **¿Cuándo llegó Cristóbal Colón a América? ¿En qué año terminó la Primera Guerra Mundial? ¿En qué año van a salir de la secundaria?**

B12 Actividad • Precios

Review the names of the items pictured and their prices with the class. Then

divide the class into cooperative learning groups of two and have them complete the activity. Have one student play the role of a customer and ask the salesclerk: **¿Cuánto cuesta esta(e) . . . ?** Have the second student play the role of the salesclerk, and respond with the price as written.

B 13 Actividad • ¡A escribir!

After the students have written the numbers, call on volunteers to read them aloud. Call on students at random to write the numbers on the board. Have the students correct any errors.

B 14 Actividad • No es así

B 15 ¿Sabes que . . . ?

Many tourists enjoy shopping in the picturesque villages and towns near Mexico City, that are well known for their handicrafts. Toluca, the capital of the state of Mexico, has a popular market on Fridays. A wide selection of regional crafts is available there, including stoneware and clay pottery, copper, metalwork, jewelry, silver, and baskets. Leather goods, textiles, and ceramics are popular purchases in Cuernavaca. Puebla's famous Talavera tiles and onyx jewelry attract shoppers from all over the world. Many of the small towns in the states of Mexico and Puebla feature the quaint "Tree of Life" candelabrum and other unique pottery items.

B 16 SE DICE ASÍ

Before class, prepare pictures of several clothing items and make price tags for them. Have the students read to themselves the expressions in the chart. For practice in asking prices, tell students to imagine that they are shopping with a friend. One of them can easily find the price tag on every item, but the other cannot and asks what the price is. Then have them discuss the price, using the expressions in the chart.

B 17 Actividad • ¿Lo compro o no?

Form cooperative learning groups of two or three. Have one student play the role of the salesclerk and the others play the roles of the customers. Using the expressions in B16 and the box in B17, the customers should select what they want to buy. Have the salesclerk help the customers make decisions. Call on groups to role-play their conversations for the class.

B 18 Actividad • ¡A escribir!

Have each student complete this activity in class or at home. Collect and correct the conversations.

B 19 Comprensión

> You'll hear different people talking about their purchases. Put a check mark in the row marked **Sí** if they found a good bargain. Check **No** if it costs too much. For example, you hear: **El suéter cuesta ocho dólares** and the response: **No vas a encontrar otro más barato.** Check the row labeled **Sí**, because it is a good bargain. The person would not find a cheaper one at another store.

1. —¿Cuánto cuesta la cámara?
   —Es muy barata. *Sí*
2. —Llevo la cartera.
   —No es una ganga, pero me gusta. *No*
3. —¡Qué bicicleta tan bonita!
   —Es muy cara. *No*
4. —Este traje vale cien dólares.
   —Es de muy buena calidad. Es una ganga. *Sí*
5. —La blusa es de seda.
   —Es demasiado cara. *No*
6. —Quiero llevar el vestido por cincuenta dólares.
   —No vale tanto. *No*
7. —A Clara le gusta el cinturón de cuero.
   —A siete dólares, es un regalo. *Sí*
8. —Las botas son muy bonitas.
   —Son muy baratas, también. *Sí*
9. —Este plato de cerámica cuesta cinco dólares.
   —No va a encontrar otro más barato. *Sí*
10. —Los guantes cuestan diez dólares.
    —No valen tanto. No pago más de cinco dólares. *No*

Now check your answers. *Read each exchange again and give the correct answer.*

B 20 **Actividad • ¿Qué precio tiene?**

For cooperative learning, form groups of two. Each group will participate in the flea market. The students may also enjoy bringing in clothing, records, or other items for the flea market. Have the students use the current rate of exchange to label the items in **pesos.**

B 21 **Actividad • En venta**

Continue working in the cooperative learning groups formed in B20. Have the students include the names of the items they are selling and a description of each item. **Suéter de lana. Talla 36. Muy buena calidad.**

B 22 **Actividad • ¿Lo llevo o no?**

Have the students take turns being the customers and the vendors. Circulate among the students and ask questions such as **¿Para quién compras** *(name of the item)***? ¿Cuánto pagaste por esto? ¿Cuántas cosas compraste?**

B 23 **Actividad • Compras y ventas**

Have the cooperative learning groups compare their purchases and sales using a chart similar to the one in the book. The groups that made the most money and those that bought the most for the least amount of money will be the winners.

SECTION C

OBJECTIVES **To exchange information:** say what you did and what you are going to do

CULTURAL BACKGROUND In the older section of Mexico City, areas are dedicated to selling one specific item. For example, near Alameda Park and

the Mexico City Cathedral are two or three streets filled with shoe stores. Behind the Zócalo, a complete area sells only baby items and children's clothing. There is also an area of approximately fifty stores where you find only wedding gowns and christening gowns.

MOTIVATING ACTIVITY   Ask the students to comment on what types of problems a customer service representative must solve. What happens when a customer returns an item to a store? What must a customer do in order to exchange something?

C1   Sección de quejas y reclamos

Explain to the students that the **Sección de quejas y reclamos** is the place in a department store where people go to complain or return items they do not want. Then introduce the word **cumpleaños** by giving the birthdays of several famous people. Ask the students the dates of their own birthdays. Bring in a receipt and an order form to introduce the words **recibo** and **pedido.**

Before class, write on the board or a transparency true-or-false statements about the dialog, such as the following.

1. El estéreo que compró el Sr. Gómez no llegó.
2. El Sr. Gómez llamó por teléfono treinta veces.
3. El Sr. Gómez subió a la oficina del segundo piso.

Allow the students to read the statements to themselves. As you play the cassette or read the dialog aloud, the students should indicate on a separate sheet of paper whether the statements are true or false. Have them listen to the dialog a second time to confirm their answers. Ask the students to correct the false statements.

Now ask individuals which statements they have corrected. If classmates disagree with the answers, have the students open their books and read the dialog silently until they find the answers. Once all the answers have been given, have the students read aloud and role-play the dialog.

CHALLENGE   Rather than distribute the list of true-or-false statements, ask the students information questions.

¿Qué pidió el Sr. Gómez?
¿Qué día es?
¿Cuántas veces habló por teléfono el Sr. Gómez?

C2   Actividad • ¡A escoger!

Have the students complete this activity in writing in class or for homework. Ask volunteers to write the sentences on the board. Ask those students to correct any errors they find. Have students exchange sentences and correct each other's work.

C3   Actividad • Para completar

The students should complete the activity orally and in writing. They may refer to the dialog in C1 if necessary.

C4   ESTRUCTURAS ESENCIALES

To present the preterit of **-er** and **-ir** verbs, follow the procedure as suggested in Unit 10, A6, page T183. Then read aloud the explanation to the students.

C5 Actividad • En la feria de la clase 🔲

Have the students complete the conversation, using the preterit of the verb **vender.** Then call on volunteers to role-play the conversation.

C6 Actividad • Quejas 🔲

Have the students follow the model to complete the activity. For writing practice, have them write complete sentences.

C7 Comprensión 🔲

Two friends are talking about a letter one of them received. First, you'll hear their entire conversation. Then, their conversation will be replayed line by line. After listening to each line, decide whether the **present tense** or the **preterit** is used, and place your check mark accordingly. For example, you hear: **¿Tú saliste con tu hermano ayer, no?** and the response: **Sí, fuimos al cine con unos chicos.** The check mark is placed in the row labeled **preterit** since the preterit tense is used.

TERESA ¿Sabes de quién es esta carta? *present*
CARLOS No, ¿por qué? ¡Oh! Llegó carta de Costa Rica, ¿no? ¿Recibiste carta de tu prima? *preterit*
TERESA Sí, ¡por fin Isabel decidió escribir! *preterit*
CARLOS ¿Viene ella para las vacaciones? *present*
TERESA No, no puede. Tiene mucho que hacer, tiene que preparar unos exámenes. *present*
CARLOS Pero ella prometió venir este año . . . ¿Tú le escribiste? ¿Contestaste su carta? *preterit*
TERESA No, no le escribí. *preterit*
        ¿Por qué no le escribes tú? *present*
CARLOS ¿Y si le escribimos una carta los dos? *present*
TERESA ¡Buena idea!

Now check your answers. *Read each exchange again and give the correct answers.*

C8 Actividad • ¿Qué pasó?

Before completing the activity, re-enter the preterit of regular **-ar** verbs. Then, for cooperative learning, form groups of two. Have the students complete the conversation, using the verbs in the box. Call on groups at random to role-play the conversation for the class.

SLOWER-PACED LEARNING Provide the infinitive of the verb for each of the spaces. Ask the students to complete the conversation by changing the verb into the correct preterit form.

C9 Actividad • ¡A escribir!

SLOWER-PACED LEARNING Provide cues for the students to use as a guide in writing what happened to Sr. Gómez. Students may also refer to C8.

C10 Actividad • Charla

After the students have completed the activity as directed, call on students at random to role-play the following situations:

You are returning a dress you bought because it's too large. You don't have the receipt.

You bought a man's bathing suit two days ago. When you opened the box, you had a woman's bathing suit instead. The customer service representative asks you to go to the clothing department.

You received a gift in a box that had the name of the store on it. You would like to exchange the gift. However, the clerk claims that the item is not from that store.

C11 SE DICE ASÍ

Re-enter the preterit of the verb **hacer** and the future tense of the verb **ir a** + *infinitive* forms. Have the students read the expressions in the chart to themselves. Ask the students what expression they would use if they wanted to know about something in the past. Then ask the students to select the expression with the verb **hacer** that they would use if they wanted to know about what their friends are going to do in the future.

C12 Actividad • Charla

Have each student work with a partner. Have them discuss what they have already done and what they are planning to do. They may use the expressions in the box as a guide.

ANSWERS:
1. —¿Corriste? —Sí, ya corrí. —No, voy a correr después.
2. —¿Caminaste? —Sí, ya caminé. —No, voy a caminar después.
3. —¿Le hablaste a tus amigos? —Sí, ya les hablé. —No, les voy a hablar después.
4. —¿Bailaste? —Sí, ya bailé. —No, voy a bailar después.
5. —¿Fuiste a la tienda? —Sí, ya fui. —No, voy a ir después.
6. —¿Escribiste? —Sí, ya escribí. —No, voy a escribir después.
7. —¿Compraste algo? —Sí, ya compré algo. —No, voy a comprar algo después.
8. —¿Estudiaste? —Sí, ya estudié. —No, voy a estudiar después.
9. —¿Comiste? —Sí, ya comí. —No, voy a comer después.
10. —¿Fuiste al parque? —Sí, ya fui. —No, voy a ir después.

C13 Actividad • La fiesta

Re-enter the direct-object pronouns. Have the students respond to the questions in C13, by replacing direct objects with direct-object pronouns whenever possible.

—¿Ya escribiste las invitaciones?
—Sí, ya las escribí.

ANSWERS:
1. Sí, ya decidí a quién invitar./No, voy a decidir a quién invitar después.
2. Sí, ya decidí el día de la fiesta./No, voy a decidir el día de la fiesta después.
3. Sí, ya hice la lista de invitados./No, voy a hacer la lista de invitados después.
4. Sí, ya escribí las invitaciones./No, voy a escribir las invitaciones después.
5. Sí, ya los llamé a todos./No, los voy a llamar a todos después.

6. Sí, ya compré la comida./No, voy a comprar la comida después.
7. Sí, ya mandé las invitaciones./No, voy a mandar las invitaciones después.
8. Sí, ya recibí los regalos./No, voy a recibir los regalos después.

C14 ## Actividad • ¡A escribir!

CHALLENGE Have the students write a paragraph describing what they did during the day. Tell them to include details, such as the time and the place. Also have them write a paragraph about what they plan to do the following day, using **ir a** + *infinitive* when necessary.

C15 ## Actividad • Charla

For cooperative learning, form groups of two or three. Have students discuss what they did last weekend and what they will do the following weekend. They may use the questions as a guide in their conversation. Then call on students from each group to report to the class.

C16 ## Comprensión

Two friends are talking about a party they're planning to attend. First, you'll hear their entire conversation. Then their conversation will be replayed line by line. After listening to each line, decide whether the **preterit tense** or the **future tense** is being used, and place your check mark accordingly. For example, you hear: **¿Vas a ir a casa de Raquel, ¿no?** and the response: **Sí, voy a ir el sábado, ¿y tú?** Since the sentence is referring to a time in the future, the check mark is placed in the row labeled **future.**

ARTURO Piedad, ¿recibiste tú la invitación de Raquel? *preterit*
PIEDAD Yo no, pero ella le mandó una invitación a mi hermano, y me invitó a mí también. *preterit*
ARTURO Entonces, tú vas a ir a la fiesta, ¿no? *future*
PIEDAD Sí, claro. ¿A cuántas personas invitó? *preterit*
ARTURO Raquel mandó como treinta invitaciones. Invitó a todo el mundo: a los chicos de la clase, a sus primos, a otros amigos . . . *preterit*
PIEDAD ¡Treinta personas! ¡Cuánta gente! No vamos a poder bailar. *future*
ARTURO Pero, sí, ¿por qué no? En el jardín. ¿Y tú le vas a llevar un regalo? *future*
PIEDAD Sí, ya le compré unos casetes, ¿y tú? *preterit*
ARTURO Yo también.
PIEDAD ¿Tú también le compraste casetes? *preterit*
ARTURO ¡Sí!, y Raquel va a tener música para escuchar mañana, tarde y noche . . . *future*

Now check your answers. *Read each exchange again and give the correct answer.*

C17 ## Actividad • ¡A escribir!

As a variation, ask the students to imagine they are living in the year 2500. They should write about what they did last weekend and what they will do the following weekend. Allow time for the students to question their classmates and complete the chart. Then have the students report their findings to the class.

OBJECTIVE   To recombine communicative functions, grammar, and vocabulary

CULTURAL BACKGROUND   In Spanish-speaking countries, the relation between the salesperson and the customer is more formal than in the United States. There, one expects the salesperson to be courteous, willing to help, and attentive. In neighborhood stores and small boutiques however, the atmosphere is friendlier. After a person has been a regular client, credit may be extended and merchandise held.

1

El cliente y el empleado

For cooperative learning, form groups of two. Have each group bring to class a few items to use while role-playing the dialog. Allow students time to practice their dialogs before calling on groups to role-play for the class.

2

Actividad • ¡A escribir!

Have the students write a summary of the conversation they had in Skills 1. Have the students who played the role of the customer write their summary from the customer's point of view. The students who played the role of salesclerk should write their summary from his or her point of view.

3

Actividad • Conversación

Have each student work with a partner to ask and answer the questions. Then call on individuals to report their partners' responses.

4

Actividad • Talleres gráficos

Have students take a few minutes to examine each cartoon. Ask them to give some information about each illustration: **¿Quién está en la primera ilustración? ¿Qué le pasó al muchacho en el dibujo dos?** Next, have the students select the best caption for each cartoon. Call on individuals to read aloud their captions.

CHALLENGE   Have the students make up original cartoons. They may use magazine pictures or illustrate the cartoons themselves.

5

Actividad • Quejas

Bring a toy telephone to class for the students to use to role-play the telephone conversation. Have the students refer to the conversation in C1, page 314, as a guide.

6

Actividad • ¡A escribir!

Have the students include the price of each item they purchased. They should write out the number: $13.00 **(trece dólares).**

7

Actividad • Charla

For further practice, ask the students to recall some pleasant experiences they have had in class. Have the students sit in a circle and complete the following sentences.

　　La mejor experiencia de esta clase fue cuando . . .
　　A causa de esta clase, voy a . . .

Have each student complete both sentences. When everyone has had the opportunity to respond, continue the conversation in Spanish.

8   **Pronunciación, lectura, dictado**

1. Listen carefully and repeat what you hear.
The sound of **g**: In Spanish when the letter **g** is followed by **e** or **i,** it is pronounced like the *h* in the English words *hen* and *him*. Listen to the following words and repeat.

> geografía   jardín   gente   naranja   abajo   Argentina

The sound of **j**: The Spanish letter **j** sounds like the *h* in the English words *hit* and *hut*. Listen to the following words and repeat.

> abajo   equipaje   jueves   José

2. Listen, and then read aloud.
To practice the sounds of **b** and **v** in Spanish, listen to the following words and sentences and repeat.

> vaso   bizcocho   invitación   venir   barato   favorito   llevar
> Ellos vivieron en Venezuela por veintinueve años.
> Le escribimos muchas veces pero nunca recibimos respuesta.

SLOWER-PACED LEARNING   The sound of **b** and **v**: In Spanish the letters **b** and **v** are pronounced exactly alike. Both sound like the *b* in the English word *boy*. When either consonant comes between vowels, it has a weaker sound than it does when beginning a word. Never pronounce these consonants like English *v*. Listen and repeat.

> bordada   vestido   blusa   voz
> vivir   aventura   corbata   abrigo

3. Write the following sentences from dictation. First listen to the sentence as it is read to you. Then you will hear the sentence again in short segments, with a pause after each segment to allow you time to write. Finally you will hear the sentence a third time so that you may check your work. Let's begin.

> Necesito *(pause)* un traje de baño *(pause)* para el verano.
> Jorge es *(pause)* un genio *(pause)* en biología.
> Julio dejó *(pause)* su tarjeta de crédito *(pause)* en la caja.

¿LO SABES?

SECTION A   For the first exercise, have the students write the questions they would ask in the **¿Lo sabes?** section of their notebooks. Then have them close their books and show that they can express their opinions by writing responses to the questions.

   After the students have completed the next three exercises, have them work in pairs to make up short dialogs in which they discuss cloth-

ing, sizes, and prices and make comparisons. In their dialogs, have them use **más** . . . **que, menos** . . . **que,** and demonstrative pronouns. The dialogs should take place between a salesclerk and a client in a department store or shopping mall.

> —Perdón señor. ¿Cuánto cuestan estos pantalones?
> —¿Éstos?
> —No, aquéllos.
> —Ésos cuestan veinticinco dólares.
> —¿Son más caros que los jeans?
> —Sí, los jeans cuestan veintidós dólares.
> —Está bien. Llevo los jeans. Gracias.

SECTION B

For the first exercise, have the students include the phrases and responses in their notebooks. Then have the students read their sentences and phrases aloud. For the second exercise, the students may prefer to name imaginary gifts and people. You might also ask the students to include the reasons for giving certain gifts to certain people.

SECTION C

For the first exercise, have the students write the phrases in their notebooks. Then call on volunteers to read them aloud.

Ask the students to work with a partner to complete the second and third exercises. Have them discuss what they did last summer and their plans for next summer.

VOCABULARIO

Juego de vocabulario. Have a student call out a word in Spanish. The next student must then say a word that begins with the last letter of the word just called out. Continue in this manner. If a student cannot think of a word, then he or she must drop out of the game. To ensure that students continue listening once they have been eliminated, have them write down the words their classmates call out. Call on them periodically to verify that the words suggested by their classmates fit the required spelling pattern.

ESTUDIO DE PALABRAS

Explain to the students that many words and expressions in Spanish are formed by adding **de: traje de baño, ir de compras.** Make a list of new words or expressions and ask the students to identify them.

> vestido de novia
> pantalones de vestir
> máquina de escribir
> estar de vacaciones

VAMOS A LEER

OBJECTIVE   To read for practice and pleasure

Antes de leer

Have the students complete this activity orally and in writing. Then continue with the reading selection.

ROPA PARA TODA LA FAMILIA

Have the students look at the illustrations and read the advertisements silently. Ask questions to check comprehension. Then play the cassette or read the advertisements aloud as the students follow along in their books. You may ask the students which item they would buy. Have them give their reasons, such as **Es de muy buena calidad.** or **Es muy barato.**

¡A escribir!

After the students have written the advertisements, display them in the classroom.

DE COMPRAS EN MÉXICO

Play the cassette or read aloud the selection as the students follow along in their books. You may wish to pause after the second paragraph to ask questions. Then continue with the rest of the selection.

Actividad • Para completar

Have the students complete the sentences in class or at home. Then call on individuals to read the answers aloud.

EL REGALO

This is the final episode of the selection. Ask the students how they would like it to end. How do they think it will end? Then play the cassette or read aloud **El regalo.** For cooperative learning, form groups of three to role-play the dialog. Then call on individuals from each group to present the dialog to the class.

Preguntas y respuestas

Have the students answer the questions orally. Remind the students to provide reasons that support their answers for sentences 2, 4, and 6.

Actividad • Charla

After the students have had time to discuss the story, call on individuals to retell the story.

Actividad • ¿Quieres cambiar la historia de Daniel y Adriana?

For homework, have the students rewrite the ending of **El regalo.** Collect and correct the papers. Have volunteers read their endings to the class.

¡Vamos de compras!

Do you like to shop? In Spanish-speaking countries, shopping can be a wonderful adventure. For very little money, you can often find beautiful clothing, handicrafts, and gifts. In the larger stores, the merchandise usually has price tags and the prices are fixed, but that's not the case in the public markets or in small shops. There you can watch lively scenes of *regateo* (bargaining), and try bargaining yourself.

In this unit you will:

SECTION A	make comparisons . . . talk about differences in quality and price
SECTION B	discuss prices . . . bargain
SECTION C	say what you did . . . talk about future plans
TRY YOUR SKILLS	use what you've learned
VAMOS A LEER	read for practice and pleasure

SECTION A

making comparisons . . . talking about differences in quality and price

*The **Palacio de Hierro** is one of the great old department stores in Mexico City. As the city grew, the store opened branches in shopping centers on the outskirts. Let's visit the super-modern **Palacio de Hierro** in **Perisur,** a shopping center on the **Periférico,** the freeway that encircles the ever-growing metropolis.*

A1   ¿Lo compramos? 📼

SEÑORA	Señorita, por favor.
VENDEDORA	¿Qué desea, señora?
SEÑORA	Ese plato de cerámica, por favor.
VENDEDORA	¿Cuál, el pequeño o el grande?
SEÑORA	Los dos . . . Este plato es más grande que ése, pero cuesta menos, ¿por qué?
VENDEDORA	El más pequeño está hecho a mano. El grande es una imitación. No es de cerámica, es de plástico.
SEÑORA	¡Oh, no! Yo quiero uno de cerámica, pero más barato que éste. ¿Y ése de allá?
VENDEDORA	Cuesta igual que el de cerámica.
SEÑORA	¡Oh! ¿Valen lo mismo? Muchas gracias.

EMILIO	¿Qué te parece, Diego? ¿Qué cinturón llevamos?
DIEGO	No sé, pero a mí me gusta más el oscuro. Es más largo y más bonito que el claro.
EMILIO	El claro no me gusta nada. El oscuro está bien, ¿no?
DIEGO	No está mal, pero es más caro que el otro.
EMILIO	¡No importa! Es bien lindo y es de cuero.

CLARA	¡Mira esta blusa! Es una preciosura. Es de algodón. Está bordada a mano. ¿La compro?
MARIANA	¡Buena idea! Voy a preguntar el precio. Por favor, señorita, ¿cuánto vale esta blusa en dólares?
VENDEDORA	Veinte dólares, señorita.
CLARA	Bueno, está bien. ¿Puedo pagar con tarjeta de crédito?
VENDEDORA	Sí, cómo no. En la caja, por favor.

1. La señora quiere ver unos platos de cerámica. 2. Ella quiere ver los dos platos. 3. El plato pequeño es más caro. 4. El plato grande es una imitación. 5. El plato grande es de plástico. 6. A Diego le gusta el cinturón más oscuro. 7. El cinturón claro es más barato que el oscuro. 8. Mariana no sabe el precio de la blusa.

A2   Actividad • ¿Es cierto o no?

Correct the following sentences to make them agree with the dialog in A1. Some of them are correct already.

1. La señora quiere ver unos platos de plástico.
2. Ella quiere ver el plato pequeño.
3. El plato pequeño es más barato.
4. El plato grande está hecho a mano.
5. El plato grande es de cerámica.
6. A Diego le gusta el cinturón más claro.
7. El cinturón claro es más pequeño que el oscuro.
8. Mariana sabe el precio de la blusa.
9. La blusa vale cincuenta dólares.
10. Clara no puede usar su tarjeta de crédito.

9. La blusa vale veinte dólares. 10. Clara puede usar su tarjeta de crédito.

A3   Actividad • ¡A escoger!

Choose the best option to complete the following sentences according to ¿Lo compramos?

1. La señora quiere comprar
   • un plato de cerámica.   • un cinturón.   • una blusa.
2. El plato pequeño cuesta más que
   • el grande.   • el de cerámica.   • el cinturón.
3. El cinturón oscuro es
   • más barato.   • más caro.   • una imitación.
4. Ellos van a llevar
   • unos platos.   • una blusa.   • un cinturón.
5. El cinturón es de
   • plástico.   • cuero.   • algodón.
6. A Clara le gusta
   • una blusa bordada.   • un cinturón.   • un plato de cerámica.
7. La blusa es de
   • plástico.   • algodón.   • cuero.
8. Clara dice que va a pagar
   • con un cheque.   • con dinero.   • con tarjeta de crédito.

A4   SE DICE ASÍ
Asking and expressing opinions

| —Y a ti, ¿qué te parece? (¿qué crees?) (¿qué piensas?) | ¡Buena idea! ¡Está(n) bien! No está(n) mal ... | (It's a) good idea! It's (They're) all right! It's not (They're not) bad ... |
| —Y a usted, ¿qué le parece? (¿qué cree?) (¿qué piensa?) | Me gusta(n) más ... No me gusta nada. No sé. No sé, pero ... | I like it (them) more ... I don't like it at all. I don't know. I don't know, but ... |

Actividad • ¿Qué te parece? Answers will vary.

You go shopping with a friend. Ask each other's opinion about what you're buying. Then write down your conversation.

—¿Qué te parece esta raqueta?

—¿Qué crees?

—¿Qué piensas?

• Está bien.

• No está mal.

• No sé, pero . . .

• Me gusta más . . .

A6 **ESTRUCTURAS ESENCIALES**
Comparisons with **más** *and* **menos**

1. In Spanish, to make comparisons with adjectives, use the following formula:

más **menos** + adjective + **que**	*more* *less* + *adjective* + *than*

El cinturón oscuro es **más** bonito **que** el claro.
The dark belt is more attractive than the light one.

El plato de plástico es **menos** caro **que** el de cerámica.
The plastic plate is less expensive than the ceramic one.

2. **Que** is the equivalent of *than* in English. It can be followed by a noun or a subject pronoun.
Compro menos ropa **que tú.** *I buy less clothing than you.*
Tú eres más alto **que yo.** *You are taller than I.*

3. Before a number or an expression of quantity, use **de** instead of **que.**
Cuesta **más de** ochenta pesos. *It costs more than eighty pesos.*
Cuesta **menos de** diez dólares. *It costs less than ten dollars.*

A7 Actividad • ¿Qué es más caro? Answers will vary.

You are at the store. Compare prices. (Use your own judgment in determining whether the first item is more or less expensive than the second item.)

cinturón / cartera —El cinturón es más barato que la cartera.
—La cartera es más cara que el cinturón.

1. zapatos / botas
2. taza / plato
3. guantes / pañuelos
4. discos / casetes

5. revistas / libros
6. cinturón / blusa
7. raqueta / bate

8. estéreo / televisión
9. tartas / pan
10. fresas / uvas

SITUACIÓN • ¿Qué ropa compramos?

abrigo

chaqueta de lana

suéter

calcetines

jeans

corbata

camisa

saco

pantalones

traje

sombrero

zapatos

vestido de algodón

falda

pañuelo de seda

blusa

traje de baño

A9 Práctica • ¡A escoger!

Choose the best option to complete these sentences according to the window display in A8.

1. La chaqueta es de
   • lana. • algodón. • seda.
2. La falda está
   • al lado de los zapatos. • a la derecha del vestido. • entre los pañuelos y las blusas.
3. Los jeans están
   • debajo del sombrero. • a la izquierda de la corbata. • detrás del traje de baño.
4. Hay pañuelos de seda de color
   • verde claro. • amarillo oscuro. • azul y blanco.
5. Las camisas son
   • blancas. • azules. • verde claro.
6. Venden vestidos de
   • seda. • lana. • algodón.
7. Los calcetines están
   • cerca de la corbata. • detrás del sombrero. • al lado del suéter.
8. Venden zapatos de color
   • verde oscuro. • marrón. • verde claro.

A10 Actividad • Voy a comprar . . .

You have some money to spend on clothes. Decide what you want to buy for yourself in the store, based on what you see in A8. After making your choices, discuss them with a classmate.

Actividad • ¡A escribir!

Write the conversation you had with your classmate in A10. Mention what you are going to buy and write about what your friend is going to buy also.

A 12 ¿Sabes que . . . ?

You want to try on one of those sweaters? **¿Qué talla necesitas?** *What size do you need?* In Spanish-speaking countries, clothing sizes are marked in the metric system. Find your sizes in the following tables and write them down where you can use them when you travel.

Tallas para señoras						
Vestidos, Trajes y Abrigos						
Métrico:	36	38	40	42	44	46
EE.UU.:	8	10	12	14	16	18
Blusas y Suéteres						
Métrico:	40 42 44 46 48 50 52					
EE.UU.:	32 34 36 38 40 42 44					
Zapatos						
Métrico:	35 35 36 37 38 38 38½ 39 40					
EE.UU.:	5 5½ 6 6½ 7 7½ 8 8½ 9					

Tallas para señores						
Trajes, Suéteres y Abrigos						
Métrico:	44 46 48 50 52 54 56					
EE.UU.:	34 36 38 40 42 44 46					
Camisas						
Métrico:	36 37 38 39 40 41 42					
EE.UU.:	14 14½ 15 15½ 16 16½ 17					
Zapatos						
Métrico:	39 40 41 42 43 43 44 44 45					
EE.UU.:	7 7½ 8 8½ 9 9½ 10 10½ 11					

A 13 Comprensión   For script and answers, see p. T202.

Listen to the conversation, then check **Sí** or **No.**

	0	1	2	3	4	5	6	7	8	9	10
Sí	✔			✔		✔			✔	✔	
No		✔	✔		✔		✔	✔			✔

A 14 Actividad • Charla

A new student enrolled in your class today. He or she doesn't know your home, family, friends, or hobbies. Using **más que** and **menos que,** talk about brothers, sisters, friends, sports figures, movies, records, songs. . . .

Ex.: Mi hermano es más delgado que yo, pero es menos inteligente que yo. Mi amiga es más alta que tú.

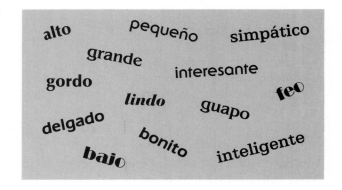

alto   pequeño   simpático   grande   interesante   gordo   lindo   guapo   feo   delgado   bonito   inteligente   bajo

SE DICE ASÍ
Asking and saying what something is made of

unos trajes **de** lana	*some wool suits* (suits of wool)
una blusa **de** seda	*a silk blouse* (blouse of silk)

To say what something is made of, use **de** + the noun naming the material.
To find out what something is made of, ask: **¿De** qué es (son)?

A 16 Actividad • ¿Qué compraste? Answers will vary.

Yesterday you went shopping. Say you bought the items listed, adding a phrase
to show what material each is made of.

un abrigo   —Ayer compré un abrigo de lana.

1. una blusa de seda/algodón   **3.** una camisa de seda/algodón   **5.** unos zapatos de cuero
2. unos calcetines de lana/seda   **4.** una cartera de cuero   **6.** una chaqueta de lana/de cuero

A 17 ESTRUCTURAS ESENCIALES   Illustrate the pronouns using classroom situations: "Este libro y
Demonstrative pronouns   aquel bolígrafo" (pointing to a book and a pen on a student's
desk).

¿Un traje?		**éste / ése / aquél.**	*this / that* (one).
¿Una falda?		**ésta / ésa / aquélla.**	
¿Unos zapatos?	Llevo	**éstos / ésos / aquéllos.**	*I'll take*
¿Unas camisas?		**éstas / ésas / aquéllas.**	*these / those.*

In Unit 9 you began to use demonstrative adjectives. Demonstrative pronouns are the same
words, with the nouns deleted. But when you write them as pronouns, add written accents.

	adjective	*noun*	*pronoun*
	este	traje ⟶	**éste.**
Llevo	esa	camisa ⟶	**ésa.**
	aquel	pañuelo ⟶	**aquél.**

A 18 Actividad • No, quiero ésa

The customer never wants what the clerk suggests. Play the role of the customer.
Work with a partner. Switch roles.

—¿Quiere **esta** blusa?

—No, quiero **ésa.**

traje	pantalones	camisas	platos	cinturón	zapatos
cartera	suéter	maleta	libro	revistas	calcetines

¿Quiere este traje? —No, ése./¿Quiere estos pantalones? No, ésos./¿Quiere estas camisas? —No, ésas./¿Quiere estos platos?
No, ésos./¿Quiere este cinturón? No, ése./¿Quiere estos zapatos? No, ésos.

¿Quiere esta cartera? No, ésa. ¿Quiere este suéter? No, ese. ¿Quiere esta maleta? No, ésa. ¿Quiere este libro? No, ése.
¿Quiere estas revistas? No, ésas. ¿Quiere estos calcetines? No, ésos.

A19 Actividad • No, aquélla 📼

Go over the items in A18, following the model given below.

—¿Lleva **esos** pañuelos?

¿Lleva ese traje? —No, aquél.
¿Lleva esos pantalones? —No, aquéllos.
¿Lleva esas camisas? —No, aquéllas.
¿Lleva esos platos? —No, aquéllos. ¿Lleva ese cinturón? —No, aquél.
¿Lleva esos zapatos? —No, aquéllos.

—No, llevo **aquéllos.**

A20 Actividad • Conversación Answers will vary.

Work with a partner. Be a difficult customer. When the clerk shows you something, ask about several other items—the more the better. Switch roles.

—Estos zapatos cuestan 30 dólares.
—¿Y ésos? ¿Y aquéllos de cuero? ¿Y ésos de tenis? ¿Y éstos blancos?

1. Esa blusa cuesta lo mismo.
2. Este plato de cerámica cuesta menos.
3. Aquel traje está hecho a mano.
4. Estos cinturones son de cuero.
5. Estas faldas son de algodón.
6. Aquellos jeans son muy baratos.
7. Estas tazas valen igual.
8. Esos suéteres son de lana.

Ex. ¿Y la azul? ¿Y aquélla de algodón? ¿Y ésta de seda? ¿Y ésa bordada a mano?

A21 Comprensión 📼 For script and answers, see p. T204.

Adjective or pronoun? Decide which of the two.

	0	1	2	3	4	5	6	7	8	9	10
Accent mark		✓	✓		✓		✓	✓			
No accent mark	✓			✓		✓			✓	✓	✓

If you buy clothes from a neighborhood shop or a vendor on the street, you can save money. Check for quality and fit and don't forget to bargain—the asking price is usually higher than the seller expects to receive.

B1   ¡Es una ganga!

Marisa y su mamá están de compras en La Lujosa, una tienda de barrio.

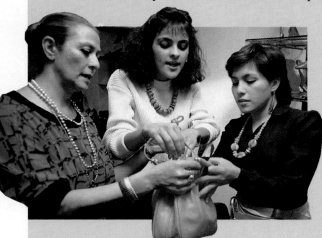

MAMÁ   ¿Le compras dos regalos a Linda, un suéter y una cartera?

MARISA   No, mamá. Compro el suéter para mí y le compro la cartera a Linda. Le mando la cartera por correo, ¿no? ¿Qué te parece? Así la recibe pronto.

MAMÁ   ¡Buena idea! Ese suéter te queda muy bien. La cartera es de muy buena calidad. ¿Sabes cuánto cuesta?

MARISA   No. ¿Le preguntamos a la vendedora?

VENDEDORA   ¿En qué puedo servirle, señorita?

MAMÁ   ¿Cuánto cuesta esta cartera?

VENDEDORA   325 pesos, señora, pero está rebajada a 280 por esta semana. Es una oferta especial. No va a encontrar otra más barata.

MAMÁ   ¡280 pesos! Es demasiado cara. Esa cartera no vale tanto. Vamos a otra tienda, Marisa.

MARISA   Por favor, mamá, ¡es una ganga! A Linda le va a encantar.

MAMÁ   No pago más de 200 pesos. (En voz baja.) Pero hijita, tú no sabes regatear. Vas a ver.

VENDEDORA   Perdón, señora. Como a su hija le gusta tanto, le dejo la cartera en 200 pesos. Más barata no puedo.

MAMÁ   Entonces, la llevamos. ¿Le puedo pagar con un cheque?

1. Marisa compra un suéter y una cartera. 2. El regalo es para Linda.
3. Le queda muy bien.
4. La cartera cuesta 325 pesos.
5. Está rebajada a 280 por esta semana.

B2   Preguntas y respuestas

Answer the following questions about B1.

1. ¿Qué compra Marisa?
2. ¿Para quién es el regalo?
3. ¿Cómo le queda el suéter a Marisa?
4. ¿Cuánto cuesta la cartera?
5. ¿A cuánto está rebajada? ¿Por cuánto tiempo?

6. ¿Van ellas a otra tienda? ¿Por qué?
7. ¿Qué piensa Marisa de la cartera?
8. ¿Sabe Marisa regatear?
9. ¿Cuánto pagan por la cartera?
10. ¿Cómo paga la señora?

6. No, no van a otra tienda, porque la vendedora le deja la cartera más barata. 7. Marisa piensa que es una ganga. 8. No, no sabe regatear. 9. Pagan 200 pesos. 10. Paga con un cheque.   **¡Vamos de compras!   307**

Pair up with a classmate. Ask each other the following questions.   Ex.

Sí, compro regalos para mi familia. Me gusta mucho, porque me gusta regatear.

1. ¿Compras regalos? ¿Te gusta comprar regalos? ¿Por qué?
2. ¿Cuándo y para quién compras regalos?
3. ¿Compras siempre los mismos regalos? ¿Por qué?
4. ¿Qué regalos compras generalmente? ¿Por qué?
5. ¿Te gusta recibir regalos? ¿Cuáles?
6. ¿Regateas generalmente? ¿Te gusta regatear? ¿Puedes regatear? ¿Dónde?

B4   ¿Sabes que . . . ?

In Mexico City, Lima, Bogotá, and other great cities in the New World, the downtown streets and even major avenues in residential sections are crowded with street vendors selling belts and bags, sweaters, blankets, and souvenirs. Theirs are usually the lowest prices in town.

B5   **ESTRUCTURAS ESENCIALES**
Indirect objects

Le escribo una carta.	*I write her a letter.*
Le escribo una carta **a mi hermana.**	*I write a letter to my sister.*

1. In Units 9 and 10, you learned that the *direct* object indicates who or what gets acted upon by the verb. In the example sentences, **una carta** is what gets written, so it is the direct object.

2. An *indirect* object is the word used to indicate who or what *benefits* from the action of the verb. In the example sentence, the letter is written for the benefit of **mi hermana**—it is written *to* or *for* her. **Hermana,** or the pronoun standing for her, is therefore the indirect object.

3. Indirect-object and direct-object pronouns are the same, except in the third person.

You may wish to illustrate use of the pronoun by acting out situations, such as: "Le doy el libro a Ud. Le doy la pluma a ella."

Stress that the "a" + phrase, used for clarification as indicated in 5, is not a substitute for the pronoun. The pronoun must be included: "**Le** escribo una carta **a mi hermana.**"

Indirect-Object Pronouns			
Singular		*Plural*	
me	(to) me	**nos**	(to) us
te	(to) you (*informal*)		
	(to) you (*formal*)		(to) you
le	(to) him	**les**	
	(to) her		(to) them (*m. + f.*)

4. Indirect-object pronouns are placed in front of the conjugated verb, even in negative sentences.

Mi hermano no me escribe cartas.

5. The indirect-object pronouns **le** and **les** require clarification when the context does not specify the person to which they refer. Spanish provides clarification by adding **a** + *personal pronoun* or

a + *name of the person*. **Le** escribo una carta. (*to whom? to him? to her?*): **Le** escribo una carta **a mi hermana.** (*to my sister*)

$$\text{Le escribo} \begin{cases} \text{a mi hermano.} \\ \text{a él.} \\ \text{a usted.} \end{cases} \qquad \text{Les escribo} \begin{cases} \text{a Marisa y a Linda.} \\ \text{a ellas.} \\ \text{a ustedes.} \end{cases}$$

B6 Actividad • ¿Qué les compras?

You've got to buy a lot of gifts. Say that you're going to buy the indicated items. Use a pronoun to mention whom the gift is for.

a mi hermano, un suéter —Le compro un suéter.

1. a la abuela, un pañuelo de seda
2. a mi amigo Raúl, discos
3. para ti, una chaqueta
4. a mis primos, corbatas
5. a mis padres, una cartera
6. para mí, un casete

1. Le compro un pañuelo de seda.
2. Le compro unos discos.
3. Te compro una chaqueta.
4. Les compro unas corbatas.
5. Les compro una cartera.
6. Me compro un casete.

B7 Actividad • ¿Lo compraste?

For answers, see p. T206.

Work with a classmate. You went shopping for everybody. Now that you're back, your classmate checks to see if you remembered everything. Answer each question **Sí** or **No**. Then write down your answers.

Mamá / la revista —¿**Le** compraste la revista?
—Sí, (No, no) **le** compré la revista.

1. Papá / el libro
2. tus hermanos / los casetes
3. tu hermana / un regalo
4. tu prima / el disco
5. tus amigos / los casetes
6. para ti / el suéter
7. tus hermanos y tu hermana / los pañuelos
8. nosotros / los guantes

B8 Comprensión

For script and answers, see p. T206.

Are the replies appropriate or inappropriate?

	0	1	2	3	4	5	6	7	8	9	10
Sí			✓		✓	✓		✓			✓
No	✓	✓		✓			✓		✓	✓	

B9 SITUACIÓN • El estéreo nuevo

Raúl quiere un estéreo nuevo . . . pero, ¿cuándo lo va a poder comprar? ¡El estéreo cuesta más de mil pesos! Raúl hace cuentas.

—Si ahorro veinticinco pesos por semana . . . son cien por mes . . . en un año puedo tener el estéreo . . . ¡No, un año es mucho tiempo! Vamos a ver . . . ahorro el doble: doscientos pesos por mes . . . en dos meses son cuatrocientos . . . sí, en cinco meses, ¡me compro el estéreo!, pero, ¿voy a poder ahorrar?

Choose the option that best completes each sentence according to B9.

1. Raúl quiere
   • una bicicleta.   • una cámara.   • un estéreo.
2. El estéreo cuesta
   • más de cien pesos.   • más de diez pesos.   • más de mil pesos.
3. Raúl hace
   • compras.   • cuentas.   • un viaje.
4. Para comprarlo, Raúl
   • tiene que estudiar.   • debe ahorrar.   • va a trabajar.
5. Veinticinco pesos por semana
   • son cien por mes.   • son diez por mes.   • son mil por mes.
6. Doscientos pesos por mes
   • son cien en dos meses.   • son cuatrocientos en dos meses.   • son mil en un mes.

B 11 ESTRUCTURAS ESENCIALES
Using the numbers 100 to 1,000

100
cien

101
ciento uno, -a

134
ciento treinta y cuatro

200
doscientos, -as

223
doscientos, -as veintitrés

300
trescientos, -as

400
cuatrocientos, -as

500
quinientos, -as

600
seiscientos, -as

700
setecientos, -as

800
ochocientos, -as

900
novecientos, -as

1,000
mil

1. In Unit 2 you saw that **uno** changes its ending to agree with the gender of the noun it modifies.

   un chico, **una** chica, veinti**ún** chicos, veinti**una** chicas
   doscientos treinta y **un** chicos, seiscientas cuarenta y **una** chicas

2. Use **cien** before a noun. It becomes **ciento** when followed by a smaller number.

   cien chicos y **cien** chicas; **ciento un** chicos y **ciento una** chicas

3. Numbers from 200 through 999 have a masculine and a feminine form. The **-os** ending of the hundreds changes to **-as** to agree with a feminine noun.

   quinient**os** chicos, quinient**as** chicas
   cuatrocient**os** tres chicos, cuatrocient**as** tres chicas

4. The word **y** is used only between the tens and the units in numbers above thirty.

   ciento treinta **y** uno   ochocientos cuarenta **y** dos   (BUT: doscientos uno)

5. Periods are often used in Spanish instead of commas to mark off thousands: 2.000 **dos mil.**

$511—quinientos once pesos; $729—setecientos veinte y nueve pesos; $618—seiscientos diez y ocho pesos; $800—ochocientos pesos; $304—trescientos cuatro pesos; $450—cuatrocientos cincuenta pesos; $200—doscientos pesos; $900—novecientos pesos; $38—treinta y ocho pesos.

B 12 Actividad • Precios

You are a clerk in a Latin American store. The customers ask for prices. Answer their questions, reading the price tags.

$ 180   —Ciento ochenta pesos

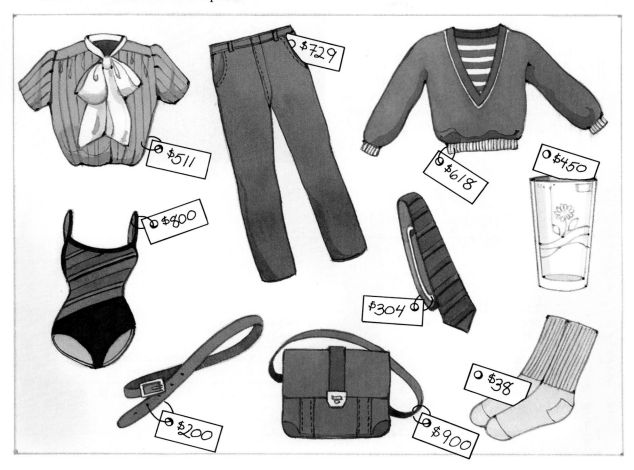

B 13 Actividad • ¡A escribir!

Write down your answers for B13, writing the quantity in Spanish. Use words, not numbers.

B 14 Actividad • No es así

It's inventory time at the store. You're working with a partner. Correct what he or she says, following the clues.

Cuatrocientos platos (tazas)   —No, son cuatrocientas tazas.

1. Cien libros (revistas)
2. Ciento un discos (cámaras)
3. Seiscientas treinta y tres chaquetas (abrigos)

1. No, son cien revistas.
2. No, son ciento una cámaras.
3. No, son seiscientos treinta y tres abrigos.

4. Mil corbatas (pañuelos)
5. Ochocientos veintiocho abrigos (faldas)
6. Doscientos pañuelos (corbatas)

4. No, son mil pañuelos.
5. No, son ochocientas veintiocho faldas.
6. No, son doscientas corbatas.

Major cities in the Spanish-speaking world
have countless small shops, large department
stores and shopping centers, and numerous
street vendors. But when you ask people
where they get their best bargains, chances
are they'll mention some special place you've
never heard of before. In Mexico City, bargain
hunters flock to **El Monte de Piedad,** a vast
pawnshop in the very center of the capital. **El
Monte de Piedad** is a good place to start your
search for almost anything; if you don't find
what you want there, you can try the
neighborhood **mercados,** government-
sponsored markets.

B 16   SE DICE ASÍ
Discussing prices, making a bargain

Cliente	Vendedor
¿Cuánto cuesta / vale? How much does it cost?	**Es un regalo.** It's practically a giveaway.
Es muy / demasiado caro. It's very / too expensive.	**Es muy barato.** It's very cheap.
No vale tanto. It's not worth that much.	**Es una ganga. Es de muy buena calidad.** It's a bargain. It's of very good quality.
No pago más de . . . I'm not paying more than . . .	**No va a encontrar uno(a) / otro(a) más barato(a).** You're not going to find a cheaper one.

B 17   Actividad • ¿Lo compro o no?

Work with two or three classmates.
One of you is the salesclerk; the
others are customers. Ask what
you want. Discuss prices. The
clerk helps the customers make
decisions.

Ex.—Quiero esa blusa de algodón.
   ¿Cuánto cuesta?
   —Noventa y cinco pesos.
   —Es demasiado cara, no la quiero. No
   vale tanto. . . .
   —Es de buena calidad, señora.

No pago más de 100 pesos

¡Es una ganga!

Es de muy buena calidad

Es muy caro

No va a encontrar otro más barato

Es un regalo

¿Cuánto cuesta?

No vale tanto

B 18   Actividad • ¡A escribir!

Write a conversation between a salesclerk and customers, using your exchanges in
B17 as a basis.

B 19 Comprensión 🎞 For script and answers, see p. T208.

B 19 Comprensión

Striking a bargain.

	0	1	2	3	4	5	6	7	8	9	10
Sí	✔	✔			✔			✔	✔	✔	
No			✔	✔		✔	✔				✔

B 20 Actividad • ¿Qué precio tiene?

Set up an imaginary flea market in class. Bring pictures of items for sale. Establish a fixed maximum price for any item beforehand.

B 21 Actividad • En venta   Answers will vary.

Make a sign with the pictures of the items you have for sale. Write in Spanish a short paragraph describing each item. Leave prices out of your sign.

B 22 Actividad • ¿Lo llevo o no?   Answers will vary.

When you find something that you like at the flea market, ask the vendor about price and quality. Compare items, and try your hand at bargaining.

B 23 Actividad • Compras y ventas   Answers will vary.

• If you sell something, write out a receipt describing the item and showing the price.

• Make a chart for yourself like the one shown below. Compare charts with your classmates. Report to the class everything you bought and sold at the flea market.

	¿Qué?	¿A quién?	¿Cuánto?
Compras			
Ventas			

When you buy something and it doesn't arrive on time, you have to complain to the store and get some action. You need to discuss what you ordered, what you said, and what you wanted.

C1 Sección de quejas y reclamos

El Sr. Gómez no recibió el estéreo que compró. Ahora está en la Sección de quejas y reclamos.

EMPLEADA	¿Señor?
SR. GÓMEZ	Sí, señorita. Aquí tengo el recibo. Ustedes me prometieron el estéreo para el día 15. Hoy es 25, . . . y no lo recibí.
EMPLEADA	El recibo, por favor. Ah, señor, ¿escribió usted una carta de reclamación?
SR. GÓMEZ	¡Señorita, por favor! Llamé por teléfono veinte veces, escribí dos cartas la semana pasada . . . , finalmente, decidí venir en persona.
EMPLEADA	¿Subió usted a la oficina del piso cinco?
SR. GÓMEZ	Sí, ya fui, me mandaron aquí.
EMPLEADA	A ver . . . un momento . . . ¿y quién le vendió el estéreo? Este pedido ya salió . . . usted va a recibir el estéreo mañana, a primera hora . . .
SR. GÓMEZ	Pero, señorita . . . Mi hijo no cumple años mañana . . . ¡su cumpleaños es hoy! ¡Y yo le prometí el estéreo!

C2 Actividad • ¡A escoger!

Choose the best option to complete the following sentences according to **Sección de quejas y reclamos** in C1.

1. El cliente está en la sección de
   • estéreos.   • recibos.   • quejas y reclamos.
2. Le prometieron el estéreo
   • para el día 25.   • para el día 15.   • para hoy.

3. El cliente
- recibió el estéreo.   • no recibió la carta.   • no recibió su pedido.

4. El señor llamó por teléfono
- dos veces.   • veinte veces.   • veinticinco veces.

5. Él escribió
- dos recibos.   • veinte veces.   • dos cartas.

6. El cliente va a recibir el estéreo
- hoy por la tarde.   • esta noche.   • mañana.

7. El cumpleaños de su hijo es
- mañana a primera hora.   • hoy.   • esta mañana.

C3 **Actividad · Para completar**

Complete these sentences to make them agree with C1.

1. Señorita, aquí tengo _____ _____ . el recibo.

2. Ustedes me prometieron _____ _____ para _____ _____ _____ . el estéreo   el día 15.

3. Hoy es 25 . . . y no lo _____ . recibí

4. Llamé por teléfono veinte veces , escribí dos cartas , _____ decidí venir en persona. finalmente

5. ¿Subió usted a la _____ del piso _____ ? oficina   piso

6. Sí, ya fui, me _____ aquí. mandaron

7. A ver . . . un _____ , este _____ ya salió. momento   pedido

8. Pero, señorita . . . ¡ No _____ _____ cumple años _____ , su cumpleaños es hoy ! mañana

C4 **ESTRUCTURAS ESENCIALES**
The preterit of -er and -ir verbs

Point out that regular "ar" and "er" verbs have the same endings in the preterit. Review the endings of "ar" verbs and tell students that now they know all preterit forms of regular verbs.

	vender *to sell*		**decidir** *to decide*	
yo	**Vendí**	mi bicicleta.	**Decidí**	escribir.
tú	**¿Vendiste**	tus periódicos?	**¿Decidiste**	subir?
usted, él, ella	**Vendió**	su coche.	**¿Decidió**	venir?
nosotros(as)	**Vendimos**	nuestros libros.	**Decidimos**	vender la casa.
vosotros(as)	**¿Vendisteis**	todo?	**¿Decidisteis**	ir?
ustedes, ellos(as)	**Vendieron**	mucho.	**Decidieron**	salir.

1. In Unit 10 you studied the preterit of regular **-ar** verbs. The preterit tense expresses completed past actions. The chart shows the preterit of **vender,** a regular **-er** verb, and **decidir,** a regular **-ir** verb.

2. You can produce the preterit forms of regular **-er** and **-ir** verbs by adding the following endings to the stem:

$$\text{í, -iste, -ió, -imos, -isteis, -ieron}$$

3. Every regular preterit form is stressed on the ending. Notice that the **yo** and **usted/él/ella** forms have written accents.

Yo **vendí** todas las corbatas.   Ella **decidió** comprar el estéreo.

1. ¿Qué vendiste tú? 2. Yo vendí bocadillos. 3. Nosotros vendimos mucho. 4. ¿Y ustedes qué vendieron? 5. Susana y yo vendimos tartas y bizcochos. 6. ¿Quién vendió discos? 7. Pablo vendió discos y casetes. 8. Y Mariana, ¿qué vendió? 9. Ella vendió calcetines. 10. Alberto y Graciela vendieron ropa también.

C5   Actividad • En la feria de la clase

The class flea market was a big success. Everybody sold something. Complete the conversation, using the preterit of **vender**.

> Raúl / libros y revistas.   —Raúl vendió libros y revistas.

1. ¿Qué / tú?
2. Yo / bocadillos.
3. Nosotros / mucho.
4. ¿Y ustedes, qué / ?
5. Susana y yo / tartas y bizcochos.

6. ¿Quién / discos?
7. Pablo / discos y casetes.
8. Y Mariana, ¿qué / ?
9. Ella / calcetines.
10. Alberto y Graciela / ropa también.

C6   Actividad • Quejas

1. Yo no recibí la cámara. 2. Tú no recibiste la guitarra. 3. Nosotros no recibimos el estéreo.

Everybody is complaining. The things people bought haven't arrived. Complete using the preterit of **recibir**. Add **no** to all your sentences.

4. Mis amigos no recibieron la bicicleta.
5. Ustedes no recibieron la computadora.
6. Usted no recibió los discos.
7. Ángel no recibió la raqueta.

> El señor López, los libros
> El señor López no recibió los libros.

1. Yo, la cámara
2. Tú, la guitarra
3. Nosotros, el estéreo

4. Mis amigos, la bicicleta
5. Ustedes, la computadora
6. Usted, los discos

7. Angel, la raqueta
8. Marisa y yo, las revistas
9. Tú, el diccionario

8. Marisa y yo no recibimos las revistas. 9. Tú no recibiste el diccionario.

C7   Comprensión

For script and answers, see p. T211.

Present or preterit?

	0	1	2	3	4	5	6	7	8	9
Present		✔		✔	✔				✔	✔
Preterit	✔		✔	✔		✔	✔			

C8   Actividad • ¿Qué pasó?

Mr. Gómez is making a complaint at the store. Write out what he says. Use the appropriate forms of these verbs in the preterit. Repetitions are allowed.

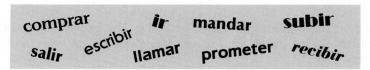

comprar   ir   mandar   subir   salir   escribir   llamar   prometer   recibir

—Señorita, yo compré un estéreo el día 15. Hoy es el 25, y yo no recibí el estéreo. El vendedor me prometió el estéreo para el día 19.
—Sí, ¿ llamó usted por teléfono?
—Sí, yo llamé la semana pasada, escribí una carta, pero no recibí el estéreo.
—¿ Subió usted a la oficina del piso cinco?
—Sí, señorita. Fui y me _____ aquí. mandaron
—Bien, señor. Su pedido ya salió . Lo va a tener mañana a primera hora.
—Pero, ¡yo lo quiero hoy!

El señor Gómez compró un estéreo el día 15. Hoy es el 25 y no recibió el estéreo. El vendedor le prometió el estéreo para el día 19. El señor Gómez llamó por teléfono a la tienda y también escribió cartas. El señor Gómez fue a la tienda, subió al quinto piso y lo mandaron a la sección de quejas y reclamos. Allí una señorita le dijo que su pedido ya salió y lo va a tener mañana. Pero el señor Gómez lo quiere para hoy.

C9 Actividad • ¡A escribir!

Use the preterit to tell what happened to Mr. Gómez according to C1. Start with:
El señor Gómez compró un estéreo el día . . .

C10 Actividad • Charla

Work with a partner. You are the customer and your partner is a clerk in the customer service department of a store. You bought something a month ago, but the store hasn't delivered your order yet. Complain. Switch roles.

C11 SE DICE ASÍ
Saying what you did and what you are going to do

—¿Qué hiciste?	—¿Qué vas a hacer?
—¿(Ya) comiste?	• Sí, ya comí.
	• No, voy a comer ahora.

You may wish to do a guided question/answer drill after "Se dice así" based on student's own experiences. "¿Qué hiciste el sábado? ¿Adónde vas mañana?" etc.

Use the preterit to say what people did. Use the **ir a** + infinitive construction to say what people are going to do. You can also use the present tense to say what people are doing in the near future: **¿Adónde vas el sábado?**

For answers, see p. T212.

C12 Actividad • Charla

Work with a partner. Talk about what you've already done today and what you're planning to do after school or tomorrow.

—¿Le hablaste a ella?

• Sí, ya le hablé.
• No, le voy a hablar después.

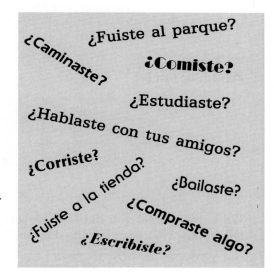

¿Fuiste al parque?
¿Caminaste?
¿Comiste?
¿Estudiaste?
¿Hablaste con tus amigos?
¿Corriste?
¿Bailaste?
¿Fuiste a la tienda?
¿Compraste algo?
¿Escribiste?

C13 Actividad • La fiesta For answers, see p. T212.

Your friend is planning a birthday party. Check to see if everything is taken care of. Work with a partner. Ask each other.

1. ¿Ya decidiste a quién invitar?
2. ¿Ya decidiste el día de la fiesta?
3. ¿Ya hiciste la lista de invitados?
4. ¿Ya escribiste las invitaciones?
5. ¿Ya llamaste a todos?
6. ¿Ya compraste la comida?
7. ¿Ya mandaste las invitaciones?
8. ¿Ya recibiste regalos?

¡Vamos de compras! 317

Actividad • ¡A escribir!   Answers will vary.

Write down what you've already done today and what you're planning to do later.

Ya comí.   Voy a mirar televisión.
Ya estudié.   Voy a salir.

C15   Actividad • Charla   Free conversation.

El fin de semana pasado y el próximo   Work with two or three classmates. Talk about what you did last weekend and what your plans for next weekend are.

—¿Adónde fueron?   —¿Adónde van a ir?
—¿Qué hicieron?   —¿Qué van a hacer?

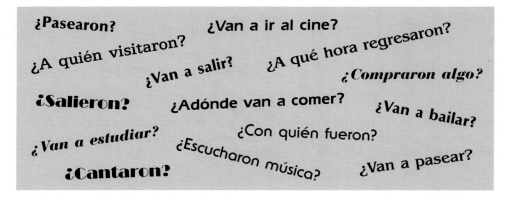

¿Pasearon?   ¿Van a ir al cine?
¿A quién visitaron?
¿Van a salir?   ¿A qué hora regresaron?
¿Salieron?   ¿Compraron algo?
¿Adónde van a comer?   ¿Van a bailar?
¿Van a estudiar?   ¿Con quién fueron?
¿Cantaron?   ¿Escucharon música?   ¿Van a pasear?

C16   Comprensión   For script and answers, see p. T213.

Preterit or future?

	0	1	2	3	4	5	6	7	8	9	10
Preterit		✔	✔		✔	✔			✔	✔	
Future	✔			✔			✔	✔			✔

C17   Actividad • ¡A escribir!   Answers will vary.

Write down what you did last weekend and what your plans for next weekend are. You can also talk about what your friends did, and about what their plans are. Follow the chart below as a model.

	El fin de semana pasado	El próximo
Yo		
José		
Carmen		
Luisa		
Felipe		

1   El cliente y el empleado

Pair off with a classmate. One of you will play the part of the client, and the other will be the salesperson. Carry out the following dialog in Spanish. Present your dialog to the class.

Client asks:
- price of item(s) he/she wants.
- what material it is made of.
- what is the lowest price to be paid.
- how good is the quality of item(s).

Salesperson says:
- price of items.
- material and quality.
- lowest possible price.
- client must buy, it's a bargain!

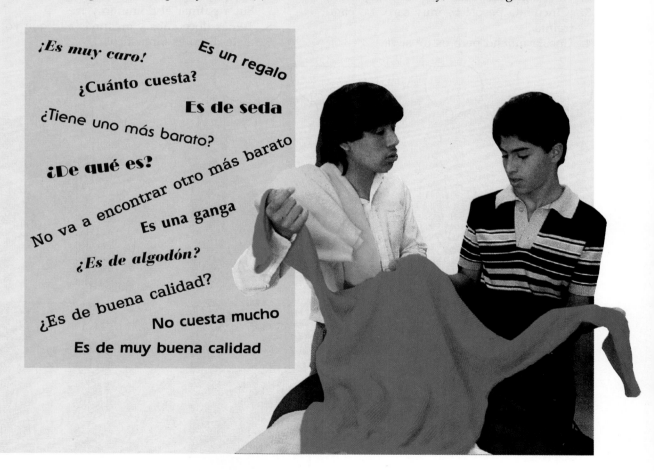

¡Es muy caro!   Es un regalo

¿Cuánto cuesta?

Es de seda

¿Tiene uno más barato?

¿De qué es?

No va a encontrar otro más barato

Es una ganga

¿Es de algodón?

¿Es de buena calidad?

No cuesta mucho

Es de muy buena calidad

2   Actividad • ¡A escribir!   Sample dialog given.

Prepare a written report based on the dialog you had with your partner.

Cliente: ¿Cuánto cuesta esta camisa?
Vendedor: 100 pesos. Pero está rebajada a 80 pesos.
Cliente: Es muy cara. No pago más de 70.
Vendedor: Es una ganga por 80 pesos y es de seda.
Cliente: 80 pesos es mucho dinero.
Vendedor: Bueno, le dejo la camisa en 75 pesos, más barato no puedo.

¡Vamos de compras!   319

Actividad • Conversación

You're coming back from a shopping trip. Work with a partner. Ask each other:

1. ¿A qué tienda fuiste?
2. ¿Es ésa tu tienda favorita? ¿Por qué?
3. ¿Compraste algo? ¿Qué?
4. ¿Cuánto pagaste?
5. ¿Piensas que pagaste mucho? ¿Por qué?
6. ¿Regateaste?

7. ¿Tú te compraste algo? ¿Qué?
8. ¿Compraste algo para tu familia? ¿Qué? ¿Para quién?
9. ¿Compraste algo para tus amigos? ¿Qué les compraste? ¿Por qué?
10. ¿Me compraste algo? ¿Qué? ¿De qué es?

4 Actividad • Talleres gráficos *Printing shop* For answers, see numbers below each illustration.

The words for today's comic strip have to be inserted into the bubbles. Tell the artist which speech goes where.

1. Ayer corrí mucho. Estoy cansada.
2. Te compré un regalo.
3. ¡Cincuenta pesos! Es muy caro. Le pago treinta.
4. Cuesta mucho pero es de seda.

5. Muchas gracias. ¿Es una bicicleta?
6. ¡Felipe!, ¿y eso?
7. Fui a patinar el domingo y . . .
8. Tienes doce años y eres más alto que yo.
9. ¡Este disco es fantástico!

5 Actividad • Quejas

While you were away traveling, you bought gifts for the whole family. Six months have passed and the presents have not arrived. Call up the company to complain. Be sure to have the list of items you bought handy. The company representative is going to ask you about your order in detail. Work with a partner. Switch roles.

6 Actividad • ¡A escribir!

The representative told you on the phone to write a letter to the company stating what you bought and when. Do it now, so you can receive your order. Start your letter with: **Señores.**

7 Actividad • Charla Free conversation.

Talk to a partner about what you did last summer and what your plans for your next summer vacation are.

—¿Adónde fuiste en el verano?

—A San Francisco, ¿y tú?

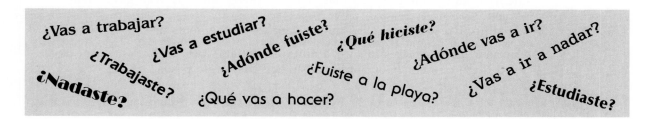

¿Vas a trabajar? ¿Vas a estudiar? ¿Adónde fuiste? ¿Qué hiciste? ¿Adónde vas a ir?

¿Trabajaste? ¿Fuiste a la playa? ¿Vas a ir a nadar?

¿Nadaste? ¿Qué vas a hacer? ¿Estudiaste?

8 Pronunciación, lectura, dictado For script, see p. T215.

1. The Spanish consonants **g** and **j** have the same sound. Listen, then read aloud.

geografía   jardín   gente   naranja   gimnasia   abajo   Argentina

2. The Spanish consonants **b** and **v** have the same sound. Listen, then read aloud.

vaso   bizcocho   invitación   venir   barato   favorito   llevar

Ellos vivieron en Venezuela por veintinueve años.
Le escribimos muchas veces pero nunca recibimos respuesta.

3. Copy the following sentences to prepare yourself to write them from dictation.

Necesito un traje de baño para el verano.
Jorge es un genio en biología.
Julio dejó su tarjeta de crédito en la caja.

¿LO SABES?

Let's review some important points you have learned in this unit.

A, B, C—Each student will create his/her own projects.

SECTION A

Do you know how to find out what other people think about something that you're going to buy or do?

Ask five questions to find out somebody else's opinion.

Can you answer those questions yourself when asked to express your opinion? ¿Está caro este plato? No, es una ganga. ¿Está barata esta blusa? Sí, y es linda. ¿Te gusta esta falda? Sí, es muy linda. ¿Es linda esta postal? No, no me gusta.

Are you able to ask the price of different items, when you are at the store?

Ask the price of five different items, then answer those questions as if you were the salesperson. ¿Cuánto cuestan estos pantalones? Cuestan 680 Ptas. ¿Cuánto cuesta esta calculadora? Cuesta $35. ¿Cuántos lápices por $2? Tres. ¿Cuánto cuesta este libro? Cuesta 500 Ptas.

Do you know how to compare the size and color of different clothing items?

Talk about a shirt, shoes, a dress, a coat, a skirt, socks, or any other clothing item you're interested in buying.

Compare those items and discuss their prices. Say what they're made of.

Ex. Esta camisa es de seda y tiene un color muy lindo. No está cara en 850 Ptas. Pero estos zapatos de cuero marrón están muy caros. No los llevo.

SECTION B

Do you know how to drive a bargain in Spanish? Está muy caro. No vale . . .

Write down five phrases you might use. No lo llevo. No pago. . . . Cuesta mucho.

Then react to your phrases as if you were the salesperson.

¡Es una ganga! Más barato no puedo. Mejor precio no existe. Es de seda. Pero es muy elegante.

Can you mention some presents you've bought and say whom you gave them to, and name presents that you've received and say who gave them to you? Compré una camisa para papá. Compré una cartera para Alicia. Compré un plato para mamá.

Make up five sentences. You might want to list the items first.

Compré un libro para mi prima. Compré una postal para Ana. ¿La blusa? Me la regaló María.

Can you discuss prices of over a hundred dollars? ¿La cámara? Me la regaló papá.

Read these numbers aloud in Spanish as if they were **pesos.**

301   525   100   436   980   762   393   219

trescientos(as) un(a) pesos/pesetas—quinientos(as) veinticinco pesos/pesetas—cien pesos/pesetas—cuatrocientos(as) treinta y seis /pesos/pesetas—novecientos(as) ochenta pesos/pesetas—setecientos(as) sesenta y dos pesos/pesetas— trescientos(as) noventa y tres pesos/pesetas—doscientos(as) diecinueve pesos/pesetas

SECTION C

Do you know how to make a complaint at the store or over the phone?

You haven't received what you've ordered. No recibí mi pedido. ¿Dónde está mi pedido?

Write down five phrases you might use to complain. ¿Por qué no recibí mi pedido? ¿Quién sabe dónde está mi pedido? ¡Escribí dos veces y todavía no recibí mi pedido!

Can you talk about what you did last summer and say what you are planning to do next summer? Each student will create his/her own project.

Make up five sentences.

Think of five questions you might ask a friend about what he or she did last summer or last weekend and what his or her plans for next summer or next weekend are.

Ex. ¿Qué hiciste el verano pasado? ¿Qué vas a hacer este verano? ¿Fuiste a la playa el verano pasado? ¿Viajaste el verano pasado? ¿Vas a España este verano?

VOCABULARIO

SECTION A

el abrigo *coat*
el algodón *cotton*
allá *(over) there*
aquél, aquélla *that one*
aquéllos, -as *those*
barato, -a *cheap*
la blusa *blouse*
bordado, -a *embroidered*
la caja *cashier's desk*
el calcetín (pl. calcetines) *sock*
la camisa *shirt*
caro, -a *expensive*
la cerámica *ceramics (material)*
claro, -a *light (in color)*
la corbata *tie*
¿cuánto vale? *how much does it cost?*
el cuero *leather*
la chaqueta *jacket*
de *made of*
de plástico *(made of) plastic*
¿de qué es? *what's it made of?*
el (de) *the one (made of)*
ése, -a *that one*
ésos, -as *those*
éste, -a *this one*
éstos, -as *these*
la falda *skirt*
hecho, -a a mano *handmade*
igual (que) *the same (as)*
los jeans *jeans*
los jóvenes *young people*
la lana *wool*
largo, -a *long*
lo mismo (que) *the same (as)*
llevar *to take*
la mano *hand*
más de . . . *more than . . .*

más . . . que *more . . . than*
más grande que *bigger than*
menos *less*
menos de . . . *less than . . .*
¡no importa! *it doesn't matter!*
no me gusta nada *I don't like it at all*
oscuro, -a *dark*
el pañuelo *handkerchief*
los pantalones *pants*
la preciosura *thing of beauty*
la ropa *clothes*
el saco *jacket*
la seda *silk*
segundo, -a *second*
el sombrero *hat*
el suéter *sweater*
la talla *size*
la tarjeta de crédito *credit card*
el traje *suit*
el traje de baño *bathing suit*
valen *they cost*
el vestido *dress*

SECTION B

ahorrar *to save*
así *that way, then*
el barrio *neighborhood*
la calidad *quality*
dejar *to allow, let*
le dejo la cartera en . . . *I'll let the purse go for . . .*
demasiado *too (much)*
doble *double*
¿en qué puedo servirle? *how may I help you?*
en voz baja *in a low voice*
encantar *to delight*
encontrar (ue) *to find*
especial *special*

estar de compras *to be shopping*
la ganga *bargain*
generalmente *generally*
hacer cuentas *to do calculations*
mandar *to send*
los números del 100 al 1000 *numbers from 100 to 1000 (see p. 310)*
la oferta *offer*
por correo *by mail*
pronto *soon*
quedar bien *it looks nice on*
rebajado, -a *reduced (in price)*
recibir *to receive*
regatear *to bargain*
servir *to serve*

SECTION C

a primera hora *as early as possible*
a ver *let's see*
el, la cliente *customer*
el cumpleaños *birthday*
cumplir años *to have a birthday*
en persona *in person*
elegante *elegant*
la feria *fair*
finalmente *finally*
el pedido *order*
el piso *floor*
prometer *to promise*
la queja *complaint*
quinto, -a *fifth*
el recibo *receipt*
la reclamación *claim*
el reclamo *claim*
la sección de quejas y reclamos *customer service department*

You may wish to have the students read the vocabulary before each section is introduced.

ESTUDIO DE PALABRAS

Make separate lists of all the items of clothing in the unit list. Add any other clothing words you know and want to remember.

---

abrigo, blusa, calcetín, camisa, corbata, falda, pañuelo, pantalones, ropa, sombrero, suéter, traje, traje de baño, vestido.

¡Vamos de compras! 323

VAMOS A LEER

Antes de leer

To practice reading for information, look at **Festival de super gangas.** In Spanish, write the important facts in the forms of notes. Try to find the Spanish equivalent for the following expressions in the ad without looking at the glosses.

1. mangas largas y cortas
1. long and short sleeves

2. colores surtidos
2. assorted colors

3. toallas de playa
3. beach towels

4. warm-up suits
4. trajes de ejercicio

5. dress shirts
5. camisas de vestir

6. giant size
4. tamaño gigante

Ropa para toda la familia

FESTIVAL DE SUPER GANGAS

GRAN° SELECCIÓN DE CAMISETAS°
Manga° Larga
Todos los tamaños°
$3.33

MEDIAS° PARA HOMBRES
Primera Calidad
Paquete° de 6
$4.99

VESTIDOS
MARCAS° FAMOSAS
Algodón, seda desde
$29.99

PIJAMAS
De primera calidad
PARA HOMBRES
Estampados° surtidos
Mangas cortas y largas
$5.99

CAMISAS DE VESTIR° PARA HOMBRES
Mangas cortas
Colores surtidos°
$4.99

PANTALONES DE VESTIR PARA HOMBRES
$9.99
Primera calidad

TOALLAS DE PLAYA°
Tamaño gigante°
colores surtidos
$2.99

TRAJES DE EJERCICIO°
Hombres, Mujeres y Niños
Estilos surtidos
Colores azul, negro y blanco
$7.99

¡A escribir!

Write a short ad for a clothing item. Mention color, size, and price. Make it sound as attractive as you can.

---

gran *great*   **camisetas** *T-shirts*   **manga** *sleeve*   **tamaños** *sizes*   **camisas de vestir** *dress shirts*   **surtidos** *assorted*
medias *socks*   **paquete** *package*   **toallas de playa** *beach towels*   **gigante** *giant*   **marcas** *brands*   **estampados** *prints*
trajes de ejercicio *warm-up suits*

De compras en México

La Ciudad de México es moderna y tradicional. Ejemplos de esta combinación son los centros comerciales de la ciudad.

En el centro°, en el Mercado de San Juan, el ambiente° es muy animado°. Desde sus puestos°, los vendedores ofrecen una gran° variedad de productos. Y como allí muchos precios no son fijos°, los mexicanos están acostumbrados a° regatear. ¡Ah . . . qué placer° cuando el vendedor rebaja° los precios!

Al oeste°, en la Zona Rosa, el ambiente es más moderado° y más quieto°. Sus tiendas elegantes ofrecen: carteras, zapatos, ropa, joyas y objetos de alfarería°. Pero la costumbre° de regatear persiste° en esta zona. Y muy a menudo, en una de estas tiendas tan modernas se oye° el intercambio° familiar de: —¿Cuánto cuesta? —¡No, es muy caro! —¡Entonces se lo dejo en . . . !

Actividad • Para completar

Complete the following sentences according to the reading

1. La Ciudad de México es <u>moderna y tradicional</u>.
2. El ambiente es muy animado en _____ .
3. Desde sus puestos los vendedores ofrecen _____ .
4. Los mexicanos están acostumbrados a _____ .
5. Es un placer cuando el vendedor <u>rebaja los precios</u>.
6. En la Zona Rosa el ambiente es <u>más moderado y quieto</u>
7. Sus tiendas elegantes ofrecen _____ .
8. La costumbre de regatear _____ .

---

centro *downtown* **ambiente** *atmosphere* **animado** *lively* **puestos** *market booths* **gran** *great* **fijos** *fixed* **estar acostumbrado (-a) a** *to be used to* **placer** *pleasure* **rebaja** *he lowers* **oeste** *west* **moderado, -a** *moderate* **quieto, -a** *quiet* **alfarería** *pottery* **costumbre** *custom* **persiste** *continues* **se oye** *one hears* **intercambio** *interchange*

2. el Mercado de San Juan.
3. una gran variedad de productos.
4. regatear

7. carteras, zapatos, ropas, joyas y objetos de alfarería.
8. persiste en esta zona.

El regalo 📼

Unos minutos después, Daniel y Adriana ya más calmados°, pueden comprender°
lo que acaba de ocurrir°. La policía arresta a la señorita Flor Gavilán—la aeromoza—
y a su cómplice°, Héctor Ríos. Omar Ramos—el joven° de El Paso—está muy complacido°.

DANIEL   ¡Llegaste en el momento preciso! ¡Nos salvaste la vida°!
ADRIANA   ¿Tú planeaste todo esto?
OMAR   No les puedo explicar° nada ahora. El héroe no soy yo. Ustedes
actuaron estupendamente°.
DANIEL   ¿Qué hacemos ahora?
OMAR   Eso depende de ustedes. Ahora, tengo que irme° . . .
ADRIANA   ¡De nuevo!
OMAR   . . . pero primero, necesito un favor.
ADRIANA   ¡Cómo no!
OMAR   ¿Me pueden devolver° la billetera°? Ustedes saben . . . cuesta mucho
reparar° un coche.

Daniel y Adriana deciden regresar a México con el canal 17. Los dos chicos están
cansados° y Adriana está muy triste°.

DANIEL   ¿Por qué estás triste? Mira, ya estamos en casa. Ahí está El Ángel,
estamos en el mismo centro de México.
ADRIANA   Sí, pero ¿qué pasa ahora? ¿Aquí termina nuestra aventura?
DANIEL   Si quieres, pongo el televisor.
ADRIANA   Ya no me interesa° el televisor. Daniel, ¡cuidado!°

En ese mismo momento unos chicos tratan de apoderarse° del televisor. El
televisor se cae y se hace trizas°.

ADRIANA   ¿Cómo? ¡El televisor no tiene nada adentro°!
DANIEL   Pero, ¿cómo funcionaba°?
ADRIANA   Yo no sé. Ya no tenemos nada. ¿Y la flor° de la canción° en la Puerta
del Sol?, ¿dónde está?
DANIEL   La flor de la canción no es una flor, Adriana. ¿No comprendes? La flor
es una mujer°, la aeromoza, Flor Gavilán. Ella es la "flor" de la Puerta del Sol.
ADRIANA   Y nosotros fuimos a Madrid con el televisor, ¡y la encontramos°!
¡Nosotros encontramos la flor, Daniel! Pero, no tenemos flores, no
tenemos nada. ¿Quién nos va a creer?
DANIEL   Vamos, yo te compro una flor.

Pero, ¿qué pasa? No pueden encontrar flores en ninguna parte°. No hay más
flores en la ciudad.

---

calmados *calmed down*   **comprender** *to understand*   **lo que acaba de ocurrir** *what just happened*   **cómplice** *accomplice*
joven *young man*   **complacido** *pleased*   **nos salvaste la vida** *you saved our lives*   **explicar** *to explain*   **actuaron**
estupendamente *you were fantastic*   **tengo que irme** *I must go*   **devolver** *to return*   **billetera** *wallet*   **reparar** *to repair*
cansados *tired*   **triste** *sad*   **no me interesa** *I don't care*   **cuidado** *be careful*   **tratan de apoderarse** *try to seize*   **se**
cae y se hace trizas *it falls and smashes into pieces*   **adentro** *inside*   **funcionaba** *worked*   **flor** *flower*   **canción** *song*
mujer *woman*   **la encontramos** *we found her*   **ninguna parte** *nowhere*

Adriana y Daniel llegan a su casa. Casi no la reconocen°. Hay flores por todas partes°, miles de flores adentro y afuera°, en las ventanas, en el patio, en la puerta. Y siguen llegando° coches, camiones°, gente en bicicleta, con todas las flores de México para ellos. ¡Adriana y Daniel son los héroes del momento! Pero, no tienen televisor. ¿Qué van a hacer ahora? Sin televisor, sus aventuras terminan . . . ¿o no?

Preguntas y respuestas

1. La policía arresta a Flor Gavilán y su cómplice Hector Ríos. 2. No, los héroes son Adriana y Daniel. Porque actuaron estupendamente. 3. Porque cuesta mucho dinero reparar un coche. 4. Adriana está muy triste porque termina su adventura. 5. Todas las flores están en casa de Adriana y Daniel.

Answer the questions according to the reading.

1. ¿A quién arresta la policía?
2. ¿Es el héroe Omar Ramos? ¿Por qué?
3. ¿Por qué necesita Omar la billetera?
4. ¿Cómo está Adriana? ¿Por qué?
5. ¿Dónde están todas las flores?
6. ¿Te gusta el final de la historia? ¿Por qué?

Actividad • Charla

Work with a partner. You should be very well acquainted with **El regalo.** Ask each other questions so that your answers retell the whole story.

—¿Quiénes son Daniel y Adriana? Son dos hermanos mexicanos.
—¿De dónde son ellos? Ellos son de México.
—¿Qué reciben los hermanos? Ellos reciben un televisor y flores al final.

Actividad • ¿Quieres cambiar la historia de Daniel y Adriana?

Imagine a different ending for **El regalo.** Write down your ending. Share it with your class.

---

la reconocen *recognize it* **por todas partes** *everywhere* **afuera** *outside* **siguen llegando** *keep coming* **camiones** *trucks*

UNIDAD 12 **Cartas de México**

Repaso

TEACHER-PREPARED MATERIALS	UNIT RESOURCES
Review 12 pictures of Mexico	**Manual de actividades,** Unit 12
	Manual de ejercicios, Unit 12
	Unit 12 Cassette
	Transparency 30
	Review Test 3

Unit 12 combines functions, grammar, and vocabulary that the students have studied in Units 9–11. This unit provides communicative and writing practice in different situations; some of the activities lend themselves to cooperative learning. If your students require further practice, you will find additional review exercises in Unit 12 of the **Manual de actividades** and **Manual de ejercicios.** On the other hand, if your students know how to use the material in Units 9–11, you may wish to omit parts of Unit 12.

OBJECTIVE   To review communicative functions, grammar, and vocabulary from Units 9–11

CULTURAL BACKGROUND   Mexico City was built on top of the capital city of the Aztecs, called Tenochtitlán. This large and beautiful city was built on an island in the middle of a lake called Texcoco. When the Spaniards arrived, the population of Tenochtitlán was over 300,000. There were more people than in the most populated city in Spain, Barcelona. The Aztec city contained many pyramids, palaces, towers, and other stone buildings. The only passage into the city was by drawbridge. The Spaniards described the city as a "vision or maybe Paradise."

Mexico City is also the home of one of the oldest universities in Spanish America, UNAM (Universidad Autónoma de México). It was founded in 1553 and, from the very beginning, was open to resident Spaniards, Creoles, mestizos, and Indians, regardless of race. It was King Charles III who insisted that one-fourth of the scholarships be allocated to the sons of Indian chiefs.

MOTIVATING ACTIVITY   Ask the students what they would do during a trip to Mexico City. What would they like to see? Where would they go?

1   Cartas a los amigos

CULTURAL BACKGROUND   Pictured at the top of page 329 is **La Torre Latino Americano** (The Latin American Tower). It is located near the **zócalo** and is one of the tallest buildings in Mexico City. At the bottom of the page is a photograph of the **Zona Rosa,** a popular tourist area in Mexico City. This area is filled with sidewalk cafés, exclusive boutiques, restaurants, and many first-class hotels.

Play the cassette or read the postcards aloud as the students follow along in their books. Have the students work in pairs and describe the photos to the class.

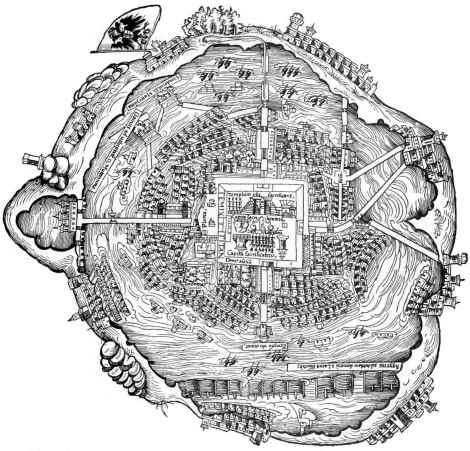

Plan of Tenochtitlán courtesy of the Mexican Government Tourism Office.

2

Actividad • ¿Es cierto o no?

Have the students complete the activity orally and in writing.

CHALLENGE The students should organize their corrected sentences in the form of a paragraph describing Gabriela and Ignacio's visit to Mexico City.

ANSWERS:
1. Fuimos en autobús hasta el Parque de Chapultepec.
2. Luego fuimos a pie por el Paseo de la Reforma hasta la Zona Rosa.
3. Pasamos un día fantástico.
4. Te mando postales, un mapa y fotos.
5. Regreso la semana próxima. ¡Qué pena!
6. Ayer pensé mucho en ti.
7. Fui a un restaurante cerca de la Zona Rosa.
8. Comimos tacos, pollo y enchiladas.
9. Costó muy barato y tocaron la guitarra.
10. Te veo la semana próxima.

3 **Actividad • Charla**

The students should work with a partner to discuss the postcards in Activity 1.

4 **Actividad • ¡A escribir!**

Before the students finish the letter, review how to say what one has already done (Unit 10, page 280). Have the students ask and tell each other what they did yesterday.

> —¿Qué hiciste ayer?
> —Fui a la casa de una amiga. ¿Y tú?

Encourage students to include as much information as possible in their letters. They should refer to the questions as a guide. After the students have completed the letters, collect their work and indicate where corrections need to be made. Return their work to them for revision. Collect the revised letters to check that the students have made the appropriate corrections. Then call on volunteers to read their letters aloud.

5 **SITUACIÓN • El diario de Gabriela** 🔲

CULTURAL BACKGROUND   **El Museo Nacional de Antropología** was opened in 1964 and is considered by many to be the best archeological museum in the world. It is located on the **Avenida de la Reforma** in front of the Chapultepec park and zoo. At the entrance to the museum lies the statue of **Tlaloc,** the rain god. It is said that on the day the statue was delivered, Mexico City experienced one of the worst rainstorms ever recorded.

Play the cassette or read the diary entry aloud as the students follow along in their books.

6 **Actividad • Para completar**

Have the students complete the sentences orally with the information from Activity 5. For writing practice, have the students write the sentences. Have them exchange papers and correct each other's work.

7 **Actividad • ¡A escoger!** 🔲

With books closed, ask the students to choose the correct word or phrase to complete each sentence.

8 **Actividad • Charla**

Have the students take turns asking and answering the questions. They should complete the activity without referring to Gabriela's diary.

9 **Actividad • Y tú, ¿adónde fuiste?**

Those students who have not visited a large city should choose a place in the Spanish-speaking world and pretend that they have taken a trip there. Have the students tell the class where they went on vacation and what they did while they were there.

10 **Conversación • El turista y el guía**

For cooperative learning, form groups of two. Assign one student the role of the tour guide and the other the role of the tourist. The "tour guide" should prepare notes on suggested places to visit, while the "tourist" should ask questions based on the suggestions in the book.

SLOWER-PACED LEARNING Brainstorm with the students phrases that they might use to complete the dialog.

Visitor	Tour guide
¿Cómo puedo ir a . . . ?	Puede tomar un taxi . . . ir a pie.
¿Dónde está . . . ?	Doblar a la derecha . . .
¿Qué hago después . . . ?	Puede ir a . . .

List the phrases on the board or a transparency, and have the students write them in their notebooks. They should refer to the list for ideas as they complete the dialog.

11 **Proyecto • Una carta**

The students should base their letter on the dialog they had in Activity 10. They should collect as much information as possible to include in the letter. Call on students at random to show the class what they plan to send.

As a variation, students may prepare a travel brochure on their favorite Spanish-speaking city. They should illustrate the brochure with magazine pictures, photographs, or drawings. They should include comments from real or imaginary people who have visited the city before.

MARTIN BAKER: La ciudad de Madrid es fantástica. Fuimos en mayo y visitamos el Museo del Prado, el Parque del Retiro, y comimos paella.

Viñeta cultural 3
Festivales

OBJECTIVES

1. To provide information on how festivals are an integral part of the culture in the Hispanic world
2. To make the student aware of the great number and variety of festivals and traditions of the Spanish-speaking world
3. To offer glimpses of the national dances of some of the countries of the Hispanic world
4. To give a general view of the culture of the Spanish-speaking people, thus providing the students with the opportunity to expand their cultural horizons

MOTIVATING ACTIVITIES

1. Ask the students to compare and contrast how Spanish-speaking people celebrate their holidays with how we celebrate ours.
2. Ask the students to find out about the national dances or feast days of some of the Spanish-speaking countries.
3. Ask the students to provide a recipe for a dish of a country in the Hispanic world.
4. Ask the students to prepare a classroom party with a Hispanic theme.

CULTURAL BACKGROUND Spain is a nation that seems to have festivals for every season and every reason.

There are three Spanish festivals which are famous throughout the world: The **Fallas** in Valencia, the **Feria de abril** in Sevilla, and the **Sanfermines** in Pamplona.

During the week preceding March 19, Valencia holds a festival known as **Las Fallas** *(the bonfire festival)*. Enormous wooden and papier mâché structures, some as tall as three story buildings called **"ninots"** are constructed in the public square. They are decorated with explosives and firecrackers and set on fire on March 19. When the structures are set on fire, the explosives ignite and the firecrackers explode—a spectacular sight against a night sky.

As famous as the **Fallas** is the April Fair in Sevilla, featuring people dressed in traditional costumes riding colorfully adorned horse carriages through the streets of Sevilla. While some ride in their carriages, others play the traditional **flamenco** and **sevillanas** along the way. This unique art form combines guitar playing, singing, chanting, dancing, and **staccato** hand clapping in a whirlwind of clicking castanets and colorful costumes.

Each year, Pamplona's **fiesta de San Fermín** on July 7 features the famous **encierros.** The youth of Pamplona, as well as a number of visitors, race through the streets ahead of the bulls which will be fought that afternoon in the bullring.

These are probably the three best-known festivals in Spain, but there is no town or village, no matter how small, which does not have a **fiesta** of its own. Many of these festivals celebrate religious holidays; others commemorate an event of local importance.

Among the most solemn occasions taking place throughout Spain is the **Semana Santa** *(Holy Week)*. During **Semana Santa** there are elaborate processions in which members of **cofradías** *(lay religious brotherhoods)* carry religious images on **pasos** *(platforms)* through the streets.

Particularly popular along northwestern Spain are the **Romerías.** These are pilgrimages made to a countryside shrine. People usually dress in local costumes and sing folk songs along the way. After the religious ceremonies are over, the people have a merry time by having a picnic and by singing and dancing to the tune of bagpipes.

Verbenas *(block festivals)* are held on the eve of a saint's day. Most common of these festivals are those of **Santiago** *(St. James)*, patron saint of Spain on July 25 and **San Juan** *(St. John)* on June 24.

Festivals are also important in the culture of Mexico, Central America, and the Caribbean. In November, Mexicans celebrate **El día de los muertos,** a feast day in honor of the dead, on which special foods and candies are prepared in the shape of skulls and skeletons. Mexicans also celebrate holidays with fireworks, candy-filled **piñatas,** and singing **mariachis.**

In Puerto Rico, the Christmas season is long and festive. It begins in early December with the singing of **aguinaldos** *(carols)* and continues through **El Día de los Reyes Magos** *(Three Kings Day)*. During the Christmas season, traditional recipes are prepared. Many families prepare the traditional well-seasoned roasted suckling pig accompanied by **pasteles,** which are made with plantains stuffed with meats and cheeses, and are very similar in shape to **tamales.**

In Central America on the eve of January 6, children place food under their bed as treats for the Three Wise Men's camels. The following morning, when they awake, they receive their gifts left by the Wise Men close to the **nacimiento** *(Nativity scene)* in their homes.

South America also has its share of festivals, many dating back to pre-Colombian times. In Bolivia, **La fiesta de la cruz** *(Feast of the Cross)* is celebrated on the first weekend in May. Hundreds of people dance in the streets wearing elaborate costumes and masks. On June 24, in Cuzco, Peru, there is the festival of the Inca sun god, **Inti Raymi.** People dance in the streets to the tunes of the **quena,** a kind of Andean reed flute, and the **charango,** a small instrument similar to a ukelele. During the night, people set bonfires in the streets, symbolizing the hope that **Inti Raymi** will protect them from the cold air of winter.

A major festival in Argentina is the National Folklore Festival in the town of Cosquín in January. During the two-week-long festival, **gauchos** perform colorful dances and **payadores** *(ballad singers)* sing songs from the Pampas.

In most of the festivals of the Spanish world, dancers perform the national dance of their respective country. Thus in Chile, it is the **cueca.** In Peru, it is the **marinera,** while in Ecuador, the **sanjuanito** is the national dance. A strong African influence is perceived in the Colombian **bambuco** and **cumbia;** the Venezuelan **joropo;** the Uruguayan **candombe;** the Cuban **rumba,** and the Dominican **merengue.**

In Spain, and throughout the Spanish-speaking world, festivals are occasions where young and old alike rejoice in their heritage.

Cartas de México

Repaso

Vista de la Ciudad de México

Ciudad de México
15 de julio

Querida Liliana:
Ayer fuimos en autobús hasta el Parque de Chapultepec. De allí caminamos por el Paseo de la Reforma hasta la Zona Rosa. Pasamos un día fantástico. Te mando postales, un mapa y fotos. Regreso la semana próxima. ¡Qué pena!
Hasta pronto, Gabriela

La Zona Rosa, Ciudad de México

Ciudad de México
20 de agosto

Querido Joaquín:
Ayer pensé mucho en ti. Fui a un restaurante mexicano cerca de la Zona Rosa. Comimos tacos, pollo y enchiladas. Todo delicioso y muy barato. Unos amigos tocaron la guitarra y todos cantamos.
Te veo la semana próxima.
Ignacio

2 Actividad • ¿Es cierto o no? For answers, see p. T219.

2 Actividad • ¿Es cierto o no?

Change the following sentences to make them true according to Gabriela's and Ignacio's letters.

1. Fuimos en autobús hasta la Zona Rosa.
2. Luego fuimos por el Paseo de la Reforma hasta el parque.
3. Pasamos un día muy aburrido.
4. Te mando postales, unos sellos y tres mapas.
5. Regreso el mes próximo. ¡Qué suerte!
6. Ayer pensé un poco en ti.
7. Fui a un restaurante en el parque.
8. Comimos tacos y chile.
9. Costó muy caro. Unos amigos tocaron el piano.
10. Te veo el año próximo.

3 Actividad • Charla

Work with a partner. Ask each other questions about what Gabriela and Ignacio did in Mexico City.

—¿Adónde fue Gabriela en autobús?
—Fue hasta el Parque de Chapultépec.

—¿Dónde comió Ignacio?
—En un restaurante cerca de la Zona Rosa.

4 Actividad • ¡A escribir! Sample letter is given.

Think of something special that you did last week, or make up an interesting trip or excursion. Then write to a friend in Spanish telling him or her what you did. You can take into account the following:

Querido Miguel:

• Where did you go? With whom?
• How? By bus, by car, on foot?
• Where did you eat? What?
• How much did it cost?
• Was there any kind of entertainment? What?
• Did you do any shopping? What did you buy?
• Did you have fun? Are you sending something with your letter? What?

La semana pasada fuimos Rosa y yo en autobús a la ciudad de Ávila. Comimos tortilla en un restaurant al aire libre. El almuerzo nos costó 1,000 pesetas. Después vimos los monumentos famosos y compramos libros sobre la ciudad. Fue muy divertido. Aquí tienes unas fotos de nosotros. Adiós.

5 SITUACIÓN • El diario de Gabriela

Martes por la noche

Queridísimo diario: Hoy por la tarde fuimos en taxi al Museo de Antropología.

MUSEO NACIONAL DE ANTROPOLOGIA

Caminamos por todas las salas.
Hay veintiséis. Después, en
la tienda compramos libros
y postales. Después del Museo
fuimos al Parque de Chapultepec.
Alquilamos un bote y paseamos.
¡Qué divertido! Comimos unos
tacos y tomamos refrescos.

6 Actividad • Para completar

Complete these sentences according to Gabriela's diary.

1. Gabriela escribe en su diario el _____ . *martes por la noche.*
2. Hoy fueron en _taxi_ al _Museo_ de Antropología
3. Caminaron por _todas_ las salas.
4. Compraron _libros_ y y _postales_.

5. Después del Museo fueron al _____ . *Parque de Chapultepec.*
6. Los chicos alquilaron _un bote_ y _pasearon_.
7. ¡Qué _____! *divertido!*
8. Comieron _tacos._ .

7 Actividad • ¡A escoger!

Choose the best option to complete the following sentences according to Gabriela's diary.

1. Fuimos al Museo de Antropología
   • en autobús.   • en taxi.   • a pie.
2. Allí caminamos por
   • el parque.   • todas las salas.   • toda la tienda.
3. También fuimos
   • a la cafetería.   • a la ciudad.   • a la tienda.
4. Después del Museo fuimos
   • a un restaurante.   • a la Zona Rosa.   • al Parque de Chapultepec.
5. Alquilamos un
   • coche.   • bote.   • autobús.
6. Comimos
   • una enchilada.   • frutas.   • unos tacos.

1. Gabriela fue al Museo de Antropología. 6. Alquilaron un bote.
2. Fue por la tarde en taxi. 7. No, pasearon.
3. Hay ventiséis salas. 8. Después comieron.
4. Compraron libros y postales. 9. Comieron tacos.
5. Fue al Parque de Chapultepec. 10. Tomaron refrescos.

8   Actividad • Charla

Pair off with a classmate. Take turns asking and answering these questions about Gabriela's diary.

1. ¿Adónde fue Gabriela el martes?
2. ¿Cuándo y cómo fue allí?
3. ¿Cuántas salas hay?
4. ¿Qué compraron en la tienda?
5. ¿Adónde fue ella después del Museo?

6. ¿Qué alquilaron allí Gabriela y sus amigos?
7. ¿Nadaron en el parque?
8. ¿Qué hicieron después?
9. ¿Qué comieron? ¿Pollo?
10. ¿Tomaron leche?

9   Actividad • Y tú, ¿adónde fuiste?   Possible answers are given.

Now think of a trip you have taken or imagined, and work with your partner on the following questions.

1. ¿A qué ciudad fuiste? ¿Cuándo?
2. ¿Con quién fuiste?
3. ¿Cómo fuiste a la ciudad?
4. ¿Visitaste un museo o viste una exhibición? ¿Cuál?

5. ¿Te gustó? ¿Por qué?
6. ¿Comiste algo? ¿Dónde y qué?
7. ¿Paseaste? ¿Caminaste?
8. ¿Compraste muchas cosas? ¿Qué?

Fui a Salamanca el mes pasado con Ana y Julio. Fuimos en autobús. Visitamos la Universidad. Me gustó mucho por su arquitectura. Paseamos por la Plaza Mayor. Comimos un bocadillo en un restaurante de la Plaza Mayor y compramos postales para nuestros amigos.

10   Conversación • El turista y el guía

Team up with a classmate. One of you will play the part of a tourist; the other will be a guide. Pick a place to visit and act out one of the following dialogs in Spanish.

Dialog 1

Visitor asks:
• what sights to see
• how to get around to the different places
• where to go for lunch

Guide suggests:
• four or five different places
• two or three means of transportation
• a soda at one of the plazas and lunch at a restaurant later

Dialog 2

Visitor asks:
• where to go after lunch
• what museum has an interesting exhibit
• what to do after the museum

Guide suggests:
• a stroll in the park or on one of the main boulevards, or a visit to a museum
• a museum and its location
• going to a park and having a soda and something to eat

11   Proyecto • Una carta   A sample letter is given.

Write a letter about your trip or excursion. Imagine you are sending it to a friend.
Say that you are enclosing postcards, maps, and pictures. Describe them in Spanish.
Make a complete folder to send your friend. Report what you're sending to the class.

Querida . . .

Ayer fuimos a Granada. Fuimos al Alcázar, un viejo palacio moro. También fuimos a la Sierra Nevada, unas montañas que siempre tienen nieve. Te mando postales del Alcázar. Una es de los jardines, otra es del palacio. Tu amigo . . .

Viñeta cultural 3

Festivales

Festivales . . . the word itself brings forth images of color, music, and dance. Spain seems to have festivals for every season and every reason. Many of the festivals celebrate religious holidays; others mark the end of winter and the beginning of spring. In Spain, and throughout the Spanish-speaking world, festivals are occasions when young and old alike rejoice in their heritage.

❶ Festival de los Mariscos en Galicia, España

❷ Festival de Santiago en Galicia, España

❸ La Muñeira, un baile popular de Galicia, España

❹ Festival de San Fermín en Pamplona, España

Festivales   333

1. La Jota, un baile folklórico en Aragón, España
2. Festival del Pilar en Aragón, España
3. Celebración del Corpus Cristi en Toledo, España
4. Un desfile de los gigantes en Toledo, España

Brilliant decorations, lively music, costumes, and fireworks are part of almost every festival in Spain. In Valencia, the end of winter is celebrated with a great festival called **Las Fallas.** Enormous wooden and papier-mâché structures, some as tall as three-story buildings, are constructed in the public square.

They are decorated with colorful explosives, while chains of smaller firecrackers hang from them in all directions. When the structures are set on fire, the explosives ignite and the firecrackers explode—a spectacular sight to see against a night sky.

1 Fallas de Valencia, España; niñas ofrecen flores a la virgen

2 Presentación de moros y cristianos en Alicante, España

3 Festival de San Juan en Alicante, España

4 Un baile folklórico en las Islas Baleares, España

5 Fiesta de San Miguel en las Islas Baleares, España

No festival in Spain is complete without flamenco dancing. This unique art form combines guitar playing, singing, chanting, dancing, and staccato hand clapping in a whirlwind of clicking castanets and colorful costumes. It is thought that this dance originated around 1500.

❶ Alegre festival en Castilla, España

❷ Bailando la Jota en Castilla, España

❸ Feria de Andalucía en Málaga, España

❹ Feria de abril en Sevilla, España

❺ El baile flamenco en Sevilla, España

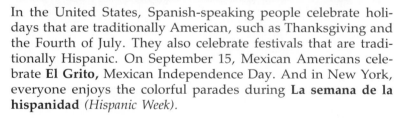

In the United States, Spanish-speaking people celebrate holidays that are traditionally American, such as Thanksgiving and the Fourth of July. They also celebrate festivals that are traditionally Hispanic. On September 15, Mexican Americans celebrate **El Grito,** Mexican Independence Day. And in New York, everyone enjoys the colorful parades during **La semana de la hispanidad** (Hispanic Week).

❶ Domingo de Ramos en St. Augustine, Florida

❷ Festival hispánico en San Antonio, Texas

❸ Una obra de teatro en español en Santa Fe, Nuevo México

❹ Festival de Lelo Lai en San Juan, Puerto Rico

❺ Fiesta mexicana en San Francisco, California

❶ Danza del Quetzal en
Puebla, México

❷ Altar en el Día de los
Muertos en México

❸ Celebración de los Tres
Reyes Magos en México

❹ Día de fiesta en Oaxaca,
México

❺ Niños con una piñata en
México

Festivals are also important in the culture of Mexico and Central America. In November, Mexicans celebrate **El Día de los Muertos,** a feast day in honor of the dead on which special foods and candies are prepared in the shape of skulls and skeletons. Mexicans also celebrate holidays with fireworks, candy-filled piñatas, and singing mariachis. Piñatas, which most people associate with Mexico, actually originated in Italy in the 1500s. The game today is played much as it was long ago. Everyone is blindfolded and given a stick with which to break the piñata. Once it is broken, a shower of toys, sweets, or other surprises comes tumbling down.

❶ Festival de Quelaquetza en Oaxaca, México

❷ Desfile de muchachas en trajes típicos en Oaxaca, México

❸ Baile de los Conquistadores en Guatemala

❹ Celebración del Día de la Raza en Costa Rica

Festivales   339

South America also has its share of festivals, many dating back to pre-Colombian times. In Bolivia, **La fiesta de la cruz** *(Feast of the Cross)* is celebrated on the first weekend in May. Hundreds of people dance in the streets wearing elaborate costumes and masks. In June, on the day of San Juan, most cities in Peru are ablaze with torches and bonfires symbolizing the hope that fires will fend off the cold air of winter.

❶ Festival del Sol en Perú

❷ Celebración religiosa en Lima, Perú

❸ Carnaval de origen pre-colombino en Oruro, Bolivia

❹ Flautista del carnaval en Oruro, Bolivia

❺ Un carnaval festivo en Corrientes, Argentina

340   **Viñeta cultural 3**

FOR REFERENCE

SUMMARY OF FUNCTIONS

The term *functions* can be defined as what you do with language—what your purpose is in speaking. Here is a list of all the functions with the expressions you have learned related to these functions. The number indicates the unit in which the expression is introduced, followed by the section letter and number in parentheses.

EXCHANGING INFORMATION

Asking and giving names
1 (B4)   ¿Cómo te llamas tú?
         Yo me llamo . . .

Asking and giving someone else's name
1 (B8)   ¿Cómo se llama él?
         Él se llama . . .
         ¿Cómo se llama ella?
         Ella se llama . . .

Asking someone's age, telling yours
6 (B5)   ¿Cuántos años tienes?
         Tengo (catorce) años

Asking and saying where people are from
1 (C6)   ¿De dónde eres tú?
         Soy de . . .
         ¿De dónde son ellos?
         Son de . . .
         ¿Tú eres de . . . ?
         Sí, soy de . . .

Asking for directions
5 (A17) ¿Dónde está(n) . . . ?
         ¿Está(n) cerca de aquí?
         ¿Está(n) lejos?

Giving directions
5 (A17) Está abajo.
         . . . lejos
5 (A15) . . . allí arriba
         . . . detrás de
         . . . a la izquierda
         . . . al lado de
         . . . a la derecha

Asking for information
2 (A10) ¿Cuándo?
         ¿Cómo?
         ¿Quién?
         ¿Qué?
         ¿Por qué?

         ¿De dónde?
7 (C8)   ¿Sabes si . . . ?
         ¿Sabes dónde . . . ?
         ¿Sabes cuándo . . . ?

Telling time
2 (B19) ¿Qué hora es?
         ¿A qué hora es . . . ?
         Es la una.
         Son las . . .
         A la una.
         A las . . .

Discussing prices
2 (C8)   ¿Cuánto cuesta(n)?
         Cuesta(n) . . .
11 (B16) ¿Cuánto vale?
         Es muy caro.
         Es demasiado caro.
         No vale tanto.
         No pago más de . . .
         Es un regalo.
         Es muy barato.
         Es una ganga.

Saying what you usually do
10 (A9) Canto a menudo.
         Casi siempre canto.

Expressing how long ago something happened
10 (A18) Isabel llegó hace
         . . . mucho tiempo.
         . . . quince días.
         . . . una hora.
         Hace un mes que Isabel llegó.

Discussing whether or not something has already been done
10 (C13) ¿Ya contestaste la carta?
         Sí, ya la contesté.
         No, no la contesté.

Saying that you know something
7 (C6)   Yo sé . . .

EXPRESSING ATTITUDES AND OPINIONS

Asking for and giving an opinion
7 (B21) ¿Qué piensas?
Pienso que (no) . . .
¿Qué crees?
Creo que (no) . . .
¿Qué te parece?
Me parece que . . .
11 (A4) ¡Buena idea!
¡Está bien!
No está mal.
Me gusta más . . .
No me gusta nada.
No sé, pero . . .

Asking what someone or something is like
6 (B17) ¿Cómo es . . . ?
¿Cómo son . . . ?

Telling how something tastes
9 (C20) ¡Qué sabrosos!
Son deliciosos.
¡Qué rico está!

Asking and saying whether people are hungry or thirsty
9 (C4) ¿Tienes sed?
Sí, tengo mucha sed.
Elena no tiene hambre ahora.
Yo sí. Tengo mucha hambre.

Asking for advice
7 (B21) ¿Qué piensas?
Pienso que (no) . . .
¿Qué crees?
Creo que (no) . . .
¿Qué te parece?
Me parece que . . .

EXPRESSING FEELINGS AND EMOTIONS

Expressing surprise
2 (B25) ¿Verdad?

Expressing agreement
3 (C1) De acuerdo.
6 (C1) Por supuesto.

Expressing disagreement
2 (B25) Al contrario.

Expressing liking
3 (A4) Me gusta . . .
9 (A15) Nos gustan . . .

Expressing dislikes
3 (A4) No me gusta . . .
9 (A15) No nos gustan . . .
11 (A4) No me gusta nada . . .

Expressing strong dislike
3 (A12) Odio . . .

Expressing preference
2 (B25) Tu materia favorita
Es mi . . . preferido(a).
3 (A12) Me gusta mucho.

Complimenting people
2 (B25) Eres un genio.
6 (B1) Es muy inteligente.
Son bien simpáticos.
Son cariñosos.
6 (B21) ¿Tu hermana? ¡Qué linda!
¿Tu hermano? ¡Qué guapo!
¡Qué chica tan linda!
¡Qué chico tan guapo!

Responding to good news
5 (A1) ¡Qué suerte!

Expressing enthusiasm
2 (B25) Es muy interesante
3 (A9) Es divertido.
3 (A12) Es estupendo.

Expressing lack of enthusiasm
3 (A9) Es horrible.
3 (A12) Es aburrido.

Expressing regret
7 (A14) ¡Qué lástima!
¡Qué pena!

PERSUADING

Making suggestions
5 (C15) ¿Por qué no comemos?
7 (B15) ¿Tienes ganas de ir al cine?
¿Vamos a ver . . . ?
¿Quieres ver . . . ?

Suggesting something else
7 (B8) Vamos a ver (una cómica).
7 (B15) No, mejor (vamos al parque).
¿Por qué no vemos . . . ?
¿Y si vemos . . . ?

SOCIALIZING

Saying hello
1 (A12) ¡Hola!
Buenos días.
Buenas tardes.
Buenas noches.

Saying goodbye
1 (A1) ¡Hasta luego!
1 (A10) ¡Hasta mañana!
1 (A12) ¡Adiós!
¡Chao!

Addressing people
1 (A10) señor + last name
señora + last name
señorita + last name
first name
11 (A1) Señorita, por favor.
¿Qué desea, señora?

Saying please, thank you, and you're welcome
1 (B6) Por favor
Gracias
De nada
3 (B1) Muchas gracias

Getting someone's attention:
getting a friend's attention
7 (C3) ¡Mira!
¡Oye!

getting a stranger's attention
1 (B8) Por favor, señor (señora, señorita)

Excusing an interruption
7 (C3) ¡Perdón!
¡Permiso, por favor!

Speaking on the phone:
answering the phone
5 (B19) ¡Diga!
¡Hola!
¡Aló!
Buenas tardes, familia + last name.

asking for someone
5 (B11) Buenas tardes, ¿el señor + last name?,
por favor.

ending a phone conversation
5 (B11) Adiós.
Hasta luego.

Introducing yourself
1 (B1) Yo me llamo . . .

Responding to an introduction
1 (B1) Yo me llamo . . . ¡Mucho gusto!
Mucho gusto.

Accepting something to eat
9 (C1) Sí, por favor.
9 (C4) Yo, sí. Tengo mucha hambre.

Declining something to eat
9 (B15) No, gracias.

Accepting an invitation
7 (A9) Sí, fantástico. ¡Vamos!

Declining an invitation
7 (A9) Lo siento, no puedo.
7 (A14) No puedo, tengo que estudiar.

Asking "How are you?":
informal
1 (A4) ¿Qué tal?
¿Cómo estás tú?

formal
1 (A16) ¿Cómo está usted?

Responding to "How are you?"
1 (A1) Regular.
¡Muy mal!
1 (A4) Bien, gracias.
5 (A10) Estoy bien, gracias.

Making somebody feel at home
6 (A10) ¡Bienvenido(a)!
¡Pasa!
¡Mucho gusto!
¡Estás en tu casa!

Accepting hospitality
6 (A10) ¡Gracias! ¡Es un placer estar aquí!
¡Igualmente, señor(a)!
¡Usted es muy amable!

Complimenting someone on food
9 (C1) . . . está perfecto(a).
. . . son deliciosos.
¡Qué rico(a) está!

GRAMMAR SUMMARY

ARTICLES

DEFINITE ARTICLES

	MASCULINE	FEMININE
SINGULAR	el chico	la chica
PLURAL	los chicos	las chicas

INDEFINITE ARTICLES

	MASCULINE	FEMININE
SINGULAR	un chico	una chica
PLURAL	unos chicos	unas chicas

CONTRACTIONS OF THE DEFINITE ARTICLE

a + el → al

de + el → del

ADJECTIVES

		MASCULINE	FEMININE
Adjectives that end in -o	SING PL	chico alto chicos altos	chica alta chicas altas
Adjectives that end in -e	SING PL	chico inteligente chicos inteligentes	chica inteligente chicas inteligentes
Adjectives that end in a consonant	SING PL	examen difícil exámenes difíciles	clase difícil clases difíciles

DEMONSTRATIVE ADJECTIVES

este			ese		
	MASCULINE	FEMININE		MASCULINE	FEMININE
SINGULAR PLURAL	este chico estos chicos	esta chica estas chicas	SINGULAR PLURAL	ese chico esos chicos	esa chica esas chicas

POSSESSIVE ADJECTIVES

SINGULAR		PLURAL	
MASCULINE	FEMININE	MASCULINE	FEMININE
mi hijo tu hijo su hijo nuestro hijo	mi hija tu hija su hija nuestra hija	mis hijos tus hijos sus hijos nuestros hijos	mis hijas tus hijas sus hijas nuestras hijas

PRONOUNS

SUBJECT PRONOUNS	DIRECT OBJECT PRONOUNS	INDIRECT OBJECT PRONOUNS	OBJECTS OF PREPOSITIONS
yo	me	me	mí
tú	te	te	ti
él, ella, Ud.	lo, la	le	él, ella, Ud.
nosotros, -as	nos	nos	nosotros, -as
ellos, ellas, Uds.	los, las	les	ellos, ellas, Uds.

NEGATION:
NEGATIVE WORDS

no
nada
nunca
ni . . . ni

INTERROGATIVES:
INTERROGATIVE WORDS

¿Cómo?	¿De dónde?
¿Cuándo?	¿Por qué?
¿Cuánto?	¿Qué?
¿Cuál?	¿Quién?

COMPARATIVES
COMPARISONS OF UNEQUAL QUANTITIES

más			más			
	+ adjective +	que		+ de +		number (expression of quantity)
menos			menos			

REGULAR VERBS

INFINITIVE	PRESENT		PRETERIT	
hablar	hablo	hablamos	hablé	hablamos
	hablas	habláis	hablaste	hablasteis
	habla	hablan	habló	hablaron
comer	como	comemos	comí	comimos
	comes	coméis	comiste	comisteis
	come	comen	comió	comieron
escribir	escribo	escribimos	escribí	escribimos
	escribes	escribís	escribiste	escribisteis
	escribe	escriben	escribió	escribieron

VERB INDEX

The alphabetical list below includes verbs with stem changes, spelling changes, or irregular forms. The page number will guide you to the verb itself or to a verb whose pattern it follows.

Verbs with Irregular Forms

Verbs listed in this section are those that do not follow the usual pattern of **-ar, -er,** and **-ir** verbs. The forms in which the changes occur are printed in **boldface** type.

CONOCER
present   **conozco,** conoces, conoce, conocemos, conocéis, conocen

DECIR
present   **digo, dices, dice,** decimos, decís, **dicen**

ESTAR
present   **estoy,** estás, está, estamos, estáis, están

HACER
present   **hago,** haces, hace, hacemos, hacéis, hacen
preterit   **hice, hiciste, hizo, hicimos, hicisteis, hicieron**

IR
present   **voy, vas, va, vamos, vais, van**
preterit   **fui, fuiste, fue, fuimos, fuisteis, fueron**

PONER
present   **pongo,** pones, pone, ponemos, ponéis, ponen

SABER
present   **sé,** sabes, sabe, sabemos, sabéis, saben

SALIR
present   **salgo,** sales, sale, salimos, salís, salen

SER
present   **soy, eres, es, somos, sois, son**

TENER
present   **tengo, tienes, tiene,** tenemos, tenéis, **tienen**

VENIR
present   **vengo, vienes, viene,** venimos, venís, **vienen**

Verbs with Stem Changes

The verbs listed in this section are stem changing. Stem changing verbs are those that have a spelling change in the root of the verb. The stem change affects the **yo, tú, él** and **ellos** forms of the present.

Present tense of stem changing verbs

-ar verbs			*-er verbs*		*-ir verbs*
e → ie **pensar**[1]	o → ue **encontrar**[2]	u → ue **jugar**	e → ie **querer**	o → ue **poder**[3]	e → i **servir**
pienso	encuentro	juego	quiero	puedo	sirvo
piensas	encuentras	juegas	quieres	puedes	sirves
piensa	encuentra	juega	quiere	puede	sirve
pensamos	encontramos	jugamos	queremos	podemos	servimos
pensáis	encontráis	jugáis	queréis	podéis	servís
piensan	encuentran	juegan	quieren	pueden	sirven

[1]**empezar (ie)** is conjugated like **pensar**
[2]**probar (ue)** and **costar (ue)** are conjugated like **encontrar**
[3]**volver (ue)** is conjugated like **poder**

NUMBERS

0	cero	18	dieciocho	60	sesenta
1	uno (un, una)	19	diecinueve	70	setenta
2	dos	20	veinte	80	ochenta
3	tres	21	veintiuno(a)	90	noventa
4	cuatro	22	veintidós	100	cien
5	cinco	23	veintitrés	101	ciento uno(a)
6	seis	24	veinticuatro	102	ciento dos
7	siete	25	veinticinco	103	ciento tres
8	ocho	26	veintiséis	200	doscientos, -as
9	nueve	27	veintisiete	201	doscientos uno(a)
10	diez	28	veintiocho	300	trescientos, -as
11	once	29	veintinueve	400	cuatrocientos, -as
12	doce	30	treinta	500	quinientos, -as
13	trece	31	treinta y uno(a)	600	seiscientos, -as
14	catorce	32	treinta y dos	700	setecientos, -as
15	quince	33	treinta y tres	800	ochocientos, -as
16	dieciséis	40	cuarenta	900	novecientos, -as
17	diecisiete	50	cincuenta	1,000	mil

ENGLISH EQUIVALENTS

The following are the English equivalents of the basic material in each section of every unit, with the exception of review units. They are not literal translations but represent what a speaker of English would say in the same situation.

1 ¡HOLA, AMIGOS!

A1 En el colegio
RAMÓN ¡Hola, Anita! ¿Cómo estás?
ANITA Muy bien, Ramón. Gracias, ¿y tú?
RAMÓN ¿Yo? Regular. ¡Hasta luego!
ANITA ¡Chao!
RAMÓN ¡Adiós!

—¿Qué tal?
—¿Yo? ¡Muy mal!
—¡Qué pena!

A10 Saludos
Carmen y el señor Colón
—Buenos días, señor.
—Buenos días, Carmen.
Jorge y la señorita López
—Buenas tardes, señorita.
—¡Adiós! Hasta mañana, Jorge.
Alicia y la señora Valdés
—Buenas noches, señora.
—Buenas noches, Alicia.
—¿Cómo estás tú?

A16 María Luisa y la profesora
SRA. VALDÉS Buenos días, María Luisa.
¿Cómo estás?
MARÍA LUISA Muy bien, señora, gracias.
¿Y cómo está usted?
SRA. VALDÉS Bien, gracias.

B1 En la escuela. En la clase.
RICARDO ¡Hola! Yo me llamo Ricardo.
¿Cómo te llamas tú?
LUPE Me llamo Lupe. ¡Mucho gusto!
RICARDO ¡Mucho gusto! Bueno . . . hasta
luego, Lupe.
LUPE Hasta luego, Ricardo.

Él se llama Ricardo.
Ella se llama Lupe.

B6 Después de la clase
En el patio de la escuela.

HI, FRIENDS!

In school
Hi, Anita! How are you?
Very well, Ramón. Thank you. And you?
Me? So-so. See you later!
So long!
Goodbye!

How are things?
(with) Me? Awful!
What a pity!

Greetings
Carmen and Mr. Colón
Good morning, sir.
Good morning, Carmen.
Jorge and Miss López
Good afternoon, miss.
Goodbye! See you tomorrow, Jorge.
Alicia and Mrs. Valdés
Good night, ma'am.
Good night, Alicia.
How are you?

María Luisa and the teacher
Good morning, María Luisa.
How are you?
Very well, ma'am, thank you.
And how are you?
Fine, thank you.

In school. In class.
Hello! My name is Ricardo.
What's your name?
My name is Lupe. Nice to meet you.
Nice to meet you! Well . . . see you
later, Lupe.
See you later, Ricardo.

His name is Ricardo.
Her name is Lupe.

After class
In the school courtyard.

ANTONIO	¡Ricardo!, ¡Ricardo!		*Ricardo!, Ricardo!*
RICARDO	¿Sí?		*Yes?*
ANTONIO	¡Oye! Por favor, ¿cómo se llama la chica nueva?		*Hey! Please, what's the new girl's name?*
RICARDO	¿Quién, la chica de Arizona?		*Who, the girl from Arizona?*
ANTONIO	No, la chica de México.		*No, the girl from Mexico.*
RICARDO	Ella se llama Lupe.		*Her name is Lupe.*
ANTONIO	¿Lupe? Gracias, Ricardo.		*Lupe? Thanks, Ricardo.*
RICARDO	De nada, Antonio.		*You're welcome, Antonio.*

C1 ¿De dónde son?

Él se llama Pedro Gómez.
Pedro es de Texas, Estados Unidos.

María Bernal y Carlos Cajal.
Ellos son de España.

Yo me llamo Pablo Matos. Soy de Puerto Rico.
¿De dónde eres tú?

Nosotras somos de México.
Yo me llamo Elena Llansó.
Ella se llama Rosa. ¿De dónde son ustedes?

Where are they from?

His name is Pedro Gómez.
Pedro is from Texas, U.S.A.

María Bernal and Carlos Cajal.
They are from Spain.

My name is Pablo Matos. I'm from Puerto Rico. Where are you from?

We are from Mexico.
My name is Elena Llansó.
Her name is Rosa. Where are you from?

2 EN LA ESCUELA

IN SCHOOL

A1 ¿Cómo vienes a la escuela?

Los estudiantes de la Escuela Secundaria Benito Juárez vienen de muchas partes de la ciudad. Muchos vienen temprano, pero no todos. Algunos vienen tarde hoy. ¿Por qué? Porque el autobús escolar número ocho tiene un problema. Pero, ¡mira!, ahí viene el autobús.

How do you get to school?

The students at the Benito Juárez Secondary School come from many parts of the city. Many come early, but not all. Some are coming late today. Why? Because school-bus number eight has a problem. But, look! Here comes the bus.

ISABEL	Andrés, ¿vienes tú en autobús con Carlos?		*Andrés, do you come by bus with Carlos?*
ANDRÉS	No, yo no vengo en autobús, vengo en auto.		*No, I don't come by bus, I come by car.*
ISABEL	Y ustedes, ¿cómo vienen?		*And you? How do you come?*
RAÚL Y MARTA	Nosotros venimos en metro.		*We come by subway.*
ISABEL	¿Y José? ¿Cuándo viene? ¿Viene él con Carlos?		*And José? When is he coming? Is he coming with Carlos?*
MARTA	Yo no sé.		*I don't know.*
ANDRÉS	Mira, ahí viene José.		*Look, here comes José.*
ISABEL	¿No viene en bicicleta?		*Isn't he coming on his bike?*
RAÚL	No, hoy viene a pie.		*No, today he is coming on foot.*
ISABEL	¡Ah, por fin viene el autobús! ¡Carlos, mi libro de inglés, por favor!		*Ah, the bus is finally coming! Carlos, my English book, please!*

B1 ¿Qué materias tienes hoy?
En el recreo.

ALBERTO	¡Hola, Enrique! ¿Tienes clase de matemáticas?		
ENRIQUE	No, tengo inglés.		

What subjects do you have today?
At recess.
Hi, Enrique! Do you have math class?

No, I have English.

ALBERTO	¿A qué hora?
ENRIQUE	A las diez. ¿Y tú?, ¿qué tienes?
ALBERTO	Hoy tengo clase de computadoras.
ENRIQUE	¿Hay muchos estudiantes?
ALBERTO	Como veinte.
ENRIQUE	Y, el profesor, ¿quién es?
ALBERTO	Tenemos una profesora: la señora Suárez. ¿Cuántas materias tienes tú?
ENRIQUE	Diez, once . . . no sé. ¿Qué hora es?
ALBERTO	¡Oh! Son casi las diez. ¡Adiós!
ENRIQUE	¡Chao!

At what time?
At ten o'clock. And you? What do you have?
Today I have computer class.
Are there a lot of students?
About twenty.
And, the teacher, who is he?
We have a female teacher, Mrs. Suárez. How many subjects do you have? (are you taking?)
Ten, eleven . . . I don't know. What time is it?
Oh! It's almost ten. Goodbye!
So long!

B4 Los números del 0 al 20

cero	once
uno	doce
dos	trece
tres	catorce
cuatro	quince
cinco	dieciséis
seis	diecisiete
siete	dieciocho
ocho	diecinueve
nueve	veinte
diez	

The numbers from 0 to 20

zero	*eleven*
one	*twelve*
two	*thirteen*
three	*fourteen*
four	*fifteen*
five	*sixteen*
six	*seventeen*
seven	*eighteen*
eight	*nineteen*
nine	*twenty*
ten	

B8 El horario de Enrique
Enrique es estudiante de la Escuela Secundaria Benito Juárez. Tiene un horario fuerte. Hay diez materias, pero no hay clases el sábado.

—Yo tengo otras materias—álgebra a las 4, biología a las 5, filosofía a las 6, francés a las 7, manualidades a las 8, química a las 9 . . .

Enrique's schedule
Enrique is a student at Benito Juárez Secondary School. He has a very heavy schedule. There are ten subjects, but there are no classes on Saturday.

"I have other subjects—algebra at four o'clock, biology at five, philosophy at six, French at seven, industrial arts at eight, chemistry at nine . . .

B25 Diferencia de opiniones

ANDRÉS	¿Qué clase tienes tú ahora?
CLARA	Biología, ¿y tú?
ANDRÉS	Historia. Con el Sr. Galván. Es mi materia preferida.
CLARA	¿Tú materia preferida? ¡Es muy aburrida! Es difícil. Hay mucha tarea.
ANDRÉS	¡Al contrario! Es fácil. Es muy interesante. Y tu materia favorita, ¿cuál es?
CLARA	Química.
ANDRÉS	Tienes bastante tarea y no es interesante, ¿verdad?
CLARA	No, es muy interesante.
ANDRÉS	¿Cuántas materias tienes?
CLARA	Tengo diez.
ANDRÉS	¿Diez? ¡Eres un genio!

Difference of opinions
What class do you have now?
Biology, and you?
History. With Mr. Galván. It's my favorite subject.

Your favorite subject? It's very boring. It's difficult. There is a lot of homework.

On the contrary! It's easy. It's very interesting. And which is your favorite subject?

Chemistry.
You have a lot of homework and it's not interesting, right?
No, it's very interesting.
How many subjects do you have?
I have ten.
Ten? You are a genius!

C1 ¿Cuánto cuesta?
En una tienda de San Juan, Puerto Rico.

How much does it cost?
In a store in San Juan, Puerto Rico.

Rosa	Miguel, ¡una regla con calculadora!	Miguel, a ruler with a calculator!
Miguel	¿Sí? ¿Cuánto cuesta?	Yes? How much does it cost?
Rosa	Catorce noventa y nueve.	Fourteen ninety–nine.
Miguel	Por favor, señor, ¿cuánto cuestan los bolígrafos? No tienen precio.	Please, sir, how much are the ballpoint pens? They don't have a price.
Vendedor	Tres por dos pesos.	Three for two dollars.
Miguel	Gracias	Thank you.
Rosa	Perdón, ¿tiene usted carteras?	Excuse me, do you have schoolbags?
Vendedora	Sí, cuestan quince pesos.	Yes, they cost fifteen dollars.
Rosa	¡Uy!, no tengo tanto. Gracias, señora.	Uf! I don't have that much. Thank you, ma'am.
Miguel	¿Qué más necesitas?	What else do you need?
Rosa	¡Dinero, por supuesto!	Money, of course!

C7 Compras para la escuela
—Por favor, ¿cuánto cuesta . . .
un cuaderno?   un lápiz?
una goma?   un marcador?
un compás?
—¡Hay rebajas! Tenemos . . . unos cuadernos, unas revistas, unas plumas, unos lápices, y unos diccionarios en venta.

Shopping for school supplies
Please, how much is . . .
a notebook?   a pencil?
an eraser?   a marker?
a compass?
There are discounts! We have some . . . notebooks, magazines, pens, pencils, and dictionaries on sale.

3 DEPORTES Y PASATIEMPOS

SPORTS AND PASTIMES

A1 ¿Qué deporte te gusta?
¿Qué deporte te gusta, Miguel?
Me gusta el béisbol.
¡No me gusta la gimnasia!

What sport do you like?
What sport do you like, Miguel?
I like baseball.
I don't like gymnastics!

También me gusta mucho el tenis.
¡Y no me gusta correr!
Pero sí me gusta montar en bicicleta.

I also like tennis very much.
And I don't like to run!
But I really like to ride my bike.

¿Qué deporte le gusta a Pedro?
A Pedro le gusta nadar.
Pero no le gusta el fútbol.

What sport does Pedro like?
Pedro likes to swim.
But he doesn't like soccer.

¿Qué deporte le gusta a Olga?
A Olga le gusta el vólibol.
Pero no le gusta el básquetbol.

What sport does Olga like?
Olga likes volleyball.
But she doesn't like basketball.

A9 Pasatiempos
—¿Qué pasatiempo le gusta a Alberto?
—A Alberto le gusta escuchar discos.
  Dice que es divertido.

Pastimes
What's Alberto's favorite pastime?
Alberto likes to listen to records.
He says it's fun.

—¿A Ofelia le gusta estudiar música y cantar?
—No, no le gusta.
  Dice que es muy aburrido.
  Le gusta patinar.

Does Ofelia like to study music and sing?
No, she doesn't like it.
She says it's very boring.
She likes to skate.

—Y a Pepe, ¿qué le gusta?
—A Pepe, le gusta tocar la guitarra y bailar.
—¿Por qué?
—Dice que es ¡estupendo!

And Pepe, what does he like?
Pepe likes to play the guitar and dance.
Why?
He says it's great!

English Equivalents   353

—¿Y a Tato y a Lola?
—A Tato le gusta tomar fotografías.
  Pero a Lola le gusta hablar por teléfono.

—¿Qué te gusta, Luisa?
—Me gusta trabajar y jugar con la computadora. ¡Es fantástico! Y también me
  gusta mirar televisión.

—Pedro, ¿te gusta mirar televisión también?
—¡No! Odio mirar televisión.
—¿Por qué?
—¡Es horrible!

And Tato and Lola?
Tato likes to take photographs.
But Lola likes to talk on the phone.

What do you like, Luisa?
I like to work and play with the computer. It's fantastic!
And I also like to watch television.

Pedro, do you like to watch television too?
No! I hate to watch television.
Why?
It's horrible!

A16 El judo

Me llamo Esteban Rodríguez. Mi pasatiempo favorito es el judo. Me gusta practicar judo. Soy cinturón azul. Después del azul vienen el cinturón marrón y el cinturón negro. En el judo hay un cinturón de color diferente para cada categoría. El blanco es para los principiantes y el negro para los más avanzados. No hay cinturón rojo. Hay siete colores en total:

blanco   amarillo   anaranjado
verde   azul   marrón   negro

Judo

My name is Esteban Rodríguez. My favorite pastime is judo. I like to practice judo. I'm a blue belt. After the blue belt, there's the brown belt and the black belt. In judo there is a different color belt for each category. White is for beginners and black is for the more advanced. There is no red belt.
There are seven colors in all:

white   yellow   orange
green   blue   brown   black

B1 ¡Un fanfarrón!

Una entrevista imaginaria
Gracias por todo, amigos. Es un honor ser el atleta del año. Pero sí, ¡es verdad! Practico todos los deportes y juego en todas las estaciones. Como todo campeón, gano muchos premios.

Me gusta mucho el invierno. ¡Soy estupendo en el hielo! Patino muy bien y . . . ¡esquiar es fantástico!

¡Ah, la primavera! ¡Soy campeón en la cancha de tenis! Ivan Lendl y yo somos amigos. Pero ahora no hablamos de Ivan.

¿Preguntas, por favor? ¿Me gusta el fútbol? Sí, pero en el otoño.
¿Con quién practico? Diego Maradona y yo practicamos mucho.

En el verano, participo en los Juegos Olímpicos. Tengo medalla de oro en natación.

¿Mi deporte favorito? ¡Ganar en todo momento! Y, ¡muchas gracias por el trofeo, amigos!

A braggart!

An imaginary interview
Thanks for everything, friends. It's an honor to be the athlete of the year. But yes, it's true! I practice all sports and play in all seasons. Like every champion, I win a lot of prizes.

I like winter very much. I'm great on ice! I skate very well and . . . skiing is fantastic!

Ah, spring! I'm a champion on the tennis court! Ivan Lendl and I are friends. But we aren't talking about Ivan now.

Questions, please? Do I like soccer? Yes, but in the fall.

Who do I practice with? Diego Maradona and I practice a lot.

During the summer, I take part in the Olympic Games. I have a gold medal in swimming.

My favorite sport? Winning every time! And, thank you very much for the trophy, friends!

C1 ¿Juegas siempre?

FELIPE ¿Te gusta jugar tenis, Sara?
SARA Sí, a veces juego. No juego a menudo.
FELIPE Yo juego siempre. Juego todos los días.

Do you always play?

Do you like playing tennis, Sara?
Yes, I play sometimes. I don't play often.
I always play. I play every day.

SARA	Necesito practicar más. ¿Jugamos un partido hoy por la tarde?	*I need to practice more. Shall we play a match today in the afternoon?*
FELIPE	Por la tarde, no. ¿Por la noche?	*Not in the afternoon. At night?*
SARA	No, nunca juego por la noche.	*No, I never play at night.*
FELIPE	¿Y mañana por la mañana?	*And tomorrow morning?*
SARA	Bueno, ¡de acuerdo! ¡Hasta mañana!	*Good, agreed! See you tomorrow!*

C9 ¿Qué tiempo hace?

How's the weather?

ANITA	¡Otro día horrible! Hace mal tiempo. Llueve y hace mucho viento.	*Another horrible day! The weather is bad. It's raining and it's windy.*
CONSUELO	Ideal para mirar televisión y escuchar discos.	*It's ideal for watching television and listening to records.*
LUISA	¡Hace frío!	*It's cold!*
CARMEN	Sí, pero no nieva. ¡Estupendo para patinar en hielo!	*Yes, but it's not snowing. It's great for ice-skating!*
FELIPE	¿Hace fresco?	*Is it cool out?*
JULIÁN	No, hace sol y hace calor. ¡Es un día magnífico!	*No, it's sunny and it's hot. It's a magnificent day!*
FELIPE	Por fin hace buen tiempo para la playa.	*At last, the weather is nice for the beach.*

5 EN EL AEROPUERTO

AT THE AIRPORT

A1 ¿Dónde está?

Un grupo de estudiantes llega a Madrid. Vienen en el vuelo 321 de Boston. Entran por la puerta 9. Están en Barajas, el aeropuerto internacional. Van primero a la sección de equipaje. Necesitan un carro para las maletas. Después, a la aduana. ¡Ya está todo! ¿Y ahora? ¡A cambiar de avión o a buscar un taxi!

Where is it?
A group of students arrives in Madrid. They come on flight 321 from Boston. They enter through gate 9. They are at Barajas, the international airport. First they go to the baggage claim area. They need a cart for the suitcases. Then, to customs. Everything's finished! And now? To change planes or look for a taxi!

BRIAN	¡Oh! Mi maleta no está. ¿Dónde está mi maleta?	*Oh! My suitcase is not here. Where is my suitcase?*
ALICE	¿Tu maleta? Allí está.	*Your suitcase? It's over there.*
BRIAN	¡Qué suerte! ¿Tienes tu cámara?	*What luck! Do you have your camera?*
ALICE	Sí, está en mi cartera. Pero, ¿dónde está mi diccionario de español? ¿Y mi mapa?	*Yes, it's in my schoolbag. But, where is my Spanish dictionary? And my map?*
BRIAN	¿Tu diccionario? No sé. ¿No está aquí?	*Your dictionary? I don't know. Isn't it here?*
ALICE	No. ¡Está con el mapa en el asiento del avión!	*No. It's with the map on the airplane seat!*
ADUANERO	Su pasaporte, por favor.	*Your passport, please.*
ALICE	Está en el bolsillo. Aquí tiene, señor.	*It's in my pocket. Here it is, sir.*
ADUANERO	Muchas gracias.	*Thank you very much.*
ALICE	De nada.	*You're welcome.*

A15 En información

Brian y Alice están en información. Tienen muchas preguntas.

At the information booth
Brian and Alice are at the information booth. They have a lot of questions.

BRIAN	Señorita, por favor, ¿dónde está la cafetería?	*Miss, where is the cafeteria please?*
EMPLEADA	La cafetería está allí arriba. ¿Tienen ustedes pesetas?	*The cafeteria is upstairs.* *Do you have pesetas?*

ALICE	No, señorita. Tenemos cheques de viajero.	No, miss. We have traveler's checks.
EMPLEADA	La casa de cambio está detrás de ustedes, a la izquierda.	The money exchange office is behind you, to the left.
BRIAN	¿Y el correo?	And the post office?
EMPLEADA	Abajo, al lado de los teléfonos y los baños.	Downstairs, next to the telephones and the bathrooms.
ALICE	¿Hay una tienda cerca de aquí?	Is there a store near here?
EMPLEADA	Sí, señorita, la tienda del aeropuerto está a la derecha.	Yes, miss, the airport store is to the right.
ALICE	Muchas gracias, señorita.	Thank you very much, miss.

B1 ¿Adónde van?

El profesor quiere saber adónde van los estudiantes. ¡Es muy difícil! Todos van a lugares diferentes.

—¿Adónde vas, Alicia?
—¡Voy a la casa de cambio!
—¿Adónde vas, Brian?
—Voy a la cafetería.
—Jennifer, ¿cómo se llama ella?
  ¿Adónde va?
—Es Gloria. Va al baño.
—George y Mary, ¿adónde van ustedes?
—Vamos a la tienda a comprar algo.

Where are they going?

The professor wants to know where the students are going. It is very difficult! They all go to different places.

Where are you going, Alicia?
I am going to the money exchange office!
Where are you going, Brian?
I am going to the cafeteria.
Jennifer, what is her name?
Where is she going?
She is Gloria. She is going to the bathroom.
George and Mary, where are you going?
We are going to the store to buy something.

B11 Conversación por teléfono

Brian llama por teléfono al señor González. ¡Hay un problema!

SR. GONZÁLEZ	¡Diga!	
BRIAN	Hola. ¿El señor González, por favor?	
SR. GONZÁLEZ	Sí, soy yo. ¿Quién habla?	
BRIAN	Brian Conally.	
SR. GONZÁLEZ	¡Brian! ¿Dónde estás? Tu vuelo llega a las diez de la noche, ¿verdad?	
BRIAN	Bueno, sí y no. El vuelo llega a las diez, pero de la mañana, no de la noche.	
SR. GONZÁLEZ	¿Entonces llegas mañana?	
BRIAN	No, ya estoy en Madrid.	
SR. GONZÁLEZ	¡Qué confusión! ¡Y son las once!	
BRIAN	¿Debo tomar un taxi?	
SR. GONZÁLEZ	No, esperas allí. Yo voy en mi coche al aeropuerto. Estoy allí dentro de una hora.	
BRIAN	Gracias, señor. Hasta luego.	
SR. GONZÁLEZ	Adiós, Brian.	

Telephone conversation

Brian calls Mr. González on the phone. There is a problem!

Hello!
Hello. Mr. González, please?

Yes, speaking. Who is calling?
Brian Conally.
Brian! Where are you? Your flight arrives at ten o'clock at night, right?

Well, yes and no. The flight arrives at ten o'clock, but in the morning, not at night.

Then you arrive tomorrow?
No, I am already in Madrid.
What a mixup! And it's eleven o'clock!

Should I take a taxi?
No, you wait there. I'm going in my car to the airport. I'll be there within an hour.

Thank you, sir. See you later.
Goodbye, Brian.

B16 ¡Hay problemas con el teléfono!
—¡La comunicación se cortó!
—¿Sí?—¿Bueno?—¡Diga!—¡Hola!—¡Aló!
—¿5237?

There are problems with the telephone!
We were cut off!
Hello!
5237?

—No, 5337. ¡Número equivocado!
—¡Hola, mamá! ¡Habla Paco!
—¡No contestan!
—¡Está ocupado!
—Buenas tardes, señorita González.

No, 5337. Wrong number!
Hello, mom! This is Paco speaking.
No answer!
It's busy!
Good afternoon, Miss González.

C1 En la sala de espera

Brian está en el aeropuerto de Barajas en Madrid. Alice y otros estudiantes del grupo esperan la llegada del vuelo para ir a León. Deben esperar una hora. ¿Qué deciden hacer?

BRIAN	¡Tengo mucha hambre! ¿Por qué no subimos a la cafetería a comer y beber algo?
ALICE	¡Estupendo! Pero primero, creo que debemos ir a la casa de cambio.
BRIAN	¿Para qué?
ALICE	Para cambiar un cheque de viajero. ¿Tú vienes, Jennifer?
JENNIFER	No, yo ya tengo pesetas.
MARK	¿Por qué no escribes a casa? Venden postales en la tienda y sellos en el correo.
JENNIFER	¿Una carta a mi familia? Ahora, no. Yo espero aquí. Tengo el periódico de hoy en español.
MARK	Yo no tengo el periódico. ¡Chao!

In the waiting area

Brian is at Barajas Airport in Madrid. Alice and other students from the group are waiting for the arrival of the flight to León. They must wait for an hour. What do they decide to do?

I am very hungry! Why don't we go up to the cafeteria to eat and drink something?

Great! But first, I think we should go to the money exchange office.
What for?
To cash a traveler's check.
Are you coming, Jennifer?
No, I have pesetas already.
Why don't you write home? They sell postcards at the store and stamps in the post office.

A letter to my family? Not now. I'll wait here. I have today's Spanish newspaper.

I don't have a newspaper. 'Bye!

6 LA FAMILIA

THE FAMILY

A1 La visita de Roberto

Roberto, un estudiante norteamericano de Los Ángeles, llega a la casa de su amigo Antonio en la Ciudad de México. Va a pasar un mes de vacaciones con la familia de Antonio.

ANTONIO	¡Mamá! ¡Mamá! ¿Dónde estás?
MAMÁ	Aquí estoy, Antonio. En la sala. ¡Bienvenido, Roberto! Pasa, por favor. ¿Cómo estás? Mucho gusto.
ROBERTO	Igualmente, señora.
MAMÁ	Estás en tu casa, Roberto.
ROBERTO	Muchas gracias, señora. Usted es muy amable. ¡Es un placer estar aquí con ustedes!
ANTONIO	Con permiso, mamá. Queremos escuchar música. Vamos a mi cuarto.
MAMÁ	¡Un momento, Antonio! ¿Dónde están las cosas de Roberto? ¿Por qué no van a su cuarto primero? Y tú, Roberto, ¿no tienes hambre? ¿Quieres comer algo? ¿Quieres un refresco?

Roberto's visit

Roberto, a North American student from Los Angeles, arrives at the home of his friend Antonio in Mexico City. He is going to spend a month of vacation with Antonio's family.

Mom! Mom! Where are you?
I'm here, Antonio. In the living room. Welcome, Roberto! Come in, please. How are you? Nice to meet you.
Likewise, ma'am.
Make yourself at home, Roberto.
Thank you very much, ma'am. You are very kind. It's a pleasure to be here with you!

Excuse us, mom. We want to listen to music. We are going to my room.

Just a moment, Antonio! Where are Roberto's things? Why don't you go to his room first? And you, Roberto, aren't you hungry? Would you like to eat something? Would you like a soda?

| ROBERTO | No, señora, muchas gracias. | No, ma'am, thank you very much. |
| ANTONIO | ¿Quieres ver tu cuarto, Roberto? | Would you like to see your room, Roberto? |

B1 Fotos de la familia

Ana María, la hermana de Antonio, y su amiga Gloria, hablan de las fotos que Ana María tiene en su cuarto. Tiene fotos de todos los miembros de la familia.

Family photos

Ana María, Antonio's sister, and her friend Gloria, talk about the photos that Ana María has in her room. She has photos of all the members of the family.

GLORIA	Tienes muchas fotografías. ¿Quién es la chica alta y morena? ¿Tu hermana?	*You have a lot of photographs. Who is the tall, dark-haired girl? Your sister?*
ANA MARÍA	No, mi hermana Consuelo es baja y rubia. Ella es Luisa, mi prima.	*No, my sister Consuelo is short and blonde. She is Luisa, my cousin.*
GLORIA	¿Cuántos años tiene?	*How old is she?*
ANA MARÍA	Quince. ¡Es un genio! Es muy inteligente.	*Fifteen. She is a genius! She is very intelligent.*
GLORIA	¡Qué fotografía tan bonita! ¿Quién es? ¿Tu padre?	*What a nice photograph! Who is it? Your father?*
ANA MARÍA	Sí, es una foto de mi papá.	*Yes, it's a photo of my dad.*
GLORIA	¡Qué guapo!	*How handsome!*
ANA MARÍA	Mira, aquí está de nuevo, con mi mamá y toda la familia.	*Look, here he is again, with my mother and all the family.*
GLORIA	La señora delgada y rubia, ¿quién es? ¡Qué linda!	*The thin, blond woman, who is she? How pretty!*
ANA MARÍA	Es mi tía Dolores, la madre de Luisa. Al lado está el esposo, mi tío José.	*She's my aunt Dolores, Luisa's mother. Her husband is beside her, my uncle José.*
GLORIA	Y aquí están tus abuelos, ¿no?	*And here are your grandparents, right?*
ANA MARÍA	Sí, los padres de mamá. Los dos son bien simpáticos y cariñosos.	*Yes, my mom's parents. They are both very nice and affectionate.*
GLORIA	¿Cuántos hijos tienen? ¿Cinco?	*How many children do they have? Five?*
ANA MARÍA	No, una hija, mi mamá, y un hijo, mi tío José. El señor pelirrojo es un amigo de ellos. Los otros cuatro son amigos también.	*No, a daughter, my mother, and a son, my uncle José. The redheaded man is a friend of theirs. The other four are also friends.*

B8 Una foto más

GLORIA	¡Qué chico tan guapo! ¿Quién es?	**One more photo** *What a handsome boy! Who is he?*
ANA MARÍA	El hijo de una amiga de mi mamá. Se llama Anselmo.	*The son of a friend of my mom. His name is Anselmo.*
GLORIA	Es muy rubio. Sus padres, ¿son los dos morenos?	*He is very blond. His parents, are they both dark-haired?*
ANA MARÍA	El señor de la foto no es su papá. Es su padrastro. Su papá murió. Ahora la mamá está casada de nuevo.	*The man in the photo is not his dad. He's his stepfather. His father died. Now his mom is married again.*

B16 ¿Cómo eres tú?

¿alto o baja?
¿gordo o delgada?
¿feo o guapa?
¿moreno, rubia o pelirroja?

What are you like?

tall or short?
fat or thin?
ugly or handsome?
dark-haired, blonde or redheaded?

¿Cómo son ustedes?	*What are you like?*
¿tontos o inteligentes?	*dumb or intelligent?*
¿antipáticas o simpáticas?	*not nice or nice?*
¿generosos o egoístas?	*generous or selfish?*
¿Y cómo eres tú, Roque?	*And what are you like, Roque?*
¿Cómo soy yo?	*What am I like?*
. . . guapo, inteligente y . . . ¡modesto!	*. . . handsome, intelligent, and . . . modest!*

C1 La casa de Antonio

Antonio y Roberto están en la casa de
Antonio.

Antonio's house

Antonio and Roberto are at Antonio's house.

ROBERTO	Me gusta mucho tu cuarto, Antonio. Es muy cómodo.	*I like your room very much, Antonio. It's very comfortable.*
ANTONIO	¿Quieres ver toda la casa?	*Would you like to see the whole house?*
ROBERTO	¡Por supuesto!	*Of course!*
ANTONIO	Bueno, ¡vamos! Empezamos por la sala de estar.	*Well, let's go! We begin in the family room.*
ROBERTO	¡Qué linda!	*How pretty!*
ANTONIO	Aquí estamos en el comedor. Y, al lado por esta puerta, la cocina.	*Here we are in the dining room. And, beside it through this door, the kitchen.*
ROBERTO	¿Y el baño?	*And the bathroom?*
ANTONIO	Tenemos tres baños. Uno a la derecha de la entrada, otro en el pasillo, y otro en el cuarto de mis padres.	*We have three bathrooms. One to the right of the entrance, another in the hall, and another in my parents' bedroom.*
ROBERTO	¿Dónde estamos ahora?	*Where are we now?*
ANTONIO	En la sala. No usamos mucho este cuarto. Es para cuando vienen visitas. Pasamos nuestro tiempo libre en la sala de estar. Es el cuarto más importante.	*In the living room. We don't use this room much. It's for when visitors come. We spend our free time in the family room. It's the most important room.*
ROBERTO	¿Entramos aquí?	*Should we go in here?*
ANTONIO	¡No, está prohibido! Es el cuarto de mis hermanas.	*No, it's off limits! It's my sisters' bedroom.*
ROBERTO	¡Ya sé! Yo también tengo hermanas. Y vivimos en un apartamento pequeño. ¿Hay un garaje?	*I know! I have sisters too. And we live in a small apartment. Is there a garage?*
ANTONIO	Sí, en el jardín, detrás de la casa. ¿Qué te parece la casa, Roberto?	*Yes, in the garden, behind the house. What do you think of the house, Roberto?*
ROBERTO	Es grande y muy bonita. ¡Y mi cuarto es estupendo!	*It's big and very pretty. And my room is great!*

7 ¡VAMOS A SALIR!

LET'S GO OUT!

A1 ¡A pasear!

Let's go for a walk!

NICOLÁS	Vamos a dar una vuelta.	*We are going for a walk.*
GRACIELA	Yo quiero tomar un helado. ¿Quieren venir?	*I want to have an ice cream. Do you want to come?*
CORINA	Sí, fantástico. ¡Vamos!	*Yes, fantastic. Let's go!*
IGNACIO	No, yo no puedo ir.	*No, I can't go.*
CORINA	¡Qué pena! ¿Qué tienes que hacer?	*What a pity! What do you have to do?*

IGNACIO	Tengo un examen mañana. Tengo que estudiar esta tarde y esta noche.	*I have a test tomorrow. I have to study this afternoon and tonight.*
NICOLÁS	Hola, Diego. ¿Qué tal? ¿Vas a la fiesta del sábado en el club?	*Hi, Diego. How are things? Are you going to the Saturday party at the club?*
DIEGO	Lo siento, no puedo.	*I'm sorry, I can't.*
NICOLÁS	¡Qué lástima! ¿Y tu hermana va?	*What a shame! Is your sister going?*
DIEGO	No, no puede. Ella tiene que trabajar el sábado.	*No, she can't. She has to work Saturday.*

A6 **¿Adónde vamos hoy?**

¿a la piscina?
¿a una discoteca?
¿al cine?
¿al parque?
¿a la playa?

Where are we going today?
to the swimming pool?
to a disco?
to the movies?
to the park?
to the beach?

A17 **¿Sales mucho?**

La revista *Juventud de hoy* entrevista a cuatro estudiantes. Ellos contestan nuestras preguntas:

¿Sales mucho?
¿Cuántas veces por semana sales?
¿Qué te gusta hacer cuando sales?

Do you go out a lot?
The magazine Today's Youth *interviews four students. They answer our questions:*

Do you go out a lot?
How many times a week do you go out?
What do you like to do when you go out?

CRISTINA
Yo salgo bastante, una o dos veces por semana. Voy al cine, a conciertos de rock, o, sencillamente, a casa de mis amigos.

I go out a lot, one or two times a week. I go to the movies, to rock concerts, or to just visit my friends.

ROBERTO
Lo que más me gusta es bailar. Yo voy a bailes y discotecas todo el tiempo. ¡Bailar es fantástico!

What I like the most is to dance. I go to dances and discos all the time. Dancing is fantastic!

RICARDO
Me gusta mucho salir a pasear con otros chicos. Salimos a menudo. Damos una vuelta, si tenemos ganas, vamos a un café, tomamos algo y hablamos mucho.

I like going out for a walk with other boys and girls. We go out often. We go for a walk, if we feel like it we go to a café, we drink something and we talk a lot.

MARTA
Yo salgo todos los domingos. También los sábados por la noche. Me gusta salir los fines de semana porque puedo volver a casa tarde. A veces voy al cine.

I go out every Sunday. Also on Saturday nights. I like to go out on weekends because I can return home late. Sometimes I go to the movies.

B1 **¿Qué vamos a ver?**

Paula y Miguel están en el Café Suárez, en Buenos Aires. Dicen que piensan ir al cine, pero, ¿qué van a ver? Miguel mira el periódico.

What are we going to see?
Paula and Miguel are in the Café Suárez, in Buenos Aires. They are saying that they're thinking of going to the movies, but what are they going to see? Miguel looks at the newspaper.

MIGUEL	¿Qué vamos a hacer? ¿Vamos al cine? ¿Qué clase de película quieres ver?	*What are we going to do? Should we go the movies? What kind of movie do you want to see?*
PAULA	¿Qué dan en el cine Belgrano?	*What are they showing at the Belgrano theater?*
MIGUEL	*Detenidos en el tiempo.* ¡Premio de oro, Mar del Plata! Creo que es una película de ciencia-ficción.	Suspended in Time. *Gold prize, Mar del Plata! I think it is a science fiction movie.*

PAULA	¿Y si vamos al Savoy? ¿Qué te parece? ¿Qué dan ahí?
MIGUEL	Mmm . . . Aquí está el programa de mañana. Van a dar *Bodas de plata*. ¿Hoy? . . . Hoy dan *Basta de ruido*.
PAULA	*¿Basta de ruido?* Me parece que es una musical. Mejor vamos al Belgrano.
MIGUEL	Bueno, entonces, vamos a ver *Detenidos en el tiempo*. ¡Vamos! La película va a empezar. Son casi las seis.

What if we go to the Savoy? What do you think? What are they showing there?
Mmm . . . Here is tomorrow's program. They are going to show Silver Wedding Anniversary. *Today? . . . Today they are showing* No More Noise.
No More Noise? *I think that is a musical. We better go to the Belgrano.*

Well, then, let's go see Suspended in Time. *Let's go! The movie is going to start. It's almost six o'clock.*

B8 Mejor una policial

TERESA	¿Vamos a ver *Sueño de amor*?
RAQUEL	No, hoy no tengo ganas de ver una película de amor.
TERESA	¿Y si vemos *El amigo de Frankenstein*?
RAQUEL	¿Una de terror? ¡No! Mejor vemos *Fantasía*.
TERESA	*Fantasía* es de dibujos animados. En el Rex dan una del oeste. ¿Qué te parece?
RAQUEL	Si quieres ver una de aventuras, aquí hay una: *Vuelo fantástico*.
TERESA	*¿Vuelo fantástico?* ¡No! Es de ciencia-ficción. Vamos a ver una cómica: *Líos locos*.
RAQUEL	*Crimen en el hielo*, ¡la mejor policial del año!
TERESA	¿Una policial? ¡Fantástico! ¡Vamos!

Better a detective film
Should we go to see Dream of Love?
No, today I don't feel like seeing a love story.

What if we see Frankenstein's Friend?
A horror movie? No! We better go see Fantasia.

Fantasia *is an animated cartoon film. They are showing a western at the Rex. What do you think?*

If you want to see an adventure film, here is one: Fantastic Flight.
Fantastic Flight? *No! It's a science fiction film. Let's go see a comedy:* Crazy Complications.

Crime on Ice, *the best detective film of the year!*

A detective film? Fantastic! Let's go!

C1 ¡Tito Ortega canta hoy!
En el autobús.

NICOLÁS	¡Mira, Paula! Ahí está Diego. ¡Hola, Diego! ¿Qué tal? ¿Conoces a Paula?
DIEGO	No. ¡Hola! ¿Cómo estás? ¿Adónde van?
PAULA	Al teatro, a escuchar a Tito Ortega.
DIEGO	¿Sí?, yo también.
NICOLÁS	¡Fantástico! Oye, Diego, ¿sabes dónde tenemos que bajar?
DIEGO	Sí, en la próxima parada, en la calle Sarmiento.

Frente al Luna Park.

DIEGO	¡Cuánta gente! ¡Permiso, por favor!
NICOLÁS	Perdón, señor. ¿Sabe si hay entradas?
SEÑOR	No, nosotros esperamos el autobús.
PAULA	Por favor, señora, ¿sabe cuál es la fila para comprar entradas?
SEÑORA	Hay entradas en la ventanilla, a la derecha, señorita.

Unos minutos más tarde.

Tito Ortega sings today!
On the bus.

Look, Paula! There is Diego. Hi, Diego! How are things? Do you know Paula?
No. Hi! How are you? Where are you going?

To the theater, to hear Tito Ortega.
Really? Me, too.
Fantastic! Listen, Diego, do you know where we have to get off?
Yes, at the next stop, at Sarmiento Street.

In front of Luna Park.

What a lot of people! Excuse me, please!
Excuse me, sir. Do you know if there are any tickets?
No, we are waiting for the bus.
Please, ma'am, do you know which is the line to buy tickets?
Tickets are at the ticket window, to the right, miss.

A few minutes later.

PAULA	¿Vienes con nosotros, Diego?	Are you coming with us, Diego?
DIEGO	No, espero a mi hermana. Ella busca a su amiga Susana.	No, I am waiting for my sister. She is looking for her friend Susana.
NICOLÁS	¡Ahí están! Vamos, el concierto va a empezar.	There they are! Let's go, the concert is going to start.

9 ¡BUEN PROVECHO!

ENJOY YOUR MEAL!

A1 ¿Qué comemos hoy?

Los señores Álvarez escriben sobre los restaurantes de San Antonio para una guía turística. ¿Qué van a comer hoy? ¿Comida española, tex-mex, del Caribe, pizza o hamburguesas?

What do we eat today?

Mr. and Mrs. Álvarez write about the restaurants of San Antonio for a tourist guide. What are they going to eat today? Spanish, Tex-Mex, Caribbean food, pizza or hamburgers?

CAMARERA	¿Desean ver el menú? El plato del día es pollo con cebolla y salsa de tomate.	Would you like to see the menu? The specialty of the day is chicken with onions and tomato sauce.
SR. ÁLVAREZ	A mí no me gustan las cebollas. ¿Hay sopa?	I don't like onions. Do you have soup?
SRA. ÁLVAREZ	Queremos probar algo típico tex-mex.	We want to try something typically Tex-Mex.
CAMARERA	¿Puede ser chile con carne?	Can it be chili con carne?
CAMARERO	¿A ustedes les gustan las enchiladas? Es una especialidad de la casa.	Do you like enchiladas? It's a specialty of the house.
SRA. ÁLVAREZ	Sí, me gustan mucho. Quiero dos de carne y una de queso.	Yes, I like them very much. I want two beef and one cheese, please.
CAMARERA	¿Y de postre, señores?	And for dessert?
SRA. ÁLVAREZ	Un helado de chocolate, por favor, y café con leche.	Chocolate ice-cream, please, and coffee with milk.
SR. ÁLVAREZ	Fruta y té con limón para mí. Estoy a dieta.	Fruit and tea with lemon for me. I'm on a diet.
SRA. ÁLVAREZ	¡Qué rápido cenamos aquí!	How quickly we eat here!
SR. ÁLVAREZ	Sí, voy a pagar la cuenta.	Yes, I'm going to pay the bill.
SRA. ÁLVAREZ	¿Cuánto dejamos de propina?	How much tip should we leave?
SR. ÁLVAREZ	¡No sé cuánto . . . ni dónde!	I don't know how much . . . or where!

¡A la mesa!

A6 Comemos por la mañana, al mediodía, por la tarde y por la noche. A la hora de la merienda, o entre comidas, lo mejor es un bocadillo y un vaso de leche o de jugo.

Por la mañana, en el desayuno, nos gusta tomar café con leche o chocolate, comer pan con mantequilla, jalea o mermelada.

Al mediodía, en el almuerzo, nos gusta un bistec o pescado, arroz, verduras, y un postre. Nuestro postre favorito es el flan. A nosotros nos gusta una comida completa.

To the table!

We eat in the morning, at noon, in the afternoon and at night. For an afternoon snack, or between meals, the best thing is a sandwich and a glass of milk or juice.

In the morning, for breakfast, we like to have coffee and milk or chocolate, eat bread with butter, jelly or marmalade.

At noon, for lunch, we like a steak or fish, rice, vegetables, and dessert. Our favorite dessert is baked custard. We like a complete meal.

En el almuerzo, a mí me gusta comer un bocadillo. Me gustan los bocadillos de jamón y queso, con lechuga, tomate y mayonesa. Las papas fritas me encantan.

Por la noche, para la cena, en casa les gusta una comida ligera: tomar sopa, comer una tortilla con ensalada, pan, queso y fruta.

For lunch, I like to eat a sandwich. I like ham and cheese sandwiches, with lettuce, tomato and mayonnaise. I love French fries.

At night, for dinner, at home they like a light meal: have some soup, eat an omelette with salad, bread, cheese and fruit.

B1 Un picnic

ELENA ¿Qué haces?
CARLOS Preparo una tortilla para el picnic.
ELENA ¡Estupendo! A todos nos gusta la tortilla. Es muy rica. ¿Te ayudo?
CARLOS ¿Por qué no cortas estas patatas y esas cebollas en trozos pequeños? Después voy a freír todo.
ELENA Bueno, a lo dicho, hecho. ¡Ay!
CARLOS ¿Por qué lloras, Elena?
ELENA ¡Son las cebollas por supuesto! Y ahora, ¿qué?
CARLOS Ahora bato los huevos, añado las patatas y las cebollas y cocino todo en esta misma sartén. Tiene que dorarse de los dos lados. ¡Y aquí está nuestra tortilla!
ELENA ¡Ay, qué hambre tengo!

A picnic
What are you doing?
I am preparing a Spanish omelette for the picnic.
Great! We all like Spanish omelette. It's delicious. Can I help you?
Why don't you cut these potatoes and those onions in small pieces? Then I will fry everything.

Well, no sooner said than done. Ah!
Why are you crying, Elena?
It's the onions of course! And now, what?

Now I beat the eggs, I add the potatoes and the onions and cook everything in the same frying pan. It has to brown on both sides. And here is our Spanish omelette!

Oh, I'm so hungry!

B3 La comida para el picnic
Miguel compra las frutas. Va a aquella frutería grande de la esquina.

—¿A cuánto están estas uvas? ¡Parecen buenísimas!

—A 500 pesos el kilo.

Alicia hace bocadillos de jamón y queso, de pollo y de atún. ¡Qué sabrosos!

—¡Alicia, estos bocadillos son deliciosos!

Sofía compra pasteles en una pastelería muy buena.

—¡Es difícil decidir! ¿Llevo esta tarta de manzanas o ese bizcocho de chocolate? ¡Mira aquel pastel con fresas!

Manuel trae los refrescos.

—Tiene el jugo, las gaseosas y el agua mineral en el coche.

— . . . ¡Ah!, y también tiene su guitarra. ¡Este picnic va a ser estupendo!

The food for the picnic
Miguel buys the fruit. He goes to that big fruit store on the corner.

How much are these grapes? They look very good!

500 pesos per kilo.

Alicia makes sandwiches of ham and cheese, chicken and tuna. How delicious!

Alicia, these sandwiches are delicious!

Sofía buys pastries at a very good pastry shop.

It's so difficult to decide! Should I take that apple tart or that chocolate cake? Look at that strawberry pie!

Manuel brings the sodas.

He has the juice, the sodas, and the mineral water in the car.

. . . Ah!, and he also has his guitar. This picnic is going to be great!

C1 Y por fin, ¡el picnic!
MIGUEL La sal, por favor. ¡Esta tortilla está perfecta! Pero, ¿dónde está Manuel con los refrescos? Tengo mucha sed.

And at last, the picnic!
The salt, please. This omelette is perfect! But, where is Manuel with the sodas? I'm very thirsty.

ELENA	¡Paciencia! Comes por tres, ¿sabes? ¡Ah, aquí viene!	Patience! You eat for three, you know? Ah, here he comes!
MANUEL	¡Hola! ¡Cuánto tráfico! ¿Pongo la mesa? ¿Dónde van los refrescos?	Hi! What a lot of traffic! Should I set the table? Where do the sodas go?
ELENA	La mesa ya está.	The table is already set.
MIGUEL	Los refrescos, aquí, por favor, a mi lado.	The sodas, here, please, beside me.
ELENA	No, a tu lado, no. Miguel, ¿por qué no pones los refrescos debajo de ese árbol?	No, not beside you. Miguel, why don't you put the sodas under that tree?
ALICIA	Debes tener hambre, Manuel. ¿Quieres un bocadillo? ¿De queso o de jamón?	You must be hungry, Manuel. Do you want a sandwich? Cheese or ham?
MANUEL	De jamón, por favor. . . . ¡Qué rico está! Gracias, Alicia.	Ham, please. . . . It's delicious! Thank you, Alicia.
CARLOS	Este picnic necesita música. Miguel, ¿por qué no pones este casete? ¿Quieres bailar, Alicia?	This picnic needs music. Miguel, why don't you play this cassette? Do you want to dance, Alicia?
ALICIA	¡Cómo no! Es mi canción favorita.	Of course! It's my favorite song.
MIGUEL	Buena idea. Vamos, Elena. Si bailas conmigo, no como más.	Good idea. Let's go, Elena. If you dance with me, I won't eat anymore.
ELENA	¡No hay más remedio! Vamos, Miguel.	I guess there's no choice! Let's go, Miguel.

C12   Ponemos la mesa

Para el desayuno pongo:

vaso para el jugo, platillo para el pan y la mantequilla
plato hondo para el cereal, cuchara y servilleta
taza con platillo, y cucharita para el azúcar

Para el almuerzo ponemos:
plato hondo para la sopa
platillo para el sandwich y servilleta
sal, pimienta, mostaza y catsup

Para la comida o para la cena ellos ponen:

platillo para la ensalada, plato llano para la comida
tenedor, cuchillo, dos cucharitas, servilleta, vaso para el agua y platillo para el postre

We set the table
For breakfast I set:

a glass for the juice, a small plate for the bread and the butter
a bowl for the cereal, a spoon and a napkin

a cup with a saucer, and a teaspoon for the sugar

For lunch we set:
a soup plate
a small plate for the sandwich and a napkin
salt, pepper, mustard and ketchup

For dinner or for supper they set:

a small plate for the salad, a dinner plate

a fork, a knife, two teaspoons, a napkin,
a water glass, and a small plate for dessert

10   UN VIAJE ESTUPENDO

A WONDERFUL TRIP

A1   El diario de Pilar
Querido diario:
   Ayer llegó carta de Marisol, mi prima de Madrid. Casi nunca canto, pero ayer canté y bailé de alegría. ¡No puedo creerlo! ¡Una invitación para pasar una semana en Madrid! Hablé con mamá. Tengo permiso. Llamé a Marisol por teléfono. Mamá habló con tía Inés. Planeamos el viaje. ¡Todo está arreglado!

Pilar's diary
Dear diary:
   Yesterday a letter arrived from Marisol, my cousin from Madrid. I almost never sing, but yesterday I sang and danced for joy. I can't believe it! An invitation to spend a week in Madrid! I talked to mom. I have permission to go. I called Marisol on the phone. Mom talked with Aunt Inés. We planned the trip. Everything's arranged!

El sábado . . . ¡a Madrid! . . . excursiones, visitas y paseos. Billy, mi amigo de Chicago, también va. ¡Qué suerte!

¿Sabes? Él ya estudió casi todos los mapas y miró los folletos de turismo. Marcó todos los lugares que quiere visitar. ¡Es tan organizado! Estoy segura que ya compró los billetes . . . y preparó las maletas . . . ¡con una semana de anticipación!

Saturday . . . to Madrid! . . . Excursions, visits and sightseeing trips. Billy, my friend from Chicago, is also going. What luck!

You know what? He already studied all the maps and looked at all the tourist brochures. He marked all the places he wants to visit. He is so organized! I'm sure he bought the tickets already . . . and prepared the suitcases . . . with a week left to go!

A14 Conversación de dos minutos

Carlos llama por teléfono a Isabel en un mal momento. Isabel está a punto de salir para el aeropuerto.

Two-minute conversation

Carlos calls Isabel on the phone at a bad time. Isabel is just about to leave for the airport.

CARLOS	¡Hola, Isabel! ¿Cómo estás?
ISABEL	¡Apuradísima! No puedo hablar ahora. Salimos para el aeropuerto dentro de dos minutos. Vamos a Barcelona.
CARLOS	¿A Barcelona?
ISABEL	Sí. Vamos a visitar a la abuela. Mamá reservó los billetes de avión la semana pasada. Papá y mamá llamaron a la abuela anoche. Papá regresó de la oficina hace una hora. El taxi ya llegó . . . y yo todavía tengo que hacer mi maleta. ¡Adiós!

Hi, Isabel! How are you?
In a big hurry! I can't talk now. We are leaving for the airport in two minutes. We are going to Barcelona.

To Barcelona?
Yes. We are going to visit Grandmother. Mom reserved the plane tickets last week. Last night Dad and Mom called Grandmother. Dad returned from the office an hour ago. The taxi has already arrived . . . and I still have to pack my suitcase.

Goodbye!

B1 Pilar llama desde Madrid

Pilar llama a su casa. Su hermana Socorro contesta el teléfono. Socorro quiere saber todo lo que pasa. Pregunta sin parar.

Pilar calls from Madrid

Pilar calls home. Her sister Socorro answers the phone. Socorro wants to know everything that's happening. She asks questions non-stop.

SOCORRO	¡Hola, Pilar! ¿Cómo estás? ¿Y Billy? ¿Cómo llegaron? ¿Les gusta Madrid?
PILAR	Estamos muy bien, Socorro. ¿Está mamá?
SOCORRO	Sí, ya viene, pero, antes, ¿qué tal el viaje? ¿Adónde fueron hoy? ¿Qué hicieron?
PILAR	Fuimos primero a casa de los tíos. Dejamos nuestras cosas allí. Hablamos mucho. Hicimos planes también.
SOCORRO	Ya sé, ya sé . . ., pero, ¿qué más hicieron?
PILAR	Hicimos muchas cosas.
SOCORRO	¿Fueron a la Gran Vía?
PILAR	No, fuimos en moto hasta la Puerta de Alcalá. Caminamos mucho. Después fuimos al Parque del Retiro. Remamos en el estanque. ¡Pasamos un día fantástico!

Hi, Pilar! How are you! And Billy? How was your arrival? Do you like Madrid?

We are very well, Socorro. Is mom there?

Yes, she is coming now, but, first, how about the trip? Where did you go today? What did you do?

We first went to our aunt's and our uncle's house. We left our things there. We talked a lot. We also made plans.

I know, I know . . ., but, what else did you do?

We did a lot of things.
Did you go to the Gran Vía?
No, we went by motorcycle to the Puerta de Alcalá. We walked a lot. Then we went to the Parque del Retiro. We went rowing in the pond. We had a fantastic day!

SOCORRO	¡Qué envidia! Aquí viene mamá. ¡Hasta mañana!
PILAR	¡Adiós, Socorro!

How I envy you! Here comes mom. Until tomorrow!

Goodbye, Socorro!

C1 Un viaje corto

La mamá de Socorro quiere saber si está todo listo para el viaje a Granada.

MAMÁ	Socorro, ¿tienes los billetes?
SOCORRO	Sí, mamá, los tengo aquí.
MAMÁ	¿Hiciste las maletas?
SOCORRO	Sí, mamá, las preparé.
MAMÁ	¿Y los regalos?
SOCORRO	Están todos.
MAMÁ	¿Te llamó tu hermano?
SOCORRO	Sí, me llamó esta mañana.
MAMÁ	¿Llamaste al taxi?
SOCORRO	Sí, ya lo llamé.
MAMÁ	Bueno, ¿qué más? . . . ¿Tiene tu papá nuestro número de teléfono?
SOCORRO	Sí, lo tiene. Mamá, ¡por favor!, ¡sólo vamos a Granada por dos días!

A short trip

Socorro's mom wants to know if everything's ready for the trip to Granada.

Socorro, do you have the tickets?
Yes, mom, I have them here.
Did you pack the suitcases?
Yes, mom, I prepared them.
And the gifts?
They are all here.
Did your brother call you?
Yes, he called me this morning.
Did you call the taxi?
Yes, I called one already.
Well, what else? . . . Does your dad have our phone number?
Yes, he has it. Mom, please!, we are only going to Granada for two days!

11 ¡VAMOS DE COMPRAS!

WE ARE GOING SHOPPING!

A1 ¿Lo compramos?

SEÑORA	Señorita, por favor.
VENDEDORA	¿Qué desea, señora?
SEÑORA	Ese plato de cerámica, por favor.
VENDEDORA	¿Cuál, el pequeño o el grande?
SEÑORA	Los dos . . . Este plato es más grande que ése, pero cuesta menos, ¿por qué?
VENDEDORA	El más pequeño está hecho a mano. El grande es una imitación. No es de cerámica, es de plástico.
SEÑORA	¡Oh, no! Yo quiero uno de cerámica, pero más barato que éste. ¿Y ése de allá?
VENDEDORA	Cuesta igual que el de cerámica.
SEÑORA	¡Oh! ¿Valen lo mismo? Muchas gracias.
EMILIO	¿Qué te parece, Diego? ¿Qué cinturón llevamos?
DIEGO	No sé, pero a mi me gusta más el oscuro. Es más largo y más bonito que el claro.
EMILIO	El claro no me gusta nada. El oscuro está bien, ¿no?
DIEGO	No está mal, pero es más caro que el otro.

Should we buy it?
Miss, please.
What would you like, ma'am?
That ceramic plate, please.
Which, the small one or the big one?
Both, . . . This plate is bigger than that one, but costs less. Why?

The small one is handmade. The big one is an imitation. It's not ceramic, it's plastic.

Oh, no! I want a ceramic one, but cheaper than this one. And that one over there?

It costs the same as the ceramic one.
Oh! They cost the same? Thank you very much.

What do you think, Diego? Which belt do we take?

I don't know, but I like the darker one more. It's longer and prettier than the lighter one.

I don't like the lighter one at all. The darker one is fine, right?
It's not bad, but it's more expensive than the other one.

EMILIO	¡No importa! Es bien lindo y es de cuero.	It doesn't matter. It's very pretty and it's leather.
CLARA	¡Mira esta blusa! Es una preciosura. Es de algodón. Está bordada a mano. ¿La compro?	Look at that blouse! It's a beauty. It's cotton. It's embroidered by hand. Should I buy it?
MARIANA	¡Buena idea! Voy a preguntar el precio. Por favor, señorita, ¿cuánto vale esta blusa en dólares?	Good idea! I'm going to ask the price. Please, miss, how much is this blouse in dollars?
VENDEDORA	Veinte dólares, señorita.	Twenty dollars, miss.
CLARA	Bueno, está bien. ¿Puedo pagar con tarjeta de crédito?	Well, that's fine. Can I pay with a credit card?
VENDEDORA	Sí, cómo no. En la caja, por favor.	Yes, of course. At the cashier, please.

A8 ¿Qué ropa compramos?

What should we buy?

abrigo	coat
chaqueta de lana	wool jacket
suéter	sweater
calcetines	socks
jeans	jeans
corbata	tie
camisa	shirt
traje	suit
saco	jacket
pantalones	pants
sombrero	hat
zapatos	shoes
vestido de algodón	cotton dress
falda	skirt
pañuelo de seda	silk handkerchief
blusa de nilón	nylon blouse
traje de baño	bathing suit

B1 ¡Es una ganga!

Marisa y su mamá están de compras en La Lujosa, una tienda de barrio.

It's a bargain!

Marisa and her mother are shopping in La Lujosa, a neighborhood store.

MAMÁ	¿Le compras dos regalos a Linda, un suéter y una cartera?	Are you buying two gifts for Linda, a sweater and a purse?
MARISA	No, mamá. Compro el suéter para mí y le compro la cartera a Linda. Le mando la cartera por correo, ¿no? ¿Qué te parece? Así la recibe pronto.	No, mom. I am buying the sweater for me and the purse for Linda. I can send her the purse by mail, right? What do you think? That way she will receive it soon.
MAMÁ	¡Buena idea! Ese suéter te queda muy bien. La cartera es de muy buena calidad. ¿Sabes cuánto cuesta?	Good idea! That sweater looks very nice on you. The purse is of very good quality. Do you know how much it costs?
MARISA	No. ¿Le preguntamos a la vendedora?	No. Should we ask the salesperson?
VENDEDORA	¿En qué puedo servirle, señorita?	How may I help you, miss?
MAMÁ	¿Cuánto cuesta esta cartera?	How much is this purse?
VENDEDORA	325 pesos, señora, pero está rebajada a 280 por esta semana. Es una oferta especial. No va a encontrar otra más barata.	325 pesos, ma'am, but it's reduced to 280 for this week. It's a special offer. You are not going to find a cheaper one.
MAMÁ	¡280 pesos! Es demasiado cara. Esa cartera no vale tanto. Vamos a otra tienda, Marisa.	280 pesos! It's too expensive. That purse isn't worth that much. Let's go to another store, Marisa.
MARISA	Por favor, mamá, ¡es una ganga! A Linda le va a encantar.	Please, mom, it's a bargain! Linda will be delighted.

MAMÁ	No pago más de 200 pesos. (En voz baja.) Pero hijita, tú no sabes regatear. Vas a ver.
VENDEDORA	Perdón, señora. Como a su hija le gusta tanto, le dejo la cartera en 200 pesos. Más barata no puedo.
MAMÁ	Entonces, la llevamos. ¿Le puedo pagar con un cheque?

I won't pay more than 200 pesos. (In a low voice.) But daughter, you don't know how to bargain. You'll see.

Excuse me, ma'am. Since your daughter likes it so much, I'll let the purse go for 200 pesos. I can't let it go any cheaper.

Then, we'll take it. Can I pay you with a check?

B9 El estéreo nuevo

Raúl quiere un estéreo nuevo . . . pero, ¿cuándo lo va a poder comprar? ¡El estéreo cuesta más de mil pesos! Raúl hace cuentas.

Si ahorro veinticinco pesos por semana . . . son cien por mes . . . en un año puedo tener el estéreo . . . ¡No, un año es mucho tiempo! Vamos a ver . . . ahorro el doble: doscientos pesos por mes . . . en dos meses son cuatrocientos . . . sí, en cinco meses, me compro el estéreo! pero, ¿voy a poder ahorrar?

The new stereo
Raúl wants a new stereo . . . but, when is he going to be able to buy it? The stereo costs more than a thousand pesos! Raúl does calculations.

If I save twenty-five pesos a week . . . that is a hundred a month . . . in a year I can have the stereo . . . No, a year is too much time! Let's see . . . I save twice as much: two hundred pesos a month . . . in two months that is four hundred . . . yes, in five months, I'll buy the stereo, but, will I be able to save?

B11 Los números del 100 al 1,000
cien
ciento uno,-a
ciento treinta y cuatro
doscientos,-as
doscientos,-as veintitrés
trescientos,-as
cuatrocientos,-as
quinientos,-as
seiscientos,-as
setecientos,-as
ochocientos,-as
novecientos,-as
mil

The numbers from 100 to 1,000
*one hundred
one hundred and one
one hundred thirty–four
two hundred
two hundred twenty–three
three hundred
four hundred
five hundred
six hundred
seven hundred
eight hundred
nine hundred
one thousand*

C1 Sección de quejas y reclamos
El Sr. Gómez no recibió el estéreo que compró. Ahora está en la Sección de quejas y reclamos.

EMPLEADA	¿Señor?
SR. GÓMEZ	Sí, señorita. Aquí tengo el recibo. Ustedes me prometieron el estéreo para el día 15. Hoy es 25, . . . y no lo recibí.
EMPLEADA	El recibo, por favor. Ah, señor, ¿escribió usted una carta de reclamación?
SR. GÓMEZ	¡Señorita, por favor! Llamé por teléfono veinte veces, escribí dos cartas la semana pasada . . . , finalmente, decidí venir en persona.

Customer Service Department
Mr. Gómez did not receive the stereo he bought. Now he is in the Customer Service Department.

Sir?
Yes, miss. Here I have the receipt. You promised me the stereo for the 15th. Today is the 25th, . . . and I have not received it.

The receipt, please. Ah, sir, did you write a letter with your claim?

Miss, please! I called on the phone twenty times, I wrote two letters last week . . ., finally, I decided to come in person.

EMPLEADA	¿Subió usted a la oficina del piso cinco?	*Did you go up to the office on the fifth floor?*
SR. GÓMEZ	Sí, ya fui, me mandaron aquí.	*Yes, I went; they sent me here.*
EMPLEADA	A ver . . . un momento . . . ¿y quién le vendió el estéreo? Este pedido ya salió . . . usted va a recibir el estéreo mañana, a primera hora.	*Let's see . . . one moment . . . and who sold you the stereo? This order left already . . . you are going to receive the stereo tomorrow, as early as possible.*
SR. GÓMEZ	Pero, señorita . . . Mi hijo no cumple años mañana . . . ¡su cumpleaños es hoy! ¡Y yo le prometí el estéreo!	*But, miss . . . My son's birthday is not tomorrow . . . his birthday is today! And I promised him the stereo!*

SPANISH-ENGLISH VOCABULARY

This vocabulary includes all the words and expressions appearing in the text of **Nuevos amigos.** Exceptions are names of people and of most countries and places.

Nouns are listed with their definite articles. Nouns referring to persons are given in the masculine and feminine form if the English is the same for both (**el aficionado, la aficionada,** fan). If the English word is different (**el abuelo,** grandfather; **la abuela,** grandmother), the words are listed separately. Adjectives are listed in the masculine singular form with the feminine ending shown after each adjective. Verbs are listed in the infinitive form. Verb forms introduced as vocabulary items are listed in the form they appeared in the text.

The number after each definition refers to the unit in which the word or expression is introduced.

The following abbreviations are used in this list: *adj.* adjective; *adv.* adverb; *com.* command; *dir.* direct; *f.* feminine; *fam.* familiar; *ind.* indicative; *inf.* infinitive; *m.* masculine; *obj.* object; *pl.* plural; *pol.* polite; *prep.* preposition; *pron.* pronoun; *sing.* singular; *sub.* subjunctive.

A

a at, to, 2
　a casa (to) home, 5; **a la derecha** on the right, 5; **a la izquierda** on the left, 5; **a la mesa** to the table, 9; **a la noche** tonight, 7; **a la una** at one o'clock, 2; **a las diez** at ten o'clock, 2; **a lo dicho, hecho** no sooner said than done, 9; **a menudo** often, 3; **a pie** on foot, 2; **a primera hora** as early as possible, 11; **¿a qué hora?** at what time?, 2; **a veces** sometimes, 3; **estar a punto de** to be on the verge of, 10; **frente a** across from, 6
a ver let's see, 11
abajo below, 5
abandonado, -a abandoned, 2
abre opens, 2
el **abrigo** coat, 11
abril April, 3
abrimos: ¿lo abrimos? do we open it?, 2
abrir to open, 2
la **abuela** grandmother, 6
el **abuelo** grandfather, 6
　los **abuelos** grandparents, 6; grandfathers, 6
aburrido, -a boring, 2
acaba de: lo que acaba de ocurrir what just happened, 11
acabado, -a finished, 6
la **academia** academy, 7
el **accesorio** accessory, 11

el **aceite** oil, 9
aceptar to accept, 7
acerca(n): se acerca(n) (they) come close, near, 6
el **ácido** acid, 2
aclamado, -a acclaimed, 7
acompañar to accompany, 10
acompañará: lo acompañará (it) will accompany you, 10
acostumbrado: estar acostumbrado, -a to be used to, 11
la **actividad** activity, 2
el **actor** actor, 1
actuar to act, 11
acuerdo: de acuerdo all right, 3
　de acuerdo con according to, 7
además besides, 5
adentro inside, 11
adiós goodbye, 1
la **adivinanza** guessing game, 6
adivinar: ¡a adivinar! guess!, 3
el **admirador, la admiradora** admirer, 7
¿adónde? (to) where? 5
la **aduana** customs, 5
el **aduanero, la aduanera** customs agent, 5
la **aeromoza, la azafata** stewardess, 5
el **aeropuerto** airport, 5
el **aficionado, la aficionada** fan, 3
afuera outside, 11
la **agencia** agency, 10
la **agenda** appointment book, 2
el, la **agente** agent, 6
agosto August, 3

agrícola agricultural, 5
el **agua** (*f.*): **el agua mineral** mineral water, 9
ahí there, 2
ahora now, 2
ahorrar to save, 11
al (a + el) to the, at the (contraction), 2
　al contrario on the contrary, 2;
　al lado de beside, next to, 5
el **álbum** album, 6
la **alegría** happiness, 10
la **alfarería** pottery, 11
el **álgebra** (*f.*) algebra, 2
algo something, 5
el **algodón** cotton, 11
alguno, -a, -os, -as some, 2
alimenticio, -a: la píldora alimenticia food capsule, 10
el **almuerzo** lunch, 2
¡aló! hello, 5
alto, -a tall, 6
allá (over) there, 11
allí there, 5
amable kind, 6
amado, -a loved, 7
amarillo, -a yellow, 3
el **ambiente** atmosphere, 11
americano, -a American, 1
el **amigo, la amiga** friend, 3
la **amistad** friendship, 10
el **amor** love, 7
amplio, -a ample, abundant, 10
amueblado, -a furnished, 6
amurallado, -a walled, 5

anaranjado, -a orange, 3
el ángel angel, 1
animado, -a lively, 11
el dibujo animado animated cartoon, 7
el animal animal, 10
anoche last night, 10
antes before, 10
la anticipación: con una semana de anticipación a week ahead of time, 10
antiguo, -a old, 10
antipático, -a not nice, 6
el anuncio ad, 10
anunciaron (they) announced, 2
añadir to add, 9
año year, 3
¿cuántos años tiene? how old are you (is he/she)? 6; **cumplir años** to have a birthday, 11; **tener . . . años** to be . . . years old, 6
apaga turns off, 2
el apartamento apartment, 6
apoderarse: tratar de apoderarse de to try to seize, 11
apretar (ie) to press, 9
aprobado, -a passing, average, 2
aprovechado, -a above average, 2
apto. (abbreviation for *apartamento*) apt., 6
apuradísimo, -a in a big hurry, 10
aquel, aquella that, 9
aquél, aquélla that one, 11
aquellos, -as those, 9
aquéllos, -as those, 11
aquí here, 5
el árbol tree, 9
el árbol genealógico family tree, 6
el archivo file, 10
arder to burn, 10
la arquitectura architecture, 5
el arte art, 5
artístico, -a artistic, 2
la educación artística art class, 2
arreglado, -a arranged, 10
arriba up (there), 5
el arroz rice, 9
asesinar to murder, 6
así so, thus, 1
se dice así this is how to say it, 1; **no es así** it's not so, 1; that way, then, 11
el asiento seat, 5
la asignatura subject, 2
el Atlántico Atlantic, 2
el, la atleta athlete, 3
atlético, -a athletic, 3
el átomo atom, 2
el atún tuna, 9
el auto car, automobile, 2
en auto by car, 2
el autobús bus, 2
el autobús escolar school bus, 2; **en autobús** by bus, 2

autónomo, -a autonomous, 2
avanzado, -a advanced, 3
la avenida avenue, 10
la aventura adventure, 7
el avión airplane, 5
ayer yesterday, 10
ayudar to help, 9
el azúcar sugar, 9
azul blue, 3

B

el bachillerato secondary education program, 2
bailar to dance, 3
el baile dance, 7
bajar to get off, 7
bajo, -a short, 6; **en voz baja** in a low voice, 11
la bala bullet, 10
el balón ball (basketball, volleyball, soccer ball), 3
el ballet ballet, 2
el banco bank, 10
el baño bathroom, 5
el traje de baño bathing suit, 11
barato, -a cheap, 11
el barrio neighborhood, 11
basado, -a based, 7
básico, -a basic, 10
el básquetbol basketball, 3
¡basta de . . .! enough . . .! 7
bastante rather, 2; a lot, 7
el bastón (*pl.* **bastones**) pole, 3
(de esquiar) ski pole, 3
el bate bat, 3
batir to beat, 9
beber to drink, 5
el béisbol baseball, 3
la bicicleta bicycle, 2
en bicicleta by bicycle, 2; **montar en bicicleta** to ride a bicycle, 3
bien well, good, fine, 1; very, 6
quedar bien to look nice (on), 11
bienvenido, -a welcome, 6
el billete ticket, 10
la billetera wallet, 11
la biología biology, 2
el bistec beefsteak, 9
el bizcocho cake, 9
blanco, -a white, 3
la blusa blouse, 11
el bocadillo snack, sandwich, 9
la boda: las bodas de plata silver wedding anniversary, 7
el boletín report card, 2
el bolígrafo ballpoint pen, 2
el bolsillo pocket, 5
bonito, -a pretty, 6
¡qué cuarto tan bonito! what a pretty room! 6
bordado, -a embroidered, 11
bordo: a bordo on board, 5
las botas boots, 3; **(de esquiar)** ski boots, 3

el botón (*pl.* **botones**) button, 9
brindar to offer, 10
la broma joke, 2
buen: ¡buen provecho! hearty appetite! 9
hace (muy) buen tiempo it's (very) nice out, 3
bueno, -a good, 1
well, 1; **¿bueno?** hello 5; **buenas noches** good evening, good night, hello, 1; **buenas tardes** good afternoon, 1; **buenos días** good morning, 1
buenísimo, -a very good, 9
buscar to look for, 5
los busca is looking for them, 7

C

la cabeza: el dolor de cabeza headache, 2
cada each, 3
caer: se cae it falls, 11
el café coffeeshop, 7; coffee, 9
la cafetería cafeteria, 5
la caja cashier's desk, 11
el calcetín (*pl.* **calcetines**) sock, 11
la calculadora calculator, 2
calentar to heat, 9
la calidad quality, 11
caliente hot, 9
la calificación grade, 2
calmado, -a calmed down, 11
el calor: hace (mucho) calor it's (very) hot out, 3
la calle street, 2
la cámara camera, 5
la camarera waitress, 9
el camarero waiter, 9
cambiado, -a changed, 7
cambiar to cash, 5; **cambiar (de)** to change, 7
el cambio: la casa de cambio money exchange office, 5
caminar to walk, 10
el camión truck, 11
la camisa shirt, 11
la camisa de vestir dress shirt, 11
la camiseta T-shirt, 11
el campeón, la campeona champion, 3
el campeonato: el Campeonato mundial de fútbol World Cup Soccer Championships, 3
el campo country, 6
el canal channel, 2
la canasta basketball hoop, 3
la canción song, 9
la cancha: la cancha de tenis tennis court, 3
cansado, -a tired, 11
cantar to sing, 3
la capital capital, 1
el carácter character, 2
la cárcel jail, 7
el Caribe Caribbean, 9
cariñoso, -a affectionate, 6

la **carne** meat, **9**
    el **chile con carne** Mexican dish of beans, ground beef and chilies, **9**
    caro, -a expensive, **11**
la **carta** letter, **5**
la **cartera** schoolbag, **2**; purse, **5**
el **carro** cart, **5**
la **casa** house, **6**; home, **5**
    a casa (to) home, **5**; **la casa de cambio** money exchange office, **5**; **estás en tu casa** make yourself at home (*fam. sing.*), **6**
casado, -a married, **6**
el **casete** cassette, **5**
casi almost, **2**
el **castellano** Castilian (language), **2**
castigado, -a punished, **7**
el **catsup** ketchup, **9**
la **categoría** category, **3**
catorce fourteen, **2**
la **cebolla** onion, **9**
la **célula** cell, **2**
la **cena** dinner, supper, **9**
    cenar to have dinner, **9**
el **centro** center, **5**
la **cerámica** ceramic (material), **11**
    cerca (de) near, **5**
el **cereal** cereal, **9**
la **cereza** cherry, **9**
    cero zero, **2**
cien, ciento a hundred, **2**
la **ciencia** science, **2**
    la **ciencia-ficción** science fiction, **7**; **las ciencias naturales** natural science, **2**; **las ciencias sociales** social science, **2**
ciento a hundred, **11**
cierto, -a certain, correct, **2**
cinco five, **2**
cincuenta fifty, **2**
el **cine** movies, **7**; movie theater, **7**
el **cinturón** (*pl.* **cinturones**) belt, **3**
el **círculo** circle, **2**
la **ciudad** city, **2**
    cívico, -a: la formación social, moral y cívica civics, **2**
claro, -a light (in color), **11**
claro of course, **10**
la **clase** classroom, **1**; class, **2**; kind, **7**
clásico, -a classic, **2**
el, la **cliente** customer, **11**
el **club** club, **7**
la **cocina** kitchen, **6**; cooking, cuisine, **9**
    cocinar to cook, **9**
el **coche** car, **5**
el **colador** colander, **9**
la **colección** collection, **10**
el **colegio** school, **1**
el **color** color, **3**
la **combinación** combination, **1**
la **comedia** comedy, **7**
el **comedor** dining room, **6**
    comenzar (ie) to start, begin, **6**

comienza a sentir starts to feel, **6**
comer to eat, **5**
comercial commercial, **10**
cómico, -a comic, comical, **7**
la **comida** food, meal, dinner, **9**
como about, **2**; as, as if, like, **3**; since, **11**
¿cómo? how? **1**
    ¿cómo es? what's he (she, it) like? **6**; **¿cómo está?** how are you? (*pol. sing.*), **1**; **¿cómo estás?** how are you? (*fam. sing.*), **1**; **¿cómo se llama él (ella)?** what's his (her) name? **1**; **¿cómo te llamas tú?** what's your name? (*fam. sing.*), **1**; **cómo no** of course, **9**
cómodo, -a comfortable, **6**
compartir to share, **6**
el **compás** (*pl.* **compases**) compass, **2**
la **competencia** competition, **3**
complacido, -a pleased, **11**
completar to complete, **1**
completo, -a complete, **9**
el, la **cómplice** accomplice, **10**
la **composición** composition, **3**
el **compositor** composer, **2**
la **compra** shopping, **2**
    estar de compras to be shopping, **11**
comprar to buy, **5**
comprender to understand, **11**
la **comprensión** comprehension, **1**
la **computadora** computer, **2**
la **comunicación: ¡la comunicación se cortó!** we were cut off! **5**
con with, **2**
    con permiso excuse me, **6**; **con una semana de anticipación** a week ahead of time, **10**; **el chile con carne** Mexican dish of beans, ground beef and chilies, **9**; **de acuerdo con** according to, **7**
el **concierto** concert, **7**
la **condición** condition, **6**
el **conductor, la conductora** conductor, **10**
la **confusión** confusion, **2**
    ¡qué confusión! what a mixup! **5**
conmigo with me, **9**
conocer (zc) to know, meet, be acquainted with, **7**
la **conquista** conquest, **7**
conseguir to get, **6**
contado: al contado cash, **6**
contestar to answer, **5**
    no contestan there's no answer, **5**
contigo with you, **6**
continuar to continue, **5**
el **contrario: al contrario** on the contrary, **2**
el **control: el control de pasaportes** passport control, **5**

controlar to control, **3**
    controlarlo to control it, **3**
convenciste; me convenciste you convinced me, **10**
conversar to converse, talk, **6**
el **copiloto** copilot, **5**
la **corbata** tie, **11**
el **corredor, -a** runner, **3**
el **correo: correos** post office, **5**; **por correo** by mail, **11**
correr to run, **3**
la **corrida** bullfighting, **3**
corro I run, **2**
cortar to cut, **9**
    ¡la comunicación se cortó! we were cut off!, **5**; **cortarlas fino** to cut (them) in thin slices, **9**
las **Cortes** Spanish Parliament, **10**
corto, -a short, **10**
la **cosa** thing, **6**
la **costa** coast, **5**
la **costumbre** custom, **11**
el **crédito: la tarjeta de crédito** credit card, **11**
creer to think, believe, **5**; **creerlo** believe it, **10**
el **crimen** crime, **7**
el, la **criminal** criminal, **7**
el **crítico, la crítica** critic, **7**
cruzar to cross, **9**
el **cuaderno** notebook, **2**
¿cuál? what? which? **2**
cualquier any, **10**
cuando when, **6**
¿cuándo? when? **2**
¿cuántas veces? how many times? **7**
¿cuánto? how much? **2**
    ¿cuánto cuesta? how much does it cost? **2**; **¿cuánto cuestan?** how much do they cost? **2**; **¿cuánto vale?** how much does it cost? **11**
¡cuánto, -a!: ¡cuánta gente! what a lot of people! **7**
¿cuántos, -as? how many? **2**
    ¿cuántos años tiene? how old are you (is he/she)? **6**
cuarenta forty, **2**
cuarto quarter hour, **2**
cuarto, -a fourth, **5**
el **cuarto** room, **6**; (abbreviation ctos.), **6**
    ¡qué cuarto tan bonito! what a pretty room! **6**
cuatro four, **2**
cuatrocientos, -as four hundred, **11**
la **cuchara** spoon, **9**
la **cucharada** tablespoonful, **9**
la **cucharita** teaspoon, **9**
el **cuchillo** knife, **9**
la **cuenta** bill, check, **9** **hacer cuentas** to do calculations, **11**
el **cuento** story, **7**
el **cuero** leather, **11**
    cuesta: it costs, 2; ¿cuánto cuesta? how much does it cost? **2**

cuestan: ¿cuánto cuestan? how much do they cost? **2**

¡cuidado! be careful!, **10**

el **cumpleaños** birthday, **11**

cumplir: cumplir años to have a birthday, **11**

CH

chao so long, 'bye, **1**

la **chaqueta** jacket, **11**

la **charla** small talk, **1**

el **cheque: el cheque de viajero** traveler's check, **5**

la **chica** girl, **1**

el **chico** boy, **1**

el **chile: el chile con carne** dish of beans, ground beef and chilies, **9**

chocar to collide, **10**

el **chocolate** chocolate, **9**

los **churros** doughnut-like pastry, **9**

D

dar: dar una película to show a movie, **7**

dar una vuelta to go for a walk, **7**

de from, **1;** of, **2;** (made) of, **11; al lado de** beside, **5; de acuerdo** all right, **3; de acuerdo con** according to, **7; de Alice: la cartera de Alice** Alice's purse, **5; de compras** shopping, **11; ¿de dónde?** from where?, **1; de él** his, **6; de ella** hers, **6; de ellas** theirs (*f.*), **6; de ellos** theirs (*m.*), **6; de la mañana** in the morning, A.M., **5; de la noche** at night, P.M., **5; de nada** you're welcome, **1; de nuevo** again, **6; de plástico** (made of) plastic, **11; de postre** for dessert, **9; de pronto** suddenly, **3; ¿de qué es?** what's it made of? **11; de repente** suddenly, **10; de usted** yours (*pol. sing.*), **6; de ustedes** yours (*pl.*), **6; el (de)** the one (made of), **11; estar a punto de** to be on the verge of, **10; estar de compras** to be shopping, **11; más de . . .** more than . . . , **11; menos de . . .** less than . . . , **11; uno, -a (de)** one, **7**

debajo (de) under, **9**

debemos we ought to, **3**

deber should, ought to, **5**

¿debo . . . ? should I . . . ?, **5**

decidir to decide, **5**

decir to say, **7**

dejan: dejan de pensar en (they) stop thinking of, **3**

dejar to leave (behind), **9;** to allow, let, **11**

le dejo la cartera en . . . I'll let the purse go for . . . , **11**

del (de + el) of the, from the (contraction), **2**

delante (de) in front (of), **5**

delgado, -a thin, **6**

delicioso, -a delicious, **9**

demás: los demás the rest, **3**

demasiado, -a too (much), **11**

dentro (de) in, within, **5**

depender to depend, **11**

el **deporte: los deportes** sports, **2**

la **derecha: a la derecha** on the right, **5**

desaparecer disappear, **6**

el **desayuno** breakfast, **9**

desde from, **3; desde . . . hasta** from . . . to, **10**

desear to like, to want, **9**

desierto, -a deserted, **2**

desmaya: se desmaya faints, **6**

desp. abbreviation for *después*, **6**

despierto: me despierto I wake up, **2**

después then, **5; después de** after, **1**

el **destino** destiny, **10**

detenido, -a suspended, **7;** detained, **5**

detrás (de) behind, **5**

devolver (ue) to return, **11**

el **día** day, **1**

buenos días good morning, **1; el plato del día** specialty of the day, **9; los días de la semana** days of the week, **2**

el **diálogo** dialog, **1**

el **diario** diary, **10**

el **dibujo** drawing, **2**

el dibujo animado animated cartoon, **7**

el **diccionario** dictionary, **2**

dice: se dice así that's the way to say it, **1**

dice it says, **2; dice que . . .** he (she) says (that) . . . , **3**

diciembre December, **3**

el **dictado** dictation, **1**

dicho: a lo dicho, hecho no sooner said than done, **9**

diecinueve nineteen, **2**

dieciocho eighteen, **2**

dieciséis sixteen, **2**

diecisiete seventeen, **2**

diez ten, **2**

a las diez at ten o'clock, **2**

diferente different, **3**

difícil difficult, **2**

¡diga! hello? **5**

digo I mean, **6**

el **dinero** money, **2**

directamente straight, **7**

el **director, la directora** director, **1**

el **disco** record, **3**

la **discoteca** disco, **7**

distinguido, -a excellent, **2**

la **diversión** diversion, pastime, **7**

divertido, -a fun, **3**

doble: ahorrar el doble to save twice as much, **11**

doce twelve, **2**

el **doctor,** (*m.*) doctor; **la doctora** (*f.*) doctor, **1**

el **dólar** dollar, **2**

el **dolor: el dolor de cabeza** headache, **2**

el **domingo** Sunday, **2**

¿dónde? where?, **1**

¿de dónde? from where? **1; ¿de dónde es ella?** where is she from?, **1**

dore: se dore to brown, **9**

dorm. abbreviation for *dormitorio*, **6**

dos two, **2**

los, las dos both, **1;** the two, **6**

doscientos, -as two hundred, **11**

dulce sweet, **9; hogar, dulce hogar** home, sweet home, **6**

E

echar: echarles to add to them, **9**

echó poured, **6**

la **educación: la educación artística** art class, **2**

la educación física physical education, **2**

EE.UU. (abbreviation for *Estados Unidos*) U.S., **1**

egoísta selfish, **6**

el **ejercicio: el traje de ejercicio** warm-up suit, **11**

el the, **1; el (de)** the one (made of), **11**

él he, **1;** him, **9; de él** his, **6**

eléctrico, -a electric, **3**

el **elefante** elephant, **10**

elegante elegant, **11**

ella she, **1;** her, it, **9**

de ella hers, **6**

ellas they, (*f.*) **1;** them, **9; de ellas** theirs, **6**

ellos they, (*m.*), **1;** them, **9**

de ellos theirs, **6**

el **embarque: la puerta de embarque** boarding gate, **5**

empezado: ha empezado it has begun, **7**

empezar (ie) to start, begin, **6**

el **empleado, la empleada** employee, **5**

la **emoción** emotion, **10**

en in, **1;** by, **2;** at, on, **5**

en auto by car, **2; en autobús** by bus, **2; en bicicleta** by bicycle, **2; en metro** by subway, **2; en persona** in person, **11; ¿en qué puedo servirle?** how may I help you? (*pol.*), **11; en serio** seriously, **7; en todo momento** every time, **3; en venta** on sale, **2; en voz baja** in a low voice, **11; estás en tu casa** make yourself at home (*fam. sing.*), **6; le dejo la cartera en . . .** I'll let the purse go for . . . , **11; patinar en hielo** to ice skate, **3**

encantar to delight, 9; **me encantan** I love them, 9

encontrar (ue) to find, 11

la **encuesta** survey, 2

la **enchilada** Mexican dish—rolled tortilla filled with meat or cheese, 9

enero January, 3

enfadado, -a angry, 11

enfrente: enfrente de in front of, 10

enorme huge, 5

la **ensalada** salad, 9

la **entidad** entity, 2

entonces then, 5

la **entrada** entrance, 6; admission ticket, 7

entrar to enter, 5; **entro a** I go in(to), 2

entre between, 5

la **entrevista** interview, 1

el **entrevistador, la entrevistadora** interviewer, 2

entrevistar to interview, 7

entro a I go in(to), 2

la **envidia: ¡qué envidia!** what envy (I feel)!, what luck! 10

el **equipaje** baggage, 5

la sección de equipaje baggage claim, 5

el **equipo** team, 3

equivocado, -a: número equivocado wrong number, 5

el **error** error, 2

es: ¿cómo es? what's he (she, it) like? 6

¿de dónde es ella? where is she from? 1; **¿de qué es?** what's it made of? 11; **es la una** it's one o'clock, 2; **es un placer . . .** it's a pleasure . . . , 6; **es verdad** it's true, 3; **no es así** it's not so, 1; **¿qué hora es?** what time is it? 2

la **escala: hacer escala** to make a stop-over, 5

escapar to escape, 6

escoger: a escoger let's choose, 1

escolar: el autobús escolar school bus, 2

el rendimiento escolar scholastic progress, 2

escondido, -a hidden, 3

escríbenos write us, 6

escribir to write, 5

¡escucha! listen!, 2

escuchar to listen, 3

escuchaste you heard, 9

la **escuela** school, 1

la escuela primaria elementary school, 2; **la escuela secundaria** secondary school, 2

la **escultura** sculpture, 2

ese, -a that, 9

ése, -a that one, 11

esos, -as those, 9

ésos, -as those, 11

esencial essential, 1

espacial: el traje espacial space suit, 10

España Spain, 1

el **español** Spanish (language), 2

se habla español Spanish is spoken here, 1

español, española Spanish, 1

especial special, 9

la **especialidad** speciality, 9

la **especie** species, 10

el **espectáculo** show, 7

espera waits, 2

la **espera: la sala de espera** waiting room, 5

esperando waiting, 7

esperar to wait (for), 5

la **esposa** wife, 6

el **esposo** husband, 6

los esposos husband and wife, 6; husbands, 6

esquiar to ski, skiing, 3

los bastones de esquiar ski poles, 3; **las botas de esquiar** ski boots, 3

la **esquina** corner (street), 9

los **esquís** skis, 3

esta this, 9; **esta noche** tonight, 7

esta tarde this afternoon, 7

está: ¿cómo está? how are you? (*pol. sing.*), 1

está ocupado it's busy, 5; **ya está todo** everything's finished, 5

estar casado, -a to be married, 6

la **estación** season, 3; station, 10

el **estacionamiento** parking, 10

el **estadio** stadium, 3

los **Estados Unidos** (abbreviation EE.UU.) United States, 1

estamos we are, 3

el **estampado** print (in clothes), 11

están they are, 3

¿están ustedes? are you? (*pl.*), 1

el **estanque** pond, 10

estar to be, 5

¿cómo está? how are you? (*pol. sing.*), 1; **¿cómo estás?** how are you? (*fam. sing.*), 1; **está ocupado, -a** busy, 5; **estamos we are**, 3; **están** they are, 3; **¿cómo están ustedes?** how are you? (*pl.*), 1; **estar a punto de** to be on the verge of, 10; **estar acostumbrado, -a** to be used to, 11; **estar de compras** to be shopping, 11; **la sala de estar** family room, 6

estás: estás en tu casa make yourself at home (*fam. sing.*), 6

¿cómo estás? how are you? (*fam. sing.*), 1

el **este** east, 1; **al este** to the east, 1

este, -a this, 9

esta noche tonight, 7; **esta tarde** this afternoon, 7

éste, -a this one, 11

el **estéreo** stereo, 11

estos, -as these, 9

éstos, -as these, 11

estoy: estoy seguro I'm sure, 2

estrecho, -a narrow, 5

la **estrella** star, 2

el **estreno** premiere, 7

la **estructura** structure, 1

el, la **estudiante** student, 2

estudiar to study, 3

el **estudio** study, 2

estupendamente wonderfully, 11

estupendo, -a great, stupendous, 3

la **etiqueta** label, 2

Europa Europe, 1

la **evaluación** evaluation, 2

el **examen** exam, test, 7

exc. abbreviation for excelente, 6

excitante exciting, 7

la **exclamación** exclamation, 6

la **excursión** excursion, pleasure trip, 10

existir to exist, 7

exótico, -a exotic, 7

la **experiencia** experience, 10

experto, -a expert, 3

explicar to explain, 11

explorar to explore, 10

la **explosión** explosion, 10

exquisito, -a exquisite, 9

extracurricular extracurricular, 2

F

fácil easy, 2

la **falda** skirt, 11

faltar: falta algo something's missing, 1; to miss, 7

las **fallas** giant figures, 10

fam. abbreviation for *familia*, 6

la **fama** fame, 10

la **familia** family, 5

familiar familiar, 11

famoso, -a famous, 5

el **fanfarrón** braggart, 3

fantástico, -a fantastic, 3

fascinante fascinating, 7

el **favor: por favor** please, 1

favorito, -a favorite, 2, 3

febrero February, 3

feo, -a ugly, 6

la **feria** fair, 11

el **festival** festival, 11

festivo, -a festive, 10

la **fiesta** party, 7

fijo, -a fixed, 11

la **fila** line, 7

la **filosofía** philosophy, 2

el **fin: el fin de semana** weekend, 7

por fin finally, 2

final final, 2

finalmente finally, 11

fino: cortarlas fino to cut (them) in thin slices, 11

la **física** physics, 2

físico, -a: la educación física physical education, 2

flaco, -a skinny, 6

el **flan** baked custard, 9

la **flor** flower, 5
el **folleto** brochure, 10
la **formación: la formación social, moral y cívica** civics, 2
la **foto** photo, 6
la **fotografía** photography, 1 photograph, 6; **tomar fotografías** to take photographs, 3
fotográfico, -a photographic, 10
el **fotógrafo, la fotógrafa** photographer, 1
el **francés** French (language), 2
Francia France, 1
la **frase** sentence; phrase, 7
freír to fry, 9
frente a across from, 6
la **fresa** strawberry, 9
fresco, -a: hace fresco it's cool out, 3
los **frijoles** beans, 9
el **frío: hace (mucho) frío** it's (very) cold out, 3
frito, -a fried, 9
la **fruta** fruit, 9
la **frutería** fruit store, 9
fuerte heavy, 2
la **función** function, 7
funcionaba it functioned, 11
funcionar to function, 11
el **fútbol** soccer, 2
el Campeonato mundial de fútbol World Cup Soccer Championship, 3
futurista futuristic, 7
el **futuro** future, 5

G

galáctico, -a galactic, 10
la **galaxia** galaxy, 10
la **gana: tener ganas de** to feel like, 7
el **ganador, la ganadora** winner, 2
ganar to win, 3
la **ganga** bargain, 11
el **garaje** garage, 6
la **gaseosa** soda, 9
el **gato** cat, 7
genealógico, -a: el árbol genealógico family tree, 6
generalmente generally, 11
generoso, -a generous, 6
el **genio** genius, 2
la **gente** people, 7
¡cuánta gente! what a lot of people! 7
la **geografía** geography, 2
la **geometría** geometry, 2
gigante giant, 11
la **gimnasia** gynmastics, 3
el **gobernador, la gobernadora** governor, 1
el **gol** goal, 3
la **goma** eraser, 2
gordo, -a fat, 6
gracias thank you, 1
muchas gracias thank you

very much, 3
gráfico, -a: el taller gráfico printing plant, 11
el **gramo** gram (0.35 ounce), 9
gran great, 5
grande large, 6
más grande que bigger than, 11
gritar to shout, 3
el **grito: el último grito** the last word, 10
el **grupo** group, 5
el **guante** glove, mitt, 3
guapo, -a handsome, 6
¡qué guapo! how handsome! 6
la **guía** guidebook, 9; **el, la guía** guide, 10
la **guitarra** guitar, 3
gustar to like, to be pleasing to, 3
le gusta you like (*pol. sing.*), he/she likes, 3; **les gusta(n)** you (they) like, 9; **me gusta** I like, 3; **no me gusta nada** I don't like it at all, 11; **nos gusta(n)** we like, 9; **te gusta** you like (*fam. sing.*), 3
el **gusto: mucho gusto** nice to meet you, 1

H

habla: se habla español Spanish is spoken here, 1
habla speaks, 2
hablan (they) speak, 1
hablar to speak, talk, 3
él habla (he's) speaking (on the phone), 5
hable: ¡qué hable! speech!, 3
hace: hace (muy) buen tiempo it's (very) nice out, 3; **hace (mucho) calor** it's (very) hot out, 3; **hace fresco** it's cool out, 3; **hace (mucho) frío** it's (very) cold out, 3; **hace (muy) mal tiempo** the weather is (very) bad, 3; **hace (mucho) sol** it's (very) sunny, 3; **hace una hora** an hour ago, 10; **hace (mucho) viento** it's (very) windy, 3
hacer to do, 5
to make 5; **hacer cuentas** to do calculations, 11; **hacer escala** to make a stopover, 5; **hacer la maleta** to pack a suitcase, 10; **¿qué puedo hacer?** what can I do? 2; **se hace trizas** it smashes into pieces, 11
hacia towards, 10
el **hambre** (*f.*): **tener (mucha) hambre** to be (very) hungry, 5
la **hamburguesa** hamburger, 1
hasta as far as, 10
desde . . . hasta from . . . to, 10; **hasta luego** see you later, 1; **hasta mañana** see you tomorrow, 1
hay there is, there are, 2

no hay más remedio it can't be helped, 9; **no hay ningún** there isn't any, 10; **¿qué hay?** what's up? 1
haz make (*com.*), 2
hecho: a lo dicho, hecho no sooner said than done, 9; **hecho, -a a mano** handmade, 11
el **helado** ice cream, 7
la **hermana** sister, 6
el **hermano** brother, 6
el hermano menor younger brother, 1; **los hermanos** brother(s) and sister(s), 6; brothers, 6
el **hielo** ice, 3
patinar en hielo to ice skate, 3
el **hierro** iron, 11
la **hija** daughter, 6
el **hijo** son, 6
los **hijos** children, 6; sons, 6
hipnotizado, -a hypnotized, 3
la **historia** history, 2; story, 7
histórico, -a historic, historical, 5
el **hogar: hogar, dulce hogar** home, sweet home, 6
la **hoguera** bonfire, 10
hola hello, 1; hello? 5
el **hombre** man, 6
hondo, -a deep, 9
el **honor** honor, 3
la **hora** time, hour, 2
a primera hora as early as possible, 11; **¿a qué hora?** at what time? 2; **hace una hora** an hour ago, 10; **¿qué hora es?** what time is it? 2
el **horario** schedule, 2
horrible horrible, 3
hoy today, 2
la **huerta** orchard, 5
el **huevo** egg, 9

I

la **idea** idea, 1
ideal ideal, 3
la **identificación** identification, 9
igual (que) the same (as), 11
igualmente likewise, 6
la **imaginación** imagination, 1
imaginario, -a imaginary, 3
la **imitación** imitation, 11
impecable impeccable, 6
importante important, 6
importar to matter, 11
¡no importa! it doesn't matter! 11
imposible impossible, 3
la **inasistencia** absence, 2
la **independencia** independence, 2
indica (it) indicates, 2
indicar to suggest, 5
industrial industrial, 5
la **información** information (booth), 5
el **informe** report, 7

el ingeniero, la ingeniera engineer, 1

el inglés English (language), 2

el ingrediente ingredient, 9

inmediatamente immediately, 10

inocente innocent, 7

inolvidable unforgettable, 10

la instrucción instruction, 7

inteligente intelligent, 6

intercambiar to exchange, 6

   intercambian miradas (they) exchange glances, 6

el intercambio interchange, 11

interesante interesting, 2

interesar to interest, 11

   no me interesa I don't care, 11

interior interior, 5

internacional international, 5

interplanetario, -a interplanetary, 10

el invasor, la invasora invader, 7

el inventario inventory, 2

el invierno winter, 3

la invitación invitation, 10

el invitado, la invitada guest, 6

invitar to invite, 6

ir to go, 5

   ¿si vamos . . .? what if we go . . .? 7; **¡vamos!** let's go! 6; **van** they go, 5

   irme: tengo que irme I must go, 11

la isla island, 1

la izquierda: a la izquierda on the left, 5

J

la jalea jelly, 9

el jamón ham, 9

el jardín garden, 6

los jeans jeans, 11

el, la joven young man, woman 9

   los jóvenes young people, 11

el judo judo, 3

el juego game, 3

   los Juegos Olímpicos Olympic Games, 3

el jueves Thursday, 2

jugar (ue) to play, 3

el jugo juice, 9

julio July, 3

junio June, 3

Júpiter Jupiter, 10

la juventud youth, 7

K

el kilo kilogram (2.2 pounds), 9

el kilómetro kilometer (.62 miles), 5

L

la the, 1; you (*pol. sing.*), her, it (*obj. pron.*), 10

lácteo, -a: la Vía Láctea Milky Way, 10

el lado side, 9; **al lado de** beside, 5

la lana wool, 11

el lápiz (*pl.* **lápices**) pencil, 2

el lapso term, 2

largo, -a long, 11

las the (*fem. pl.*), 2; you (*pl.*), them (*obj. pron.*), 10

la lástima: ¡qué lástima! what a shame! 7

lavar: lavarlas to wash (them), 9

le you (*pol. sing.*), him, her, (*indir. obj.*) 9

   le gusta you like (*pol. sing.*), he/she likes, 3

la lectura reading, 1

la leche milk, 9

la lechuga lettuce, 9

leer to read, 1

las legumbres vegetables, 10

lejos (de) far (from), 5

les you (*pl.*), them (*obj. pron.*), 9

   les gusta (n) you (they) like, 9

levanta: se levanta gets up (*sing.*), 6

libre free, 6

   los ratos libres, 2; **el tiempo libre** free time, 6

el libro book, 2

ligero, -a light (meal), 9

el limón lemon, 9

lindo, -a pretty, 6

el lío complication, 7

la lista list, 11

listo, -a ready, 10

la literatura literature, 2

el litro liter (1.05 quarts), 9

lo you (*pol. sing.*), him, it (*dir. obj.*), 10

   ¿lo abrimos? do we open it?, 2; **lo mejor** the best (thing), 9; **lo mismo** the same thing, 7; **lo mismo (que)** the same (as), 11; **lo que** what, that, 7; **lo que pasa** what's happening, 10; **¿lo sabes?** do you know it? (*fam. sing.*) 1; **lo siento** I'm sorry, 7; **por lo menos** at least, 7

loco, -a crazy, 7

el locutor, la locutora announcer, 2; newscaster, 3

los the (*m. pl.*), 2; you (*pl.*), them, 10

   luego: hasta luego see you later, 1

el lugar place, 5

lunar lunar, 10

el lunes Monday, 2

la luz (*pl.* **luces**) light, 10

LL

llamar to call, 5

   ¿cómo se llama él (ella)? what's his (her) name? 1; **¿cómo te llamas tú?** what's your name? (*fam. sing.*), 1

llano, -a flat, 9

la llegada arrival, 5

llegando: siguen llegando (they)

keep coming, 11

llegar to arrive, 5

llego I arrive, 2

llevar to take, 9

llorar to cry, 9

llueve it's raining, 3

M

la madrastra stepmother, 6

la madre mother, 6

magnífico, -a magnificent, 3

el mago, la maga wizard, 7

mal bad, 1

   hace (muy) mal tiempo the weather is (very) bad, 3; **muy mal** awful, terrible, 1

la maleta suitcase, 5

   hacer la maleta to pack a suitcase, 10

la mamá mom, 1

mandar to send, 11

la manga sleeve, 11

la mano hand, 11

la mantequilla butter, 9

las manualidades industrial arts, 2

la manzana apple, 9

mañana tomorrow, 3

   hasta mañana see you tomorrow, 1

la mañana morning, 3

   de la mañana in the morning, A.M., 5; **por la mañana** in the morning, 3

el mapa map, 5

el mar sea, 1

   el Mar Mediterráneo Mediterranean Sea, 2

la marca brand, 11

el marcador felt-tip marker, 2

marcar to mark, 10

los mariachis Mexican band of strolling musicians, 9

los mariscos seafood, 10

Marte Mars, 7

el martes Tuesday, 2

marzo March, 3

marrón brown, 3

más more, else, 2

   most, 6; **más de . . .** more than . . ., 11; **más grande que** bigger than, 11; **más o menos** so-so, 1; **más . . . que** more . . . than, 11; **más tarde** later, 7; **no hay más remedio** it can't be helped, 9; **¿qué más necesitas?** what else do you need? (*fam. sing.*), 2

las matemáticas mathematics, 2

la materia subject, 2

mayo May, 3

la mayonesa mayonnaise, 9

mayor older, 6

me me, 9, 10

   me gusta I like, 3; **me llamo . . .** my name is . . ., 1; **no me gusta nada** I don't like it at all, 11

la **medalla de oro** gold medal, 3
la **medianoche** midnight, 10
las **medias** socks, 11
el **mediodía** noon, 9
mediterráneo, -a Mediterranean, 2
    el **Mar Mediterráneo** Mediterranean Sea, 2
mejor better, 7
    best, 7; **mejor . . .** it would be better to . . ., 7; **lo mejor** the best (thing), 9
el **melocotón** peach, 9
la **melodía** melody, 2
el **melón** melon, 9
menor younger, 1
    el **hermano menor** younger brother, 1
menos less, 1
    más o menos so-so, 1; **menos de . . .** less than . . ., 11; **por lo menos** at least, 7
el **mensaje** message, 9
el **menú** menu, 9
menudo: a menudo often, 3
el **mercado** market, 11
la **merienda** snack, light meal in the afternoon, 9
la **mermelada** marmalade, 9
el **mes** month, 3
la **mesa** table, 9
    a la mesa to the table, 9
    poner la mesa to set the table, 9
la **meta** finish line, 3
métrico, -a metric, 11
el **metro** subway, 2; **en metro** by subway, 2
mexicano, -a Mexican (adj.), 9
mexicano americanos Mexican Americans, 1
la **mezcla** mixture, 7
mi my, 2
mí me, 9
el **miércoles** Wednesday, 2
mil a thousand, 11
el **minuto** minute, 7
¡mira! look! (com.), 2
la **mirada** glance, look, 6
    intercambian miradas (they) exchange glances, 6
mirar to look at, watch, 3
    ¡mira! look! 2
    ¿me miras? are you looking at me? (fam. sing.), 3; **miran: se miran** (they) look at each other, 7
la **misión** mission, 7
mismo, -a same, 9
    lo mismo the same thing, 7; **lo mismo (que)** the same (as), 11
el **misterio** mystery, 3
moderado, -a moderate, 11
moderno, -a modern, 11
modesto, -a modest, 6
el **mole** spicy chocolate sauce, 9
el **momento** moment, 2
    en todo momento every time, 3;

un momento just a moment, 6
el **monstruo** monster, 10
montar to ride, 3
    montar en bicicleta to ride a bicycle, 3
el **Monte de Piedad** pawnshop in Mexico City, 11
moral: la formación social, moral y cívica civics, 2
moreno, -a dark (hair, complexion), 6
la **mostaza** mustard, 9
la **moto** motorcycle, 10
mover (ue) to move, 9; **moverlas** to move (pl. f.), 9
mucho a lot (adv.), 3
mucho, -a a lot (of), 2
    mucho gusto nice to meet you, 1; **mucho tiempo** a long time, 10
muchos, -as many, a lot (of), 2
    muchas gracias thank you very much, 3
la **mujer** woman, 10
mundial: el Campeonato mundial de fútbol World Cup Soccer Championship, 3
el **mundo** world, 3; **todo el mundo** everybody, 1
murió: se murió he's dead, 6
el **museo** museum, 10
la **música** music, 2
musical musical, 7
el **músico, la música** musician, 7
muy very, 1; **muy mal** awful, terrible, 1

N

nada nothing, 1
    de nada you're welcome, 1; **no me gusta nada** I don't like it at all, 11
nadar to swim, 3
nadie no one, nobody, 7
    nadie más nobody else, 2
la **naranja** orange, 9
la **natación** swimming, 3
natural: las ciencias naturales natural science, 2
la **nave** (space)ship, 10
necesitar to need, 3
    necesitas you need (fam. sing.), 2; **¿qué más necesitas?** what else do you need? (fam. sing.), 2
negro, -a black, 3
nervioso, -a nervous, 2
ni . . . ni neither . . . nor, 9
nieva it's snowing, 3
el **nilón** nylon, 11
ningún: no hay ningún there isn't any, 10
ninguna: en ninguna parte nowhere, 11
el **nitrógeno** nitrogen, 2
no no, 1; not, 2; **¿no?** right? 6
    no contestan there's no an-

swer, 5; **no es así** it's not so, 1; **no hay más remedio** it can't be helped, 9; **¡no importa!** it doesn't matter! 11; **no me gusta nada** I don't like it at all, 11; **¿por qué no . . .?** why don't we . . .? 5; **yo no** not me, 5
la **noche** night, 3
    a la noche at night, 7; **buenas noches** good evening, good night, 1; **de la noche** at night, P.M., 5; **esta noche** tonight, 7; **por la noche** at night, 3
el **nombre** name, 3
el **norte** north, 5; **al norte** to the north, 1
norteamericano, -a North American, 6
nos us, 9; **nos gusta(n)** we like, 9
nosotras we (f.) 1; us (f.), 9
nosotros we (m. or m. and f.), 11; us (m. or m. and f.), 9; **de nosotros** about us, 6
notable very good, 2
las **noticias** news, 2
el **noticiero** newsreel, 7
novecientos, -as nine hundred, 11
noventa ninety, 2
la **novia** girlfriend, 3
noviembre November, 3
el **núcleo** nucleus, 2
nuestro, -a, -os, -as our, 6
nueve nine, 2
nuevo, -a new, 1
    de nuevo again, 6
el **número** number, 2
    size, 11; **número equivocado** wrong number, 5
nunca never, 3

O

o or, 2
el **objeto** object, 11
el **Océano Pacífico** Pacific Ocean, 2
octubre October, 3
ocupado, -a: está ocupado it's busy, 5
ocurrir: lo que acaba de ocurrir what just happened, 11
ochenta eighty, 2
ocho eight, 2
ochocientos, -as eight hundred, 11
odiar to hate, 3; **odio** I hate, 3
el **oeste** west, 1
    al oeste to the west, 1; **la película del oeste** Western (movie), 7
la **oferta** offer, 11
oficial official, 7
la **oficina** office, 10
ofrecer to offer, 11
olímpico, -a: los Juegos Olímpicos Olympic Games, 3
olvidar to forget, 10

no olvides don't forget, **10**
once eleven, **2**
la **opinión** opinion, **2**
ordenar to put in order, **7**
organizado, -a organized, **10**
original original, **10**
la **orilla** shore, **5**
el **oro** gold, **3**
    la **medalla de oro** gold medal, **3**
os you (*fam. pl.*), **11**
oscuro, -a dark, **11**
el **otoño** fall, autumn, **3**
otro, -a other, another, **2**
    otra vez again, **5**
el **oxígeno** oxygen, **2**
¡oye! hey! **1**; **se oye** one hears, **11**

P

la **paciencia** patience, **9**
el **padrastro** stepfather, **6**
    los **padrastros** stepparents, **6**; stepfathers, **6**
el **padre** father, **6**
    los **padres** parents, **6**; fathers, **6**
la **paella valenciana** hearty saffron-flavored dish of rice, meat, seafood and vegetables, **9**
pagar to pay, **9**
el **país** country, **1**
la **palabra** word, **1**
el **palacio** palace, **11**
el **pan** bread, **9**
Panamá Panama, **1**
los **pantalones** pants, **11**
el **pañuelo** handkerchief, **11**
la **papa** potato **las papas fritas** french fries, **9**
el **papá** dad, **6**
el **paquete** package, parcel, **11**
para to, in order to, for, **3**
    ¿para qué? for what? what for? **5**
la **parada** stop, **7**
paralizado, -a paralyzed, **10**
parar to stop, **10**
parecer to seem; **¿qué te parece . . .?** what do you think of . . .? (*fam. sing.*), **6**
el **parque** park, **7**
la **parte** part, **1**
    en ninguna parte nowhere, **11**; **por todas partes** everywhere, **11**
participar to participate, to take part, **3**
    participar de to share in, **10**
la **partícula** particle, **2**
el **partido** game, match, **3**
pasa: ¿qué pasa? what's happening, **1**
    todo lo que pasa everything that's happening, **10**
pasado, -a last, past, **10**

la **semana pasada** last week, **10**
el **pasado** past, **5**
el **pasajero, la pasajera** passenger, **5**
el **pasaporte** passport, **5**
    el **control de pasaportes** passport control, **5**
pasar to spend (time), **6**; to come in, **6**; to happen, **9**; to pass by, **9**; **pasa** come in, **6**; **pasar por** to pass through, **3**
el **pasatiempo** pastime, **3**
pasear to go for a walk, **7**
el **paseo** stroll, walk, **1**; sightseeing trip, **7**
el **pasillo** hall, **6**
el **paso** step, **3**
el **pastel** cake; pie, **9**
la **pastelería** pastry, pastry shop, **9**
la **patata** potato (Spain), **9**
patear to kick, **3**
patinar to skate, **3**
    patinar en hielo to ice skate, **3**
el **patio** inner courtyard, patio, **1**
el **pedido** order, **11**
pedir (i) to ask (for something), order, **9**
pegue: para que no se pegue so it doesn't stick, **9**
pelar to peel, **9**
la **película** film, movie, **7**
    dar una película to show a movie, **7**; **la película de terror** horror movie, **7**; **la película del oeste** Western, **7**; **la película policial** detective movie, **7**
peligroso, -a dangerous, **3**
pelirrojo, -a redheaded, **6**
la **pelota** ball (baseball, tennis ball), **3**
la **pena: ¡qué pena!** what a pity! **1**
pensar (ie) to think, plan, **7**
    dejan de pensar en they stop thinking of, **3**
pequeño, -a small, little, **6**
la **pera** pear, **9**
la **perdición** doom, **7**
perdón excuse me, **2**
perfecto, -a perfect, **9**
el **periódico** newspaper, **5**
el, la **periodista** journalist, **3**
el **permiso** permission, **10**
    con permiso excuse me, **6**; **permiso** excuse me, **7**
pero but, **2**
persistir to continue, **11**
la **persona** person, **11**
    en persona in person, **11**
Perú Peru, **1**
el **pescado** fish, **9**
la **peseta** monetary unit of Spain, **5**
el **peso** monetary unit of Mexico, Colombia and Chile, **9**
el **picnic** picnic, **9**
el **pie** foot, **2**
    a pie on foot, **2**
la **piedad: el Monte de Piedad** pawnshop in Mexico City, **11**

el, la **pijama** pajamas, **11**
la **pila** battery, **2**
la **píldora: la píldora alimenticia** food capsule, **10**
el **piloto** pilot, **5**
la **pimienta** pepper, **9**
pintoresco, -a picturesque, **5**
la **pintura** painting, **2**
la **piña** pineapple, **9**
la **piscina** pool, **7**
el **piso** floor, story, **11**
la **pizza** pizza, **9**
el **placer** pleasure, **11**
    es un placer . . . it's a pleasure . . ., **6**
el **plan** plan, **10**
planear to plan, **10**
el **planeta** planet, **10**
el **plano** floor plan, **6**
el **plástico** plastic, **11**
    de plástico made of plastic, **11**
la **plata** silver, **7**
    las bodas de plata silver wedding anniversary, **7**
el **plátano** banana, plantain, **9**
el **platillo** saucer, small plate, **9**
    el **plato hondo** soup dish, bowl, **9**
el **plato** dish, plate, **9**
    el **plato del día** specialty of the day, **9**
la **playa** beach, **3**
la **pluma** fountain pen, **2**
pobre poor, **2**
poco, -a little, **2**
    poco tiempo a short time, **10**
podemos: podemos ver we can see, **5**
poder (ue) to be able, can, **7**
    ¿en qué puedo servirle? how may I help you? (*pol.*), **11**; **puedes** you can (*fam. sing.*), **6**; **¿qué puedo hacer?** what can I do? **2**
la **policía** police, **5**
policial: la película policial detective movie, **7**
el **pollo** chicken, **9**
poner to put, **9**
    poner la mesa to set the table, **9**
por for, **2**; along, **3**; through, **5**
    por correo by mail, **11**; **por favor** please, **1**; **por fin** finally, at last, **2**; **por la mañana** in the morning, **3**; **por la noche** at night, **3**; **por la tarde** in the afternoon, **3**; **por lo menos** at least, **7**; **¿por qué?** why? **2**; **¿por qué no . . .?** why don't we . . .? **5**; **por semana** per week, **7**; **¡por supuesto!** of course! **6**; **por teléfono** on the telephone, **3**
porque because, **2**
portátil portable, **2**
la **posición** position, **2**
la **postal** postcard, **5**

el **postre** dessert, 9
  de **postre** for dessert, 9
practicar to practice, play, 3
el **precio** price, 2
preciso, -a precise, 11
la **preciosura** thing of beauty, 11
preferido, -a favorite, 2
la **pregunta** question, 3
preguntar to ask, 10
el **premio** prize, 3
prende turns on, 3
prender to turn on (an appliance), 3
preocupado, -a worried, 7
preparar to prepare, 9
la **presentación** introduction, 1
el **presidente, la presidenta** president, 2
previo, -a previous, last, 2
primario, -a: la escuela primaria elementary school, 2
la **primavera** spring, 3
primer, -o, -a first, 1
  a primera hora as early as possible, 11
primero first, 5
el **primo, la prima** cousin, 3
principal main, 9
el, la **principiante** beginner, 3
probar to try, 9
el **producto** product, 11
el **profesor, la profesora** teacher, 1
el **programa** program, show, 7
prohibido, -a forbidden, 6
prometer to promise, 11
pronto soon, 10
  de pronto suddenly, 3
el **pronto** down payment, 6
la **pronunciación** pronunciation, 1
la **propiedad: propiedades** real estate, 6
la **propina** tip, 9
el **provecho: ¡buen provecho!** hearty appetite! 9
próximo, -a next, 7
el **proyecto** project, plan, 1
puedes you can (*fam. sing.*), 6
puedo: ¿en qué puedo servirle? how may I help you? (*pol.*), 11
  ¿qué puedo hacer? what can I do? 2
la **puerta** door, 6; gate, 5
  la Puerta del Sol famous plaza in Madrid, 9; **tocan a la puerta** (they) are knocking at the door, 1
el **puerto** port, 5
el **puesto** market booth, 11
el **punto** point, 10
  estar a punto de to be on the verge of, 10
púrpura purple, 7

Q

que that, 5
  dice que . . . he (she) says (that) . . ., 3; **igual (que)** the same (as), 11; **lo que** what,

that, 7; **lo mismo (que)** the same (as), 11; **más (grande) que** (bigger) than, 11; **más . . . que** more . . . than, 11; **tener que** to have to, 7
¿qué? what, 2
  ¿qué hay? what's up?, 1; **¿qué hora es?** what time is it?, 2; **¿qué más necesitas?** what else do you need? (*fam. sing.*), 2; **¿qué pasa?** what's happening?, 1; **¿qué tal?** how are things?, 1; **¿qué te parece . . .?** what do you think of . . .? (*fam. sing.*), 6; **¿qué tiempo hace?** what's the weather?, 3; **¿a qué hora?** at what time?, 2; **¿de qué es?** what's it made of?, 11; **¿en qué puedo servirle?** how may I help you? (*pol.*), 11; **¿para qué?** for what?, 5; **¿por qué?** why?, 2; **¿por qué no . . .?** why don't we . . .?, 5
¡qué . . .!: ¡qué confusión! what a mixup! 5
  ¡qué cuarto tan bonito! what a pretty room! 6; **¡qué envidia!** what envy (I feel)!, what luck! 10; **¡qué guapo!** how handsome! 6; **¡qué lástima!** what a shame! 7; **¡qué pena!** what a pity! 1; **¡qué suerte!** what luck! 5
¡que hable! speech! 3
quedar: quedar bien to look nice on (clothing), 11
la **queja** complaint, 11
  la sección de quejas y reclamos customer service department, 11
quemar to burn, 10
  se queman they are burned, 10
querer (ie) to want, 6
  quiere he wants, 5
querido, -a dear, 10
el **queso** cheese, 9
¿quién? who? 1
quiere he wants, 5
quieto, -a quiet, 11
quinto, -a fifth, 11
la **química** chemistry, 2
quince fifteen, 2
quinientos, -as five hundred, 11
quitar to throw out, 9

R

el **radio** radio, 3
rápido quickly, 2
la **raqueta** racquet, 3
el **Rastro** flea market in Madrid, 10
el **rato** short time, 2
  los ratos libres free time, 2
la **razón: tener razón** to be right, 5
la **reacción** reaction, 1
la **rebaja** discount, 2
  rebajado, -a reduced (in price), 11

rebajar to lower the price, 11
recibir to receive, 11
el **recibo** receipt, 11
recitar to recite, 6
la **reclamación** claim, 11
el **reclamo** claim, 11
  la sección de quejas y reclamos customer service department, 11
reconocer (zc) to recognize, 10
el **recreo** recess, 2
el **rectángulo** rectangle, 2
recuerdos regards, 1
la **red** net, 3
la **referencia** reference, 6
el **refresco** soda, 6
el **refugio** refuge, 9
el **regalo** present, gift, 1
regateando bargaining, 11
  regatear to bargain, 11
el **regateo** bargaining, 11
regional regional, 3
la **regla** ruler, 2
regresar to return, 10
regular so-so, 1
el **rehén** (*pl.* **rehenes**) hostage, 5
la **religión** religion, 2
remar to row, 10
el **remedio: no hay más remedio** it can't be helped, 9
el **remitente** sender, 2
el **rendimiento: el rendimiento escolar** scholastic progress, 2
reparar to repair, 11
el **repaso** review, 4
repente: de repente suddenly, 10
la **repetición** repetition, 2
el **reportero, la reportera** reporter, 3
la **reproducción** reproduction, 10
la **república** republic, 2
reservar to reserve, 10
resistir to resist, 7
la **respuesta** answer, 1
el **restaurante** restaurant, 9
la **revista** magazine, 2
revuelto, -a scrambled, 9
el **rey** king, 10
  rico, -a tasty, delicious (food), 9
el **rincón** corner, 7
el **río** river, 5
el **robot** robot, 10
el **rock** rock (music), 7
  romano, -a Roman, 5
la **ropa** clothes, 11
  rosa pink, 9
la **rosa** rose, 1
  rubio, -a fair, blonde, 6
la **rueda** wheel, 10
el **ruido** noise, 7
la **ruta** route, 10
la **rutina** routine, 10

S

el **sábado** Saturday, 2
saber to know (a fact), 5; (+ inf) to know how (+ inf), 7

¿lo sabes? do you know it? (*fam. sing.*), **1; ¿sabes que . . .?** do you know that . . .? (*fam. sing.*), **1; ¡ya sé!** I know it! **6; yo no sé** I don't know, **2**

sabes: ¿lo sabes? do you know it? (*fam. sing.*) **1**

sabroso, -a tasty, delicious, **9**

el **saco** jacket, **11**

la **sal** salt, **9**

la **sala** living room, **6**

    la sala de espera waiting area, **5; la sala de estar** family room, **6**

sale (he or she) goes out, leaves, **3**

salen (they) leave, **3**

salir to go out, leave, **7**

la **salsa** sauce, **9**

saludar to greet, **10**

saludos greetings, **1**

salvar to save, **10**

    le salvaron la vida they saved his life, **10**

la **sandía** watermelon, **9**

el **sandwich** sandwich, **9**

la **sartén** frying pan, **9**

se: se dice así this is how you say it, **1;**

    ¿cómo se llama él (ella)? what's his (her) name? **1; ¡la comunicación se cortó!** we were cut off! **5; se habla español** Spanish is spoken here, **1; se llama . . .** his (her) name is . . ., **1**

sé: ¡ya sé! I know it! **6**

    yo no sé I don't know, **2**

la **sección** department, **11**

    la sección de equipaje baggage claim, **5; la sección de quejas y reclamos** customer service department, **11**

secreto, -a secret, **7**

el **secuestro** hijacking, **5**

secundario, -a: la escuela secundaria secondary school, **2**

la **sed: tener (mucha) sed** to be (very) thirsty, **9**

la **seda** silk, **11**

seguimos: ¿la seguimos? do we follow her?, **10**

siguen (they) follow, **5**

    siguen llegando (they) keep coming, **11**

segundo, -a second, **8**

seguro, -a sure, **1**

seis six, **2**

seiscientos, -as six hundred, **11**

la **selección** selection, **11**

el **sello** stamp, **5**

la **semana** week, **2**

    con una semana de anticipación a week ahead of time, **10; el fin de semana** weekend, **7; por semana** per week, **7; la semana pasada** last week, **10**

sencillamente simply, **7**

sensacional sensational, **7**

sentado, -a (en) seated (at), **6**

sentir (ie) to feel, **6**

    comienza a sentir starts to feel, (*sing.*) **6; lo siento** I'm sorry, **7**

el **señor** (abbreviation Sr.) Mr., sir, **1; man**, **6**

la **señora** (abbreviation Sra.) Mrs., ma'am, **1; woman**, **6**

la **señorita** (abbreviation Srta.) Miss, **1**

septiembre September, **3**

ser to be, **1**

    ¿cómo es? what's he (she, it) like? **6; ¿de dónde es ella?** where is she from? **1; ¿de qué es?** what's it made of? **11; es la una** it's one o'clock, **2; es un placer . . .** it's a pleasure . . ., **6; es verdad** it's true, **3; ¿qué hora es?** what time is it? **2; son las diez** it's ten o'clock, **2**

serio: en serio seriously, **7**

la **servilleta** napkin, **9**

servir (i) to serve, **11**

    ¿en qué puedo servirle? how may I help you? (*pol.*), **11**

sesenta sixty, **2**

setecientos, -as seven hundred, **11**

si if, **7; ¿si vamos . . .?** what if we go . . .? **7**

sí yes, **1; really**, **3**

siempre always, **7**

siento: lo siento I'm sorry, **7**

siete seven, **2**

siguen (they) follow, **5**

    siguen llegando (they) keep coming, **11**

siguiente following, **7**

simpático, -a nice, **6**

sin without; **sin parar** without stopping, **10**

singular singular, **7**

la **situación** situation, **1**

sobre about, **9**

sobresaliente excellent, **2**

la **sobrina** niece, **6**

el **sobrino** nephew

    los sobrinos nephew(s) and niece(s), **6; nephews**, **6**

social: las ciencias sociales social science, **2**

    la formación social, moral y cívica civics, **2**

¡socorro! help!, **2**

el **sol: hace (mucho) sol** it's (very) sunny, **3; sun**, **4**

    la Puerta del Sol famous plaza in Madrid, **9**

sólo only, **1**

la **solución** solution, **2**

el **sombrero** hat, **11**

son: son las diez it's ten o'clock, **2**

el **sonido** sound, **7**

la **sopa** soup, **9**

la **sorpresa** surprise, **1**

el **sótano** basement, **6**

Sr. (abbreviation of *señor*) Mr., **1**

Sra. (abbreviation of *señora*) Mrs., Ma'am, **1**

Srta. (abbreviation of *señorita*) Miss, **1**

su(s) your (*pol. sing.*), his, her, its, **5; their**, **6**

subir to go up, **5; subir a** to get on, **5; to get into**, **10**

el **suburbio** suburb, **1**

suculento, -a succulent, **10**

Suramérica South America, **1**

el **sueño** dream, **7**

la **suerte: ¡qué suerte!** what luck! **5**

el **suéter** sweater, **11**

super super, **11**

supuesto, -a: ¡por supuesto! of course! **6**

el **sur** south, **1; al sur** to the south, **1**

el **suroeste** southwest, **1**

    al suroeste to the southwest, **1**

surtidos, -as assorted, **11**

suspenso suspended, below average, **2**

sustituir to substitute, **5**

T

el **taco** Mexican dish—folded tortilla filled with ground beef, tomatoes, lettuce, etc., **9**

tal: ¿qué tal? how are things? **1; tal vez** perhaps, **9**

el **talento** talent, **2**

la **talla** size, **11**

el **taller: el taller gráfico** printing plant, **11**

el **tamaño** size, **11**

    también also, too, **3**

    tan so, **6; ¡qué cuarto tan bonito!** what a pretty room! **6**

tanto, -a so (as, that) much, **2**

las **tapas** appetizer, **9**

tarde late, **6**

    más tarde later, **7**

la **tarde** afternoon, **3**

    buenas tardes good afternoon, **1; esta tarde** this afternoon, **7; por la tarde** in the afternoon, **3**

la **tarea** homework, **2**

la **tarjeta** card, **11**

    la tarjeta de crédito credit card, **11**

la **tarta** tart, pastry, **9**

el **taxi** taxi, **5**

la **taza** cup, **9**

te you (*fam. sing.*), **9**

    ¿cómo te llamas tú? what's your name? (*fam. sing.*), **1; te gusta** you like (*fam. sing.*), **3**

el **té** tea, **9**

el **teatro** theater, **7**

telefónico, -a telephone, **5**

el **teléfono** telephone, **3**

    por teléfono on the telephone, **3**

la **televisión** television, **2**
el **televisor** television set, **2**
el **templo** temple, **7**
temprano early, **2**
el **tenedor** fork, **9**
tener to have, **2**
¿**cuántos años tiene?** how old are you (is he/she)? **6**; **tener . . . años** to be . . . years old, **6**; **tener ganas de** to feel like, **7**; **tener (mucha) hambre** to be (very) hungry, **5**; **tener que** to have to, **7**; **tener razón** to be right, **5**; **tener (mucha) sed** to be (very) thirsty, **9**; **tiene** it has, **2**
tengo: tengo que irme I must go, **11**
el **tenis** tennis, **3**
la cancha de tenis tennis court, **3**; **los zapatos de tenis** tennis shoes, **3**
la **tentación** temptation, **7**
tercer, -o, -a third, **12**
termina it's over, **2**
terminan they finish, **3**
terminar to finish, **10**
el **terror: la película de terror** horror movie, **7**
el **testimonio** testimony, **5**
texano, -a Texan, **9**
ti you (*fam. sing.*), **9**
la **tía** aunt, **6**
el **tiempo** weather, **3**
time, **6**; **hace (muy) buen tiempo** it's (very) nice out, **3**; **hace (muy) mal tiempo** the weather is (very) bad, **3**; **mucho tiempo** a long time, **10**; **poco tiempo** a short time, **10**; ¿**qué tiempo hace?** what's the weather? **3**; **el tiempo libre** free time, **6**; **todo el tiempo** all the time, **7**
la **tienda** store, **2**
tiene it has, **2**
¿**cuántos años tiene?** how old is (he/she)? **6**
el **tigre** tiger, **1**
el **tío** uncle, **6**
los tíos uncle(s) and aunt(s), **6**; uncles, **6**
típico, -a typical, **9**
las **tiras cómicas** comic strips, **2**
la **toalla** towel, **11**
tocan: tocan a la puerta (they are) knocking at the door, **1**
tocar to play (a musical instrument), **3**
todavía still, **10**
todo, -a all, **7**; every, **3**
whole, **6**; **en todo momento** every time, **3**; **todo el mundo** everybody, **1**; **todo el tiempo** all the time, **7**
todo everything, **3**
ya está todo everything's finished, **5**; **todo lo que pasa**

everything that's happening, **10**
todos, -as all, every, **3**; whole, **6**
todos los días every day, **3**
tomar to take, **3**;
to have (to eat or drink), **7**;
tomar fotografías to take photographs, **3**
tomo: lo tomo I take it, **2**
el **tomate** tomato, **9**
tonto, -a dumb, **6**; fool, **1**
la **tortilla** Mexican flat corn cake, **9**; Spanish omelette, **9**
el **total** total, **3**
trabajar to work, **3**
trabaje: que trabaje who works (*sub.*), **11**
tradicional traditional, **11**
trae brings, **9**
la **tragedia** tragedy, **1**
el **tráfico** traffic, **9**
la **tragedia** tragedy, **1**
el **traje** suit, **11**
el traje de baño bathing suit, **11**; **el traje de ejercicio** warm-up suit, **11**; **el traje espacial** space suit, **10**
el **transbordador** carrier, **10**
trasmitir to broadcast, **5**
tratar de to try to, **11**
tratar de apoderarse to try to seize, **11**
trataron de they tried to, **11**
trece thirteen, **2**
treinta thirty, **2**
tres three, **2**
trescientos, -as three hundred, **11**
el **triángulo** triangle, **2**
triste sad, **11**
trizas: se hace trizas it smashes into pieces, **11**
el **trofeo** trophy, **3**
el **trozo** piece, **9**
tu(s) your (*fam. sing.*), **2**
tú you (*fam. sing.*), **1**
el **turismo** tourism, **10**
el, la **turista** tourist, **12**
turístico, -a: la guía turística tourist guidebook, **9**

U

Ud. (abbreviation of *usted*) you (*pol. sing.*), **1**
Uds. (abbreviation of *ustedes*) you (*pl.*), **1**
último, -a: el último grito the last word, **10**
un a, an, **2**
un momento just a moment, **6**
una a, an, **2**
a la una at one o'clock, **2**; **es la una** it's one o'clock, **2**; **una vez** once, **7**
la **unidad** unit, **1**
uno one, **2**
uno, -a (de) one (of), **7**
unos, -as some, **2**

usar to use, **6**
usted (Ud.) you (*pol. sing.*), **1, 9**
de usted your, **6**
ustedes (Uds.) you (*pl.*), **1**
de ustedes your, **6**
la **uva** grape, **9**

V

las **vacaciones** vacation, **6**
vale it costs, **11**
¿**cuánto vale?** how much does it cost? **11**
valen they cost, **11**
valenciano, -a from Valencia, **10**
la paella valenciana hearty saffron-flavored dish of rice, meat, seafood and vegetables, **9**
vamos let's go, **6**
¿**si vamos . . . ?** what if we go . . . ? **7**; **vamos a casa** let's go home, **3**; **vamos a leer** let's read, **1**; **vamos a ver** let's see, **2**
van they go, **5**
la **variedad** variety, **10**
vario, -a various, **2**
el **vaso** glass, **9**
váyanse (*com.*) go away, **6**
el **vecino, la vecina** neighbor, **1**
el **vehículo** vehicle, **10**
veinte twenty, **2**
el **vendedor, la vendedora** salesperson, **2**
vender to sell, **5**
venir to come, **2**
la **venta: en venta** on sale, **2**
la **ventanilla** ticket window, **7**
ver to see, **6**
vamos a ver let's see, **2**
el **verano** summer, **3**
la **verdad:** ¿**verdad?** really? **2** right? **5**; **es verdad** it's true, **3**
verdadero, -a true, **7**
verde green, **3**
la **verdura** green vegetable, **9**
el **vestido** dress, **11**
vestir: la camisa de vestir dress shirt, **11**
la **vez** (*pl.* **veces**) time, **7**
a veces sometimes, **3**; **dos veces** twice, **7**; **otra vez** again, **5**; **tal vez** perhaps, **9**; **una vez** once, **7**
la **vía: la Vía Láctea** Milky Way, **10**
el **viaje** trip, **10**
el **viajero: el cheque de viajero** traveler's check, **5**
la **vida** life, **10**
le salvaron la vida they saved his life, **10**
el **viento: hace (mucho) viento** it's (very) windy, **3**
el **viernes** Friday, **2**
la **viñeta** vignette, **1**
violeta violet, **10**
la **visita** visit; visitor, **6**
visitar to visit, **10**
¡**viva!** long live!, **10**

vivir to live, **6**
vivo I live, **1**
el **vocabulario** vocabulary, **1**
el **volibol** volleyball, **3**
voltearla turn it over, **9**
volver (ue) to return, **7**
vosotras you (*f., fam. pl.*), **1**
vosotros you (*m., fam. pl.*), **1**
voy a I am going to (to indicate intention), **7**
la **voz: en voz baja** in a low voice, **11**

el **vuelo** flight, **5**
la **vuelta: dar una vuelta** to go for a walk, **7**
vuestro, -a, -os, -as your (*fam. pl.*), **6**

Y

y and, **1**
ya already, **2**; now, **10**; **ya está todo** everything's finished, **5**; **¡ya sé!** I know it! **6**; **ya viene** he (she) is coming, **10**
yo I, **1**
yo no not me, **5**; **yo no sé** I don't know, **2**

Z

el **zapato** shoe, **3**
los **zapatos de tenis** tennis shoes, **3**
la **zona** zone, **11**
el **zoológico** zoo, **10**

ENGLISH-SPANISH VOCABULARY

This vocabulary includes all the active words in the text of **Nuevos amigos**. These are the words listed in the vocabulary at the end of each unit. Spanish nouns are listed with the definite article. Spanish expressions are listed under the English words that the student would be most likely to look up.

The following abbreviations are used in this list: *adj.* adjective; *adv.* adverb; *com.* command; *dir.* direct; *f.* feminine; *fam.* familiar; *ind.* indicative; *inf.* infinitive; *m.* masculine; *obj.* object; *pl.* plural; *pol.* polite; *prep.* preposition; *pron.* pronoun; *sing.* singular; *sub.* subjunctive.

A

a un, una, 2
above average (grade) aprovechado, -a, 2
about como, 2; sobre, 9
academy la academia, 7
accessory el accesorio, 11
acquainted: be acquainted with conocer, 7
across: across from frente a, 6
activity la actividad, 1
to **add** añadir, 9
admission: admission ticket la entrada, 7
advanced avanzado, -a, 3
adventure la aventura, 7
affectionate cariñoso, -a, 6
after después de, 1
afternoon la tarde, 3; **good afternoon** buenas tardes, 1; **in the afternoon** por la tarde, 3; **this afternoon** esta tarde, 7
again de nuevo, 6
agent: customs agent el aduanero, 5
ago: an hour ago hace una hora, 10
ahead: a week ahead of time con una semana de anticipación, 10
airplane el avión, 5
airport el aeropuerto, 5
algebra el álgebra (*f.*), 2
all todos, 2; todo, -a, -os, -as, 3, 7; **all right** de acuerdo, 3; **all the time** todo el tiempo, 7; **I don't like it at all** no me gusta nada, 11
to **allow** dejar, 11
almost casi, 2
already ya, 5
also también, 3
always siempre, 3
A.M. de la mañana, 5
American: North American norteamericano, -a, 6
and y, 1
angry enfadado, -a, 11
animated: animated cartoon el dibujo animado, 7

anniversary: silver wedding anniversary las bodas de plata, 7
another otro, -a, -os, -as, 2, 3
to **answer** contestar, 5; **there's no answer** no contestan, 5
apartment el apartamento, 6
apple la manzana, 9
April abril, 3
arranged arreglado, -a, 10
arrival la llegada, 5
to **arrive** llegar, 5
art: industrial arts las manualidades, 2
as como, 3; **as early as possible** a primera hora, 11; **as far as** hasta, 10; **as much** tanto, -a, 2; **the same as** igual que, 11, lo mismo que, 11
to **ask** preguntar, 10
at a, 2; en, 5; **at night** por la noche, 3, de la noche, 5, a la noche, 7; **at one o'clock** a la una, 2; **at ten o'clock** a las diez, 1; **at the . . .** al (a + el), 2; **at what time?** ¿a qué hora? 2
athlete el, la atleta, 3
August agosto, 3
aunt la tía, 6; **uncles and aunts** los tíos, 6
automobile el auto, 2
autonomous autónomo, -a, 2
autumn el otoño, 3
awful muy mal, 1

B

bad mal, 1
baggage el equipaje, 5; **baggage claim** la sección de equipaje, 5
ball el balón (basketball, volleyball, soccer ball), 3; la pelota (baseball, tennis ball), 3
ballet el ballet, 2
ballpoint: ballpoint pen el bolígrafo, 2
banana el plátano, 9
bargain la ganga, 11
to **bargain** regatear, 11

baseball el béisbol, 3; (the ball) la pelota, 3
basketball el básquetbol, 3; (the ball) el balón, 3; **basketball hoop** la canasta, 3
bat el bate, 3
bathing: bathing suit el traje de baño, 11
bathroom el baño, 5
to **be** ser, 1; estar, 5; **be able** poder (ue), 7; **be (very) hungry** tener (mucha) hambre, 5; **be on the verge of** estar a punto de, 10; **be pleasing to** gustar, 3; **be shopping** estar de compras, 11; **be . . . years old** tener . . . años, 6; **be (very) thirsty** tener (mucha) sed, 9; **be married** estar casado, 6
beach la playa, 3
beans los frijoles, 9
to **beat** batir, 9
beauty: thing of beauty la preciosura, 11
because porque, 2
beefsteak el bistec, 9
before antes, 10
beginner el, la principiante, 3
behind detrás de, 5
below abajo, 5; **below average (grade)** suspenso, 2
belt el cinturón (*pl.* cinturones), 3
beside al lado de, 5
best mejor, 7; **the best (thing)** lo mejor, 9
better mejor, 7; **it would be better to . . .** mejor . . ., 7
between entre, 5
bicycle la bicicleta, 2; **by bicycle** en bicicleta, 2; **to ride a bicycle** montar en bicicleta, 3
bigger: bigger than más grande que, 11
bill la cuenta, 9
biology la biología, 2
birthday el cumpleaños, 11; **to have a birthday** cumplir años, 11
black negro, -a, 3
blonde rubio, -a, 6

blouse la blusa, 11
blue azul, 3
book el libro, 2
boot la bota, 3; **ski boots** las botas de esquiar, 3
booth: information booth la información, 5
boring aburrido, -a, 2
boy el chico, 1
braggart el fanfarrón, 3
bread el pan, 9
breakfast el desayuno, 9
brings trae, 9
brochure el folleto, 10
brother el hermano, 6; **brother(s) and sister(s)** los hermanos, 6
brown marrón, 3
to brown dorar, 9
bus el autobús, 2; **by bus** en autobús, 2; **school bus** el autobús escolar, 2
busy: it's busy está ocupado, 5
but pero, 2
butter la mantequilla, 9
to buy comprar, 5
by en, 2; **by bicycle** en bicicleta, 2; **by bus** en autobús, 2; **by car** en auto, 2; **by mail** por correo, 11; **by subway** en metro, 2
'bye chao, 1

C

café el café, 7
cafeteria la cafetería, 5
cake el pastel; el bizcocho, 9
calculation: to do calculations hacer cuentas, 11
calculator la calculadora, 2
to call llamar, 5
camera la cámara, 5
can poder (ue), 7
car el auto, 2; el coche, 5; **by car** en auto, 2
card la tarjeta, 11; **credit card** la tarjeta de crédito, 11
Caribbean el Caribe, 9
cart el carro, 5
cartoon el dibujo animado, 7
to cash cambiar, 5
cashier: cashier's desk la caja, 11
cassette el casete, 9
category la categoría, 3
ceramics la cerámica (art), 2; (material), 11
cereal el cereal, 9
champion el campeón, la campeona, 3
to change cambiar de, 5
character carácter, 2
cheap barato, -a, 11
check la cuenta, 9; **traveler's check** el cheque de viajero, 5
cheese el queso, 9
chemistry la química, 2
cherry la cereza, 9
chicken el pollo, 9
children los hijos, 6

chocolate el chocolate, 9
to choose: let's choose a escoger, 1
city la ciudad, 2
claim el reclamo, 11; **baggage claim** la sección de equipaje, 5
class la clase, 2
classroom la clase, 1
clothes la ropa, 11
club el club, 7
coat el abrigo, 11
coffee el café, 9
coffeeshop el café, 7
cold: it's (very) cold out hace (mucho) frío, 3
color el color, 3
to come venir, 2; **to come in** pasar, 6
comfortable cómodo, -a, 6
comic(al) cómico, -a, 2
comic strips las tiras cómicas, 2
compass el compás (pl. compases), 2
complaint la queja, 11
complete completo, -a, 9
complication el lío, 7
computer la computadora, 2
concert el concierto, 7
contrary: on the contrary al contrario, 2
to cook cocinar, 9
cooking la cocina, 9
cool: it's cool out hace fresco, 3
corner la esquina, 9
cost: how much do they cost? ¿cuánto cuestan? 2; **how much does it cost?** ¿cuánto cuesta? 2, ¿cuánto vale?, 11; **it costs** cuesta, 2, vale, 11; **they cost** cuestan, 2, valen, 11
cotton el algodón, 11
course: of course! ¡por supuesto! 6; ¡cómo no! 11
court: tennis court la cancha de tenis, 3
courtyard: inner courtyard el patio, 1
crazy loco, -a, 7
credit: credit card la tarjeta de crédito, 11
crime el crimen, 7
to cry llorar, 9
cuisine la cocina, 9
cup la taza, 9
custard (baked) el flan, 9
customer el, la cliente, 11; **customer service department** la sección de quejas y reclamos, 11
customs la aduana, 5; **customs agent** el aduanero, 5
to cut cortar, 9

D

dad el papá, 6
dance el baile, 7
to dance bailar, 3
dark oscuro, -a, 11; **dark hair, complexion** moreno, -a, 6
daughter la hija, 6

day el día, 1; **every day** todos los días, 3; **specialty of the day** el plato del día, 9
dear querido, -a, 10
December diciembre, 3
to decide decidir, 5
deep hondo, -a, 9
delicious delicioso, -a, 9; rico, -a, 9; sabroso, -a, 9
to delight encantar, 11
department la sección, 11; **customer service department** la sección de quejas y reclamos, 11
desk: cashier's desk la caja, 11
dessert el postre, 9; **for dessert** de postre, 9
detective: detective movie la película policial, 7
diary el diario, 10
dictionary el diccionario, 2
diet la dieta, 9
difference la diferencia, 2
different diferente, 3
difficult difícil, 2
dining: dining room el comedor, 6
dinner la cena, 9; la comida, 9; **to have dinner** cenar, 9
disco la discoteca, 7
discount la rebaja, 11
dish el plato, 9
to do hacer, 5, 9; **do calculations** hacer cuentas, 11
door la puerta, 6
dollar el dólar, 2
double doble, 11
drawing el dibujo, 2
dress el vestido, 11
to drink beber, 5
dumb tonto, -a, 6

E

each cada, 3
early temprano, 2; **as early as possible** a primera hora, 11
easy fácil, 2
to eat comer, 5
education: physical education la educación física, 2
egg el huevo, 9
eight ocho, 2; **eight hundred** ochocientos, -as, 11
eighteen dieciocho, 2
eighty ochenta, 2
eleven once, 2
else más, 2; **what else?** ¿qué más? 2
embroidered bordado, -a, 11
employee el empleado, la empleada,
English (language) el inglés, 2
enough bastante, 2
to enter entrar, 5
entrance la entrada, 6
envy la envidia, 10; **what envy (I feel)!** ¡qué envidia! 10
eraser la goma, 2
evaluation la evaluación, 2

evening: good evening buenas noches, **1**

every todo, -a, -os, as, **3**; **every day** todos los días, **3**; **every time** en todo momento, **3**

everything todo, **3**; **everything's finished** ya está todo, **5**

exam el examen, **7**

excellent excelente, so-bre-sa-lien-te, **2**

exchange: money exchange la casa de cambio, **5**

excursion la excursión, **10**

excuse: excuse me perdón, **2**; con permiso, **6**; permiso, **7**

expensive caro, -a, **11**

extracurricular extracurricular, **2**

F

fair la feria, **11**

fall el otoño, **3**

family la familia, **6**; **family room** la sala de estar, **6**

fantastic fantástico, -a, **3**

far: far from lejos de, **5**; **as far as** hasta, **10**

fat gordo, -a, **6**

father el padre, **6**

favorite favorito, -a, **2**, **3**; preferido, -a, **2**

February febrero, **3**

to feel: feel like tener ganas de, **7**

fifteen quince, **2**

fifth quinto, -a (*adj.*), **11**

fifty cincuenta, **2**

film la película, **7**

finally por fin, **2**; finalmente, **11**

to find encontrar (ue), **11**

fine bien, **1**

to finish terminar, **10**

first primero, **5**; primero, -o, -a, **11**

fish el pescado, **9**

five cinco, **2**; **five hundred** quinientos, -as, **11**

flat llano, -a, **9**

flight el vuelo, **5**

floor el piso, **11**

food la comida, **9**

foot el pie, **2**; **on foot** a pie, **2**

for por, **2**; para, **3**; **for what?** ¿para qué? **5**

fork el tenedor, **9**

forty cuarenta, **2**

four cuatro, **2**; **four hundred** cuatrocientos, -as, **11**

fourteen catorce, **2**

free: free time el tiempo libre, **6**

French (language) el francés, **2**; **french fries** papas fritas, **9**

Friday el viernes, **2**

friend el amigo, la amiga, **3**

from de, **1**; desde, **10**

front: in front (of) delante (de), **5**

fruit la fruta, **9**; **fruit store** la frutería, **9**

to fry freír, **9**

frying pan la sartén, **9**

fun divertido, -a, **3**

funny gracioso, -a, **9**

G

game el juego, **3**; el partido, **3**; **Olympic Games** los Juegos Olímpicos, **3**

garage el garaje, **6**

garden el jardín, **6**

gate la puerta, **5**

generally generalmente, **11**

generous generoso, -a, **6**

genius el genio, **2**

geography la geografía, **2**

geometry la geometría, **2**

to get: get off bajar, **7**

girl la chica, **1**

glass el vaso, **9**

glove el guante, **3**

to go ir, **5**; **go for a walk** dar una vuelta, **7**; pasear, **7**; **go out** salir, **7**; **go up** subir, **5**

gold el oro, **3**; **gold medal** la medalla de oro, **3**

good bueno, -a, **1**; bien, **1**; **good afternoon** buenas tardes, **1**; **good evening** buenas noches, **1**; **good morning** buenos días, **1**; **good night** buenas noches, **1**; **very good** buenísimo, -a, **9**

goodbye adiós, **1**

grandfather el abuelo, **6**

grandmother la abuela, **6**

grandparents los abuelos, **6**

grape la uva, **9**

great estupendo, -a, **3**

green verde, **9**; **green vegetable** la verdura, **9**

group el grupo, **5**

to guess: guess! ¡a adivinar! **3**

guidebook la guía, **9**

guitar la guitarra, **3**

gymnastics la gimnasia, **3**

H

hall el pasillo, **6**

ham el jamón, **9**

hamburger la hamburguesa, **9**

hand la mano, **11**

handkerchief el pañuelo, **11**

handmade hecho, -a a mano, **11**

handsome guapo, -a, **6**

happiness la alegría, **10**

hard difícil, **2**

hat sombrero, **11**

hate: I hate odio, **3**

to have tener, **2**; (to eat or drink) tomar, **7**; **have a birthday** cumplir años, **11**; **have dinner** cenar, **9**; **have to** tener que, **7**

he él, **1**

heavy fuerte, **2**

hello hola, **1**; **hello? (on the phone)** ¡aló!, ¿bueno?, ¡diga!, ¿hola? **5**

to help ayudar, **9**; **help!** ¡socorro!, **2**; **how may I help you?** ¿en qué puedo servirle? (*pol. sing.*), **11**; **it can't be helped** no hay más remedio, **9**

her (*poss.*) su(s), **5**; de ella, **6**

her le (*indir. obj.*), **9**; ella (*obj. of prep.*), **9**; (*dir. obj.*) la, **10**

here aquí, **5**

hey! ¡oye! **1**

him él (*obj. of prep.*), **9**; le (*indir. obj.*), **9**; lo (*dir. obj.*), **10**

his su(s), **5**; de él, **6**

history la historia, **2**

home la casa, **6**; **(to) home** a casa, **5**; **make yourself at home** estás en tu casa (*fam. sing.*), **6**

homework la tarea, **2**

hoop: basketball hoop la canasta, **3**

horrible horrible, **3**

horror: horror movie la película de terror, **7**

hot: it's (very) hot out hace (mucho) calor, **3**

hour la hora, **2**; **an hour ago** hace una hora, **10**

house la casa, **6**

how? ¿cómo? **1**; **how are things?** ¿qué tal? **1**; **how are you?** ¿cómo está? (*pol. sing.*), **1**, ¿cómo estás? (*fam. sing.*), **1**; **how old is (he/she)?** ¿cuántos años tiene? **6**

how!: how handsome! ¡qué guapo! **6**

how: how many? ¿cuántos, -as? **2**; **how many times?** ¿cuántas veces?, **7**

how: how much? ¿cuánto? **2**; **how much do they cost?** ¿cuánto cuestan? **2**; **how much does it cost?** ¿cuánto cuesta? **2**, ¿cuánto vale? **11**

hundred cien, **2**, ciento, **11**; **eight hundred** ochocientos, -as, **11**; **five hundred** quinientos, -as, **11**; **nine hundred** novecientos, -as, **11**; **seven hundred** setecientos, -as, **11**; **six hundred** seiscientos, -as, **11**; **three hundred** trescientos, -as, **11**; **two hundred** doscientos, -as, **11**

hungry: to be (very) hungry tener (mucha) hambre, **5**

hurry: in a big hurry apuradísimo, -a, **10**

husband el esposo, **6**; **husband and wife** los esposos, **6**

I

I yo, **1**

ice el hielo, **3**

ice cream el helado, **7**

to ice skate patinar en hielo, **3**

idea la idea, **9**

ideal ideal, 3

if si, 7; **what if we go . . .?** ¿si vamos . . .? 7

important importante, 6

in en, 1; **in front of** delante de, 5; **in order to** para, 3; **in person** en persona, 11

information: information booth la información, 5

intelligent inteligente, 6

interesting interesante, 2

international internacional, 5

to **interview** entrevistar, 7

invitation la invitación, 10

to **invite** invitar, 6

it (*obj. of prep.*) él, ella, 9; (*indir. obj.*) le, 9; (*dir. obj.*) lo, la, 10

item el artículo, 11

its su(s), 5

J

jacket la chaqueta, el saco, 11

January enero, 3

jeans los jeans, 11

jelly la jalea, 9

to **jog** correr, 3

judo el judo, 3

juice el jugo, 9

July julio, 3

June junio, 3

K

ketchup el catsup, 9

kilo(gram) el kilo (2.2 pounds), 9

kind amable, 6; la clase, 7

kitchen la cocina, 6

knife el cuchillo, 9

to **know** conocer, 7; **know a fact** saber, 7; **know how** (+ inf) saber (+ inf), 7; **I don't know** yo no sé, 2; **I know it!** ¡ya sé! 6

L

large grande, 11

last pasado, -a, 10; **last night** anoche, 10; **last week** la semana pasada, 11

late tarde, 2

later más tarde, 7; **see you later** hasta luego, 1

leather el cuero, 11

to **leave (behind)** dejar, 9

left: on the left a la izquierda, 5

lemon el limón, 9

less menos, 11; **less than . . .** menos de . . ., 11

let dejar, 11; **I'll let the purse go for . . .** le dejo la cartera en . . ., 11

let's: let's go! ¡vamos! (*com.*), 6; **let's see** a ver, 11

letter la carta, 5

lettuce la lechuga, 9

light (in color) claro, -a, 11; **(meal)** ligero, -a, 9

like como, 3

to **like** gustar, 3; **he (she) likes** le gusta, 3; **I don't like it at all** no me gusta nada, 11; **I like** me gusta, 3; **they like** les gusta(n), 9; **we like** nos gusta(n), 9; **you like** te gusta (*fam. sing.*), 3, le gusta (*pol. sing.*), 3, les gusta (*pl.*), 9

likewise igualmente, 6

limit: off limits prohibido, -a, 6

line la fila, 7

list la lista, 11

to **listen (to)** escuchar, 3

little pequeño, -a, 6; **a little** poca, 2

to **live** vivir, 6

living room la sala, 6

long: a long time mucho tiempo, 10

to **look: look at** mirar, 3; **look!** ¡mira! (*com.*), 2; **look for** buscar, 5; **look nice on** quedar bien, 11

lot: a lot mucho, 3

lot: a lot (of) mucho, -a, -os, -as, 2

love el amor, 7

luck: what luck! ¡qué suerte!, 5; ¡qué envidia! 10

lunch el almuerzo, 2

M

ma'am la señora, 1

made: made of de, 11; **made of plastic** de plástico, 11; **what's it made of?** ¿de qué es?, 11

magazine la revista, 2

magnificent magnífico, -a, 3

mail: by mail por correo, 11

main principal, 9

to **make** hacer, 5, 9; **make yourself at home** estás en tu casa (*fam. sing.*), 6

man el hombre, 2; el señor, 6

many muchos, -as, 2; **how many?** ¿cuántos, -as? 2

map el mapa, 5

March marzo, 3

to **mark** marcar, 10

marker el marcador, 2

market el mercado, 11

marmalade la mermelada, 9

married casado, -a, 6

match el partido, 3

mathematics las matemáticas, 2

matter: it doesn't matter! ¡no importa! 11

May mayo, 3

mayonnaise la mayonesa, 9

me mí (*obj. of prep.*), 9; me (*indir. obj.*), 9; me (*dir. obj.*), 10; **not me** yo no, 5; **with me** conmigo, 9

meal la comida, 9

meat la carne, 9

medal la medalla, 3; **gold medal** la medalla de oro, 3

to **meet** conocer, 7; **nice to meet you** mucho gusto, 1

melon el melón, 9

menu el menú, 9

Mexican mexicano, -a, 1

Mexican Americans mexicano americanos, 1

Mexico México, 1

milk la leche, 9

minute el minuto, 7

Miss la señorita, 1

mitt el guante, 3

mixup: what a mixup! ¡qué confusión! 5

mom la mamá, 5

moment: just a moment un momento, 6

Monday el lunes, 2

money el dinero, 2; **money exchange** la casa de cambio, 5

month el mes, 3

more más, 6; **more . . . than** más . . . que, 11; **more than . . .** más de . . ., 11

morning la mañana, 3; **good morning** buenos días, 1; **in the morning** por la mañana, 3, de la mañana, 5

most más, 6

mother la madre, 6

motorcycle la moto, 10

movie la película, 7; **detective movie** la película policial, 7; **horror movie** la película de terror, 7; **to show a movie** dar una película, 7; **Western** la película del oeste, 7

movies el cine, 7

Mr. (abbreviation of *señor*), 1

Mrs. (abbreviation of *señora*), 1

much: as much tanto, -a, 2; **how much** ¿cuánto?, 2; **how much do they cost?** ¿cuánto cuestan?, 2; **how much does it cost?** ¿cuánto cuesta? 2, ¿cuánto vale? 11; **so much** tanto, -a, 2; **that much** tanto, -a, 2

musical película musical, 7

music la música, 2

mustard la mostaza, 9

my mi, 2

N

name: his (her) name is . . . se llama . . ., 1; **my name is . . .** me llamo, 1; **what's his (her) name?** ¿cómo se llama él (ella)? 1

napkin la servilleta, 9

near cerca (de), 5

to **need** necesitar, 3

neighborhood el barrio, 11

neither ni, 9

net la red, 3

never nunca, 3

new nuevo, -a, 1

newspaper el periódico, 5

next próximo, -a, 7

nice simpático, -a, 7; **it's (very) nice out** hace (muy) buen tiempo, 3; **to look nice on (clothing)** quedar bien, 11; **nice to meet you** mucho gusto, 1; **not nice** antipático, -a, 6

night la noche, 3; **at night** por la noche, 3; de la noche, 5; a la noche, 7; **good night** buenas noches, 1; **last night** anoche, 10

nine nueve, 2; **nine hundred** novecientos, -as, 11

nineteen diecinueve, 2

ninety noventa, 2

no no, 1

noise el ruido, 7

noon el mediodía, 9

nor ni, 9

North American norteamericano, -a, 6

not no, 2; **not me** yo no, 5

notebook el cuaderno, 2

November noviembre, 3

now ahora, 2

number el número, 2; **wrong number** el número equivocado, 5

nylon el nilón, 11

O

o'clock: at one o'clock a la una, 2; **at ten o'clock** a las diez, 2; **it's one o'clock** es la una, 2; **it's ten o'clock** son las diez, 2

October octubre, 3

of de, 2; **of the** del (de+el), 2; **of course!** ¡por supuesto! 6

off: get off bajar, 7; **off limits** prohibido, -a, 6

offer la oferta, 11

office la oficina, 10

official oficial, 7

often a menudo, 3

old: to be . . . years old tener . . . años, 6; **how old are you (is he/she)?** ¿cuántos años tiene? 6

Olympic: Olympic Games los Juegos Olímpicos, 3

on en, 5; **on foot** a pie, 2; **on sale** en venta, 2; **on the contrary** al contrario, 2; **on the left** a la izquierda, 5; **on the right** a la derecha, 5; **on the telephone** por teléfono, 3

once una vez, 7

one un, una, 2

one uno, -a (de), 2, 7; **that one** ése, -a, 11; aquél, aquélla, 11; **the one (made of)** el (de), 11; **this one** éste, -a, 11

onion la cebolla, 9

only sólo (*adv.*), 1

opinion la opinión, 2

or o, 7

orange (color) anaranjado, -a, 3

orange la naranja, 9

orchard la huerta, 5

order el pedido, 11; **in order to** para, 3

organized organizado, -a, 10

other otro, -a, -os, -as, 2, 3

our nuestro, -a, -os, -as, 6

over: over there allá, 11

P

pack (a suitcase) hacer la maleta, 10

painting la pintura, 2

pan: frying pan la sartén, 9

Panama Panamá, 1

pants los pantalones, 11

parents los padres, 6

park el parque, 7

part la parte, 2

to participate participar, 3

party la fiesta, 7

passing (grade) aprobado, -a, 2

passport el pasaporte, 5

pastime el pasatiempo, 3

pastry la pastelería, la tarta, 9; **pastry shop** la pastelería, 9

patience la paciencia, 9

to pay pagar, 9

peach el melocotón, 9

pear la pera, 9

pen: ballpoint pen el bolígrafo, 2; **fountain pen** la pluma, 2

pencil el lápiz (*pl.* lápices), 2

people la gente, 7

pepper la pimienta, 9

per: per week por semana, 7

perfect perfecto, -a, 9

permission el permiso, 10

person: in person en persona, 11

Peru Perú, 1

philosophy la filosofía, 2

photo la foto, 6

photograph la fotografía, 6; **take photographs** tomar fotografías, 3

photography la fotografía, 2

physical: physical education la educación física, 2

physics la física, 2

picnic el picnic, 9

pie el pastel, 9

piece el trozo, 9

pineapple la piña, 9

pink rosa, 9

pity: what a pity! ¡qué pena! 1; ¡qué lástima! 7

pizza la pizza, 9

place el lugar, 5

plantain el plátano, 9

plan el plan, 10

to plan pensar (ie), 7; planear, 10

plastic el plástico, 11; **made of plastic** de plástico, 11

plate el plato, 9; **small plate** el platillo, 9

to play jugar (ue), 3; **(a sport)** practicar, 3; **(a musical instrument)** tocar, 9

please por favor, 1

pleasing: to be pleasing to gustar, 3

pleasure el placer, 11; **it's a pleasure** es un placer, 6

P.M. de la noche, 5

pocket el bolsillo, 5

pole el bastón, 3; **ski poles** los bastones de esquiar, 3

pond el estanque, 10

pool la piscina, 7

possible: as early as possible a primera hora, 11

post office correos, 5

postcard la postal, 5

potato la patata (Spain), 9

to practice practicar, 3

to prepare preparar, 9

present el regalo, 10

pretty bonito, -a, 6; lindo, -a, 6

price el precio, 2

prize el premio, 3

problem el problema, 2

program el programa, 7

to promise prometer, 11

Puerto Rico Puerto Rico, 1

purse la cartera, 5

to put poner, 9

Q

quality la calidad, 11

question la pregunta, 3

quickly rápido, 2

R

racquet la raqueta, 3

to rain: it's raining llueve, 2

rather bastante, 2

ready listo, -a, 10

really? ¿verdad? 2

receipt el recibo, 11

to receive recibir, 11

recess el recreo, 2

record el disco, 2

redheaded pelirrojo, -a, 6

reduced (in price) rebajado, -a, 11

to reserve reservar, 10

rest: the rest los demás, 3

restaurant el restaurante, 9

to return volver (ue), 7; regresar, 10

rice el arroz, 9

to ride: ride a bicycle montar en bicicleta, 3

right: all right de acuerdo, 3; **on the right** a la derecha, 5

right? ¿verdad? 5; ¿no? 5

rock (music) el rock, 7

room el cuarto, 6; **dining room** el comedor, 6; **family room** la sala de estar, 6; **living room** la sala, 6; **waiting room** la sala de espera, 5

to row remar, 10

ruler la regla, 2

to run correr, 3

S

salad la ensalada, **9**
sale: on sale en venta, **2**
salesperson el vendedor, la vendedora, **2**
salt la sal, **9**
same mismo, -a, **9; the same as** igual que, **11**, lo mismo que, **11**
sandwich el bocadillo, **9**; el sandwich, **9**
Saturday el sábado, **2**
sauce la salsa, **9**
saucer el platillo, **9**
to **save** ahorrar, **11**
to **say** decir, **7**
schedule el horario, **2**
school la escuela, **1; high school** el colegio, **1; school bus** el autobús escolar, **2; elementary school** escuela primaria, **2; secondary school** la escuela secundaria, **2**
schoolbag la cartera, **2**
science la ciencia, **2; natural science** las ciencias naturales, **2; science fiction** la ciencia-ficción, **7; social science** las ciencias sociales, **2**
sculpture la escultura, **2**
season la estación, **3**
seat el asiento, **5**
second segundo, -a, **11**
secondary: secondary school la escuela secundaria, **2**
to **see** ver, **6; see you later** hasta luego, **1; see you tomorrow** hasta mañana, **1**
to **seem** parecer, **9**
selfish egoísta, **6**
to **sell** vender, **5**
to **send** mandar, **11**
September septiembre, **3**
to **serve** servir, **11**
service: customer service department la sección de quejas, **11**
to **set: set the table** poner la mesa, **9**
seven siete, **2; seven hundred** setecientos, -as, **11**
seventeen diecisiete, **2**
shame: what a shame! ¡qué lástima!, **7**
she ella, **1**
shirt la camisa, **11; dress shirt** la camisa de vestir, **11**
shoe el zapato, **3; tennis shoes** los zapatos de tenis, **3**
shop: pastry shop la pastelería, **9**
shopping la compra, **2; to be shopping** estar de compras, **11**
short bajo, -a, **6;** corto, -a, **10; a short time** poco tiempo, **10**
should deber, **5; should I . . .?** ¿debo . . .?, **5**
to **show: show a movie** dar una película, **7**
side el lado, **9**
sight la vista, **5**
sightseeing trip el paseo, **10**

silk la seda, **11**
silver la plata, **7; silver wedding anniversary** las bodas de plata, **7**
simply sencillamente, **7**
since como, **11**
to **sing** cantar, **3**
sir el señor (abbreviation Sr.), **1**
sister la hermana, **6; brother(s) and sister(s)** los hermanos, **6**
six seis, **2; six hundred** seiscientos, -as, **11**
sixteen dieciséis, **2**
sixty sesenta, **2**
size el tamaño, **9;** la talla, **11**
to **skate** patinar, **3; to ice skate** patinar en hielo, **3**
ski: skis los esquís, **3; ski boots** las botas de esquiar, **3; ski poles** los bastones de esquiar, **3**
to **ski** esquiar, **3**
skiing esquiar, **3**
skirt la falda, **11**
small pequeño, -a, **6**
snack el bocadillo, **9;** la merienda, **9**
to **snow: it's snowing** nieva, **3**
so tan, **6; so much** tanto, -a, **2; so long** chao, **1**
soccer el fútbol, **3; soccer ball** el balón, **3**
social: social science las ciencias sociales, **2**
sock el calcetín (*pl.* calcetines), **11**
soda el refresco, **6;** la gaseosa, **9**
some algunos, -as, **2;** unos, -as, **2**
something algo, **5**
sometimes a veces, **3**
son el hijo, **6**
song la canción, **9**
so-so regular, **1**
sorry: I'm sorry lo siento, **7**
soup la sopa, **9**
Spain España, **1**
Spanish español, española, **5; (language)** el español, **2**
to **speak** hablar, **3; (he's) speaking (on the phone)** él habla, **5**
special especial, **11**
specialty la especialidad, **9; specialty of the day** el plato del día, **9**
to **spend: spend time** pasar, **6**
spoon la cuchara, **9**
sports los deportes, **2**
spring la primavera, **3**
stamp el sello, **5**
to **start** empezar (ie) comenzar, **6**
stepfather el padrastro, **6**
stepmother la madrastra, **6**
stepparents los padrastros, **6**
stereo el estéreo, **11**
stewardess aeromoza, azafata, **5**
still todavía, **10**
stop la parada, **7**
to **stop** parar, **10**
store la tienda, **2; fruit store** la frutería, **9**
story la historia, **7; love story (movie)** la película de amor, **7**

strawberry la fresa, **9**
student el, la estudiante, **2**
to **study** estudiar, **3**
subject la materia, **2**
subway el metro, **2; by subway** en metro, **2**
sugar el azúcar, **9**
suit el traje, **11; bathing suit** el traje de baño, **11**
suitcase la maleta, **5; to pack a suitcase** hacer la maleta, **10**
summer el verano, **3**
Sunday el domingo, **2**
sunny: it's (very) sunny hace (mucho) sol, **3**
supper cena, **11**
sure seguro, -a, **10**
suspended suspenso, **2;** detenido, -a, **7**
sweater el suéter, **11**
to **swim** nadar, **3**
swimming la natación, **3**

T

table la mesa, **9; to set the table** poner la mesa, **9**
to **take** llevar, **9 (eat or drink)** tomar, **5; take photographs** tomar fotografías, **3**
to **talk** hablar, **3**
tall alto, -a, **6**
tart la tarta, pastry, **9**
tasty rico, -a, **9;** sabroso, -a, **9**
taxi el taxi, **5**
tea el té, **9**
teacher el profesor, la profesora, **1**
teaspoon la cucharita, **9**
telephone el teléfono, **3; on the telephone** por teléfono, **3**
television la televisión, **2**
ten diez, **2**
tennis el tenis, **3; tennis ball** la pelota, **3; tennis court** la cancha de tenis, **3**
terrible muy mal, **1**
than: less than . . . menos de . . ., **11; more . . . than** más . . . que, **11; more than . . .** más de . . ., **11**
thank: thank you gracias, **1; thank you very much** muchas gracias, **3**
that ese, -a, **9;** aquel, aquella, **9; that one** ése, -a, **11,** aquél, aquella, **11**
that que, **5;** lo que, **7**
that: that much tanto, -a, **2; that way** así, **11**
the el, la, **1;** los (*m. pl.*), las (*f. pl.*), **2**
theater el teatro, **7**
theirs su(s), **6;** de ellos, de ellas, **6**
them les (*m. and f.*), **9;** ellos, ellas, **9;** los, las, (*obj. prep.*), **10**
then después, **5; then** entonces, **5**

there allí, 5; **over there** allá, 11
there: there is, there are hay, 2
these estos, -as, 9; éstos, -as, 11
they ellos, ellas, 1
thin delgado, -a, 6
thing la cosa, 6
to think creer, 5; pensar (ie), 7; **what do you think of . . .?** ¿qué te parece . . .? (*fam. sing.*), 6
thirsty: to be (very) thirsty tener (mucha) sed, 9
thirteen trece, 2
thirty treinta, 2
this este, -a, 9; **this afternoon** esta tarde, 7; **this one** éste, -a, 11
those esos, -as, 9; aquellos, -as, 9
thousand mil, 11
three tres, 2; **three hundred** trescientos, -as, 11
through por, 5
Thursday el jueves, 2
ticket el billete, 10; **ticket window** la ventanilla, 7
tie la corbata, 11
time la hora, 2; el tiempo, 6; la vez (*pl.* veces), 7; **a long time** mucho tiempo, 10; **a short time** poco tiempo, 10; **all the time** todo el tiempo, 7; **a week ahead of time** con una semana de anticipación, 10; **at what time?** ¿a qué hora? 2; **free time** el tiempo libre, 6; **to spend time** pasar, 6; **what time is it?** ¿qué hora es? 2
tip la propina, 9
tired cansado, -a, 11
to a, 2; para, 3; **to the** al (a + el), 2; **to where?** ¿adónde? 5
today hoy, 2
tomato el tomate, 9
tomorrow mañana, 3; **see you tomorrow** hasta mañana, 1
tonight esta noche, 7
too también, 3; **too much** demasiado -a, 6
total el total, 3
tourism el turismo, 10
tourist el, la turista, 11; turístico, -a, 9
traffic el tráfico, 9
traveler: traveler's check el cheque de viajero, 5
tree el árbol, 9
trip el viaje, 10; **pleasure trip** la excursión, 10
trophy el trofeo, 3
true: it's true es verdad, 3
to try probar, 9
Tuesday el martes, 2
tuna el atún, 9
twelve doce, 2
twenty veinte, 2
twice dos veces, 7
two dos, 2; **the two** los, las dos, 6; **two hundred** doscientos, -as, 11
typical típico, -a, 9

U

ugly feo, -a, 6
uncle el tío, 6; **uncles and aunts** los tíos, 6
under debajo (de), 9
United States los Estados Unidos (abbreviation EE.UU.), 1
up (there) arriba, 5
us nos, 9; nosotros, nosotras, 9
to use usar, 6

V

vacation las vacaciones, 6
very muy, 1; bien, 6; **very good** buenísimo, -a, 9; **very good (grade)** notable, 2
vegetable: green vegetable la verdura, 9
verge: to be on the verge of estar a punto de, 10
vignette la viñeta, 1
visit la visita, 6
visitor la visita, 6
voice: in a low voice en voz baja, 11
volleyball el volibol, 3; **(the ball)** el balón, 3

W

to wait (for) esperar, 5
waiter el camarero, 9
waiting: waiting area la sala de espera, 5
waitress la camarera, 9
to walk caminar, 10
to want querer (ie), 6
to watch mirar, 3
water el agua (*f.*), 9
watermelon la sandía, 9
we nosotros, nosotras, 1
weather el tiempo, 3; **the weather is very bad** hace muy mal tiempo, 3; **what's the weather?** ¿qué tiempo hace? 3
wedding: silver wedding anniversary las bodas de plata, 7
Wednesday el miércoles, 2
week la semana, 2; **last week** la semana pasada, 10; **per week** por semana, 7
weekend el fin de semana, 7
welcome bienvenido, -a, 6; **you're welcome** de nada, 1
well bueno, -a, 1; bien, 1
Western (movie) la película del oeste, 7
what lo que, 7
what? ¿cuál? 2; ¿qué? 2; **at what time?** ¿a qué hora? 2; **what else?** ¿qué más? 2; **what for?** ¿para qué? 5; **what if we go . . .?** ¿si vamos . . .? 7; **what's his (her) name?** ¿cómo se llama él (ella)? 1; **what's the weather?** ¿qué tiempo hace? 3
what!: what a lot of people! ¡cuánta gente! 7; **what a mixup!** ¡qué confusión! 5; **what a pity!** ¡qué pena! 1, ¡qué lástima! 7; **what a pretty room!** ¡qué cuarto tan bonito! 6; **what a shame!** ¡qué lástima! 7; **what envy I feel!** ¡qué envidia! 10; **what luck!** ¡qué suerte! 5, ¡qué envidia! 10
when cuando, 6
when? ¿cuándo? 2
where? ¿dónde? 1; **to where?** ¿adónde? 5
white blanco, -a, 3
who? ¿quién? 1
whole todo, -a, -os, -as, 6
why? ¿por qué? 2; **why don't we . . .?** ¿por qué no . . .? 5
wide largo, -a, 11
wife la esposa, 6; **husband and wife** los esposos, 6
to win ganar, 3
window: ticket window la ventanilla, 7
windy: it's (very) windy hace (mucho) viento, 3
winter el invierno, 3
to wish desear, 11
with con, 2; **with me** conmigo, 9
without sin, 10
woman la señora, 6
wool la lana, 11
to work trabajar, 3
to write escribir, 5
wrong: wrong number el número equivocado, 5

Y

year el año, 3
yellow amarillo, -a, 3
yes sí, 1
yesterday ayer, 10
you (*subj.*) tú (*fam. sing.*), 1; usted (*pol. sing.*) (abbreviation Ud.), 1; vosotros, vosotras (*fam. pl.*); ustedes (*pl.*) (abbreviation Uds.), 1
you (*dir. obj.*) te (*fam. sing.*), 10; lo, la (*pol. sing.*), 10; los, las (*pl.*), 10; os (*fam. pl.*), 11
you (*indir. obj.*) te (*fam. sing.*), 9; le (*pol. sing.*), 9; les (*pl.*), 9; os (*fam. pl,*), 11
you (*obj. of prep.*) ti (*fam. sing.*), 9; usted (*pol. sing.*), 9; ustedes (*pl..*), 9
young: young people los jóvenes, 11
your(s) tu(s) (*fam. sing.*), 2; su(s) (*pol. sing. and pl.*), 5; vuestro, -a, -os, -as (*fam. pl.*), 6; de usted (*pol. sing.*), 6; de ustedes (*pol. pl.*), 6
youth la juventud, 7

Z

zero cero, 2

English-Spanish Vocabulary 389

INDEX

The numbers and letters after each entry refer to the unit and section where the entry first appears.

ir: present tense, 5 (B3); ir + a + infinitive to express future time, 7 (B3); preterit, 10 (B10)

irregular verbs: present tense of ser, 1 (C10); venir, 2 (A5); tener, 2 (B13); estar, 5 (A10); ir, 5 (B3); querer, 6 (A6); salir, 7 (A21); conocer, 7 (C13); poder, 9 (C8); pensar, 7 (B18); saber, 7 (C6); hacer, 9 (B5); poner, 9 (C8); jugar, 3 (B17); empezar, 7 (B18); preterit tense of hacer, 10 (B5); ir, 5 (B3); see also: regular verbs and stem-changing verbs

jugar (u-ue): pres. tense, 3 (B16)

llamarse: pres. tense, 1 (B4)

más/menos . . . que: 11 (A6)

mucho: with certain weather expressions, 3 (C11)

negation: with no, 2 (A12); position of negative in sentence, 2 (A12); with verb gustar, 3 (A4); with ir + a + infinitive, 7 (B3)

nouns: gender, 1 (B15); number, 2 (C3); plural, 2 (C3); agreement with definite article, 1 (B15); agreement with adjective, 1 (B15)

number: of nouns, 2 (C3); of definite article, 2 (C11); subject pronoun, 1 (C10)

numbers: cardinal numbers from 0 to 20, 2 (B4); cardinal numbers from 21 to 100, 2 (C14); cardinal numbers from 100 to 1,000, 11 (B11)

object pronouns: direct object pronoun, 7 (C10); indirect object pronoun, 11 (B5)

pensar (e-ie): present tense, 7 (B18)

planear: preterit, 10 (A6)

plural: of nouns, 2 (C3); of definite article, 2 (C11); of indefinite article, 2 (C11); see also nouns, agreement

poder (o-ue): present tense, 7 (A3)

poner: present tense, 9 (C8)

¿por qué?: 2 (A10)

possession: expressed with de, 6 (C10); see also possessive adjectives

possessive adjectives: mi-tu-su, 5 (A4); agreement with noun, 5 (A4); mis-tus-sus, 6 (C10); nuestro (vuestro) -a, -os, -as, 6 (C10); agreement in number and gender, position, 6 (C10)

prepositional pronouns: forms and use, 9 (A11)

prepositions: a, 11 (B5); de, 6 (C10)

present tense: forms and use of regular -ar verbs, 3 (B3); forms and use of regular -er and -ir verbs, 5 (C8); to indicate the future, 7 (B3); see also: regular verbs, irregular verbs, and stem-changing verbs

preterit tense: defined, 10 (A6); regular -ar verbs, 10 (A6); hacer, 10 (B5); ir, 10 (B10); regular -er and -ir verbs, 11 (C4); see also: regular verbs, irregular verbs, and stem-changing verbs

pronouns: subject pronoun, 1 (C10); used after prepositions, 6 (C10), 11 (B5)

pronunciation: find in Try Your Skills section; consonants h and ñ, 1; sound of ll and ch, 2; vowels a, e, and o, 3; vowels i and u, 5; c before a, e and u, 6; qu before e or i, 6; g before a, o, and u, 7; sound of r, 9; sound of z and s, 10; sound b and v, 11; g before e or i, 11

¿qué?: 1 (A17)

querer (e-ie): present tense, 6 (A6)

¿quién?: 2 (A10)

regular verbs: agreement with subject, 3 (B3); present of regular -ar verbs, 3 (B3); present of regular -er and -ir verbs, 5 (C8); preterit of regular -ar verbs, 10 (A6); preterit of regular -er and -ir verbs, 11 (C4); see also: irregular verbs, stem-changing verbs

saber: pres. tense, 7 (C6); saber vs. conocer, 7 (C13)

salir: pres. tense, 7 (A21)

ser: pres. tense, 1 (C10); used with national origin, 1 (C10)

stem-changing verbs: explained, 6 (A6); jugar (u-ue), 3 (B16); querer (e-ie), 6 (A6), poder (o-ue), 7 (A3); pensar (e-ie), 7 (B18); empezar (e-ie), 7 (B18)

subject pronouns: forms and use, 1 (C10); tú vs. usted, 1 (A17)

tener: pres. tense, 2 (B13); to ask or express age, 6 (B5); tener + que + infinitive to express obligation, 7 (A11); expressions with tener, 9 (C4)

tener + que + infinitive: to express obligation, 7 (A11)

time: asking or telling time (o'clock), 2 (B19); expressions with hacer (. . . ago), 10 (A18)

tú: usage, 1 (A17); tú vs. usted, 1 (A17)

usted: usage, 1 (C10); usted vs. tú, 1 (A17)

ustedes: usage, 1 (C10)

vender: preterit, 11 (C4)

venir: pres. tense, 2 (A5)

verbs: see: irregular verbs, regular verbs, and stem changing-verbs

y: use with numbers, 2 (C17)

Assoc.; 233(bl), Ian Strange/Photo Researchers; 233(br), Jacques Jangoux/Peter Arnold, Inc.; 234(t), F. Gohier/Photo Researchers; 234(cl), Joe Viesti; 234(cr), Peter Menzel; 234(b), F. Gohier/Photo Researchers; 235(t), HBJ Photo/Daniel Aubry; 235(c), HBJ Photo/Daniel Aubry; 235(b), HBJ Photo/Peter Menzel

UNIT 9, 236, HBJ Photo/Daniel Aubry; 237(tl), HBJ Photo; 237(tr), HBJ Photo/Oscar Buitrago; 237(b), HBJ Photo/Daniel Aubry; 239(t), HBJ Photo/Bob Daemmrich; 239(b), HBJ Photo; 244(all), HBJ Photo/Earl Kogler; 246(both), HBJ Photo/Daniel Aubry; 250, HBJ Photo/Rodney Jones; 252(both), HBJ Photo; 258, HBJ Photo/Mark Antman; 259, HBJ Photo/Daniel Aubry; 261(tl), HBJ Photo/Stephanie Maze; 261(tr), Stuart Cohen; 261(bl), HBJ Photo/Mark Antman; 261(br), Anne Heimann/The Stock Market; 264, HBJ Photo; 265, HBJ Photo

UNIT 10, 268, HBJ Photo/Daniel Aubry; 269(all), HBJ Photo/Daniel Aubry; 270, HBJ Photo/Rodney Jones; 271(both), A. G. E. Fotostock/Wheeler Pictures; 274(both), HBJ Photo/Daniel Aubry; 275(both), Joe Viesti; 277(t), Bruce Hayes/Photo Researchers; 277(cl), Luis Villota/The Stock Market; 244(c), A. G. E. Fotostock/Wheeler Pictures; 277(cr), Stephanie Maze/Woodfin Camp & Assoc.; 277(b), HBJ Photo; 278(all), HBJ Photo/Rodney Jones; 279, Robert Frerck/Woodfin Camp & Assoc.; 282(l), Joe Viesti; 282(lc), Peter Menzel/Wheeler Pictures; 282(rc), Stephanie Maze; 282(r), Joe Viesti; 284(all), HBJ Photo/Daniel Aubry; 285(all), A. G. E. Fotostock/Wheeler Pictures; 288(t), HBJ Photo; 288(b), A. G. E. Fotostock/Wheeler Pictures; 290(l), Joe Viesti; 290(r), HBJ Photo; 294(l), A. G. E. Fotostock/Wheeler Pictures; 294(r), Claudia Parks/The Stock Market; 295, Dr. Jean Lorre/Photo Researchers

UNIT 11, 298, HBJ Photo/Peter Menzel; 299(tl), HBJ Photo; 299(tr), HBJ Photo; 299(b), HBJ Photo/Stephanie Maze; 300(t), HBJ Photo/Stephanie Maze; 300(c), HBJ Photo/Arturo Salinas; 300(b), HBJ Photo/Stephanie Maze; 306(all), HBJ Photo/Stephanie Maze; 307, HBJ Photo/Stephanie Maze; 308, HBJ Photo/Stephanie Maze; 309, HBJ Photo/Stephanie Maze; 312, HBJ Photo/Stephanie Maze; 313(l), Benn Mitchell; 313(r), HBJ Photo/Stephanie Maze; 314, HBJ Photo/Stephanie Maze; 319, HBJ Photo/Stephanie Maze; 321, HBJ Photo/Stephanie Maze; 325(l), Jules Bucher/Photo Researchers; 325(r), Benn Mitchell

UNIT 12, 328, HBJ Photo/Gerhard Gscheidle; 329(both), Benn Mitchell; 330, Stuart Cohen/The Stock Market; 331(l), G. Schiff/Photo Researchers; 331(r), Benn Mitchell; 331(b), Benn Mitchell; 332, Stuart Cohen; 333(t), Joe Viesti; 333(cl), Luis Castañeda/The Image Bank; 333(cr), Luis Castañeda/The Image Bank; 333(b), Craig Aurness/Woodfin Camp & Assoc.; 334(tl), Luis Castañeda/The Image Bank; 334(tr), Joe Viesti; 334(bl), Luis Castañeda/The Image Bank; 334(br), Robert Frerck/The Stock Market; 335(tl), Luis Castañeda/The Image Bank; 335(tr), Luis Castañeda/The Image Bank; 335(cl), Jonathan Blair/Woodfin Camp & Assoc.; 335(cr), Joe Viesti; 335(b), Joe Viesti; 336(tl), Joe Viesti; 336(tr), Joe Viesti; 336(cl), Joe Viesti; 336(cr), Luis Villota/The Stock Market; 336(b), Claudia Parks/The Stock Market; 337(tl), M. C. Magruder/The Image Bank; 337(tr), David Hiser/The Image Bank; 337(cl), John Lewis Stage/The Image Bank; 337(cr), Gary Cralle/The Image Bank; 337(b), Harvey Lloyd/Peter Arnold, Inc.; 338(tl), Paolo Gori/The Image Bank; 338(tr), David Hiser/The Image Bank; 338(cl), John Dominis/Wheeler Pictures; 338(cr), Gerhard Gscheidle/Peter Arnold, Inc.; 338(b), John Dominis/Wheeler Pictures; 339(all), Joe Viesti; 340(tl), Enrique Shore/Woodfin Camp & Assoc.; 340(tr), Luis Villota/The Stock Market; 340(cl), Joe Viesti; 340(cr), Joe Viesti; 340(b), Joe Viesti

ART CREDITS   Agustín Fernández: 16, 32, 33, 37, 38, 40, 42, 62, 64, 67, 81(b), 95(b), 96, 97, 99, 100, 107, 123, 124, 137, 143, 147, 174, 202, 205, 210, 238, 245, 247, 249, 257, 306 and 320
Manuel García: 56, 57, 88, 89, 116, 117, 118, 119, 160, 162, 188, 190, 191, 220, 221, 266, 267, 296, 297 and 327
Len Ebert: 17, 73, 74, 76, 77, 81(c), 101, 240, 253, 255, 303 and 311
Anita Lovitt: 106, 270, 283 and 324
Susan Dietrich: 142, 179 and 182